HANDBOOK OF AMERICAN POPULAR CULTURE

HANDBOOK OF AMERICAN POPULAR CULTURE

Second Edition, Revised and Enlarged

Propaganda–Women

Edited by M. THOMAS INGE

Greenwood Press
NEW YORK
WESTPORT, CONNECTICUT
LONDON

Library of Congress Cataloging-in-Publication Data

Handbook of American popular culture / edited by M. Thomas Inge.—
2nd ed., rev. and enlarged.
  p. cm.
  Includes index.
  ISBN 0–313–25406–0 (lib. bdg. : alk. paper)
  1. United States—Popular culture.   2. United States—Popular
culture—History—Sources.   3. United States—Popular culture—
Bibliography.   I. Inge, M. Thomas.
  E169.1.H2643   1989
  306'.4'0973—dc19   88–39092

British Library Cataloguing in Publication Data is available.

Library of Congress Catalog Card Number: 88–39092
ISBN: 0–313–25406–0
ISBN: 0–313–27241–7 (v. 1)
ISBN: 0–313–27242–5 (v. 2)
ISBN: 0–313–27243–3 (v. 3)

First published in 1989

Greenwood Press, Inc.
88 Post Road West, Westport, Connecticut   06881

Printed in the United States of America

Copyright Acknowledgment

The editor and publisher gratefully acknowledge permission to reprint material from the
following copyrighted source.

William Howland Kenney. "Jazz: A Bibliographical Essay" (*American Studies International*,
25, April 1987, Vol. XXV, No. 1).

For Tonette

*Mistress of herself
though china fall.*

Contents

x   Contents

About the Contributors

ROBERT S. ALLEY is Professor of Humanities and Chair of Area Studies at the University of Richmond. His publications include *The Producer's Medium,* written with Horace Newcomb, and *Television: Ethics for Hire?* In 1977 he produced and wrote the PBS film, *Television: For Better or Worse.* He has co-directed several symposia dealing with television and its portrayal of women. He is currently working on two books with his colleague, Irby Brown, one dealing with the role of women on television, the other on "The Mary Tyler Moore Show."

ROY M. ANKER is Professor of English at Calvin College in Grand Rapids, Michigan, where he teaches courses in literature, film, and popular religion. He is currently completing a book surveying the role of the self-help tradition in American popular religion and culture.

ROBERT A. ARMOUR is Professor of English at Virginia Commonwealth University, a fellow at VCU's Center for Educational Development and Faculty Resources, and co-director of the Central Virginia Faculty Consortium. He has published widely on literature, film, and popular culture. His most recent book is *The Gods and Myths of Ancient Egypt.*

EVELYN BECK is a staff writer for the Anderson *Independent-Mail,* a daily South Carolina newspaper. She has taught English at Florida State University, Clemson University, and Tri-County Technical College. She has published fiction and is a freelance writer for a number of regional and national publications.

MICHAEL J. BELL is Associate Professor of American Studies and Anthropology and the Chairman of the American Studies Department at Grinnell College, Grinnell, Iowa. He is the author of *The World from Brown's Lounge: An Ethnography of Black Middle Class Play* as well as numerous articles on Afro-American performance styles, workers' culture, and the history of critical theory.

BILL BENNETT, jazz critic and former production coordinator for the Smithsonian Collection of Recordings, is now employed in the Technical Systems Sector of Hewlett Packard in California.

MICHAEL L. BERGER is Professor in the Division of Human Development at St. Mary's College of Maryland. His research interests center on the impact of technology on society and human behavior, especially as it relates to automotive history. He is the author of *The Devil Wagon in God's Country: The Automobile and Social Change in Rural America, 1893–1929* and is currently completing *The Automobile: A Reference Guide* for Greenwood Press.

VICKI L. BERGER is Head of the Collections Branch and Curator of Textiles at the North Carolina Museum of History in Raleigh. Her professional service includes active membership in the Costume Society of America, Popular Culture Association, and the North Carolina Museums Council. Before Joining the Museum of History, Dr. Berger taught clothing and textiles at East Carolina University where she was the recipient of the ECU Alumni Association's Award for Teaching Excellence.

JAMES J. BEST is Associate Professor of Political Science at Kent State University, where he also teaches a course on the history of American illustration for the American Studies Program. He is the author of *American Popular Illustration* and is currently completing a book dealing with the social, economic, and cultural context of the Golden Age of American illustration.

MARK W. BOOTH is Professor and Chairman of the English Department at the University of Wyoming. He has written *The Experience of Songs,* a study of the nature and uses of folk, popular, and literary song verse, and *American Popular Music: A Reference Guide.* He has also written about and teaches courses in eighteenth-century English literature.

JOHN BRYANT is Associate Professor of English at Hofstra University. His articles on Melville have appeared in *American Literature, Nineteenth-*

Century Fiction, Philological Quarterly, and *Melville Society Extracts.* Editor and contributor to *The Companion to Melville Studies* (1986), he is also at work on *American Repose,* a book-length study of Melville's comic sensibility. His work on television sitcoms has appeared in *Journal of Popular Culture* and *Studies in American Humor.* Of an evening, he will fiddle with a stamp collection that he has maintained since the age of ten.

CHARLES CAMP has served as Maryland State Folklorist at the Maryland State Arts Council since 1976. He served as Executive Secretary/Treasurer of the American Folklore Society from 1980 through 1985 and has published more than forty articles on traditional music, crafts, architecture, and cookery in various scholarly journals. Among his activities at the Arts Council have been the production of three documentary films, four exhibitions on regional folk artists, and eight festivals. He has taught courses on food and culture in American life at the University of Maryland and Indiana University.

LORETTA CARRILLO is Lecturer in the Romance Studies Department at Cornell University. She has published articles on dance, fashion, and U. S. Hispanic popular culture.

ROBERT K. DODGE is Professor of English at the University of Nevada, Las Vegas, where he teaches American literature. He is co-editor of *Voices from Wah Kon-tah,* and of *New and Old Voices of Wah Kon-tah,* anthologies of poetry by contemporary native Americans. He is editor of *Early American Almanac Humor* and is currently working on two indexes of almanacs of the early American republic to be published by Greenwood Press.

MAURICE DUKE is Professor of English at Virginia Commonwealth University in Richmond and the author and editor of books and articles on American literature. He was for twelve years the Book Page editor and a weekly book columnist for the Richmond Times-Dispatch. Professing a lifelong interest in automobiles—he thinks he has owned about fifty—Duke was for five years a licensed amateur race car driver, competing often on tracks from Charlotte Motor Speedway to Pocono. In addition, he worked briefly as a volunteer pit crew member for a professional team for several Daytona International Speedway races. Duke is currently at work on a historical anthology of the Chesapeake Bay, on which he regularly sails.

KATHERINE FISHBURN is Professor of English at Michigan State University, where she teaches courses in women's literature, feminist critical theory, modern American fiction, and contemporary literature. She is author of *Richard Wright's Hero, Women in Popular Culture, The Unexpected Universe of Doris Lessing,* and *Doris Lessing: Life, Work and Criticism.* Recent essays of hers have appeared in *Science-Fiction Studies, Studies in the Novel, Regionalism and the Female Imagination,* and *Doris Lessing: The Alchemy of Survival.* She is currently at work on a full-length study of Buchi Emecheta's fiction, and she serves as the managing editor of the *Doris Lessing Newsletter.*

JEANIE K. FORTE is Assistant Professor of English at the University of Tennessee, Knoxville. Her research interests include women's performance art, women in film, feminist theory, and modern drama. Her publications include articles in *Theatre Journal, Theater, High Performance,* and *Women and Performance;* her book, *Women in Performance Art: Feminism and Postmodernism,* is forthcoming from Indiana University Press.

ROBERT GALBREATH is Assistant University Librarian for Collection Management at Loyola University of Chicago. An intellectual historian by training, his research interests focus on modern occultism, gnosticism, and visionary and apocalyptic literature. He edited *The Occult: Studies and Evaluations,* contributed chapters to such books as *The Occult in America* and *The End of the World,* and has published articles and essays in the *Journal of Religion, Political Theory, Science-Fiction Studies,* and elsewhere.

MARILYN J. GIBBS is Assistant Professor of Health and Sport Science at the University of Richmond, where she teaches professional preparation courses for the undergraduate program and sport sociology for the sport management graduate program. Her research interests are in pedagogy, sport administration, as well as sport and the arts. She has published material on the concepts of teaching sport and sport poetry.

THOMAS A. GREENFIELD is Dean of Arts and Sciences and Professor of English at Bellarmine College. He is the author of *Radio: A Reference Guide* (Greenwood Press), the editor of *Scholar and Educator,* and a regular reviewer for *Comparative Drama.* In 1983 his book, *Work and the Work Ethic in American Drama, 1920–1970,* was nominated for the Freedley Award for the outstanding book in Theater Arts.

CLAUDIUS W. GRIFFIN is Professor of English at Virginia Commonwealth University. He has published essays on teaching composition, edited a collection of essays on writing across the curriculum, and written a textbook on business writing. He is currently working on a book about teaching Shakespeare through film and performance.

PATSY G. HAMMONTREE is Assistant Professor of English at the University of Tennessee, Knoxville. She is the author of *Elvis Presley* (Greenwood Press), and her publications have appeared in the *Southern Quarterly,* the *Country Music Journal,* and the *Association for Communication Administration Bulletin.* She is working on a bio-bibliography about Shirley Temple Black for Greenwood Press and a drama anthology for Harcourt Brace Jovanovich.

ROBERT J. HIGGS is Professor of English at East Tennessee State University, where he teaches courses in Appalachian and Southern literature and the literature of sports. He is the author of *Laurel and Thorn: The Athlete in American Literature* (1981) and *Sports: A Reference Guide* (1982) and co-editor with Neil D. Isaacs of *The Sporting Spirit: Athletes in Literature and Life* (1977). He is presently at work on a book on sports and religion entitled *God in the Stadium, Muscle in the Church.*

THOMAS W. HOFFER is Professor of Communication and a filmmaker at the College of Communication, Florida State University, Tallahassee. His film, video, and print publications include studies in American television docudrama, broadcasting, Vietnam and Southeast Asia, Florida regional folklore, music and medical technology, Florida and American film history, aging, and national defense. He is author of *Animation: A Reference Guide* (Greenwood Press, 1981), an encyclopedic organization of the literature in cel, stop-action, drawing-on-film, and computer technologies, and is completing a book-length treatment of docudrama in American television for Greenwood Press. He is President of a videocassette production and packaging company, Dunecrest Video Corporation, Eastpoint, Florida.

LISA N. HOWORTH is Instructor in Art History at the University of Mississippi and a research bibliographer at the Center for the Study of Southern Culture. With the Center and the United States Information Agency, she has written and produced a series of slide and videotape programs on American art, and she is co-editor of a forthcoming bibliographic guide to the blues. She has contributed articles on popular culture and architecture to the *Encyclopedia of Southern Culture.*

M. THOMAS INGE is Robert Emory Blackwell Professor of Humanities at Randolph-Macon College in Ashland, Virginia. He has edited many reference guides in popular culture for Greenwood Press, including the *Handbook of American Popular Literature.* In addition to his research on the history, development, and appreciation of comic strips and comic books, he is general editor of the "Studies in Popular Culture" series for the University Press of Mississippi.

ROBERT H. JANKE is Associate Professor in the School of the Arts, Virginia Commonwealth University, where he teaches and serves as director of the school's program in speech communication. He is a past president of the Virginia Speech Communication Association, and his work includes articles published in *The Speech Communication Teacher, Perceptual and Motor Skills,* and *The Ideabook: For Teaching the Basic Speech Communication Course.*

ANNE HUDSON JONES is Associate Professor of Literature and Medicine at the Institute for the Medical Humanities of the University of Texas Medical Branch at Galveston. She is the editor of *Literature and Medicine: Images of Healers* (1983) and *Images of Nurses: Perspectives from History, Art, and Literature* (1988), and the author of numerous articles on various aspects of literature and medicine. Since 1985 she has been editor of the annual journal *Literature and Medicine,* published by Johns Hopkins University Press.

ELIZABETH BARNABY KEENEY is Lecturer on the History of Science and Allston Burr Senior Tutor at Harvard University. Her teaching and research interests focus on popular science and medicine in nineteenth-century America. She is currently working on a history of botany as popular culture in America.

WILLIAM HOWLAND KENNEY III is Associate Professor of History and Coordinator of the American Studies Program at Kent State University. His scholarly articles have appeared in *American Studies, American Music, American Studies International,* and the *Black Perspective in Music.* He is General Editor of the monographic series "Jazz: History, Culture & Criticism" at Wayne State University Press and is presently at work on a cultural history of jazz in Chicago, 1906–1930.

RICHARD N. MASTELLER is Associate Professor of English at Whitman College, where he teaches American literature and participates in an interdisciplinary General Studies program. Trained in American Studies, he has published in *The New England Quarterly* (with Jean Carwile Masteller), *Prospects: An Annual of American Cultural Studies,* and *Smithsonian Studies in American Art.* He organized the photographic exhibition, "Auto as Icon," for the International Museum of Photography at George Eastman House and recently completed the exhibition and catalogue, *"We, the People?" Satiric Prints of the 1930s,* with support from the Washington Commission for the Humanities and the Swann Foundation. His teaching and research interests include the 1930s, the 1960s, photographic history, and twentieth-century American literature.

DONALD A. McQUADE is Professor of English at the University of California, Berkeley. He has written extensively on American literature and culture. His publications on advertising include *Popular Writing in America*

(1973, 1988) and *Edsels, Luckies, and Frigidaires: Advertising the American Way* (1979). In 1985–86 he served as the guest curator of an exhibition on advertising and American social history at the Smithsonian Institution's Cooper-Hewitt Museum in New York. Most recently, he has contributed to the *Columbia Literary History of the United States* and served as both general and contributing editor to *The Harper American Literature*, a two-volume comprehensive regathering and reassessment of the American literary canon. He is currently at work on *The Culture of Efficiency*, a study of the impact of Frederick Taylor's principles of scientific management on twentieth-century American culture.

BERNARD MERGEN is Professor of American Civilization at George Washington University and associate editor of the *American Quarterly*. His research interests include the history of children's play, material culture, and environmental history. He is the author of *Play and Playthings: A Reference Guide* and *Recreational Vehicles and Travel: A Resource Guide*. Currently he is working on a cultural and technological history of snow in America.

ARTHUR H. MILLER, JR., is College Librarian at Lake Forest College. He supervises the Elliott Donnelley Railroad Collection in the college's Donnelley Library and is a member of the American Studies Program committee. He has taught in the American Studies Program and has published articles on library topics.

RICHARD ALAN NELSON Is Professor and Public Relations Sequence Head in the A. Q. Miller School of Journalism and Mass Communications at Kansas State University, following a long academic association with the University of Houston. Accredited by the Public Relations Society of America, he regularly serves as a consultant to business and government. Nelson is on the editorial board of *American journalism* and authored numerous refereed articles. In addition, Nelson is the author of *Florida and the American Motion Picture Industry, 1898–1980* and co-author of *Issues Management: Corporate Public Policymaking in an Information Society*, and is completing *Propaganda: A Reference Guide* for Greenwood Press.

NANCY POGEL is Professor of American Thought and Language at Michigan State University. Her articles and reviews on American humor, film comedy, and women in popular culture appear in *Literature/Film Quarterly*, *MidAmerica, American Literature,The Dictionary of Literary Biography*, and *American Women by Women*. She is the author of *Woody Allen* (Twayne, 1987). With Paul P. Somers, Jr., she has written a chapter on "Literary Humor" in *Humor in America* (Greenwood Press, 1988). She is currently working on a book about women in film comedy. She has been named an American Council on Education Fellow for 1988–89.

ANNE E. ROWE is Professor of English at Florida State University, Tallahassee. Her research interests are in Southern literature. She is the author of *The Enchanted Country: Northern Writers in the South, 1865–1910*, and *The*

Idea of Florida in the American Literary Imagination. She is presently at work on a book on the Southern domestic novel.

DOROTHY S. SCHMIDT is Associate Professor of English at Pan American University. Founder of Pan American University Press as well as the small presses riverSedge and Double SS Press, she is also an advisor for the prize-winning student literary magazine, *Gallery.*

RICHARD A. SCHWARZLOSE is Professor in the Medill School of Journalism, Northwestern University, where he teaches media history, law and ethics, and press-government relations. His articles on these subjects have appeared in several academic and trade publications. His *Newspapers: A Reference Guide* was published in 1987 by Greenwood Press, and a two-volume history of the American wire services is scheduled for publication. He spent seven years as a reporter and telegraph editor in daily newspaper journalism.

NICHOLAS A. SHARP is Director of Nontraditional Studies at Virginia Commonwealth University. Primarily interested in the relationships of language, literature, and values, he has published articles and essays on Shakespeare, Renaissance literature, popular culture, and adult education.

JOSEPH W. SLADE is Director of the Communications Center and Chairman of the Department of Media Arts at Long Island University, Brooklyn Campus. He is editor of *The Markham Review,* an interdisciplinary journal of American culture, and co-editor of the forthcoming *Essays on Science, Technology, and Literature.* Author of *Thomas Pynchon* (1974) and some sixty articles on communications, film, television, American literature, technology, and other subjects, he is currently working on two books, the first a study of the Maxim family of inventors and the second a history of the clandestine cinema.

PAUL SOMERS, JR., is Professor of American Thought and Language at Michigan State University and Contributing Editor to *National Lampoon.* He has published short stories and numerous articles on American literature and humor. He is the author of *Johnson J. Hooper* (1984).

STEVEN S. TIGNER is Professor of Philosophy at the University of Toledo. His non-magical research interests and publications lie mainly in ancient Greek philosophy and philology and in moral education. He was founding editor of the *Journal of Magic History* and has lectured widely on magic and fraud in human culture as well as on numerous other topics in the liberal arts.

JAMES VON SCHILLING is Assistant Professor in the Humanities Division of Northampton Community College in Bethlehem, Pennsylvania, where he teaches writing and journalism. A semiprofessional musician on weekends, he has written on contemporary music for the *Popular Culture Reader, Creem,* and other publications, and has taught popular music at Bowling Green State University.

FAYE NELL VOWELL is Associate Vice President for Academic Affairs at Emporia State University. She compiled the section on black Americans for *A Comprehensive Bibliography for the Study of American Minorities,* edited by Wayne C. Miller. Her current research interests are the Chicano novel and minorities on the Great Plains. As part of a National Endowment for the Humanities grant, she has written and directed a number of educational television programs about minorities on the Great Plains.

RICHARD F. WELCH is Associate Professor of Communication at Kennesaw State College, Georgia, where he teaches journalism and public address. He is the Chair of the Mass Communication and Public Relations Division of the Popular Culture Association and is presently working on a book about Hollywood's vision of the Vietnam War. He has worked as a reporter, advertising copywriter and photographer, and corporate advertising supervisor and was co-owner of a communication research firm.

MICHAEL G. WESSELLS is Associate Professor of psychology and Assistant Dean of Academic Planning at Randolph-Macon College. He studied computers and culture on a Kellogg Fellowship from 1983–1986 and has taught numerous courses for faculty and students on social and ethical issues in the use of computers. He is the author of *Computer, Self and Society,* published by Prentice-Hall.

J. CAROL WILLIAMS was formerly Assistant Professor of Philosophy and Religious Studies at Virginia Commonwealth University. Her philosophical articles on perception and semantics have appeared in the *Southern Journal of Philosophy* and *Man and World.* She has also written several essays on aspects of death ranging from images of death in popular music to the rhetoric of the funeral industry. She is now an attorney practicing in Washington, D.C.

ELIZABETH WILLIAMSON is a freelance writer and an adjunct Instructor of English at Camden County Community College in Blackwood, New Jersey. She is married to an ad man and has two small sons who want to write jingles when they grow up.

DON B. WILMETH, Professor of Theatre and English at Brown University, administered the Program and then the Department of Theatre, Speech and Dance there for thirteen years until 1987. The author, editor, or co-editor of nine books,including the award-winning *George Frederick Cooke* (1980), his most recent projects have included co-editing *The Cambridge Guide to World Theatre* (1988), writing the text for *Mud Show: American Tent Circus Life* (1988), and compiling and editing documents for the period 1865–1915 for Cambridge University Press's series on theatre documents. He is advisory editor for four journals, was book review editor for *Theatre Journal,* and theater editor/columnist for the magazine *Usa Today.* In 1982 he was selected as a Guggenheim Fellow.

RICHARD GUY WILSON is Professor of Architectural History at the University of Virginia. His specialty is American and European architecture of the nineteenth and twentieth centuries. He has been the curator of a number of museum exhibitions and author of books and articles, among them *The American Renaissance, 1876–1917* (1979), *McKim, Mead and White Architects* (1983), *The AIA Gold Medal* (1984), *The Machine Age in America* (1986), as well as a contributor to *"The Art That Is Life" : The Arts and Crafts Movement in America* (1987).

Propaganda

RICHARD ALAN NELSON

However unclearly we perceive it, propaganda—especially when cloaked as education or information—influences our understanding of the world around us. Each one of us has been indoctrinated since childhood, and daily we continue to be bombarded with intrusive messages attempting to inform, manipulate, motivate, redirect, and even placate us.

Propaganda is worth studying for numerous reasons, if only because it so permeates American culture and institutions. Widespread technological diffusion and urbanization, prerequisites at the core of contemporary mass society, are essential components explaining the emergence of propaganda as an everyday factor in the American experience. The growth of propaganda in modern life has resulted largely from applied usage of certain inventive media developments over the last two centuries (including high-speed print, telegraphy, films, radio, television, and, more recently, satellites) which provided governments and private interests with an unprecedented mind manipulation arsenal useful in times of both war and peace.

The impact of propaganda seems self-evident today, although this has not always been the case. While public opinion was recognized as an important component of the American political experiment, most nineteenth-century political theorists felt that governing institutions reflected rather than directed popular attitudes. Struggles by Populist, muckraker, and other reform forces used media to bring about middle-class awareness and helped spur change. But the blatant manipulation of news and public opinion during World War I through persuasive campaigns by government and various special interests was a revelation to scholars, forcing an abandonment of prior theories about a benign public-private compact. Disillusioned by the distortion practiced by the warring powers for often inconsistent and changing war aims, they began applying critical perspectives to understand better those patterns shaping social influence.

Most propaganda research in the 1920s and 1930s was largely impressionistic, pacifistic, and aimed at educating a broad public about the continuing dangers presented by the persuasion industries. This revisionist line of inquiry, drawing upon rhetorical scholarship and progressive ideology, came to be known as "propaganda analysis." However, such research emphases presented a problem for those who sought to investigate propaganda more dispassionately. Gradually, influenced by the increasing precision of the social sciences, those in this competing school turned to statistical and experimental methodologies. Abandoning the term *propaganda analysis* entirely, they preferred to define themselves as empirical communication researchers. Over time this emphasis on quantifiable documentation has become the dominant paradigm or approach to research. As a result, contemporary studies of power groups and propaganda using qualitative historical-critical research tools tend to be written by Marxist, libertarian, and other ideologically motivated scholars still actively committed to social change.

Many people give little thought to their culture, assuming that most of life is just "there." We now know that propaganda plays a great role in shaping mass society's "psychic economy" as part of a broader "culture industry"—terms popularized by Marxist philosopher and art theoretician Theodor Wiesengrund-Adorno (1903–69). In fact there is a social, economic, and political context to the institutions and power relationships in a nation as diverse as the United States. Culture, particularly popular culture, is of importance in the study of propaganda since it reflects the indigenous nature of a people and incorporates the cumulative short-term and long-term residual influence of mass-mediated messages in the collective national consciousness.

In discussing ideology, thinkers such as Marx have also been correct in their observation that we are dominated by ideas that bear no accurate relationship to the reality we live. One reason is that in a "propaganda environment," opinion and belief are manipulated by social managers more interested in control than freedom. Where propaganda is widespread, cultural conditioning occurs so that the illusion of choice is maintained while truly independent thought is discouraged. The result is a channeling away from broadly participatory processes, what some have termed a cynical short-circuiting of critical thinking through subversion of political and economic discourse, into more predictable "rituals" where prepackaged commodities ranging from candidates to products are not so much chosen as rubber-stamped. Certainly, an objective observer is forced to conclude that we live at a time when propaganda—far from abating—is becoming an increasingly pervasive force in democratic as well as totalitarian states. For example, almost all governments maintain that they legitimately represent the will of the people. But this means that whether they be a capitalist democracy or a people's republic, their leaderships must devote vast resources to "engineering" and maintaining that consent.

Despite the continuing role played by commercial advertising and political propaganda in defining our national culture and institutions, Americans by and large bear a traditional antipathy toward the idea (if not the practice) of propaganda. The sobering thought that arises in preparing a topical reference guide such as this is that, notwithstanding an overwhelmingly negative literature condemning propaganda as inimical to freedom (an argument which itself is open to question, but which nevertheless represents a consensus of published opinion), very little has been done to control its spread. That the term continues to hold a strongly pejorative—even sinister—connotation is somewhat surprising since it was Americans who pioneered the implementation of attitudinal methodologies, mass-marketing strategies, and media technologies now considered essential to widespread persuasive communication.

What, then, constitutes propaganda? Unfortunately, there is no easy answer. Although we have progressed beyond the insular "us versus them" belief that propaganda is something only our enemies engage in (facetiously described as the other side's case put so convincingly as to be annoying!), a definition remains largely a matter of perspective. Writers on the topic regularly devote entire chapters to this one problem due to the imprecision of propaganda and related terms such as *ideology, persuasion,* and *rhetoric.* Propaganda has been interpreted variously to include such functions as advertising, public relations, publicity, political communication, special interest lobbying, radical agitation, psychological warfare, and even education. There is, however, general agreement that propaganda is a form of manipulative communication designed to elicit some predetermined response.

We can divide such persuasive communication into activities that require impersonal use of media as a way of linking sender to audience and those conducted interpersonally. Messages can also be conveniently separated into those that encourage us to buy a commercial product and those that seek to direct our belief structure and personality in a more fundamental way. While not all persuasive communication is equally embracive, pervasive, or effective in what the persuader asks us to think or do, nevertheless we can agree that propaganda is purposive. In many cases, the job of today's propagandist involves not so much changing minds as finding the right audience in order to reinforce and extend existing attitudes.

Some have seen propaganda as the organized spreading of special doctrines, beliefs, ideas, or information to promote or injure a nation, cause, or group. This is perhaps too generic, however. For purposes of this chapter, *propaganda is defined as the systematic attempt to influence the emotions, attitudes, opinions, and actions of specified target audiences for ideological, political, or commercial purposes through the controlled transmission of one-sided messages via mass and direct media channels.*

As we have seen, part of the confusion in terminology stems from the interdisciplinary nature and differing emphases of propaganda studies. Some authors argue that all propaganda is corrosive and a menace, whereas a minority state that propaganda is a neutral tool which can be put to either good or bad uses depending on the purpose of the source. A number of books have focused on the use of propaganda by governments in wartime; others choose a broad historical rather than case study approach. Another way of looking at propaganda favored by social scientists and linguists codifies and analyzes in "cookbook" form various motivational devices and techniques used by propagandists (such as the "glittering generality"). A fourth methodology often used by psychologically oriented communications researchers tests various hypotheses about attitude formation and behavioral change. These are loosely grouped under the banner of "persuasion" studies. Because we still lack clear theoretical bases for understanding the persuasive process, these conclusions (particularly those evaluating the effectiveness of propaganda) remain tentative and are not necessarily generalizable to mass groups. Despite scientific trappings, for example, we still cannot predict with absolute certainty that a particular campaign design will lead to the desired results in a target population.

HISTORIC OUTLINE

One can trace the origins of propaganda to remote antiquity. More than 2,500 years ago Chinese strategist Sun Tzu was writing in *The Art of War* about the military importance of manipulating information. Plato points out that the foundations of ancient democracy were connected with the emergence of professional communicators skilled in using language to move other people to action. The Greeks were among the first to see the need for selecting spokesmen to represent various interest groups in the community; they called a person who could effect one-to-many argumentation a *rhetor*. In the *Phaedrus* the famed philosopher defines the practice of rhetoric as "a universal art of winning the mind by arguments, which means not merely arguments in the courts of justice and all other sorts of public councils, but in private conference as well." Aristotle was Plato's pupil and, although they disagreed on some fundamental principles, Aristotle's *Rhetoric* even today remains a valuable guide to propaganda techniques despite the passage of more than two millennia.

By the Middle Ages, the introduction of the printing press in Europe and the spread of literacy were encouraging greater use of books and tracts designed to sway opinion. Much of this literature was religious, particularly by independent Protestants boldly attempting to get Biblical scriptures and doctrinal commentaries into the hands of the common people. This was perceived as a radical threat to royal governments and state religious unity, with many of the reformers sentenced to torture and death for their publishing activities. The term *propaganda* was first used widely by the Roman Catholic Church in 1622, with the founding of the Congregatio de propaganda fide (Congregation for the Propagation of Faith) during the Counter-Reformation.

Drawing on this European heritage, religionists coming to America during the prerevolutionary period became active publishers not only of biblical texts but also of literature extolling the virtues of the new land. In this endeavor they were joined by wealthy colonial trading companies, which issued a number of misleading promotional advertisements designed to encourage settlement of their commercial plantations. The political foundations for modern propaganda emerged late in the eighteenth century, when the idea of inalienable rights advanced during the Enlightenment found flower in the colonial republics. The use of printing technologies in America allowed for expression both supportive and critical of the Crown. The now famous "JOIN, or DIE" political cartoon by Benjamin Franklin appeared in a 1754 issue of the *Pennsylvania Gazette* urging the people of the colonies to unite in fighting the French and Indian War. Little more than twenty years later, the Declaration of Independence, penned by Thomas Jefferson, was widely distributed. This proved itself a masterful propaganda document not only by clearly expressing the philosophy of the Revolution in language that all colonists could understand, but also by justifying the American cause overseas and presaging the rise in importance of public opinion.

One should remember, however, that the American Revolution was not a spontaneous popular uprising. Contrary to myth, it was in reality the work of a small group of dedicated persuaders who created our first national propaganda and agitation campaign in order to overthrow a monarchical government. Even today the work of James Otis, Samuel Adams, Patrick Henry, Benjamin Franklin, and Thomas Paine (whose *Common Sense* in 1776 and *The American Crisis* in 1776–83 helped cement opposition to the Crown) continues to be studied by propaganda researchers. Among the techniques these radical pamphleteers inaugurated that are still utilized in contemporary ideological communication are (1) the realization that propaganda, to be effective, requires organization (the Sons of Liberty and Committees of Correspondence acted as conduits for revolutionary propaganda throughout the colonies); (2) the creation of the identifiable emotive symbols (the Liberty Tree) and slogans ("Don't tread on me" and "Taxation without representation is tyranny"), which simplify issues and arouse emotions; (3) the utilization of publicity and staged events (such as the Boston Tea Party) to attract media attention and enlist support of key cooperators (religious leaders whose sermons were widely published and distributed); (4) the exploitation of differences rather than emphasizing similarities of specified groups as well as mass audiences with monolithic reportage on a sustained and unrelenting basis through control of key organs of opinion (press, pamphlets, broadsides, even songs). The "Patriots" proved expert at publicizing their grievances first so as to establish the agenda for debate, while simultaneously discrediting their Loyalist opponents.

During the period of controversy surrounding adoption of the federal Constitution to replace the Articles of Confederation after the war, a series of newspaper articles now known collectively as *The Federalist Papers* (1787–88) were anonymously prepared by Alexander Hamilton, James Madison, and John Jay to sell Americans on the new government. These proved an effective instrument of propaganda among opinion leaders as well as a thoughtful political treatise of more lasting interest. The freedoms secured by the Constitution led to the development early in the nineteenth century of clearly defined political parties and special interest organizations which readily adopted propaganda techniques and technologies for their own purposes. Leading American propagandists of the early 1800s include Theodore Dwight, an effective spokesman for the Federalist cause, and Amos Kendall, who served as Andrew Jackson's chief advisor and later earned the title of "first presidential public relations man."

Fears of undue foreign influence in the new republic led to a series of "anti" campaigns (anti-Illuminati, anti-Mason, anti-Catholic, anti-Irish, anti-Jewish, anti-Mormon, and so on), which even today flourish sporadically. Early propaganda books, typified by Rebecca Reed's *Six Months in a Convent,* which first appeared in 1835, helped to focus hatred and were often underwritten by interests anxious to control immigrant blocs politically and keep their wages artificially low. The outstanding propaganda novel of the century was Harriet Beecher Stowe's powerful indictment of slavery, *Uncle Tom's Cabin* (1851), which sold an unprecedented 300,000 copies during its first year of publication and contributed significantly to the Abolitionist movement. Proslavery forces were also active in the period up through the Civil War, issuing tracts and lobbying for support in Congress. In this they were secretly aided by "manifest destiny" expansionists in the North, who flooded the country with literature designed to raise patriotic fervor for war with Mexico. In a real sense, words as much as bullets helped to win the West.

As sectional differences became more pronounced and a war between the states inevitable, leaders in both the North and South recognized the importance of propaganda to the struggle. Particularly in the north, where the war remained unpopular (there were draft riots in New York in 1863, and the so-called Copperhead movement fielded peace candidates as late as 1864), propaganda was utilized to mobilize public opinion both at home and abroad. Many of the trappings of contemporary journalism such as the press conference, press pass, and author by-line were instituted by military leaders in order to censor battle reportage unfavorable to the Union. Lincoln also personally dispatched up to one hundred special agents to Britain along with a boatload of foodstuffs for unemployed English cotton textile workers so as to counter propaganda gains made by the Confederacy. In the North, too, the art of pamphleteering was advanced by the unceasing efforts of private organizations such as the Loyal Publication Society and the Union League Board of Publications.

The full impact of industrialism and the importance of public opinion began to be felt by 1865. Public opinion, which was at first narrowly defined to include only educated white male landowners, gradually came to be extended to the middle and lower working classes (and later, in the twentieth century, to women and minorities, changes themselves brought about in part by propaganda). Groups such as the Fenian Brotherhood, a body of Irish patriots and exiles organized in 1857 to bring about Ireland's revolutionary independence from England, sought to mobilize sympathy in the United States by becoming more active in issuing propaganda following the Civil War. In the Fenians' case, they sought to energize anti-British sentiment by staging an invasion of Canada with 800–900 men in 1866, actually capturing Fort Erie in an uprising leaders hoped would inflame annexationist sentiment in the United States. Even though military success proved fleeting, the Brotherhood organization was not suppressed, and its propagandistic activities for some time contributed to Canadian-U.S. border tensions.

Growing urbanism was accompanied by sweeping improvements in communication, which extended the power of the press as a corridor into the minds of millions. In the era of yellow journalism (roughly 1890–1914) much of the news was, as it is today, artificial; that is, created and promoted by the news media, which reported the stories as bona fide events. Although the impact of the press as a propaganda organ dates back before the Revolution, by this period the chains of publications controlled by press barons such as William Randolph Hearst had unrivaled influence on American thought. His *New York Journal* is largely credited with exciting the United States to challenge Spain over Cuba in 1898. Besides quadrupling Hearst's circulation, the events leading up to the war also marked the first time motion pictures were utilized meaningfully for propagandistic purposes. Highly patriotic short films such as *Tearing Down the Spanish Flag!* (1898) electrified U.S. audiences when the hated European emblem was replaced by "Old Glory." The tremendous popular success of this picture (although it was actually shot on a rooftop in New York) spawned a host of imitators once actual hostilities broke out. Since cameramen were often prohibited from gaining access to authentic battleground footage because of military censorship, much of the visual "reportage," such as the series released under the title *The Campaign in Cuba* (1898), was surreptitiously filmed in the wilds of New Jersey. Screen propaganda already had shown flagrant disregard for truth, but this proved secondary to audiences who clamored for the lifelike images on the screen. This power of "actuality" and "documentary" freed propagandists for the first time from nearly complete reliance on publications and the printed word.

As the United States emerged to become a more important twentieth-century international political factor, European nations competing for continental leadership soon realized that the United States could play a pivotal role in the next war. As early as 1910, Germany began an active propaganda campaign to counteract pro-British biases in the leading organs of U.S. opinion. With the outbreak of hostilities in Europe, both Irish-American and German-American propagandists such as George Sylvester Viereck sought to combat the much more pervasive pro-intervention views spread by English agents working through a well-organized network of native sympathizers, press contacts, cultural exchanges, and business and banking ties. Overcoming isolationist impulses thanks to clumsy German diplomacy, American gullibility, and the huge investments made in United Kingdom war bonds by U.S. financial interests, the British view prevailed. The country was successfully maneuvered into collective hatred of all things German through widespread dissemination of maliciously false (but effective) "anti-Hun" atrocity stories and other propaganda.

Even though the United States was the last major power to enter the war, it ironically was the first belligerent to establish an open, fully coordinated propaganda unit, known as the Committee on Public Information (CPI). Headed by advertising executive George Creel, the CPI was given the commission to "sell the War to America." To do this, the CPI organized a national speakers' bureau of "four-minute men" who galvanized audiences with carefully timed short propaganda messages supporting Liberty Bond sales drives. Recognizing the power of the screen, the Creel Committee also arranged for cooperation between the private film industry (including newsreel companies) and the military. The poster also emerged at this time as an effective mass war medium, and individual governments flooded their nations with millions of propaganda posters designed to muster public support for total victory. Among the American artists who lent themselves to the war effort were Norman Rockwell, James Montgomery Flagg (whose "I Want You For U.S. Army" Uncle Sam recruiting poster is the best-known example from the period), and Charles Dana Gibson (creator of the "Gibson Girl"). Under CPI auspices alone, more than 100 million enthusiastically patriotic posters and other publications were distributed.

Although in the end much of the propaganda effort by Creel and his Allied counterparts proved (like Wilson's famous "Fourteen Points" as the basis for a just peace) more hyperbole than fact, World War I is important historically because it commemorates the inaugural deployment of contemporary mass propaganda. While the history of propaganda is indelibly linked to war, the seemingly interminable stalemate that marked most of the years of fighting propelled propaganda to the forefront as an important tool of government for sustaining homeland morale and maintaining ties of alliance. With the end of the war, however, Americans' desire to return to "normalcy" led to the quick disbanding of the CPI and a limiting of U.S. government propaganda efforts. On the other hand, during the 1920s and 1930s privately originated propaganda increased as numerous pressure groups formed in attempts to influence individual thought and actions as well as to affect government policies by harnessing mass opinion swelled by newly enfranchised women voters.

Later, when the social upheavals wrought by the Great Depression led to installation of an activist Democratic administration promising a "New Deal," official U.S. propaganda took off once more. The expansion of government powers and the introduction of new social security, public works, labor, housing, agricultural, military, and other policies required unparalleled peacetime publicity, with federal authorities committed to mobilizing a shared public consensus. Motion picture advertising (which had already been used for partisan political purposes) was extended, and the Roosevelt leadership further commissioned the filming of a number of documentary films with strong social messages. *The Plow that Broke the Plains* (1936) and *The River* (1937), for example, both pointed to the need for government intervention in conserving natural resources, and their success helped establish a federally controlled U.S. Film Service. Perhaps the most controversial of the early New Deal propaganda campaigns involved the National Recovery Administration (NRA). The totalitarian methods favored by NRA administrators, including enforced display of the blue NRA eagle emblem by "cooperating" businesses, were seen by many as a threat to American democratic principles. Partially on the basis of the propagandistic excesses of its supporters, the NRA was declared unconstitutional and nullified by the Supreme Court.

World propaganda had already entered a new phase with the successes of the Communists in Russia and the National Socialists in Germany. Attention to propaganda issues was further exacerbated by the uncertain economic climate of the period and increases in the West of ideological movements willing to utilize propaganda unhesitatingly for both internal and external distribution. As early as 1919–20, the United States had been engulfed in a "Red Scare," but despite this temporary setback Marxist propaganda continued to circulate with growing effectiveness among disenchanted American intellectuals and workers. The sheer amount of propaganda issued by the totalitarian states forced the leading democracies (notably Britain and the United States) to respond with a series of investigations and by upgrading their own intelligence and propaganda apparatuses. Much of the latter was again interventionist in nature, particularly after 1939 and the outbreak of World War II in Europe. Until Pearl Harbor, U.S. antiwar sentiment (epitomized by the America First Committee and the radio sermons of Catholic firebrand preacher Father Charles Edward Coughlin) openly competed against the line promoted by Anglophile organizations such as the Fight for Freedom Committee. Even as early as 1938, the United States was moving to shore up its position in Latin America by forming a Division of Cultural Relations in the Department of State which rigorously issued propaganda designed to portray the United States as an altruistic benefactor in a common struggle against possible foreign aggression. That same year Congress also passed the Foreign Agents Registration Act, specifying that individuals and organizations engaged in disseminating propaganda or related activities on behalf of another country must file public reports with the Justice Department's Criminal Division. While the act includes some exemptions for commercial, religious, academic, scientific, and artistic pursuits, it has tended to be used arbitrarily as a way of controlling domestic dissent and limiting access to print and visual political materials produced outside the United States.

With the coming of World War II, official American propaganda efforts were mostly directed by the Office of War Information (OWI), which was responsible for internal and external information. The Office of Strategic Services (OSS) conducted clandestine anti-Axis psychological warfare or so-called black propaganda programs as well as more conventional spy missions. Coordinating the European operations of the OWI and OSS for military needs was the Psychological Warfare Division at Allied Supreme Headquarters. There were marked differences between U.S. propaganda and that of the Axis powers, who generally proved more adept at utilizing the latest advances in technology until battlefield reverses curtailed their effectiveness. National Socialist magazines such as *Signal* were published in lavish color versions in all the major languages of Europe (including English). Similarly, well-produced German newsreels and documentaries were masterful propaganda devices screened widely not only in the Greater Reich and occupied Europe, but also in many neutral countries (among them the United States prior to 1942). Much of the enemy effort, however, relied heavily on radio. The sarcastic broadcasts of "Lord Haw Haw" (William Joyce) and "Axis Sally" from Germany, "Tokyo Rose" and "The Zero Hour" from Japan, and American expatriate poet Ezra Pound from Italy were listened to widely by U.S. servicemen. Apart from Allied counterbroadcasts, the Allies utilized a number of other propaganda methods—notably air-dropped leaflets. How effective these were in undermining enemy morale is still debated, but there is no doubt that internally the overall U.S. propaganda effort was successful.

On the home front, the major media willingly cooperated in the war effort. The Hollywood studios actively collaborated with federal authorities in grinding out hundreds of racist anti-Japanese and anti-German war epics. In the changed political climate after the war, some pro-Soviet films also made at this time were to prove more controversial. Numerous government agencies, including the Treasury Department, took to the airwaves with highly propagandistic patriotic radio programs such as "Treasury Star Parade" (1943–44) to sell war bonds and maintain enthusiasm for continuing the fight. Newspapers and newsreels, too, carried regular government-inspired reports and voluntarily censored potentially demoralizing news. Gigantic posters dominated factories and military shipyards to spur production, and even comic books and pulp literature were enlisted to put the country on a war footing unenvisioned even in the darkest and most regimented days of World War I.

With the defeat of fascist Italy, Germany, and Japan, U.S. propaganda took on a new direction. Largely because of the struggle with the Soviet Union for postwar dominance, much of the official propaganda issued by the United States since the mid-1940s has been directed at Eastern Europe and the emerging Third World states. The Voice of America, which transmits news, entertainment, and propaganda worldwide in dozens of languages, is a division of the United States Information Agency (USIA, briefly renamed the United States International Communication Agency during the Carter administration). The USIA also supervises the anti-Castro Radio Marti, maintains information offices and libraries in approximately sixty countries, and operates an extensive press and broadcast assistance service. Secret operations are usually the function of the Central Intelligence Agency (CIA), which for years helped to support the ostensibly private anticommunist Radio Free Europe and Radio Liberty broadcasts.

Many other government departments and divisions are responsible for information gathering and/or communication. Today the federal government, rather than any Madison Avenue firm or corporate entity, constitutes the single greatest "propaganda machine" in the United States. Despite cutback attempts in the Reagan presidency, specialists in an estimated forty-seven different federal agencies currently spend over $2.5 billion each year attempting to influence the way Americans think. The government, for example, is the nation's leading publisher and film producer, distributing thousands of magazines and books, hundreds of motion pictures and video cassettes, and countless press releases annually. The Treasury Department continues to underwrite production of special video episodes for internal government use, using some of Hollywood's top television series stars to promote purchases of Savings Bonds by federal employees. Taxpayers are also underwriting the military as one of the country's largest advertisers, whose messages urge young people to join up—not to preserve peace or ensure foreign policy objectives, but rather so recruits can "find a great place to start" to "be all you can be."

Earlier government intervention in the broadcast advertising marketplace helped to spur development of so-called public service announcements (PSAs) that continue to ask the public to support a variety of "approved" causes ranging from the innocuous to the controversial. Despite deregulatory elimination of many controversial communication restrictions, agencies such as the Federal Trade Commission and the Federal Communications Commission retain great powers over media and ancillary industries. Uncertainty exists about how far broadcast deregulation should go and whether electronic communicators should have the same First Amendment rights as their print counterparts. The convergence of communications and computer technologies as well as widespread group ownership of media properties in several fields is blurring the once clear distinction between print and broadcast, important legally as well as in popular culture terms. National newspapers such as the *Wall Street Journal* and *USA Today,* for example, now daily use satellites to get copies of their lithographed pages to printing plants across the country for localized editing and distribution. Should related technologies such as teletext and videotex (which use print on video screens) be regulated according to broadcast or print standards? Taking advantage of these uncertainties and the cutback in governmental controls, so-called hate groups have allegedly been more actively using electronic media in recent years. At the same time, one questionable impact of the FCC-authored "Fairness Doctrine" (which remained in effect until 1987 and may yet be reimposed) was to restrict discussions of major issues and limit the content of serious broadcast advertising (such as "advertorials" and "informationals." The experience in deciding such questions leaves open the possibility of greater (rather than less) government intervention in American media over the long term.

What of the future of propaganda in America? It is somewhat interesting to note that the elitist critics who most decry propaganda tend to view it as a direct form of indoctrination mindlessly swallowed by the mass audience. Implied is a personal superiority by virtue of their intellectual isolation from the naive propaganda consumer. This is a false and dangerously parochial dichotomy because wealthy intellectuals are just as susceptible to well-targeted propaganda as are the poor or ignorant. The naive assumptions voiced by some that federal controls and "rational education" would somehow neutralize "irrational propaganda" have not been borne out by experience, nor are they likely to be in coming years.

For numerous private groups operating nationally, the battle of propaganda is as much as anything a fight for access to political decision makers and the channels of mass dissemination. Political action committees, trade and education groups, foundations, and other organizations that must compete and lobby for support are often forced to rely on the techniques of propaganda if they are successfully to reach their own institutional goals. Increased use of direct mail and new technological breakthroughs may well open additional doors and opportunities for ideational propagandists, as well as those more interested in purely commercial advertising and public relations marketing efforts.

As we enter the 1990s, we can expect additional refinements in propaganda technique. Indeed, by the end of the century the previous work chronicled in this bibliographic essay may unfortunately seem like child's play. The relatively new concept of "narrowcasting" to highly specialized, homogeneous audiences will allow for cost-effective message placement to specific population subgroups on an unprecedented scale. Widespread private ownership of audio and video cassette players, for example, encouraged "Pat" Robertson to distribute free tapes (or "electronic campaign buttons") to targeted voting groups with his message unedited by network newscasters. The result: political professionals were surprised by the unexpected early caucus voter turnouts for Robertson in the 1988 Republican presidential nomination race.

Other new telecommunications technologies (including international direct satellite-to-home transmission and extension of optic two-way capacity) promise to redefine our informational environment dramatically in ways only dimly perceived. The revolution in information technology is making classical closed-door diplomacy less viable, as nations begin responding to internal challenges by counteracting propaganda from outsider groups and expanding their own initiatives directed at various "publics" in other countries. As United States Information Agency Director Charles Wick pointed out at a "Public Diplomacy in the Information Age" meeting in 1987, "Today the success or failure of foreign policy undertakings is frequently affected more profoundly by what people think and say than by the workings of judical diplomacy." Some recent examples include the the training of Afghan rebels to use minicams to document for Western newscasts the armed struggle during the 1980s against the Soviet occupation; improvements in broadcast technology that make it possible for American USIA satellite television as well as radio to reach around the world and cut through the Iron Curtain; the new, aggressive image campaign by Mikhail Gorbachev to undercut NATO and restructure the European and American political landscape by presenting a more open view of Soviet life and decision making; and the largely private distribution of cassette tapes, which can result in a revolution such as the one that brought Ayatollah Khomeini to power in Iran.

Like all powerful forces, propaganda must be understood and wisely used if an unintended disastrous backlash is to be avoided. For example, the possibilities for genetic alteration and cloning are expanding. Combined with the specter of controlled mind-altering drugs and gases, this, frighteningly, may lead some to seek a permanent redirection of society through media-supported biochemical means. As a neutral weaponry system, propaganda can be used either to support or to combat this horrific possibility. If uncertain economic and social conditions in the United States worsen, some no doubt will be tempted to embrace these developments to impose order through more totalitarian controls. So beware when the rights of various organizations to communicate—even organizations you dislike— are restricted "in the public interest," for this will mean that access to information is being interfered with, possibly prefiguring a drift toward an authoritarian dictatorship.

At the same time, propaganda is now such an indelible part of life that it may take on a less heinous stature as more individuals come to see that one-sided communication can be an essential component not only of free speech, but of civilization itself. Indeed, given the pluralistic nature of con- temporary society, some forms of propagandistic social engineering may be necessary if we hope to reach consensus on the many vital (but perhaps controversial) issues facing us. Raucous views are not so much the problem as not having the opportunity to publicly dispute them. The best antidote to abuse continues to be the absolutely free libertarian marketplace of ideas endorsed by America's Founding Fathers, who more than two centuries ago recognized that the common good is advanced most effectively when private individuals and organizations are allowed to compete openly in pursuing their own self-interests.

Just as in Shakespeare's day, we are still players living on a world stage. Unlike his plays, though, our scenario remains unfinished. Only one cer- tainly exists—we have entered an exciting new era for the propagandists, but a challenging and potentially haunting one for the rest of us.

REFERENCE WORKS

Given the divergent sources of propaganda, its literature is enormous. Relevant references run into the tens of thousands. Obviously, an intro- ductory guide cannot hope to provide more than a representative overview of the more important works and collections. The appended bibliography, however, lists a number of specialized studies cited in the text which are definitive for their topic or offer interesting insights on propaganda in Amer- ica. Included are selected books, doctoral dissertations, master's theses, and government documents, along with pertinent journals and magazine arti- cles.

Despite propaganda's long history and the large number of publications devoted to its analysis, serious study of the phenomenon has largely been limited to the last seventy years. Most pre-World War I reference works (including the venerable *Encyclopedia Britannica*) do not even mention the topic. However, the widespread utilization of propaganda in World War I and the extension of radical ideology in the 1920s led a number of thoughtful writers to reflect on the problems as well as the promises of propaganda.

The late political scientist Harold D. Lasswell may well be referred to as the father of propaganda study in the United States. His doctoral disser- tation, published as *Propaganda Technique in the World War* in 1927 (more recently reissued as *Propaganda Technique in World War I*), even led one critic to suggest that such "a Machiavellian textbook... should be destroyed." Lasswell's importance stems from the fact that he made a number of contributions toward the development of a comprehensive theoretical basis for analyzing propaganda. This book holds continuing interest because it provides an objective overview of the structure and strategies utilized by the propaganda services in the belligerent governments. Lasswell was one of the first to observe that the propagandist usually works within a specific culture in which strategies are circumscribed by the availability of media; the value norms of targeted audiences, which limit the variance of messages from current norms; and other pre-existing constraints that are not necessarily universal in character. He further notes that war, by extending beyond established frontiers, forces the military propagandist to adapt or fail. The new edition includes a valuable introduction by Lasswell and Jackson A. Giddens summarizing the field after fifty years of subsequent research. Unfortunately, the appended bibliography remains unannotated, and the index is inadequate.

Despite these shortcomings, a number of later studies issued during the revisionist period of the 1930s built upon Lasswell without substantially altering his conclusions. Today much of the work appears rather primitive. One glaring weakness of the pioneering propaganda scholars was their cursory treatment of the origin and historical development of propaganda in the United States. Even today, there are relatively few in-depth documentary analyses detailing the historicity of the propaganda phenomenon. Nevertheless, it was only after Lasswell's ground-breaking work that the first serious questions were raised and tentative answers proposed about the nature of attitude change and the effects of persuasive communications. Lasswell himself later turned to the problems of methodology in *World Revolutionary Propaganda* (1939, co-authored by Dorothy Blumenstock) and received support from the Rockefeller Foundation to develop a statistical method of content analysis. An outstanding overview essay describing the underlying reasons for his and others' significant shift away from propaganda to communication analysis is found in J. Michael Sproule's essay "Propaganda Studies in American Social Science."

Another useful jumping-off point is the three-volume *Propaganda and Communication in World History* series (1979–80), edited by Lasswell, Daniel Lerner, and Hans Speier. Volume 1, subtitled "The Symbolic Instrument in Early Times," covers the period before the emergence of America as a nation. However, Volume 2, subtitled "The Emergence of Public Opinion in the West," includes nineteen essays (many original to the work) that begin with the invention of the printing press and trace the development of mass communication and symbol management to the present day. Volume 3 features fourteen chapters on "A Pluralizing World in Formation" which analyze contemporary marketing, advertising, public relations, and media planning from a social science perspective. Lasswell concludes this last volume with a prophetic look at the future of world communication and propaganda, written shortly before his death in 1978. Each volume has its own introduction, a comprehensive index, and brief biographies of contributors. But while virtually a who's who forum for leading political and communication scholars, these compendiums suffer from the weaknesses common to all anthologies by not being a true encyclopedia of propaganda—a work sorely needed despite the welcome new addition to the literature of *The International Encyclopedia of Communications,* edited by Erik Barnouw.

The Fine Art of Propaganda: A Study of Father Coughlin's Speeches, edited by Alfred McClung Lee and Elizabeth Briant Lee, remains one of the most significant books on propaganda ever published. First issued in 1939 and now available in several reprint editions, the work cuts across several fields. Although only 140 pages, the book's influence stems from its clear organizational analysis and labeling of the seven chief devices utilized by professional propagandists (such as "name calling" and "band wagon"). Updating this seminal study, Alfred McClung Lee in 1952 published the probing *How to Understand Propaganda.* Rather than taking a communication-oriented approach, Lee describes how we are all consumers of propaganda. Using numerous illustrations taken from the popular press, he writes that the only way to combat propaganda is to recognize it. Although Lee typically sees propaganda as an often debilitating force assaulting individual free will, he nevertheless points out that propaganda is also used to achieve a variety of desirable socioeconomic and political ends. A similar emphasis is found in *The Analysis of Propaganda* by William Hummel and Keith Huntress. After offering a general introduction and describing how propaganda can be detected in everyday life, the authors provide a justification for its further study. A rather eclectic reader, ranging from writings by Benjamin Franklin to those of John Steinbeck, is appended. Unfortunately, there is no bibliography, and the book is disappointing when contrasted to the publications by Alfred and Elizabeth Lee.

The leading theoretical analyses of propaganda today are Terence H. Qualter's *Opinion Control in the Democracies* (1985) and Jacques Ellul's *Propaganda: The Formation of Men's Attitudes,* published twenty years earlier. Both challenge many traditional notions (that education is the antidote to propaganda, that there are significant differences between so-called democratic and totalitarian propagandas, that the principal purpose of propaganda is to change belief rather than reinforce existing attitudes or motivate people to action) and provide a theoretical base from which to examine it as an important social force. In particular, the brilliant French theorist presents a convincing case for the corrosive effect of propaganda despite its necessity. After an introductory review of major trends in propaganda analysis, Ellul describes the primary characteristics and categories of propaganda as he sees them, discusses the underlying conditions that contribute to the widespread existence of propaganda, analyzes the necessity of propaganda for individuals and states, and reviews the results of propaganda. Two appendixes probe the effectiveness and limits of propaganda and dissect the brainwashing techniques used in Mao's China. Included are a bibliography and index. No illustrations and a lack of statistical data are the major weaknesses of the work (he argues that small-group experiments are unnecessary if we are to understand the psychology of propaganda), but clearly Ellul— like Qualter—is obligatory reading. In an interesting attempt at making this more relevant for Americans, Robert W. Raspberry's *The "Technique" of Political Lying* applies Ellul's propaganda theories, using the Watergate incident as its primary case study.

For those looking for a solid one-stop guide to the entire field, a major book has appeared: Garth S. Jowett and Victoria O'Donnell's *Propaganda and Persuasion.* Their work fills an important void in the literature. The authors' attempt to distinguish between persuasion and propaganda is useful but bound to be somewhat controversial, since others use the terms almost interchangeably. Although arguing that Ellul's views about propaganda's pervasiveness are too inclusive, Jowett and O'Donnell are also forced to be somewhat expansive in labeling the subtleties of social influence that propaganda incorporates. Aside from these criticisms and a few minor factual errors (for example, Charles I rather than James II was beheaded after being deposed, p. 51), this is a major contribution that will certainly help stimulate a revival of propaganda studies. Indeed, *Propaganda and Persuasion* is ideally suited as a primer to the subject and should be the starting text of choice for most classes on the subject. The authors present an overview of the history of propaganda, a review of the social scientific research on its effects, and an examination of its applications. Early chapters offer an original, systematic analysis and evaluation of propaganda from a communication perspective. This is followed by five detailed case studies of propaganda in modern times: the banning of cigarette advertising on radio and television, religious evangelism on television (which needs updating in a second edition because of recent developments), the *Pueblo* incident, the controversy over legalized abortion, and South African activities in the United States. The model and accompanying narrative describing the process and social-historical context for propaganda is very well done. A useful bibliography, index, and illustrations are appended.

Oliver Thomson's *Mass Persuasion in History: A Historical Analysis of the Development of Propaganda Techniques* is another compact primer valuable for beginning students because of its brevity. After a thoughtful introduction to the problems of historical analysis, Thomson divides propaganda into seven main categories ranked according to the objectives of the propagandist (political, economic, war/military, diplomatic, didactic, ideological, and escapist aimed at achieving social acquiescence). He treats message construction in terms of style, structure, and theme, then follows it with a pragmatic review of propagandistic philosophy and methodologies used for determining effectiveness. Also useful, given the transient nature and un-availability of much propaganda product, is a photographic section illustrating appended historical case studies ranging from the Roman Empire through the mobilization propaganda of the Western democracies. The work is faulted, though, by the limited bibliography and index.

Unfortunately, the more detailed *3000 Jahre Politische Propaganda* (3000 Years of Political Propaganda) by Alfred Sturminger remains untranslated. Although this profusely illustrated work concentrates on the history of propaganda in Europe, it is useful for its inclusion of such media as postage stamps and cancellations as propaganda tools. Besides art, another interesting section traces pro- and anti-religious propaganda. Standard bibliographic data and indexing facilitate the book's use.

The title of Frederick E. Lumley's *The Propaganda Menace* adequately describes his attitude to the practice. Unlike others, who typically lament the barrage of distortion while neglecting historical precedent, Lumley devotes considerable space to the prior development of propaganda. Considering that he wrote over fifty years ago, the book holds up well and reflects credibly on his scholarship. One of its valuable attributes is the division into specific topic areas. In addition to the obligatory "Propaganda and War" section, later chapters discuss politics, race, education, and religion as forums for persuasive communication. His fear that then-current trends would make propaganda an increasingly powerful factor in society has been borne out. Lumley's somewhat depressing conclusion that the only antidote for propaganda is the ability to think straight seems as true as ever. One oversight is that no illustrations or photographs are used.

Following closely in Lumley's tradition is Michael Choukas's *Propaganda Comes of Age*. Choukas, who holds a doctoral degree from Columbia University, writes with some authority since he served in the propaganda arm of the OSS during World War II. In tracing the evolution of the vast domestic propaganda network in this country, he argues that, because of its deliberately manipulative nature, propaganda is not an informational tool. Rather, says Choukas, propaganda and democracy are at odds, and without strong controls on advertising, lobbying, and so forth the country faces a totalitarian future. Nevertheless, he approves of propaganda directed at foreign audiences in pursuit of governmental policies. The book is enhanced by numerous cartoons, advertisements, leaflets, and so on, but these are not always keyed directly to the text. A serious deficiency is the lack of an index or bibliography.

Despite a rather sensational title, Robert Sobel's *The Manipulators: America in the Media Age* is a serious—if flawed—look at the development of U.S. communications. Writing from a passionate fear that the media are contributing to national instability by the blurring of fact and fiction, Sobel has compiled a big book (458 pages) that documents the emergence of America's newspapers, the role of the university as a training ground for the journalistic elite, the wartime propaganda blitz of the Committee on Public Information, the anti-Axis co-optation of the motion picture industry, and the rise of television and other new technologies as a force in contemporary society. More than simply a history, Sobel raises important questions about the future of our propagandistic culture. The value of this work as a scholarly reference, however, is undermined by the inclusion of numerous careless factual errors which work to negate the credibility of Sobel's argumentation.

Also of interest is Barry Marks's doctoral dissertation, "The Idea of Propaganda in America" (1957), which traces the origin of the concept of propaganda as a malevolent new social force after World War I, analyzes the "marriage" of propaganda and anti-intellectualism as a challenge to democracy, and treats the influence of propagandistic impact in American progressive education. Marks's study certainly deserves a wider audience.

Two books sharing the same title, *Public Opinion and Propaganda,* by Frederick C. Irion and Leonard W. Doob, respectively, were both geared to the college market, but given the dramatic changes in media statistics and sociological perspectives have become rather dated. Irion also lacks a bibliography. Each, however, has some historic interest because of the wealth of detail included; thus they are recommended for overviews of the field up to the date of their publication. Doob, particularly, has been an important figure in U.S. propaganda studies since the publication of his *Propaganda: Its Psychology and Technique.* Less useful for the specialist is *Propaganda Handbook* by D. Lincoln Harter and John Sullivan. The book reflects the Cold War period in which it appeared and, despite the embracive title, is rather simplistic. Largely based on secondary sources, its major strength is in synthesis of more original work.

Among the first to catalog the growing literature systematically were Kimball Young and Raymond D. Lawrence, whose annotated *Bibliography on Censorship and Propaganda,* issued serially in 1928, is still useful for early newspaper and magazine citations dating from the nineteenth century not usually found in later compendiums.

Expanding upon this pioneering work were Harold D. Lasswell, Ralph D. Casey, and Bruce L. Smith, whose *Propaganda and Promotional Activities: An Annotated Bibliography* quickly became a standard reference upon publication in 1935 and remains an indispensable guide to the seminal literature. A 1969 reissue includes a new introduction by Lasswell summarizing his thoughts after nearly forty years of propaganda study. Lasswell (whose communication formula "who says what, in which channel, to whom, with what effect?" remains the basic starting point for most empirical studies) notes that despite scientific advances we are still without a comprehensive theory that can accurately explain as well as analyze human behavior—including the interplay of propaganda. Originally prepared for the Social Science Research Council, the bibliography has seven divisions. Theories of propaganda management are discussed in a thirty-five-page section, which is followed by references to the propagandas of governments, international agencies, political parties, and other organizations classified by type (business, labor, professional, and so on). Later sections classify propaganda according to the response sought, the symbols manipulated, and the channels used. Also listed are early measurement studies and references that describe the impact of propaganda and censorship on modern society. An author-subject index is appended, helping to compensate for the somewhat loose topical categorization.

The same authors (but with Bruce L. Smith listed first) updated this in 1946 with *Propaganda, Communication, and Public Opinion: A Comprehensive Reference Guide,* which includes four essays on the science of mass communication and within a similar organizational framework provides an excellent selectively annotated bibliography of 2,558 books and articles published for the most part between 1934 and 1943. Bruce L. Smith has additionally co-authored with Chitra M. Smith the supplemental *International Communication and Political Opinion: A Guide to the Literature.* This features another 2,500 entries (among them government documents and unpublished studies) released between 1943 and 1955. Stress is placed on the international and political aspects of propaganda. Both of the above works include author and subject indexes.

Reference should also be made to Harwood L. Childs, *A Reference Guide to the Study of Public Opinion* (1934), which is organized topically and continues to hold interest despite the lack of annotations, and to the brief *List of Bibliographies on Propaganda* prepared for publication by the U.S. Library of Congress in 1940. Warren C. Price's *The Literature of Journalism: An Annotated Bibliography* includes a short section devoted specifically to selected books and articles on "public opinion, propaganda, and public relations" (177 citations). Again, a subject-author index provides cross-references. Price supplements this volume with *An Annotated Journalism Bibliography: 1958–1968,* co-authored with Calder M. Pickett. This work has 2,172 listings (most not related specifically to propaganda) organized alphabetically by author rather than subject. To compensate for this stylistic change, the index has been expanded to fifty pages.

Of more direct relevance are Scott M. Cutlip's *A Public Relations Bibliography to 1965,* with 6,000 entries organized topically; Robert L. Bishop's *Public Relations: A Comprehensive Bibliography—Articles and Books on Public Relations, Communication Theory, Public Opinion, and Propaganda, 1964–1972,* which follows Cutlip with another 4,500 subject-divided citations; and the subsequent annual updates by Bishop and Albert Walker that appear in special issues of *Public Relations Review.* Even though more than 300 periodical and other sources were searched in compiling the Cutlip-Bishop-Walker bibliographies, there are, unfortunately, still numerous omissions. The more recent Walker-prepared guides, for example, appear far less comprehensive, particularly in the area of government and think-tank reports. Each follows a similar format, indexing author names and government agencies as well as listing occasional names of companies and countries.

Researchers interested in government publications on the topic of propaganda should not overlook George D. Brightbill's *Communications and the United States Congress: A Selectively Annotated Bibliography of Committee Hearings, 1870–1976*, which provides chronologically arranged guidance to some 1,100 titles issued by the House and Senate. Material on censorship is included, although publishing references are not. This work is further limited because documents, reports, and committee prints are also excluded. William W. Buchanan and Edna A. Kanely, *Cumulative Subject Index to the Monthly Catalog of United States Government Publications 1900–1971*, published by Carrollton Press, is invaluable for wading through the wealth of available material. Neglected by many researchers has been another Carrollton service called the "Declassified Documents Reference System." The basic collection includes 16,000 official documents made available through the Freedom of Information Act. These are summarized, indexed, photo-duplicated on microfilm, and supplied to subscribing research libraries with annual updates (1976 to the present). The importance of the system is that it includes sensitive material previously unavailable to the public, taken directly from the files of the CIA, the FBI, and other government agencies.

A very different orientation is found in *Marxism and the Mass Media: Towards a Basic Bibliography*, issued intermittently by the International Mass Media Research Center (1972 to present) as part of an ongoing periodical series whose purpose is to compile a global, multilingual, annotated bibliography of left studies on all aspects of communication (including propaganda). As a result this reference journal covers ground often overlooked by others. Affiliated researchers to the center have additionally prepared *Marxist Readings: A Bibliography of over 4,000 Books, Pamphlets, and Reprints in English, German and Italian—Volume 1*, a source worth reviewing. Also of considerable reference value is Thomas F. Gordon and Mary Ellen Verna's *Mass Communication Effects and Processes: A Comprehensive Bibliography, 1950–1975*. The bibliography, although not annotated, has a useful narrative introduction to the literature and features over 2,700 citations arranged alphabetically by author. The subject index is detailed, and there is an unusual index of secondary authors which allows the user to find specific citations.

On political propaganda, see *Political Campaign Communications: A Bibliography and Guide to the Literature* (1974) by Lynda Lee Kaid, Keith R. Sanders, and Robert O. Hirsch, the first comprehensive summarization of the literature in this specialized area. Included is an annotated introduction to the fifty most important reference books plus an unannotated supplemental listing of hundreds of relevant periodical citations, updated in 1985 and 1986 by two followup books. Dan Nimmo (whose earlier *The Political*

Persuaders: The Techniques of Modern Election Campaigns is still required reading for understanding the importance of image over issue in determining most electoral outcomes) has also recently published a helpful analysis entitled *Political Communication and Public Opinion in America.* This latter work presents a useful summary of available knowledge with comments on the general area of political communication as well as the roles played by expert communicators, the language and symbols manipulated, persuasion (including propaganda, advertising, and rhetoric), media channels, and other contemporary pragmatic approaches to influencing voter behavior.

In *Information Sources in Advertising History* (1979), edited by Richard W. Pollay, four essays assess the literature and discuss sources, but the book's centerpiece is an annotated bibliography of 1,600 titles arranged by subject, with strength in literature prior to 1940. Although "propaganda" as such is not one of the topics, related areas such as the psychology and sociology of advertising, marketing, public relations, and broadcasting are covered. Two directories list professional associations and describe special collections and archival holdings.

General overviews of the history and literature of propaganda (often prepared by leading authorities) can be found in most encyclopedias. Among the more complete and analytical are those of Harwood L. Childs in *Collier's Encyclopedia,* W. E. Barber in *Dictionary of American History,* Jackson Giddens in *Encyclopedia Americana,* Harold D. Lasswell in *Encyclopaedia Britannica* and the classic first edition of the *Encyclopaedia of the Social Sciences* found in most good reference libraries, Bruce L. Smith in *The New Encyclopaedia Britannica* and the *International Encyclopedia of the Social Sciences,* and Horst Reimann in *Marxism, Communism and Western Society: A Comparative Encyclopedia.*

Researchers interested in the more recent serious periodical literature should also consult the basic volume and yearly updates entitled *Public Opinion, Mass Behavior and Political Psychology* issued as part of the Political Science, Government, and Public Policy series published since 1967. Through use of a computerized keyword system, literally thousands of citations appearing in social and behavioral science literature are cataloged under the heading "Edu/Prop . . . Education, Propaganda, Persuasion." This is well worth reviewing.

Standard business indexes list media/business topics. Recent publications can also be searched using keywords and the unique cross-referenced citation listings of *Social Sciences Citation Index,* and the *Arts and Humanities Citation Index,* supplemented by up-to-date title page reprints in *Current Contents/ Social and Behavioral Sciences* and *Current Contents/Arts and Humanities.* Other reference guides regularly summarizing current propaganda writing include *America: History and Life, Communication Abstracts, Historical Abstracts, International Political Science Abstracts, Sociological Abstracts,* and *Topicator* (for advertising).

The *Insider Newsletter*, published by the Heritage Foundation, is a particularly useful free monthly summary of recent conservative and libertarian
publications, conferences, and legal cases. In contrast, the slicker magazine-
format *Propaganda Review*, produced by the Media Alliance (a San Francisco–
based collective of left-oriented media professionals), serves as an interesting
forum for critiques of the pervasive "propaganda environment." Writers
cover topics ranging from public relations/advertising campaigns to disinformation activities by intelligence agencies. This replaces an earlier tab-
loid predecessor, *Propaganda Analysis Review* (1985–87).

Communication Booknotes, published monthly by policy academic Christopher Sterling at George Washington University, is another effective and
timely source; in addition to thoughtful commentary on new publications,
it devotes one issue per year to federally issued literature (including reports
by propaganda agencies such as the USIA). See also selected articles and
the review sections of journals such as *Critical Studies in Mass Communication,
Historical Journal of Film, Radio and Television, Journal of Broadcasting and
Electronic Media, Journal of Communication, Journalism Quarterly, Political Communication and Persuasion: An International Journal, Public Affairs Review*, and
Quarterly Review of Doublespeak.

Countless articles, monographs, and books have also appeared under
the catch-all heading "persuasion research." This, like public opinion,
often involves surveys and experimental control studies reported in psychology, sociology, political science, and communications journals. One
distinction made is that, although all propaganda attempts to persuade,
not all persuasion is propaganda. As a result, much of this material is directed to an empirical audience and is thus far removed from the popular
culture literature. (Major exceptions include Vance Packard's popularized
The Hidden Persuaders, first published in 1957, and Wilson Bryant Key's
pseudoscientific *The Subliminal Seduction: Ad Media's Manipulation of a
Not So Innocent America.*) The student of propaganda in America, however, should at least be aware that this body of research writing exists
and may want to cross-reference it with a review of the broader rhetorical and ideological literature which can be given here no more than cursory discussion.

Useful in distinguishing between persuasion, propaganda, debate, brain-
washing, and coercion is the introductory chapter in Austin J. Freeley,
Argumentation and Debate: Critical Thinking for Reasoned Decision Making.
Although not as structurally integrated as one would hope, *Introduction to
Rhetorical Theory* by Gerard A. Hauser does provide a rather useful compilation summarizing the literature of rhetorical theory. On the other hand,
Richard M. Weaver's *The Ethics of Rhetoric* is a classical study that insists
that analyzing rhetoric can reveal the degree to which a person's or organization's use of language expresses or betrays their underlying values. "The
use of language is, in short, an ethical undertaking, bearing with it high

obligations to the true and the good." *Iconology: Image, Text, Ideology* by W.J.T. Mitchell argues that distinctions between images and words reflect ideological values and interests of a culture rather than any naturally based differences. The book then critiques the question of ideology itself. This is heavy reading, not for the beginner without solid grounding in philosophy. Similarly, *The Concept of Ideology and Political Analysis: A Critical Examination of Its Usage by Marx, Lenin, and Mannheim,* authored by Walter Carlsnaes, tries to come to grips with the widely used but imprecise term *ideology.* This unenviable task is complicated by the almost endless variety of meanings applied by those writing about the topic, particularly in the literature of the left.

Fortunately, there are several guides to help the neophyte interested in bridging these gaps for a fuller discussion of the literature dealing specifically with persuasion. Two useful critical introductions are "Persuasion" by Gerald R. Miller and "Persuasion Research: Review and Commentary" by Miller and Michael Burgoon, which complement "Persuasion, Resistance, and Attitude Change" by William J. McGuire.

Among the more widely circulated general works, all of which provide an overview of this specialized field, are Erwin P. Bettinghaus and Michael J. Cody, *Persuasive Communication;* Winston Brembeck and William Howell, *Persuasion: A Means of Social Influence;* Gary Cronkhite, *Persuasion: Speech and Behavioral Change,* which has a particularly thoughtful analysis; George N. Gordon, *Persuasion: The Theory and Practice of Manipulative Communication;* Carl Hovland and others, *Communication and Persuasion;* Marvin Karlins and Herbert Abelson, *Persuasion: How Opinions and Attitudes Are Changed;* Andrew King, *Power and Communication;* Charles U. Larson, *Persuasion: Reception and Responsibility;* Wayne Minnick, *The Art of Persuasion;* Michael Roloff and Gerald R. Miller, editors, *Persuasion: New Directions in Theory and Research;* Herbert W. Simons, *Persuasion: Understanding, Practice and Analysis;* Mary John Smith, *Persuasion and Human Action: A Review and Critique of Social Influence Theories;* Wayne N. Thompson, *The Process of Persuasion: Principles and Readings;* and Philip Zimbardo, Ebbe B. Ebbeson, and Christina Maslach, *Influencing Attitudes and Changing Behavior.* Gary C. Woodward and Robert E. Denton, Jr.'s *Persuasion and Influence in American Life* is a recent comprehensive text describing the processes that apply both for constructing and analyzing persuasive messages used by businesses, politicians, and others.

Among the newer persuasion periodicals that should be referenced are *Human Communication Research* and *Social Science Monitor.* The latter, which is aimed at public relations and advertising executives, summarizes findings from behavioral science journals that have implications for the pragmatist interested in "getting the right information into the right minds." Hugh Rank's *The Pitch* evaluates the typical five-part strategy used by most advertisers to get attention, build confidence, stimulate desire, press urgency, and seek an action response. Later, in *The Pep Talk*, he similarly reviews the common patterns of political persuasion. Both are worthwhile attempts to create a contemporary pedagogy of propaganda analysis, using numerous illustrations to reinforce understanding of the often non-rational structures utilized in such persuasive messages. Also of relevance is Steuart Henderson Britt's *Psychological Principles of Marketing and Consumer Behavior*, which collates a wealth of data. Now must reading for the contemporary propagandist, his book is organized to describe both what happens in the psyche of a person exposed to directed communication and how the mass of available empirical data can be more effectively applied in persuasive campaigns.

Anthologies and Reprints

Thirty-one of the most important books issued originally between 1920 and 1962 have now been made available in an International Propaganda and Communications collection by Arno Press. Included are a number of seminal studies cited elsewhere in this book. Greenwood Press also has reprinted a variety of titles on mass persuasion covering the fields of public opinion, advertising, and psychology. A particular service is making Gallup poll data from 1935 on conveniently available. In addition, publication has begun on a one-volume annual, *Index to International Public Opinion,* edited by Elizabeth and Philip Hastings, with comprehensive worldwide coverage of polling data issued by more than fifty leading research organizations.

Despite earlier citations of several excellent reference anthologies, no definitive collation of propaganda essays exists. Given the breadth of the literature, such a work is probably impossible. Among the first to study the relationship of pressure groups and propaganda was Harwood Childs, who assembled a series of topical papers by twenty-eight leading authorities and students for a special issue of the *Annals* of the American Academy of Political and Social Sciences in May 1935. Much of this was previously unpublished and, although somewhat dated, continues to have historical and theoretical interest. By the 1950s, as a result of the propaganda onslaught in World War II and the beginnings of the Cold War, a number of readers began to appear. These include *Propaganda in War and Crisis: Materials for American Foreign Policy,* edited by Daniel Lerner, *America's Weapons of Psychological Warfare,* edited by R. E. Summers, and *Political Opinion and Propaganda: A Book of Readings,* edited by Daniel Katz and other noted researchers for the Society for the Psychological Study of Social Issues.

Most such books are geared to the needs of undergraduates, offering a rather eclectic review of public opinion and propaganda as a social science discipline. Updating these with more recent material are massive works such as *Reader in Public Opinion and Communication,* edited by Bernard Berelson and Morris Janowitz, and *Voice of the People: Readings in Public Opinion and Propaganda* by Reo M. Christenson and Robert O. McWilliams. For the less academic, *Language in Uniform: A Reader on Propaganda,* edited by Nick Aaron Ford, and *Propaganda, Polls, and Public Opinion: Are the People Manipulated?,* compiled by Malcolm Mitchell, provide a more directed and simplified introduction.

Teaching About Doublespeak is a useful primer prepared for classroom use by Daniel Dietrich. Published by the National Council of Teachers of English, it includes a number of readings designed to make students more informed about their daily intake of propaganda (including advertising). A useful sixteen-page bibliography is appended. Note should also be made of the collection of articles "On Propaganda" in the Summer 1979 issue of *ETC.: A Review of General Semantics.* Authors include Jacques Ellul on "The Role of Persuasion in a Technical Society," Thomas Steinfatt on "Evaluating Approaches to Propaganda Analysis," Elizabeth Briant Lee and Alfred McClung Lee on "The Fine Art of Propaganda Analysis—Then and Now," and others. Journals such as *Public Opinion Quarterly* also occasionally devote entire issues to the subject of propaganda (some earlier *POQ* compilations are included in the Arno Press collection cited above). For more on available advertising reprints, see the chapter on "Advertising" elsewhere in this *Handbook.*

HISTORY AND CRITICISM

Since numerous studies exist covering specialized topical areas and historical periods, subdivisions have been included in this section to enable readers to identify more easily what is most useful for their particular research interests.

Revolutionary War Period

The American Revolution was a conflict of political ideals in which both warring sides were convinced of the rightness of their cause. Conveniently available in reprint is *A Short Narrative of the Horrid Massacre in Boston,* first prepared in 1770 by a partisan committee chaired by James Bowdoin. Featured are eyewitness interviews of ninety-six military men, citizens, and others who testified about their experiences on that fateful day when a group of frightened British soldiers opened fire on a threatening crowd of demonstrators, killing or wounding eleven. Perhaps overemphasized is the impact of actions taken in cities such as Boston on the rest of the colonies, a fault remedied by Robert W. Smith in his unpublished thesis "What Came After?: News Diffusion and the Significance of the Boston Massacre in Six American Colonies, 1770–1775." Smith traces the media coverage of the "massacre" and concludes that the Patriotic view of the British army as a major threat to liberty had meaning only for Massachusetts and was relatively unimportant in terms of its propaganda value outside the Bay Colony.

Philip Davidson's *Propaganda and the American Revolution, 1763–1783* remains the standard history of American propaganda before and during the Revolution. Included are sections on Whig and Patriotic propaganda, as well as the efforts of the Tory-Loyalist counterattack. Although the topical arrangement at times results in some repetition, Davidson's careful scholarship not only forms a solid contribution to the study of the early American experience but also points to the many similarities to be found within all modern revolutionary movements. Challenging many supposed facts about U.S. history (since much of what we "know" about the Revolution has derived from the propaganda of that era), the author stresses the importance of ideas in deciding the conflict of arms.

Supplementing Davidson, by concentrating more directly on the actual war years, is the revised edition of *Broadsides & Bayonets: The Propaganda War of the American Revolution* by Carl Berger. Unlike most studies, which focus primarily on pamphlets and newspapers, Berger explores other efforts involving "secret arts and machinations" to influence the course of the war. Particularly interesting are the chapters entitled "American Propaganda and the Struggle for Canada," "The Campaign to Win the Indians' Allegiance," "The Incitement of Negro Insurrection," and "Overseas Propaganda." The notes and bibliography are useful as well. Readers interested in a related aspect of the revolutionary struggle should also refer to "Lafayette as a Tool of American Propaganda," a neglected doctoral study completed by Marguerite Bloxom in 1970.

Useful guides to available original propaganda publications of the pre-Constitutional period include Charles F. Heartman, compiler, *The Cradle of the United States, 1765–1789: Five Hundred Contemporary Broadsides, Pamphlets, and a Few Books Pertaining to the History of the Stamp Act, the Boston Massacre and Other Pre-Revolutionary Troubles, the War for Independence and the Adoption of the Federal Constitution;* Ruth Lampham, compiler, *Check List of American Revolutionary War Pamphlets in the Newberry Library;* and the unattributed *Manuscripts of the American Revolution in the Boston Public Library: A Descriptive Catalog.* Heartman had one of the finest collections of its type, alphabetically listing each item "bibliographically, historically and sometimes sentimentally" with an index to materials issued anonymously. Lampham similarly describes 754 tracts issued by American and British sources between 1750 and 1786, including a specific section devoted to revolutionary propaganda held by the Chicago research facility. The Boston collection has the advantage of being larger because of the more recent date of collation but otherwise differs little from its predecessors. Useful insights and references to contemporary materials are also found in Bernard Bailyn's *Ideological Origins of the American Revolution,* which complements his earlier *Pamphlets of the American Revolution, 1750–1776.* The latter reprints original texts selected on the basis of representativeness, contemporary fame, originality of thought, literary distinction, and/or importance of the author.

Of the American propagandists, Samuel Adams and Thomas Paine have been written about the most. John C. Miller's *Sam Adams: Pioneer in Propaganda* supersedes Ralph Volney Harlow's *Samuel Adams, Promoter of the American Revolution: A Study in Psychology and Politics* as the standard biographical reference for Adams's propagandistic career. Miller draws a picture of the "father of the American Revolution" that is not entirely flattering. The omission of an introduction (which would have been useful in appraising Adams's significance) and a bibliography weakens an otherwise fine book. The later edition does add a brief one-page bibliography of works appearing after 1941, but for details one must struggle through the footnotes. While Harlow takes an intriguing Freudian approach in interpreting Adams's motivations and psyche, he tends at times to be inaccurate in detail and biased in his use of supporting evidence. Among early works, *The Life and Public Services of Samuel Adams* by great-grandson William Vincent Wells is of interest. Published in three volumes in 1865, the biography is naturally laudatory but nonetheless demonstrates careful and thorough attention to research as well as a wealth of fascinating minutiae. Of the newer studies, see John R. Galvin, *Three Men of Boston,* which focuses on the interrelationship among Adams, James Otis, and Governor Thomas Hutchinson; Stewart Beach, *Samuel Adams: The Fateful Years, 1764–1776;* and Cass Canfield, *Sam Adams' Revolution (1765–1776),* published in the Bicentennial. While Galvin offers an excellent interpretive account, Canfield unfortunately tells us little we do not already know about Adams. Beach, drawing extensively from Adams's state papers, correspondence, and political essays, believes he was neither the extremist nor as violent as he is depicted in more conventional biographies. By approaching the Revolution through the eyes of Adams, Beach presents a reappraisal of the whole period which cannot simply be shunted aside. Although lacking footnotes, the book has a particularly useful bibliographic essay which is must reading for anyone interested in Adams and the Revolution. Note also that *The Writings of Samuel Adams 1764–1802* were collected and edited by Harry Alonzo Cushing in four volumes appearing between 1904 and 1908. Only Adams's own surviving writings appear. Letters from others to him, although numerous in the manuscript collections, are not included.

The materials on Paine are, if anything, more voluminous. The basic biography is the 500-page *Paine,* by David Freeman Hawke, who has written knowledgeably about the colonial era in numerous other books. Paine, despite an active public career in America and Europe, proves to be a surprisingly introspective and exceedingly private man. Because few of Paine's personal papers survive, the task of the historian is at once complicated and simplified—complicated, because questions must remain unanswered and details undiscovered; simplified, because most of the remaining Paine materials have been collected under one roof. In readable, even exciting style, Hawke traces Paine's life from his humble origins working as a ladies corset maker in Britain to his spectacular rise as a major revolutionary pamphleteer in America and France, through his later imprisonment and bittersweet return to the United States he helped create. The bibliography, albeit extensive, lacks references to publishers and cities of publication for all citations, an unfortunate omission. Other studies of interest include the overly journalistic but still fascinating *Tom Paine: America's Godfather, 1737–1809* by W. E. Woodward (featuring a chapter entitled "Paine as Propagandist"); Arnold Kinsey King, "Thomas Paine in America, 1774–1787," an unpublished 1952 dissertation which exhaustively covers Paine's revolutionary influence; and Alfred Owen Aldridge, *Man of Reason: The Life of Thomas Paine,* which points out that Paine's writings were important not because of his style but because of the substantive appeal and compelling logic they employed. Aldridge includes full chapter notes and fleshes out his narrative with information overlooked by previous researchers.

Recent biographies such as Samuel Edwards's *Rebels! A Biography of Tom Paine* and *Tom Paine* by Jerome D. Wilson and William F. Ricketson are designed more for the popular market. Wilson and Ricketson do, however, include a useful select annotated bibliography; Edwards's book, on the other hand, despite pretensions as an authoritative text, lacks documentation and is rather free in handling sources. Better are Audrey Williamson's *Thomas Paine: His Life, Work and Times* and Eric Foner's *Tom Paine and Revolutionary America.* Williamson includes newly researched details about Paine's life and benefits not only from a rather comprehensive treatment but also the author's British perspective. Foner, rather than pursuing a traditional biography, explores key moments in Paine's career. He suggests that Paine's influence was not merely propagandistic but transcended narrow economic interests when he became an innovative political communicator who really believed in the utopian vision of an egalitarian American society.

No complete collection of Paine's public and private writings is as yet available. *The Writings of Thomas Paine,* collected and edited by Moncure Daniel Conway in four volumes from 1894 to 1896, filled a gap at the time of publication but is now superseded by later works such as the ten-volume large-print *The Life and Works of Thomas Paine,* edited by William van der Weyde and published in 1925; and Philip S. Foner's *The Complete Writings of Thomas Paine,* issued in two volumes in 1945. Unfortunately, all are seriously flawed. Although Foner's is perhaps the most comprehensive, occasional misdating of letters, editorial deletions, a topical organization that makes it difficult to work chronologically, the inclusion of an inadequate index, and the failure to collate all available Paine material point to the need for a new and truly definitive collection. Numerous student editions of Paine's political writings also exist. Among the best, because of its useful introduction to Paine's career with full explanatory notes, is *Common Sense and Other Political Writings* (1953), edited by Nelson F. Adkins.

Propaganda in a New Nation, 1785–1825

The years between the Revolutionary and Civil wars saw great change, yet they remain among the most neglected in the history of U.S. propaganda. The outstanding document influencing the constitutional debate is, of course, *The Federalist Papers* by Alexander Hamilton, James Madison, and John Jay. A number of editions of the collected papers exist, but the most used reference text is that edited by Clinton Rossiter based on what is known as the McLean edition of 1788. Included is an informative introduction describing the political and social background, an expanded table of contents with a brief precis for each of the eighty-five essays, an appendix containing the Constitution with cross-references to pertinent sections within the papers, and an index of ideas which helps search out the major political concepts. See also John Heller's unpublished "The Selling of the Constitution: The Federalist Papers Viewed as an Advertising Campaign." After tracing the historical development of constitutionalism in the United States, Heller describes the reasons advanced for adopting the Constitution contained within the papers and provides factual data on the authors. Using a content analysis, Heller concludes that the advocacy methodology of the proponents strongly resembles issue-oriented advertising campaigns common today.

Most of the other important scholarly materials commenting on U.S. propaganda in this period appear in journals or remain unpublished. Of value in terms of background, however, is Gustavus Myers's monumental *History of Bigotry in the United States,* which gives a very serviceable guide to not only the immediate post-revolutionary period but more modern eras as well. The footnotes are extensive, although one wishes that they had been organized into a bibliography.

Emergence of Political Parties and Factions, 1826–1860

The Antimasonic party was the first influential minor or third party in the United States and introduced the technique of the national presidential nominating convention to the nation in 1831. The avowed goal of its members was the destruction of Freemasonry and all secret societies because of Masonry's alleged subversive, unchristian, undemocratic character and activities. Later the Antimasonry Crusade was incorporated into the reform wing of the Whig party and declined as more pressing issues, such as slavery, came to dominate national attention. Its story is well told by William Preston Vaughn in *The Antimasonic Party in the United States, 1826–1843.* This remains the best reference source, although specialists interested in political rhetoric should review Leland M. Griffin's doctoral dissertation, "The Antimasonic Persuasion: A Study of Public Address in the American Antimasonic Movement, 1826–1838." For comparison, see also Powrie Vaux Doctor's "Amos Kendall, Propagandist of Jacksonian Democracy."

An in-depth scholarly study exploring every aspect of the struggle to rid the country of slavery is contained in Dwight Lowell Dumond's *Antislavery: The Crusade for Freedom in America.* For the student of propaganda, the book details the organization and development of antislavery societies, the continuing communication efforts to win over public opinion by activists such as William Lloyd Garrison, and the emergence of partisan activity in the Liberty party that eventually led "free soilers" to fuse their interests by forming the Republican party. In contrast, Joel H. Silbey argues in a series of provocative revisionist essays that slavery was not the most important issue in American politics in the period just prior to the outbreak of war in 1861. In *The Partisan Imperative: The Dynamics of American Politics Before the Civil War* he discusses the importance of local issues, ethnic and religious attitudes, and the role of the national parties in influencing the drift toward secession. For background, see James Constantine's 1953 doctoral dissertation, "The African Slave Trade: A Study of Eighteenth Century Propaganda and Public Controversy," which thoroughly covers the topic.

The Civil War

Every American war has brought a heated debate over the extent to which national security will permit protesters to exercise constitutional guarantees of free speech. Frank L. Klement's *The Limits of Dissent: Clement L. Vallandigham and the Civil War* is an intellectual biography of the passionate critic who led the pro-peace faction in the North opposed to Lincoln's policies by insisting that no circumstance—not even a divisive war—could deprive a citizen of the right to oppose governmental decisions freely and openly. In the resulting fiercely fought propaganda battle for mass opinion, Vallandigham risked everything—including arrest, imprisonment, and exile—to defend free speech for all. "Valiant Val" became a symbol of the dissenter; his case raises civil rights questions of continuing relevance today as documented in this important book.

The North-South conflict has the "advantage" of being the first major war fought in the United States when there was general literacy. Given the strong philosophical and ideological differences between the northern and southern leaderships, the increasing presence of large numbers of foreign-born immigrants who needed to be "Americanized," and the lack of enthusiasm for the war among large segments of the nonsecessionist population, it is not surprising that the staple of pre-twentieth-century propagandists—pamphlets and broadsides—proliferated in the effort to rally support for what, it soon was realized would be a protracted fight.

For northern publications see *Union Pamphlets of the Civil War, 1861–1865,* compiled in two volumes by Frank B. Freidel. This is the standard introduction to this material, reprinting fifty-two selected texts. Organization here is similar to that employed for the Revolutionary War collection edited by Bailyn. Each pamphlet appears in its entirety, along with appendixes and associated matter (including a fact-filled introduction supplemented by representative illustrations). Numerous works on the life of Harriet Beecher Stowe are not included here, but reference should be made to "Generative Forces in Union Propaganda: A Study in Civil War Pressure Groups" by George Winston Smith, written in 1940 during another era of crisis; and to "The Pictorial Reporting and Propaganda of the Civil War" by William F. Thompson, Jr., a fascinating exploration of the role played by wartime illustrators, photographers, cartoonists, and commercial artists in shaping northern public opinion.

The Confederacy also issued literally thousands of imprints. Fortunately, guides and catalogs do exist to assist the researcher in locating pertinent references. Basic works include Marjorie Lyle Crandall, *Confederate Imprints: A Check List Based Principally on the Collection of the Boston Athenaeum*, in two volumes, with 5,121 citations; Richard Harwell, *More Confederate Imprints*, two volumes, with 1,773 citations; and Ray O. Hummel, Jr., *Southeastern Broadsides Before 1877: A Bibliography*, with over 5,000 entries. Although not every publication can be classified as propaganda, each guide contains references to official publications by state as well as by topic area for unofficial publications ("Slavery and the Negro," "Religious Tracts," and so on), an author index, and authoritative introductions. Of specialized interest is Charles P. Cullop's *Confederate Propaganda in Europe, 1861–1865*. The work is currently unique, features a six-page bibliography, but is only 160 pages long.

Following the defeat of the Confederacy, post–Civil War reactionaries formed the Ku Klux Klan as a political and social movement to reestablish white supremacy in the South, but soon its influence began to be felt nationwide and has not yet died out. There are many books on the Klan, but a serviceable introduction and overview is found in *Hooded Americanism: The History of the Ku Klux Klan* by David M. Chalmers, now out in a third edition.

Spanish-American War

Not surprisingly, the flashpoint of propaganda studies in the years between the Civil War and World War I is yet another armed conflict—the Spanish-American War. Two basic references are Marcus M. Wilkerson, *Public Opinion and the Spanish-American War: A Study in War Propaganda*, and Joseph E. Wisan, *The Cuban Crisis as Reflected in the New York Press, 1895–1898*. Of the two, Wisan's book is by far the more complete, but each has contrasting insights on the role played by such New York papers as the *Journal* and *World* in whipping up interventionist enthusiasm. Wilkerson is particularly damning in his indictment of the publishers, whose primary concern was circulation rather than human rights. Often overlooked, however, is the role played by Cuban nationalists in encouraging U.S. involvement. See, for example, the article by George Auxier, "The Propaganda Activities of the Cuban Junta in Precipitating the Spanish-American War, 1895–1898," which appeared in the *Hispanic American Historical Review*.

Rise of Populism, Progressivism, and the Muckrakers

Set against the power of rawboned industrialization were two movements that sought to constrain the increasingly unbridled power of business and finance. The muckrakers were journalistic supporters of the Progressives, the middle-class counterpart to the more agrarian Populists. The efforts of these reformers were fostered by the growing numbers of magazines seeking to enlarge their circulations, particularly during the first two decades of this century. For example, *McClure's Magazine* became the leading outlet for reformist material. Muckraking investigative reporters such as David Graham Phillips, Frank Norris, Lincoln Steffens, Upton Sinclair, Ida Tarbell, and others rallied to expose irresponsibility rampant in industry, as in Tarbell's damning *History of the Standard Oil Company* and Steffens's *The Shame of the Cities*. Books such as Norris's *The Pit* (1903) and Sinclair's *The Jungle* (1906) fostered a national discussion which led to passage of the Pure Food and Drug Act and the Federal Meat Inspection Act of 1906, two major victories for Progressive reform.

Indeed, the Progressive movement influenced American life so decisively from the 1890s through World War I that historians have labeled the period the Progressive Era. Benjamin Parke DeWitt's *The Progressive Movement: A Non-partisan, Comprehensive Discussion of Current Tendencies in American Politics,* first published in 1915 and now reprinted with a new introduction by Arthur Mann, despite often being overlooked by later scholars, remains a particularly useful contemporary analysis of Progressivism's manifestations in various political parties. Although a true believer in the reform effort, DeWitt wrote soberly and without sentimentalism about its impact on the U.S. political scene. Compare this to the cogent outline found in *The Progressive Movement: Its Principles and Its Programme* by Samuel Duncan-Clark, published in 1913, and the more recent reassessment in Robert M. Cruden's *Ministers of Reform: The Progressives' Achievement in American Civilization, 1889–1920*.

About the same time, Populism culminated in the formation of yet another party organization that despite a relatively brief existence in the 1890s had a lasting effect on American politics and society. An outstanding biography-history of the life of the movement's foremost spokesman is *Populism and Politics: William Alfred Peffer and the People's Party* by Peter H. Argersinger. The book documents how Populism succumbed to the very factors in American politics that it sought to destroy: prejudice, corruption, indifference, expediency, and elite manipulation.

Increasingly sophisticated lobby efforts by middle-class reformers and labor interests over time encouraged a rethinking of the public interest. For example, the rising importance of public relations, as Walter Lippmann notes in *Drift and Mastery,* by 1914 reflected dramatic changes not only in the public perception of business but also in management attitudes toward corporate social responsibility. Readers further interested in the propaganda of the Populist and Progressive movements should consult *Progressivism and Muckraking* by Louis Filler, part of a bibliographic series issued by the R. R. Bowker Company. While the emphasis is on in-print materials, there is much valuable commentary and annotation for the person interested in these traditional undercurrents in U.S. history extending from early roots to the contemporary political and news scenes. Appended are useful author, subject, and title indexes.

World War I

The "war to end all wars" failed to accomplish that goal but does mark a major break with the past. The public lies about national aims, the wasteful policy of attrition, and the wearing down of social barriers as the carnage continued help explain the onset of postwar disillusionment. Each side emphasized propaganda but differed in its approach toward the United States. An excellent resource is "German Propaganda in the United States, 1914–1917," a doctoral dissertation completed by David Hirst at Northwestern University in 1962. It identifies the major propaganda agencies and their leaders and also analyzes pro-German reportage as it appeared in books, films, pamphlets, periodicals, and newspapers (including the New York *Evening Mail,* secretly purchased by representatives of the Kaiser in 1915). A graduate thesis by Elizabeth Gaines, *"The Fatherland:* An American Vehicle for German Propaganda, 1914–1917," presents an independent analysis of another publication. Gaines's review indicates that the four major propaganda themes stressed by George S. Viereck's publication were maintaining U.S. neutrality, promoting closer U.S.-German political and commercial ties, warning of the dangers of an entangling alliance with Great Britain, and exposing the pro-Ally bias of U.S. news media.

In studying various movements, one often overlooks the people behind the propaganda. This is unfortunate, for very often these men and women prove more interesting than the dogmas they attempt to spread. A case in point is Phyllis Keller's unusual *States of Belonging: German-American Intellectuals and the First World War.* Keller tracks the impact of World War I as a decisive turning point for individuals representative of Western civilization in her illuminating combination of cultural, governmental, and psychological history. She explores the conflicting group loyalties and allegiances of three similar men who chose different political paths: Viereck, the poet-publicist embracing the German side; Hugo Munsterberg, opting for the middle of the road; and Hermann Hagedorn, also a writer, turning to American superpatriotism. Viereck himself later published several works in which he describes his career. See, for example, his *Spreading Germs of Hate* and *My Flesh and Blood: A Lyric Autobiography with Indiscreet Annotations*.

Unlike the Germans, who attempted to keep the United States out of the war, leaders in the United Kingdom sought U.S. intervention. Their ultimate success is chronicled in Horace C. Peterson's *Propaganda for War: The Campaign Against American Neutrality, 1914–1917*, James D. Squires's *British Propaganda at Home and in the United States from 1914 to 1917*, and Cate Haste's *Keep the Home Fires Burning: Propaganda in the First World War*. Of the three, Peterson's remains the most definitive and despite the passage of years holds up well in its basic approach. Extensive notes and ten pages of bibliographic references are also useful, although the index is inadequate. Squires's slim book is largely a summary of other works but presents a serviceable and occasionally brilliant outline of the topic. While Haste emphasizes internal propaganda in Britain rather than that designed for overseas consumption, the book benefits from inclusion of thirty-seven illustrations and particularly incisive chapters describing the nature of propaganda in World War I, the impact of prewar images on later propaganda efforts, the organizational machinery used by the British government to mobilize the press and other propaganda cooperators, and the long-term implications that the propaganda onslaught unleashed by England had for postwar stability. This latter theme is treated in greater depth by George C. Bruntz in *Allied Propaganda and the Collapse of the German Empire in 1918*, which despite occasional lapses in the quality of the translation from the original German is objective and well documented. See also the representative studies by Victor S. Mamatey, *The United States and East Central Europe, 1914–1918: A Study in Wilsonian Diplomacy and Propaganda*, which utilizes printed sources, State Department files, plus diaries of key governmental officials and foreign materials to describe the contradictory U.S. policies and propaganda messages that contributed to the breakup of the Hapsburg Empire; Arthur Posonby, *Falsehood in War-time*, which, although brief, exposes the fabrications, distortions, and official-unofficial lies circulated by the belligerent powers; James M. Read, *Atrocity Propaganda, 1914–1919*, an excellent, comprehensive summary of the motives, methods, and notorious untruths widely disseminated during the war and after; Albert R. Buchanan, "European Propaganda and American Public Opinion, 1914–1917," a dissertation; and George T. Blakey, *Historians on the Homefront: American Propagandists for the Great War*.

The American propaganda effort spearheaded by George Creel is well recounted in a number of works. The standard history, *Words that Won the*

War: The Story of the Committee on Public Information, 1917–1919 by James
R. Mock and Cedric Larson, is based on the papers of the CPI now in the
National Archives. The authors trace the background on American public
opinion and the coming of wartime censorship, the committee's use of
various media in cooperating with educators, labor organizations, and corporate leaders to create an effective internal propaganda campaign, as well
as "the fight for the mind of mankind" overseas. Although there is no
bibliography as such, the notes are well organized and are supplemented
with numerous illustrations. A more recent scholarly reinterpretation of the
CPI is contained in Stephen L. Vaughn's *Holding Fast the Inner Lines: Democracy, Nationalism, and the Committee on Public Information*. This 397-page
tome, issued as a supplementary volume to the Papers of Woodrow Wilson
series, concentrates on the domestic operations of the CPI. While covering
much of the same ground as Mock and Larson, the book is an important
addition to the literature of propaganda administration. An extensive bibliography is appended, along with an intriguing twenty-page comparative
essay on primary and secondary sources.

While the overall communicative structure of advertising changed over
time, as Robert L. Craig documents in his doctoral dissertation, many
individuals such as Creel willingly defended the need for government involvement in the emerging field. The CPI leader proudly recounts his
experiences in *How We Advertised America: The First Telling of the Amazing
Story of the Committee on Public Information that Carried the Gospel of Americanism to Every Corner of the Globe*. Despite Creel's jingoism, evident from
the title he chose, this is an important work since Creel reveals the congressional attempt to suppress his public report describing the true nature of
the CPI's propaganda activities. Creel himself was unapologetic for his
wartime activities and details the history of the CPI's domestic and foreign
sections along with an account of the unhappy period of demobilization.
A documentary listing of CPI publications along with photographs and an
index make this a valuable reference. Creel also later wrote an autobiography, *Rebel at Large: Recollections of Fifty Crowded Years*, in which he reviews
his World War I experiences.

For further reference readers may wish to peruse "American Foreign
Propaganda in World War I," a relevant doctoral study by Jackson Giddens;
and Kent and Gretchen Kreuter's *An American Dissenter: The Life of Algie
Martin Simons, 1870–1950*, a fascinating biography tracing the intellectual
odyssey of one of the journalists who founded the American Socialist Movement. Simons's subsequent disillusionment led him to work in World War
I for the ultra-patriotic CPI and later as a researcher and pamphleteer attacking health insurance on behalf of the American Medical Association.

The Interwar Period, 1919–1941

The Bolshevik victory in Russia and other radical uprisings in Europe
following World War I caused the United States to be swept by a wave of

fear that revolution could similarly happen here. This paranoia was fueled by release of sensational propaganda emanating from supposedly responsible governmental agencies as much as by left- and right-wing extremist groups. The standard account of this phenomenon is Robert Murray's meticulously researched *Red Scare: A Study in National Hysteria, 1919–1920*. Although the federal government conducted several hearings and issued a report on foreign propaganda activities in the United States (see the bibliography for a selective listing of important U.S. documents on communist and Nazi propaganda), the most complete and detailed published repository of radical propaganda literature is found in a four-volume report released in 1920 by a New York State Senate committee chaired by Clayton R. Lusk. The resulting *Revolutionary Radicalism: Its History, Purpose, and Tactics* ("Lusk Report") totals 10,983 pages and is a unique collation of original documents, manifestos, and the like. Care, however, must be maintained in utilizing this collection since the conclusions reached by the committee members on the basis of their investigation are open to question.

While much has been written about the growth of the Ku Klux Klan during these years, relatively little has been said about the propaganda methods utilized by its leaders in building their organization. John Shotwell's thesis, "Crystalizing Public Hatred: Ku Klux Klan Public Relations in the Early 1920s," is the first detailed study of the effective, though sometimes nefarious, campaign waged by the Klan to influence key opinion leaders and elites.

Also of interest is Ralph Droz Casey's pioneering doctoral study of propaganda in the 1928 election. Most of the key studies chronicling the very effective use of mass communication by the Franklin D. Roosevelt administration for political purposes are referenced below and in a later section on media. Worth noting here is "The Propaganda Program of the National Recovery Administration," Carol Jean Holgren's unpublished 1962 thesis investigating the NRA as an example of government abuse of its public trust during the 1930s. This is must reading for the topic, particularly for its treatment of the New Deal program as a harbinger of a type of American fascism.

Isolationism vs. Interventionism

A book by Justus Doenecke, *Anti-interventionism: A Bibliographical Introduction to Isolationism and Pacifism from World War I to the Early Cold War*, provides a long-needed critical overview to the literature. This is the place to start in sorting out what has been written about those opposed to "foreign military adventures." Readers interested in the interventionist versus isolationist controversy leading up to the U.S. alliance with Britain and the Soviet Union also might wish to consult Selig Adler, *The Isolationist Impulse: Its Twentieth Century Reaction*. It is an accessible, classic text that attempts to place the history of American isolationism in context with other developments and forces active in the world. The book serves as a good narrative to the philosophy that connected La Follette's Progressive party with later developments such as the Nye Committee antiwar investigation of 1934 and the subsequent Neutrality Law that (unsuccessfully) sought to keep America out of overseas conflicts. Special attention is given to Charles Lindbergh's involvement with the America First Committee and the post– World War II reemergence of isolationism, culminating in the dramatic anticommunist hearings chaired by Senator Joseph McCarthy in the 1950s. While Adler is not particularly sympathetic with the conservative and Populist views that underscored isolationist thought, he does summarize well the key underlying issues that troubled American society while the nation rose to prominence as a world power. The notes and bibliography are still pertinent.

Adler's reading of history should be compared to Harold Lavine and James Wechsler, *War Propaganda and the United States,* originally prepared for the Institute for Propaganda Analysis in 1940 and subsequently reprinted in several editions; Walter Johnson, *The Battle Against Isolation;* Letty Bergstrom, "The Battle for America: German-English Language Propaganda in the U.S. from 1933 to 1941;" Jane Schwar, "Interventionist Propaganda and Pressure Groups in the United States, 1937–1941," a detailed 1973 doctoral study of prewar organizations actively encouraging U.S. involvement in Europe; and Michele Flynn Stenejhem, *An American First: John T. Flynn and the America First Committee.* The latter details the career and philosophy of one of the nation's leading revisionist journalists, concentrating on the 1940–41 period, when Flynn sought to strengthen the U.S. commitment to neutrality. Six appendixes, more than one hundred cited references, and an extensive bibliography help provide access to other relevant works. Also of some interest is Larry Ceplair's *Under the Shadow of War: Fascism, Anti-Fascism, and Marxists, 1918–1939,* which analyzes the failure of the antifascist movement during the interwar years; and Alan Brinkley's *Voices of Protest: Huey Long, Father Coughlin and the Great Depression,* a highly praised study of "two fascinating, disturbing political figures whose brief but vast popularity explains much about Depression-age America."

World War II

Of course, everything changed following the attack on Pearl Harbor by the Japanese. The resulting avalanche of books can overwhelm the reader interested in pursuing propaganda issues from the war years. Two of the more interesting, in that they concentrate on propaganda as a creative cultural phenomenon, are John Morton Blum's *V Was for Victory: Politics and American Culture During World War II* and Richard R. Lingeman's *Don't You Know There's a War On? The American Home Front, 1941–1945.* The former is an intriguing (if somewhat fawning) look at the legacy of FDR's presidency in shaping American popular culture. The first fifty pages detail the efforts by the Office of War Information to sell the war domestically. Also discussed in this serious account written by a Yale history professor are other official (and unofficial) propaganda activities, including, a particularly trenchant review of wartime popular novels. Despite the catchy title of Lingeman's book, his is more than simply a nostalgic overview. Written in an evocative style, *There's a War On* is a solidly researched and richly detailed history of the war years. Included is a discussion of the propagandistic and escapist purposes to which books, motion pictures, comics, and music were put in cooperation with the government.

Several excellent studies covering visual aspects of the propaganda war have appeared in recent years, among them J. Darracott and B. Loftus, *Second World War Posters;* Denis Judd, *Posters of World War Two;* Anthony Rhodes, *Propaganda—The Art of Persuasion: World War II;* and Zbynek Zeman, *Selling the War: Art and Propaganda in World War II.* Darracott and Loftus concentrate on materials from the Imperial War Museum. Although there are some inaccuracies as well as mediocre integration of the lengthy text and pictorial matter, Judd does provide a basic introduction to the use of posters. Rhodes tends to follow a similar organization to that of Judd (with long sections by country, including the United States), but coverage is broader, with more than 270 color and a like number of black-and-white illustrations superbly reproduced in a lavish oversize 9″ x 12″ volume. Rhodes also gives attention to recordings, radio, and the cinema as propaganda channels, noting how different nations dealt with common themes. Additionally, there is an afterword by Daniel Lerner on the American psychological warfare campaign against Germany and a fifteen-page filmographic essay, as well as a short bibliography and complete index. Zeman, an authority on Nazi propaganda, reprints one hundred of the most effective wartime posters issued by Allied and Axis propagandists (with an emphasis on European rather than American contributions). The strength of the work is in his analysis of what such visual propaganda reveals about the political, military, and moral conditions that lay behind it. The text itself is brief, supplemented with a limited bibliography and index.

Highly critical of U.S. policy is Benjamin Colby's *'Twas a Famous Victory: Deception and Propaganda in the War with Germany.* The author argues in common with several other revisionist historians that Roosevelt deliberately deceived the American people by telling them that American survival—like Britain's—depended on U.S. entry into the war. After reviewing administration cover-ups of Soviet atrocities and distortions of Hitler's true war aims, Colby asserts that Roosevelt bears the blame for the needless deaths of thousands of GIs through his propaganda policy designed to cause war. Mobilization of American media (through such institutions as the OWI, the Writers War Board, and the Hollywood studios), again to create hatred of the Germans and build enthusiasm for the alliance with the Soviets, is also covered. Colby, a former *New York Times* and Associated Press staff journalist, organizes his case well but relies largely on secondary sources for his evidence. That there was a secret conspiracy between Roosevelt and Churchill, however, is now known. The links between the highly clandestine British Security Coordination organization and the American OSS were revealed following the declassification of a number of sensitive wartime documents in recent years. The standard recitals include R. Harris Smith, *OSS: The Secret History of America's First Central Intelligence Agency,* and Bradley F. Smith, *The Shadow Warriors: O.S.S. and the Origins of the C.I.A.* For an authoritative account of British intelligence and propaganda activities both before and during World War II, see William Stevenson's *A Man Called Intrepid: The Secret War.*

Four major studies document the history of the OWI. See Allan M. Winkler, *The Politics of Propaganda: The Office of War Information, 1942–1945;* Lamar MacKay, "Domestic Operations of the Office of War Information in World War II;" Robert L. Bishop, "The Overseas Branch of the Office of War Information;" and Sydney Weinberg's massive "Wartime Propaganda in a Democracy: America's Twentieth Century Information Agencies." Winkler's text, drawn heavily from original documents in the National Archives, is organized into four chapters describing the OWI's origins, its use of propaganda at home (where the OWI was prohibited from distributing materials directly to the public), political propaganda abroad, and overseas military propaganda. As all four authors make clear, the OWI was limited by its temporary wartime mandate and the fact that it had powerful congressional enemies. Also hampering the agency (which at its height had 11,000 employees) were the lack of clear-cut U.S. goals other than unconditional victory, the failure to develop long-range policies for the postwar period, personality conflicts within the OWI itself, and continued public distrust of government-issued propaganda. Bishop's study is particularly useful for its discussion of the operations of the Voice of America, directed originally by OWI's Overseas Branch.

In a heavily annotated (and at times repetitious) history with the virtues and weaknesses common to doctoral studies converted to books, Leila J. Rupp's *Mobilizing Women for War: German and American Propaganda, 1939–1945* nevertheless adds dimension to our understanding of the effectiveness of mobilization propaganda. Rupp contrasts the image of women carried within popular periodicals and other media with the reality of wartime conditions in both countries. Working from a feminist perspective, she demonstrates that such propaganda was more extensive in the United States and proved critically important in converting women to industrial work so that men could be freed to fight overseas. Scrupulous documentation and a wide-ranging use of sources is confirmed by an extensive fifty-page bibliography.

The U.S. military's postwar de-Nazification efforts at reeducating the German people to support democracy are reported in Albert Norman's *Our German Policy: Propaganda and Culture*. The focus of the book, which relies heavily on primary sources acquired by the author while a member of the occupation government, is a history of the policies and practices applied by U.S. forces in reshaping the media and cultural institutions of a defeated Germany. The Western allies slowly abandoned all systematic reeducation attempts and eventually resorted to a series of piecemeal measures. More recent scholarship investigating this period is found in "Propaganda and the Control of Information in Occupied Germany: The U.S. Information Control Division at Radio Frankfort 1945–1949," a Ph.D. dissertation completed by Lawrence Raymond Hartenian at Rutgers University in 1984; and in *The Political Re-education of Germany and Her Allies After World War II*, edited by Nicholas Pronay and Keith Wilson.

Psychological Warfare

Propaganda as a manipulative art naturally has an interest in psychology and human attitudes. An offshoot of World War II, the Korea and Vietnam conflicts, and the establishment of a permanent U.S. governmental news and propaganda ministry in the United States Information Agency has been increased emphasis on what is known as psychological warfare or psy-war. A basic introduction is Terence H. Qualter's *Propaganda and Psychological Warfare*, which offers both a philosophical and historical treatment of the subject. Daniel Lerner's *Sykewar: Psychological Warfare Against Germany, D-Day to VE-Day* is the definitive history of Allied wartime efforts in the European theater by an actively involved scholar. Chapters discuss policy, personnel, media, operations, and effectiveness. See also Charles G. Cruickshank's *The Fourth Arm: Psychological Warfare 1938–1945*, emphasizing the British perspective. Writers such as Murray Dyer in *The Weapon on the Wall: Rethinking Psychological Warfare* and Robert T. Holt and Robert W. van de Velde in *Strategic Psychological Operations and American Foreign Policy* have questioned the assumptions underlying American propaganda and psy-war overseas by arguing that U.S. naïveté and overreliance on military aspects of political communication undercut the effectiveness of messages to other peoples. Other basic references include Paul Linebarger's *Psychological Warfare*, a very useful summary of thinking on the topic through time of publication, and William E. Dougherty and Morris Janowitz's *Psychological Warfare Casebook*, which during the Vietnam years served as the chief psy-warrior text. Updating these are Joseph J. McDonough's "Analysis of Official U.S. Military Psychological Warfare Efforts in the Vietnam Conflict," Phillip Paul Katz's *A Systematic Approach to Psyop Information*, and the 1982 book edited by Ron D. McLaurin called *Military Propaganda: Psychological Warfare and Operations*. Less valuable is Charles Roetter's historical *The Art of Psychological Warfare, 1914–1945,* which lacks notes or bibliography and is rather shallow in its coverage.

A review of case studies makes it clear that the "hypodermic theory" model (a blatant campaign organized from the top down in order to inject the populace with information) does not work particularly well and in no way guarantees message reception, understanding, acceptance, or desired action. This points to the central problem facing psychological warfare and propaganda researchers: how does one adequately measure effectiveness? In contrast to advertising—where syndicated research is widely available because of the competitive needs of media, agencies, and clients—when one wades through the mass of military propaganda literature generated since World War I, this area is usually glibly, simplistically, and inadequately addressed. Even in the Korean conflict, very little evaluation was carried out. Since Vietnam, however, the beginnings of a true social science effort to evaluate the output of psychological warfare message systems and activities have been evident.

Recommended reading includes Edward Hunter's *Brainwashing: The Story of the Men Who Defied It,* a lucidly reported popular account of the horror techniques used against American POWs in Korea; more recently supplemented by Edgar Schein and others, *Coercive Persuasion: A Socio-Psychological Analysis of the "Brainwashing" of American Civilian Prisoners by the Chinese Communists;* Alan W. Scheflin and Edward M. Opton, Jr., *The Mind Manipulators;* and John Marks's shocking *The Search for the "Manchurian Candidate" : The CIA and Mind Control—The Story of the Agency's Secret Efforts to Control Human Behavior.* Schein notes that the essential prerequisite is to close off the outside environment. Once this condition is met, as in a POW camp or closed psychiatric ward, all kinds of successful manipulations are possible. This is one reason why the United States placed so much reliance on broadcasting in Vietnam in order to break down the local communication structure and replace it with a tightly controlled new one. However, as Thomas William Hoffer points out in his massive two-volume dissertation, "Broadcasting in an Insurgency Environment: USIA in Vietnam, 1965–1970," U.S. advisors underestimated competing propaganda strategies used by the insurgents, who acted effectively to limit U.S.–South Vietnam efforts. Adding to the value of Hoffer's analysis are extensive appendixes which reprint a number of rare government reports, memoranda, and other documents. Also worthwhile is Peter Braestrup's massive two-volume analysis of media performance, *Big Story! How the American Press and Television Reported and Interpreted the Crises of Tet 1968 in Vietnam and Washington.*

United States Information Agency

For a quick introduction and independent overview see the special report "USIA: A Battered but Powerful Propaganda Tool" in *U.S. News & World*

Report. Note that the USIA operates an Office of Public Liaison (Washington, D.C. 20547). This publishes a free newsletter called *USIA Update* and provides fact sheets and other materials describing current agency activities. Since 1953 the USIA has also issued a series of reports to Congress that contain a wealth of statistical and policy information on operations of the agency, including Voice of America broadcasting (see below). Also of interest are the independent oversight studies prepared by the General Accounting Office for congressional hearings on budget requests before the House Committee on Foreign Affairs, often providing extensive coverage of current issues.

Many of the relevant data, along with an expert introduction to working with government documents, have been collected in *The Mass Media: Aspen Institute Guide to Communication Industry Trends* by Christopher H. Sterling and Timothy R. Haight. Dr. Sterling, as noted earlier, also edits an indispensable monthly review of new literature called *Communication Booknotes,* which features a special annual issue summarizing the major government studies from the previous year of interest to researchers.

Of the available histories, the most valuable books on the USIA include Robert Elder's *The Information Machine: The United States Information Agency and American Foreign Policy,* John W. Henderson's *The United States Information Agency,* and Leo Bogart's *Premises for Propaganda: The United States Information Agency's Operating Assumptions in the Cold War.* The latter, for example, is based on 142 interviews with key USIA personnel conducted during the 1950s. The book is actually an abridgment of a five-volume report that remained restricted for more than twenty years. These sources are further supplemented by personalized subjective accounts such as Edward W. Barrett's *Truth Is Our Weapon* and Thomas C. Sorenson's *The Word War: The Story of American Propaganda.* Critical studies of the USIA also include George N. Gordon and Irving A. Falk, *The War of Ideas: America's International Identity Crisis,* Eugene W. Castle's polemical *Billions, Blunders and Baloney: The Fantastic Story of How Uncle Sam Is Squandering Your Money Overseas,* and L. Skvortsov, *The Ideology and Tactics of Anti-Communism,* which contains an interesting section entitled "The Aims and Tactics of Propaganda," written from a pro-Soviet perspective.

The Voice of America, Radio Free Europe, Radio Liberty, Radio Marti, Worldnet, and Other Broadcasting Efforts

The success of Voice of America encouraged other post–1945 efforts once the Cold War got under way. Former OSS officers used secret CIA funding to establish Radio Free Europe (1950) and Radio Liberty several years later. Much of this history is summarized in an important 1983 work by Sig Mickelson, *America's Other Voice: The Story of Radio Free Europe and Radio*

Liberty. The former president of CBS News, who headed RFE/RL from 1975 to 1978, argues the widely presented case that such broadcasts provide not propaganda but "free information" to censored societies behind the Iron Curtain.

In recent years there has been a greater effort—particularly by the USIA—to upgrade communications equipment and take advantage of new technological advances. Worldnet, for example, is an interactive audiovisual satellite service competing against Soviet efforts to influence media coverage affecting public opinion in Europe and Asia. USIA's Express File was inaugurated in 1987 to transmit news and information about the United States directly into the newsrooms of foreign news organizations (wire services, newspapers, magazines, and broadcasters) over the communications circuits of United Press International (UPI). To limit potential criticism, the Express File is clearly labeled as USIA material. An estimated 130 million adults listen to direct broadcasts by the Voice of America at least once a week, according to a 1986 survey released by the USIA, an increase of 11 million people over 1985. Not included in the figures are audiences for the VOA-operated Radio Marti (broadcasting to Cuba), VOA Europe, or rebroadcasts of VOA programs on foreign radio stations.

In the absence of definitive legal controls over international radio broadcasting, nations may engage in diplomacy, jamming, counter-propaganda, and other responses. For standard overviews of U.S. government radio and television propaganda, consult David Abshire, *International Broadcasting: A New Dimension in Western Diplomacy;* Julian Hale, *Radio Power: Propaganda and International Broadcasting;* Maury Lisann, *Broadcasting to the Soviet Union: International Politics and Radio;* K.R.M. Short, *Western Broadcasting over the Iron Curtain;* plus a number of other government reports and unpublished scholarly works listed in the bibliography. The Broad for International Broadcasting, for example, now coordinates the various nonmilitary overseas radio and television services operated by the government. It has issued a series of useful *Annual Reports* (1974 to the present), which, when combined with the published record of the House of Representatives Committee on Foreign Affairs *Oversight Hearings,* document activities of Radio Liberty and Radio Free Europe.

Broadcasting to Latin America by U.S. interests dates back to the 1920s, as pointed out by Fred Fejes in *Imperialism, Media and the Good Neighbor: New Deal Foreign Policy and United States Shortwave Broadcasting to Latin America,* published in 1986. Unfortunately, Fejes's work is not definitive, for he overlooks several major collections of source material and inadequately documents his claims of U.S. dominance. Worse, he fails to explore the actual content of American broadcasts and nowhere defines imprecise terminology such as "cultural diplomacy" or "propaganda." Two independent views on the more current Radio Marti experience are Hazel G. Warlaumont's 1986 thesis, "Radio Marti and the U.S.-Cuban Radio War:

Strategies Used in the Absence of Definitive Legal Controls over International Broadcasting as Compared with Strategies Used in the U.S.-USSR Radio War," and Howard H. Frederick's *Cuban-American Radio Wars: Ideology in International Telecommunications*. Both present the story of pro- and anti-Castro radiocasts, although the latter book reflects a leftist "progressive" approach to content analysis in propounding a "theory of inter-ideological state propaganda apparatuses."

Other Recent Latin American Developments

Beginning in 1985, the State Department engaged in a secret effort to generate congressional and public support for President Reagan's Central American policies. As part of this campaign, the State Department's Office of Public Diplomacy for Latin America and the Caribbean began awarding numerous contracts to outside public relations consultants to help "favorably influence" the image of the Nicaraguan Contra rebels. A National Security Council memo outlining some of these activities by Oliver North to National Security Adviser Robert McFarlane, "Timing and the Nicaraguan Resistance Vote," dated March 20, 1985, was released two years later as a result of the Iran-Contra hearings. A reprint of the complete memo and twelve-page confidential chronology is available from *Propaganda Review* in San Francisco. In 1987 these and related covert "white propaganda" activities were held by the General Accounting Office, the investigative arm of Congress, to violate congressional restrictions curbing the use of federal funds for publicity or propaganda purposes.

Much of this government effort (which also included authorizing the FBI to conduct surveillance on individuals prominently associated with support for immigration amnesty for Salvadorans and other Latin American refugees) stemmed from frustrations by federal policymakers over the successful propaganda efforts of pro-Sandinista supporters in the United States. See, for example, two monographs by the leftist Institute for Media Analysis published in 1987: *The Reagan Administration and Nicaragua: How Washington Constructs Its Case for Counterrevolution in Central America* by professors Noam Chomsky, Morris Morley, James Petras, and Michael Parenti; and *Packaging the Contras: A Case of CIA Disinformation* by Edgar Chamorro, former dean at the University of Central America and a direct descendant of four Nicaraguan presidents. Both argue that the U.S. government manipulated journalists and media institutions to create a false image of the "freedom fighter" rebels as "the democratic alternative" to Daniel Ortega's government. Three critical, yet well-documented, recent briefs upholding the administration's position include James L. Tyson, *Prophets or Useful Idiots? Church Organizations Attacking U.S. Central America Policy;* J. Michael Waller, "CISPES: A Terrorist Propaganda Network"; and Allan C. Brownfeld and J. Michael Waller, *The Revolution Lobby*. Are religious groups lobbying for radical political causes? Yes, says Tyson, who reports on the extensive propaganda and support network American churches have provided the Sandinista regime in Nicaragua as well as to Cuban-supported insurgencies in El Salvador and throughout Central America. The other studies by Waller listed above present overviews of the various organizations supporting dovish policy toward Latin America and the Caribbean, particularly their communication efforts to affect political decision making.

Intelligence

Decoding the garbled terminology of government-orchestrated propaganda campaigns and intelligence operations often requires a guidebook. Three paperbacks that help are Henry S.A. Becket, *The Dictionary of Espionage: Spookspeak into English* incorporating little-known facts and interesting anecdotes in clear definitions to over 2,000 words of tradecraft used by covert organizations worldwide; Bob Burton, *Top Secret: A Clandestine Operator's Glossary of Terms,* identifying more than 800 common espionage terms; and Roy Colby, *A Communese-English Dictionary,* containing over 1,000 Marxian expressions and idioms de-semanticized for anticommunist audiences. Compare the latter book to the more sympathetic *A Dictionary of Marxist Thought,* edited by Tom Bottomore. While propaganda is inexplicably neglected here, a useful review of ideology is included. So while these works are not necessarily individually definitive, they have collectively proven helpful.

For an in-depth, "up close and personal" introduction to the major superpowers, readers should consult Jeffrey T. Richelson's *The U.S. Intelligence Community* and *Sword and Shield: Soviet Intelligence and Security Apparatus.* These superb companion volumes dispense with rhetorical excess to document the organizational structure and activities that each country would prefer to remain hidden. While differing in philosophy and approach, both powers agree that they have a right to manipulate mass opinion and intervene in the affairs of other countries. Although the CIA gets most of the publicity, actually the American intelligence community is much broader and includes numerous lesser-known agencies described here. Depending on point of view, you will either be reassured or concerned over the extent of activities ranging from information gathering, to policy/issue management, to covert activities (including propaganda) that government employees undertake to enforce U.S. interests. Soviet propaganda measures are directed by the Politburo and Central Party Secretariat through an International Information Department linking various news organizations and embassy information departments; an International Department operating clandestine radio stations in addition to coordinating foreign communist parties, front organizations, and friendship societies; and the KGB, specializing in more direct active measures. These are must reading for the serious student. Richelson's *American Espionage and the Soviet Target*, published in 1987, is also recommended.

Other provocative studies include James Bamford's very revealing *The Puzzle Palace: A Report on NSA, America's Most Secret Agency*, republished by Penguin Books in 1983 with a new afterword outlining government attempts to quash the book. Philip Agee's *Inside the Company: A CIA Diary* created an uproar when first published in 1975 by chronicling the author's growing estrangement as it described classified operations in which he participated. Very downbeat is Agee's latest book, co-edited with Louis Wolf. *Dirty Work: The CIA in Western Europe* exposes the seamy side of American espionage, including the secret portfolio of dirty work done under the guise of national security—from the routine planting of phony news stories to assassinations and the overthrow of governments. Jonathan Kwitny's *The Crimes of Patriots: A True Tale of Dope, Dirty Money, and the CIA* also persuasively argues that a secret government does exist, actively engaging in widespread corruption and media manipulation. One of the more balanced books by disgruntled former agents incorporating newly declassified materials is the updated 1983 version of *The CIA and the Cult of Intelligence* by Victor Marchetti and John D. Marks.

For a controversial overview of the William Casey era, see Bob Woodward's *Veil: The Secret Wars of the CIA, 1981–1987*. He gives the impression that "ideological overdrive" by Casey on the subject of Soviet active measures led the United States wrongfully to upgrade its own propaganda efforts. This supplements—yet contrasts with—the views of Ernest W. Lefever and Roy Godson, who concentrate on the troubled 1974–79 period in *The CIA and the American Ethic: An Unfinished Debate*. The authors say that the arguments over CIA activities have proven inadequate. They believe that national media (led by the commercial television networks, which regularly criticized the CIA while giving scant attention to Soviet KGB activities) and individual congressmen were strongly influenced by an aggressive and well-financed "anti-intelligence lobby" determined to diminish American clandestine operations and covert action. Subsequently this distorted flow of information resulted in congressional restrictions which temporarily crippled CIA intelligence capabilities.

That lobby has not disappeared. The Institute for Media Analysis (IMA), for example, is a New York–based nonprofit organization formed in 1986. The IMA is devoted to monitoring, analyzing, and reporting on propaganda and disinformation, making available a newsletter entitled *Right to Know* and specialized monographs as noted above. Co-directors Ellen Ray and Bill Schaap are also the publishers of *Covert Action Information Bulletin*, which for more than a decade has critically covered the role of the intelligence community in the "worldwide power struggle."

Knowing what to believe can prove a serious problem. One example involves the attack on a Korean Airlines passenger plane by Soviet fighter defense forces, killing all on board, including a U.S. Congressman. This proved a propaganda bonanza for the Reagan administration. But what actually occurred? Detailed studies include R. W. Johnson's *Shootdown: Flight 007 and the American Connection,* which indicates, in a chapter titled "The Media War," that U.S. officials misled the public and engaged in cover-up; it is well complemented by Seymour M. Hersh's *"The Target Is Destroyed"—What Really Happened to Flight 007 and What America Knew About It.* The updated 1987 edition outlines a controversial, carefully researched account of the plane's secret spy mission describing "how intelligence is collected and abused as well as used."

Disinformation and Deception

Disinformation, according to Ladislav Bittman, is a false message leaked to the opponents in order to deceive the decision-makers or the public. It works because it is deliberately designed to confirm the darkest suspicions of the recipients. It serves to convince people to believe what they already want to believe. Bittman should know, as he was intimately involved with creating such campaigns as deputy commander of the disinformation department of the Czechoslovak intelligence service. After the Soviet invasion of his country in 1968, Bittman left and received political asylum in the United States, where he now is on the faculty of Boston University. His two books, *The KGB and Soviet Disinformation: An Insider's View* and *The Deception Game,* are authoritative introductions to the theory and Marxist application of intelligence, black propaganda, and disinformation. Also valuable reading from specialists expert in the field is *Dezinformatsia: Active Measures in Soviet Strategy* by Richard H. Shultz and Roy Godson. Recent developments can be followed in *Disinformation and Subversion Update,* a new weekly newsletter addressing various themes relating to Soviet active measures campaigns and perceived incorrect reporting in the U.S. media.

Several KGB-initiated disinformation coups in 1980 proved the susceptivity of U.S. and world media to cleverly planted false stories. One involved a forged "Presidential Review Memorandum NSC 46" supposedly urging a tilt of U.S. policy toward total support for South Africa, complete with a program to monitor and divide American blacks to neutralize their political influence on this issue. Copies of the supposed document were widely circulated to black U.N. delegates and U.S. media outlets. Subsequent denials by confused Carter White House staffers proved so lame that they enhanced the credibility of the forgery. Another forged document, a State Department "dissent" paper that year recommended what was called the "Zimbabwe option" in El Salvador. This suggested that the United States could limit Soviet and Cuban influence by aiding the Marxist opposition to win them to the American side. A number of leftist columnists encouraged the administration to heed the recommendations before the window of opportunity to influence the guerrillas was lost. Only later was it shown to be a Soviet-manipulated disinformation campaign.

More specifically focusing on KGB activities inside the United States are several in-depth studies: John Barron's *KGB: The Secret Work of Soviet Secret Agents* and the more recent *KGB Today: The Hidden Hand* are well-documented essential reading for those interested in digging below the surface to study systematic Soviet attempts to influence U.S. mass opinion. James L. Tyson, *Target America: The Influence of Communist Propaganda on U.S. Media,* by the former research director of Time-Life International, is also a highly regarded conservative critique outlining the extent of communist influence in American mass communication. *Soviet Hypocrisy and Western Gullibility* by Sydney Hook, Vladimir Bukovsky, and Paul Hollander discusses the susceptibility of intellectuals, religious leaders, and politicians to Soviet propaganda, and even lies about totalitarianism in the twentieth century. Each essayist, writing from personal experience, decries what is called the hypocrisy of Soviet life and information, and the silly—but by no means harmless—gullibility of many Westerners to the ideology of Marx and the *glasnost* of Gorbachev.

Soviet Influence Activities, issued in 1987 by the U.S. Department of State's Bureau of Intelligence and Research, describes active measures by the USSR in America and names Soviet front groups spreading disinformation aimed at discrediting the United States. The Soviet AIDS disinformation campaign as well as propaganda about the USSR's role in Afghanistan are examined in great detail. This complements *Contemporary Soviet Propaganda and Information,* a 337-page report summarizing the research findings of experts brought together by the U.S. Department of State and the Central Intelligence Agency in 1985; and *Soviet Covert Action (The Forgery Offensive)* and *Soviet Active Measures,* published records of oversight hearings conducted in 1980 and 1982 by the U.S. House of Representatives Permanent Select Committee on Intelligence.

Terrorism/Counterterrorism

Terrorism has often been described as "propaganda of the deed"—a strategy used by activists when their socially acceptable information efforts are inadequate to effect change. However, it was not until 1970 that the term *terrorism* first entered the *New York Times Index.* Selecting the term *terrorist* rather than other options such as "freedom fighter," "member of a liberation front," "resistance leader," or even "guerrilla" implies that the specific action is illegitimate or criminal. On the other hand, use of one of the alternative labels encourages the reader, viewer, or listener to accept a particular incident—even if it involves kidnapping, bombing, or killing—as a legitimate attention-getting tactic in an unequal struggle for social justice.

Clearly, terrorism is not simply going to wither away. A solid introductory grounding to the phenomenon is found in *The Terrorism Reader*, edited in a new edition by Walter Laqueur and Yonah Alexander. The history of terrorism, including contemporary developments, is well covered. This should be compared to *Alchemists of Revolution: Terrorism in the Modern World* by Richard E. Rubenstein, offering "a clear-eyed look at the terrorist mentality, its origins, and consequences;" *The Never-Ending War: Terrorism in the 80's* by Christopher Dobson and Ronald Payne, with a who's who guide to terrorism today; and *Beating International Terrorism: An Action Strategy for Preemption and Punishment* by Stephen Sloan, which, despite being a short monograph, clearly defines issues and terminology before opting for military control of American antiterrorist activities.

Television has often been accused of promoting the cause of terrorist violence. Although written from a British perspective, or perhaps because of it, *Televising "Terrorism": Political Violence in Popular Culture* by Philip Schlesinger, Graham Murdock, and Philip Elliot might be profitably read by students and analysts in the United States. After discussing the work of critics on both the left and right, the book argues for a more sophisticated understanding of the way in which television coverage of terrorism is conducted. The authors also outline an approach to analysis that incorporates not only factual news coverage but also fictional representations that could be usefully applied in an American context.

Claire Sterling, *The Terror Network: The Secret War of International Terrorism*, and Edward S. Herman, *The Real Terror Network: Terrorism in Fact and Propaganda* come to opposite conclusions. Sterling's book supports the conservative position that most terrorism movements are globally interlocked and manipulated by KGB agent provocateurs to support Soviet aims indirectly. Herman disputes this U.S. government-supported "official" account, arguing that Sterling and those like her are right-wing Cold Warriors dispensing pseudo-scientific disinformation to direct attention away from American-backed state terrorism in Latin America, Israel, South Africa, Indonesia, and other countries.

Also of interest is *Low Intensity Warfare: Counterinsurgency, Proinsurgency, and Antiterrorism in the 80s,* edited by Michael Klare and Peter Kornbluh. This brings together eight experts who investigate the nature and future of American warfighting capabilities as they are reoriented toward unconventional conflict situations in the Third World—what the Pentagon calls "low-intensity warfare." The contributors are associated with three important Washington-based policy analysis centers: the Institute for Policy Studies, the Center for Defense Information, and the Carnegie Endowment for International Peace.

Ongoing scholarship is reported in *Terrorism*, a major new journal published by Taylor and Francis. This presents the results of original research by social scientists, humanists, public officials, and diplomats on the types, causes, consequences, control, and management of all forms of terrorism. The approach is interdisciplinary, with articles examining the historical, legal, sociological, psychological, philosophical, political, biological, and economic aspects of the subject.

Political Definitions

Dictionary of Modern Political Ideologies, edited by Michael A. Riff, is a sourcebook tracing the origins of most modern ideologies to ideas born of the European Enlightenment, particularly in the tumult of the French Revolution and its aftermath. Rather than simply offering a chronological history of various Western political movements, the contributors discuss the subsequent development of these ideas and their manifestation in approximately 200 distinct "isms" today. See also *Beyond Liberal and Conservative* by William S. Maddox and Stuart A. Lilie, which shows the need to incorporate populist and libertarian categories in demographic research if ideological diversity in the political terrain is to be effectively analyzed in the future. Another reference to consult is *Right Minds: A Sourcebook of American Conservative Thought* by Gregory Wolfe. This features a detailed bibliography of important conservative writings and serves as a convenient desktop reference to leaders, organizations, foundations, publishers, etc. (including addresses and phone numbers). More conventional is Louis Filler, *Dictionary of American Conservatism,* which should be consulted, but does not really live up to its jacket billing as "the first complete guide to issues, people, events, organizations." For example, it includes Jimmy Carter but leaves out Willis Carto and Liberty Lobby.

Pressure/Power Special Interest Groups and Lobbying

If you have been in a major American air terminus, you have likely encountered dedicated individuals distributing attractive books, magazines, and *The New Federalist* newspaper—all literature representing the political philosophies of Lyndon LaRouche and his supporters. Given the growth of the government sector in our society, it is not surprising that such special interests attempt to influence the opinions of selected audiences. Lobbying actually is protected in the First Amendment, a right jealously guarded by those seeking redress of grievances. For example, opponents of Judge Robert Bork's nomination to the Supreme Court conducted an unprecedented public campaign to prevent his confirmation in 1987. Heavy news coverage resulted from updated releases of polling data and a steady stream of other media events. Grass-roots contact with senators was encouraged in broadcast and print ads as well as through sophisticated computerized phone lists used to direct calls to targeted homes. Organizational supporters of Bork such as We the People were outraged and responded by charging that the anti-Bork forces spent millions of dollars to create a hate campaign. Bork opponents such as the American Civil Liberties Union and the National Organization of Women shrugged off the criticism as sour grapes and said that they were clarifying the record to encourage democratic citizen participation in a decision with far-reaching social implications.

Literally hundreds of other policy think tanks such as the conservative Heritage Foundation or the liberal Brookings Institution compete for influence in government, media, and public opinion. Heritage, for example, sponsors seminars, liaisons with other like-minded organizations and academics, produces an *Annual Guide to Public Policy Experts,* coordinates testimony, lobbies, conducts studies, sponsors a booth at media trade conventions such as the annual meeting of the Radio-Television News Directors Association, and produces a wide variety of "audience positioned" informational materials. These range from a newsletter such as *Heritage Today,* summarizing activities and collating reprints of news articles mentioning the foundation and its members, to a prestige academic-style intellectual journal, *Policy Review,* to position papers and backgrounders on topical subjects and critical issues such as trade, national security, Taiwan, and the United Nations, to books on the merits of enterprise zones. Similarly, *Policy Analysis* is an interesting libertarian think-tank publication by the feisty Cato Institute, typically poking holes in conventional public policy arguments through well thought out summaries and alternative proposals.

Among the first to study this relationship of pressure groups and propaganda in depth was Harwood Childs, who assembled a series of topical papers by twenty-eight leading authorities and students for a special issue of the *Annals* of the American Academy of Political and Social Sciences in May 1935. Much of this was previously unpublished; although somewhat dated, it continues to have historical and theoretical interest. Also of historical relevance are *Interest Groups in American Politics* by L. Harmon Ziegler and Wayne C. Peak, and *Pressure Groups in American Politics* by H. R. Mahood.

For current detailed overviews of 250 leading advocacy groups supplemented with commentaries by noted policy experts, see the latest edition of *Public Interest Profiles,* edited by Douglas J. Bergner of the Foundation for Public Affairs. *The Washington Lobby,* updated regularly and published by the staff of *Congressional Quarterly,* also provides an unbiased comprehensive overview of contemporary lobbying tactics in the United States. Introductory material includes a compact history of lobbying and federal attempts to regulate it. Additional sections describe how the executive branch lobbies in behalf of the White House; trace the development and impact of political action committees (PACs); profile major business, labor, and public interest lobbies; and analyze the work of foreign lobbyist organizations working in the United States. There is an index and a detailed bibliography of pertinent books, articles, and documents. All in all, *The Washington Lobby* is mandatory reading for its subject.

If you ever wondered why Congress couldn't balance the budget and why money keeps getting spent on projects and programs you don't like, William Ashworth's *Under the Influence: Congress, Lobbies, and the American Pork-Barrel System* has the answer. The answer, of course, is that the pork barrel isn't just dams and other public works. It involves almost every decision made by Congress, particularly when questions of the public interest are raised. This is a no-nonsense guide to the reality of Washington lobbying and how self-interests couch their rhetoric to influence public policy. Additional information is in the report prepared by the Congressional Research Service for the U.S. Senate's Committee on Government Affairs, *Congress and Pressure Groups: Lobbying in a Modern Democracy,* published in 1986.

Detailed case studies can be especially instructive, as is the case with the fascinating *Showdown at Gucci Gulch: Lawmakers, Lobbyists, and the Unlikely Triumph of Tax Reform* by Jeffrey H. Birnbaum and Alan S. Murray. Probably the best, and most critical, survey of how the process can be manipulated by sophisticated insiders, however, is found in *Destroying Democracy: How Government Funds Partisan Politics* by James T. Bennett and Thomas J. DiLorenzo. They document how every year governments give hundreds of millions of taxpayer dollars to organizations that use the money for political advocacy—lobbying, campaigning, grass-roots organizing, and more. Although Congress has prohibited the use of federal funds for political activities and lobbying, abuses of the law are widespread and flagrant. A 1987 study by the Postal Rate Commission, for example, found that 21 percent of nonprofit subsidized mail contains political advocacy.

Equally controversial is the impact of foreign lobbyists, who have often proved very adept at representing their national interests in American corridors of power. For example, in 1974 Arab nations began a coordinated program outlined in a highly confidential document, "Public Affairs Program for the Arab World," to spend as much as $15 million annually employing a network of Washington lobbyists, influential lawyers, public relations experts, political consultants, and other highly paid specialists to shift American public opinion away from the Israelis. How successful they have been is argued in *Pro-Arab Propaganda in America: Vehicles and Voices,* a research brief published by the Anti-Defamation League of B'nai B'rith. Contrast this with the challenging anti-Zionist thesis in *They Dare to Speak Out: People and Institutions Confront Israel's Lobby* by former Congressman Paul Findley.

Joining the traditional corridor lobbyists (an estimated 15,000 currently work Capitol Hill pleading causes for their clients) are increasing numbers of PACs which utilize all available channels from personal contact to direct mail and advocacy advertising in order to create support for their business, labor, or ideological agenda. Corporations are barred by law from making direct political contributions, but following a 1974 ruling of the Federal Election Commission which said that there was nothing illegal about businesses soliciting voluntary donations from employees for electoral purposes, the number of business PACs alone jumped from less than 100 to nearly 4,000. *National Trade and Professional Associations of the United States* has annual listings of more than 6,000 groups. While PACs are excluded from this work, they do appear in a companion directory issued yearly called *Washington Representatives*. Another useful research reference is the *Encyclopedia of Associations,* updated continuously and published in multiple volumes. This is the most complete guide to nonprofit membership organizations with national scope. Listed are the name, location, size, objectives, and other useful data for over 14,000 organizations. All of the above are thoroughly cross-referenced. Current editors are Karin E. Keak and Susan Boyles Martin.

Several recent studies analyze the rise and status of important contemporary movements. *Persuasion and Social Movements* by Charles J. Stewart, Craig Smith, and Robert E. Denton, Jr., synthesizes previous research in the study of persuasion and applies the findings to investigations of current social movements (the radical right and pro-life movements) and nontraditional discourse (songs, slogans, and obscenities). Also worth looking at is Irwin Unger's *The Movement: A History of the American New Left, 1959–1972,* a concise, objective survey of the emergence and decline of the romanticized student political rebellion against middle-class values characterized by rock and roll, posters of Che Guevara, and marches against the war in Vietnam. Some of this same moral enthusiasm has been applied to tackling the problems of racism and poverty. See, for example, Robert Tomshoi's survey of the Hispanic immigration struggle in the sympathetic *The American Sanctuary Movement*.

Taking a very different topic, Joni Lovenduski and Joyce Outshoorn have edited *The New Politics of Abortion*. This is a useful guide to understanding the complexities of abortion arguments, networks, and pressure group activities as they influence political agendas here in the United States and Europe. Similarly, *The New Women's Movement: Feminism and Political Power in Europe and the U.S.A.,* edited by Drude Dahlerup, concentrates on how decentralized, grass-roots organizing has been able to effect political change. Mary Frances Berry's *Why ERA Failed: Politics, Women's Rights, and the Amending Process of the Constitution* is a balanced analysis of the ERA campaign, placing its rise and fall in constitutional, political, and ideological contexts.

While the scandals facing some prominent televangelists have dominated the headlines, much religious activity of interest to propaganda researchers is happening behind the scenes. For specialized—if biased—looks at some of the more controversial organizations and activists, see Dave Hunt, *The Cult Explosion;* Marilyn Ferguson, *The Aquarian Conspiracy: Personal and Social Transformation in the 1980s;* and Constance Cumby, *The Hidden Dangers of the Rainbow: The New Age Movement and Our Coming Age of Barbarism.*

Public Relations, Advertising, and Issues Management

The art of opinion molding is practiced in even the most primitive tribes, with evidence reaching back to the earliest written records. But advertising and public relations, as specialized research-based vocations concerned with image building, did not develop as recognized professions until relatively recently. The rise of the Western democracies, including the United States, meant that greater attention needed to be paid public opinion both in expanding markets for consumer goods and informing political policies reflecting a national consensus. Thus the growth in public relations parallels the rise of advertising as key components of twentieth-century society.

Business leaders realize that public opinion and government regulation are likely to be a major part of corporate decision making for the future despite the often capricious nature of public opinion. We seem to be in a period of accelerating change and uncertainty. But because no single clear-cut public interest standard exists, any attempt to influence issue development and policy implementation is open to controversy. For example, business critics such as Michael Schudson in *Advertising, the Uneasy Persuasion* warn that "deep pocket" corporate advocacy can distort the public policy process and result in dangerous "information inequality." Other commentators argue that such communication is narrowing the gap between corporate performance and public expectations by harmonizing corporate practices to public interests.

Art Stevens's *The Persuasion Explosion: Your Guide to the Power and Influence of Contemporary Public Relations,* sounds like an exposé. While essentially anecdotal, the author's breezy style and use of numerous examples to illustrate his thesis that public relations is a necessary part of society make for a useful quick-read introduction to modern PR practices. In terms of basic public relations textbooks, the market is flooded with them. Among the best and most widely taught from are the latest editions of Otis Baskin and Craig Aronoff, *Public Relations: The Profession and the Practice* ; Scott M. Cutlip, Allen H. Center, and Glen M. Broom, *Effective Public Relations;* S. Watson Dunn, *Public Relations: A Contemporary Approach,* with a more marketing-oriented focus; James E. Grunig and Todd Hunt, *Managing Public Relations,* structured to emphasize systems theory; and Doug Newsom, Alan Scott, and Judy Vanslyke Turk, *This Is PR.*

The historical development of public relations is generally covered in these texts, but numerous lacunae need to be filled in by specialists. The earliest public relations practitioners—individuals such as James Ellsworth,

George Michaelis, and Ivy Lee—were former journalists whose newspaper background made them valuable press agents for big business. Over time, however, they saw the need to shape as well as explain corporate policy. Edward L. Bernays, the nephew of Freud who rejected individual psychotherapy to concentrate on linking psychological principles to practical mass applications, helped focus attention on how meaningful public relationships might be collectively engineered with his seminal books *Crystalizing Public Opinion* and *Propaganda*.

Among the more intriguing published studies tracing the development of public relations as a managerial function, led by defenders of railroads and utilities against labor unrest and political hostility, is Alan R. Raucher's *Public Relations and Business, 1900–1929*. While Raucher outlines some of the ethical problems facing these corporate defenders, his approach is essentially sympathetic. Much more critical is Marvin N. Olasky, who argues for the elimination of public relations entirely. Olasky takes on Bernays and argues that the ongoing purpose of most corporate public relations has been to erect a mask of social responsibility behind which management can ruthlessly collude with government to stifle competition. Writing in *Corporate Public Relations: A New Historical Perspective*, Olasky uses a number of case studies to paint a sad portrait of continuing manipulation and to raise ongoing questions about the ethical role of business in American society today.

Olasky's pessimistic conclusions are open to question, however, even though today the new bottom line is public acceptance; this has necessitated a radical shift from the traditional adherence to profitmaking at any cost to a more socially responsible balance of interests. Though corporate attempts at issues management occurred as early as the nineteenth century, evidence is mounting that it is evolving into a specialized strategic planning process requiring broader organizational involvement than traditional public relations/affairs campaigns. These important developments stem from the desire by executive leaderships to integrate with long-term social changes through proactive—as compared to reactive—intervention in the public interest process. Issues management functions include (1) integrating public policy issues analysis and audits into corporate strategic planning; (2) monitoring standards of corporate performance to discover the opinions and values key publics hold which may affect corporate operations: (3) developing and implementing codes of corporate social accountability; (4) assisting senior management decision making, particularly in readjusting corporate goals and operating policies vis-à-vis public opinion; (5) identifying, prioritizing, and analyzing empirically those issues of greatest operational, financial, and political significance to the organization; (6) creating multidimensional proactive and reactive response plans from among the range of available issue change strategy options; (7) communicating on issues important to various key publics to direct opinion and stall or mitigate the development and effects of undesirable regulation; and (8) evaluating the impact of these efforts to make ongoing improvements in recommendations to the management core.

A still timely and comprehensive introduction to what business advocates are doing is found in *The Public Affairs Handbook*, edited by Joseph S. Nagelschmidt. The forty-one successful practitioners featured draw upon their experience to describe the evolution of the public affairs function, explain how such departments are commonly structured, reveal the ways public policy issues are identified by government/business political relations specialists, and discuss resulting grass-roots mobilization programs. This should be updated and contrasted with S. Prakash Sethi's more critical *Advocacy Advertising and Large Corporations: Social Conflict, Big Business Image, the News Media, and Public Policy;* his *Handbook of Advocacy Advertising: Concepts, Strategies, and Applications,* offering numerous case histories and hundreds of illustrated examples from the print and broadcast media; and *Business and Public Policy: Dimensions of Conflict and Cooperation,* co-edited by Sethi and Cecilia McHugh Falbe.

W. Howard Chase (a founding father of both the Public Relations Society of America and the Issues Management Association) and Raymond P. Ewing (at Allstate Insurance Companies) pioneered in applying futures research and developing contemporary advocacy advertising. Chase's *Issue Management: Origins of the Future* and Ewing's *Managing the New Bottom Line: Issues Management for Senior Executives* are excellent insider-written primers directed at a management audience. Drawing upon years of practical experience, they explain and illustrate step by step the basics of identifying potential public policy issues, analyzing them, selecting from appropriate change strategy options, creating action programs, and conducting continuing evaluation. More in-depth in terms of outlining the actual methods and techniques used by successful practitioners is the highly recommended *Issues Management: How You Can Plan, Organize, and Manage for the Future* by Joseph F. Coates, Vary T. Coates, Jennifer Jarratt, and Lisa Heinz. The book also contains numerous charts and graphs. *Issues Management: Corporate Public Policymaking in an Information Society* by Robert L. Heath and Richard Alan Nelson is more scholarly. After reviewing the history and practice of issues management, Heath and Nelson demonstrate that efforts by business to communicate to targeted audiences—even when propagandistic—are an important antidote to information imbalance created by artificial government regulatory restrictions on business speech. Coverage of broadcast Fairness Doctrine and IRS deductibility issues is particularly detailed, and an impressive reference and case law bibliography is appended. In conjunction with leading practitioners and scholars, Heath in 1988 extended research in the area by editing *Strategic Issues Management: How Organizations Influence and Respond to Public Interests and Policies.* This offers specific advice on creating a comprehensive corporate survival strategy for the 1990s.

Oscar H. Gandy, Jr.'s *Beyond Agenda Setting: Information Subsidies and Public Policy* takes a different approach in examining advocacy attempts. *Beyond Agenda Setting* is a thought-provoking, but at times strident, analysis of the often successful manipulations applied to mass media and other communication channels by corporations, bureaucrats, politicians, and consumer advocates. Gandy warns that organizations are successfully using indirect as well as more open means to influence the outcome of policy debates to their—not necessarily the public's—advantage. The book begins with a discussion of agenda setting as it is traditionally explored. Building on insights from political economy and decision theory, the author then provides numerous illustrations and examples which describe the flow of information and influence in the areas of science, technology, education, and social service delivery. Interestingly integrated are discussions of corporate issue advertising, government information as subsidized news, the growth of television docudrama as a replacement for the documentary, and information inequity. The final chapter identifies problems and possible goals for structured research into the ideological role of information subsidies in the public policy process. The extensive bibliography includes congressional hearings, corporate publications, and research reports.

Propaganda and Education, authored by William Wishart Biddle in 1932, was an early exploration of the business linkage between propaganda and education. It has been updated with the issuance of *Hucksters in the Classroom: A Review of Industry Propaganda in Schools* by Sheila Harty. Published by the Ralph Nader-organized Center for the Study of Responsible Law, the book examines four major areas of current controversy (nutrition education, nuclear power advocacy, environmental education, and economics education). A major conclusion is that American school teachers have been largely dependent on business-produced educational materials. Harty is particularly critical of sponsored films and videos distributed by organizations such as Modern Talking Picture Service. For more on the role of sponsored film from a less strident perspective, see Jay E. Gordon, *Motion Picture Production for Industry,* and Walter Klein, *The Sponsored Film.*

Labor Union Propaganda

In contrast, *Labor's New Voice: Unions and the Mass Media* by Sara U. Douglas is an important study of public relations activities by unions. The book explores relevant history, legal and regulatory factors, economic constraints, and short-and long-term goals—incorporating several case studies to show how the labor movement in recent years has again been more active in advocacy communication. An important theme throughout is access. The publisher of the book is Ablex, based in Norwood, New Jersey, which has fast become an important source of information for critical studies in the field of communications and information science. While the slant is usually politically leftist, the research is well documented and often at the cutting edge of developments of interest to students of propaganda.

It is important to note that federal, state, and local governments have historically worked to support corporate interests by suppressing more radical labor organizations. Various means, including deportation of foreign-born leaders, have been utilized at different times. Eldridge Foster Dowell's *History of Criminal Syndicalism Legislation in the United States,* first published in 1939, is a valuable pioneering study of legal attempts to suppress radical worker movements such as the Industrial Workers of the World (IWW or "Wobblies"). *The Price of Vigilance* by Joan Jensen traces in scholarly style the history of the American Protective League, a World War I–period business organization which promoted vigilante action to combat militant labor groups. Similarly, Louis F. Post's *The Deportations Delirium,* originally appearing in 1923, features disclosures by the assistant secretary of labor on anti-radical raids of 1919–20. However, William Preston, Jr.'s *Aliens and Dissenters* is the benchmark study, standing as the basic work on this subject. Preston utilized correspondence in the National Archives to document federal acquiescence to pressure by business groups for repression of activist labor organizations during World War I and after. Following publication of the book in 1963, FBI director J. Edgar Hoover ordered a review of archival holdings which restricted access to some of the cited materials and removed other "sensitive" materials from public files.

Contemporary revelations that the FBI investigated organizations outspokenly opposed to the Reagan administration's Central American policies are newsworthy but not particularly unique, as we have seen. Frank J. Donner's *The Age of Surveillance: The Aims and Methods of America's Political Intelligence System* is a devastating critique of the limits of democracy written by a noted attorney while director of the American Civil Liberties Project on Political Surveillance. This monumental book rather chillingly documents how from the Red Scare of World War I to the Watergate scandals of the 1970s continuing (often illegal) attempts were made to suppress political dissenters and other movements seeking social change. These clandestine campaigns against Americans were conducted by officials of their own government. Although left-leaning progressives were often targeted, legal activities by rightist organizations also were regularly victimized by disinformation. The exercise of civil liberties by potentially subversive individuals and organizations highlights the ongoing constitutional tension between investigative information gathering and more aggressive uses of surveillance to disrupt political free speech. Also worth reading in this same vein is Athan Theoharis's *Spying on Americans: Political Surveillance from Hoover to the Huston Plan.* This is a solid history of the abuses of the American domestic intelligence system from 1936, when President Franklin Roosevelt verbally authorized investigation of fascist and communist activities, until 1978, when proposals were made to lift existing restrictions under White House direction. An eye-opening chapter is devoted to exposing a variety of government political counterintelligence programs (COINTELPROs) secretly conducted to neutralize opposition to federal policies.

In studying labor history and propaganda, a number of useful reference guides to workers' movements exist. Since the amount of overlap material is relatively small, serious researchers should consult them all. Among the most important are Gulik, Ockert, and Wallace's *History and Theories of Working Class Movements—A Select Bibliography;* two bibliographies by the Institute of Labor and Industrial Relations at the University of Illinois entitled *American Labor in Journals of History* and *Labor History in the United States;* James McBrearty's *American Labor History and Comparative Labor Movements—A Selected Bibliography* (which includes a brief but intriguing section on labor novels); Maurice Neufeld's *A Representative Bibliography of American Labor History;* and Gerald Friedberg's annotated "Sources for the Study of Socialism in America, 1901–1919." Also helpful are two pamphlets: John Evansohn et al.'s *Literature of the American Working Class,* and a descriptive introduction to the "Wobblies" prepared by IWW members entitled "A Reading List on IWW History," with pro-union citations on a variety of topic areas.

The standard labor history, sympathetic to the aspirations of workers, is Philip S. Foner's multivolume *History of the Labor Movement in the United States.* Also important in analyzing labor theory and ideology, especially its more radically politicized elements, are several master's theses and doctoral studies, including Thomas Howard McEnroe, "The International Workers of the World: Theories, Organizational Problems and Appeals as Revealed Principally in *Industrial Worker*"; Donald Barnes, "Ideology of the IWW"; and John Crow, "Ideology and Organization."

Most IWW magazines were not archived by libraries when first published, but Greenwood Press has conveniently republished a number of key journals in bound form with introductions by recognized academic labor historians. These include *International Socialist Review* (Chicago, 1900–1918), *Industrial Union Bulletin* (Chicago, 1907–9), *Industrial Worker* (Spokane, 1909–13), *One Big Union Monthly* (Chicago, 1919–28), *Industrial Pioneer* (Chicago, 1921–26), and *Industrial Unionist* (Portland, Oregon, 1925–26). *Rebel Voices, an IWW Anthology,* edited by Joyce Kornbluh, draws from the files of these IWW publications and other hard to come by materials to reproduce a representative sample of articles, poems, photographs, and cartoons.

Contemporary journals with valuable labor material include *Labor History* (1960-present), the resurrected *Industrial Worker, Radical America,* and other publications. For example, an interesting reminiscence on IWW use of colorful stickers for organizing is well discussed in an illustrated article in *American West* by Tony Bubka.

Free Speech, the Mass Media, and Propaganda

Surveys reveal that most people in the United States endorse freedom of speech for the views they believe in but welcome censorship of positions they oppose. This general misunderstanding of the rationale for constitutional speech guarantees and the ongoing history of attempted controls point to a continuing need for defenders of the First Amendment to articulate its worth even when media are used as a conduit for propaganda.

For a history lesson see Thomas L. Tedford's *Freedom of Speech in the United States,* an important new book summarizing the history of control on free speech, stressing the ethical responsibilities of sender and receiver. Valuable appendixes explain the federal court system, chart underlying First Amendment theory, and index 310 key cases. For an overview of some major historical turning points, see Craig R. Smith's *The Fight for Freedom of Expression: Three Case Studies,* written by a leading contemporary media civil libertarian. The case studies involve events surrounding passage of the Alien and Sedition Acts of 1798, the Reconstruction Acts following the Civil War, and the Subversive Activities Control Act of 1950, which set the stage for Senator Joseph McCarthy's anti-communist investigations. Appendixes include reprints of pertinent documents and speeches.

More detailed is Leonard W. Levy's *Emergence of a Free Press,* a greatly revised and enlarged edition of his landmark 1960 book, *Legacy of Suppression.* That work created a storm of controversy when it was first published by challenging the absolutist position on the freedom of the press. He maintained that it was not the intention of the framers of the First Amendment to overturn the common law of seditious libel, the principal means of suppressing political dissent. On the basis of further research, however, Levy has revised some of his earlier views and deepened others. He now contends that the early press was far more robust in its criticisms of public officials and policies than existing laws and theoretical tradition would seem to have allowed. That makes the new book a major source work, now much more supportive of the libertarian absolutist view. Thomas C. Leonard's *The Power of the Press: The Birth of American Political Reporting* is a pioneering look at the birth of political journalism. It traces the rise of political reporting, beginning with the exposés that helped trigger the revolution in 1776 through the emergence of muckraking at the beginning of the twentieth century. Supplementing these is Jeffery A. Smith, *Printers and Press Freedom: The Ideology of Early American Journalism,* which tracks the origins of the freedom-of-the-press clause in the First Amendment and includes discussion of how "libertarian press theory" was translated into practice by Benjamin Franklin and others.

The Press as a Propaganda Conduit

The continuing interaction of politics, media, and propaganda is well documented in such historical works as the popularized *Political Power and the Press* by CBS Washington bureau manager William Small; *The Press, Politics, and Patronage: The American Government's Use of Newspapers, 1789–1875* by Culver Smith; the early muckraking *Our Press Gang; or, A Complete Exposition of the Corruptions and Crimes of the American Newspapers,* first published in 1859 by Lambert A. Wilmer; the similarly outspoken report on the early twentieth-century press, *The Brass Check: A Study in American Journalism* by Upton Sinclair; and the engrossing analysis of the death of truth in wartime by Phillip Knightley entitled *The First Casualty—From the Crimea to Vietnam: The War Correspondent as Hero, Propagandist, and Myth Maker,* which supplements Oscar W. Riegel's gloomily prophetic *Mobilizing for Chaos: The Story of the New Propaganda.* See also George Seldes's angry exposé of corrupt media, *The Facts Are . . . A Guide to Falsehood and Propaganda in the Press and Radio,* and Kent Cooper's *The Right to Know: An Exposition of the Evils of News Suppression and Propaganda.* Less satisfying is David Wise's *The Politics of Lying: Government Deception, Secrecy and Power.* Overly dramatic in tone (befitting Wise's experience as a journalist) and somewhat simplistic in analysis, the book provides a rather vitriolic view of the Nixon administration's attempts to manipulate public opinion by ahistorically condemning it as the first to condone habitual lying. Wise's basic problem is that he fails to recognize the failings of the news media themselves and is guilty of many of the same faults he criticizes, such as concealing sources. Also refer to C. Richard Hofstetter's *Bias in the News: Network Television Coverage of the 1972 Election Campaign,* which argues that McGovern—not Nixon—was the real media victim. For a contrasting view see Victor Lasky, *It Didn't Start with Watergate.*

The up-to-date *The Interplay of Influence: Mass Media and Their Publics in News, Advertising, Politics,* by Kathleen Hall Jamieson and Karlyn Kohrs Campbell, explains how key mass media systems interact with society and respond to a variety of commercial, political, group, self-imposed, and other pressures. A number of case studies document the commercial limitations and persuasive nature of news, audience analysis, advertising, and political versus product campaigns. The book encourages readers to go beyond claims of media manipulation to become activists themselves. W. Lance Bennett's textbook *News: The Politics of Illusion* presents a well-documented critique of the news to demonstrate how government leaders, journalists, and the general public all contribute to the illusory nature of mass media reporting in the United States—particularly how mass prejudices and stereotypes are reinforced.

Much of the recent criticism has emanated from conservative authors who perceive a deliberate leftist bias in media (particularly broadcasting).

Representative publications include *Distortion by Design:—The Story of America's Liberal Press* by the Reverend Billy James Hargis; *The News Twisters* and *How CBS Tried to Kill a Book,* both by *TV Guide* columnist Edith Efron, which detail controversies in the early 1970s over her findings that there were indeed anti-Nixon media tendencies at the three major networks; Joseph Keeley's somewhat rambling *The Left Leaning Antenna: Political Bias in Television;* Tim La Haye's pro-Christian exploration of humanism's "stranglehold" on the media in *The Hidden Censors;* and the work of Accuracy in Media (AIM), a Washington-based conservative watchdog organization. See particularly AIM chairman Reed Irvine's collection of columns entitled *Media Mischief and Misdeeds. The Media Elite: America's New Powerbrokers* by S. Robert Lichter, Stanley Rothman, and Linda S. Lichter is the most scientific and serious of the books demonstrating that journalists working for the major national media share common political perspectives and exercise growing influence over public opinion. To keep tabs on their current research, the Lichters edit *Media Monitor,* a research publication of the Center for Media and Public Affairs.

In contrast, Martin Linsky's *Impact: How the Press Affects Federal Policymaking* and the companion volume he co-authored with Jonathan Moore, Wendy O'Donnell, and David Whitman, *How the Press Affects Federal Policymaking: Six Case Studies,* attempt to demonstrate that the press are neither passive, detached observers of government nor liberal interventionists who heavy-handedly impose their views through selective reporting. Linsky and his collaborators do agree, however, that the media act to frame issues and influence government policy. Cases cover three administrations and include the 1969 reorganization of the Postal Department, the resignation of Vice President Agnew, the decision of President Carter not to deploy the neutron bomb, the Love Canal chemical tragedy, the struggle over Bob Jones University's attempt to retain tax exemption, and the 1984 case on the suspension of Social Security disability reviews. Although rich in anecdotes, the books lack any theoretical underpinning, which weakens their presentation.

A timely and important series, Presidents and the Press, co-published by the White Burkett Miller Center of Public Affairs and the University of Virginia, includes several studies of interest. Blaire Atherton French, *The Presidential Press Conference: Its History and Role in the American Political System,* is a monograph answering questions about the origins of the press conference and how and why it came to be as we find it today. *The White House Press on the Presidency: News Management and Co-option,* by Frank Cormier, James Deakin, and Helen Thomas, offers "insider" opinion by three senior White House correspondents about how the news media are co-opted by the officials they cover. Also included as an appendix is a reprint of *The Report of the Commission on Presidential Press Conferences.* Finally, John E. Mueller's *War, Presidents and Public Opinion* is a minor classic presenting rigorous reanalysis of public opinion on the wars in Korea and Vietnam.

In showing how polling results were often misused, the author develops many unconventional conclusions including, for example, the argument that the press and the antiwar movement probably had little special impact on attitudes toward the Vietnam conflict.

Dale Minor's *The Information War* is a practical primer on how the government has intervened in the news process. Drawing on his experience as a Pacifica Radio correspondent, Minor traces the cynical cooperation (and occasional confrontation) between government and media gatekeepers in manipulating, censoring, and directing the news for their own corrupt practices. Events in Vietnam form the backdrop for much of Minor's report. Specialized analyses of contemporary U.S. military propaganda activities include former U.S. Senator J. William Fulbright's *The Pentagon Propaganda Machine* and a post-Vietnam update by Juergen Arthur Heise titled *Minimum Disclosure: How the Pentagon Manipulates the News*. This latter work is based on the author's personal encounters with military information officers.

For a variety of views, see a current reader. One that raises fundamental questions about how the mass media shape public opinion and serve as propaganda conduits is *When Information Counts: Grading the Media*, edited by Bernard Rubin. Herbert I. Schiller's *The Mind Managers*, written in the early 1970s, is still useful to counteract the more chauvinistic "us versus them" views, angrily surveying the role the communications industry plays as a purveyor of propaganda. Updating the work of thoughtful leftist critics such as Schiller and George Seldes is Ben H. Bagdikian's *The Media Monopoly*, which presents an insightful and readable introduction to how news is being used by propagandists. Contrast these views with those of the equally critical Michael Parenti in *Inventing Reality: The Politics of the Mass Media*. Parenti is angry, too, in outlining a provocative thesis. However, he says that a continuing pattern of press misrepresentation works to uphold capitalistic ideological values while distorting Marxist criticisms which might lead to a more genuine discourse on what needs to be done to change the world for the better. The book is worth reading. Another Marxian perspective is provided in James Aronson's now dated *Packaging the News: A Critical Survey of Press, Radio, TV*.

Also of interest is Robert Cirino's mildly left critique, *Don't Blame the People: How the News Media Use Bias, Distortion and Censorship to Manipulate Public Opinion*. See particularly the chapter titled "The Importance of Propaganda." Cirino argues that the news media manipulated attitudes toward the Vietnam War, minorities, car safety, crime, abortion, pollution, safety, population increase, dissenters, the hazards of smoking, and hunger in America—not to serve liberal causes, but to serve the mass media's and the corporate establishment's own profit-making and political interests. For these reasons the author, a history teacher, blames the news media and not the people (hence the book's title) for what he sees as the mistaken priorities and policies that have made America unnecessarily pay so high a price in lives, resources, environmental quality, and worldwide respect. In another work by Cirino called *We're Being More than Entertained,* rather than simply decrying the propagandistic nature of mass media, he creatively allows the reader to construct his or her own "propaganda detector." The book encourages rewriting of scripts using four basic political viewpoints (liberal, conservative, socialist, and libertarian) to study the impact of various social and political objectives on what we see. Overall this is an unusual, fun, and perceptive short analysis of the so-called entertainment industry.

International News Issues

As an antidote to unwavering acceptance of U.S. government or media claims, one might want to read the booklet *The Big Lie: Analysis of U.S. Press Coverage of the Grenada Invasion,* published by the International Organization of Journalists in cooperation with the National Alliance of Third World Journalists. Author Glen Ford, a former host and producer for the syndicated television news program "America's Black Forum," argues that despite minor differences with the government, American reporters served U.S. ruling class interests by deceitfully setting up the Cubans as villains and romantically justifying the resulting military aggression against the Grenadan government as a "rescue mission."

Ze'ev Chafets's *Double Vision: How the Press Distorts America's View of the Middle East,* by the former director of the Israeli Government Press Office during the Menachem Begin administration, argues that a closed and impenetrable Arab world, by restricting correspondent access (a fact reporters generally do not mention), and a relatively open Israel (with the largest number of foreign correspondents per capita of any country in the world) create the impression of an Israel constantly in turmoil and a relatively dull Arab world where basically nothing is going on. For a more official U.S. view, see the House Committee on Foreign Affairs hearing summary *The Media, Diplomacy and Terrorism in the Middle East,* which analyzes the role of television network coverage in unwittingly aiding terrorists.

William A. Hachten and C. Anthony Giffard comprehensively document the history of legal and political constraints on the press in South Africa in *The Press and Apartheid: Repression and Propaganda in South Africa,* with a description of media conditions current to the date of publication. Of particular interest is the chapter on "Muldergate," which details the South African Information Department's failed efforts to influence U.S. political opinion by secretly acquiring control of the *Washington Star* through bankrolling sympathetic conservative American media owner John McGoff.

Taking a less narrow topical approach, *The World News Prism: Changing Media, Clashing Ideologies* by William A. Hachten traces the growth of the global news network, especially the impact of developing technology in placing new pressures on both news organizations and governments. A new chapter in the second edition on public diplomacy and propaganda provides a good introduction to international radio and the ongoing efforts of governments to influence world opinion by manipulating foreign news media. The ever prolific Herbert I. Schiller weighs in with another important related book, *Information and the Crisis Economy,* which portrays the future information society as a nightmare rather than a blessing.

Beyond the scope of this chapter are studies attacking American television and film exports as a form of "media imperialism." Along with similar critiques decrying Western domination of the major world news and information agencies, they provide a fascinating perspective on the cultural and propaganda implications of media. Most of the fundamental issues and supporting documents are collected in *The New International Information and Communication Order,* edited by Kaarle Nordenstreng et al. Readers interested in exploring the topic further can do so by referring to Jeremy Tunstall's *The Media Are American: Anglo-American Media in the World* and other current international communications literature (particularly recent Unesco reports and the English-language issues of *The Democratic Journalist* published in Czechoslovakia).

Films that Lie

During the period of U.S. neutrality before World War II, motion pictures were already established as propaganda vehicles attempting to sway public opinion, a trend accelerated by the CPI's wartime involvement and subsequent governmental utilization of Hollywood in World War II and Korea. Current estimates of federal propaganda film work range as high as $500 million a year. (This figure omits commercial, educational, state-financed, and privately produced "sponsored" motion pictures). Again the literature is large, and a bibliographic review must be selective. A basic starting point is *Politics and Film,* a collation of available secondary sources with refreshingly objective perspective by Leif Furhammer and Folke Isaksson, which traces the troubled origins of movie propaganda, details the fervently patriotic efforts of 1914–18 through more current releases, and includes a well-organized analysis of the aesthetics and principles of the genre. Kevin Brownlow's *The War, the West and the Wilderness* is a massive study of silent films. The largest section of the book, more than 200 pages, examines the motion picture in the Spanish-American War and World War I. In addition to published material, the author conducted interviews with many newsreel and propaganda filmmakers active in the period and had access to previously unpublished letters, diaries, and logbooks. The work is lavishly illustrated, with excellent notes and a detailed index. A thoughtful study of the overuse of war themes by motion picture propaganda, with recommendations on how the screen might have been used for more uplifting purposes, is found in William Marston Seabury's *Motion Picture Problems: The Cinema and the*

League of Nations. Also of interest is Winifred Johnston's *Memo on the Movies: War Propaganda, 1914–1939,* a short but nonetheless intriguing polemical study of how "peace-loving people" "turned to ways of hate" by filmic distortion. One might compare it to more recent critiques of television as a propaganda medium.

The upheavals wrought by the two world wars and the continuing struggle between the Soviet Union and United States for international influence have spurred ongoing interest by scholars in the impact of communications on public opinion. Much of what we know about information control and the psychology of propaganda stems from earlier efforts by Harold Lasswell and others to describe propaganda techniques and analyze both private and government attempts to mobilize targeted publics and populations. One value of propaganda analysis is to be predictive of emerging trends, particularly for those of us who see the future in terms of the past. While the propaganda literature is large, a need exists for more in-depth historical studies of official propaganda by democratic and other powers in war and peace, drawing upon new research advances and the wealth of recently declassified state documents.

That is the value of Nicholas Pronay and D. W. Spring, *Propaganda, Politics and Film, 1918–1945,* and K.R.M. Short, *Film & Radio Propaganda in World War II.* These two books, each edited by a leading world scholar, bring together specialists of the first rank in the field of propaganda and communication to make an important contribution to our current knowledge of the workings and effects of propaganda. Both are organized logically. Pronay and Spring divide their volume into four parts: the official projection of Britain, film propaganda in Britain and France between the world wars, film propaganda in Britain in World War II, and the projection of the Soviet Union. Short similarly utilizes four sectional groupings, but is far more expansive in the range of topical coverage. An introduction to propaganda in international politics by Philip Taylor is followed by aspects of the allied experience ranging from racial ambiguities and attempts in American films at fighting anti-Semitism to broadcasts by Radio Luxembourg in 1944–45; then the book's coverage moves to propaganda in fascist Europe, and concludes with Japanese persuasive communication. The twenty eight chapters (thirteen and fifteen, respectively) stem from papers presented at international conferences in which co-participation by academicians and individuals personally involved in government propaganda efforts took place.

One wishes the two books had been jointly released, for not only do they share similar perspectives but a number of authors have integrative essays appearing in each volume. Among them are studies by Pronay (on news as propaganda and other topics), David Ellwood (who examines cultural propaganda by Britain and then turns southward to report on fascist propaganda from Italy), Elizabeth Strebel (on prewar and Vichy cinema),

Sergie Drobashenko (describing Soviet film), and Taylor (on interwar propaganda efforts).

While such collaborative publications are often uneven, through expert editing both volumes demonstrate unusual coherence and focus as references. Pronay, Spring, and Short (at the time all senior lecturers in history at major British universities) were well qualified for the task. Short, particularly, is well known for his *Films as History* and as editor of the influential *Historical Journal of Film, Radio and Television*. Pronay, like Spring, has held leadership positions in the InterUniversity History Film Consortium and is widely published, including co-authorship with Frances Thorpe of *British Official Films in the Second World War: A Descriptive Catalogue*.

Although all countries to some extent engage in propaganda, the British early proved particularly adept at using media for political mobilization—a point later noted by Hitler in *Mein Kampf* when outlining the communication strategy he would ultimately impose on Germany. British politics is confusing to many Europeans as well as Americans, and Pronay provides a useful introduction to the turbulent social context of interwar Britain in *Propaganda, Politics and Film*. He describes how a variety of class factors influenced continued reliance on propaganda—despite claims to the contrary—by politicians worried that democratic institutions might well collapse from powerful internal as well as external evolutionary and revolutionary challenges. This is supplemented by Pronay's informative evaluation in Short of the role played by leftist documentarists in pushing socialist causes while working in the British Ministry of Information under Conservative party administrations.

Pronay's views are also well complemented by Philip Taylor's lead essay appearing in *Film & Radio Propaganda in World War II*. As Taylor observes, the "communications revolution" we are now experiencing parallels the technological innovations of the 1920s and 1930s beyond mass print which spurred greater usage of broadcasting, newsreels, and feature motion pictures as propaganda tools during a crisis period of world history. Taylor outlines developments in various industrial countries including the United Kingdom, arguing that Britain's decline as a power forced it to exploit the new media but with questionable effectiveness (particularly in the United States and the Soviet Union). Ultimately, he says, "Truth was a casualty long before the actual fighting began."

Recognizing that some contributing authors might resent the term, the books are nevertheless revisionist in that many of the articles reflect changing views on the nature of propaganda. They agree that once war began propaganda was practiced widely by both Allied and Axis governments. Several authors point to the lack of unified policy in France, the United States, and other bellingerents, which led to contradictory propaganda campaign efforts and resulting uncertainty as to the long-term effects on intended audiences.

Generally speaking, however, Pronay, Taylor, and most of their fellow contributors fail to agree on a clear definition of propaganda—usually equating the term uncertainly with political communication. This umbrella usage is not atypical, given the imprecision and vagaries associated with its use. Commonly, "propaganda" is used as a pejorative appellation for the communication efforts of others, while the euphemism "information" is retained for one's own activities. Thus the value of Kenneth Short's insightful commentary on the problems "propaganda" has caused both for scholars and lexicologists attempting to grapple with its ambiguity. While recognizing that there are differences in propaganda styles, particularly between totalitarian one-party states and those nations with multiple political/economic/religious social organizations, Short realistically points out that "propaganda," "information," and "education" are often used interchangeably to mean "persuasion" in democracies as well as dictatorships. Indeed, he argues, because of the need to build social consensus through ideological conditioning, "a world in which *propagandas* compete for dominance and allegiance would appear to be our earthly lot."

Even though some chapters are not particularly illuminating because of the wealth of previously available material (for example, David Welch's review of wartime newsreels by National Socialist Germany offers little new), overall *Film and Radio Propaganda in World War II* is greatly strengthened by analyses of Italian, Japanese, and French topics not well covered in English. Gordon Daniel's interesting overview of Japanese domestic radio and cinema propaganda from 1937 to 1945 reports on the sustained emphasis placed on social continuity despite wartime stress. This is coupled with the unusually frank insider assessment by Namikawa Ryo of the Imperial government's Central Information Bureau and Japanese short-wave transmissions such as the "Zero Hour" broadcast to Allied troops in the Pacific. Even topics well covered elsewhere, such as David Culbert's review of the social engineering aspects of the American *Why We Fight* series, receive fresh analysis.

There are some things to criticize in the two books, among them: occasional typographical errors, the failure except in one instance to publish organizational charts clearly defining the chain of command and linkages in various propaganda agencies, the lack of photographs, no comprehensive frontispiece listing of figures and tables, inconsistent inclusion of filmographies which would have been useful for most chapters instead of only a few, the decision not to append glossaries of terms and biographical details on key personalities mentioned in the text, and the elimination of comprehensive reference bibliographies (instead each chapter has endnotes). For the most part these excisions are likely victims of the publishers' need to keep production costs within reasonable limits, and such complaints are minor in comparison to the value of each volume. In addition to suggesting the diversity of methodological approaches useful in the study of film and broadcast, both books reinforce the importance of understanding the process of dissemination and control of information. They certainly are must reading for propaganda historians and contemporary researchers seeking to learn from the past rather than repeat it.

The documentary film is an ideal vehicle for propaganda, for it combines the advantages of believability through "reality" and image manipulation (subject/shot selection plus control over the audience response to the screen dialectic via edit juxtapositioning). A number of outlets such as Third World Cinema Group, October Films, Tricontinental Film Center, and Films for Social Change arose out of the student protests in the 1960s to distribute noncommerical documentaries in actively creating a "new consciousness." Tricontinental, for example, found itself the target of a U.S. Justice Department order in 1976 to register as a "foreign agent" under the provisions of the Foreign Agents Registration Act of 1938. The law requires that registered organizations must attach a "foreign propaganda" label to their printed materials and similarly identify films with a preceding leader. In addition, all officers and employees are required to register, organizational records must be kept open to FBI investigation, and sales and rental data, including the names and addresses of customers, must be filed with the government. These and similar rules are now undergoing various legal challenges.

The interrelationship of the "factual" motion picture and propaganda is further explored in a number of other published studies. These include Thomas Bohn, *An Historical and Descriptive Analysis of the "Why We Fight" Series;* Raymond Fielding, *The American Newsreel: 1911–1967;* Richard Dyer MacCann, *The People's Films: A Political History of U.S. Government Motion Pictures;* Richard A. Maynard, *Propaganda on Film: A Nation at War,* a basic reader comparing Soviet, German, and U.S. responses to film propaganda; Tom Perlmutter, *War Movies;* Clyde Jeavons, *A Pictorial History of War Films;;* Joe Morella, Edward Z. Epstein, and John Griggs, *The Films of World War II;* Ken Jones and Arthur McClure, *Hollywood at War: The American Motion Picture Industry and World War II,* with a useful introductory essay and filmography of over 400 releases; and Roger Manvell, *Films and the Second World War,* in which Manvell provides parallels between what actually was happening in the world and how that was presented in film. All told, from 1939 to 1945 some 2,500 pictures were released in the United States. Valuable additions to the literature are the more recent *Mission to Moscow: The Feature Film as Official Propaganda,* edited by David Culbert, and *Hollywood Goes to War: How Politics, Profits, and Propaganda Shaped World War II Movies* by Clayton R. Koppes and Gregory D. Black. Unfortunately, publication has been delayed on *Film and Propaganda in America: A Documentary History,* also edited by Culbert. Projected are four volumes of new textual analysis and photographs to be supplemented with a "fifth volume" on microfiche which, when completed, will provide a veritable archive of original documents and other materials reproduced in affordable format.

Continuing interest in the topic is also reflected by the growing number of critical histories and anthologies. Lewis Jacobs's *The Documentary Tradition* collates a wide variety of works by theoreticians, critics, and filmmakers to survey mostly American and European developments. Arranged chronologically in five decade-long sections starting in 1922, it serves as a useful—though incomplete—summary. Richard M. Barsam's two major works in this area—*Nonfiction Film: A Critical History* and *Nonfiction Film: Theory and Criticism*—have been criticized for promoting a dichotomy between art and politics in arguing that documentaries can be analyzed in terms of their artistic qualities irrespective of the ideology of the filmmaker. Nevertheless, for the beginning student they are serviceable introductions to the field and incorporate adequate—if predictable—discussion of major topics related to war propaganda and government films by the USIA and other agencies. More extensive and detailed (reflecting his background as a media—as compared to simply film—historian) is Erik Barnouw's *Documentary: A History of the Non-fiction Film,* which focuses on the different roles that documentary films and filmmakers have played in society. The illustrations are thoughtful and help the text chronicle major developments in the history of documentary and its use as a forum for the socially committed. Coverage outside America is also more extensive than the books above. The short (115 pages) *About Documentary: Anthropology on Film* by Robert Edmunds is worth noting for its discussion of the fallacy of the notion of objectivity in film. Its primary value is for someone interested in teaching documentary. The book features an introduction by Lewis Jacobs and incorporates a course outline, filmography, and bibliography.

F. D. Klingender and Stuart Legg's *Money Behind the Screen,* first published in 1937, documents the economic consolidation of the major studios that saw them all come under the financial control of either Morgan or Rockefeller interests by the mid-thirties. This helps amplify explanations of the continuing cooperation between the motion picture industry and the federal government, evident in features and numerous patriotic shorts made by the studios over the years to demonstrate their patriotism. Propaganda documentaries such as *Why Korea?* (1951, Twentieth Century Fox-Movietone News) were distributed without charge, in this case to bolster Truman administration foreign policy intervention. The same basic theme was again used in *Why Viet Nam?,* a 1965 Defense Department production which revived Cold War rhetoric and analyses. Among the more ambitious anti-communist films was *Red Nightmare* (Warner Brothers, 1962; reissued 1965), produced under the personal supervision of Jack L. Warner. Narrated by television star-producer Jack Webb and featuring popular actors such as Jack Kelley and Robert Conrad, such educational pictures helped cement a long-lasting formal alliance with Pentagon project co-sponsors such as the

Department of Defense Directorate for the Armed Forces and Educational Information.

In part these releases were designed to combat the image of Hollywood as a virtual Soviet enclave. Among those leading the charge against communism was Myron C. Fagan, who edited the Cinema Educational Guild's *News-Bulletin* (first published in 1949) and later authored *Red Treason on Broadway: Stage, Television, Radio, Red Treason in Hollywood,* and *Documentation of the Red Stars in Hollywood* to focus attention on the use of front tactics by leftist media groups. Fagan, a prolific playwright with successes, found himself out of favor as his work became more political. Concerned that entertainment industry and Jewish organizations seemed to be moving further to the left, Fagan authored two controversial plays: *Thieves Paradise* (about travails in Iron Curtain Bulgaria) and *Red Rainbow* (an exposé of communist infiltration in America). His subsequent blacklisting (as an anti-communist) led him into pamphleteering for a cleanup of Hollywood and Broadway. He heartily endorsed calls for investigation of un-American practices in numerous publications issued by his Cinema Educational Guild (originally known briefly as Citizens United for American Principles), which operated from the late forties until the sixties. His oversize paperback books contain a fascinating combination of personal observation, historical philosophizing, and reprints from news items, books, and government reports. Differing perspectives can be found in alternative journals such as *Cinéaste, Jump Cut,* and *Cultural Correspondence: A Journal of Popular and Left Culture,* important sources of Marxist media ideology and history. They often feature interviews with leading activists which supplement more standard book-length studies.

American Radio and Television Broadcasting

The essential starting point for study of American broadcasting, tracing the history of radio and television from 1900 to 1970, is the 1,200-page trilogy *(A Tower in Babel, The Golden Web,* and *The Image Empire)* by Erik Barnouw. Each volume contains a wealth of material including texts of significant documents, chronology, and full bibliography. Although not particularly sympathetic to the media moguls, Barnouw avoids open editorializing until end-of-book summaries. The widespread popularity of broadcasting only underscores the importance of the long and largely successful struggle by corporate, military, and civilian government agencies to control the medium. The growth of the industry, move to commercial sponsorship, formation of the networks, emergence of "public interest" regulatory bodies co-opted by industry, limitations on private broadcasters in wartime, and official government propaganda "information" programming efforts ranging from the Armed Forces Radio and Television Service to Radio Free Europe, Radio Free Asia, Radio Liberation, and the Voice of America are all well discussed here. The result is a monument to scholarship. Interestingly, the wartime cooperation with the government proved profitable: in 1939 the industry as a whole earned 67.1 percent before-tax profits; by 1944 the figure was 222.6 percent which helped underwrite the move of the radio networks into television.

Richard W. Steele's *Propaganda in an Open Society: The Roosevelt Administration and the Media, 1933–41* is more useful for the footnotes than the narrative. Ultimately the book fails to hang together, and in actuality is more a series of articles than a coherent analysis. This is unfortunate, since there is a wealth of material here on news management and attempts to create a national propaganda agency. Readers should compare this to David Culbert's more satisfying *News for Everyman: Radio and Foreign Affairs in Thirties America* and Qualter's *Opinion Control in the Democracies,* cited earlier. On communism and television, the literature is well summarized in J. Fred McDonald's *Television and the Red Menace.* Additional studies related to broadcasting are described in *Television: A Guide to the Literature* by Mary B. Cassata and Thomas Skill, as well as in other chapters of this *Handbook.*

Political Advertising

A good place to begin is *Political Communication in America* by Robert E. Denton, Jr., and Gary C. Woodward. This encyclopedic overview of history, theory, and practices ranges from presidential marketing to mass media effects on contemporary politics. All in all, it is an excellent primer on how the "engineering of consensus" occurs. See also Robert G. Meadow's *Politics as Communication,* a useful, left-oriented introduction to the theories of political communication. It discusses how manipulation of political image and myth via news, advertising, and entertainment are expanding through new technologies.

Kathleen Hall Jamieson's *Packaging the Presidency: A History and Criticism of Presidential Campaign Advertising* is somewhat misleadingly titled. Actually the book concentrates on the 1952–80 campaigns, although an introductory chapter provides an overview of early practices through the 1940s. The themes, issues, candidates, agencies, finances, media, images, and slogans of each campaign are identified. *The Spot: The Rise of Political Advertising on Television* is now a standard reference work. But while widely praised, this is not an exhaustive scholarly treatment even in its revised edition. Authors Edwin Diamond and Stephen Bates still largely gloss over motion picture and radio broadcasting origins to such advertising; they also leave room for more thorough investigation, particularly of non-presidential television campaigns.

Of related interest is David Paletz, Robert Pearson, and Donald Willis, *Politics in Public Service Advertising on Television,* which notes the growing role of and the highly politicized atmosphere surrounding production and airing of corporate "advertorials" and nonprofit PSAs. Access to major media is dominated by the private Advertising Council, established in 1942 to support the war effort. Since then it has publicized information and positions for hundreds of organizations on such wide-ranging issues as drunken driving prevention, savings bonds, Social Security, safety belt education, the U.S. Bicentennial, the United Nations, and world hunger problems. In 1987 alone, more than $1.1 billion in free broadcast airtime and print advertising space was contributed to the Ad Council's "public service" campaigns. See also *Public Communication Campaigns,* edited by Ronald E. Rice and William J. Paisley. Following three chapters that provide historical and theoretical linkages to the long tradition of non-partisan mobilization via mass communication in America, the book presents seven case studies of various public service campaigns, and concludes with ways to analyze how these social marketing efforts can be measured in terms of effectiveness. The bibliography and index are valuable.

Music as Propaganda

Popular music has always reflected political and cultural attitudes. Advertisers, of course, use music to sell products because of its unique ability to establish mood. In recent years, rock-and-roll artists in particular have used their songs as a forum to communicate ideas, expressing their protests in styles ranging from folk to heavy metal to Christian rock. However, overtly partisan music tends to be confined to a more narrow spectrum of specialized recordings. A number of companies such as Brass Tacks Music of New Haven, Connecticut, market records and cassettes with radical political messages—in this case albums such as *Paint the Town Red* with songs such as the "Young Communist League Song" and "You Ain't Done Nothing if You Ain't Been Called a Red." See Philip S. Foner's *American Labor Songs of the Nineteenth Century.* However, the best overall information source for further study is Arnold Perris's *Music as Propaganda,* published by Greenwood Press.

RESEARCH COLLECTIONS

Much of the material of the propagandist is ephemeral. Leaflets, broadsides, banners, posters, pamphlets, broadcasts, commercials, and even motion pictures are not designed to be long-lasting. The propagandist usually is time-bound and concerned with effecting specific, measurable goals rather than creating permanent monuments to "truth." Therefore, specialized reference and research collections are critical for serious historical research involving the propaganda activities of particular organizations, agencies, and individuals. Unfortunately, important materials are widely scattered.

The difficulty is compounded because reference aids and guides to special collections are inadequately cross-referenced.

With this caveat, the logical place to begin the study of American propaganda is in Washington, D.C. Indispensable in working one's way through the maze of government records is the U.S. National Archives and Records Services's *Guide to the National Archives of the United States,* issued in 1974. All photographic and paper holdings in the National Archives are organized by government agency "Record Groups" (RG), now numbering over 400. A list of record groups is available on request from the archives; many RGs have printed "preliminary inventories" of real value in tracking down specific documents, manuscripts, and other materials. Demonstrating the extent of media involvement, an estimated seventy-five federal agencies have made motion pictures at one time or another. The National Archives now houses over 35,000 sound recordings, 50,000 reels of film, and more than 4.5 million photographic items. Among the more important RGs relating to federal propaganda and informational activities are the following:

RG 44—Office of Government Reports (OGR). This office acted as a clearinghouse for government information and helped coordinate homefront aspects of the defense and war effort in World War II until being consolidated with other agencies to form the Office of War Information in 1942. Later, the OGR was briefly reestablished to provide motion picture advertising and liaison services. Within this large collection, for example, are the records of the Office of the Coordinator of Government Films, 1941–42; still photos and posters issued by the OWI's Division of Public Inquiries, 1942–45 (14,150 items); and other pertinent propaganda materials from the Division of Press Intelligence, which issued summaries and digests of radio and press comments.

RG 63—Committee on Public Information (CPI). More than 110 linear feet of reports, correspondence, posters, bulletins, speeches, films, clippings, and other documentation detailing both the domestic and foreign work of the CPI from 1917 to 1919 are housed in this collection. Included are materials describing the anti-Bolshevik propaganda campaign conducted by the United States in Russia following the collapse of the Czarist regime.

RG 111—Office of the Chief Signal Officer. Preserved here are propaganda and informational films and newsreels made by the Signal Corps since World War I, the immense bulk of production files for World War II releases, plus other related post–1945 material.

RG 131—Office of Alien Property. Minutes, reports, pamphlets, press releases, periodicals, films, and other documents seized from German and Italian organizations operating in the United States (such as the German-American Bund) at the time of American entry into World War II are collected in this record group. For a comprehensive introduction to the more general topic of "Germany and German Film, 1930–1945" and attempts to sway American audiences, see the comprehensive three-part research bibliography by Richard Alan Nelson published by the *Journal of the University Film Association* in 1977–78.

RG 200—National Archives Gift Collection. This is a motion picture and newsreel treasure house covering the years from 1919 to 1967. Included in the collection are issues of the *Official War Review, March of Time, Paramount News, Ford Animated Weekly* (1914–21), and eight commercial films investigated by a Senate subcommittee just prior to Pearl Harbor for their alleged war propaganda. The useful *Guide to the Ford Film Collection in the National Archives* by Mayfield Bray, documenting the auto manufacturer's motion picture interests, appeared in 1970.

RG 208—Office of War Information. This is the main source of OWI documentation. Among the extensive holdings are a complete run of *Victory* magazine, 1943–46.

RG 216—Office of Censorship. The records of this office, established by executive order to coordinate U.S. press censorship in World War II, still have restricted entry, suggesting that such activities must have been more extensive and coordinated than commonly recognized.

RG 226—Office of Strategic Services,. The major archival depository for the OSS. The long-classified U.S. War Department's *War Report of the O.S.S.,* however, was published in 1976 and provides a revealing look at the organization's clandestine psychological operations.

RG 229—Office of Inter-American Coordinator. Records here describe Nelson Rockefeller's work in promoting a favorable U.S. image in Latin America during World War II, particularly through the efforts of the Walt Disney studios.

RG 262—Foreign Broadcast Intelligence Service. Contained are 512 cubic feet of documents from the period 1940–47. Included are English translations of monitored foreign broadcasts and actual recordings by U.S. citizens such as Edward Delaney, Douglas Chandler, and Fred Kaltenback aired over German radio. Tokyo Rose broadcasts from Japan and speeches by Allied leaders are also preserved. Note that the Center for Research Libraries in Chicago has microfilm copies of the *Daily Report of Foreign Radio Broadcasts* (1941-) transcribed into English, Voice of America broadcast scripts in English (1953-present), foreign broadcasts monitored by CBS (1939–45), and other related wide-ranging deposits of potential interest.

RG 306—United States Information Agency. These consist primarily of audiovisual materials, including sound recordings (387 items) issued by the Voice of America from 1950 to 1965. However, unclassified materials relating to USIA's later role in Vietnam are also now available for study.

The National Audio-Visual Center operated by the National Archives and Record Service also rents and/or sells prints of more than 9,000 motion pictures produced by the federal government since the 1930s. Included are many classic propaganda films from World War II, as well as more recent USIA productions. The USIA maintains its own library in Washington,

D.C., with a large clipping and document collection (much of it devoted to the persuasive efforts of the USIA and its predecessor organizations). Note should also be made of the State Department library, which has tightly restricted entry into its large holdings, including extensive propaganda documentation. The Library of Congress, however, tends to be much more cooperative with independent researchers and offers a wealth of material for the propaganda historian. The *Catalog of Holdings, the American Film Institute Collection and the United Artists Collection at the Library of Congress* lists the 14,124 motion pictures acquisitioned through September 1977. Most of these are commercial features, but a number are of interest for their political messages. The Rare Book Division, by way of further illustration, has a very large collection of early political broadsides (including over 250 relating to the Continental Congress and the Constitutional Convention of 1787). The Prints and Photographs Division is also rich with posters and political cartoons of all periods, as well as World War II photos issued by the OWI and others. On deposit at the Library of Congress are many important collections of private papers, such as those of CPI director George Creel. The library also houses the records of the National Board for Historical Service (which in World War I conducted an enemy press intelligence service), the Elmer Gertz Papers (with important materials relating to the career of George Viereck), and a series of bound volumes containing pamphlets issued by U.S. radical groups since the early 1900s.

The National Association of Broadcasters' Library and Information Center is an important reference service administered by the NAB's Public Affairs and Communications Department in Washington, D.C. In nearby Lexington, Virginia, the George C. Marshall Research Foundation and Library boasts much more than the general's private papers (themselves of great interest). There is also a small but excellent twentieth-century war poster collection (nearly 700 issued in the United States, Germany, and France), over 6,000 uncataloged U.S. Signal Corps and OWI photos, and other military propaganda materials. A useful illustrated guide to the poster holdings written by Anthony Crawford, with an informed sixteen-page introduction by former OWI propaganda analyst O. W. Riegel, was published in 1979. For more on other available resources, see *Scholars' Guide to Washington D.C. Film and Video Collections* by Rowan, Culbert, Cripps, and Lichty; and *Scholars' Guide to Washington, D.C. for Audio Resources* by James Heintze.

As to the country as a whole, also refer to *The Directory of Archives and Manuscript Repositories,* published by the National Historical Publications and Records Commission. This is a guide to 3,200 archives and manuscript repositories in the United States, arranged by state and town. Additional access is provided by a name-subject index, as well as special lists of different types of repositories. Bibliographic references accompany some of the entries.

Outside the greater Washington area, New York offers perhaps the single greatest concentration of library research materials for the study of American propaganda. The Radio Free Europe/Radio Liberty Reference Library in New York City is open to the public by appointment. Although its abundant holdings largely document current developments in the Soviet Union, there are also runs of RFE/RL publications and other pertinent materials detailing international broadcast propaganda. All in all, this is an exceptional research library which attracts scholars from across the globe interested in Soviet studies. Note that the papers of Frank Altschul, former chairman of Radio Free Europe, are in the Lehman Collection at Columbia University.

Anti- and pro-Semitic propaganda from here and abroad is collected at the four major Jewish libraries in New York City: the Jacob Alson Memorial Library of the Anti-Defamation League of B'nai B'rith, the Blaustein Library of the American Jewish Committee, the YIVO Institute for Jewish Research Library and Archives, and the Zionist Archives and Library. The Jewish Division of the New York Public Library also has a large collection of extremist literature. The American Jewish Archives (AJA) in Cincinnati is another source worth consulting as it includes the papers of important figures such as Jacob Schiff, Samuel Untermeyer, Felix Warburg, and Isaac Wise. The records of the House Special Committee on Un-American Activities, 1934–39, focusing on Nazi propaganda in the United States, have been donated to the AJA by the family of Representative Samuel Dickstein. Similarly, an extensive collection of anti-Jewish propaganda materials issued between 1922 and 1967 is on deposit at the Minnesota Historical Society.

The New York Public Library's American History Division additionally houses a plethora of political propaganda materials, including party pamphlets, presidential campaign buttons, posters, ribbons, coins, and similar material (cataloged on over one hundred cards). Its research libraries also have a strong advertising collection, and regular deposit of newer publications and materials from groups such as the Advertising Council (which has had great agenda-setting influence on national "public service" issues). There are also twenty-nine Civil War enlistment posters and bound photographic volumes of over 2,000 World War I posters. The Bancroft Collection of original manuscripts from the American Revolution at the library includes the papers of the Boston Committee of Correspondence. The New York Public Library also has the papers of Samuel Adams and his grandson, Samuel Adams Wells. While considerable, these personal effects of Adams represent only a small portion of his total correspondence since much of what he wrote suffered from neglect or was destroyed in an effort to protect his reputation. Wells's papers consist of his manuscript notes and partial drafts for an unfinished biography of his grandfather, later utilized by subsequent writers. (Specialized materials on Samuel Adams and other revolutionary leaders can also be reviewed at the Massachusetts Historical Society Research Library in Boston.)

Other materials at the New York Public Library of interest to propaganda researchers include wide-ranging anti-slavery materials (including runs of early abolitionist propaganda periodicals such as the *Anti-Slavery Reporter*), over 11,000 pamphlets from World War I (many of them propagandistic; see also the Socialism Collection), a number of psychological warfare leaflets distributed in Europe and Asia during World War II, and substantial holdings of press releases and other publications issued by various government information services (such as those of the U.S. Central Intelligence Group from the years 1942–47). Note that the papers of the Institute for Propaganda Analysis, long held privately by Alfred McClung Lee, have also recently been donated to the New York Public Library. Other materials on the institute can be consulted in the Kirtley F. Mather Collection, Harvard University Archives, Cambridge, Massachusetts. Mather was secretary for the institute.

For students of radical literature, the Tamiment Labor History Collection of New York University's Bobst Library is a mecca. There are extensive holdings of AFL-CIO materials, and the Oral History of the American Left Project serves as a repository for veterans of radicalism in unions, politics, and culture. A free guide can be obtained on request. Also in New York, the American Institute for Marxist Studies, headed for many years by Herbert Aptheker, has an interesting collection of "progressive" literature and publishes the bimonthly *AIMS Newsletter* (1964–) describing current activities in the field of Marxist thought, including bibliographical listings of interest to students of left propaganda.

The New York Historical Society tends to take a longer view and so is another source for early revolutionary and Civil War propaganda broadsides. The society also houses the Landauer Collection of American Advertising—more than one million pictorial items demonstrating the power and art of U.S. business propaganda. Nearby, the library at Fairleigh Dickinson University in Madison, New Jersey, has been the official depository of the Outdoor Advertising Industry since 1972. Manuscripts, pamphlets, slides, photographs, and even full-sized billboards make up this most unusual collection.

Brooklyn College of the City University of New York is the home of the papers of Norman Cousins. These cover the years 1942–58 and include his work with the OWI. The school's Department of Television and Radio also houses an unusual collection of black-and-white television commercials produced between 1948 and 1958. Across town, the Museum of Broadcasting (founded in 1976 with seed money from CBS) has already acquired a number of historical materials, including copies of World War II Axis English-language propaganda programs. It is also establishing a collection of landmark radio and television commercials that will be the only one of its kind to be thoroughly accessible to the public. Supplementing these is the University of Arizona's Bureau of Audio-Visual Services Archive Collection of Television Commercials, which includes more than 2,000 spots, mostly from the 1960s to the present. See also the holdings of the American Advertising Museum in Portland, Oregon. The collection contains more than 1,700 original advertising prints dating from 1673, impressive runs of pertinent trade journals, and a representative selection of broadcast commercials tracing back to the early 1920s. Of related interest is the Broadcast Promotion Association Archive in the Telecommunications Department Library at San Diego State University. This is the world's largest collection of tape, film, and print materials created by radio and television professionals to promote and advertise stations and programs.

The Public Relations Society of America operates a Research Information Center from its New York offices. This lending and reference library is primarily for members, but the library and vertical file holdings are open to the public. Although "propaganda" is not a specific subject area, related topics (particularly those of interest to contemporary public relations practitioners) are well covered. The New York State Library in Albany contains extensive propaganda poster holdings from World War I (including the Benjamin Walworth Arnold Collection), World War II (with civilian and war industries issues featured), the United Nations, and a number of other miscellaneous items. Also archived there are records of the now defunct New York State Board of Censors (1910–66), which reviewed all films screened in the state. Scripts were required for purposes of rating and approval, and copies of these (which number over 70,000) have been indexed by title and transferred to the jurisdiction of the library's Manuscripts and Special Collections Division. Unfortunately, photocopying is restricted, but the collection forms a unique reference for the polemical as well as the purely entertainment film. The Sarah Lawrence Library in Bronxville also reportedly has propaganda-related materials.

The Rockefeller Archive Center in Pocantico Hills, New York, contains family and business papers of interest to students of Rockefeller-endowed organizations and people. Among the presidential libraries, the Franklin D. Roosevelt Library in Hyde Park is well organized and has collections and other manuscripts indispensable for research into the 1933–45 New Deal period. A useful pamphlet describing historical materials in the library is available on request. Except for the Rutherford B. Hayes Library in Fremont, Ohio, the other presidential collections are administered by the National Archives and continue to receive relevant documents and publications. These include the Herbert Hoover Library in West Branch, Iowa; the Harry S. Truman Library in Independence, Missouri; the Dwight D. Eisenhower Library in Abilene, Kansas; the Lyndon B. Johnson Library in Austin, Texas; the John F. Kennedy Library in Dorchester, Massachusetts; the Gerald R. Ford Library in Ann Arbor, Michigan; plus the future Jimmy Carter Library in Atlanta and Ronald Reagan Library in California. Unfortunately, in the Johnson and Kennedy complexes a number of propaganda and psychological warfare documents from the Vietnam period remain classified. The difficulty former President Nixon has had in locating a home for his library, including disputes over who owns what materials, further restricts serious political communication research for these years. For helpful suggestions, see the step-by-step advice of Kathleen Turner on getting started.

The presidential libraries also house political advertisements. For example, copies of selected Democratic ads for 1956–64 are found in the Lyndon B. Johnson Library and for 1952–68 in the John F. Kennedy Library. Fortunately, there are numerous other locations for campaign propaganda. The Kanter Political Archives at the University of Oklahoma is a particularly important collection, especially for broadcast materials—the place to head to if you only can go to one source. Materials in the archives, collected over more than thirty years by Julian Kanter, come from all across the country and represent candidates for every office from president to city council member. The collection today consists of more than 10,000 television spots and uncounted radio announcements. Rarities include a cartoon for Eisenhower, with a "We Like Ike" soundtrack song—the only animated commercial ever made by the Disney Studio for a political campaign. Some of the other major archives include the University of Rhode Island, which has complete sets of the Eisenhower-Stevenson 1952 spots in the Wood and Devlin Collections, supplemented by a large number of later polispots, mostly from presidential campaigns. The Television Archives of the News Study Group in the Department of Political Science at the Massachusetts Institute of Technology has collected hundreds of commercials plus other political television materials. All of this is available on videotape for public inspection. In addition, a number of VHS compilations are beginning to appear for home and teaching use. Among the best is a sixty-minute documentary hosted by former Senator Eugene McCarthy entitled *The Classics of Political Television Advertising* (Washington, D.C.: Campaigns and Elections, 1986). David Beiler has written a very informative accompanying viewer's guide to this outstanding collection.

Befitting its historic revolutionary heritage, Pennsylvania boasts several important propaganda collections. The American Philosophical Library in Philadelphia houses the vast Richard Gimbel Collection, formerly at Yale University, of published and unpublished materials by and about Thomas Paine. Other documents have been added to make this the single greatest reference center for the study of Paine's life and work. The Historical Society of Pennsylvania has cataloged the papers of U.S. Senator Jonathan Roberts (1771–1854), which are rich for study of national political history in the post-revolutionary/pre–Civil War period (particularly the agitation for war with England in 1812 and controversies relating to the charter of the Bank of the United States).

The World War II Collection in the library of the Historical Society of Pennsylvania is also strong in broadsides, posters, and other forms of federal publicity and propaganda issued by U.S. government agencies. One of the country's largest collections of war posters and radical-racist literature is found nearby at the Balch Institute in Philadelphia. Temple University's Rare Books and Manuscripts Room also stores over 3,000 U.S. and foreign war posters dating from 1914 through the end of the Vietnam conflict. A card guide exists for World War I issues. The university's Contemporary Culture Center has equally impressive holdings of alternative and radical left- and right-wing press ephemera and polemical writings. These are supplemented by microfilm documents and taped interviews with neo-Nazi leaders and others.

See also the Quaker Collection at Haverford College in Pennsylvania, which includes the records (1821–57) of the Indian Society of Anti-Slavery Friends and the diary of William Charles Allen, which discusses at some length the effect of propaganda on American public attitudes in World War I. Swarthmore College, besides material from World War I, also holds propaganda materials issued by the Women's Information League for Peace and Freedom, the League of Nations Association, and the Emergency Peace Campaign of 1937. The Harry S. Baird Papers in the U.S. Army Military History Research Collection at Carlisle Barracks, Pennsylvania, include a scrapbook of propaganda leaflets dropped over Japan in World War II. For other related materials consult the librarian directly.

Another useful source is the Thomas Newcommen Memorial Library and Museum in Exton, Pennsylvania, one of the finest specialized business and industrial history libraries in the world. Since propaganda has depended so closely upon technological advances, this library, with its extensive corporate documentation, should be canvassed by those interested in business elites' relationship to mass persuasion.

Cambridge and Boston are rightly regarded as among our greatest library centers. In addition to the John F. Kennedy Library, one can consult the Widener Library at Harvard, which has a simply overwhelming collection of Americana primary and secondary materials dating back to the seventeenth century. Researchers working in Cambridge should also visit the Edward L. Bernays Public Relations Library, which features one of the nation's largest propaganda collections. Because of its leadership role in recognizing public relations as an academic discipline, Boston University also has strong propaganda holdings including a number of war posters.

The papers of veteran newscaster Edward R. Murrow and his personal library (with much describing his years as USIA director) are now at the Murrow Center of public Diplomacy, Fletcher School of Law and Diplomacy, Tufts University in Medford, Massachusetts. These contain scripts, research notes, and correspondence and are now available on fifty reels from Microfilming Corporation of America, a *New York Times* company. See the printed *Edward R. Murrow Papers, 1927–1965: A Guide to the Microfilm Edition* for more information.

In other New England institutions, the Yale University holdings in New Haven, Connecticut, make it one of the premier library collections in the United States. Besides general references, of interest are the extensive holdings of twentieth-century war posters plus the papers of Ezra Pound (whose propaganda broadcasts from Italy favorably comparing Mussolini to Thomas Jefferson were held by the victorious Allies to be clear proof of his insanity).

Rhode Island's history as an anti-slavery capital is reflected in the Harris Collection on the American Civil War and Slavery, archived at the Providence Public Library. It includes propaganda pamphlets, books, periodicals, broadsheet music, and other eighteenth- and nineteenth-century materials reflecting both sides of the controversy. Archiving more than eighty-five editions of *Uncle Tom's Cabin* in fourteen languages is typical of the thoroughness of the collection. Use is restricted, however, as is photocopying. Benefiting from the trend to microfilm scarce documents has been the Anti-Slavery Collection at Oberlin College in Ohio, now widely available.

The Newberry Library in Chicago, Northwestern University Library in Evanston, and the Illinois Historical Society Library at the University of Illinois in Urbana all have important holdings dealing with U.S. radicalism and related social, political, and labor struggles. Newberry's is perhaps the strongest for the nineteenth century. The files of the Church League of America in Wheaton, Illinois, offer an unusually detailed clipping collection of materials documenting communist and leftist propaganda in the United States. Included in this conservative research and lobby organization are complete sets of the hearings and reports issued by the U.S. House and California State Un-American Activities committees. Large holdings of right-wing political literature, documentation on controversial public relations pioneer Ivy Lee, and propaganda from World War I (including twelve file drawers of correspondence and business records from the Council on Books in Wartime) are now housed at the Princeton University Library in New Jersey. For researchers interested in acquiring reasonably priced works by radical rightist authors, many of which are out of print or unavailable elsewhere because of what the distributors call a "historical blackout," an indispensable source is the Sons of Liberty, P.O. Box 214, Metairie, Louisiana 70004. A free booklist of hundreds of titles is available.

The University of Kansas also encompasses strong holdings in radical ephemera from the United States, much of which is cataloged. The Leon Josephson Collection there of pamphlets on modern socialism is particularly definitive with regard to the Communist Party of America. The University of Michigan has an excellent radical literature collection (except for Populism) dating from the nineteenth century. These include recordings of rightist figures in addition to limited collections of World War I posters (320 items) and election advertisements dating from the 1950s (500-plus items from the United States, Canada, and Europe). Note should additionally be made of the Archives of Labor and Urban Affairs in the Walter P. Reuther Library, Wayne State University, Detroit, where materials relevant to labor struggles as well as interesting collections such as the papers of Heber Blankenhorn (a journalist and economist who played an important role in World War II army psychological warfare efforts) are on deposit.

The State Historical Society of Wisconsin is yet another surprising source of documents and audiovisual material, particularly in relation to communist propaganda in the motion picture industry. Papers of Dalton Trumbo, Albert Maltz, Melvyn Douglas, Samuel Ornitz, the Progressive Citizens of America/Hollywood Democratic Committee, plus Robert Morris and Robert Kenny (lawyers who defended the Hollywood 10) are all available at the Wisconsin Center for Theatre Research, sponsored jointly by the society and the University of Wisconsin at Madison Department of Communication Arts. Other extensive film and television material is located there, including episodes of the controversial FBI-supported "I Led Three Lives" program aired during the McCarthy era of the 1950s. The papers of Frank Early Mason, also in the society's collections, contain private records of his radio propaganda activities as special assistant to the secretary of the navy in World War II. The university's School of Journalism and Mass Communication additionally operates a reading room with vertical file holdings on propaganda and public opinion. The University of Wisconsin campus at Milwaukee houses in its library an interesting collection of propaganda-related materials documenting third-party movements in U.S. politics.

Other state libraries such as the one at the University of Iowa maintain important reference archives. For example, at Iowa one can consult runs of more than 900 propaganda periodicals issued by right-wing groups since the 1920s. The basic collection is now available on microfilm for purchase by other research centers. The University of Iowa also holds the letters, papers (including a confidential psychiatric report), and legal documents of German-American propagandist George Sylvester Viereck. Nearly 1,300 items are included, covering the years 1896–1959, which reflect his long activist career (including representation of the National Socialist government prior to World War II). The American Archives of the Factual Film at Iowa State University now has close to 2,000 "sponsored" films in its collection and is the only major repository of its kind for business, educational, and informational motion pictures prepared for private distribution.

The University of Nebraska at Lincoln is another source for limited-circulation materials. The Rare Books and Special Collections Room there has posters, pamphlets, clippings, and other fugitive propaganda issues from World War II numbering over 1,000 items. The papers of Horace C. Peterson archived in the University of Oklahoma Library include original references used in writing his book *Propaganda for War: The Campaign Against*

American Neutrality, 1914–1917, supplemented by reviews and other documentation of reaction to publication. Of a different nature are the sixty-nine microfilm reels of administrative records for the *Congregatio de propaganda fide* covering Catholic activities in the Americas and Great Britain from 1622 to 1865, housed, appropriately, at the University of Notre Dame Archives. A guide to these documents by Finbar Kenneally has been published.

In the South, the U.S. Infantry Museum at Fort Benning (Columbus, Georgia) includes a collection of posters and other militaria from both world wars. The U.S. Army Institute for Military Assistance Library (formerly the Special Warfare School Library) at Fort Bragg, North Carolina, has more than 45,000 pamphlets and documents related to military strategy and counterintelligence (including propaganda leaflets from World War II and Korea). The University of Louisville's Belknap Campus Library and Allen Hite Art Institute have strong U.S. government-issue poster holdings from both world wars, Red Cross posters from the 1915–21 period, and numerous posters issued by the anti–Vietnam War movement. The University of Georgia Library has a noted Confederate Imprint Collection with eighty broadsides and other persuasive documents (official and unofficial) issued between 1861 and 1865.

The Vanderbilt Television News Archive in Nashville is a unique collection of nearly 10,000 hours of videotaped news and public affairs programs issued since August 1968 (indexed and abstracted since 1972). Disputes over news bias and propaganda in electronic journalism can at last be objectively researched, with individual programs and complications available at nominal cost for noncommercial purposes. A regional News Archive center also exists at George Washington University in Washington, D.C. The Purdue University Public Affairs Video Archive in West Lafayette, Indiana, began recording Cable-Satellite Public Affairs Network (C-SPAN) programming in October 1987. The archive is developing a catalog that will list C-SPAN material by type of event, content, and time reference. Educators can purchase unedited C-SPAN airings or single-subject packaged tapes.

In Texas, several centers other than the Lyndon B. Johnson Presidential Library are of interest. The University of Texas Library at Austin, for example, owns the Frances Harvey Papers, which discuss use of newspaper propaganda in the Southwest following the Civil War. The Edward A. Peden papers at the University of Texas-Austin trace his work distributing U.S. propaganda materials in Germany after World War I.

One of the finer specialized collections of atheist, free-thought, and anti-church propaganda in the country is the Society of Separationists Library in Austin, Texas. Unfortunately, the books and other materials are not properly cataloged because of financial constraints and are displayed in rather haphazard condition. The Library of the American Association for the Advancement of Atheism in San Diego, California, reflects similar interests and encompasses another useful reference center for this topic. Researchers, however, are requested to make prior arrangements before traveling to the library. More narrow is the Richard Alan Nelson Mormon Film and Television Collection, which supplements other archived communications holdings at Brigham Young University in Provo, Utah, to document pro- and anti-Mormon media portrayals over the years.

In contrast, the Hoover Institution of War, Revolution, and Peace at Stanford University is the largest private repository in the United States. Its library, begun in 1919, alone houses over 1.25 million book volumes dealing with all aspects of modern social, economic, and political change. However, it is for the library's collection of propaganda posters (more than 50,000), letters, leaflets, newspapers, rare photos, diaries, personal records, and limited-circulation street propaganda that Hoover Institution is justly famed. Several surveys of holdings and library catalogs have been published, indicating the importance of this research treasure house.

Another Northern California resource is the Pacific Studies Center (founded in 1969) in Mountain View, which maintains a library with information files covering a wide variety of propaganda-related titles. The center also publishes the bimonthly *Pacific Research,* a critical journal focusing on U.S. foreign policy and power structure studies concerning the activities of multinational corporations. The DataCenter is an unusual user-supported library and information center in Oakland, California, which collects, organizes, and provides access to a treasure trove of information on economic, social, and political issues. It also offers specialized search, clipping, and other services. PeaceNet, a San Francisco–based computer network for "progressives," links users throughout the United States and in over seventy countries. It offers electronic mail, on-line bulletin boards, data bases, and Telex services to share information.

For the historian, access to scarce left radical propaganda is possible at the Southern California Library for Social Studies and Research in Los Angeles. More than 15,000 volumes on Marxism, a like number of rare pamphlets dating back more than eighty-five years, over 2,000 tape recordings of contemporary anti-establishment leaders ranging from Angela Davis to Martin Luther King, Jr., plus 150,000 news clips broken down into 800 categories (including propaganda) and selected news films made in the 1930s are arranged for easy use. Also maintained are files documenting hundreds of labor, social, and political campaigns and groups active before World War I.

California State University, Fullerton, has a small but interesting Freedom Center of Political Ephemera which has runs of over 800 labor publications dating from the late 1800s, election propaganda and campaign buttons from the twentieth century, and the nearly complete papers of the League of Nations. Yet another archive is found at the University of California at

Davis, whose library has a substantial collection of over 6,000 pamphlets issued by U.S. radical and social change organizations (1890 to the present) and a more limited number of U.S. and Japanese war posters from the 1940s. The University of Wyoming similarly has literally thousands of collections of papers, many relating to propaganda (such as those of Lyman Munson, Frank Capra's boss for the *Why We Fight* motion picture series). Also of interest is the collection of U.S. and French World War I propaganda posters (over 1,000) and pamphlets on file at the Tacoma, Washington, Public Library. An unusually comprehensive resource is the KIRO-CBS Collection of Broadcasts of the World War II Years and After, in the Phonoarchive of the University of Washington, which preserves inclusive sound recordings of one radio network's fare during the 1940s. A guide to this collection exists, prepared by Milo Ryan.

This brief overview of available materials gives some idea of the immensity of the topic. Not all sources for the study of American propaganda, however, are to be found within the United States. The Imperial War Museum in London is a major propaganda research center. The museum's library is very strong in twentieth-century pamphlets, film (with over 37 million feet from the two world wars and an increasing collection of post–1945 footage, including Vietnam), art work (the poster collection exceeds 50,000 items, among them significant U.S. issues), and photographs, as well as standard book and clipping file materials. Another British contact is the Psywar Society of England, headed by Reginald Auckland, which publishes a fact-filled journal called *The Falling Leaf* and acts as a clearinghouse for psychological warfare memorabilia collectors. Auckland, for example, has a personal collection of over 9,000 items (including many rare U.S. Army leaflets). On the continent, the Radical Communication Research Library at the Institute of Social Studies, The Hague, Netherlands (formerly the International Mass Media Research Center Library in Bagnolet, France) library , serves as a documentary archive for those interested in worldwide Marxist studies involving all aspects of communications (including propaganda). The center also publishes useful bibliographical catalogs.

BIBLIOGRAPHY

Books, Articles, and Unpublished Scholarly Works

Abshire, David. *International Broadcasting: A New Dimension in Western Diplomacy.* Beverly Hills, Calif.: Sage, 1976.

Adams, Samuel. *The Writings of Samuel Adams 1764–1802.* 4 vols. Collected and edited by Harry Alonzo Cushing. New York: Putnam's, 1904–8.

Adler, Selig. *The Isolationist Impulse: Its Twentieth Century Reaction.* New York: Free Press, 1966.

Agee, Philip. *Inside the Company: A CIA Diary.* New York: Stonehill, 1975.

Agee, Philip, and Louis Wolf, eds. *Dirty Work: The CIA in Western Europe.* Secaucus, N.J.: L. Stuart, 1978.

Aldridge, Alfred Owen. *Man of Reason: The Life of Thomas Paine*. Philadelphia: J. B. Lippincott, 1959.

Altschull, J. Herbert. *Agents of Power: The Role of the News Media in Human Affairs*. White Plains, N.Y.: Longman, 1984.

Altheide, David L., and John M. Johnson. *Bureaucratic Propaganda*. Boston: Allyn and Bacon, 1980.

Archival and Manuscript Materials at the Hoover Institution on War, Revolution and Peace: A Checklist of Major Collections. Stanford, Calif.: Hoover Institution Press, 1978.

Argersinger, Peter H. *Populism and Politics: William Alfred Peffer and the People's Party*. Lexington: University Press of Kentucky, 1974.

Aristotle. *Rhetoric*. Translated by Lane Cooper. New York: Appleton-Century, 1932.

Armor, John C. *Substance and Shadows: The Original Meaning of Freedom of the Press*. Washington, D.C.: Freedom of Expression Foundation, 1984.

Aronson, James. *Packaging the News: A Critical Survey of Press, Radio, TV*. New York: International, 1971.

Ashworth, William. *Under the Influence: Congress, Lobbies, and the American Pork-Barrel System*. New York: Hawthorn/Dutton, 1981.

Auxier, George. "The Propaganda Activities of the Cuban Junta in Precipitating the Spanish American War, 1895–1898." *Hispanic American Historical Review*, 19 (August 1939), 286–305.

Bagdikian, Ben H. *The Media Monopoly*. Boston: Beacon Press, 1983.

Bailey, R N. "Issues Management: A Survey of Contemporary Practice." Master's thesis, University of Florida, 1983.

Bailyn, Bernard. *Ideological Origins of the American Revolution*. Cambridge, Mass.: Belknap Press of Harvard University Press, 1967.

———, ed. *Pamphlets of the American Revolution, 1750–1776*. Cambridge, Mass.: Belknap Press of Harvard University Press, 1965.

Bamford, James. *The Puzzle Palace: A Report on NSA, America's Most Secret Agency*. New York: Penguin Books, 1983.

Barber, W. E. "Propaganda." In *Dictionary of American History*. Rev. ed. New York: Scribner's, 1976, V: 41–43.

Barghoorn, Frederick C. *Soviet Foreign Propaganda*. Princeton, N.J.: Princeton University Press, 1964.

Barnes, Donald. "Ideology of the IWW." Ph.D. dissertation, Washington State University, 1962.

Barnouw, Erik. *Documentary: A History of the Non-fiction Film*. New York: Oxford University Press, 1974.

———. *The Golden Web: A History of Broadcasting in the United States, 1933–1953*. New York: Oxford University Press, 1968.

———. *The Image Empire: A History of Broadcasting in the United States from 1953*. New York: Oxford University Press, 1970.

———. *A Tower in Babel: A History of Broadcasting in the United States to 1933*. New York: Oxford University Press, 1966.

———, ed.-in-chief. *The International Encyclopedia of Communications*. 4 vols. New York: Oxford University Press, 1989.

Barrett, Edward W. *Truth Is Our Weapon*. New York: Funk and Wagnalls, 1953.

Barron, John. *KGB: The Secret Work of Soviet Secret Agents*. New York: Reader's Digest Press, 1974.

————. *KGB Today: The Hidden Hand*. New York: Reader's Digest Press, 1983.

Barsam, Richard M. *Nonfiction Film: A Critical History*. New York: E. P. Dutton, 1973.

————, ed. *Nonfiction Film: Theory and Criticism*. New York: E. P. Dutton, 1976.

Bartlett, F. C. *Political Propaganda*. Cambridge, England: Cambridge University Press, 1940. Reprint. New York: Octagon, 1973.

Baskin, Otis, and Craig Aronoff. *Public Relations: The Profession and the Practice*. 2nd ed. Dubuque, Iowa: William C. Brown, 1988.

Beach, Stewart. *Samuel Adams: The Fateful Years, 1764–1776*. New York: Dodd, Mead, 1965.

Becket, Henry S.A. *The Dictionary of Espionage: Spookspeak into English*. New York: Dell, 1987.

Beiler, David. *The Classics of Political Television Advertising: A Viewers Guide*. Washington, D.C.: Campaigns and Elections, 1986. This accompanies a sixty-minute VHS videotape documentary hosted by former Senator Eugene McCarthy.

Bennett, James T., and Thomas J. DiLorenzo. *Destroying Democracy: How Government Funds Partisan Politics*. Washington, D.C.: Cato Institute, 1985.

Bennett, W. Lance. *News: The Politics of Illusion*. 2nd ed. White Plains, N.Y.: Longman, 1988.

Berelson, Bernard, and Morris Janowitz. *Reader in Public Opinion and Communication*. 2nd ed. New York: Free Press, 1966.

Berger, Carl. *Broadsides & Bayonets: The Propaganda War of the American Revolution*. Rev. ed. San Rafael, Calif.: Presidio Press, 1976.

Bergner, Douglas J., ed. *Public Interest Profiles, 1986–1987*. 5th ed. Washington, D.C.: Foundation for Public Affairs, 1986.

Bergstrom, Letty. "The Battle for America: German-English Language Propaganda in the U.S. from 1933 to 1941." Master's thesis, Northwestern University, 1948.

Bernays, Edward L. *Crystalizing Public Opinion*. New York: Boni and Liveright, 1923. 2nd ed. New York: Liveright, 1961.

————. *Propaganda*. New York: Horace Liveright, 1928.

Berry, Mary Frances. *Why ERA Failed: Politics, Women's Rights, and the Amending Process of the Constitution*. Bloomington: Indiana University Press, 1986.

Bettinghaus, Erwin P., and Michael J. Cody. *Persuasive Communication*. 4th ed. New York: Holt, Rinehart and Winston, 1987.

Biddle, William Wishart. *Propaganda and Education*. New York: Teachers College Press, Columbia University, 1932.

Birnbaum, Jeffrey H., and Alan S. Murray. *Showdown at Gucci Gulch: Lawmakers, Lobbyists, and the Unlikely Triumph of Tax Reform*. New York: Random House, 1987.

Bishop, Robert L. "The Overseas Branch of the Office of War Information." Ph.D. dissertation, University of Wisconsin at Madison, 1966.

————. *Public Relations: A Comprehensive Bibliography—Articles and Books on Public Relations, Communication Theory, Public Opinion, and Propaganda, 1964–1972*. Ann Arbor: University of Michigan Press, 1974.

————. "Public Relations: A Comprehensive Bibliography of Articles and Books on Public Relations, Communication Theory, Public Opinion, and Propaganda, 1973–1974." *Public Relations Review,* 1 (Winter Supplement 1975–76), 1–200.

————. "Public Relations: A Comprehensive Bibliography of Articles and Books on Public Relations, Communication Theory, Public Opinion, and Propaganda, 1975." *Public Relations Review,* 3 (Summer 1977), 1–145.

Bittman, Ladislav. *The Deception Game.* Syracuse, N.Y.: Syracuse University Research Corp. 1972.

————. *The KGB and Soviet Disinformation: An Insider's View.* Washington, D.C.: Pergamon-Brassey's 1985.

Blakey, George T. *Historians on the Homefront: American Propagandists for the Great War.* Lexington: University of Kentucky Press, 1970.

Bloxom, Marguerite. "Lafayette as a Tool of American Propaganda." Ph.D. dissertation, University of Maryland, 1970.

Blum, John Morton. *V Was for Victory: Politics and American Culture During World War II.* New York: Harcourt Brace Jovanovich, 1976.

Bogart, Leo. *Premises for Propaganda: The United States Information Agency's Operating Assumptions in the Cold War.* New York: Free Press, 1976.

Bohn, Thomas. *An Historical and Descriptive Analysis of the "Why We Fight" Series.* New York: Arno Press, 1977.

Bottomore, Tom, ed. *A Dictionary of Marxist Thought.* Cambridge, Mass.: Harvard University Press, 1983.

Bowdoin, James, Joseph Warren, and Samuel Pemberton. *A Short Narrative of the Horrid Massacre in Boston, Perpetrated in the Evening of the Fifth Day of March, 1770, by Soldiers of the 29th Regiment, which with the 14th Regiment were then Quartered There; with Some Observations on the State of Things Prior to that Catastrophe.* Boston: Town of Boston, 1770. Republished with notes and illustrations. New York: John Doggett, Jr., 1849. Photo-republication of 1849 ed. Williamstown, Mass.: Corner House, 1973.

Braestrup, Peter. *Big Story! How the American Press and Television Reported and Interpreted the Crises of Tet 1968 in Vietnam and Washington.* 2 vols. Boulder, Colo.: Westview Press, 1977.

Brembeck, Winston, and William Howell. *Persuasion: A Means of Social Influence.* 2nd ed. Englewood Cliffs, N.J.: Prentice-Hall, 1976.

Brightbill, George D. *Communications and the United States Congress: A Selectively Annotated Bibliography of Committee Hearings, 1870–1976.* Washington, D.C.: Broadcast Education Association, 1978.

Brinkley, Alan. *Voices of Protest: Huey Long, Father Coughlin and the Great Depression.* New York: Alfred A. Knopf, 1982.

Britt, Steuart Henderson. *Psychological Principles of Marketing and Consumer Behavior.* Lexington, Mass.: Lexington Books/Heath, 1978.

Brownfeld, Allan C., and J. Michael Waller. *The Revolution Lobby.* Washington, D.C.: Council for Inter-American Security and the Inter-American Security Educational Institute, 1985.

Brownlow, Kevin. *The War, the West and the Wilderness.* New York: Alfred A. Knopf, 1979.

Bruntz, George C. *Allied Propaganda and the Collapse of the German Empire in 1918.* Stanford, Calif.: Stanford University Press, 1938.

Bubka, Tony. "Time to Organize!: The IWW Stickerettes." *American West,* 5 (January 1968), 21–27, 73.

Buchanan, Albert R. "European Propaganda and American Public Opinion, 1914–1917." Ph.D. dissertation, Stanford University, 1935.

Buchanan, William W., and Edna A. Kanely, comps. *Cumulative Subject Index to the Monthly Catalog of United States Government Publications 1900–1971.* 15 vols. Washington, D.C.: Carrollton Press, 1973–75.

Buchholz, Rogene. *Essentials of Public Policy for Management.* Englewood Cliffs, N.J.: Prentice-Hall, 1985.

Burton, Bob. *Top Secret: A Clandestine Operator's Glossary of Terms.* New York: Berkley Books, 1987.

Canfield, Cass. *Sam Adams' Revolution (1765–1776).* New York: Harper and Row, 1976.

Carlsnaes, Walter. *The Concept of Ideology and Political Analysis: A Critical Examination of Its Usage by Marx, Lenin, and Mannheim.* Westport, Conn.: Greenwood Press, 1981.

Carroll, Wallace. *Persuade or Perish.* Boston: Houghton Mifflin, 1948.

Casey, Ralph Droz. "Propaganda Technique in the 1928 Presidential Campaign." Ph.D. dissertation, University of Wisconsin, 1929.

Cassata, Mary B., and Thomas Skill. *Television: A Guide to the Literature.* Phoenix: Oryx Press, 1985.

Castle, Eugene W. *Billions, Blunders and Baloney: The Fantastic Story of How Uncle Sam Is Squandering Your Money Overseas.* New York: Devin-Adair, 1955.

Ceplair, Larry. *Under the Shadow of War: Fascism, Anti-Fascism, and Marxists, 1918–1939.* New York: Columbia University Press, 1987.

Chafets, Ze'ev. *Double Vision: How the Press Distorts America's View of the Middle East.* New York: William Morrow, 1985.

Chaitkin, Anton. *Treason in America from Aaron Burr to Averell Harriman.* 2nd ed. New York: New Benjamin Franklin House, 1985.

Chalmers, David M. *Hooded Americanism: The History of the Ku Klux Klan.* 3rd ed. Durham, N.C.: Duke University Press, 1987.

Chamorro, Edgar. *Packaging the Contras: A Case of CIA Disinformation.* New York: Institute for Media Analysis, 1987.

Chase, W. Howard. *Issue Management: Origins of the Future.* Stamford, Conn.: Issue Action Publications, 1984.

Childs, Harwood L. *An Introduction to Public Opinion.* New York: Wiley, 1940.

———. "Propaganda." In *Collier's Encyclopedia.* New York: Macmillan, 1979, XIX: 410–17.

———. *A Reference Guide to the Study of Public Opinion.* Princeton, N.J.: Princeton University Press, 1934. Reprint. Ann Arbor, Mich.: Gryphon Books, 1971.

———, ed. "Pressure Groups and Propaganda." *Annals* of the American Academy of Political and Social Sciences, 179 (May 1935). Special issue.

Childs, Harwood L., and John B. Whitton, eds. *Propaganda by Short Wave* (1942). Bound with C. A. Rigby's *The War on Short Waves* (1943) in a new joint edition as part of the International Propaganda and Communication series. New York: Arno Press, 1972.

Chomsky, Noam, Morris Morley, James Petras, and Michael Parenti. *The Reagan Administration and Nicaragua: How Washington Constructs Its Case for Counterrevolution in Central America.* New York: Institute for Media Analysis, 1987.

Choukas, Michael. *Propaganda Comes of Age.* Washington, D.C.: Public Affairs Press, 1965.

Christenson, Reo M., and Robert O. McWilliams, comps. *Voice of the People: Readings in Public Opinion and Propaganda.* 2nd ed. New York: McGraw-Hill, 1967.

Cigler, Allan J., and Burdett A. Loomis, eds. *Interest Group Politics.* 2nd ed. Washington, D.C.: Congressional Quarterly Books, 1986.

Cirino, Robert. *Don't Blame the People: How the News Media Use Bias, Distortion and Censorship to Manipulate Public Opinion.* New York: Vintage/Random House, 1972.

———. *We're Being More than Entertained.* Honolulu: Lighthouse Press, 1977.

Coates, Joseph F., Vary T. Coates, Jennifer Jarratt, and Lisa Heinz. *Issues Management: How You Can Plan, Organize, and Manage for the Future.* Mt. Airy, Md.: Lomond, 1986.

Colby, Benjamin. *'Twas a Famous Victory: Deception and Propaganda in the War with Germany.* New Rochelle, N.Y.: Arlington House, 1974.

Colby, Roy. *A Communese-English Dictionary.* Boston: Western Islands, 1972.

Congressional Quarterly. *The Washington Lobby.* 5th ed. Washington, D.C.: Congressional Quarterly Books, 1987.

Constantine, James. "The African Slave Trade: A Study of Eighteenth Century Propaganda and Public Controversy." Ph.D. dissertation, Indiana University, 1953.

Conway, Moncure D. *The Life of Thomas Paine.* 2 vols. New York: Putnam's, 1892. Reprint. New York: Benjamin Blom, 1969.

Cooper, Kent. *The Right to Know: An Exposition of the Evils of News Suppression and Propaganda.* New York: Farrar, Straus, and Cudahy, 1956.

Cormier, Frank, James Deakin, and Helen Thomas. *The White House Press on the Presidency: News Management and Co-option.* Lanham, Md.: University Press of America, 1983.

Craig, Robert L. "The Changing Communicative Structure of Advertisements, 1850–1930." Ph.D. dissertation, University of Iowa, 1985.

Crandall, Marjorie Lyle. *Confederate Imprints: A Check List Based Principally on the Collection of the Boston Athenaeum.* 2 vols. Boston: Boston Athenaeum, 1955.

Crawford, Anthony R., ed. *Posters of World War I and World War II in the George C. Marshall Research Foundation.* Charlottesville: University Press of Virginia, 1979.

Creel, George. *How We Advertised America: The First Telling of the Amazing Story of the Committee on Public Information that Carried the Gospel of Americanism to Every Corner of the Globe.* New York: Harper and Brothers, 1920. Reprint. New York: Arno Press, 1972.

———. *Rebel at Large: Recollections of Fifty Crowded Years.* New York: Putnam's, 1947.

Cronkhite, Gary. *Persuasion: Speech and Behavioral Change.* Indianapolis: Bobbs-Merrill, 1969.

Crow, John. "Ideology and Organization." Master's thesis, University of Chicago, 1958.

Cruickshank, Charles G. *The Fourth Arm: Psychological Warfare 1938–1945*. London: Davis-Poynter, 1977.

Crunden, Robert M. *Ministers of Reform: The Progressives' Achievement in American Civilization, 1889–1920*. New York: Basic Books, 1982.

Culbert, David. *News for Everyman: Radio and Foreign Affairs in Thirties America*. Westport, Conn.: Greenwood Press, 1976.

——, ed.-in-chief. *Film and Propaganda in America: A Documentary History*. 5 vols. Text and microfiche. Westport, Conn.: Greenwood Press, forthcoming.

——, ed. *Mission to Moscow: The Feature Film as Propaganda*. Madison: University of Wisconsin Press, 1980.

Cullop, Charles P. *Confederate Propaganda in Europe, 1861–1865*. Coral Gables, Fla.: University of Miami Press, 1969.

Cumby, Constance. *The Hidden Dangers of the Rainbow: The New Age Movement and Our Coming Age of Barbarism*. Rev. ed. Shreveport, La.: Huntington House, 1983.

Cutlip, Scott M. *A Public Relations Bibliography to 1965*. 2nd ed. Madison: University of Wisconsin Press, 1965.

Cutlip, Scott M., Allen H. Center, and Glen M. Broom. *Effective Public Relations*. 6th ed. Englewood Cliffs, N.J.: Prentice-Hall, 1985.

Dahlerup, Drude, ed. *The New Women's Movement: Feminism and Political Power in Europe and the U.S.A.* Newbury Park, Calif.: Sage, 1987.

Darracott, J., and B. Loftus. *Second World War Posters*. London: Imperial War Museum, 1972.

Davidson, Philip. *Propaganda and the American Revolution, 1763–1783*. Chapel Hill: University of North Carolina Press, 1941. Reprinted as *Propaganda in the American Revolution*. New York: W. W. Norton, 1973.

de Borchgrave, Arnaud, and Robert Moss. *The Spike*. New York: Avon Books, 1981.

Denton, Robert E. Jr., and Gary C. Woodward. *Political Communication in America*. New York: Praeger, 1985.

DeWitt, Benjamin Parke. *The Progressive Movement: A Non-partisan, Comprehensive Discussion of Current Tendencies in American Politics*. New York: Macmillan, 1915. Republished with a new introduction by Arthur Mann. Seattle: University of Washington Press, 1968.

Diamond, Edwin, and Stephen Bates. *The Spot: The Rise of Political Advertising on Television*. Cambridge, Mass.: MIT Press, 1984. Rev. ed. 1988.

Dietrich, Daniel, ed. *Teaching About Doublespeak*. Urbana, Ill.: National Council of Teachers of English, 1976.

Dizard, Wilson P., Jr. *The Coming Information Age: An Overview of Technology, Economics and Politics*. 2nd ed. White Plains, N.Y.: Longman, 1985.

Dobson, Christopher, and Ronald Payne. *The Never-Ending War: Terrorism in the Eighties*. New York: Facts on File, 1987.

Doctor, Powrie Vaux. "Amos Kendall, Propagandist of Jacksonian Democracy." Ph.D. dissertation, Georgetown University, 1940.

Doenecke, Justus. *Anti-interventionism: A Bibliographical Introduction to Isolationism and Pacifism from World War I to the Early Cold War.* New York: Garland, 1987.

Donner, Frank J. *The Age of Surveillance: The Aims and Methods of America's Political Intelligence System.* New York: Vintage Books, 1981.

Doob, Leonard W. *Propaganda: Its Psychology and Technique.* New York: Holt, 1935.

————. *Public Opinion and Propaganda.* 2nd ed. Hamden, Conn.: Archon Books, 1966.

Dougherty, William E., and Morris Janowitz. *Psychological Warfare Casebook.* Baltimore: Johns Hopkins University Press, 1958.

Douglas, Sara U. *Labor's New Voice: Unions and the Mass Media.* Norwood, N.J.: Ablex, 1986.

Dowell, Eldridge Foster. *History of Criminal Syndicalism Legislation in the United States.* Studies in Historical and Political Science, Series LVII, No. 1. Baltimore: Johns Hopkins University, 1939. Reprint ed. New York: Da Capo Press, 1970.

Dumond, Dwight Lowell. *Antislavery: The Crusade for Freedom in America.* New York: W. W. Norton, 1966.

Duncan-Clark, Samuel. *The Progressive Movement: Its Principles and Its Programme.* Boston: Small, Maynard, 1913.

Dunham, Donald C. *Kremlin Target: U.S.A.; Conquest by Propaganda.* New York: I. Washburn, 1961.

Dunn, S. Watson. *Public Relations: A Contemporary Approach.* Homewood, Ill.: Irwin, 1986.

Dyer, Murray. *The Weapon on the Wall: Rethinking Psychological Warfare.* Baltimore: Johns Hopkins University Press, 1959.

Edmunds, Robert. *About Documentary: Anthropology on Film.* Dayton, Ohio: Pflaum, 1974.

Edward R. Murrow Papers, 1927–1965: A Guide to the Microfilm Edition. Sanford, N.C.: Microfilming Corporation of America, 1981.

Edwards, Samuel. *Rebel! A Biography of Tom Paine.* New York: Praeger, 1974.

Efron, Edith. *The News Twisters.* Los Angeles: Nash, 1971.

Efron, Edith, and Clytia Chambers. *How CBS Tried to Kill a Book.* Los Angeles: Nash, 1972.

Elder, Robert. *The Information Machine: The United States Information Agency and American Foreign Policy.* Syracuse, N.Y.: Syracuse University Press, 1968.

Ellul, Jacques. *Propaganda: The Formation of Men's Attitudes.* New York: Alfred A. Knopf, 1965. Reprint. New York: Vintage Books, 1973.

Evans, Frank Bowen, ed. *Worldwide Communist Propaganda Activities.* New York: Macmillan, 1955.

Evansohn, John, et al. *Literature of the American Working Class.* San Francisco: Bay Area Radical Education Project, [1969].

Ewing, Raymond P. *Managing the New Bottom Line: Issues Management for Senior Executives.* Homewood, Ill.: Dow Jones-Irwin, 1988.

Fagan, Myron C. *Documentation of the Red Stars in Hollywood.* Hollywood, Calif.: Cinema Educational Guild, [ca. 1950].

————. *Red Treason in Hollywood.* Hollywood, Calif.: Cinema Educational Guild, 1949.

————. *Red Treason on Broadway: Stage, Television, Radio.* Hollywood, Calif.: Cinema Educational Guild, 1954.

Fejes, Fred. *Imperialism, Media and the Good Neighbor: New Deal Foreign Policy and United States Shortwave Broadcasting to Latin America.* Norwood, N.J.: Ablex, 1986.

————. *The U.S. in Third World Communications: Latin America, 1900–1945.* Journalism Monographs, No. 86. Columbia, S.C.: Association for Education in Journalism and Mass Communication, November 1983.

Ferguson, Marilyn. *The Aquarian Conspiracy: Personal and Social Transformation in the 1980s.* Updated ed. Los Angeles: J. P. Tarcher, 1987.

Fielding, Raymond. *The American Newsreel: 1911–1967.* Norman: University of Oklahoma Press, 1972.

Filler, Louis. *Dictionary of American Conservatism.* New York: Philosophical Library, 1987.

————. *Progressivism and Muckraking.* New York: R. R. Bowker, 1976.

Findley, Paul. *They Dare to Speak Out: People and Institutions Confront Israel's Lobby.* Westport, Conn.: Lawrence Hill, 1985.

Fitzgerald, Richard. "The Images of Power in American Political Cartoons." *Praxis: A Journal of Radical Perspectives on the Arts,* 1 (Winter 1976), 1–8.

Foner, Eric. *Tom Paine and Revolutionary America.* New York: Oxford University Press, 1976.

Foner, Philip S. *History of the Labor Movement in the United States.* 6 vols. New York: International Publishers, 1947–82.

————, ed. *American Labor Songs of the Nineteenth Century.* Urbana: University of Illinois Press, 1975.

Ford, Glen. *The Big Lie: Analysis of U.S. Press Coverage of the Grenada Invasion.* Prague: International Organization of Journalists in cooperation with the National Alliance of Third World Journalists, 1985.

Ford, Nick Aaron. *Language in Uniform: A Reader on Propaganda.* New York: Odyssey Press, 1967.

Fraser, Lindley. *Propaganda.* New York: Oxford University Press, 1957.

Frederick, Howard H. *Cuban-American Radio Wars: Ideology in International Telecommunications.* Norwood, N.J.: Ablex, 1986.

Freeley, Austin J. *Argumentation and Debate: Critical Thinking for Reasoned Decision Making.* 6th ed. Belmont, Calif.: Wadsworth, 1986.

Freidel, Frank. B., comp. *Union Pamphlets of the Civil War, 1861–1865.* Cambridge, Mass.: Belknap Press of the Harvard University Press, 1967.

French, Blaire Atherton. *The Presidential Press Conference: Its History and Role in the American Political System.* Lanham, Md.: University Press of America, 1982.

Friedberg, Gerald. "Sources for the Study of Socialism in America, 1901–1919." *Labor History,* 6 (Spring 1965), 159–65.

Fulbright, J. William. *The Pentagon Propaganda Machine.* New York: Liveright, 1970.

Furhammar, Leif, and Folke Isaksson. *Politics and Film.* New York: Praeger, 1971.

Gaines, Elizabeth. *"The Fatherland: An American Vehicle for German Propaganda, 1914–1917."* Master's thesis, Indiana University, 1971.

Galvin, John R. *Three Men of Boston.* New York: Crowell, 1976.

Gandy, Oscar H., Jr. *Beyond Agenda Setting: Information Subsidies and Public Policy.* Norwood, N.J.: Ablex, 1982.

Giddens, Jackson. "American Foreign Propaganda in World War I." Ph.D. dissertation, Fletcher School of Law and Diplomacy, Tufts University, 1967.

———. "Propaganda." In *The Encyclopedia Americana*. International ed. Danbury, Conn.: Americana, 1979, xxii: 656–60.

Giffard, C. Anthony. *UNESCO and the Media*. White Plains, N.Y.: Longman, 1988.

Gimbel, Richard. *Thomas Paine: A Bibliographical Check List of "Common Sense," with an Account of Its Publication*. New Haven: Yale University Press, 1956.

Gipson, Henry Clay. *Films in Business and Industry*. New York: McGraw-Hill, 1947.

Glazier, Kenneth M., and James R. Hobson. *International and English-Language Collections: A Survey of the Holdings at the Hoover Institution on War, Revolution and Peace*. Stanford, Calif.: Hoover Institution Press, 1971.

Goehlert, Robert U., and Fenton S. Martin. *The American Presidency: A Bibliography*. Washington, D.C.: Congressional Quarterly Books, 1987.

———. *American Presidents: A Bibliography*. Washington, D.C.: Congressional Quarterly Books, 1987.

Gordon, George N. *Persuasion: The Theory and Practice of Manipulative Communication*. New York: Hastings House, 1971.

Gordon, George N., and Irving A. Falk. *The War of Ideas: America's International Identity Crisis*. New York: Hastings House, 1973.

Gordon, George N., and William Hodapp. *The Idea Invaders*. New York: Hastings House, 1963.

Gordon, Jay E. *Motion Picture Production for Industry*. New York: Macmillan, 1961.

Gordon, Thomas F., and Mary Ellen Verna. *Mass Communication Effects and Processes: A Comprehensive Bibliography, 1950–1975*. Beverly Hills, Calif.: Sage, 1978.

Gould, Frederick James. *Thomas Paine (1737–1809)*. Boston: Small, Maynard, 1925.

Graber, Doris A. *Mass Media and American Politics*. 3rd ed. Washington D.C.: Congressional Quarterly Books, 1988.

———, ed. *Media Power in Politics*. Washington, D.C.: Congressional Quarterly Books, 1984.

Greenstadt, Melvin. "A Critical Survey of United States Government Films in World War I." Master's thesis, University of Southern California, 1949.

Griffin, Leland M. "The Antimasonic Persuasion: A Study of Public Address in the American Antimasonic Movement, 1826–1838." Ph.D. dissertation, Cornell University, 1950.

Grunig, James E., and Todd Hunt. *Managing Public Relations*. New York: Holt, Rinehart and Winston, 1984.

Gulik, Charles, Roy Ockert, and Raymond Wallace. *History and Theories of Working Class Movements—A Select Bibliography*. Berkeley: Institute of Industrial Relations, University of California, 1955.

Hachten, William A. *The World News Prism: Changing Media, Clashing Ideologies*. 2nd ed. Ames: Iowa State University Press, 1987.

Hachten, William A., and C. Anthony Giffard. *The Press and Apartheid: Repression and Propaganda in South Africa*. Madison: University of Wisconsin Press, 1984.

Hale, Julian. *Radio Power: Propaganda and International Broadcasting*. Philadelphia: Temple University Press, 1975.

Hamilton, Alexander, James Madison, and John Jay. *The Federalist Papers*. Introduction by Clinton Rossiter. New York: New American Library/Mentor Books, 1961.

Hapgood, Norman, ed. *Professional Patriots: An Exposure of the Personalities, Methods and Objectives Involved in the Organized Effort to Exploit Patriotic Impulses in These United States During and After the Late War.* New York: Boni, 1927.

Hargis, Billy James. *Distortion by Design: The Story of America's Liberal Press.* Tulsa, Okla.: Christian Crusade, 1965.

Harlow, Ralph Volney. *Samuel Adams, Promoter of the American Revolution: A Study in Psychology and Politics.* New York: Holt, 1923.

Hartenian, Lawrence Raymond. "Propaganda and the Control of Information in Occupied Germany: The U.S. Information Control Division at Radio Frankfort 1945–1949." Ph.D. dissertation, Rutgers University, 1984.

Harter, D. Lincoln, and John Sullivan. *Propaganda Handbook.* Philadelphia: Twentieth Century, 1953.

Harty, Sheila. *Hucksters in the Classroom: A Review of Industry Propaganda in Schools.* Washington, D.C.: Center for the Study of Responsible Law, 1980.

Harwell, Richard. *More Confederate Imprints.* 2 vols. Richmond: Virginia State Library, 1957.

Haste, Cate. *Keep the Home Fires Burning: Propaganda in the First World War.* London: Alien Lane/Penguin Books, 1977.

Hauser, Gerard A. *Introduction to Rhetorical Theory.* New York: Harper and Row, 1986.

Hawke, David Freeman. *Paine.* New York: Harper and Row, 1974.

Heartman, Charles F., comp. *The Cradle of the United States, 1765–1789: Five Hundred Contemporary Broadsides, Pamphlets, and a Few Books Pertaining to the History of the Stamp Act, the Boston Massacre and Other Pre-Revolutionary Troubles, the War for Independence and the Adoption of the Federal Constitution.* Perth Amboy, N.J.: Privately printed, 1922.

Heath, Robert L., et al. *Strategic Issues Management: How Organizations Influence and Respond to Public Interests and Policies.* San Francisco: Jossey-Bass, 1988.

Heath, Robert L., and Richard Alan Nelson. *Issues Management: Corporate Public Policymaking in an Information Society.* Beverly Hills, Calif.: Sage, 1986.

Heintze, James R. *Scholars' Guide to Washington, D.C. for Audio Resources: Sound Recordings in the Arts, Humanities and Social, Physical and Life Sciences.* Washington, D.C.: Smithsonian Institution Press, 1985.

Heise, Juergen Arthur. *Minimum Disclosure: How the Pentagon Manipulates the News.* New York: W. W. Norton, 1979.

Heller, John. "The Selling of the Constitution: The Federalist Papers Viewed as an Advertising Campaign." Master's thesis, University of Florida, 1974.

Henderson, John W. *The United States Information Agency.* New York: Praeger, 1969.

Herman, Edward S. *The Real Terror Network: Terrorism in Fact and Propaganda.* Boston: South End Press, 1982.

Hersh, Seymour M. *"The Target Is Destroyed"—What Really Happened to Flight 007 and What America Knew About It.* Updated ed., with new preface. New York: Vintage Books, 1987.

Hirst, David. "German Propaganda in the United States, 1914–1917." Ph.D. dissertation, Northwestern University, 1962.

Hitler, Adolf. *Mein Kampf.* Unexpurgated annotated translation. New York: Reynal and Hitchcock, 1940. Sentry Edition, Ralph Manheim translation. Boston: Houghton Mifflin, 1943.

Hoffer, Thomas William. "Broadcasting in an Insurgency Environment: USIA in Vietnam, 1965–1970." Ph.D. dissertation, University of Wisconsin, 1972.

Hofstetter, C. Richard. *Bias in the News: Network Television Coverage of the 1972 Election Campaign*. Columbus: Ohio State University Press, 1976.

Holgren, Carol Jean. "The Propaganda Program of the National Recovery Administration." Master's thesis, University of Washington, 1962.

Holt, Robert T., and Robert W. van de Velde. *Strategic Psychological Operations and American Foreign Policy*. Chicago: University of Chicago Press, 1960.

Hook, Sydney, Vladimir Bukovsky, and Paul Hollander. *Soviet Hypocrisy and Western Gullibility*. Lanham Md.:University Press of America, 1987.

Hosmer, James K. *Samuel Adams*. Boston: Houghton Mifflin, 1917.

Hovland, Carl, et al. *Communication and Persuasion*. New Haven: Yale University Press, 1953.

Howe, Quincy. *England Expects Every American to Do His Duty*. New York: Simon and Schuster, 1937.

Howe, Russell Warren, and Sarah Hays Trott. *The Power Peddlers: How Lobbyists Mold America's Foreign Policy*. Garden City, N.Y.: Doubleday, 1977.

Hummel, Ray O., Jr. *Southeastern Broadsides Before 1877: A Bibliography*. Richmond: Virginia State Library, 1971.

Hummel, William, and Keith Huntress. *The Analysis of Propaganda*. New York: William Sloane, 1949.

Hunt, Dave. *The Cult Explosion*. Eugene, Ore.: Harvest House, 1980.

Hunter, Edward. *Brainwashing: The Story of the Men Who Defied It*. New York: Farrar, Straus and Cudahy, 1956.

Industrial Workers of the World. *IWW Little Red Songbook*. Chicago: Industrial Workers of the World, n.d.

————. "A Reading List on IWW History." Rev. pamphlet. Chicago: Industrial Workers of the World, August 1973.

Institute of Labor and Industrial Relations. *American Labor in Journals of History*. Urbana: Institute of Labor and Industrial Relations, University of Illinois, 1962.

————. *Labor History in the United States*. Urbana: Institute of Labor and Industrial Relations, University of Illinois, 1961.

International Propaganda/Communications: Selections from the Public Opinion Quarterly. New York: Arno Press, 1972.

Irion, Frederick C. *Public Opinion and Propaganda*. New York: Crowell, 1950.

Irvine, Reed. *Media Mischief and Misdeeds*. Chicago: Regnery Gateway, 1984.

Irwin, Will. *Propaganda and the News; or, What Makes You Think So?* New York: McGraw-Hill, 1936. Reprint. Westport, Conn.: Greenwood Press, 1970.

Jacobs, Lewis, ed. *The Documentary Tradition*. New York: Hopkinson and Blake, 1971.

Jamieson, Kathleen Hall. *Packaging the Presidency: A History and Criticism of Presidential Campaign Advertising*. New York: Oxford University Press, 1984.

Jamieson, Kathleen Hall, and Karlyn Kohrs Campbell. *The Interplay of Influence: Mass Media and Their Publics in News, Advertising, Politics*. 2nd ed. Belmont, Calif.: Wadsworth, 1988.

Jeavons, Clyde. *A Pictorial History of War Films*. Secaucus, N.J.: Citadel Press, 1974.

Jensen, Joan. *The Price of Vigilance*. New York: Rand McNally, 1968.

Johnson, R. W. *Shootdown: Flight 007 and the American Connection*. New York: Penguin Books, 1986.

Johnson, Walter. *The Battle Against Isolation*. Chicago: University of Chicago Press, 1944.

Johnston, Winifred. *Memo on the Movies: War Propaganda, 1914–1939*. Norman, Okla.: Cooperative Books, 1939.

Jones, Ken and Arthur McClure. *Hollywood at War: The American Motion Picture Industry and World War II*. New York: Castle Books, 1973.

Jowett, Garth S., and Victoria O'Donnell. *Propaganda and Persuasion*. Newbury Park, Calif.: Sage, 1986.

Judd, Denis. *Posters of World War Two*. New York: St. Martin's Press, 1973.

Kaid, Lynda Lee, Keith R. Sanders, and Robert O. Hirsch. *Political Campaign Communications: A Bibliography and Guide to the Literature*. Metuchen, N.J.: Scarecrow Press, 1974.

Kaid, Lynda Lee, and Anne J. Wadsworth. *Political Campaign Communications: A Bibliography and Guide to the Literature, 1973–1982*. Metuchen, N.J.: Scarecrow Press, 1985.

Kaid, Lynda Lee, et al., eds. *New Perspectives on Political Advertising*. Carbondale: Southern Illinois University Press, 1986.

Karlins, Marvin, and Herbert Abelson. *Persuasion: How Opinions and Attitudes Are Changed*. 2nd ed. New York: Springer, 1970.

Katz, Daniel, et al. *Public Opinion and Propaganda: A Book of Readings*. New York: Dryden, 1954.

Katz, Phillip Paul. *A Systematic Approach to Psyop Information*. Washington, D.C.: Center for Research in Social Systems, 1970.

Keeley, Joseph. *The Left-Leaning Antenna: Political Bias in Television*. New Rochelle, N.Y.: Arlington House, 1971.

Keller, Phyllis. *States of Belonging: German-American Intellectuals and the First World War*. Cambridge, Mass.: Harvard University Press, 1979.

Kenneally, Finbar. *United States Documents in the Propaganda Fide Archives: A Calendar*. 7 vols. Washington, D.C.: Academy of American Franciscan History, 1966–71.

Key, Wilson Bryant. *The Subliminal Seduction: Ad Media's Manipulation of a Not So Innocent America*. Englewood Cliffs, N.J.: Prentice-Hall, 1973.

King, Andrew. *Power and Communication*. Prospect Heights, Ill.: Waveland Press, 1987.

King, Arnold Kinsey. "Thomas Paine in America, 1774–1787." Ph.D. dissertation, University of Chicago, 1952.

Klare, Michael, and Peter Kornbluh, eds. *Low Intensity Warfare: Counterinsurgency, Proinsurgency, and Antiterrorism in the 80s*. New York: Random House/Pantheon, 1988.

Klein, Walter. *The Sponsored Film*. New York: Hastings House, 1976.

Klement, Frank L. *The Limits of Dissent: Clement L. Vallandigham and the Civil War*. Lexington: University Press of Kentucky, 1970.

Klingender, F. D., and Stuart Legg. *Money Behind the Screen*. London: Lawrence and Wishart, 1937.

Knightley, Phillip. *The First Casualty—From the Crimea to Vietnam: The War Correspondent as Hero, Propagandist, and Myth Maker.* New York: Harcourt Brace Jovanovich, 1976.

Koek, Karin E., and Susan Boyles Martin, eds. *Encylopedia of Associations, 1988.* 22nd ed. 4 vols. Detroit: Gale Research, 1987.

Koppes, Clayton R., and Gregory D. Black. *Hollywood Goes to War: How Politics, Profits, and Propaganda Shaped World War II Movies.* New York: Free Press, 1987.

Kornbluh, Joyce L., ed. *Rebel Voices, an IWW Anthology.* Ann Arbor: University of Michigan Press, 1964. Rev. ed. Chicago: Charles H. Kerr, 1985.

Kreuter, Kent, and Gretchen Kreuter. *An American Dissenter: The Life of Algie Martin Simons, 1870–1950.* Lexington: University Press of Kentucky, 1969.

Kwitny, Jonathan. *The Crimes of Patriots: A True Tale of Dope, Dirty Money, and the CIA.* New York: W. W. Norton, 1987.

La Haye, Tim. *The Hidden Censors.* Old Tappan, N.J.: Fleming H. Ravell Co., 1984.

Lampham, Ruth, comp. *Check List of American Revolutionary War Pamphlets in the Newberry Library.* Chicago: Newberry Library, 1922.

Laqueur, Walter, and Yonah Alexander, eds. *The Terrorism Reader.* Rev. ed. New York: NAL Penguin, 1987.

Larson, Charles U. *Persuasion: Reception and Responsibility.* 4th ed. Belmont, Calif.: Wadsworth, 1986.

Lasky, Victor. *It Didn't Start with Watergate.* New York: Dell, 1978.

Lasswell, Harold D. "Propaganda." In *Encyclopaedia Britannica.* Chicago: Encyclopaedia Britannica, 1973, XVIII: 624–39.

———. "Propaganda." In *Encyclopaedia of the Social Sciences.* New York: Macmillan, 1933, XII: 521–28.

———. *Propaganda Technique in the World War.* London: Kegan Paul, Trench, Trubner, 1927. Reprinted as *Propaganda Technique in World War I.* Cambridge, Mass.: MIT Press, 1971.

Lasswell, Harold D., and Dorothy Blumenstock. *World Revolutionary Propaganda.* New York: Alfred A. Knopf, 1939.

Lasswell, Harold D., Ralph D. Casey, and Bruce L. Smith. *Propaganda and Promotional Activities: An Annotated Bibliography.* Minneapolis: University of Minnesota Press, 1935. Reprint. Chicago: University of Chicago Press, 1969.

Lasswell, Harold D., Daniel Lerner, and Hans Speier, eds. *Propaganda and Communication in World History, Volume 1: The Symbolic Instrument in Early Times.* Honolulu: University Press of Hawaii, 1979.

———. *Propaganda and Communication in World History, Volume 2: The Emergence of Public Opinion in the West.* Honolulu: University Press of Hawaii, 1979.

———. *Propaganda and Communication in World History, Volume 3: A Pluralizing World in Formation.* Honolulu: University Press of Hawaii, 1980.

Lavine, Harold, and James Wechsler. *War Propaganda and the United States.* New Haven: Yale University Press for the Institute for Propaganda Analysis, 1940. Reprint. New York: Arno Press, 1972.

Lee, Alfred McClung. *How to Understand Propaganda.* New York: Holt, Rinehart, 1952.

Lee, Alfred McClung, and Elizabeth Briant Lee. *The Fine Art of Propaganda: A Study of Father Coughlin's Speeches.* New York: Harcourt, Brace, 1939. Reprint. New York: Octagon, 1972; San Francisco: International Society for General Semantics, 1979.

Lefever, Ernest W., and Roy Godson. *The CIA and the American Ethic: An Unfinished Debate.* Washington, D.C.: Ethics and Public Policy Center of Georgetown University, 1979.

Leonard, Thomas C. *The Power of the Press: The Birth of American Political Reporting.* New York: Oxford University Press, 1986.

Lerner, Daniel. "Propaganda." In *Funk and Wagnalls Standard Reference Encyclopedia.* New York: Standard Reference Works, 1959, xx: 7266–68.

———. *Sykewar: Psychological Warfare Against Germany, D-Day to VE-Day.* New York: George W. Stewart, 1949.

———, ed. *Propaganda in War and Crisis: Materials for American Foreign Policy.* New York: George W. Stewart, 1951. Reprint. New York: Arno Press, 1972.

Levy, Leonard W. *Emergence of a Free Press.* New York: Oxford University Press, 1985.

———. *Legacy of Suppression: Freedom of Speech and Press in Early American History.* Cambridge, Mass.: Belknap Press of Harvard University Press, 1960.

Lichter, S. Robert, Stanley Rothman, and Linda S. Lichter. *The Media Elite: America's New Powerbrokers.* Bethesda, Md.: Adler and Adler, 1986.

Linebarger, Paul. *Psychological Warfare.* 2nd ed. Washington, D.C.: Combat Forces Press, 1954. Reprint. New York: Arno Press, 1972.

Lingeman, Richard R. *Don't You Know There's a War On? The American Home Front, 1941–1945.* New York: Putnam's, 1970.

Linsky, Martin. *Impact: How the Press Affects Federal Policymaking.* New York: W. W. Norton, 1986.

Linsky, Martin, Jonathan Moore, Wendy O'Donnell, and David Whitman. *How the Press Affects Federal Policymaking: Six Case Studies.* New York: W. W. Norton, 1986.

Lippmann, Walter. *Drift and Mastery: An Attempt to Diagnose the Current Unrest.* Englewood Cliffs, N.J.: Prentice-Hall, 1961.

———. *Public Opinion.* New York: Harcourt, Brace, 1922. Rev. ed. New York: Free Press, 1965.

Lisann, Maury. *Broadcasting to the Soviet Union: International Politics and Radio.* New York: Praeger, 1975.

Lovenduski, Joni, and Joyce Outshoorn, eds. *The New Politics of Abortion.* Newbury Park, Calif.: Sage, 1986.

Lowenthal, Leo, and Norbert Guterman. *Prophets of Deceit: A Study of the Techniques of the American Agitator.* 2nd ed. Palo Alto, Calif.: Pacific Books, 1970.

Lumley, Frederick E. *The Propaganda Menace.* New York: Century, 1933.

McBrearty, James. *American Labor History and Comparative Labor Movements—A Selected Bibliography.* Tucson: University of Arizona Press, 1973.

MacCann, Richard Dyer. *The People's Films: A Political History of U.S. Government Motion Pictures.* New York: Hastings House, 1973.

McDonald, J. Fred. *Television and the Red Menace: The Video Road to Vietnam.* New York: Praeger, 1985.

McDonough, Joseph J. "Analysis of Official U.S. Military Psychological Warfare Efforts in the Vietnam Conflict." Master's thesis, Boston University, 1968.

McEnroe, Thomas Howard. "The International Workers of the World: Theories, Organizational Problems and Appeals as Revealed Principally in the *Industrial Worker.*" Ph.D. dissertation, University of Minnesota, 1960.

McGuire, William J. "Persuasion, Resistance, and Attitude Change." In *Handbook of Communication.* Edited by Ithiel de Sola Pool, Wilbur Schramm, et al. Chicago: Rand McNally, 1973, pp. 216–52.

MacKay, Lamar. "Domestic Operations of the Office of War Information in World War II." Ph.D. dissertation, University of Wisconsin, 1966.

McLaurin, Ron D., ed. *Military Propaganda: Psychological Warfare and Operations.* New York: Praeger, 1982.

Maddox, William S., and Stuart A. Lilie. *Beyond Liberal and Conservative.* Washington, D.C.: Cato Institute, 1984.

Mahood, H. R. *Pressure Groups in American Politics.* New York: Scribner's, 1967.

Mamatey, Victor S. *The United States and East Central Europe, 1914–1918: A Study in Wilsonian Diplomacy and Propaganda.* Princeton, N.J.: Princeton University Press, 1957.

Manuscripts of the American Revolution in the Boston Public Library: A Descriptive Catalog. Boston: G. K. Hall, 1968.

Manvell, Roger. *Films and the Second World War.* New York: Dell, 1974.

Marchetti, Victor, and John D. Marks. *The CIA and the Cult of Intelligence.* Updated paperback ed. New York: Laurel/Dell, 1983.

Marks, Barry. "The Idea of Propaganda in America." Ph.D. dissertation, University of Minnesota, 1957.

Marks, John. *The Search for the "Manchurian Candidate": The CIA and Mind Control— The Story of the Agency's Secret Efforts to Control Human Behavior.* New York: Times Books, 1979.

Marxist Readings: A Bibliography of over 4,000 Books, Pamphlets, and Reprints in English, German and Italian—Volume 1. Bagnolet, France: Critiques Livres, 1970.

Maynard, Richard A. *Propaganda on Film: A Nation at War.* Rochelle Park, N.J.: Hayden Books, 1975.

Meadow, Robert G. *Politics as Communication.* Norwood, N.J.: Ablex, 1980.

Mickelson, Sig. *America's Other Voice: The Story of Radio Free Europe and Radio Liberty.* New York: Praeger, 1983.

Miller, Gerald R. "Persuasion." In Charles R. Berger and Steven H. Chaffee, eds., *Handbook of Communication Science.* Newbury Park, Calif.: Sage, 1987.

Miller, Gerald R., and Michael Burgoon. "Persuasion Research: Review and Commentary." In *Communication Yearbook 2.* Edited by Brent Ruben. New Brunswick, N.J.: Transaction Books, 1978, pp. 29–47.

Miller, John C. *Sam Adams: Pioneer in Propaganda.* Stanford, Calif.: Stanford University Press, 1936.

Minnick, Wayne. *The Art of Persuasion.* 2nd ed. Boston: Houghton Mifflin, 1968.

Minor, Dale. *The Information War.* New York: Hawthorn Books, 1970.

Mitchell, Malcolm. *Propaganda, Polls, and Public Opinion: Are the People Manipulated?* Englewood Cliffs, N.J.: Prentice-Hall, 1970.

Mitchell, W. J. T. *Iconology: Image, Text, Ideology.* Chicago: University of Chicago Press, 1986.

Mock, James R., and Cedric Larson. *Words That Won the War: The Story of the*

Committee on Public Information, 1917–1919. Princeton, N.J.: Princeton University Press, 1939. Reprint. New York: Russell and Russell, 1968.

Morella, Joe, Edward Z. Epstein, and John Griggs. *The Films of World War II.* New York: Citadel Press, 1973.

Mueller, John E. *War, Presidents and Public Opinion.* New York: Wiley, 1973. Reprint. Lanham, Md.: University Press of America, 1985.

Murray, Robert. *Red Scare: A Study in National Hysteria, 1919–1920.* Minneapolis: University of Minnesota Press, 1955. Reprint. New York: McGraw-Hill, 1964.

Murty, B. S. *Propaganda and World Public Order: The Legal Regulation of the Ideological Instrument of Coercion.* New Haven: Yale University Press, 1968.

Myers, Gustavus. *History of Bigotry in the United States.* Rev. ed. New York: Capricorn Books, 1960.

Nagelschmidt, Joseph S., ed. *The Public Affairs Handbook.* New York: Amacom, 1982.

Neilson, Francis. *Escort of Lies: War Propaganda.* Brooklyn, N.Y.: Revisionist Press, 1979.

Nelson, Richard Alan. "Commercial Propaganda in the Silent Film: A Case Study of *A Mormon Maid* (1917)." *Film History: An International Journal,* (1987), 149–62.

———. "Germany and the German Film, 1930–1945: An Annotated Research Bibliography. Part I: Books, Dissertations, and Pamphlets." *Journal of the University Film Association* 29 (Winter 1977), 45–66.

———. "Germany and the German Film, 1930–1945: An Annotated Research Bibliography. Part II: Articles and Periodicals." *Journal of the University Film Association,* 29 (Spring 1977), 67–80.

———. "Germany and the German Film, 1930–1945: An Annotated Research Bibliography. Part III: Research Libraries, Archives, and Other Sources." *Journal of the University Film Association,* 30 (Winter 1978), 53–72.

———. "Mormons as Silent Cinema Villains: Propaganda and Entertainment." *Historical Journal of Film, Radio and Television,* 4 (March 1984), 3–14.

Neufeld, Maurice. *A Representative Bibliography of American Labor History.* Ithaca, N.Y.: Cornell University Press, 1964.

Newsom, Doug, Alan Scott, and Judy Vanslyke Turk. *This Is PR: The Realities of Public Relations.* 4th ed. Belmont, Calif.: Wadsworth, 1985.

Nimmo, Dan. *Political Communication and Public Opinion in America.* Santa Monica, Calif.: Goodyear, 1978.

———. *The Political Persuaders: The Techniques of Modern Election Campaigns.* Englewood Cliffs, N.J.: Prentice-Hall, 1970.

Nordenstreng, Kaarle, E. G. Manet, and W. Kleinwächter. *The New International Information and Communication Order.* Prague: International Organization of Journalists, 1987.

Norman, Albert. *Our German Policy: Propaganda and Culture.* New York: Vintage Books, 1951.

Norris, Frank. *The Pit: A Story of Chicago.* New York: Doubleday, 1903.

Olasky, Marvin N. *Corporate Public Relations: A New Historical Perspective.* Hillsdale N.J.: Lawrence Erlbaum Associates, 1988.

"On Propaganda." *ETC.: A Review of General Semantics,* 36 (Summer 1979). Special issue.

Packard, Vance. *The Hidden Persuaders.* New York: McKay, 1957. Rev. ed. New York: Pocket Books, 1980.

Paine, Thomas. *Common Sense and Other Political Writings.* Edited by Nelson F. Adkins. Indianapolis: Bobbs-Merrill, 1953.

———. *The Complete Writings of Thomas Paine.* Edited by Philip S. Foner. 2 vols. New York: Citadel Press, 1945.

———. *The Life and Works of Thomas Paine.* Edited by William van der Weyde. 10 vols. New Rochelle, N.Y.: Thomas Paine National Historical Association, 1925.

———. *The Writings of Thomas Paine.* Edited by Moncure Daniel Conway. 4 vols. New York: Putnam's, 1894–96. Reprint. New York: AMS Press, 1967.

Paletz, David, Roberta Pearson, and Donald Willis. *Politics in Public Service Advertising on Television.* New York: Praeger, 1977.

Parenti, Michael. *Inventing Reality: The Politics of the Mass Media.* New York: St. Martin's Press, 1986.

Perlmutter, Tom. *War Movies.* New York: Castle Books, 1974.

Perris, Arnold. *Music as Propaganda.* Westport, Conn.: Greenwood Press, 1985.

Peterson, Horace C. *Propaganda for War: The Campaign Against American Neutrality, 1914–1917.* Norman: University of Oklahoma Press, 1939. Reprint. Port Washington, N.Y.: Kennikat Press, 1968.

Philippe, Robert. *Political Graphics: Art as a Weapon.* New York: Abbeville Press, 1982.

Pirsein, Robert W. *The Voice of America.* New York: Arno Press, 1979.

Plato. *Phaedrus.* Edited by R. Hackworth. Cambridge, England: Cambridge University Press, 1972.

Pollay, Richard W., ed. *Information Sources in Advertising History.* Westport, Conn.: Greenwood Press, 1979.

Pool, Ithiel de Sola, Wilbur Schramm, et al, eds. *Handbook of Communication.* Chicago: Rand McNally, 1973.

Posonby, Arthur. *Falsehood in War-time.* New York: E. P. Dutton, 1928.

Post, Louis F. *The Deportations Delirium of Nineteen-Twenty: A Personal Narrative of an Historic Official Experience.* Chicago: Charles H. Kerr, 1923. Reprint. New York: Da Capo Press, 1970.

Preston, William, Jr., *Aliens and Dissenters: Federal Suppression of Radicals, 1903–1933.* Cambridge, Mass.: Harvard University Press, 1963. Reprint. New York: Harper and Row, 1963.

Price, Warren C. *The Literature of Journalism: An Annotated Bibliography.* Minneapolis: University of Minnesota Press, 1959.

Price, Warren C., and Calder M. Pickett. *An Annotated Journalism Bibliography: 1958–1968.* Minneapolis: University of Minnesota Press, 1970.

Pro-Arab Propaganda in America: Vehicles and Voices. New York: Anti-Defamation League of B'nai B'rith, 1983.

Pronay, Nicholas and D. W. Spring, eds. *Propaganda, Politics and Film, 1918–1945.* Atlantic Highlands, N.J.: Humanities Press, 1982.

Pronay, Nicholas, and Keith Wilson, eds. *The Political Re-education of Germany and Her Allies After World War II.* London: Croom Helm, 1985.

Public Opinion, Mass Behavior and Political Psychology. Vol. 6 of the Political Science, Government, and Public Policy Series. Princeton, N.J.: Princeton Research/ IFI/Plenum Data, 1967. With annual supplements, 1967-.

Qualter, Terence H. *Opinion Control in the Democracies.* New York: St. Martin's Press, 1985.

————. *Propaganda and Psychological Warfare.* New York: Random House, 1962.

Rank, Hugh. *The Pep Talk: How to Analyze Political Language.* Park Forest, Ill.: Counter-Propaganda Press, 1984.

————. *The Pitch: How to Analyze Advertising.* Park Forest, Ill.: Counter-Propaganda Press, 1982.

Raspberry, Robert W. *The "Technique" of Political Lying.* Washington, D.C.: University Press of America, 1981.

Raucher, Alan R. *Public Relations and Business, 1900–1929.* Baltimore: Johns Hopkins University Press, 1968.

Read, James M. *Atrocity Propaganda, 1914–1919.* New Haven: Yale University Press, 1941. Reprint. New York: Arno Press, 1972.

Reed, Rebecca Theresa. *Six Months in a Convent.* Boston: Rusell, Odiorne and Metcalf, 1835.

Reimann, Horst. "Propaganda" and "Public Opinion." In *Marxism, Communism and Western Society: A Comparative Encyclopedia.* London: Herder and Herder, 1973, vii: 67–68, 113–23.

Rhodes, Anthony. *Propaganda—The Art of Persuasion: World War II.* New York: Chelsea House, 1976. Reprint. Secaucus, N.J.: Wellfleet Press, 1987.

Rice, Ronald E., and William J. Paisley, eds. *Public Communication Campaigns.* Beverly Hills, Calif.: Sage, 1981.

Richelson, Jeffrey T. *American Espionage and the Soviet Target.* New York: William Morrow, 1987.

————. *Sword and Shield: Soviet Intelligence and Security Apparatus.* Cambridge, Mass.: Ballinger, 1986.

————. *The U.S. Intelligence Community.* Cambridge, Mass.: Ballinger, 1985.

Riegel, Oscar W. *Mobilizing for Chaos: The Story of the New Propaganda.* New Haven: Yale University Press, 1934. Reprint. New York: Arno Press, 1972.

Riff, Michael A., ed. *Dictionary of Modern Political Ideologies.* New York: St. Martin's Press, 1987.

Robison, John. *Proofs of a Conspiracy Against All the Religions and Governments of Europe, Carried on in Secret Meetings of Free Masons, Illuminati, and Reading Societies, Collected from Good Authorities.* 4th ed. New York: George Forman, 1798. Reprint, with new introduction. Boston and Los Angeles: Western Islands, 1967.

Roetter, Charles. *The Art of Psychological Warfare, 1914–1945.* New York: Stein and Day, 1974.

Roloff, Michael, and Gerald R. Miller, eds. *Persuasion: New Directions in Theory and Research.* Beverly Hills, Calif.: Sage 1980.

Rowan, B. G., with D. Culbert and consultants T. Cripps and L. Lichty. *Scholars' Guide to Washington D.C. Film and Video Collections.* Washington, D.C.: Smithsonian Institution Press and Woodrow Wilson International Center for Scholars, 1980.

Rubenstein, Richard E. *Alchemists of Revolution: Terrorism in the Modern World*. New York: Basic Books, 1987.

Rubin, Bernard, ed. *When Information Counts: Grading the Media*. Lexington, Mass.: Lexington Books, 1985.

Rupp, Leila J. *Mobilizing Women for War: German and American Propaganda, 1939– 1945*. Princeton, N.J.: Princeton University Press, 1978.

Ryan, Milo. *History in Sound: A Descriptive Listing of the KIRO-CBS Collection of Broadcasts of the World War II Years and After, in the Phonoarchive of the University of Washington*. Seattle: University of Washington Press, 1963.

Salisbury, Allen. *The Civil War and the American System*. New York: Campaigner Publications, 1978.

Scheflin, Alan W., and Edward M. Opton, Jr. *The Mind Manipulators: A Non-Fiction Account*. New York: Paddington Press, 1978.

Schein, Edgar, et al. *Coercive Persuasion: A Socio-Psychological Analysis of the "Brain-washing" of American Civilian Prisoners by the Chinese Communists*. New York: W. W. Norton, 1971.

Schiller, Herbert I. *Information and the Crisis Economy*. New York: Oxford University Press, 1986.

———. *The Mind Managers*. Boston: Beacon Press, 1973.

Schlesinger, Philip, Graham Murdock, and Philip Elliott. *Televising "Terrorism" : Political Violence in Popular Culture*. London: Comedia Publishing Group, 1983.

Schudson, Michael. *Advertising, the Uneasy Persuasion*. New York: Basic Books, 1985.

Schwar, Jane. "Interventionist Propaganda and Pressure Groups in the United States, 1937–1941." Ph.D. dissertation, Ohio State University, 1973.

Seabury, William Marston. *Motion Picture Problems: The Cinema and the League of Nations*. New York: Avondale Press, 1929. Reprint. New York: Arno Press, 1978.

Seldes, George. *The Facts Are . . . A Guide to Falsehood and Propaganda in the Press and Radio*. New York: In Fact, 1942.

Sethi, S. Prakash. *Advocacy Advertising and Large Corporations: Social Conflict, Big Business Image, the News Media, and Public Policy*. Lexington, Mass.: Lexington Books/Heath, 1977.

———. *Handbook of Advocacy Advertising: Concepts, Strategies, and Applications*. Cambridge, Mass.: Ballinger/Harper and Row, 1987.

Sethi, S. Prakash, and Cecilia McHugh Falbe, eds. *Business and Public Policy: Dimensions of Conflict and Cooperation*. Lexington, Mass.: Lexington Books/D. C. Heath, 1987.

Severin, Werner J., and James W. Tankard, Jr. *Communication Theories: Origins— Methods—Uses*. New York: Hastings House, 1979.

Shaheen, Jack G. *The TV Arab*. Bowling Green, Ohio: Bowling Green State University Popular Press, 1984.

Short, K.R.M., ed. *Film and Radio Propaganda in World War II*. Knoxville: University of Tennessee Press, 1983.

———, ed. *Films as History*. Knoxville: University of Tennessee Press, 1981.

———, ed. *Western Broadcasting over the Iron Curtain*. London: Croom Helm, 1986.

Shotwell, John. "Crystalizing Public Hatred: Ku Klux Klan Public Relations in the Early 1920s." Master's thesis, University of Wisconsin at Madison, 1974.

Shultz, Richard H., and Roy Godson. *Dezinformatsia: Active Measures in Soviet Strategy*. Washington, D.C.: Pergamon-Brassey's, 1984.

Silbey, Joel H. *The Partisan Imperative: The Dynamics of American Politics Before the Civil War*. New York: Oxford University Press, 1985.

Simons, Herbert W. *Persuasion: Understanding, Practice and Analysis*. 2nd ed. New York: Random House, 1986.

Sinclair, Upton. *The Brass Check: A Study in American Journalism*. Pasadena, Calif.: Privately printed, 1919. Reprint. New York: Arno Press, 1974.

———. *The Jungle*. New York: Doubleday, 1906.

Skvortsov, L. *The Ideology and Tactics of Anti-Communism*. Moscow: Progress, 1969.

Sloan, Stephen. *Beating International Terrorism: An Action Strategy for Preemption and Punishment*. Maxwell Air Force Base, Ala.: Air University Press, December 1986.

Small, William. *Political Power and the Press*. New York: W.W. Norton, 1972.

Smith, Bradley F. *The Shadow Warriors: O.S.S. and the Origins of the C.I.A.* New York: Basic Books, 1983.

Smith, Bruce L. "Propaganda." In *International Encyclopedia of the Social Sciences*. New York: Macmillan, 1968, XII: 579–89.

———. "Propaganda." In *The New Encyclopaedia Britannica*. Macropaedia. Chicago: Encyclopedia Britannica, 1974, XV: 36–45.

Smith, Bruce L., Harold D. Lasswell, and Ralph D. Casey. *Propaganda, Communication, and Public Opinion: A Comprehensive Reference Guide*. Princeton, N.J.: Princeton University Press, 1946.

Smith, Bruce L., and Chitra M. Smith. *International Communication and Political Opinion: A Guide to the Literature*. Princeton, N.J.: Princeton University Press, 1956. Reprint. Westport, Conn.: Greenwood Press, 1972.

Smith, Craig R. *The Fight for Freedom of Expression: Three Case Studies*. Washington, D.C.: Institute for Freedom of Communication, 1985.

Smith, Culver. *The Press, Politics, and Patronage: The American Government's Use of Newspapers, 1789–1875*. Athens: University of Georgia Press, 1977.

Smith, George Winston. "Generative Forces in Union Propaganda: A Study in Civil War Pressure Groups." Ph.D. dissertation, University of Wisconsin, 1940.

Smith, Jeffrey A. *Printers and Press Freedom: The Ideology of Early American Journalism*. New York: Oxford University Press, 1987.

Smith, Mary John. *Persuasion and Human Action: A Review and Critique of Social Influence Theories*. Belmont, Calif.: Wadsworth, 1982.

Smith, R. Harris. *OSS: The Secret History of America's First Central Intelligence Agency*. Berkeley: University of California Press, 1972.

Smith, Robert W. "What Came After?: News Diffusion and the Significance of the Boston Massacre in Six American Colonies, 1770–1775." Ph.D. dissertation, University of Wisconsin at Madison, 1972.

Sobel, Robert. *The Manipulators: America in the Media Age*. Garden City, N.Y.: Doubleday, 1976.

Sorensen, Thomas C. *The Word War: The Story of American Propaganda*. New York: Harper and Row, 1968.

Spannaus, Nancy, and Christopher White. *The Political Economy of the American Revolution*. New York: Campaigner Publications, 1977.

Sproule, J. Michael. "Propaganda Studies in American Social Science: The Rise and Fall of the Critical Paradigm." *Quarterly Journal of Speech*, 73 (February 1987), 60–78.

Squires, James D. *British Propaganda at Home and in the United States from 1914 to 1917*. Cambridge, Mass.: Harvard University Press, 1935.

Steele, Richard W. *Propaganda in an Open Society: The Roosevelt Administration and the Media, 1933–41*. Westport, Conn.: Greenwood Press, 1985.

Steffens, Lincoln. *The Shame of the Cities*. New York: McClure, Phillips, 1904.

Stenejhem, Michele Flynn. *An American First: John T. Flynn and the American First Committee*. New Rochelle, N.Y.: Arlington House, 1976.

Sterling, Christopher H., and Timothy R. Haight. *The Mass Media: Aspen Institute Guide to Communication Industry Trends*. New York: Praeger, 1978.

Sterling, Claire. *The Terror Network: The Secret War of International Terrorism*. London: Weidenfeld and Nicolson, 1981.

Stevens, Art. *The Persuasion Explosion: Your Guide to the Power and Influence of Contemporary Public Relations*. Washington, D.C.: Acropolis Books, 1985.

Stevenson, William. *A Man Called Intrepid: The Secret War*. New York: Harcourt Brace Jovanovich, 1976.

Stewart, Charles J., Craig Smith, and Robert E. Denton, Jr. *Persuasion and Social Movements*. Prospect Heights, Ill.: Waveland Press, 1984.

Stoetzer, Carlos. *Postage Stamps as Propaganda*. Washington, D.C.: Public Affairs Press, 1953.

Stowe, Harriet Beecher. *The Annotated Uncle Tom's Cabin*. Edited, with an introduction by Phillip Van Doren Stern. New York: Eriksson, 1964.

Stridsberg, A. B., in conjunction with International Advertising Association. *Controversy Advertising: How Advertisers Present Points of View in Public Affairs*. New York: Hastings House, 1977.

Sturminger, Alfred. *3000 Jahre Politische Propaganda*. Vienna: Herold, 1960.

Summers, R. E., ed. *America's Weapons of Psychological Warfare*. New York: H. W. Wilson, 1951.

Tarbell, Ida. *The History of the Standard Oil Company*. New York: McClure, Phillips, 1904.

Tedford, Thomas L. *Freedom of Speech in the United States*. New York: Random House, 1985. Carbondale: Southern Illinois University Press, 1985.

Theoharis, Athan. *Spying on Americans: Political Surveillance from Hoover to the Huston Plan*. Philadelphia: Temple University Press, 1978.

Thompson, Wayne N. *The Process of Persuasion: Principles and Readings*. New York: Harper and Row, 1975.

Thompson, William F. "The Pictorial Reporting and Propaganda of the Civil War." Ph.D. dissertation, University of Wisconsin, 1959.

Thomson, Charles. *Overseas Information Service of the United States Government*. Washington, D.C.: Brookings Institution, 1948.

Thomson, Oliver. *Mass Persuasion in History: A Historical Analysis of the Development of Propaganda Techniques*. Edinburgh: Paul Harris Publishing, 1977.

Thorpe, Frances, and Nicholas Pronay, with Clive Coultass. *British Official Films in the Second World War: A Descriptive Catalogue.* Santa Barbara, Calif.: Clio Press, 1980.

Tomshoi, Robert. *The American Sanctuary Movement.* Austin: Texas Monthly Press, 1987.

Tunstall, Jeremy. *The Media Are American: Anglo-American Media in the World.* New York: Columbia University Press, 1977.

Turner, Kathleen J. "The Presidential Libraries as Research Facilities: An Analysis of Resources for Rhetorical Scholarship." *Communication Education,* 35 (July 1986), 243–53.

Tyson, James L. *Prophets or Useful Idiots? Church Organizations Attacking U.S. Central America Policy.* Washington, D.C.: Council for the Defense of Freedom, 1987.

———. *Target America: The Influence of Communist Propaganda on U.S. Media.* Chicago: Regnery Gateway, 1981.

Tzu, Sun. *Sun Tzu, the Art of War.* Translated by Samuel Griffith. London: Oxford University Press, 1963.

Unger, Irwin. *The Movement: A History of the American New Left, 1959–1972.* New York: Dodd, Mead, 1974.

"USIA: A Battered but Powerful Propaganda Tool." Special Report. *U.S. News and World Report* (March 5, 1984), 58–61.

Vaughn, Stephen L. *Holding Fast the Inner Lines: Democracy, Nationalism, and the Committee on Public Information.* Chapel Hill: University of North Carolina Press, 1980.

Vaughn, William Preston. *The Antimasonic Party in the United States, 1826–1843.* Lexington: University Press of Kentucky, 1983.

Viereck, George S. *My Flesh and Blood: A Lyric Autobiography with Indiscreet Annotations.* New York: Horace Liveright, 1931.

———. *Spreading Germs of Hate.* New York: Horace Liveright, 1930.

Walker, Albert. "Public Relations Bibliography: Sixth Edition, 1976–77." *Public Relations Review,* 4 (Winter 1978), 1–94. Subsequent annual updates appear in the Winter issues of *Public Relations Review,* 1979–.

Waller, J. Michael. "CISPES: A Terrorist Propaganda Network." Special Report. Washington, D.C.: Council for Inter-American Security, 1984.

Warlaumont, Hazel G. "Radio Marti and the U.S.-Cuban Radio War: Strategies Used in the Absence of Definitive Legal Controls over International Broadcasting as Compared with Strategies Used in the U.S.-USSR Radio War." Master's thesis, California State University-Fullerton, 1986.

Weaver, Richard M. *The Ethics of Rhetoric.* Chicago: Henry Regnery, 1953. Reprint. Davis, Calif.: Hermagoras Press, 1985.

Weinberg, Sydney. "Wartime Propaganda in a Democracy: America's Twentieth Century Information Agencies." Ph.D. dissertation, Columbia University, 1969.

Wells, William Vincent. *The Life and Public Services of Samuel Adams.* 3 vols. Boston: Little, Brown, 1865.

White, Carol. *The New Dark Ages Conspiracy: Britain's Plot to Destroy Civilization.* New York: New Benjamin Franklin House, 1980.

Wilkerson, Marcus M. *Public Opinion and the Spanish-American War: A Study in War Propaganda.* Baton Rouge: Louisiana State University Press, 1932.

Williamson, Audrey. *Thomas Paine: His Life, Work and Times*. London: Allen and Unwin, 1973.

Wilmer, Lambert A. *Our Press Gang; or, a Complete Exposition of the Corruptions and Crimes of the American Newspapers*. Philadelphia: J. T. Lloyd, 1859. Reprint. New York: Arno Press, 1970.

Wilson, Jerome D., and William F. Ricketson. *Tom Paine*. Boston: Twayne/Hall, 1978.

Winkler, Allan M. *The Politics of Propaganda: The Office of War Information, 1942–1945*. New Haven: Yale University Press, 1978.

Wisan, Joseph. *The Cuban Crisis as Reflected in the New York Press, 1895–1898*. New York: Columbia University Press, 1934. Reprint. New York: Octagon Books, 1965.

Wise, David. *The Politics of Lying: Government Deception, Secrecy and Power*. New York: Vintage Books, 1973.

Wolfe, Gregory. *Right Minds: A Sourcebook of American Conservative Thought*. Chicago: Regnery Gateway, 1987.

Woodward, Bob. *Veil: The Secret Wars of the CIA, 1981–1987*. New York: Simon and Schuster, 1987.

Woodward, Gary C., and Robert E. Denton, Jr. *Persuasion and Influence in American Life*. Prospect Heights, Ill.: Waveland Press, 1988.

Woodward, W. E. *Tom Paine: America's Godfather, 1737–1809*. New York: E. P. Dutton, 1945.

Wright, Quincy, ed. *Public Opinion and World-Politics*. Chicago: University of Chicago Press, 1933. Reprint. New York: Arno Press, 1972.

Young, Kimball, and Raymond D. Lawrence. *Bibliography on Censorship and Propaganda*. University of Oregon Journalism Series, No. 1. Eugene: University of Oregon Press, 1928.

Zeman, Zbynek. *Selling the War: Art and Propaganda in World War II*. London: Orbis, 1978.

Ziegler, L. Harmon, and Wayne C. Peak. *Interest Groups in American Politics*. 2nd ed. Englewood Cliffs, N.J.: Prentice-Hall, 1972.

Zimbardo, Philip, Ebbe B. Ebbesen, and Christina Maslach. *Influencing Attitudes and Changing Behavior*. 2nd ed. New York: Random House, 1977.

State and Federal Government Documents

American Film Institute. *Catalog of Holdings, the American Film Institute Collection and the United Artists Collection at the Library of Congress*. Washington, D.C.: American Film Institute, 1978.

"Declassified Documents Reference System." Official U.S. documents photoduplicated, summarized, and indexed from Freedom of Information requests. Washington, D.C.: Carrollton Press, 1976–.

National Historical Publications and Records Commission. *The Directory of Archives and Manuscript Repositories*. Washington, D.C.: National Historical Publications and Records Commission, 1978.

New York State Senate. Lusk Committee. *Revolutionary Radicalism: Its History, Purpose, and Tactics*. 4 vols. Albany, N.Y.: J. B. Lyon, 1920.

The Psychological Warfare Division, Supreme Headquarters, Allied Expeditionary Force. An Account of Its Operations in the Western European Campaign, 1944–45. Bad Homburg, Germany: S.H.A.E.F., 1945.

U.S. Advisory Commission on Public Diplomacy. *Public Diplomacy: Lessons from the Washington Summit.* Washington, D.C.: U.S. Advisory Commission on Public Diplomacy, March 1988.

U.S. Arms Control and Disarmament Agency. *Soviet Propaganda Campaign Against NATO,* by Charles A. Sorrels. Washington, D.C.: U.S. Arms Control and Disarmament Agency, October 1983.

U.S. Board for International Broadcasting. *Annual Report.* Washington, D.C.: Government Printing Office, 1974–.

U.S. Committee on Public Information. *Complete Report of the Chairman of the Committee on Public Information: 1917, 1918, 1919,* by George Creel ("Creel Report"). Washington, D.C.: Government Printing Office, 1920. Reprint. New York: Da Capo Press, 1972.

U.S. Congress. General Accounting Office. *Suggestions to Improve Management of Radio Free Europe/Radio Liberty.* Report No. ID–76–55. Washington, D.C.: General Accounting Office, June 25, 1976.

———. *Telling America's Story to the World—Problems and Issues.* Report No. B–118654. Washington, D.C.: General Accounting Office, March 25, 1974.

U.S. Congress. House. Committee on Foreign Affairs. *Authorizing Appropriations for Fiscal Years 1980–81 for the Department of State, the International Communication Agency, and the Board for International Broadcasting. Hearings. February 1979.* Washington, D.C.: Government Printing Office, 1979.

———. *The Media, Diplomacy and Terrorism in the Middle East, Hearing July 30, 1985.* Washington, D.C.: Government Printing Office, 1985.

———. *Oversight of the Broad for International Broadcasting. Hearing, June 17, 1986.* Washington, D.C.: Government Printing Office, 1986.

———. *Oversight of the Bureau of International Communications and Information Policy. Hearing, June 16, 1986.* Washington, D.C.: Government Printing Office, 1986. (Note: First extensive coverage of what until recently had been a smaller office in the Department of State.)

———. *Radio Free Europe and Radio Liberty, September 14, 21, 1971.* Washington, D.C.: Government Printing Office, 1972.

———. *Soviet Active Measures. Hearings Before the Subcommittee on European Affairs, September 12–13, 1985.* Washington, D.C.: Government Printing Office, 1985.

———. *USIA: Authorization for Fiscal Year 1973. March, May, 1972.* Washington, D.C.: Government Printing Office, 1972.

———. *U.S. Information Agency Operations.* 2 parts. *Part I: Survey of the U.S. Information Service, December 1972; Part II: Hearings on the United States Information Agency, July 1970, September-October 1971.* Washington, D.C.: Government Printing Office, 1973.

———. *Winning the Cold War: The U.S. Ideological Offensive.* Hearings Before the Subcommittee on International Organizations and Movements of the Committee on Foreign Affairs. 9 parts. Washington, D.C.: Government Printing Office, 1963–66.

U.S. Congress. House. Committee on Un-American Activities. *Annual Reports.* Washington, D.C.: Government Printing Office, 1946–69.

———. *Cumulative Index to Publications of the Committee on Un-American Activities, 1938–1954.* Washington, D.C.: Government Printing Office, January 29, 1955.

———. *Supplement to Cumulative Index to Publications of the Committee on Un-American Activities, 1950 Through 1960.* Washington, D.C.: Government Printing Office, June 1961. (Note: Between 1945 and 1969, when the House Un-American Activities Committee (HUAC) became the Internal Security Committee, approximately 600 publications were issued covering a variety of "un-American" activities. These include transcripts of public hearings, reports, and other documents. Many deal specifically with the effects of subversive propaganda. Rather than list each here, readers are recommended to consult the HUAC indexes, previously cited guides to U.S. government publications, and general studies critically analyzing the work of the committee.)

U.S. Congress. House. Permanent Select Committee on Intelligence. *Soviet Active Measures. Hearings, July 13–14, 1982.* Washington, D.C.: Government Printing Office, 1982.

———. Subcommittee on Oversight. *Soviet Covert Action (The Forgery Offensive). Hearings, February 6 and 19, 1980.* Washington, D.C.: Government Printing Office, 1980. (Note: Includes the "Central Intelligence Agency Study: Soviet Covert Action and Propaganda.")

U.S. Congress. House. Special Committee on Un-American Activities. *Appendixes.* 9 parts. Washington, D.C.: Government Printing Office, 1940–44. See particularly Part 3, *Preliminary Report on Totalitarian Propaganda in the United States* (1941); and Part 9, *Communist Front Organizations* (Committee Print, 1944).

———. *Hearings.* 16 vols. Washington, D.C.: Government Printing Office, 1938–43.

———. *Investigation of Nazi and Other Propaganda.* Report No. 153. Washington, D.C.: Government Printing Office, 1935.

———. *Investigation of Nazi Propaganda Activities and Investigation of Certain Other Propaganda Activities. Public Hearings.* 6 vols. Washington, D.C.: Government Printing Office, 1934.

———. *Investigation of Un-American Activities and Propaganda.* House Report No. 2. Washington, D.C.: Government Printing Office, January 3, 1939.

———. *Investigation of Un-American Activities and Propaganda.* House Report No. 1476. Washington, D.C.: Government Printing Office, January 3, 1940.

———. *Investigation of Un-American Activities and Propaganda.* House Report No. 1. Washington, D.C.: Government Printing Office, January 3, 1941.

U.S. Congress. House. Special Committee to Investigate Communism in the United States. *Hearings.* 6 parts. Washington, D.C.: Government Printing Office, 1930.

———. *Investigation of Communist Propaganda.* Report No. 2290. Washington, D.C.: Government Printing Office, 1931.

U.S. Congress. Senate. Committee on Foreign Relations. *Foreign Relations Authorization Act, Fiscal Years 1980 and 1981.* Washington, D.C.: Government Printing Office, March 1979.

———. *Foreign Relations Authorization Act. Hearings.* Washington, D.C.: Government Printing Office, April 1977. (Note: Includes Board for International Broadcasting and USIA. See earlier and subsequent years, as well as publications listed below for other related source information.)

———. *Russian Propaganda. Hearings Before a Subcommittee of the Senate Committee on Foreign Relations Pursuant to S. Res. 263.* Washington, D.C.: Government Printing Office, 1920.

U.S. Congress. Senate. Committee on Government Affairs. *Congress and Pressure Groups: Lobbying in a Modern Democracy,* by Congressional Research Service. Washington, D.C.: Government Printing Office (Committee Print, Senate Print 99–161), June 1986.

U.S. Congress. Senate. Committee on Interstate Commerce. *Propaganda in Motion Pictures. Hearings Before a Subcommittee of the Senate Committee on Interstate Commerce Pursuant to S. Res. 152.* Washington, D.C.: Government Printing Office (Committee Print), 1942.

U.S. Congress. Senate. Committee on the Judiciary. *Bolshevik Propaganda. Hearings Before a Subcommittee of the Committee on the Judiciary, Feb. 11, 1919 to March 10, 1919.* Washington, D.C.: Government Printing Office, 1919.

———. *Brewing and Liquor Interests and German and Bolshevik Propaganda. Report, Doc. No. 61.* Washington, D.C.: Government Printing Office, 1919.

———. *The Technique of Soviet Propaganda. A Study Presented by the Subcommittee to Investigate the Administration of the Internal Security Act and Other Internal Security Laws of the Committee on the Judiciary,* by Suzanne Labin. Washington, D.C.: Government Printing Office, 1960.

U.S. Department of State. *Memorandum on the Postwar International Information Program of the United States,* by Arthur W. MacMahon. Publication 2348. Washington, D.C.: Government Printing Office, 1945. Reprint. New York: Arno Press, 1972.

U.S. Department of State. Bureau of Intelligence and Research, Active Measures Analysis and Response. *Soviet Influence Activities.* Washington, D.C.: Department of State, 1987.

U.S. Department of State. Bureau of Public Affairs. *Soviet Active Measures: An Update.* Special Reports No. 101 and 110. Washington, D.C.: Department of State, July 1982 and September 1983.

U.S. Department of State. International Information Program. *Telling America's Story Abroad: The State Department's Information and Educational Exchange Program.* Washington, D.C.: Government Printing Office, 1951.

———. *The Voice of America: 1950–1951.* Washington, D.C.: Department of State, 1951.

U.S. Department of State. Library Division. *Psychological Warfare in Support of Military Operations: A Bibliography of Selected Materials with Annotations.* Washington, D.C.: Department of State, Library Division, 1951.

U.S. Department of State and Central Intelligence Agency. *Contemporary Soviet Propaganda and Information: A Conference Report, Airlie, Virginia, June 25–27, 1985.* Publication 9536. Washington, D.C.: Department of State, Bureau of Intelligence and Research, Office of the Executive Director, March 1987.

U.S. Foreign Broadcast Intelligence Service. *The Daily Report of Foreign Radio Broadcasts.* Washington, D.C.: Foreign Broadcast Intelligence Service, 1940–47.

U.S. Information Agency. *Propaganda and Information: An Annotated Bibliography*. Washington, D.C.: USIA Library, July 1973.

———. *Report to the Congress*, nos. 5, 10–11, 38. Washington, D.C.: Government Printing Office, 1955, 1958, 1972.

———. *Report to the Congress*, nos. 43–46. Washington, D.C.: Government Printing Office, 1974–78.

———. *Review of Operations*, nos. 1–4, 6–9, 12–32, 35. Washingon, D.C.: Government Printing Office, 1953–55, 1956–57, 1959–60, 1970.

———. *Semiannual Report to the Congress*, nos. 34, 36–37, 39–42. Washington, D.C.: Government Printing Office, 1970, 1971, 1972–74.

———. *Semiannual Review of Operations*, no. 33. Washington, D.C.: Government Printing Office, 1969.

———. *Soviet Foreign Propaganda: An Annotated Bibliography*, by Anne Boyer. Washington, D.C.: USIA Library, 1971.

———. *The United States Information Agency: A Bibliography*. 2nd ed. Washington, D.C.: USIA Library, 1976.

U.S. International Communication Agency. Office of Congressional and Public Liaison. *International Communication Agency Fact Sheet*. Washington, D.C.: USICA, October 1979.

———. *Report to Congress 1978–1979*. Washington, D.C.: Government Printing Office, 1980.

U.S. Library of Congress. *A List of Bibliographies on Propaganda*, by Grace Hadley Fuller. Compiled under the direction of Florence S. Hellman. Washington, D.C.: Library of Congress, Division of Bibliography, 1940.

U.S. National Archives and Records Service. *Guide to the Ford Film Collection in the National Archives*, by Mayfield Bray. Washington, D.C.: National Archives and Records Service, General Services Administration, 1970.

———. *Guide to the National Archives of the United States*. Washington, D.C.: National Archives and Records Service, 1974.

U.S. National Security Council. "Timing and the Nicaraguan Resistance Vote." Secret NSC memo and 12-page confidential chronology from Oliver L. North to Robert C. McFarlane, March 20, 1985. Reprint. San Francisco: *Propaganda Review*, 1987.

U.S. War Department. *Guide to the Use of Information Materials*. War Department Pamphlet, no. 20–3. Washington, D.C.: Government Printing Office, September 1944.

———. Strategic Services Unit. History Project. Office of the Assistant Secretary of War. *War Report of the O. S. S. (Office of Strategic Services)*, vol. 1; *The Overseas Targets: War Report of the O. S. S. (Office of Strategic Services)*, vol. 2. Previously classified and unavailable. Reprinted with a new introduction by Kermit Roosevelt. New York: Walker, 1976.

Periodicals and Annuals

AIMS Newsletter. New York, 1964–.

America: History and Life. Santa Barbara, Calif., 1964–.

Annals of the American Academy of Political and Social Sciences. Newbury Park, Calif., 1891–.

Annual Guide to Public Policy Experts. Washington, D.C.: Heritage Foundation, 1982-.

Anti-Slavery Reporter. New York, 1825–32; 1840–44.

Arts and Humanities Citation Index. Philadelphia, 1976-.

Business and Home TV Screen (formerly *Business Screen*). New York, 1939–77.

Cinéaste. New York, 1967-.

Communication Abstracts. Newbury Park, Calif., 1978-.

Communication Booknotes (formerly *Mass Media Booknotes*). Washington, D.C., 1969-.

Communication Monographs (formerly *Speech Monographs*). Annandale, Va., 1934-.

Communication Research: An International Quarterly. Newbury Park, Calif., 1974-.

Covert Action Information Bulletin. Washington, D.C., 1978-.

Critical Studies in Mass Communication. Annandale, Va., 1984-.

Cultural Correspondence: A Journal of Popular and Left Culture. New York, 1976-.

Current Contents/Arts and Humanities. Philadelphia, 1979-.

Current Contents/Social and Behavioral Sciences. Philadelphia, 1969-.

The Democratic Journalist (English-language ed.). Prague, Czechoslovakia, 1953-.

Disinformation and Subversion Update. Washington, D.C., 1988-.

The Falling Leaf. Birmingham, England, 1958-.

The Gallup Poll, 1935-. Wilmington, Del.: Scholarly Resources, 1972-. Annual.

The Gallup Report (formerly *Gallup Opinion Index* and *Gallup Political Index*). Princeton, N.J., 1965-.

Heritage Today. Washington, D.C., 1984-.

Historical Abstracts. Santa Barbara, Calif., 1955-.

Historical Journal of Film, Radio and Television. Oxford, England, 1981-.

Human Communication Research. Newbury Park, Calif., 1974-.

Index to International Public Opinion, 1978-. Westport, Conn.: Greenwood Press, 1980-. Annual.

Industrial Pioneer. Chicago, 1921–26.

*Industrial Union Bulletin.*Chicago, 1907–9.

Industrial Unionist. Portland, Ore., 1925–26.

Industrial Worker. Spokane, 1909–13.

Industrial Worker. Chicago, 1909-.

In Fact. New York, 1940–50.

The Insider Newsletter. Washington, D.C., 1980-.

Insurgent Sociologist. Eugene, Ore., 1969-.

International Historic Films Videocassette Catalog. Chicago, 1982-.

International Political Science Abstracts. Oxford/Paris, 1951-.

International Socialist Review. Chicago, 1900–1918.

International Socialist Review. New York, 1939-.

Journal of Broadcasting and Electronic Media (formerly *Journal of Broadcasting*). Washington, D.C., 1956-.

Journal of Communication. Philadelphia, 1951-.

Journal of Historical Review. Torrance, Calif., 1980-.

JQ: Journalism Quarterly. Columbus, S.C., 1924-.

Jump Cut. Berkeley, 1974-.

Labor History. New York, 1960-.

McClure's Magazine. New York, 1890–1918.
Marxism and the Mass Media: Towards a Basic Bibliography. Bagnolet, France, and New York, 1972-88.
Media Monitor. Washington, D.C., 1987-.
National Trade and Professional Associations of the United States. Washington, D.C.: Columbia Books, 1966-. Annual.
The New Federalist. Leesburg, Va., 1987-.
News-Bulletin. Hollywood, Calif., 1949–65.
New Solidarity. New York, 1973–87.
One Big Union Monthly. Chicago, 1919–28.
Pacific Research. Mountain View, Calif., 1969-.
Policy Analysis.Washington, D.C.: Cato Institute, 1981-.
Policy Review. Washington, D.C: Heritage Foundation, 1976-.
Political Communication and Persuasion: An International Journal. New York, 1981-.
Praxis: A Journal of Cultural Criticism. Los Angeles, 1975-.
Propaganda Analysis. New York, 1937–41.
Propaganda Analysis Review. San Francisco, 1985–87.
Propaganda Review. San Francisco, 1987-.
Psychological Abstracts. Washington, D.C., 1927-.
Public Affairs Review. Washington, D.C., 1980-.
Public Opinion Quarterly. Chicago, 1937-.
Public Relations Review. College Park, Md., 1975-.
Quarterly Journal of Speech. Annandale, Va., 1915-.
Quarterly Review of Doublespeak. Urbana, Ill., 1973-.
Radical America. Somerville, Mass., 1967-.
Radical History Review. New York, 1973-.
Radio Free Europe Research Reports on Eastern Europe. Munich and New York, 1956-.
Right to Know. New York: Institute for Media Analysis, 1988-.
Signal. Paris, 1940–44. Berlin, 1944–45. (Published in some twenty languages, including English.)
Socialist Review (formerly *Socialist Revolution* and *Studies on the Left*, 1959–67). Berkeley, 1970-.
Social Science Monitor. College Park, Md., 1979-.
Social Sciences Citation Index, 1956-. Philadelphia, 1972-.
Sociological Abstracts. San Diego, 1953-.
The Spotlight. Washington, D.C., 1975-.
Terrorism. New York, 1988-.
Topicator: Classified Article Guide to the Advertising/Communications/Marketing Periodical Press. Clackamas, Ore., 1967-.
USIA Update: News from the United States Information Agency. Washington, D.C.
Victory. Washington, D.C.: Office of War Information, 1943–46.
Washington Representatives. Washington, D.C.: Columbia Books, 1977-. Annual.

Radio

THOMAS A. GREENFIELD
and NICHOLAS A. SHARP

Since its earliest days, radio has been widely recognized as a tremendously potent force in American culture. Educators were among the medium's first and most enthusiastic exploiters (see S. E. Frost, Jr., *Education's Own Stations: The History of Broadcast Licenses Issued to Educational Institutions*), and the earliest "broadcast pioneers"—Guglielmo Marconi, Lee De Forest, Reginald Fessenden, David Sarnoff—felt strongly that radio would improve the level of American taste by offering every citizen the finest of the world's music, poetry, and drama. In 1910, for instance, De Forest broadcast Caruso and the entire Metropolitan Opera Company as a demonstration of radio's ability to spread Culture (with a capital C) throughout the land. Less than four years after Fessenden had first used a microphone, the medium's artistic potential was being recognized.

Not surprisingly, therefore, the literature of radio is copious and virtually co-natal with the medium itself. Even excluding the technical and engineering literature (which dates back to Hertz and other pre-Marconi experimenters), a thorough bibliographer will find newspaper and magazine speculations about "wireless telephony"—even television—scattered here and there throughout the last decade of the nineteenth century. The legal and bureaucratic literature of litigation and regulation dates to Marconi's patent documents in 1896, and by World War I these writings had already assumed huge proportions; moreover, their importance in gauging radio's effect on popular culture cannot be ignored. If the United States Navy, for instance, had been allowed to retain full control of radio's development after 1918, as seemed to be a real possibility at the time (see *History of*

Communications-Electronics in the United States Navy, prepared by Captain S. L. Howeth, there would never have been a Herbert Hoover to cooperate with the major broadcasters in the development of commercial program patterns.

In this chapter, however, the concentration is on neither the educational, technical, nor bureaucratic aspects of radio. Rather, the focus is on the programming and the personalities connected with radio's development as an entertainment medium. Though an occasional nod is bent toward the international setting within which radio has developed, primary attention is given to the American scene, particularly to comedy, drama, music, and variety show broadcasting. Inevitably, some attention is given to news, sports, and "high culture" broadcasting—all of which are at least partially entertainment. Moreover, much of the material reviewed here concerns history, not the contemporary scene. Radio's "golden age," the years of its most obvious and dominating impact on the culture of everyday Americans, came in the 1930s and 1940s.

Even in this comparatively limited field, however, it is not possible to attempt a comprehensive bibliography within the confines of this chapter. The first issue of *Radio Broadcast* appeared in 1922, and by 1950 there were literally scores of daily, weekly, monthly, and quarterly publications devoted exclusively or primarily to radio programming. Every newspaper and general interest magazine of the 1930s and 1940s had regular columnists assigned to cover radio, and the most popular programs generated dozens of spin-off book publications every year—Gertrude Berg's *The Rise of the Goldbergs* and Phillips H. Lord's *Seth Parker's Sunday Evening Meeting: An Entertainment in One Act* are just two examples. A fuller bibliographical treatment of the subject may be found in Thomas Greenfield's *Radio: A Reference Guide*.

HISTORIC OUTLINE

It is not easy to summarize the history of radio. In its early days the medium grew so rapidly and in such diverse ways that time still has not fully clarified what things were important and what were merely interesting. One thing, however, is obvious. Radio in America has gone through three developmental stages: the "pioneer period" from the 1890s through the mid-1920s, the "golden age" of network programs in the 1930s and the 1940s, and the "television age," which began in the late 1940s and is still in progress. From the viewpoint of the "old-time radio" fans, this pattern is almost tragic, representing periods of adventurous youth, glorious maturity, and pitiable decay. From a less partisan position, however, the pattern looks better. It shows a medium that went through a period of early technological and commercial development, then through a boom period of unstable and rapid growth, and finally achieved a secure place in the structure of American business and culture.

The pioneer years can be traced to Heinrich Hertz and the other pre-Marconi investigators of the nineteenth century. For our purposes, however, radio really began in 1895 when the young Italian inventor, Guglielmo Marconi, took his wireless telegraph to England. Customs inspectors smashed his prototype (they thought it was a bomb), but he rebuilt it, obtained British patents, and soon had commercial backers. Before the turn of the century, he had used Morse code to broadcast the results of the America's Cup yacht race, and virtually all of the major Western powers were investigating wireless for military and naval communications.

During the next decade, Reginald Fessenden, Lee De Forest, and scores of other inventors and enthusiasts developed technical improvements—the microphone, the vacuum tube, various crystal receivers—which made radio both inexpensive and exciting.

During World War I, the United States Navy took over almost exclusive control of American radio. It severely limited the use of the medium but made rapid technological progress. Then, in 1919, radio stations again became independent, and the mass production of commercial radio equipment became profitable. General Electric formed the Radio Corporation of America (RCA), which took over Marconi's original American company with the idea that the big profits would lie in the production of radio parts. They were not really thinking of broadcasting as anything but a marketing device to help sell radio receivers. The other big electrical companies like Westinghouse and American Telephone and Telegraph had similar ideas. Each of them set up broadcasting stations in order to put interesting things on the air, believing (rightly) that they could sell more receivers that way.

Many other people, however, were also interested in broadcasting. Amateurs broadcast from their garages and basements for the pure joy of contacting people in distant places. Newspapers set up stations to broadcast election results, sporting events, and other notable occurrences because they hoped to sell more newspapers by whetting the public's interest. By the early 1920s, dance bands and Broadway plays were being broadcast live from the cramped, ill-equipped studios of pioneer stations such as WJZ and KDKA, and many stations were beginning to broadcast on regular schedules. Meanwhile, performers were beginning to agitate for payment when they performed on radio.

By 1925, the American Society of Composers, Artists, and Performers (ASCAP) was insisting on pay scales for radio performances. The National Association of Broadcasters had been formed to protect the interests of station owners, and local stations were using telephone lines to achieve multistation broadcasts of major events. In Chicago, Detroit, Pittsburgh, and other areas, not to mention New York, stations had established their own regular programs of drama, comedy, and vaudeville, many of them with commercial sponsors. Broadcasting had become a business of its own.

In 1926, the General Electric Corporation, Westinghouse, and the Radio Corporation of America formed the National Broadcasting Company (NBC). The network system was born. Within a year, the Columbia Broadcasting System (CBS) was also operating. NBC contracted to supply each local station with a certain number of programs, most of which originated in New York. Local stations still had considerable time at their own disposal, but they had to carry the programs that NBC sent them. NBC, in turn, sold air time to sponsors. The sponsors were to supply the programs; the network simply used its facilities to broadcast whatever program the sponsors wanted. Sponsors, in turn, wanted to use air time to sell products, and they turned to advertising agencies to produce shows that would sell their wares. The result was that certain advertising agencies became the major employers of actors, singers, directors, writers, and all the other show business professions. Only Hollywood and Broadway could complete as talent markets. Vaudeville died, but radio grew and grew.

Programming patterns on the networks developed rapidly. At first, comedy-variety shows dominated, and sponsored programs were heard largely at night. In 1929, when Freeman Gosden and Charles Correll took their local Chicago program to New York, "Amos n' Andy" became radio's first nationwide phenomenon. Soon, other shows with a continued story line and consistent characters became standard nighttime fare, though the variety show performers like Eddie Cantor, Ed Wynn, and Al Jolson continued to be the biggest crowd pleasers.

In a relatively short time, the "Amos n' Andy" concept was metamorphosed into a form designed for daytime listeners, mainly housewives. The daily, fifteen-minute soap opera was born, and within a few years it became almost the only thing that the networks could carry during the day. There were always sponsors for a soap opera.

During the middle and late 1930s, the networks began to discover that they had programming capabilities of their own. They did not have to rely on advertising firms for programs. All of the networks had certain time periods which no sponsor was using, and the networks had to sustain their programming with fillers. So they began using that time for programs, such as the "Columbia Workshop," which were showcases for experimentation. Archibald MacLeish's verse-drama, The Fall of the City, for instance, was written for and performed as part of sustaining-time programming. Programs stressing new, dynamic approaches to history, current events, and the arts were developed, and in some cases they became hits. In turn, they stimulated sponsors to develop programs; for example, Time magazine developed "The March of Time," which recreated current events through dramatization.

During the late 1930s two more networks were formed. The American

Broadcasting Company (ABC) was formed when antitrust actions forced RCA to give up NBC, and NBC was forced to become one network rather than two; ABC had formerly been the NBC "blue" network, which supplemented the larger, more popular "red" network. Also, the Mutual Broadcasting System (MBS) was formed as a more or less cooperative venture among stations that wanted more independence than they would be allowed as part of NBC or CBS and yet needed the greater range of programming and services that only a network could provide.

By 1940, the basic programming patterns were set, and they continued through World War II with very little major change. But in the late 1940s, commercial television became a reality. By 1950, television was cutting heavily into radio's market. Network radio tried to respond with some new, creative concepts, such as "Monitor," a weekend program of interviews, satire, and new features. Basically, the entertainment role that network radio programs had filled for two decades was being thoroughly assumed by television. Radio programming, except for news, reverted primarily to the owners of individual stations. Pioneer stations became "Top–40" stations just to survive.

Today, radio programming is still basically a local station phenomenon, though more and more stations find they must turn to prepackaged models ("beautiful music," "adult rock," etc.) to compete for advertising dollars. The networks sponsor a few shows, mostly in the soft "news you can use" genre (CBS's "Tax Tips" is one example), but radio is again a local medium.

Radio is no longer the big business that it was in 1940. It is, however, still a vital, important factor in our society. Like its budgets, radio's pretensions and ambitions have become smaller. Yet it continues to be a medium of essential communication, especially at the local level. Its broadcasts of community events, its occasionally heated talk shows featuring local luminaries, and its constant barrage of local advertisements make it an integral part of most people's lives. Radio fills a crucial need in our society, and as long as it does, it will continue to be a major part of America's popular culture.

REFERENCE WORKS

As of now, there exists no single authoritative or comprehensive bibliography of radio broadcasting materials. However, there are a number of useful bibliographic sources for the study of radio; some of these sources are indispensable.

Eleanor Blum's *Basic Books in the Mass Media: An Annotated, Selected Booklist Covering General Communications, Book Publishing, Broadcasting, Film, Magazines, Newspapers, Advertising, Indexes, and Scholarly and Professional Periodicals* is exactly what it claims to be. The third chapter includes 123 entries on broadcasting, many of them exclusively on radio, and all entries give broad, general treatment to various aspects of the subject. Her annotations are succinct, thorough, and useful. The exact cannons governing her selections of material are admittedly vague, and her concern is almost entirely with book-length materials, but for a generalist's overview of the whole field, her selections of histories, handbooks, and bibliographies provide an excellent starting point. She includes subject and author-title indexes.

For the person with a specific interest in the "golden age," Oscar Rose's *Radio Broadcasting and Television: An Annotated Bibliography* offers a useful starting point for works produced during the 1930s and 1940s. It is far from an ideal starting point, to be sure. He ignores any number of important works, such as Arnheim's critical study of radio as a formal aesthetic mode (noted in the "History and Criticism section"), and he displays a remarkable blindness toward some performers and programs, especially those connected with variety shows. On the other hand, he includes items that might well escape a modern person's thinking; he devotes a subsection of his list to novels and plays with radio backgrounds, for instance, and since many of them are by noted radio personalities (for example, Fielden Farrington's *The Big Noise* and Mary Margaret McBride's *Tune in for Elizabeth: Career Story of a Radio Interviewer*), they add a significant viewpoint to the study of the medium. Rose's subject headings are practical and useful, and his inclusion of an index and of annotations for each item makes his work quite useful.

G. Howard Poteet's *Published Radio, Television, and Film Scripts* devotes 125 pages to radio dramas available in printed form. Scripts are cataloged alphabetically by title of the program on which they were aired. He analyzes anthologies and lists their contents by title or program of the individual work. It seems to be a thorough piece of work for published scripts and is an important tool for anyone with an aesthetic or critical bent.

Two substantial works are of real utility to those who seek recorded versions of radio programming. Michael R. Pitts's *Radio Soundtracks: A Reference Guide* is the closest thing to a comprehensive guide that has yet appeared. Even so, it is far from complete, as Pitts himself points out. It is, however, a reasonably thorough treatment of commercially available tapes and records of radio shows, including both the generally available materials and those that circulate more exclusively among collectors and enthusiasts. It does not attempt to cover the recordings available in research libraries only. Though it is small, the booklet is relatively complex and takes some getting used to; the complexities of the field seem to require relatively subtle classification. The index, however, is thorough, and the introduction is clear and informative, both about the book itself and about the legal and technical pitfalls awaiting those who venture into soundtracks. The prolific Marietta Chicorel has produced a huge three-volume set (Numbers 7, 7a, and 7b of the Chicorel Index series) entitled *Chicorel Index to the*

Spoken Arts on Discs, Tapes, and Cassettes. Though the focus of the work is broadly on drama and oratory, she has included numerous radio programs among the materials, and she has covered several items that are not mentioned by Pitts. This set of interlocking bibliographies is complex and requires a good deal of effort to use, but it is of real value for students of poetry and drama on radio.

Though its British focus puts it beyond the pale of this essay, the British Broadcasting Corporation's *British Broadcasting 1922–1972: A Selective Bibliography,* edited by John Houle, is worth mentioning as a highly selected listing of interesting readings. It is the third of the BBC's bibliographies on broadcasting (the earlier ones appeared in 1948 and 1958) and is in some ways a model of how an introductory bibliography can be both thorough and brief. Such a work would be useful in America.

Before looking at serial bibliographies, we should also note one important fact regarding book-length publications. Some of the most valuable bibliographies for radio are available only as appendixes to scholarly studies in the area of mass communication. The nearest thing America has yet produced to a bibliography of the history of broadcasting is the set of bibliographies at the end of each volume of Erik Barnouw's three-volume *History of Broadcasting in the United States.* The shortest of them lists over 200 major items, both published and unpublished, and they are a major starting point for any historical item-hunting that a person might wish to do. Similarly, the bibliography in David Holbrook Culbert's *News for Everyman: Radio and Foreign Affairs in Thirties America* constitutes a major resource for any investigation into the history of news broadcasting. This work started as a dissertation (which explains some of its quirks of style and organization), but the thoroughness of the research bore real fruit in the bibliographic essays which constitute Part 3 of the bibliography. The bibliographies included in some other books are also of real value, and until someone produces a truly sophisticated bibliography in the field, they will continue to serve as major resources.

A number of periodicals have published bibliographic information that is important to the study of radio. In the early 1970s Kenneth Harwood compiled "World Bibliography of Selected Periodicals on Broadcasting (Revised)," in the Association of Professional Broadcasting Education's official quarterly, *Journal of Broadcasting* (now *Journal of Broadcasting and Electronic Media*). The article revises the original 1961 "World Bibliography," which listed more than 500 periodicals, and it both updated the listing and made it more useful. It includes more than seventy periodicals published in the United States, and while it gives only the most limited information about each of them, it is useful because of its clear concern with professional and scholarly material, not just popular and "fan" publications.

The *Journal of Broadcasting and Electronic Media* is useful also for its regular inclusion of a "Books Received" feature, which amounts to a bibliographic listing of serious items on broadcasting published during each quarter of the year.

An extremely useful publication is *Communication Booknotes,* which Christopher H. Sterling releases on a regular basis from George Washington University. Begun in 1969 as *Broadcast Bibliophile's Booknotes,* it changed its name in 1974, but it has continually provided excellent brief reviews and synopses of publications in the whole broadcasting field, including radio.

Other bibliographies, of course, are available, but with the items cited, it should be possible to get a good start on almost any bibliographic problem in the field of radio and popular culture.

Aside from bibliographies and standard reference works (encyclopedias, biographical dictionaries, etc., many of which include substantial articles on radio and radio personalities), there are a number of publications that offer general information on radio programming. *Broadcasting Yearbook,* for instance, has been published annually since 1935 by *Broadcasting.* Each issue includes directories of radio stations, both commercial and educational, and brief histories of ownership, licensure, and so on, for each station. Virtually an almanac of information about broadcasting companies, organizations, and networks, each issue includes a bibliography of the year's outstanding books in the field and numerous pieces of statistical information. Feature articles on items of topical interest are included, too.

Another important reference publication is *Radio Annual,* which was put out by *Radio Daily* of New York from 1938 to 1964. Typically, much of the information in each issue of this handbook concerns names and addresses of key personnel at networks, advertising agencies, and radio stations in the major markets. Also, listings of programming information, statistical data on radio listeners, and numerous short articles on current topics of interest are included in each issue.

For the late 1930s, the *Radio Directory,* issued by *Variety,* is a primary source. Edited by Edgar Grunwald, it appeared four times between 1937 and 1941 but did not reappear after World War II. Like the other annuals, it is a compendium of varied information, but its emphasis is especially on advertisers, producers, and artists. When it is remembered that during these years the bulk of commercially successful programs were produced entirely by advertising agencies (networks themselves produced only the shows that used unsponsored or sustaining time), the interest in advertising personnel becomes understandable. Most important, the *Variety Radio Directory* includes brief entries about hundreds of radio performers, writers, and directors, giving primary attention to their achievements in entertainment aspects of the medium.

Other useful reference books are also available. Sydney Head and Christopher H. Sterling's *Broadcasting in America: A Survey of Electronic Media* is a thorough, carefully researched treatment of the technological, historical, and economic structure of American broadcasting. It pays special attention to the place of radio and television in the total spectrum of the mass media, and it is especially concerned with the effects of advertising. This is the fifth edition of a survey publication begun by Head in 1956.

A similar work, but with an international focus, is Walter B. Emery's *National and International Systems of Broadcasting: Their History, Operation, and Control*. Organized by continent, then subclassified into regions and, finally, nations, the work surveys the entire world. Each nation is considered in terms of the history, regulation, and current status of its national broadcast system.

Two works in the H. W. Wilson Reference Shelf series deserve mention in this category. Poyntz Tyler edited *Television and Radio* and Herbert L. Marx, Jr., edited *Television and Radio in American Life*. Each draws from the general circulation periodicals of its day to anthologize approximately twenty articles on the state of the art of broadcasting. Each includes a brief bibliograhpy as well. Surprisingly, the Tyler book is the more useful to radio scholars because it includes several pieces on the demise of network radio drama, but each offers an interesting view of informal public opinion in its day.

Within the last several years, the "nostalgia market" has prepared the way for three extremely important reference volumes concerning "golden age" radio. The most comprehensive of these is John Dunning's *Tune in Yesterday: The Ultimate Encyclopedia of Old Time Radio 1925–1976*. This large, illustrated volume focuses on drama, comedy, and variety programs carried by the major networks during the 1930s and 1940s. It pays attention to band leaders, newscasters, and local programs only to the extent that they became prominent on a national level. Though the preface specifically disclaims any intention of being complete, Dunning's work is remarkably thorough. His entries, organized alphabetically by program title, range from ten lines to five pages, and they include good, brief coverage of all aspects of the programs. He wisely chose to include an index.

While Dunning's is the largest and best encyclopedia for old radio, Frank Buxton and Bill Owen can claim the first. Their *The Big Broadcast 1920–1950* is a revised, expanded, and polished edition of their earlier *Radio's Golden Age: The Programs and Personalities*. Their system of listing programs by exact title has established itself as the norm (that is, "The Romance of Helen Trent" is cataloged among the R's not the H's or T's), and their effort was a truly pioneering achievement. On the other hand, their work reveals some idiosyncrasies. Some programs listed include the program title, the type of program (mystery, variety, etc.), the announcer's standard opening, and nothing else. Amount and type of information vary drastically from entry to entry, and critical pieces of information, such as dates, network changes, and sponsor shifts, are not always included. On the other hand, the revised edition includes substantial articles on "announcers," "cowboys," and other topical entries, and these are excellent supplements to some of the briefer entries. They include an index and a bibliography.

Dunning and Buxton and Owen are the primary encyclopedias for old network programs, but Ron Lackmann's *Remember Radio* deserves mention in this category, too. Though it was obviously intended for the coffee tables of nostalgia buffs, not the library shelves of scholars, it does include some useful information. Primarily, it is a scrapbook of news and publicity photographs of major network radio figures, but it also includes examples of other radioana—program notes, news stories, and so on—and since it has a moderately thorough index, it is of some modest utility.

Also along historical lines, Harrison B. Summers's *A Thirty Year History of Programs Carried on National Radio Networks in the United States 1926–1956* is an excellent chronological analysis of network programs. It includes every program carried by the four major networks (NBC, CBS, ABC, and MBS) and analyzes them into a fairly complex set of categories and sub-categories. Drama, for instance, is subdivided into numerous headings such as "thriller drama" and "detective drama." Then, in a year-by-year analysis, each program is set down in tabular form, giving title, sponsors, seasons on the air, network, length, day and hour, and ratings. The work is not, in fact, a history; it is a chronological log involving virtually no narrative; but it is a crucial source of information, and its reprinting by Arno Press as part of the Arno-New York Times series History of Broadcasting: Radio to Television has made it readily available in most university libraries.

A work with more contemporary value is the *Radio Programming Profile*. Published by BF Communications Service in Glen Head, New York, it appeared originally in 1968 and has been revised quarterly since then. Focusing on the one hundred top markets in the United States, it offers hour-by-hour analyses of stations' programming and identifies their type of programming, primary audience, and policies and practices. Though intended for advertisers, it is useful for scholars interested in the impact of radio programming in modern society.

A similarly useful publication is the annual booklet put out by the National Association of Broadcasters, *Dimensions of Radio*. Essentially a statistical handbook, it analyzes station revenues, audience patterns, buying trends, and similar information of interest to station owners and operators.

A work of more tightly defined interest is Bernard E. Garnett's *How Soulful Is Soul Radio?* Looking specifically at programming patterns among stations with a substantially black audience, it is a logical starting point for anyone concerned with radio's relationship to Afro-American culture.

Finally, some mention should be made of the large number of books, many of them college textbooks, on the subject of radio station management, including programming. These works examine radio from a station operator's viewpoint, and they are probably the easiest way for non-professionals to get a sense of how and why programming patterns take the shapes they do. J. Raleigh Gaines's *Modern Radio Programming* is a commercial radio operator's how-to book, and it is especially useful because of its glossary of broadcast terms and its index. Another useful book of this sort is *Radio Broadcasting: An Introduction to the Sound Medium,* edited by Robert L. Hilliard. The chapter entitled "Producing and Directing" (by Earl R. Wynne) gives excellent treatment of the constraints and conventions of radio performance. *Modern Radio Station Practices* by Joseph S. Johnson and Kenneth K. Jones, includes a bibliography, a glossary, the complete Radio Code, and profiles of fourteen commercial stations as well as the usual chapters on operation. There are dozens of other works with similar purpose, the earliest of them dating to the 1930s, and each has its own manner and, to a greater or lesser degree, its own value in explaining how and why radio functions the way it does.

RESEARCH COLLECTIONS

Radio is blessed with numerous excellent research collections, both public and private. Not surprisingly, these tend to be clustered in California, the northern Midwest, and the section of the Eastern seaboard from Boston to Washington, D.C. There are exceptions, of course, as a look at Lee Ash's *Subject Collections: A Guide to Special Book Collections and Subject Emphasis as Reported by University, College, Public, and Special Libraries and Museums in the United States of America and Canada* or *The Directory of Special Libraries and Information Centers,* edited by Margaret Labash Young, Harold Chester Young, and Anthony T. Kruzas, will reveal. For the most part, however, research opportunities in the South, the Southwest, and the Great Plains are comparatively limited. Private collectors and enthusiasts, of course, are to be found throughout the country, and their resources, especially their collections of recorded radio shows, are not to be dismissed lightly. These sources are, however, relatively difficult to track down and not easy to access without actually making a trip to see the materials.

The Washington, D.C., area has several collections of special note. From a bibliographer's point of view the most important of these is the Broadcast Pioneers Library in the National Association of Broadcasters Building at 18th and N Streets. While the library contains a substantial collection of primary material, especially of clippings and industry records (the "Hedges files"), its more important role is to serve as a clearinghouse and reference center for materials of all sorts connected with radio broadcasting. It features a very sophisticated data retrieval system, and it has a staff devoted to researching in the area of broadcast history.

The Smithsonian is obviously a primary research center, especially the Clark Collection of Radioana in the Museum of History and Technology Branch Library. The Clark Collection is especially strong on very early radio developments. The Manuscript Division of the Library of Congress also has substantial radio materials, including the Eric Sevareid papers.

The special Motion Picture, Broadcasting and Recorded Sound Division of the Library of Congress not only has one of the major research holdings in the country but, owing to its location in the newer James Madison Building, also offers a far more congenial research and study area than does the august but somewhat cramped old Library of Congress building across the street. In addition, the National Association of Broadcasters (NAB) has its own library collection; it is located conveniently in the NAB building with the Broadcast Pioneers Library, although the two are not affiliated with one another.

Just outside Washington in Fairfax, Virginia, George Mason University houses the Federal Theatre Project Research Center, which has a huge collection of scripts and research materials prepared by the radio branch of Roosevelt's WPA-sponsored Federal Theatre Project.

In New York, the Theater Collection of the New York Public Library has a large collection of books and periodicals relating to all aspects of the radio industry. ABC, CBS, and NBC have their official libraries and archives located in New York. These are not public libraries in the conventional sense, but staff members do respond to inquiries, and the networks have a history of working cooperatively with scholars.

The centerpiece of New York's offerings is the Museum of Broadcasting on East 53rd Street. The museum has a Radio Collection of 10,000 cassette tape programs available for listening by the public. (There are also 8,000 taped television programs.) The holdings in the museum are virtually all tape holdings; it is not a manuscript or book library.

The David Sarnoff Library in Princeton, New Jersey, is a major source of information on the business aspect of radio, and in Philadelphia, Temple University Library houses a substantial collection of scripts and other radioana.

In the Midwest, the best-known and probably most widely used research center is the Wisconsin Historical Society's Library in Madison. Its Division of Archives and Manuscripts contains a collection of several thousand recordings (discs) of network radio shows, and the library also has the National Association of Broadcasters papers as well as other substantial holdings in the form of private and corporate papers of various radio personalities and organizations. The newly opened (1987) Museum of Broadcast Communications in Chicago boasts a well-cataloged collection of over 45,000 radio shows with listening facilities available for public use. It also contains substantial film and tape holdings for television and advertising.

In California, the most important collections are at UCLA's libraries. UCLA houses the National Academy of Television Arts and Sciences Television Library, which includes, among many other things, a Jack Benny Collection. Also, UCLA's Theater Arts Library has a collection of over

1,500 radio scripts and a major collection of books and periodicals. Also in California, the North American Radio Archives Library is located in San Francisco. The archives include tapes of 15,000 radio programs and substantial slide, script, and book holdings.

In addition to public research centers, there are hundreds, perhaps thousands, of private collectors who are willing to share their enthusiasm and resources, and many of them belong to various organizations, such as the Pacific Broadcasts Pioneers and the Society to Preserve and Encourage Radio Drama, Variety, and Comedy (an organization which goes by the delightful acronym SPERDVAC).

HISTORY AND CRITICISM

Histories of broadcasting are so many and so varied that a good-sized bibliography could be devoted exclusively to this one type of literature. They come in a variety of types ranging from the ponderously academic and scholarly to the breezily informal and anecdotal, and when biography, autobiography, and memoir are included, as they should be, the number of works legitimately identifiable as radio history swells to the hundreds. Obviously, this essay will not attempt comprehensive treatment, but a representative selection should indicate the nature of the field.

The premier work on radio history is certainly Erik Barnouw's three-volume *History of Broadcasting in the United States*. Volume 1, entitled *A Tower in Babel*, appeared in 1966 and covers the period from Marconi's first experiments to 1933. Volume 2, *The Golden Web*, covers the "golden age" and the rise of television up to 1953. Volume 3 focuses primarily on television but covers the decline of network radio as well; entitled *The Image Empire*, it also covers the experiments and efforts made by local stations and small groups through the mid-1960s. Barnouw writes well, and his volumes are enlivened by many of the more remarkable anecdotes and stories about radio personalities and programs, but his real concern is with the development of the total broadcast system. His analyses of the development of regulatory policies, corporate structures, technical developments, and dominating personalities are remarkably thorough and lucid. His concern with programming, however, develops entirely from his interest in the larger pattern. With the exception of occasional digressions on such crucially significant phenomena as the popularity of "Amos 'n' Andy" or the rise of news broadcasting during the late 1930s, he seldom offers more than summary analyses of programming patterns during any given period of time, and even then he is concerned primarily with the effects of programming developments in the larger patterns of radio's relationship to society. Barnouw's scholarly thoroughness, however, makes him indispensable, and his inclusion of bibliographies, indexes, chronological tables, and summaries of regulations and laws makes his volumes absolutely central to any inquiry into radio's history.

Barnouw's book stands at the end of a long line of radio histories, each of them unique in its own way. Among the most important of these are Gleason L. Archer's *A History of Radio to 1926* and *Big Business and Radio*. Archer's concern, like Barnouw's, is essentially an academic interest in the development of the total broadcasting spectrum, especially in the roles of RCA and NBC. A more enjoyable, more "popular" approach is that of Francis Chase, Jr. His *Sound and Fury: An Informal History of Broadcasting* concentrates heavily on the development of programming and the effects of personalities on radio shows. Since his book was intended for popular consumption during radio's heyday, he has few negative remarks to make about anyone. But he is an excellent raconteur, and his retelling of stories, such as the reason that "Grand Ole Opry" became a four-hour show (in order to give "Uncle Jimmy" Thompson time to get his fiddle warmed up) cannot be found in any other source. E. P. J. Shurick's *The First Quarter Century of American Broadcasting* is another important early history of radio. Its strength lies in its demonstration of how programming capability in news and information grew with the earliest technological advances in radio broadcasting. J. Fred MacDonald's *Don't Touch That Dial: Radio Programming in American Life from 1920 to 1960* is a superb scholarly history and criticism of radio programming (drama, mystery, soap opera, adventure, etc.) and is probably the best single treatment of radio programming of the "golden age" currently available.

Abel Green and Joe Laurie, Jr., also produced an excellent light history of radio based on *Variety*'s coverage of the medium. *Show Biz: From Vaude to Video* covers the whole spectrum of the entertainment field during the first half of the twentieth century, but much of its attention is fixed on radio. It stresses the most sensational events of the time, such as Mae West's "lewd" Adam and Eve sketch during the "Chase and Sanborn Hour" in 1937, but it gives decade-by-decade attention to the development of the medium from the performers' viewpoints, and there is no other book-length work which offers a similar approach.

Another popular book, really a folio-sized coffee-table book, is Lowell Thomas's *Magic Dials: The Story of Radio and Television*. Though the book is filled with impressive but meaningless color photographs, the text is a brief, no-nonsense history of the medium, written in Thomas's characteristic style. Though uncritical in its assumption that the American system of broadcasting is perfect, it is a better piece of writing than its format would lead one to expect.

Irving Settel's *A Pictorial History of Radio* is another coffee-table book. More than anything else, it is a conglomeration of old publicity photos and news shots, but the text is readable, and it is reasonably thorough in its coverage of radio personalities from the 1930s and 1940s.

One of the best popular histories is Sam J. Slate and Joe Cook's collaboration, called *It Sounds Impossible*. Both Slate and Cook were active in radio during the 1930s, 1940s, and 1950s, and they frequently include firsthand reminiscences about programs and personalities. Their primary concern, however, is to present a topical history of radio programming. They include chapters on soap opera, comedy, and so on, each one emphasizing the pioneer developers in the form. Their real usefulness is the detail with which they analyze program patterns. For instance, they include some of the few substantial essays on pathos programming ("Queen for a Day," etc.), and their close involvement with various announcers, directors, and writers gives them a tremendous fund of anecdotal material.

More recently, nostalgia has influenced some of the popular histories. Jim Harmon, for instance, has written *The Great Radio Heroes* and *The Great Radio Comedians,* both of which are prefaced with an unabashed appeal to the reader's yearning for the good ol' days. Nevertheless, Harmon does a good job of pulling together interesting information about the actors, writers, sponsors, and distributors of "Gangbusters," "Inner Sanctum," "The Shadow," etc. He seems to have an endless store of plot summaries, and his critical sense is quite acute. His approach is idiosyncratic and personal, but it is not dilettantish, and the books rank as serious contributions to the field. Similarly, nostalgia (or at least the urge to exploit the nostalgia market) seems to have been the starting point for Madeleine Edmondson and David Round's book *The Soaps: Daytime Serials of Radio and TV*. Actually, the book is a serious study of the aesthetic and historical development of soap operas, the first 120 pages of which focus on radio. The tone, however, is light, and the appeal is clearly to the reader's fond memories of happier times. The book offers information on the kingpins of radio soap opera (Irma Phillips, Elaine Carrington, and Frank and Anne Hummert) and the various developments in their formula. It also offers interesting critical hypotheses for the various successes and failures within the form.

Similar but more scholarly (though that may be too strong a term) is Raymond William Stedman's *The Serials: Suspense and Drama by Installment.* Stedman's real concern in this large, illustrated volume is the whole pop aesthetic of the cliff-hanger from its first transmutation out of the serialized novel into pulp, film, radio, comic books, and television. Much of his attention goes to radio programs, however, and he takes a scholar's interest in such questions as the history of the writers. He includes a substantial bibliography, indexes, and an appendix listing daytime network serial dramas.

Within the general field of popular history, two more works deserve some mention. Lloyd R. Morris's *Not So Long Ago* and Robert Campbell's *The Golden Years of Broadcasting: A Celebration of the First 50 Years of Radio and TV on NBC* are both of value in their own ways. Morris's book is a general account of radio and is useful as such. Campbell's work is, as the title indicates, unremittingly celebratory of the virtues and accomplishments of the National Broadcasting Company. Large and heavily illustrated, it is filled with minor facts and details about the growth of NBC. Despite its frothiness, it is a useful book.

Some serious historical work in the field of radio has focused less on national and network developments than on individual stations. Actually, this is a reasonable way for things to have gone. Radio stations are relatively concrete, stable phenomena with clear histories and a distinctly real existence. Networks, on the other hand, are essentially corporate entities made up of legal contracts and cable linkages. Conceptually and historically, networks are much more difficult to deal with than are actual broadcasting stations. Moreover, since many stations had established themselves as creative, vital programming entities long before RCA created NBC, it is not surprising that many stations are proudly conscious of their histories as separate entities from any network.

Probably the best-known work on an individual station is William Peck Banning's *Commercial Broadcasting Pioneer: The WEAF Experiment 1922–1926*. WEAF was AT&T's broadcast outlet in the early 1920s and was deeply involved in the development of both the "toll" broadcasting concept and early multistation hookups using cables. Banning's study is a scholarly and thorough analysis of early attempts to commercialize radio.

A number of other station histories have been written from a more partisan viewpoint, frequently by principals in a station's development. Elliott M. Sanger, for instance, wrote *Rebel in Radio: The Story of WQXR*. Sanger was general manager of the "radio station of the *New York Times*" for nearly thirty years, and his tracing of the station's development from a garage-based hobby to the best-known classical music station in the country is told with some understandable bias. Similarly, Steve Post's *Playing in the FM Band: A Personal Account of Free Radio* tells the story of listener-sponsored Pacifica radio's New York station from the viewpoint of an advocate and primary participant in the "underground" or "counterculture" programming for which the station became widely known. More commercial but no less biased is Dick Perry's *Not Just a Sound: The Story of WLW*. This strange book offers a laudatory history of "the nation's station," the huge 500,000 watt WLW (which broadcast during the 1920s and 1930s from its Cincinnati tower with ten times the power of any other station in the country) and fan-oriented biographies of AVCO Broadcasting's six popular television personalities. The first part of the book, up to page 120, is of real interest to radio fans. The latter part is not.

In general, station history collections are hard to come by. Of course, individual stations often have histories written about themselves, but access to these works can be difficult. The Broadcast Pioneers Library in Washington has over seventy published and unpublished station histories. Broadcast Pro-File in California will provide brief station histories on any station for a nominal fee. Of course, basic information on station incorporation and licensing is available from the FCC.

For the development of radio news there is really one primary source from which almost any inquiry can be launched. David Holbrook Culbert's *News for Everyman: Radio and Foreign Affairs in Thirties America* is a book of limited scope, focusing on the careers of six news commentators who came to prominence during the last years of the 1930s. The twenty-page bibliographic essay that he includes with the volume, however, is so thorough that it amounts to a guidebook for research into the historical development of newscasting. Although most of the networks seem to have published promotional pieces, such as NBC's *The Fourth Chime,* which tells a glorified version of NBC's news operation from the 1930s through World War II and includes biographies of various newsmen, Culbert's sane evaluation of various sources is the most reliable guide to information sources on the news.

Other important books in the history of radio news include Charles Siepmann's *Radio's Second Chance,* which provides solid analysis of some of the earliest efforts at radio news broadcasting, as does Mitchell V. Charnley's *News by Radio.* These general histories of radio news provide a groundwork for the many biographies and autobiographies that are to be found, such as Abel Alan Schechter's *I Live on Air* and Paul White's *News on the Air*—respective memoirs of NBC and CBS newsmen trying to make radio news work during the early 1930s. Although the aforementioned work by Culbert provides excellent bibliographical information on the major news commentators, two books about the inestimable Edward R. Murrow deserve special mention. A. M. Sperber's massive *Murrow: His Life and Times* is almost unwieldy in its thoroughness, but it is without question the definitive work on the man who all but created modern broadcast news. Also, Murrow's own *This Is London,* a collection of many of the London-based reports prior to World War II, is notable as a rich, though not complete, collection of Murrow's historic 1939–40 coverage of the bombing of London. The intensity of Murrow's writing holds up, and the style is so remarkably unique that even reading the transcripts evokes clear memory of his voice.

The very broad field of music programming has produced several valuable books. Among the premiere books is Tom DeLong's *The Mighty Music Box: The Golden Age of Musical Radio,* a highly successful effort to cover the history of music programming from classical to country to all forms of popular music. Disappointing only in his sketchy handling of jazz, DeLong is probably the best single source for the general history of radio music programming. More narrow in scope but more thorough in analysis in Philip Eberly's *Music in the Air: America's Changing Tastes in Popular Music,* which treats not only contemporary music but also the FM–Top 40 formats, jazz, swing, and black popular music of the 1920s and 1930s. Eberly offers some useful social insights, as he deftly negotiates the tricky issue of middle-class taste and the evolution of American popular music. Other useful histories and criticism in the overtrodden field of radio and rock music include David Ewen's *History of Popular Music*.

No discussion of radio music would be complete without a source on the payola scandals. Without question, the best source on the history of payola and its evolution through the natural tensions between radio programmers and music producers (first sheet music producers and then record companies) is Russell Sanjet's splendid book *From Print to Plastic: Publishing and Promoting America's Popular Music*. Sanjet traces the scandals of 1959 to their earliest roots in the ASCAP/BMI feuds.

The far less fertile field of radio and classical music does offer useful resources, including Irving Sablosky's *American Music*, which discusses lucidly the role of radio in forming the transition between nineteenth- and twentieth-century serious music. John Briggs's *Requiem for a Yellow Brick Brewery: A History of the Metropolitan Opera* treats at length how the Met's desire for an audience and radio's early desire for respectability helped forge a sixty-year relationship. Of course, the major biographies of Arturo Toscanini, such as Howard Taubman's *Maestro: The Life of Arturo Toscanini*, devote large sections to Sarnoff's bold decision to bring class and the flammable Toscanini to NBC—a relationship that lasted for seventeen intense and fascinating years.

The best book on radio and country music, which has lost forever its early status as regional or novelty programming, is Nick Tosches's *Country: The Biggest Music in America*. The low-brow title notwithstanding, this is a serious study of country music, highlighting the early influence of key radio stations and disc jockeys and their role in the maturity of both the music and the country music industry.

Biography and autobiography are a major form of historical information about radio, and scores of works have been produced about the stars of network shows. Frequently, as with Charles J. Correl and Freeman Godsen's *All About Amos 'n Andy,* biography is not only romanticized but also confounded with fictional biography of radio characters associated with performers. Also, many of the biographical works produced during radio's heyday are manifestly unreliable, being designed more to tell the fans what they wanted to hear than to convey significant information. Robert Eichberg's *Radio Stars of Today: Behind the Scenes in Broadcasting* is an example of such a work.

On the other hand, first-rate biographical materials are becoming more readily available. Two books on David Sarnoff, for instance, open real channels of understanding about this incredibly influential man. Eugene Lyons's *David Sarnoff: A Biography* is a thorough and sympathetic study of the outlines of Sarnoff's career, and the anthology of Sarnoff's own writings—speeches, memoranda, reports and so on—collected in *Looking Ahead:*

The Papers of David Sarnoff constitutes a major addition to biographical studies.

Autobiography and memoirs are also excellent sources of history, provided they are taken with the appropriate dosage of salt, and they have always been popular with publishers. Fred Allen's *Treadmill to Oblivion*, for instance, includes not only inside information but also some genuinely penetrating criticism of the medium and its personalities. Allen's comments on the way that Ed Wynne and Eddie Cantor used visual comedy to become stars of an aural medium, for example, shed real light on the aesthetics of early variety programs and comedy.

Frequently, the reminiscences of behind-the-scenes people shed more light than the memoirs of better-known personalities. Carroll Carroll's *None of Your Business; or, My Life with J. Walter Thompson (Confessions of a Renegade Radio Writer)* gives some real insight into what it was like to work in program production during the years when advertising agencies were the primary producers of commercially successful shows. Though he later became a radio columnist, Carroll speaks with authority about how the interplay of sponsor, star, agency, network, and audience shaped the creation of a successful program in the 1930s. Ben Gross's *I Looked and I Listened: Informal Recollections of Radio and Television* offers a journalist's view of how programs and personalities took their unique shapes. Joseph Julian's *This Was Radio: A Personal Memoir* offers a lucid and rancorless account of radio from an actor's point of view, and he is particularly enlightening about how the networks responded to Joseph McCarthy's efforts to "clean up" the media in the early 1950s. A truly singular book about the creation of one of radio's most spectacular programs is Kenneth Koch's *The Panic Broadcast: Portrait of an Event*, which tells about the "Mercury Theater on the Air" production of H. G. Wells's *War of the Worlds*, narrated by Orson Welles. Koch wrote the script (which is included in the book), and his account of the preparation and aftermath of the production makes fascinating reading for anyone concerned with this famous broadcast's genesis.

Announcers are a phenomenon unique to radio and television, and their memoirs give a very special perspective on the medium. Ubiquitous as they are, announcers become involved in wider ranges of programming—sports, news, quiz shows, drama—than any other persons who are actually heard on the air. Red Barber, for instance, concentrates on sports announcers in his *The Broadcasters*, but his memoirs touch upon a wide range of prominent figures in radio history. Ted Husing's *Ten Years Before the Mike* has a similarly wide-ranging set of interests, especially if read in conjunction with the maudlin autobiography *My Eyes Are in My Heart*, which was based on the "This Is Your Life" television show done after Husing lost his sight due to a brain tumor. Graham McNamee, the first genuinely famous radio sportscaster, wrote an autobiography in 1926, entitled *You're on the Air*. McNamee's writing, although burdened by spates of self-congratulation, not only provides some substantial insights into early radio history but also stands as both product of and resource on the nature of early radio "celebrity." Lindsey Nelson, the erstwhile voice of the New York Mets, is the author of two books, one of which (*Hello, I'm Lindsay Nelson*) offers several engaging chapters on his life among the vagabond radio broadcasters in the 1930s and 1940s.

Other contemporary radio personalities have produced interesting books about themselves and their medium. Gene Klavan's *We Die at Dawn: The True Life Story of America's No. 1 Radio Team, or No. 2, or No. 3, Klavan and Finch,* is of interest as an example of how the relatively low-prestige position of disc jockey can become a springboard to creative, popular broadcasting. Similarly, Herman Weiskopf's *On Three: Inside the Sports Huddle* offers some good insights as to how an essentially local program can achieve a wide following through a dynamic approach.

While radio is long on historical account, it is rather short on criticism. Surprisingly few book-length works have ever been published with the intention of explaining, analyzing, or improving the artistic dimensions of the medium, and the majority of those critical studies exhibit surprisingly naive notions about the medium. In a way, this dearth of criticism is hard to explain. The foundations for an effective, sophisticated aesthetic of radio were set down in the 1930s by the art critic Rudolf Arnheim, and the importance of his work was clearly recognized within the intellectual community, if not by professional broadcasters. No less a personage than Herbert Read collaborated with Margaret Ludwig in translating Arnheim's *Radio* for the English-speaking world. Admittedly, Arnheim's formalist aesthetic depends too much on analogy to the perceptual processes of vision, but Arnheim was onto a potentially enlightening approach to the art of radio, and his aesthetic theories still offer a profoundly intelligent means of understanding the beauty in such creations as the "pure" noise of Fibber McGee's closet or the Great Gildersleeve's giggle. Yet no one seems to have read Arnheim, or if they did, they avoided letting any influence show.

Much more representative of most radio criticism is Erik Barnouw's *Mass Communications: Television, Radio, Film, Press; The Media and Their Practice in the United States of America.* Insightful and intelligent, Barnouw offers some extremely useful points for understanding how radio functions and its proper nature as both an aesthetic form and a communications medium. He points to its unique ability to serve an active audience, for instance, and its inherent leaning toward narrative rather than dramatic presentations. For an understanding of the craftsmanship of radio and the processes by which programs are brought into being, he is unsurpassed as a critic; but he is basically uninterested in the more philosophical questions raised by an aesthetician such as Arnheim. Various other critics have also written good, intelligent books about radio as seen from a non-academic point of view.

Journalists have been among the best. John Crosby, for instance, was the New York *Herald's* radio critic after World War II, and his *Out of the Blue: A Book About Radio and Television* collects some of his most provocative and enjoyable comments. A sort of William Hazlitt of the airways, he wrote well, and his comments on such productions as the Maurice Evans and Dorothy McQuire broadcast of *Romeo and Juliet* and the annual Easter Parade in New York City are examples of truly acute critical sense combined with a real enthusiasm for the medium. Similarly, Albert N. Williams's *Listening: A Collection of Critical Articles on Radio* collects columns and articles originally written for the *Saturday Review of Literature*. Unlike Crosby, Williams is at his best when he looks at the principles and policies governing network program patterns rather than individual shows or persons, and his commentary sheds real light on the character and style of various network programming policies.

Gilbert Seldes wrote two excellent books concerning radio, and he brings to his trenchant criticisms both the bite of the satirist and the affection of a practitioner. In *The Great Audience,* Seldes is heavily concerned with radio, and he scourges the medium for such things as its penchant to write scripts "in order to be forgotten" (so that the audience will tune in for the next show). On the other hand, Seldes was one of the first people to argue seriously that soap opera was an original and serious literary form, and his praise of Rhymer's "Vic and Sade" reveals his fundamental optimism about radio as an artistic medium. In *The Public Arts,* Seldes treats radio along with all the other mass entertainment media, but he notices such important facts as that radio was the turning point at which Americans began to regard entertainment not as a privilege of leisure but as a right to which they were entitled.

No treatment of criticism would be complete without some mention of Marshall McLuhan. A listing of all of the works published on, by, and about McLuhan would require a substantial bibliography in itself, so we can restrict our attention to *The Gutenberg Galaxy* and *Understanding Media: The Extensions of Man.* In these two works, McLuhan lays out his vision of man's extension and definition of himself through his communications media. In *Understanding Media* he sheds constant light, punctuated by occasional shadows of obscurity, on the essential natures of all the electronic media, and his chapter on radio looks harder at the whole medium than anything since Arnheim. To be sure, his vision of radio as "tribal drums" carrying the electrical impulses of the social nervous system was not so totally unprecedented as some have thought it; but it was new and radical enough to influence substantially the thinking of even so seasoned a critic as Raymond Swing (see, for example, Swing's essay entitled "Radio: The Languishing Giant," *Saturday Review,* August 12, 1967, reprinted in William M. Hammel's *The Popular Arts in America: A Reader)*. Having once read

McLuhan, no one will ever again see radio in quite the same way, and his comments are certainly among the most influential remarks ever made by a critic.

Besides this essentially artistic and academic criticism, there is also a large and important body of criticism produced by social scientists. Much of this material is of relatively little concern to students of popular culture, being slanted toward marketing and advertising interests of the narrowest variety. Much of it, however, attacks broad social and psychological questions of real importance to historians and critics. Two names of paramount importance in this field are Hadley Cantril and Paul F. Lazarsfeld. Cantril and Gordon W. Alport, for instance, wrote *The Psychology of Radio,* which was the first major attempt to analyze the psychological process by which listeners respond to radio. Cantril also published (with Hazel Gaudet and Herta Herzog) *The Invasion from Mars: A Study in the Psychology of Panic,* which was merely the first of a long list of scholarly and critical publications about Orson Welles's phenomenal Halloween prank. Cantril is best known as a public opinion researcher, of course, and he was among the earliest people to develop scientific methodologies for dealing with radio audiences.

Even more prolific than Cantril, Paul F. Lazarsfeld was probably the most assiduous sociological researcher of the "golden age." In *Radio and the Printed Page,* subtitled *An Introduction to the Study of Radio and Its Role in the Communication of Ideas,* he discussed the nature of the complex interplay between the aural medium and the visual media of books and newspapers. Vitiated by the lack of a sophisticated concept of information as a measurable substance, Lazarsfeld's study is yet interesting for its attempt to see radio as a medium of exchange and change in opinion. Lazarsfeld also worked with Frank N. Stanton to edit two volumes of *Radio Research,* which attempted to digest developments in the field, and he later worked on two studies of public opinion about radio. With Harry Field he produced a report of an extensive survey of public opinion on radio entitled *The People Look at Radio.* Two years later he worked with Patricia Kendall to produce a follow-up study entitled *Radio Listening in America: The People Look at Radio—Again.* In both studies, he was primarily interested in both the content of programming and the nature of public response to programs and advertisement. Characteristically, he was also interested in the effect of criticism on public response.

Since the late 1940s, social scientists have tended to focus their attention on television as the primary grounds for research, and in this trend they are typical of all criticism. With the exception of occasional anomalies, more criticism today subsumes radio within a larger concern with television, and thus the field of radio criticism is a relatively dead issue with most periodicals and publishers.

Research into the effects of radio on American popular culture will always be complicated. The interplay of business, government, technology, and art, for instance, causes part of the creative tension within which radio has always existed, and this is an extremely difficult interplay to understand. To what extent, for instance, did the combined development of transistor technology and low import taxes for Japanese products influence the direction of radio programming in the 1950s? Perhaps no one will ever answer such questions, yet they are of real importance in our understanding of American civilization, and it is to be hoped that as bibliography in the field becomes more sophisticated, scholars will become increasingly able to find the information they need in order to get closer to the answers.

BIBLIOGRAPHY

Books and Articles

Allen, Fred. *Treadmill to Oblivion*. Boston: Little, Brown, 1954.

Archer, Gleason L. *Big Business and Radio*. New York: American Historical Society, 1939.

————. *A History of Radio to 1926*. New York: American Historical Society, 1938.

Arnheim, Rudolf. *Radio*. Translated by Margaret Ludwig and Herbert Read. London: Faber and Faber, 1936.

Ash, Lee. *Subject Collections: A Guide to Special Book Collections and Subject Emphases as Reported by University, College, Public, and Special Libraries and Museums in the United States of America and Canada*. 5th ed. New York: R. R. Bowker, 1985.

Banning, William Peck. *Commercial Broadcasting Pioneer: The WEAF Experiment 1922–1926*. Cambridge, Mass.: Harvard University Press, 1946.

Barber, Walter L. ("Red"). *The Broadcasters*. New York: Dial Press, 1970.

Barnouw, Erik. *History of Broadcasting in the United States*. 3 vols. New York: Oxford University Press, 1966–70.

————. *Mass Communications: Television, Radio, Film, Press; The Media and Their Practice in the United States of America*. New York: Rinehart, 1956.

Berg, Gertrude. *The Rise of the Goldbergs*. New York: Barse and Co., 1931.

Blum, Eleanor. *Basic Books in the Mass Media: An Annotated, Selected Booklist Covering General Communications, Book Publishing, Broadcasting, Editorial Journalism Film, Magazines,* and *Advertising. Indexes, and Scholarly and Professional Periodicals* Urbana: University of Illinois Press, 1980.

Briggs, John. *Requiem for a Yellow Brick Brewery: A History of the Metropolitan Opera*. Boston: Little, Brown, 1969.

Buxton, Frank, and Bill Owen. *The Big Broadcast 1920–1950*. New York: Viking, 1972.

————. *Radio's Golden Age: The Programs and the Personalities*. New York: Easton Valley Press, 1966.

Campbell, Robert. *The Golden Years of Broadcasting: A Celebration of the First 50 Years of Radio and TV on NBC*. New York: Scribner's, 1972.

Cantril, Hadley, and Gordon W. Allport. *The Psychology of Radio*. New York: Harper and Brothers, 1935.

Cantril, Hadley, Hazel Gaudet, and Herta Herzog. *The Invasion from Mars: A Study in the Psychology of Panic.* Princeton, N.J.: Princeton University Press, 1940.

Carroll, Carroll. *None of Your Business; or, My Life with J. Walter Thompson (Confessions of a Renegade Radio Writer).* New York: Cowles, 1970.

Carson, Gerald. *The Roguish World of Dr. Brinkley.* New York: Holt, Rinehart and Winston, 1960.

Charnley, Mitchell V. *News by Radio.* New York: Macmillan, 1948.

Chase, Francis, Jr. *Sound and Fury: An Informal History of Broadcasting.* New York: Harper and Brothers, 1942.

Chicorel, Marietta, ed. *Chicorel Index to the Spoken Arts on Discs, Tapes, and Cassettes.* 3 vols. Chicorel Index Series, vols. 7, 7a, 7b. New York: Chicorel Library Publishing Corp., 1973–74.

Correl, Charles J., and Freeman Gosden. *All About Amos n' Andy.* New York: Rand McNally, 1929.

Crosby, John. *Out of the Blue: A Book About Radio and Television.* New York: Simon and Schuster, 1952.

Culbert, David H. *News for Everyman: Radio and Foreign Affairs in Thirties America.* Westport, Conn.: Greenwood Press, 1976.

DeLong, Tom. *The Mighty Music Box: The Golden Age of Musical Radio.* Los Angeles: Amber Crest Books, 1980.

Dunning, John. *Tune In Yesterday: The Ultimate Encyclopedia of Old Time Radio 1925–1976.* Englewood Cliffs, N.J.: Prentice-Hall, 1976.

Eberly, Philip. *Music in the Air: America's Changing Tastes in Popular Music.* New York: Hastings House, 1982.

Edmondson, Madeleine, and David Round. *The Soaps: Daytime Serials of Radio and TV.* New York: Stein and Day, 1973.

Eichberg, Robert. *Radio Stars of Today, Behind the Scenes in Broadcasting.* Boston: L. C. Page, 1937.

Emery, Walter B. *National and International Systems of Broadcasting: Their History, Operation, and Control.* East Lansing: Michigan State University Press, 1969.

Evans, James F. *Prairie Farmer and WLS: The Burridge D. Butler Years.* Urbana: University of Illinois Press, 1969.

Ewen, David. *History of Popular Music.* New York: Barnes and Noble, 1961.

Farrington, Fielden. *The Big Noise.* New York: Crown, 1946.

Frost, S. E., Jr. *Education's Own Stations: The History of Broadcast Licenses Issued to Educational Institutions.* Chicago: University of Chicago Press, 1937.

Gaines, J. Raleigh. *Modern Radio Programming.* Blue Ridge Summit, Pa.: TAB Books, 1973.

Garnett, Bernard E. *How Soulful Is Soul Radio?* Nashville, Tenn.: Race Relations Institute, 1970.

Green, Abel, and Joe Laurie, Jr. *Show Biz: From Vaude to Video.* New York: Henry Holt, 1951.

Greenfield, Thomas A. *Radio: A Reference Guide.* Westport, Conn.: Greenwood Press, 1989.

Gross, Ben. *I Looked and I Listened: Informal Recollections of Radio and Television.* New York: Random House, 1954.

Harmon, Jim. *The Great Radio Comedians.* Garden City, N.Y.: Doubleday, 1970.

———. *The Great Radio Heroes.* Garden City, N.Y.: Doubleday, 1967.

Harwood, Kenneth. "World Bibliography of Selected Periodicals on Broadcasting (Revised)." *Journal of Broadcasting,* 16 (1972), 131–46.

Head, Sydney, and Christopher H. Sterling. *Broadcasting in America: A Survey of Electronic Media.* 5th ed. Boston: Houghton Mifflin, 1987.

Hilliard, Robert L., ed. *Radio Broadcasting: An Introduction to the Sound Medium.* New York: Hastings House, 1967.

Houle, John, ed. *British Broadcasting 1922–1972: A Selective Bibliography.* London: British Broadcasting Corporation, 1972.

Howeth, S. L. *History of Communications-Electronics in the United States Navy.* Washington, D.C.: Government Printing Office, 1963.

Husing, Ted. *My Eyes Are in My Heart.* New York: Simon and Schuster, 1941.

———. *Ten Years Before the Mike.* New York: Farrar and Rinehart, 1935.

Jackson, Paul T. *Collector's Contact Guide 1975.* Record Collectors' Sourcebook Series, No. 3. Peoria, Ill.: Recorded Sound Research, 1975.

Johnson, Joseph S., and Kenneth K. Jones. *Modern Radio Station Practices.* Belmont, Calif.: Wadsworth, 1972.

Julian, Joseph. *This Was Radio: A Personal Memoir.* New York: Viking, 1975.

Klavan, Gene. *We Die at Dawn: The True Life Story of America's No. 1 Radio Team, or No. 2, or No. 3, Klavan and Finch.* Garden City, N.Y.: Doubleday, 1964.

Koch, Kenneth. *The Panic Broadcast: Portrait of an Event.* Boston: Little, Brown, 1970.

Lackmann, Ron. *Remember Radio.* New York: G. P. Putnam's Sons, 1970.

Lazarsfeld, Paul F. *Radio and the Printed Page: An Introduction to the Study of Radio and Its Role in the Communication of Ideas.* New York: Duell and Sloan, 1940.

Lazarsfeld, Paul F., and Harry Field. *The People Look at Radio.* Chapel Hill: University of North Carolina Press, 1946.

Lazarsfeld, Paul F., and Patricia L. Kendall. *Radio Listening in America: The People Look at Radio—Again.* Englewood Cliffs, N.J.: Prentice-Hall, 1948.

Lazarsfeld, Paul F., and Frank N. Stanton, eds. *Radio Research 1941.* New York: Duell, Sloan and Pearce, 1942.

———. eds. *Radio Research 1942–43.* New York: Duell, Sloan and Pearce, 1944.

Lord, Phillips H. *Seth Parker's Sunday Evening Meeting: An Entertainment in One Act.* New York: Samuel French, 1930.

Lyons, Eugene. *David Sarnoff: A Biography.* New York: Harper and Row, 1966.

McBride, Mary Margaret. *Tune in for Elizabeth: Career Story of a Radio Interviewer.* New York: Dodd, Mead, 1945.

MacDonald, J. Fred. *Don't Touch That Dial: Radio Programming in American Life from 1920 to 1960.* Chicago: Hall, 1979.

McLuhan, Marshall. *The Gutenberg Galaxy: The Making of Typographic Man.* Toronto: University of Toronto Press, 1965.

———. *Understanding Media: The Extensions of Man.* New York: McGraw-Hill, 1964.

McNamee, Graham, with Robert Gordon Anderson. *You're on the Air.* New York: Harper Brothers, 1926.

Marx, Herbert Lewis, Jr., ed. *Television and Radio in American Life.* The Reference Shelf, Vol. 25, No. 2. New York: H. W. Wilson, 1953.

Morris, Lloyd R. *Not So Long Ago.* New York: Random House, 1949.

Murrow, Edward R. *This Is London.* New York: Simon and Schuster, 1941.

National Broadcasting Company. *The Fourth Chime*. New York: National Broadcasting Company, 1944.

Nelson, Lindsay. *Hello, Everybody, I'm Lindsay Nelson*. New York: William Morrow, 1985.

Perry, Dick. *Not Just a Sound: The Story of WLW*. Englewood Cliffs, N.J.: Prentice-Hall, 1971.

Pitts, Michael R. *Radio Soundtracks: A Reference Guide*. Metuchen, N.J.: Scarecrow Press, 1976.

Post, Steve. *Playing in the FM Band: A Personal Account of Free Radio*. New York: Viking, 1974.

Poteet, G. Howard. *Published Radio, Television, and Film Scripts*. Troy, N.Y.: Whitston, 1975.

Rose, Oscar. *Radio Broadcasting and Television: An Annotated Bibliography*. New York: H. W. Wilson, 1947.

Sablosky, Irving. *American Music*. Chicago: University of Chicago Press, 1969.

Sanger, Elliott M. *Rebel in Radio: The Story of WQXR*. New York: Hastings House, 1973.

Sanjet, Russell. *From Print to Plastic: Publishing and Promoting America's Popular Music 1900–1980*. Brooklyn, N.Y.: Institute for Studies in American Music, 1983.

Sarnoff, David. *Looking Ahead: The Papers of David Sarnoff*. New York: McGraw-Hill, 1968.

Schechter, Abel Alan. *I Live on Air*. New York: Frederick A Stokes, 1941.

Seldes, Gilbert. *The Great Audience*. Reprint. Westport, Conn.: Greenwood Press, 1970.

———. *The Public Arts*. New York: Simon and Schuster, 1956.

Settle, Irving. *A Pictorial History of Radio*. New York: Grosset and Dunlap, 1960.

Shurick, E. P. J. *The First Quarter Century of American Broadcasting*. Kansas City, Mo.: Midland, 1946.

Siepmann, Charles. *Radio's Second Chance*. Boston: Little, Brown, 1946.

Slate, Sam J., and Joe Cook. *It Sounds Impossible*. New York: Macmillan, 1963.

Sperber, A. M. *Murrow: His Life and Times*. New York: Freundlich Books, 1986.

Stedman, Raymond William. *The Serials: Suspense and Drama by Installment*. Norman: University of Oklahoma Press, 1971.

Summers, Harrison B. *A Thirty Year History of Programs Carried on National Radio Networks in the United States 1926–1956*. Columbus: Ohio State University Press, 1958.

Swing, Raymond. "Radio: The Languishing Giant." In *The Popular Arts in America: A Reader*. Edited by William M. Hammel. New York: Harcourt Brace Jovanovich, 1972, pp. 238–45.

Taubman, Howard. *Maestro: The Life of Arturo Toscanini*. New York: Simon and Schuster, 1961.

Thomas, Lowell. *Magic Dials: The Story of Radio and Television*. New York: Lee Furman, 1939.

Tosches, Nick. *Country: The Biggest Music in America*. New York: Stein and Day, 1977.

Tyler, Poyntz, ed. *Television and Radio*. The Reference Shelf, Vol. 36, No. 2. New York: H. W. Wilson, 1961.

Weiskopf, Herman. *On Three: Inside the Sports Huddle*. Boston: Little, Brown, 1975.

White, Paul W. *News On the Air*. New York: Harcourt, Brace, 1947.

Williams, Albert N. *Listening: A Collection of Critical Articles on Radio*. Reprint. Freeport, N.Y.: Books for Libraries Press, 1968.

Young, Margaret Labash, Harold Chester Young, and Anthony T. Kruzas, eds. *Directory of Special Libraries and Information Centers*. 4th ed. Detroit: Gale, Research 1977.

Periodicals

Broadcast Bibliophile's Booknotes. Philadelphia, 1969–74.

Broadcasting. Washington, D.C., 1931-.

Broadcasting Yearbook. Washington, D.C., 1935-.

Communication Booknotes. Washington, D.C., 1982-.

Dimensions of Radio. Washington, D.C., 1960-.

Journal of Broadcasting and Electronic Media (originally *Journal of Broadcasting*). Washington, D.C., 1956-.

Journal of Popular Culture. Bowling Green, Ohio, 1966-.

Mass Media Booknotes (originally *Broadcast Bibliophiles Booknotes*). Washington, D.C., 1974-82.

Radio Annual. New York, 1938–64.

Radio Broadcast. New York, 1922–30.

Radio Daily. New York, 1937–64.

Radio Directory. New York, 1938–41.

Radio Programming Profile. Glen Head, N.Y., 1968–74.

Records and the Recording Industry

JAMES VON SCHILLING

"I was never taken so aback in my life," was Thomas Alva Edison's reaction to the initial sounds coming from the machine he had hastily designed to repeat the spoken word, its first words being Edison's own rendition of "Mary Had a Little Lamb." Amazing as that premiere performance of the first phonograph must have been in 1876, even to its inventor, perhaps much more amazing has been its performance in the hundred-plus years since. The phonograph has survived patent struggles and labor disputes, two world wars and a Great Depression, the breakup of monopolies and the breakdown of distribution systems, the advent of motion pictures, radio, and television, along with the rise and fall of musical tastes, styles, and superstars. At times the industry's sales may have dipped, and there were even moments when the phonograph seemed on its last leg and tipping over, but the general trend for over a century has been continuous growth in product, audience, and profits.

Even in recent times, some argued that the emergence of home video technology posed a serious threat to the record industry. But this argument ignored two of the basic principles that have governed the complex history of recorded music. First, the industry has survived and prospered partly by taking advantage of any new medium that appeared to be its rival, or even conquerer. When radio boomed in the 1920s, for example, it seemed to mark the demise of the record industry. Aided by the onset of the Depression, radio was making the notion of *paying* to hear music at home obsolete, or at least foolish. Within a few years, though, radio had introduced America to "swing" music, a style so popular it triggered as a side-effect a whole new boom in record buying. Similarly, the later notion that television might doom the record industry was disproved in the aftermath of the 1964 appearances of the Beatles on the "Ed Sullivan Show," if not the appearances of Elvis Presley on the same show a decade earlier. And so, not surprisingly, the video revolution of the 1980s actually helped rescue the recording industry from an economic slump, with album and cassette sales spurred by "music videos" of performers shown on television.

The second principle behind the remarkable growth and survival of the record industry reaches all the way back to Edison's reaction to his "child's" first words. At the very heart of recorded music's relationship to American culture has been its power to take each of us aback, as Edison was, throughout our personal lives. Historians of the phonograph have noted that each new development in recording technology was heralded as introducing the ultimate in lifelike sound, only to be rendered hopelessly "tinny" by newer technologies, sometimes just a few years later. This suggests we take such claims (for example, the current publicity about digital recording) with a certain skepticism, but it also illustrates an important point. Despite how inferior the recording techniques and results of the past may seem to us now, they created powerful emotional experiences for the audiences of their time. The essential bond has always been between the listener and the recorded sound, and everything else—the technology, the marketing, the profits—has resulted from that bond and its basic power.

In other words, recorded sound does something of great significance to people, and so it has for over one hundred years of American culture. The variety of styles and performers that have been recorded, as well as the variety of audiences that have been affected by these recordings, makes it difficult to determine exactly what this significance is and where its real power resides. "It's got a good beat and you can dance to it," goes the classic explanation for what makes a rock-and-roll record a memorable experience to its audience, but that hardly works with recordings of other genres: jazz, country, Broadway, opera, and so forth. Regardless of genre, however, all recordings do one thing in common: they capture in time a unique combination of music, performance, and artistry and then enable us to make this "timepiece" part of our personal experience.

When we purchase a record, we generally have little knowledge of the history, technology, or economics behind it. But all that may be incidental; the essence of recorded music may simply be the personal actions of bringing that record home, slitting the cellophane "shrink jacket," placing the disc on the turntable, starting the electricity and machinery, and then experiencing internally the timepiece of music, performance, and artistry awaiting us in the grooves. A nursery rhyme in his own voice took Edison aback; today it may require a multi-tracked, million-dollar electronic production, but the results are the same. We are taken hold of, and a truly memorable recording will transcend all the history, technology, and business and not let us back into that other world—at least until the music ends.

HISTORIC OUTLINE

Thomas Edison invented the phonograph the way Columbus discovered America—accidentally, while looking for something else entirely. Edison was actually seeking to improve the newly emerging telephone system by making it more accessible to the middle and lower classes in America. Home telephone equipment was expensive back in 1876; Edison hoped to design a machine for recording messages, with the results capable of being replayed and transmitted at a centrally located telephone. Precisely why anybody would need to record the message beforehand rather than simply speak into the centrally located phone (for instance, today's public telephones) has never been completely established, not that it really mattered. Edison's idea, which was rendered into a working mechanism by an assistant, John Kruesi, in November 1876, quickly took on new applications when introduced to the public the following year. Edison himself soon envisioned a list of ten general uses for his invention, of which only the tenth dealt with telephones. The others included "letter writing and all kinds of dictation," "reproduction of music" (fourth on his list), and "clocks that announce in accurate speech the time for going home, going to meals, etc."[1]

At first the phonograph generated great publicity as Edison's assistants conducted public demonstrations around the country. But by 1880 Edison had rechanneled his energies and redirected his laboratory toward a new idea, the electric lightbulb, and the phonograph slipped into a state of suspended animation for most of the decade. In October 1887, however, Edison switched gears again, "confessing" to America that, despite his apparent fixation on what he called "the electric business," "Nevertheless, the phonograph has been more or less constantly in my mind."[2] Edison's apparent fickleness was, in reality, a shrewd businessman's response to a rapidly changing commercial climate, as his short-lived monopoly over the machine, the industry, and its future was about to end.

Edison's invention was facing a stiff, serious competitor in 1887, the Alexander Graham Bell-sponsored Graphophone; the following year yet a third rival emerged, Emile Berliner's gramophone. The stage was set for the next thirty years of the fledging industry's history and a series of complex, exhaustive struggles among the pioneering individuals and companies that emerged from these first three rivals. From a technological perspective, the machine that eventually dominated the market after this "Thirty Years War" was a far cry from Edison's mechanism. Instead, it more closely resembled Emile Berliner's gramophone, recording on discs rather than Edison's cylinder products.

From a business viewpoint, two major companies survived out of the dozen or so that played key roles during these early years; although the ranks of "majors" have changed throughout the decades, these two have always made the list. The first company, Victor Talking Machine, came to life in 1901, when Eldridge R. Johnson, who had been Berliner's equipment supplier, staked his own claim in the industry. Twenty-five years later Johnson sold his controlling interest in Victor for $28 million to a firm that soon merged with the Radio Corporation of America (RCA). Columbia Phonograph, the other permanent leg of the record industry, had its origins way back in 1878, as a subsidiary distributor for Bell's Graphophone. Columbia suffered through periods of hard times and one clear case of bankruptcy. Propped up in 1923 by new owners, it survived the Depression and eventually found a safe haven in the early 1930s under the corporate umbrella of RCA's arch-rival, the Columbia Broadcasting System (CBS).

From a musical standpoint, no single style dominated these early years of the record industry as rock music has since the 1950s. Rather, the catalogs of the pioneer companies featured everything from the arias of Enrico Caruso to the popular ditties of George W. Johnson, "The Whistling Coon." Popular music in general, though, clearly dominated the market, no doubt partly because many early phonographs were coin-operated and served as amusements in public locations. But classical performers, particularly opera stars (orchestras fared poorly under the early recording techniques), became crucial weapons in the fierce publicity battles fought between the pioneer companies. Signing a top European tenor or soprano could help establish a company as an industry leader, even though the bulk of that company's sales were likely to fall in the popular market.

Linked so closely to America's popular culture, though, the record industry was subject to the fluctuations of public taste. The medium experienced its first real boom during the Dance Mania of the mid-1910s. Victor scored a coup by signing the period's ballroom royalty, Vernon and Irene Castle, to "supervise" the recording of dance music, while Columbia trumpeted its own expert, G. Hepburn Wilson, who "dances while the band makes the record." Sales of newly designed phonograph consoles, with prices ranging up to $2,000, soared in the United States and Europe and continued strong through the early 1920s, aided by a popular, shocking, and liberating style of music and dance: hot jazz.

But the focus of popular culture shifted unexpectedly in the mid-1920s to a new medium for speech and music—the radio—with one clear technical advantage over the phonograph. The radio was electric: the amplification processes involved in radio transmission produced sounds far superior in quality to the mechanical diaphragm and stylus system that the early phonograph employed. That technological edge gave radio a jump-start and forced the record industry to adapt by adding radio sets to its consoles and developing electrical recording and playback processes itself. But these changes weren't enough to carry the record industry through a second upheaval later that decade, as the Great Depression placed phonograph records on its list of obviously expendable purchases.

Record sales by 1932 had dropped incredibly—to just 6 percent of the 1927 rate—and sales of phonographs sank to similar depths. The industry did climb back, of course, but doing so took the rest of the decade and involved a number of factors, not the least of which was the New Deal's gradual restoration of consumer confidence in general. Within the industry itself, though, several key developments aided the recovery, most notably the sudden leap to sales prominence of Decca Records, founded by an American, Jack Kapp, and financed by a London stockbroker. With the current industry "majors"—Victor, Columbia, and Brunswick—all selling their discs for seventy-five cents apiece, Decca managed to corral some top performers and peddle their records for only thirty-five cents. "Decca Scoops Music World" headlined their ads, and they did indeed scoop up such pop stars as Bing Crosby, the Mills Brothers, and the Dorseys for their roster. RCA-Victor also contributed significantly to the recovery by marketing a popular, budget-priced phonograph called the Duo, Jr., designed to use the home radio for amplification.

Perhaps the biggest boost to the record industry, though, came from America's popular culture, as the "hot jazz" craze of the 1920s settled into a more mainstream, socially acceptable style of entertainment. America thus entered the "Swing" or "Big Band" era, when purchasing the latest tunes by Benny Goodman, Glenn Miller, Harry James, and others became a basic part of life for a whole generation of young Americans. Radio may have popularized the music in the first place, and jukeboxes whetted the public's appetite, but actually owning an "In the Mood" 78 rpm to play in the parlor was the next best thing to jitter-bugging in front of the bandstand. Sales of records picked up slowly at first and then dramatically, reaching a peak of 127 million in 1941—and then the bubble burst again.

At first the problem this time was World War II and the restrictions imposed on the record industry: all manufacturers of electrical equipment were redirected to the war effort, and 70 percent of the nation's shellac resources (from which records were being produced) were devoted to strictly military purposes. But a heavier bomb fell on the homefront in the summer of 1942, when the American Federation of Musicians (AFM) voted to strike the record industry on the grounds that recorded music was putting the professional musician out of business, or at least severely curtailing the need for live performances. With its sales concentrated solely in the popular market, Decca suffered the most by not being able to record the latest styles and hits (which could still be heard in live performances on the radio) and was forced to capitulate the following year. The terms of the Decca agreement involved the payment of royalties to the AFM, for the support of unemployed musicians, for every record sold. Columbia and RCA held out for a second year but eventually " surrendered" on the same day Germany signed its peace pact with the Allies.

With conflicts both national and international finally settling down, the record industry may have anticipated a relatively calm postwar period. Instead, the following decade featured an upheaval in technology, a disruption of the industry's economic structure, and a shift in American popular culture of earthquake proportions. The revolution in technology surfaced to the public as the "Battle of the Speeds," with the new 33 1/3 rpm album from CBS in one corner and the new 45 rpm "single" from RCA in the other. Actually, a great deal more than different turntable speeds was involved since Peter Goldmark, the CBS engineer who developed the long-playing 33 1/3 album, had virtually reinvented the entire recording and production process along the way. Nothing would ever be the same after Goldmark's album caught on with the public: not the recording studio, with its dramatically improved microphone system; not the records themselves, with their contents expanded up to ten times the two- or three-minute span of the old 78; not even the industry's long-established hierarchy, with Columbia now the leader and RCA playing "catch up." Countering with its own 45, RCA weakly described the little disc's virtues as the ideal form for the popular single. They were in luck, though, as a figure emerged in America's popular culture (conveniently signed to an RCA contract) who would link the 45, with its oversized hole and its undersized playing time, to millions of young people from that point on: the "Hillbilly Cat" from Tupelo, Mississippi—Elvis Presley.

RCA may have reaped the most benefits from the rise of Elvis Presley from "Hillbilly Cat" to superstardom, but the fact is that neither Elvis, Chuck Berry, Little Richard, the Coasters, nor any of the pioneers of rock and roll would have affected our popular culture had it not been for a new force that developed in the postwar record industry: the independent record company, or "indie." These businesses ranked far below the "majors" in total sales, production and promotional budgets, as well as access to distribution (the majors at that time being RCA, Columbia, Decca, Capitol, Mercury, and MGM). Yet, for several key reasons, such relatively small-scale operations as Chess, Savoy, and Atlantic Records came to assume a position of great importance and, in fact, permanently changed the direction of popular music and the entire record industry. First and perhaps foremost, these independent companies recorded black music performed by black artists in a style that was known as rhythm and blues ("R&B"), out of which developed rock and roll. With but a few exceptions (for example, Louis Jordan on Decca), the majors either disavowed black music entirely, shunted it onto less-supported subsidiary labels, or recorded black artists like Nat King Cole who were closer to the white mainstream.

In neglecting to record rhythm-and-blues performers, the majors were simply following a pattern that had been established and reestablished throughout the century, in which black artists influenced—and often determined—the course of America's popular music, but white artists profited commercially once the new music reached the public. From the industry's viewpoint, the history of recorded music up to that point had clearly shown that any new music emerging from the black subculture could be directed into the mainstream by the majors, with the ensuing profits diverted from the original sources. Such had been the case with hot jazz and swing music; thus, there was every reason to believe that the system would prevail with rhythm and blues, despite the presence of the independent companies. After all, the majors in the early 1950s were holding a tight grip over all possible distribution routes—jukeboxes, radio airplay, record stores, sheet music— or so they thought. As it turned out, the majors failed to assess two additional factors, one sociological, the other commerical, that nearly toppled the whole system.

In sociological terms, the majors failed to adjust to the new realities of America's racial structure, for World War II had brought blacks and whites into much greater proximity. This was clearly the case in America's northern cities, where thousands of southern blacks had relocated during the war to seek jobs and had remained afterwards. Segregation and discrimination were still in force, but the music of a people can sometimes penetrate where the people themselves cannot, especially if an ideal commercial means for that penetration exists. In this case, the music—rhythm and blues—found the perfect means in a handful of young and daring radio disc jockeys, such as Alan Freed, Hal Jackson, and Bill Randle, who felt its power and promoted it to anyone who would listen, black or white. Thus, radio undermined the ability of the majors to orchestrate this new popular music, for the one thing RCA, Columbia, and the others couldn't control was the tuning of the American teenager's bedroom or car radio.

Yet, considering all that the majors *could* control, it is a testimony to the power of rhythm and blues that performers such as Chuck Berry, Fats Domino, Ray Charles, the Coasters, Little Richard, Frankie Lymon, and Bo Diddley—all recording for indies—ever managed to gain a white audience. The majors had direct influence, and often outright control, over the entire production, promotion, and distribution stages in the life of most popular tunes up through the 1950s, and they used all their power to fight for the continued success of their performers, many of whom were holdovers from the Big Band era. Their most infamous tactic was the "cover" record: a white version of a black hit, quickly recorded, released, and promoted in the mainstream white markets and on leading white radio stations (for example, Perry Como's cover of "Kokomo," originally recorded by Gene and Eunice). One especially heavy-handed tactic involved public denunciation of the new music by established mainstream figures; Frank Sinatra, for example, used the words "brutal, ugly, desperate, vicious" to describe rock and roll at a 1958 congressional hearing. With less publicity, but perhaps more effectiveness, the industry developed a third key tactic: revamping their commercial operations and strengthening their promotion departments, especially involving radio airplay. The majors now recognized the importance of releasing pop singles quickly, to capitalize on popular trends, and of marketing their releases thoroughly from coast to coast.

In the short run, the majors lost the struggle with the indies. The number of hit singles produced by independent companies at the close of the 1950s was twice that of the majors, a remarkable shift from the immediate postwar years, when only 5 out of 162 million-sellers belonged to indies. In the long run, though, the majors won the fight, as few of the independent companies survived the 1960s and the industry retrenchment that decade brought. Once again, the forces behind the new shift were numerous and complex. A well-publicized factor was the 1960 congressional investigation into record industry "payola," or the bribing of radio disc jockeys by record personnel to spur airplay for new releases. The big losers in the scandal weren't the major record companies but the free-wheeling rock-and-roll disc jockeys who had played such key roles in the rise of the new music, especially Alan Freed, whose career and personal life crumbled after the hearings. The indies themselves suffered, too, losing whatever respectability they might have gained during the 1950s. Also, any curtailment of payola activities would hurt the indies more than the majors, who could still rely on their own extensive distribution systems and, in the case of RCA and Columbia, their own nationwide home record clubs.

In addition, the style of popular music had by then progressed from the early years of rock and roll and in a direction that benefited the mainstream industry. With a surprising number of rock pioneers removed from the scene for various reasons (Elvis Presley drafted, Chuck Berry jailed), the sound was decidedly less black R&B and more white "pop." Top hits, for example, were recorded by numerous television situation-comedy stars, ranging from Shelley Fabares to Walter Brennan. Another portion of the market belonged to the young performers who recorded for the Philadelphia-centered labels associated with Dick Clark's "American Bandstand" television show. Few members of either group remained successful through the mid-1960s; however, their brief tenure at the top clearly presaged two trends that have characterized the record industry ever since. First, the record industry had developed economically to the point where cross-ownership and conglomeration were influencing the musical results, that is, television's nonsingers owed their recording careers to the tangled webs being weaved during the 1960s among the various entertainment industries. Second, the record industry was now profiting heavily from the "cult of personality" approach to producing and marketing performers. Whether it was the pompadoured teenage idol or the cashmere-sweatered girl-next-door, the *image* of the performing artist was selling records, perhaps more than the music or performance itself.

Neither trend was exactly new to the record industry. After all, RCA and CBS had been media conglomerates for decades, and numerous recording stars had developed careers in other entertainment fields or had public images that boosted their sales. But it was during the 1960s that the record industry's corporate structure and its promotional apparatus became as important, if not more so, than the recording technology or the music itself. Under such conditions, the companies that did the best weren't necessarily the most inventive or even the most talented, but rather the ones with the strongest economic bases and skills of promotion.

A company whose rise to major status typified the changes in the industry was Warner Records, an independent purchased in the 1960s by Kinney Services, a New York-based conglomerate. With a stock of reasonably talented young performers (based largely in southern California), but with lots of promotional campaigning and enough capital to support its own operations and also acquire Atlantic and Elektra Records, Warner spent the 1960s climbing toward the top of the industry in sales. Warner is often cited as the company best illustrating how the "baby boom" generation and their fixation on popular music brought enormous growth and success to the record industry during the 1960s. Although this sociological approach has obvious validity, it misses the equally obvious point that neither Warner nor the other 1960s majors could have capitalized on the boom and the fixation without their corporate structures and promotional efforts.

Even the Beatles, when viewed in retrospect, were not as spontaneously welcomed by American youth as our popular myths would have us believe. In 1963, the year before "Beatlemania" struck our shores, several Beatles singles were released in the United States on independent labels and caused little reaction. It wasn't until a major company, Capitol, bought the distribution rights and launched one of the most extensive promotional campaigns in the history of recorded music that the Beatles attracted their massive following. In other words, Beatlemania—along with the other waves of popular music intensity during the last two decades—developed from a combination of factors all present in contemporary America: an unusually large population of young people; the close links that have existed between popular music and the social and emotional lives of young Americans, at least since the mid-1950s and the advent of rock music, although probably extending back through the "swing" and "hot jazz" years; and the existence of well-financed, promotion-oriented record companies to feed huge amounts of product to the vast young audience.

With a large collection of albums and an expensive stereo now important status symbols among American youth, with records now sold everywhere from local supermarkets to coast-to-coast chain stores, and with top performers now rating "cover story" prominence in our national news magazines, it is no surprise that the record industry has climbed past both the radio and the motion picture industry in total annual income. Whether the products on which that climb has been based—the recorded music of the 1960s, 1970s, and 1980s—truly deserve so much promotion, sales, and recognition is subject to debate. Some would draw an imaginary line in the 1970s to separate the "good" from the "bad"—1960s rock, for example, from 1970s disco. Some would draw the line a few years earlier or later, and others would make a distinction throughout both decades between "genuine" popular music expression and "hyped" record industry product.

Still others would argue that all such lines and distinctions are more a reflection of social- and peer-group attitudes than of the relative quality of any of the music. According to this line of thinking, most recorded music since 1960, when the majors began operating on a grander economic scale, has been fashioned with the same basic principles in mind. The ever-present goal has been to maximize profits, as the media conglomerates to which all leading record companies now belong attempt to support current and future acquisitions with all the money generated by all the music. Thus, every trend—even the hint of a trend—is picked up by the industry, worked into salable products, heavily promoted, and eventually dropped by the wayside when a new trend emerges. In the 1970s and 1980s, trends that followed this pattern included country-rock, punk rock, new wave, heavy metal, disco, and—still in the promotion stage at this writing—rap and new age music.

The medium of recorded music today is in many ways vastly different from even just one generation past. Total sales of record albums, for example, now run second to sales of prerecorded cassettes and are being matched by total sales of the latest in recording technology, compact discs. This latter product, introduced in the early 1980s, combines computer and laser technology to create wearproof, smaller-sized albums with clear and dynamically strong sounds.

Indeed, yesterday's hi-fi in the parlor may now be today's compact disc player in the dashboard, complete with laser beam and computer chips. The music itself may have passed through synthesizers, equalizers, digital analyzers, and even satellite transponders before reaching the compact disc as an embossed spiral of electronic dots, written in binary computer code. And before reaching the radio stations and retail outlets, the disc's commercial potential may have been debated by market researchers, video producers, and top executives of multinational conglomerates (e.g., RCA, with its origins as the first record company, Victor Talking Machine, is now a subsidiary of West Germany's Bertelsmann A. G.).

Today's top albums earn "gold" and "platinum" status not after weeks of high sales but often right at the point of release; some albums cost over $1 million to produce, sell over 10 million units, and bring in over $100 million in gross profits. Today's top recording stars influence fashions, hair styles, sexual mores, drug usage, even social and political decision making. And today's industry scandals are less likely to involve small sums of money paid to free-wheeling disc jockeys than millions of dollars raked in by well-organized "pirates" of illegally copied records and tapes.

In other ways, though, the more things have changed, the more they've remained the same. It took Thomas Edison only months to begin speculating how his new invention, originally a telephone accessory, might expand into new fields and directions: the expansion continues. The industry's early years featured intensely fought struggles between competing companies: the struggles continue with all their intensity. Those first recordings were a mixed lot, mostly based on popular tastes and often disdained by cultural critics: the mixture continues, along with the popular emphasis and critical disdain. And from "Mary Had a Little Lamb" up through Madonna, the sounds of music and voice on record have continued to hold a power all their own, transcending changes in technology and styles of performance. For the future, we can expect both technology and styles to continue changing, with the power remaining strong. It has been over a century now since America played its first record; right now, despite all that has happened to the culture and the industry during those hundred years, there is no sign that the music is about to end.

REFERENCE WORKS

The subject of reference works in the field of records and the recording industry is in itself a revealing topic. For example, there are numerous books that list records falling within certain styles of music, such as rock or jazz, but no book that attempts to bring together all styles. Many books are intended as reference sources for information about performers, but no one has yet published a reference book about record companies. And although two authors have put together guides to that most elaborate of phonographs, the jukebox, no such work exists for the study of the phonograph in general.

The most common reference work on recorded music is the discography, which comes in all styles, years, and sizes. Some discographies might more accurately be labeled "cylinderographies," for they deal solely with the early years of the record industry and the wax cylinders produced for Edison's machines: Brian Rust's *Discography of Historical Records on Cylinders and 78s* and Allen Koenigsberg's *Edison Cylinder Records: 1889–1912*. Other discographies concentrate on smaller movements within the realm of popular music, such as *Blues* and *Gospel Records,* by John Godrich and Robert M. W. Dixon, and one book narrows its focus to just one recording group, *All Together Now: The First Complete Beatles Discography: 1961–1975,* by Walter J. Podrazik and Harry Castleman. A discography of so-called new wave and punk music, *The New Trouser Press Record Guide,* edited by Ira A. Robbins, is now available, as are discographies devoted to key independent record labels, such as Chess and Atlantic Records, compiled by Michael Ruppli for Greenwood Press.

A subgenre of the discography is the chronological listing of record releases, usually hit singles and albums. The work of one researcher in this field is particularly noteworthy: Joel Whitburn, who has compiled a series of books listing top pop and rhythm-and-blues records of the last few decades. Less extensive works in this subgenre have also been compiled by Joe Edwards (*Top 10's and Trivia of Rock & Roll and Rhythm & Blues: 1950–1973*) and H. Kandy Rhode (*The Gold of Rock & Roll: 1955–1967*).

An excellent discography of popular music in general is Dean Tudor's *Popular Music: An Annotated Guide to Recordings,* with more selective listings compiled by Frank Hoffman (*The Cash Box Single Charts: 1950–1981*), Don Tyler (*Hit Parade: 1920–1955*), and Joseph Murrells (*Million Selling Records: From the 1900s to the 1980s*). Nelson George's *Top of the Charts: The Most Complete Listing Ever* is a final example of this genre, although the title is misleading as it only covers the 1970–81 period.

Another variation on the discography is the guide to record prices, with the leading figure being Steve Propes, author of *Those Oldies But Goodies; A Guide to 50's Record Collecting, Golden Oldies: A Guide to 60's Record Collecting,* and *Golden Goodies*—indispensable works for the pop record collector.

The second leading category of reference works is the so-called encyclopedia, which attempts to catalog information about performers, styles, and other popular-music topics. Roger D. Kinkle's four-volume work, *The Complete Encyclopedia of Popular Music and Jazz,* is perhaps the best example of how extensive and valuable such a work can be. Other outstanding compilations of assorted facts, figures, and anecdotes include Leonard Feather's updated *Encyclopedia of Jazz; The Rolling Stone Illustrated History of Rock 'n' Roll,* edited by Jim Miller; and *Encyclopedia of Country and Western Music,* by L. Brown and G. Fredrich. An interesting variation on the "encyclopedia" theme is the *Rock Almanac,* by Stephen Nugent and Charlie Gillet, which uses a chronological format to present its wealth of material. Norm N. Nite, a disc jockey specializing in the "oldies" format, has published a three-volume set entitled *Rock On: The Illustrated Encyclopedia of Rock n' Roll,* while Michael Ochs has compiled a cocktail-table collection of photographs entitled *Rock Archives: A Photographer's Journey Through the First Two Decades of Rock & Roll.* Also contributing to the genre of reference works is Arnold Shaw, a major writer in this field, with his *Dictionary of American Pop/Rock.*

The remaining reference works within the field of recorded music fall under a variety of categories. The editors of *Rolling Stone,* for example, have published two critical guides to rock albums based on the reviews from their own publication: *The Rolling Stone Record Book,* edited by Dave

Marsh, and *The Rolling Stone Record Review* by the *Rolling Stone* staff. Also dealing with critical reviews is the *Annual Index to Popular Music Record Reviews,* compiled by Andrew D. Armitage and Dean Tudor. Another potentially valuable resource is published by the National Academy of Recording Arts and Sciences, *The Grammy Awards Book,* with lists of current and past award winners in a variety of categories. Finally, as mentioned above, two works have been published as guides to one of the great entertainment bargains left in America, the jukebox: Cynthia A. Hoover's *Music Machines—American Style* and J. Krivine's *Juke Box Saturday Night.*

RESEARCH COLLECTIONS

For those to whom popular music is something of a religion, the third floor of the Main Library at Bowling Green State University is nothing short of Mecca, for housed there in the flatlands of Ohio is the best collection of purely popular music in the country. The Sound Recording Archives, closely linked to the Center for the Study of Popular Culture, was developed on a shoestring budget by William L. Schurk with the object of collecting an actual copy of every popular record ever made. So far Schurk has put together upwards of a quarter of a million LP albums, singles, old 78s, and Edison cylinders. Other libraries may house more jazz or folk or country records, but no single collection has Bowling Green's range and variety—with the exception of the Library of Congress, which is not a strictly popular archive. Schurk's secret in building such a collection on a limited budget has been to take full advantage of donations, trading opportunities, auctions, and sales. His holdings in rock and roll and obscure, limited issues are particularly noteworthy, as are his extremely rare "soundies," musical motion picture shorts used in a form of early 1940s jukebox.

Another strong asset of the Bowling Green collection is its accessibility to the public. Although the stacks themselves are closed, with all records handled only by the staff, listening facilities make it possible for the user to hear virtually any request in a matter of minutes. The Audio Center provides taping services for the university community and research opportunities, under certain conditions, for outside groups and individuals. The center also maintains a diverse collection of reference materials, including discographies, industry promotional material, record sleeves, and back issues of most popular music magazines.

The Library of Congress in Washington, D.C., began collecting popular and classical records in 1924, largely through the donations of Victor and the other early major companies. The industry donations continued for decades, while the library's Music Division began developing special collections in folk music and in such government recordings as the World War II "V-discs." In 1972, legislation brought recorded music within the provisions of the copyright law, with one result being that most record companies began automatically submitting most new releases to the library's Recorded Sound Division. Today, the Recorded Sound Division has accumulated the world's largest collection, with over a million recordings and additional tens of thousands acquired each year. An important boost to the library's collection developed when a private citizen donated some 40,000 discs and 500 cylinders of mostly pre-1926 material. According to the library, these new holdings are particularly strong in popular music, especially jazz, humor, minstrel, and vaudeville recordings.

The services provided by the Library of Congress for the recorded music researcher are numerous and include the production of listening tapes, under certain strict conditions, by the division's own recording laboratory. The division is also involved in record production on a small-scale commercial basis, with special anthologies of some of its holdings available to the general public. Limited listening facilities are provided on the premises for researchers and advanced students, who are advised to schedule time well in advance. Also, catalogs of recordings and of printed works on music are distributed twice a year through the library's Descriptive Cataloguing Division, as well as lists of all records received for copyright purposes from 1972 on, the latter service provided by the library's Copyright Office and the U.S. Government Printing Office.

Another major collection of classical and popular recorded music, the Rodgers and Hammerstein Archives of Recorded Sound, is housed at the New York Public Library's Performing Arts Research Center at Lincoln Center. The library itself had been building a collection since the 1930s, but it took a large grant from the Rodgers and Hammerstein Foundation to create the efficient, extensive, multiservice facilities that presently exist. The archives hold well over 300,000 recordings on disc and tape, serving about 4,000 users every year. The recordings range from Edison cylinders to commercial classical and popular discs to dramatic and recitative material. A significant percentage of the collection was acquired from WNEW-AM, a top New York popular radio station.

Like Bowling Green's archives, the Rodgers and Hammerstein Archives offer easy public access to their recording collections through the use of headphones and listening carrels, although their taping services have been discontinued due to staffing shortages. Also like the Bowling Green collection, the Lincoln Center facility contains assorted reference material on the record industry, including industry catalogs, clipping files, and scores of related periodicals. In addition, examples of early phonographs and gramophones are displayed throughout the archives.

Other noteworthy collections specialize in certain types of popular music. The John Edwards Memorial Foundation, for example, at UCLA's Folklore and Mythology Center, collects "those forms of American folk music disseminated by commercial media such as print, sound recordings, films, radio and television. These forms include the music referred to as cowboy, western, country and western, old time, hillbilly, bluegrass, mountain, country, cajun, sacred, gospel, race, blues, rhythm and blues, folk and folk rock." The foundation not only collects recordings and various material related to these musical genres, it also reissues "historically significant" out-of-print records as well.

A major collection of jazz records, with some 50,000 LPs and 78s, is housed at the Institute for Jazz Studies at Rutgers University's Newark campus. The institute, which offers an academic program and publishes the *Journal of Jazz Studies,* also maintains a book collection, clipping files, and back issues of various jazz and jazz-related magazines. Listening facilities are available; in addition, taping services are offered for the researcher (who must supply the blank tape). For the specialist interested in New Orleans jazz, unusually strong collections are maintained at the Archives of New Orleans Jazz at Tulane University (over 10,000 recordings) and at the New Orleans Jazz Museum and Archives (close to 5,000 recordings). Finally, a significant new collection is being developed at the New York Public Library's Schomburg Center, which specializes in black culture. The collection so far includes over 10,000 records from a wide range of styles—R&B, jazz, Caribbean, contemporary, classical, and traditional and modern African. Along with listening carrels, the center's new facilities will make available videotaped performances and interviews featuring both past and present black recording artists.

HISTORY AND CRITICISM

The definitive story of the record industry and recorded music has yet to be written. For reasons that perhaps might best be explored by popular culture theorists, this vital and significant medium has spawned countless works of limited scope but none that attempts to deal with the entire picture—historic, economic, social, cultural, and artistic. A leading candidate at this point is Roland Gelatt's *The Fabulous Phonograph—1877–1977,* first written in 1954, amended in 1965, and amended again for the Bicentennial in 1976. As a basic history of the industry's formative years, and especially of the complex machinations that led to the emergence of the disc system and the early major companies, Gelatt's work cannot be faulted. For the popular culturalist, though, the book is flawed by its strong classical-music slant. Gelatt focuses, for example, on the signing of numerous operatic performers and the recording of countless symphonic works, while brushing past the overwhelming majority of recorded performances and record sales, which feature popular styles. The chapters added in the newer versions attempt to cover developments in popular recorded music from Elvis on but without the depth and detailing of Gelatt's earlier sections on the industry's infancy and adolescence.

For an almost exactly opposite approach, the popular culture researcher should consider *Rock 'n' Roll Is Here to Pay,* by Steve Chapple and Reebee Garofalo. This 1978 work takes a radical, semi-Marxist look at the record industry, supporting its controversial arguments (for example, that the industry has been and still is racist) with scores of facts, figures, quotations, and anecdotes. As the title indicates, the work focuses on the industry's rock years, with scant treatment of the periods Gelatt covers in great detail. But the title is somewhat deceiving in that Chapple and Garofalo range beyond rock music to study other dimensions of the industry, such as media conglomeration. Its political slant aside, *Rock 'n' Roll Is Here to Pay* is an important, eye-opening study often focusing on significant but usually neglected aspects of the medium and industry.

A third work, combined with those of Gelatt and Chapple and Garofalo, would comprise a fairly good introduction to recorded music and the record industry: R. Serge Denisoff's *Solid Gold.* Professor Denisoff, of the Sociology Department at Bowling Green State University, combines his first-hand experiences within the industry with his discipline's frame of reference to explore the roles and organizational workings of the medium. The focus is on contemporary rock, with the approach objective (as befits a sociologically oriented work) and the range of subjects fairly extensive: for example, industry promotional activities and generational attitudes toward music performers. Perhaps the work's strongest chapters are those delineating the "life" of a record, from concept to recording to marketing to promoting.

A new version of *Solid Gold,* entitled *Tarnished Gold,* was published in 1986, written by Denisoff with the assistance of William Schurk, who oversees Bowling Green's vast record collection. As noteworthy a book on the record industry as *Solid Gold* was, the new version is even better—with excellent chapters on the industry of the late 1970s and early 1980s, including discussions of MTV (music video television) and recent controversies over song lyrics and home-taping. Indeed, *Tarnished Gold* might well be the most thorough exploration of the modern record industry now in print.

Several other books deserve recognition as works that, by themselves, explore a wide range of topics in the field of recorded music. *Billboard,* in honor of both the nation's and the industry's anniversary, published *Music/Records/200* in 1976, featuring a series of informative, well-written essays on various styles and aspects of popular music. Another excellent business-related work is *The Making of Superstars: Artists and Executives of the Rock Music Business,* by Robert Stephen Spitz. The book is basically a collection of narrative essays on the workings of the music industry, based on the words of the industry people themselves. The classic text on the record industry as a business is Sidney Shemel and M. William Krasilovsky's *This Business of Music,* a fine work that is now in its fifth edition. For those interested in a career within the record industry, David Baskerville's *Music Business Handbook and Career Guide* is a good introductory work. For a more technical perspective tracing the history of records, phonographs, and the recording process, Oliver Read and Walter L. Welch's *From Tin Foil to Stereo* is the most extensive work currently available.

Two noteworthy books take a more chronological approach and, although their main intent is to present the history of popular music, provide valuable insight into the growth of the record industry and the power of recorded music. Tony Palmer's *All You Need Is Love: The Story of Popular Music* is a colorful, photo-laden work which blends the history of popular music in the United States and Great Britain with the cultural history of both countries. Somewhat similar in approach but with a stronger dose of social history is Ian Whitcomb's *After the Ball: Pop Music from Rag to Rock.* Whitcomb writes from the perspective of a one-shot pop star, having recorded a hit song himself during the 1960s. The chapter on his own career in the record industry provides an interesting conclusion to this intelligent, well-written critical work.

Another category of general introductory works deserves consideration: the collection of essays. The most outstanding examples currently available have one thing in common: they all focus on rock music and the rock record industry. Three of them feature essays culled from the pages of *Rolling Stone,* the leading journal of contemporary music for over a decade: *The Rolling Stone Reader, The Rolling Stone Rock 'n' Roll Reader,* and *What's That Sound?,* the first edited by the Rolling Stone staff and the latter pair edited by Ben Fong-Torres. Two other fine collections of essays, both edited by Jonathan Eisen, can be considered almost relics, for they were both published before *Rolling Stone* achieved dominance in rock criticism. The books are entitled *The Age of Rock* and *The Age of Rock 2;* published in 1969 and 1970, their titles are (perhaps surprisingly) still appropriate.

Some of the most revealing and readable books about the record industry are those written by insiders, industry people, usually with the help of professional writers. A perfect example of this genre is *Clive: Inside the Record Business,* by the ex-director of Columbia Records, Clive Davis (with the help of James Willwerth). The career of Clive Davis is fascinating not just because of the performing stars he discovered, nurtured, and/or helped popularize (for example, Janis Joplin, Bob Dylan) but because of what his own quick rise from lawyer to media mogul reveals about the industry's motives and priorities. Davis's even quicker fall from power—he lost his title, job, office, and limousine in less than an hour—makes for an unforgettable and controversial climax to the book, although Davis has since returned to the profession as head of his own successful record company.

Dick Clark's version of his career, *Rock, Roll & Remember,* should be read in conjunction with works more critical of his intentions and accomplishments, such as Chapple and Garofalo's *Rock 'n' Roll Is Here to Pay.* The balanced picture perhaps best explains how someone can remain both boyish and successful in such a high-pressured, trendy business for a total of five decades—so far. Of particular interest in Clark's work are the chapters concerning his testimony before Congress in the payola scandal. Somehow, Clark managed to confess to building an intricate, self-serving web of holdings in the music industry and at the same time be declared a fine example of American ideals, while others less fortunate saw their careers destroyed.

Another major figure in the record industry with a recently published autobiography is John Hammond, author of *John Hammond on Record*. Hammond's claim to fame as an industry executive has been his uncanny knack for discovering and nurturing, at early stages in their careers, top recording stars and performers, artists ranging from Billie Holiday to Bob Dylan. Hammond's book focuses more on jazz than any other style of music, reflecting the focus of his career as an "a&r" ("artists and repertoire") executive and record producer. Another autobiography that deals mainly with the jazz world is Dave Dexter's *Playback*. Dexter, a prominent figure in the radio industry, relates his colorful, celebrity-studded career as a disc jockey and jazz promoter. One of the more controversial autobiographies has been *Nothing Personal: Reliving Rock in the Sixties,* written by Al Kooper and Ben Edmunds. Kooper is best known as a rock "sideman," having backed up performers ranging from Gary Lewis and the Playboys to (once again) Bob Dylan. Kooper, who also helped found the jazz-rock group Blood, Sweat, and Tears, aroused critics and fellow musicians with his autobiography, which is far more candid and less ingratiating than most books of this genre.

Al Kooper's autobiography is also unusual in that, as a contemporary rock performer, he remains one of the few to have already written his memoirs. The long-awaited autobiography of Chuck Berry, entitled *Chuck Berry: The Autobiography,* like his music, sparkles with life and images. Also, Howard DeWitt's *Chuck Berry's Rock 'N' Roll Music* gives another perspective on the life and career of this seminal figure in recorded music. Perhaps the practice will become widespread within a decade or so, but, in the meantime, the best resource for the researcher interested in the personal reflections of rock artists is a two-volume set of interviews, once again culled by the *Rolling Stone* staff from the pages of the magazine: *The Rolling Stone Interviews* and *The Rolling Stone Interviews, Vol. 2.* A recent addition to this genre is Bill Flanagan's *Written in My Soul,* which compiles interviews with some of rock music's most prominent songwriters, including Chuck Berry, Bob Dylan, Mick Jagger, Sting, and David Byrne.

Related to the insider genre of record industry writings is the inside book written by an "outsider," a professional author purporting to reveal some aspect of the industry's workings. A number of these books can be considered relatively "light," such as Mike Jahn's *How to Make a Hit Record* and Sharon Lawrence's *So You Want to Be a Rock & Roll Star,* aimed at and best suited for the teenage market. But other inside works serve as excellent resources—well written, well researched, and usually full of colorful incidents and details. *Making Tracks: Atlantic Records and the Growth of a Multi-*

Billion Dollar Industry, by Charlie Gillett, focuses on just one record company, Atlantic (once an independent, now under the Warner corporate umbrella), but that company pioneered rhythm and blues and has always featured trend-setting and colorful performers and other personnel. Two additional recommended works also focus on a single important record company: Colin Escott and Martin Hawkins's *Catalyst,* an aptly titled study of Sun Records, the small Memphis operation that brought the world Elvis Presley, Carl Perkins, Jerry Lee Lewis, and Johnny Cash, and David Morse's *Motown and the Arrival of Black Music,* exploring America's only black-owned and black-operated record company. Peter Benjaminson's *The Story of Motown* also focuses on the label that symbolized black music for much of the 1960s and 1970s.

Several important works approach the record industry from the perspective of the performer or group under contract, with a style more new journalistic than biographical. Bob Greene explores the bizarre world of the rock group Alice Cooper in *Billion Dollar Baby,* going so far as to actually participate as a member of the performing stage show (he was assaulted nightly while wearing a Santa Claus costume). David Walley's choice of subject matter is no less bizarre in *No Commercial Potential; The Saga of Frank Zappa and the Mothers of Invention.* In *S. T. P.: A Journey Through America with the Rolling Stones,* Robert Greenfield narrows the focus even further: studying not just a single group but that group on a single tour of U.S. cities.

One of the most interesting works within this genre focuses, unlike the others, on a group that never quite made it to the upper levels of music stardom, Commander Cody & His Lost Planet Airmen, a rock/country/western-swing band of the 1970s. The book, Geoffrey Stokes's *Starmaking Machinery,* gives a good sense of all the costs, both personal and financial, entailed in the quest for success in the record industry. Two other works that deal with overwhelming personal and financial costs focus on perhaps the most successful recording group of all time, the Beatles: Richard DiLello's *The Longest Cocktail Party* and *Apple to the Core,* by Peter McCabe and D. R. Schonfeld. Both works chronicle the amazing speed and complications involved in the late 1960s personal breakup and financial collapse of the group that seemed destined to survive at least a whole generation.

The Beatles, as can be expected, have generated a number of works, most of which can be classified as biographies, and some of those relatively superficial. Besides the two mentioned above, other noteworthy Beatles books include the "authorized" biography, Hunter Davies's *The Beatles;* an exhaustive collection of memorabilia entitled *The Beatles Forever,* by Nicholas Schaffner; and a collection of interviews with the group's most outspoken and controversial member, Jann Wenner's *Lennon Remembers,* from the pages of *Rolling Stone.* Perhaps second only to the Beatles in number of biographical studies is Elvis Presley, or, as Paul Lichter describes him in the title of his extensive study, *The Boy Who Dared to Rock: The Definitive Elvis*. Up until his death, the definitive Presley biography was Jerry Hopkins's *Elvis: A Biography,* written earlier in the 1970s. With the seamier sides of his personal life beginning to emerge as the shock of his sudden death wears off, doubtless many new studies will emerge as well, although all will suffer from the same handicap: trying to fathom someone who became so public he felt compelled to make most of his life as private as possible. Thus, unfortunately, we can expect no "Presley Remembers" from this fascinating American who, in "daring to rock," brought recorded music and popular culture in general into a new era.

Several noteworthy biographies have been written about other rock stars who died in the midst of their careers. John Goldrosen has contributed a thoroughly researched study of the life of Buddy Holly, the pioneering rock-and-roll star of the 1950s. The recent film biography of Holly was based ever so loosely on Goldrosen's book, which is entitled *Buddy Holly: His Life and Music.* Chris Welch's *Hendrix: A Biography* deals with the life and career of the late-1960s superstar, guitarist Jimi Hendrix, while *Buried Alive* is Myra Friedman's chronicle of the equally tragic life of rock vocalist Janis Joplin. On the other hand, rock music's most famous producer, Phil Spector, is alive and well and the subject of an excellent biography/insider work: *Out of His Head: The Sound of Phil Spector,* by Richard Williams.

Ray Charles, the acknowledged genius of soul music, is also alive and well and has so far inspired two biographical works, Sharon Bell Mathis's *Ray Charles* and *Brother Ray,* by Ray Charles himself, with the assistance of David Ritz. Both works are a bit better than the average paperback biography, which is often written for the high school market and borders on the edge of public relations material. Also above average is Dave Marsh's recent work on the life and career of one of the recording industry's newest superstars, Bruce Springsteen, a white vocalist in the R&B tradition; the biography is entitled *Born to Run.* Springsteen's continued success in the 1980s has inspired a new look at his life by Dave Marsh, *Glory Days,* as well as a quasi-"art book" entitled *Springsteen,* by Robert Hilburn.

That same black rhythm-and-blues tradition has not only inspired scores of white performing careers, it has also inspired a number of fine critical works. Perhaps the best in the field is Charlie Gillett's *The Sound of the City,* an extensive historical and sociological study of the development, production, and spread of the music that gave us (or perhaps *is*) rock and roll. Even more sociological is Charles Keil's *Urban Blues,* which examines the value systems and cultural practices behind the music, as well as the music itself and some of its leading performers, such as Bobby Bland and B. B. King. A book that deals more with the recordings and performers themselves is Lynn E. McCutcheon's *Rhythm and Blues,* an excellent source of discographical information on this style of music.

One of the most prolific and important writers in the whole field of popular music is Arnold Shaw, whose works manage to bridge the gap between the academic resource text and the mass-market paperback. Two of Shaw's best works deal with black music: *The World of Soul: Black America's Contribution to the Pop Music Scene* and *Honkers and Shouters: The Golden Years of Rhythm and Blues.* (Shaw has also contributed perhaps the most outstanding study of popular music and the record industry in the 1950s, the decade that became a turning point in the history of recorded music; Shaw's book is entitled *The Rockin' Fifties.*) Another of the best writers in the field, also contributing a major work that focuses on R&B, is rock critic Robert Palmer, a regular contributor to the *New York Times.* Palmer's book, *Baby, That Was Rock & Roll: The Legendary Lieber and Stoller,* tells the story of the R&B songwriting and producing duo Jerry Lieber and Mike Stoller, two white men who helped create some of the freshest, most memorable records of the 1950s, including "Yakety Yak" and "Jailhouse Rock." Two other noteworthy books also deal with the lives and careers of white recording artists who chose to follow the black R&B style: Edward K. Engel's *White and Still All Right* and Philip Groia's *They All Sang on the Corner: New York City's Rhythm & Blues Vocal Groups of the 1950's.* Both works focus on the "doo-wop" singers and groups, vocal harmonists whose style took its name from the repeated phrase someone in the background would invariably be singing.

Continuing the trend in the 1980s of excellent works on black recorded music are Peter Guralnick's *Sweet Soul Music* and Gerri Hirshey's *Nowhere to Run.* In both cases, highly skilled and intelligent writers focus their energies on the music, lives, and recording careers of famous and not-so-famous black performers, with Guralnick narrowing in on southern soul and Memphis's Stax Records. Also new in the 1980s is another work by Arnold Shaw, an overview entitled *Black Popular Music in America.*

Other styles of recorded music that have inspired numerous critical works include swing or Big Band music, with the current leading critical study being Albert McCarthy's *Big Band Jazz,* and country music, which has produced a number of excellent books. The most authoritative study is probably Bill Malone's *Country Music USA,* closely followed by the previously mentioned *Encyclopedia of Country & Western Music* by L. Brown and G. Fredrich and Nick Tosches's *Country: The Biggest Music in America.* Also of interest is Larry Wacholtz's *Inside Country Music.* Two noteworthy books deal with fascinating subdivisions of the country music industry: Charles R. Townsend's *San Antonio Rose: The Life and Music of Bob Wills,* focusing on "western swing" (a combination of country and big band music that helped spawn rock and roll), and Michael Bane's *The Outlaws: Revolution in Country Music,* which explores the Waylon Jennings–Willie Nelson world of progressive country.

Although disco music accounted for a large percentage of the record industry's business during the late 1970s, no one has yet contributed a noteworthy study of the disco industry, its recordings, or its performers. On the other hand, it took Latin music almost a century of influencing American popular recordings before it managed to inspire a critical study: John Storm Roberts's *The Latin Tinge: The Impact of Latin American Music on the United States,* published in 1979. Roberts is another example of the exceptional writer in this field who has made a point of studying black and black-influenced styles. A recent book on Latin music (which gave us the rumba, samba, tango, mambo, cha-cha, bugaloo, bamba, and even the hustle) is *Hot Sauces: Latin and Caribbean Pop* by Billy Bergman. Punk and new wave music, phenomena of the late 1970s and the 1980s, have thus far spawned several authoritative books, including Caroline Coon's *1988: The New Wave Punk Rock Explosion,* David Bianco's *Who's New Wave in Music,* and Stuart Coupe and Glenn Baker's *The New Rock 'N' Roll.* Another recent publication, *New Sounds* by John Schaffer, focuses on "new age" music (an easy-listening form of jazz), while Michael Shore's *Music Video: A Consumer's Guide* explores perhaps the most important record industry trend of the 1980s.

Final recognition must be given to a pair of young writers whose works belong to no particular category, and perhaps for that reason come closest to achieving what the best records themselves do: transcend all the history, technology, and commercialism to reach some powerful, culturally significant emotional level. The writers are Greil Marcus, author of *Mystery Train: Images of America in Rock 'n' Roll Music,* and Michael Lydon, author of *Rock Folk: Portraits from the Rock 'n' Roll Pantheon* and *Boogie Lightning.* Their writings have little in common other than their avoidance of what most authors in this field dwell on and their focus instead on recorded music as both a cultural product and a personal experience. For that reason, and not because their books are excellent sources of information, they have both contributed significantly to our understanding of recorded music. For it may be that, in the long run, those approaches which explore the range of human experiences involved in this medium, from performing to listening, will best explain why recordings have the power to reach so deeply inside us.

NOTES

1. Roland Gelatt, *The Fabulous Phonograph—1877–1977* (New York: Collier, 1977), p. 29.
2. Ibid., p. 36.

BIBLIOGRAPHY

Books

Albertson, Chris. *Bessie.* New York: Stein and Day, 1972.
Armitage, Andrew D., and Dean Tudor. *Annual Index to Popular Music Record Reviews.* Metuchen, N.J.: Scarecrow Press, 1972–77.

Baggelaar, Kristin, and Donald Milton. *Folk Music: More Than a Song*. New York: Crowell, 1976.

Bane, Michael. *The Outlaws: Revolution in Country Music*. New York: Doubleday/ Dolphin, 1978.

Baskerville, David. *Music Business Handbook and Career Guide*. Los Angeles: Sherwood, 1982.

Benjaminson, Peter. *The Story of Motown*. New York: Grove Press, 1979.

Bergman, Billy. *Hot Sauces: Latin and Caribbean Pop*. New York: Quill, 1985.

Berman, Jay. *The Fifties Book*. New York: Berkley Medallion, 1974.

Berry, Chuck. *Chuck Berry: The Autobiography*. New York: Harmony Books, 1987.

Berry, Peter E. *". . . And the Hits Just Keep on Comin'"* Syracuse, N.Y.: Syracuse University Press, 1977.

Bianco, David. *Who's New Wave in Music: An Illustrated Encyclopedia*. Ann Arbor, Mich.: Pierian Press, 1985.

Billboard. *Music/Records/200*. New York: Billboard, 1976.

Broadcast Music, Incorporated. *Pop Hits: 1940–1966*. New York: BMI, 1967.

———. *Rhythm and Blues*. New York: BMI, 1969.

Brown, L., and G. Fredrich. *Encyclopedia of Country & Western Music*. New York: Tower Books, 1971.

Carr, Roy. *The Rolling Stones: An Illustrated Record*. New York: Harmony Books, 1976.

Carr, Roy, and Steve Clarke. *Fleetwood Mac: Rumours 'N'Fax*. New York: Harmony Books, 1978.

Carr, Roy, and Tony Tyler. *The Beatles Illustrated Record*. New York: Harmony Books, 1975.

Cash, Johnny. *Man in Black*. Grand Rapids, Mich.: Londewar, 1975.

Chapple, Steve, and Reebee Garofalo. *Rock 'n' Roll Is Here to Pay*. Chicago: Nelson-Hall, 1978.

Charles, Ray, with David Ritz. *Brother Ray*. New York: Dial Press, 1978.

Charters, Samuel. *The Bluesmen*. New York: Oak, 1967.

———. *Robert Johnson*. New York: Oak, 1973.

Christgau, Robert. *Any Old Way You Choose It*. Baltimore: Penguin Books, 1973.

———. *Christgau's Record Guide: Rock Albums of the Seventies*. New York: Ticknor and Fields, 1981.

Clark, Dick. *Rock, Roll & Remember*. New York: Crowell, 1976.

Coon, Caroline. *1988: The New Wave Punk Rock Explosion*. New York: Hawthorn Books, 1978.

Cooper, B. Lee. *Popular Music Handbook*. Littleton, Colo.: Libraries Unlimited, 1984.

Cooper, David Edwin. *International Bibliography of Discographies: Classical Music and Jazz & Blues*. Littleton, Colo.: Libraries Unlimited, 1975.

Coupe, Stuart, and Glenn A. Baker. *The New Rock 'N' Roll*. New York: St. Martin's Press, 1983.

Dalton, David, and Lenny Kaye. *Rock 100*. New York: Grosset and Dunlap, 1977.

Davies, Hunter. *The Beatles*. New York: McGraw-Hill, 1985.

Davis, Clive. *Clive: Inside the Record Business*. New York: William Morrow, 1975.

Denisoff, R. Serge. *Solid Gold*. New Brunswick, N.J.: Transaction Books, 1975.

Denisoff, R. Serge, and Richard A. Peterson, eds. *The Sounds of Social Change*. Chicago: Rand McNally, 1972.

Denisoff, R. Serge, and William L. Schurk. *Tarnished Gold*. New Brunswick, N.J.: Transaction Books, 1987.

DeWitt, Howard A. *Chuck Berry's Rock 'N' Roll Music*. Ann Arbor, Mich.: Pierian Press, 1985.

Dexter, Dave. *The Jazz Story*. Englewood Cliffs, N.J.: Prentice-Hall, 1964.

———. *Playback*. New York: Billboard, 1976.

DiLello, Richard. *The Longest Cocktail Party*. Chicago: Playboy Press, 1972.

Dimmick, Mary Laverne. *The Rolling Stones: An Annotated Bibliography*. Pittsburgh: University of Pittsburgh Press, 1979.

Dixon, Robert M. W., and John Godrich. *Recording the Blues*. New York: Stein and Day, 1970.

Edwards, Joe. *Top 10's and Trivia of Rock & Roll and Rhythm & Blues: 1950–1973*. St. Louis: Blueberry Hill, 1974.

Eisen, Jonathan, ed. *The Age of Rock*. New York: Vintage Books, 1969.

———, ed. *The Age of Rock 2*. New York: Vintage Books, 1970.

Ellington, Edward Kennedy. *Music Is My Mistress*. New York: Doubleday, 1973.

Engel, Edward K. *White and Still All Right*. N.p.: Crackerjack Press, 1977.

Engel, Lyle K. *Popular Record Directory*. New York: Fawcett, 1958.

Epstein, Brian. *A Cellarful of Noise*. New York: Doubleday, 1964.

Escott, Colin, and Martin Hawkins. *Catalyst*. London: Aquarius Books, 1975.

Ewen, David. *History of Popular Music*. New York: Barnes and Noble, 1961.

Feather, Leonard. *Encyclopedia of Jazz*. New York: Bonanza Books, 1960.

The Fifty Year Story of RCA Records. New York: Radio Corporation of America, 1953.

Flanagan, Bill. *Written in My Soul: Rock's Great Songwriters Talk About Creating Their Music*. Chicago: Contemporary Books, 1986.

Fong-Torres, Ben, ed. *The Rolling Stone Rock 'n' Roll Reader*. New York: Bantam Books, 1974.

———, ed. *What's That Sound?* New York: Anchor Press, 1976.

Friedman, Myra. *Buried Alive*. New York: Bantam Books, 1974.

Gelatt, Roland. *The Fabulous Phonograph–1877–1977*. New York: Collier, 1977.

George, Nelson. *Top of the Charts: The Most Complete Listing Ever*. Piscataway, N.J.: New Century, 1983.

Gibb, Barry, Robin Gibb, Maurice Gibb, and David Leaf. *BeeGees: The Authorized Biography*. New York: Dell, 1979.

Gillett, Charlie. *Making Tracks: Atlantic Records and the Growth of a Multi-Billion Dollar Industry*. New York: E. P Dutton, 1983.

———. *The Sound of the City*. New York: Outerbridge and Dientsfrey, 1972.

Godrich, John, and Robert M. W. Dixon. *Blues and Gospel Records*. London: Storyville, 1969.

Goldrosen, John. *Buddy Holly: His Life and Music*. Bowling Green, Ohio: Popular Press, 1975.

Goldstein, Richard. *Goldstein's Greatest Hits*. Englewood Cliffs, N.J.: Prentice-Hall, 1970.

The Grammy Awards Book. Hollywood: National Academy of Recording Arts and Sciences, 1978.

Greene, Bob. *Billion Dollar Baby*. New York: Signet, 1975.

Greenfield, Robert. *S.T.P.: A Journey Through America with the Rolling Stones*. New York: E. P. Dutton, 1974.

Grissim, John. *Country Music: White Man's Blues*. New York: Paperback Library, 1970.

Groia, Philip. *They All Sang on the Corner: New York City's Rhythm & Blues Vocal Groups of the 1950's*. New York: Edmund, 1973.

Guralnick, Peter. *Feel Like Going Home*. New York: E. P. Dutton, 1971.

———. *Sweet Soul Music: Rhythm and Blues and the Southern Dream of Freedom*. New York: Harper and Row, 1986.

Hammond, John. *John Hammond on Record*. New York: Ridge Press, 1977.

Harry, Bill, ed. *Mersey Beat: The Beginning of the Beatles*. London: Omnibus, 1977.

Heckman, Don. "Five Decades of Rhythm and Blues." In *BMI: The Many Worlds of Music*. New York: Broadcast Music, 1969.

Hemphill, Paul. *The Nashville Sound: Bright Lights and Country Music*. New York: Simon and Schuster, 1970.

Hilburn, Robert. *Springsteen*. New York: Rolling Stone Press, 1985.

Hirsch, Paul. *The Structure of the Popular Music Industry*. Ann Arbor, Mich.: University of Michigan Press, 1969.

Hirshey, Gerri. *Nowhere to Run: The Story of Soul Music*. New York: Times Books, 1984.

Hoffman, Frank. *The Cash Box Singles Charts: 1950–1981*. Metuchen, N.J.: Scarecrow Press, 1983.

Holiday, Billie, and William Duffy. *Lady Sings the Blues*. New York: Doubleday, 1956.

Hoover, Cynthia A. *Music Machines—American Style*. Washington, D.C.: Smithsonian Institution Press, 1975.

Hopkins, Jerry. *Elvis: A Biography*. New York: Simon and Schuster, 1975.

———. *Festival*. New York: Macmillan, 1971.

Horstman, Dorothy. *Sing Your Heart Out, Country Boy*. New York: Dutton, 1975.

Hurst, Walter E. *The Music Industry Book: How to Make Money in the Music Industry*. Hollywood, Calif.: Seven Arts Press, 1963.

Jahn, Mike. *How to Make a Hit Record*. Scarsdale, N.Y.: Bradbury Press, 1976.

———. *Rock: From Elvis Presley to the Rolling Stones*. New York: Quadrangle Books, 1973.

Jasper, Tony. *Paul McCartney and Wings*. Secaucus, N.J.: Chartwell, 1977.

Jones, LeRoi. *Black Music*. New York: William Morrow, 1967.

Karshner, Roger. *The Music Machine*. Los Angeles: Nash, 1971.

Kaufman, Murry. *Murry the K Tells It Like It Is, Baby*. New York: Holt, Rinehart and Winston, 1966.

Keil, Charles. *Urban Blues*. Chicago: University of Chicago Press, 1970.

Kimball, Robert, and William Bolcom. *Reminiscing with Sissle and Blake*. New York: Viking, 1973.

Kinkle, Roger D. *The Complete Encyclopedia of Popular Music and Jazz: 1900–1950*. 4 vols. New Rochelle, N.Y.: Arlington House, 1974.

Koenigsberg, Allen. *Edison Cylinder Records: 1889–1912*. New York: Stellar Productions, 1969.

Kooper, Al, and Ben Edmunds. *Nothing Personal: Reliving Rock in the Sixties*. New York: Stein and Day, 1975.

Krivine, J. *Juke Box Saturday Night*. Secaucus, N.J.: Chartwell, 1977.

Laing, Dave. *The Sound of Our Time*. Chicago: Quadrangle Books, 1969.

Landau, Jon. *It's Too Late to Stop Now: A Rock and Roll Journal*. San Francisco: Straight Arrow Books, 1972.

Lawrence, Sharon. *So You Want to Be a Rock & Roll Star*. New York: Dell, 1976.

Leadbitter, Mike, and Neil Slaven. *Blues Records, 1943–1966*. New York: Oak, 1968.

Leaf, David. *The Beach Boys and the California Myth*. New York: Grosset and Dunlap, 1978.

Leonard, Neil. *Jazz and the White Americans*. Chicago: University of Chicago Press, 1962.

Lichter, Paul. *The Boy Who Dared to Rock: The Definitive Elvis*. Garden City, N.Y.: Doubleday, 1978.

Logan, Nick, and Bob Woffinden. *Illustrated Encyclopedia of Rock*. New York: Harmony Books, 1977.

Lydon, Michael. *Boogie Lightning*. New York: Dial Press, 1974.

———. *Rock Folk: Portraits from the Rock 'n' Roll Pantheon*. New York: Dial Press, 1971.

McCabe, Peter, and D. R. Schonfeld. *Apple to the Core*. New York: Pocket Books, 1972.

McCarthy, Albert. *Big Band Jazz*. New York: Berkley, 1977.

McCutcheon, Lynn E. *Rhythm and Blues*. Arlington, Va.: Beatty, 1971.

Malone, Bill. *Country Music USA*. Austin: University of Texas Press, 1974.

Marcus, Greil. *Mystery Train: Images of America in Rock 'n' Roll Music*. New York: E. P. Dutton, 1974.

———. *Stranded: Rock and Roll for a Desert Island*. New York: Alfred A. Knopf, 1979.

———, ed. *Rock and Roll Will Stand*. Boston: Beacon, 1969.

Marsh, Dave. *Born to Run*. New York: Hawthorn Books, 1979.

———. *Glory Days*. New York: Pantheon, 1986.

———, ed. *The Rolling Stone Record Book*. New York: Rolling Stone Press, 1979.

Mathis, Sharon Bell. *Ray Charles*. New York: Crowell, 1973.

Mattfield, Julius. *Variety Music Cavalcade*. Englewood Cliffs, N.J.: Prentice-Hall, 1964.

Millar, Bill. *The Drifters: The Rise and Fall of the Black Vocal Group*. London: Studio Vista, 1971.

Miller, Jim, ed. *The Rolling Stone Illustrated History of Rock 'n' Roll*. New York: Random House, 1980.

Moore, Jerrold Northrop. *A Matter of Records*. New York: Taplinger, 1976.

Morse, David. *Motown and the Arrival of Black Music*. New York: Macmillan, 1971.

Murrells, Joseph. *Million Selling Records: From the 1900s to the 1980s*. New York: Arco, 1984.

The Music Industry: Markets and Methods for the Seventies. New York: Billboard, 1970.

Nassour, Ellis, and Richard Broderick. *Rock Opera: The Creation of Jesus Christ*

Superstar from Record Album to Broadway Show to Motion Picture. New York: Hawthorn Books, 1973.

Nite, Norm N. *Rock On: The Illustrated Encyclopedia of Rock 'n' Roll*. 3 vols. New York: Harper and Row, 1985.

Nugent, Stephen, and Charlie Gillett. *Rock Almanac*. Garden City, N.Y.: Doubleday, 1978.

Ochs, Michael. *Rock Archives: A Photographer's Journey Through the First Two Decades of Rock and Roll*. Garden City, N.Y.: Doubleday, 1984.

Oliver, Paul. *The Story of the Blues*. New York: Chilton Book, 1969.

Orloff, Katherine. *Rock 'n' Roll Lady*. Freeport, N.Y.: Nash, 1974.

Osbourne, Jerry. *Record Album Price Guide*. Phoenix, Ariz.: O'Sullivan, Woodside, 1977.

———. *Record Collector's Price Guide*. Phoenix, Ariz.: O'Sullivan, Woodside, 1976.

Palmer, Robert. *Baby, That Was Rock & Roll: The Legendary Lieber & Stoller*. New York: Harcourt Brace Jovanovich, 1978.

Palmer, Tony. *All You Need Is Love: The Story of Popular Music*. New York: Grossman, 1976.

Passman, Arnold. *The Deejays*. New York: Macmillan, 1971.

Pleasants, Henry. *Serious Music and All That Jazz*. New York: Simon and Schuster, 1969.

Podrazik, Walter J., and Harry Castleman. *All Together Now: The First Complete Beatles Discography: 1961–1975*. Ann Arbor, Mich.: Pierian Press, 1975.

———. *The Beatles Again?* Ann Arbor, Mich.: Pierian Press, 1977.

Propes, Steve. *Golden Goodies*. Radnor, Pa.: Chilton Book, 1975.

———. *Golden Oldies: A Guide to 60's Record Collecting*. Radnor, Pa.: Chilton Book, 1974.

———. *Those Oldies But Goodies: A Guide to 50's Record Collecting*. New York: Collier, 1973.

Randle, Bill. *The American Popular Music Discography: 1920–30*. Bowling Green, Ohio: Popular Press, 1974.

Read, Oliver, and Walter L. Welch. *From Tin Foil to Stereo*. New York: Bobbs-Merrill, 1959.

Rhode, H. Kandy. *The Gold of Rock & Roll: 1955–1967*. New York: Arbor House, 1970.

Robbins, Ira A. *The New Trouser Press Record Guide*. New York: Scribner's, 1985.

Roberts, John Storm. *The Latin Tinge: The Impact of Latin American Music on the United States*. New York: Oxford University Press, 1979.

Robinson, Richard, ed. *Rock Revolution*. New York: Popular Library, 1976.

Rolling Stone. *The Rolling Stone Interviews*. New York: Paperback Library, 1971.

———. *The Rolling Stone Interviews, Vol. 2*. New York: Paperback Library, 1973.

———. *The Rolling Stone Reader*. New York: Warner Paperback Library, 1974.

———. *The Rolling Stone Record Review*. New York: Pocket Books, 1971.

Rooney, James. *Bossmen: Bill Monroe and Muddy Waters*. New York: Dial Press, 1971.

Rowe, Mike. *Chicago Breakdown,* New York: Drake, 1975.

Roxon, Lillian, ed. *Lillian Roxon's Rock Encyclopedia*. New York: Grosset and Dunlap, 1969.

Rublowsky, John. *Popular Music*. New York: Basic Books, 1967.

Ruppli, Michael. *Atlantic Records: A Discography*. Westport, Conn.: Greenwood Press, 1979.

————. *The Chess Labels: A Discography*. Westport, Conn.: Greenwood Press, 1983.

————. *The Prestige Label: A Discography*. Westport, Conn.: Greenwood Press, 1980.

Russcol, Herbert. *The Liberation of Sound*. Englewood, N.J.: Prentice-Hall, 1972.

Rust, Brian. *Discography of Historical Records on Cylinders and 78s*. Westport, Conn.: Greenwood Press, 1979.

Scaduto, Tony. *Mick Jagger: Everybody's Lucifer*. New York: Berkley Medallion, 1975.

Schaffer, John. *New Sounds*. New York: Harper and Row, 1981.

Schaffner, Nicholas. *The Beatles Forever*. Harrisburg, Pa.: Cameron House, 1977.

Schicke, C. A. *Revolution in Sound: A Biography of the Recording Industry*. Boston: Little, Brown, 1974.

Shapiro, Nat, ed. *Popular Music: An Annotated Index of American Popular Songs*. New York: Adrian Press, 1964.

Shaw, Arnold. *Black Popular Music in America*. New York: Shimer, 1986.

————. *Dictionary of American Pop/Rock*. New York: Shimer, 1982.

————. *Honkers and Shouters: The Golden Years of Rhythm and Blues*. New York: Macmillan, 1978.

————. *The Rockin' Fifties:* New York: Macmillan, 1974.

————. *Sinatra*. New York: W. H. Allen, 1968.

————. *The World of Soul: Black America's Contribution to the Pop Music Scene*. New York: Cowles Book, 1970.

Shemel, Sidney, and M. William Krasilovsky. *This Business of Music*. New York: Billboard, 1985.

Shore, Michael. *Music Video: A Consumer's Guide*. New York: Ballantine, 1987.

Spitz, Robert Stephen. *The Making of Superstars: Artists and Executives of the Rock Music Business*. Garden City, N.Y.: Anchor Press, 1978.

Stewart-Baxter, Derrick. *Ma Rainey and the Classic Blues Singers*. New York: Stein and Day, 1970.

Stokes, Geoffrey. *Starmaking Machinery*. New York: Vintage Books, 1977.

Taylor, Derek. *As Time Goes By*. San Francisco: Straight Arrow Books, 1973.

Tosches, Nick. *Country: The Biggest Music in America*. New York: Stein and Day, 1977.

————. *Unsung Heroes of Rock 'N' Roll*. New York: Scribner's, 1984.

Townsend, Charles R. *San Antonio Rose: The Life and Music of Bob Wills*. Urbana, Ill.: University of Illinois Press, 1976.

Tudor, Dean. *Popular Music: An Annotated Guide to Recordings*. Littleton, Colo.: Libraries Unlimited, 1983.

Tyler, Don. *Hit Parade: 1920–1955*. New York: Quill, 1985.

Ulanov, Barry. *Handbook of Jazz*. New York: Viking Press, 1960.

Vassal, Jacques. *Electric Children: Roots and Branches of Modern Folkrock*. New York: Taplinger, 1975.

Wacholtz, Larry E. *Inside Country Music*. New York: Billboard, 1986.

Walley, David. *No Commercial Potential: The Saga of Frank Zappa and the Mothers of Invention*. New York: Outerbridge, 1972.

Ward, Ed, Geoffrey Stokes, and Ken Tucker. *Rock of Ages: The Rolling Stone History of Rock and Roll*. New York: Summit, 1986.

Welch, Chris. *Hendrix: A Biography*. New York: Flash Books, 1973.

Wenner, Jann. *Lennon Remembers*. San Francisco: Straight Arrow Books, 1971.

Whitburn, Joel. *Top Pop Records: 1940–1955*. Menomonee Falls, Wis.: Record Research, 1973.

———. *Top Pop Records: 1955–1973:* Menomonee Falls, Wis.: Record Research, 1973.

———. *Top Rhythm & Blues Records: 1949–1971*. Menomonee Falls, Wis.: Record Research, 1973.

Whitcomb, Ian. *After the Ball: Pop Music from Rag to Rock*. New York: Simon and Schuster, 1972.

Williams, Allan, and William Marshall. *The Man Who Gave the Beatles Away*. New York: Macmillan, 1975.

Williams, Richard. *Out of His Head: The Sound of Phil Spector*. New York: Outer bridge and Lazard, 1972.

Young, Jean, and Jim Young. *Succeeding in the Big World of Music*. Boston: Little, Brown, 1977.

Regionalism

ANNE E. ROWE

Although regionalism in literature and the arts has long been the subject of numerous studies by scholars and critics, only in the past two decades has any significant attention been given to regionalism as it relates to popular culture. A survey of the handbooks and anthologies of popular culture reveals increasing concern with regionalism. Similarly, papers presented at sections on regionalism at meetings of the Popular Culture Association generally have treated individual writers of a particular region rather than focusing on regionalism as a force. Recently, however, a number of articles on popular culture and regionalism have appeared, and formal theories concerning regionalism in popular culture are steadily being developed.

The chief thrust of this chapter is to survey the studies that have been made of regionalism and to define where these studies have intersected with those of popular culture. A seminal work that treats regionalism as it relates to popular culture is Jack Temple Kirby's *Media-Made Dixie: The South in the American Imagination,* an exploration of the image of the South as it has been created and presented in the popular media. *Geography, the Media and Popular Culture,* edited by Jacquelin Burgess and John R. Gold, also explores the importance of the relationship between a place and its culture. These books point the way to future studies to be undertaken in regionalism in popular culture.

Much of the recent important work on regionalism and popular culture has appeared in such journals as *Studies in Popular Culture* and the *Journal of Popular Culture.* The latter has devoted several in-depth sections to the topic. For example, Volume 11 (Spring 1978) contains a number of essays on cultural geography and popular culture. Volume 16 (Winter 1982) is devoted to the topic "The South and Popular Culture." The Western novel has also been the subject of several numbers of the *Journal of Popular Culture,* including Volume 4 (Fall 1970).

With the advent of the *Journal of Regional Cultures* in 1981, the subject of regionalism and popular culture has finally begun to receive the treatment it deserves. Volume 1 (Fall/Winter 1981) treats the South. Other issues include Volume 4 (Spring/Summer 1984), which contains essays on Florida, including Jerome Stern's perceptive essay, "Florida as Popular Culture." A recent issue, Volumes 4–5 (Fall/Winter 1984; Spring/Summer 1985) contains essays on the topic "New Jersey Culture: The View from the Disciplines." With the increasing attention given to regionalism and popular culture in these journals, it seems likely that book-length studies of the subject will also grow in number.

HISTORIC OUTLINE

Although an awareness of regions or sections has existed in America from the colonial period to the present, regionalism in literature and the arts generally refers to two periods: the local color period of the late nineteenth century and regionalism of the 1930s and after.

The beginning of the local color movement is usually cited as 1868, when Bret Harte began publishing stories of California mining camps in the *Overland Monthly.* Many provincial sketches and stories appeared in large-circulation magazines during the 1870s, and the local color vogue reached its height during the 1880s and 1890s, tapering off near the end of the century.

Only after the end of the Civil War, when it became clear that the battle for nationalism had been won, was there a dramatic growth of interest in the many sectional differences of the United States. Local color writing, which emphasized the unique setting of a particular region and reproduced the dialect, customs, provincial types, and other qualities of that region, seemed to satisfy the desire of the American people to take a nostalgic look at the good old days of the preindustrialized, prewar period. Thus, much local color writing was rural-based but intended for city consumption. Local color writing grew out of every region, and representative local colorists included Mary E. Wilkins Freeman and Sarah Orne Jewett of New England, Bret Harte of the West, and George Washington Cable and Thomas Nelson Page of the South. After the fall of the Confederacy there was much national interest in and curiosity about the South, and southern local colorists were heavily represented in nationally circulated magazines.

Local color writing usually appeared as short stories. Plots were highly contrived and characterization was generally superficial, characters usually not transcending the stereotype. Because of these limitations, local color writing of this period is looked upon today as having been more a popular than an artistic success.

In contrast to the term *local color,* regionalism refers to an intellectual movement of the 1930s which posited that each of the regions of the United States is a geographical, cultural, and economic entity. This new concept of regionalism, which was as much sociological as literary, was apparent particularly in the South. The publication of *I'll Take My Stand: The South and the Agrarian Tradition* by Twelve Southerners in 1930 expressed the desire of its authors to resist standardization and to preserve, as far as possible, an agrarian-based culture. Although the Agrarians, as they were called, including John Crowe Ransom, Robert Penn Warren, Donald Davidson, Allen Tate, and others, did not believe that the South could remain an entirely agricultural society, they argued for a set of values that supported a human rather than a machine-dominated society.

During the 1930s a number of works appeared that explored the relationship of the regions to the literary and social culture of America. Carey McWilliams, *The New Regionalism in American Literature,* was an early attempt at defining regionalism. *The Attack on Leviathan: Regionalism and Nationalism in the United States* by Donald Davidson posited an agrarian point of view. *American Regionalism: A Cultural-Historical Approach to National Integration* by Howard W. Odum and Harry Estill Moore argued for an integration of cultural, geographical, and historical factors.

One of the most important literary movements related to regionalism in the 1930s was the Southern Renaissance, out of which came the work of William Faulkner, Thomas Wolfe, Robert Penn Warren, Eudora Welty, and others. In novels, short stories, poetry, and essays, the literary productivity of the South loomed great. Other major writers of the 1930s, Willa Cather and John Steinbeck, for example, also employed a regional base for their works. The important distinction to be made, then, between local color and regionalism is that the latter brought much more breadth and depth to the depiction of a cultural region.

Regionalism as a cultural force has continued to receive attention since the 1930s. For some artists and critics regionalism has a pejorative connotation; it implies limitation. Regionalism, it is argued, must necessarily limit the universal message of the work of art. Proponents of regionalism argue, perhaps more convincingly, that all art must come out of a particular region or culture. That it does so in no way limits its universal statement. For example, although most of Faulkner's work is set in Mississippi, its meaning extends far beyond the boundaries of that state.

Most recently regionalism has aroused the interests of students of popular culture. Although the development of a formal theory concerning regionalism in popular culture is only in the beginning stages, a number of explorations of the relationship between a region and its culture have been undertaken. A challenging aspect of this study is the fact that with the increasing standardization of the media—television shows that are broadcast nationally, top ten radio programming, films that are released simultaneously in all parts of the country—the question of how many regional distinctions will continue to exist during the remaining decades of this century becomes especially important.

REFERENCE WORKS

Although many works provide bibliographical information on regional writings and a number of general guides to popular culture are available, there is still relatively little reference material devoted specifically to regionalism in popular culture. Standard sources for critical material dealing with earlier regional studies are three volumes compiled by Lewis Leary, *Articles on American Literature, 1900–1950, Articles on American Literature, 1950–1967,* and *Articles on American Literature, 1968–1975.* These volumes have special sections on regionalism which provide an invaluable listing of the articles pertaining to the topic. Another standard research tool, edited by Robert E. Spiller et al., is *The Literary History of the United States,* which contains chapters on the various sections of the United States as well as extensive bibliographical material on regionalism, including general studies, New England, New York to Delaware, the South and the Deep South, the Midwest, the Southwest, the Pacific Northwest, and California and the Far West. Other useful bibliographical works on regionalism, although limited to the South, are Louis D. Rubin, Jr., *A Bibliographical Guide to the Study of Southern Literature,* and the volume that updates it, *Southern Literature, 1968–1975: A Checklist of Scholarship,* edited by Jerry T. Williams.

RESEARCH COLLECTIONS

The description of research collections that follows must of necessity be eclectic because no comprehensive index to library holdings in popular culture is available. Much of the material cited here includes manuscript holdings of regional materials, only a portion of which pertain to popular culture as such.

Volume 6 of the Popular Culture Association *Newsletter,* edited by Michael T. Marsden, contains a compilation of popular culture holdings of various sizes related to regionalism. A representative listing follows. The Oral History Collection at Brookens Library in Springfield, Illinois, emphasizes regional history of Springfield and Central Illinois. Lees Junior College Library, Jackson, Kentucky, has an Appalachian Oral History Project which includes 600 taped interviews with mountain residents. Louisiana State University Library, Baton Rouge, has a collection of Acadian folk material and folk music. Northern Arizona University Library, Flagstaff, has a collection of Western pulp novels and Western pulp magazines. Northern Arizona University English Department has original tape recordings of southwestern folksongs and ballads.

One of the most extensive collections of western Americana is found in the Bancroft Library of the University of California at Berkeley. The collection includes manuscripts assembled by Hubert Howe Bancroft which center on the history of California and Mexico. Also contained in the Bancroft Library are regional oral history materials including "personal reminiscences of Northern Californians who have made significant contributions to the cultural, economic, intellectual, and social life of the West, particularly the San Francisco Bay region." Norlin Library of the University of Colorado at Boulder has published Ellen Arguimbau's *A Guide to Manuscript Collections: Western Historical Collections,* which describes the 480 individual collections of material relating to western culture.

The *Subject Directory of Special Libraries and Information Centers,* edited by Margaret Labash Young, Harold Chester Young, and Anthony T. Kruzas, provides listings of many collections that relate, in part at least, to regionalism in popular culture. For example, Beik Library, Appalachian State University, Boone, North Carolina, has an Appalachian Regional Collection (music library). The Sam Houston State University Library, Huntsville, Texas, has a collection of 10,000 volumes of Texana and Confederate materials. The Indiana University Lilly Library, Bloomington, contains the Ellison Far West Collection. The Walter Havighurst Special Collections Library at Miami University, Oxford, Ohio, has 4,220 volumes pertaining to Ohio Valley history. Johnson Camden Library at Morehead State University, Morehead, Kentucky, holds a Kentucky Collection of 2,560 volumes. The library of the Pacific-Union Club, San Francisco, has a special collection of 2,000 items of Californiana. The Special Collections Department of Rutgers University, New Brunswick, New Jersey, has a special collection of New Jerseyana. The Special Collections Department of the University of Arizona Library, Tuscon, contains collections of southwest material. The Department of Special Collections in the University of California at Los Angeles Research Library contains a Southern California Regional Oral History Interviews Collection. The Special Collections Library of the University of Idaho, Moscow, has a collection of Pacific Northwest materials. The Kerlan Collection of the University of Minnesota Library, Minneapolis, includes a collection of Minnesota authors and settings. The Special Collections Department/University Archives of the University of Nevada's Reno Library has a collection of material on Nevada and the West. The library of the University of Texas at El Paso contains several collections, the most prominent being the Sonnichsen Collection of Southwestern Literature and Fiction (1,200 books and papers), the McNeely Collection of southwestern and Mexican works, and the Southern Pacific Collection (500 boxes). The Virginia Commonwealth University James Branch Cabell Library, Richmond, has a collection of contemporary Virginia authors. The Pacific Northwest Collection of the University of Washington, Seattle, has materials relating to the anthropology, history, economics, and social conditions of the Pacific Northwest, including Washington, Oregon, Idaho, western Montana, Yukon, British Columbia, and Alaska.

During the 1930s and 1940s, when regional writing was at its peak, southern writers dominated the market. Listed below are some special collections of southern regional materials listed in Thomas H. English, *Roads to Research: Distinguished Library Collections of the Southeast*. The Aldermann Library of the University of Virginia, Charlottesville, has a large collection of writings of southern authors. The George W. Cable Collection of Tulane University includes more than 20,000 items, among them letters, manuscripts, and typescripts. The Joel Chandler Harris Collection at Emory University is very large and includes an extensive manuscript collection. The Joint University Libraries at Vanderbilt University in Nashville, Tennessee, have a collection of the Fugitive Group. The University of Florida Library has the Marjorie Kinnan Rawlings Collection and a collection of Floridiana. The Southern Historical Collection at the University of North Carolina at Chapel Hill has over 3.6 million items which are private records pertaining to southern culture and history. The George Washington Flowers Collection of Southern Americana at Duke University has over 2.5 million items covering the entire South for every period of its history. The Georgiana Collection in the University of Georgia Library at Athens provides a record of all phases of history and culture from the colonial period to the present. In the Department of Archives and Manuscripts at the Louisiana State University Library are nearly three million items related to contemporary life in the Lower Mississippi Valley for the past 200 years. The North Carolina Collection at the University of North Carolina at Chapel Hill has more than 200,000 items relating to every aspect of life in North Carolina. A collection of Tennesseana is held at the Manuscript Division of the Tennessee State Library and Archives.

Special Collections in Libraries of the Southeast, edited by J. B. Howell, cites a collection of 500 cheap editions of fiction, "displayed for sale in railway bookstalls from the mid-19th century,"[1] in the Robert W. Woodruff Library at Emory University. Hutchins Library of Berea College at Berea, Kentucky, has a collection of "8,000 volumes and 250 linear feet of archival and manuscript materials relating to the history and culture of the Southern highlands."[2] The collection includes books, pamphlets, manuscripts, photographs, tapes, and films. Another extensive collection is the Folk-lore, Folk-life and Oral History Archives at the Helm-Cravens Library of Western Kentucky University, Bowling Green. The Mississippi Department of Archives and History, Jackson, has a collection of Mississippiana including the Works Progress Administration Collection of material assembled by WPA workers on the history and culture of Mississippi. At the University of Mississippi Library in University is the Mississippi Collection, consisting of 20,000 cataloged volumes as well as thousands of uncataloged items pertaining to the culture and history of the state. The Carol Grotnes Belk Library at Appalachian State University, Boone, North Carolina, contains the William Leonard Eury Appalachian Collection comprising over 10,000 volumes, clippings, slides, oral history tapes, original manuscripts, and four extensive collections of ballads. The Library and Media Center of the Country Music Foundation, Nashville, Tennessee, has "70,000 recordings, 2,500 tapes including 150 oral tapes, 2,500 volumes, 2,000 song books, 750 films, 6,000 photographs and extensive files of biographical sketches and newspaper clippings," making this collection "the largest ever assembled in the field of country music."[3]

What is most obvious about the listing above is that it refers to large collections of regional material only a portion of which may constitute popular culture. The task of cataloging popular culture material in these and other collections has yet to be done.

HISTORY AND CRITICISM

The works treated below are arranged chronologically, and the majority of those focusing strictly on popular culture appear among the more recent critical works. The earlier works cited are important to the understanding of the concept of regionalism as it has influenced American life and art.

Provincial Types in American Fiction by Horace Spencer Fiske, published in 1907, is an early work describing various types of American provincial life as treated since the Civil War by writers in New England, the South, the Midwest, and the Far West. Fiske describes provincial types in fiction according to region, and there are separate introductory sections for each of the regions as well as explication and discussion of the stories by these authors.

Another early work, *The New Regionalism in American Literature,* by Carey McWilliams, published in 1930, reflects the growing interest in regionalism. McWilliams provides useful discussions of early journals and collections of writings of the various regions. He concludes that regional writers are trying to create a sense of community through their work.

A seminal study of regionalism in many aspects—geographical and political as well as cultural—is Howard W. Odum and Harry Estill Moore, *American Regionalism: A Cultural-Historical Approach to National Integration.* Odum and Moore find that "the older authentic literary regionalism stands in direct opposition to our premise of regionalism as a constituent part of the whole and as a tool for national integration of all parts of the nation."[4] Part 1 traces the general rise and incidence in American regionalism; part 2 provides a theoretical-historical account from the perspective of the social sciences; and part 3 enumerates and describes each region. Important to our consideration here is the fact that Odum and Moore make a distinction between local color and regionalism. Local color they find to be a pejorative term, whereas regionalism has positive connotations. They also note, "Next to metropolitan regionalism and sectionalism the rise and characterization of American regionalism has perhaps been more often identified with literary regionalism than with anything else."[5]

An important early statement about regionalism from a perspective very different from that of Odum and Moore is made by Donald Davidson in his collection of essays, *The Attack on Leviathan: Regionalism and Nationalism in the United States*. Davidson's premise is that in attacking Leviathan (the monolithic nationalism in writing), artists and others are "seeking . . . a definition of the terms on which America may have both the diversity and the unity that gives soundness to a tradition."[6] In a chapter entitled "Regionalism in the Arts," Davidson argues that artistic regionalism "is like the regionalism of the social scientists in so far as it is a new attempt to meet an old problem. . . . To one wing of American criticism regionalists seem to subscribe to some narrow and confining principle of art." Some regionalists, on the other hand, "are too ready to elevate the word *regional* . . . into a slogan and a panacea."[7] In an essay entitled "Regionalism and Nationalism in American Literature," Davidson concludes, "The national literature is the compound of the regional impulses, not antithetical to them, but embracing them and living in them as the roots, branch, and flower of its being."[8]

The Tennessee Valley Authority: A National Experiment in Regionalism by Clarence Lewis Hodge is a study of the significance of the Tennessee Valley Authority as a new regional unit in the field of government. Hodge's central premise is that "regionalism is a trend the importance of which has been inadequately recognized by students in the field of government."[9] Although this work does not address regionalism in popular culture as such, it is important for stressing the concept of regionalism as a major influence in people's lives.

Regionalism in America, edited by Merrill Jensen, provides important historical information. Part 1 treats the development and use of the concept of regionalism from its beginnings in the eighteenth century until the present. Part 2 offers an account of three historic regions of the United States: the South, Spanish Southwest, and Pacific Northwest. Part 3 surveys regionalism in American culture and includes a survey of literature, architecture, painting, and linguistics. This section of Jensen's book is of special interest because it treats a variety of genres and disciplines in terms of their regional qualities. Part 4 surveys contributions of those who have dealt with regionalism as a practical concept. Part 5, "The Limitations and the Promise of Regionalism," contains essays arguing for the continuation of discrete regions and for regionalism as leading to the integration of regions.

Mass Culture: Popular Arts in America, edited by Bernard Rosenberg and

David Manning White, is a reader that deals with the interplay between the mass media and society. Its fifty-one contributors include literary critics, social scientists, journalists, and art critics. Although it does not address regionalism specifically, the reader does contain useful essays on mass literature (books, detective fiction, magazines, comic books, and cartoon scripts), motion pictures, television, and radio.

Leo Lowenthal's *Literature, Popular Culture, and Society* provides in its introduction a historical account of popular culture, which Lowenthal says is "probably as old as human civilization."[10] Four chapters deal with literature as commodity, and the final chapter treats literature as art. Although not focused on regionalism, the historical account of popular culture is useful.

Regionalism and Beyond: Essays of Randall Stewart, edited by George Core, excludes a consideration of popular literature but does treat American regions extensively, including New England and the Tidewater and Frontier South. Another work appearing in 1968, *Frontiers of American Culture,* edited by Ray B. Browne, Richard H. Crowder, Virgil L. Lokke, and William T. Stafford, contains an essay by Leslie Fiedler entitled "The New Western: Or, the Return of the Vanishing American," in which Fiedler posits that "geography in the United States is mythological. From the earliest times, at any rate, American writers have tended to define their own country— and, much of our literature has, consequently, tended to define itself— topologically, as it were, in terms of the four cardinal directions: mythicized North, South, East and West."[11] Another essay in the collection, Richard M. Dorson's, "Folklore in Relation to American Studies," comments on the humor of the Old Southwest and finds that it is "clearly an expression of the popular culture.... One reason... this humorous literature disappeared from sight when its vogue had passed was its lack of recognition or even awareness by highbrow literary critics."[12] Dorson argues that the folklorist can correct the overly exclusive definition of southwest humor made by literary historians.

Challenges in American Culture, edited by Ray B. Browne, Larry N. Landrum, and William K. Bottorff, is a potpourri of popular culture interests. Related to the study of regionalism in popular culture is an essay by Esther K. Birdsall, "The FWP and the Popular Press." Birdsall gives a brief history of the Federal Writers Project, which "spent 27,189,370 dollars to fill seven twelve foot shelves in the library of the Department of the Interior with publications ranging from the state guides to pamphlets of regional interest," and discusses contemporary reaction to the FWP.[13]

Raymond D. Gastil in *Cultural Regions of the United States* cites the greater interest in regionalism in the 1930s as compared with today. Gastil draws on studies of dialect, house styles and architecture, settlement patterns, regional history, and so forth, to demonstrate that "there is still much more life in American regionalism than many of us believed."[14] Gastil describes cultural regions of the United States and concludes that we have exaggerated the disappearance of regionalism.

Western Popular Theatre, edited by David Mayer and Kenneth Richards, is the proceedings of a symposium sponsored by the Manchester University Department of Drama and contains a paper of interest to students of regionalism in popular culture. "The Wild West Exhibition and the Drama of Civilization" by William Brasmer traces the history of the development of the Wild West exhibit.

Floyd C. Watkins, *In Time and Place: Some Origins of American Fiction,* analyzes eight novels, "each of [which] treats a particular culture or a diversity of cultures and reveals the author's ignorance or knowledge in his use of the ways of the communities."[15] The novels are of the South, the Southwest, and the prairies, and one (*The Grapes of Wrath*) begins in Oklahoma and ends in California.

Jeffrey Schrank's *Snap, Crackle, and Popular Taste: The Illusion of Free Choice in America* contains a chapter entitled "The Packaged Environment: Illusions of Quality and Culture," which discusses kitsch as "a package of phony culture. Kitsch is something ordinary, cheap or simply mass produced but packaged to appear as culture or art with a capital A."[16] *Snap, Crackle, and Popular Taste* deals not so much with regionalism as with its replacement—a packaged sameness that may be found in every part of the United States.

Marshall W. Fishwick's *Springlore in Virginia* treats a very specific aspect of regionalism in popular culture: the culture that grows up around springs. Fishwick defines springlore as "what we know, think, and say about flowing waters, springs and spas, and the people who gather around them. Springs can and do serve as healing places, stage sets, touchstones, cyphers, icons— even tombstones of a class or culture."[17] Fishwick's book focuses on a close cluster of Virginia springs and discusses the culture of the South as it relates to these springs.

Another project that treats regionalism in popular culture is the special issue of the *Journal of Popular Culture,* "In-Depth: Cultural Geography and Popular Culture," edited by Alvar Carlson. In an essay titled "The Contributions of Cultural Geographers to the Study of Popular Culture," Carlson points out that "cultural geographers, knowingly or unknowingly, have long had an interest in some aspects of popular culture, although the discipline of popular culture was formally established only within the last decade."[18] Following Carlson's essay are twelve articles treating topics ranging from a geographical examination of alcoholic drink in the United States to massage parlors in the nation's capital.

Media-Made Dixie: The South in the American Imagination by Jack Temple Kirby is one of the few extended works specifically to evaluate regionalism in popular culture. Kirby states that the main object of his inquiry is the "*popular* historical images of the South since the advent of feature movies and annual best-seller lists."[19] Kirby surveys the images of the South in the mass communication media, including films, best sellers, popular histories, school texts, television, music, radio, drama, sports, and advertising.

Several recent studies offer perceptive analyses of regionalism and art of the 1930s. Joseph S. Czestochowski's *John Steuart Curry and Grant Wood: A Portrait of Rural America* contains prints of representative art of the period and analyzes the role of these two artists. Mary Scholz Guedon's *Regionalist Art: Thomas Hart Benton, John Steuart Curry, and Grant Wood: A Guide to the Literature* is an annotated bibliography of regionalism in art during the 1920s and 1930s. M. Sue Kendall's *Rethinking Regionalism: John Steuart Curry and the Kansas Mural Controversy* uses a case study, the confrontation between the artist and the region he depicted, to explore the relationship between art and culture and to "suggest several ways in which we need a rethinking of the phenomenon of regionalism in American art."[20]

Finally, *Regionalism and the Female Imagination,* edited by Emily Toth, contains essays treating women writers and a variety of regions: New England, the Midwest, the Appalachian Mountain region, and the South. Of special interest are essays in a section of the book entitled "Psychology, Religion, and Regionalism." Works such as Toth's point the way to increasingly specialized treatments of culture and region.

ANTHOLOGIES AND REPRINTS

Because regionalism in popular culture is such an all-inclusive topic, only a sampling of representative anthologies will be treated. The discussion below is based on a sampling of works that contain local color and regional stories. A full listing, of course, would number in the hundreds. A selective list is included in the bibliography at the end of this chapter.

Some early regional anthologies include *American Local-Color Stories,* edited by Harry R. Warfel and G. Harrison Orians, which has selections from the works of thirty-eight writers. Kendall B. Taft's *Minor Knickerbockers: Representative Selections, with Introduction, Bibliography, and Notes* contains selections of the work of early New York writers. Robert Penn Warren's *A Southern Harvest: Short Stories by Southern Writers* is a good anthology of southern writing. Midwestern and western anthologies are represented by Benjamin S. Parker's *Poets and Poetry of Indiana;* Mary H. Marable and Elaine Boylan's *A Handbook of Oklahoma Writers;* Thomas M. Pearce and A. P. Thomason's *Southwesterners Write;* Stewart Hall Holbrook's *Promised Land: A Collection of Northwest Writing;* and Levette J. Davidson and Prudence Bostwick's *The Literature of the Rocky Mountain West, 1803–1903.*

The Southwest in Literature: An Anthology for High Schools, edited by Mabel Major and Rebecca W. Smith and published in 1929, is representative of early anthologies intended for school use. The editors state that the purpose of the anthology "is to inspire in the teachers and pupils who use it a proud recognition of how much really good literature and art have already been produced about the Southwest; and to arouse in them a desire to write and to sing and to paint the beauties and the truths of the land which is their own."[21] The anthology is divided into sections describing early pioneers, cowboys, Indians, and inheritors of Old Spain, and includes songs, poems, and short stories.

Tall Tales of the Southwest: An Anthology of Southern and Southwestern Humor, 1830–1860, edited by Franklin J. Meine and published in 1930, collects stories written between 1830 and 1860 and provides brief biographical sketches and bibliographical information for each writer. Meine's introduction gives a historical account of the development of frontier humor. Of special interest is a summary of the range of subjects treated in southwest humor. A distinction must be made, of course, between humor of the Old Southwest, as treated here, including the old southwest frontier—Alabama, Mississippi, western Georgia—and the modern Southwest.

Claude M. Simpson's *The Local Colorists: American Short Stories, 1857–1900* is a seminal study of the local color period. Representative writers of the Northeast, Midwest, South, and West are included, and Simpson's introduction to the collection provides what has become a standard definition of local color. A historical account of the rise of the local color movement is included as well.

Walter Blair's *Native American Humor,* first published in 1937 and published in a revised edition in 1960, is also a standard work. The first half of the book contains essays dealing with nineteenth-century developments in American humor, which Blair groups as follows: changing attitudes of humorists toward comic native characters, changes in humorous techniques, and changing reader attitudes toward this humor. Representative selections of Down East humor (1830–67), humor of the Old Southwest (1830–67), literary comedians (1855–1900), local colorists (1869–1900), and writings of Mark Twain are included.

E. N. Brandt has edited *The Saturday Evening Post Reader of Western Stories.* The collection, published in 1960, contains eighteen short stories and two novelettes. Brandt's preface catalogs the "many Wests—the West of the explorers, the West of the Mountain Men and the Indian Wars, the West of the wagon trains, the gold seekers, the homesteaders, the ranchers, and the cowboys. Each one has had its faithful chroniclers."[22]

Another work published in 1960, *Southern Stories,* edited by Arlin Turner, chronologically presents stories by southern writers. In his introduction Turner provides a brief historical outline of the development of the short story in southern writing and says that, for southerners, "the regional affiliation is conspicuous."[23]

Representative of contemporary editions of the works of a single regional writer is M. Thomas Inge's edition of *Sut Lovingood's Yarns* by George Washington Harris. Inge provides an extensive introduction to Harris's life and gives the publication history of his work. Inge considers Harris probably the foremost writer of the southwest humor school and includes in his edition the best of the Sut Lovingood sketches written between 1854 and 1869.[24]

A book that is representative of the works published in the past decade that collect popular culture materials is Ray B. Browne's *The Alabama Folk Lyric: A Study in Origins and Media of Dissemination*. Browne provides a working definition for the folk song and notes that the songs collected in this work are part of a collection of 2,500 ballads and songs made in the summers of 1951, 1952, and 1953, a collection which Browne describes as one of the largest ever assembled for any state. The 192 pieces included in this work (328, counting variants) represent all classes and geographical sections of the state.

NOTES

1. J. B. Howell, ed., *Special Collections in Libraries of the Southeast* (Jackson, Miss.: Howick House, 1978), p. 82.

2. Howell, pp. 112–13.

3. Howell, p. 293.

4. Howard W. Odum and Harry Estill Moore, *American Regionalism: A Cultural-Historical Approach to National Integration* (New York: Holt, 1938), p. vi.

5. Odum and Moore, p. 168.

6. Donald Davidson, *The Attack on Leviathan: Regionalism and Nationalism in the United States* (Chapel Hill: University of North Carolina Press, 1938), p. 12.

7. Davidson, p. 65.

8. Davidson, pp. 232–33.

9. Clarence Lewis Hodge, *The Tennessee Valley Authority: A National Experiment in Regionalism* (New York: American University Press, 1938. Reprint. New York: Russell and Russell, 1968), p. vii.

10. Leo Lowenthal, *Literature, Popular Culture, and Society* (Englewood Cliffs, N.J.: Prentice-Hall, 1961), p. xvii.

11. Leslie A. Fiedler, "The New Western: or, The Return of the Vanishing American," in *Frontiers of American Culture,* ed. Roy B. Browne, Richard H. Crowder, Virgil L. Lokke, and William T. Stafford (Lafayette, Ind.: Purdue Research Foundation, 1968), p. 114.

12. Richard M. Dorson, "Folklore in Relation to American Studies," in *Frontiers of American Culture,* ed. Roy B. Browne, Richard H. Crowder, Virgil L. Lokke, and William T. Stafford (Lafayette, Ind.: Purdue Research Foundation, 1968), p. 183.

13. Esther K. Birdsall, "The FWP and the Popular Press," in *Challenges in American Culture,* ed. Roy B. Browne, Larry N. Landrum, and William W. Bottorff (Bowling Green, Ohio: Bowling Green University Popular Press, 1970), p. 101.

14. Nathan Glazer, "Foreword" in Raymond D. Gastil, *Cultural Regions of the United States* (Seattle: University of Washington Press, 1975), p. viii.

15. Floyd C. Watkins, *In Time and Place: Some Origins of American Fiction* (Athens: University of Georgia Press, 1977), p. ix.

16. Jeffrey Schrank, *Snap, Crackle, and Popular Taste: The Illusion of Free Choice in America* (New York: Dell, 1977), p. 117.

17. Marshall W. Fishwick, *Springlore in Virginia* (Bowling Green, Ohio: Bowling Green University Popular Press, 1978), p. 2.

18. Alvar Carlson, "The Contribution of Cultural Geographers to the Study of Popular Culture," in "In Depth: Cultural Geography and Popular Culture," ed. Alvar Carson, special issue, *Journal of Popular Culture,* II (Spring 1978), 830.

19. Jack Temple Kirby, *Media-Made Dixie: The South in the American Imagination* (Baton Rouge: Louisiana State University Press, 1978), p. xiv.

20. M. Sue Kendall, *Rethinking Regionalism: John Steward Curry and the Kansas Mural Controversy* (Washington, D.C.: Smithsonian Institution Press, 1986), p. 14.

21. Mabel Major and Rebecca W. Smith, eds., *The Southwest in Literature: An Anthology for High Schools* (New York: Macmillan, 1929), p. vii.

22. E. N. Brandt, ed., *The Saturday Evening Post Reader of Western Stories* (Garden City, N.Y.: Doubleday, 1960), p. [vii].

23. Arlin Turner, ed., *Southern Stories,* 2nd ed. (New York: Holt, Rinehart and Winston, 1965), p. xiii.

24. M. Thomas Inge, ed., *Sut Lovingood's Yarns* by George Washington Harris (New Haven, Conn.: College and University Press, 1966), p. 10.

BIBLIOGRAPHY

Books and Articles

Arguimbau, Ellen, comp., and John A. Brennan, ed. *A Guide to Manuscript Collections: Western Historical Collections.* Boulder: Western Historical Collections, University of Colorado, 1977.

Bargainnier, Earl F. "The Falconhurst Series: A New Popular Image of the Old South." *Journal of Popular Culture,* 10 (Fall 1976), 298–314.

Bigsby, C. W. E., ed. *Approaches to Popular Culture.* Bowling Green, Ohio: Bowling Green University Press, 1976.

Boney, Nash. "The American South." *Journal of Popular Culture,* 10 (Fall 1976), 290–97.

Browne, Ray B. *The Alabama Folk Lyric: A Study in Origins and Media of Dissemination.* Bowling Green, Ohio: Bowling Green University Popular Press, 1979.

Browne, Ray B., Richard H. Crowder, Virgil L. Lokke, and William T. Stafford, eds. *Frontiers of American Culture.* Lafayette, Ind.: Purdue Research Foundation, 1968.

Browne, Ray B., Larry N. Landrum, and William K. Bottorff. *Challenges in American Culture.* Bowling Green, Ohio: Bowling Green University Popular Press, 1970.

Burgess, Jacquelin, and John R. Gold, eds. *Geography, the Media, and Popular Culture.* London: Croom Helm, 1985.

Carlson, Alvar W. "Cultural Geography and Popular Culture." *Journal of Popular Culture,* 9 (Fall 1975), 482–83.

————, ed. "In-Depth: Cultural Geography and Popular Culture." *Journal of Popular Culture,* 11 (Spring 1978), 829–997 (12 articles).

Core, George, ed. *Regionalism and Beyond: Essays of Randall Stewart.* Nashville, Tenn.: Vanderbilt University Press, 1968.

Czestochowski, Joseph S. *John Steuart Curry and Grant Wood: A Portrait of Rural America.* Columbia: University of Missouri Press, 1981.

Davidson, Donald. *The Attack on Leviathan: Regionalism and Nationalism in the United States.* Chapel Hill: University of North Carolina Press, 1938.

Engler, Richard E., Jr. *The Challenge of Diversity.* New York: Harper and Row, 1964.

English, Thomas H. *Roads to Research: Distinguished Library Collections of the Southeast.* Athens: University of Georgia Press, 1968.

Fishwick, Marshall W. *Springlore in Virginia.* Bowling Green, Ohio: Bowling Green University Popular Press, 1978.

Fiske, Horace Spencer. *Provincial Types in American Fiction.* Chautauqua, N.Y.: Chautauqua Press, 1907.

Gastil, Raymond D. *Cultural Regions of the United States.* Seattle: University of Washington Press, 1975.

Guedon, Mary Scholz. *Regionalist Art: Thomas Hart Benton, John Steuart Curry, and Grant Wood: A Guide to the Literature.* Metuchen, N.J.: Scarecrow Press, 1982.

Hodge, Clarence Lewis. *The Tennessee Valley Authority: A National Experiment in Regionalism.* New York: American University Press, 1938. Reprint. New York: Russell and Russell, 1968.

Howell, J. B., ed. *Special Collections in Libraries of the Southeast.* Jackson, Miss.: Howick House, 1978.

Jensen, Merrill, ed. *Regionalism in America.* Madison: University of Wisconsin Press, 1951.

Kendall, M. Sue. *Rethinking Regionalism: John Steuart Curry and the Kansas Mural Controversy.* Washington, D.C.: Smithsonian Institution Press, 1986.

Kirby, Jack Temple. *Media-Made Dixie: The South in the American Imagination.* Baton Rouge: Louisiana State University Press, 1978. Rev. ed. Athens: University of Georgia Press, 1987.

Leary, Lewis. *Articles on American Literature, 1900–1950.* Durham, N.C.: Duke University Press, 1954.

————. *Articles on American Literature, 1950–1967.* Durham, N.C.: Duke University Press, 1970.

————. *Articles on American Literature, 1968–1975.* Durham, N.C.: Duke University Press, 1979.

Lowenthal, Leo. *Literature, Popular Culture, and Society.* Englewood Cliffs, N.J.: Prentice-Hall, 1961.

McWilliams, Carey. *The New Regionalism in American Literature.* Seattle: University of Washington Book Store, 1930. Reprint. Folcroft, Pa.: Folcroft Library Editions, 1974.

Marsden, Michael T., ed. "National Finding List of Popular Culture Holdings Special Collections." *Popular Culture Association Newletter,* 6 (March 1977).

Mayer, David, and Kenneth Richard, eds. *Western Popular Theatre*. London: Methuen, 1977.

Odum, Howard W., and Harry Estill Moore. *American Regionalism: A Cultural-Historical Approach to National Integration*. New York: Holt, 1938.

Rosenberg, Bernard, and David Manning White, eds. *Mass Culture: Popular Arts in America*. Glencoe, Ill.: Free Press, 1957.

Rubin, Louis D., Jr. *A Bibliographical Guide to the Study of Southern Literature*. Baton Rouge: Louisiana State University Press, 1969.

Schrank, Jeffrey. *Snap, Crackle, and Popular Taste: The Illusion of Free Choice in America*. New York: Dell, 1977.

Simpson, Claude M., ed. *The Local Colorists: American Short Stories, 1857–1900*. New York: Harper and Row, 1960.

Spiller, Robert E., Willard Thorp, Thomas H. Johnson, Henry Seidel Canby, and Richard M. Ludwig, eds. *Literary History of the United States*. 2 vols. 3rd rev. ed. New York: Macmillan, 1963.

Stern, Jerome. "Florida as Popular Culture." *Journal of Regional Cultures*, 4 (Spring/Summer 1984), 1–14.

Toth, Emily, ed. *Regionalism and the Female Imagination: A Collection of Essays*. New York: Human Sciences Press, 1985.

Twelve Southerners. *I'll Take My Stand: The South and the Agrarian Tradition*. New York: Harper and Brothers, 1930.

Vance, Mary A., ed. *Regionalism: Monographs*. Monticello, Ill.: Vance Bibliographies, 1987.

Watkins, Floyd C. *In Time and Place: Some Origins of American Fiction*. Athens: University of Georgia Press, 1977.

Williams, Jerry T., ed. *Southern Literature, 1968–1975: A Checklist of Scholarship*. Boston: G. K. Hall, 1978.

Wolfe, Margaret Ripley. "The Southern Lady: Long Suffering Counterpart of the Good Ole' Boy." *Journal of Popular Culture*, 11 (Summer 1977), 18–27.

Young, Margaret Labash, Harold Chester Young, and Anthony T. Kruzas, eds. *Subject Directory of Special Libraries and Information Centers*. Detroit: Gale Research, 1975.

Anthologies

Blair, Walter. *Native American Humor*. New York: American Book, 1937. Rev. ed. San Francisco: Chandler, 1960.

Brandt, E. N., ed. *The Saturday Evening Post Reader of Western Stories*. Garden City, N.Y.: Doubleday, 1960.

Browne, Ray B., ed. *The Alabama Folk Lyric: A Study in Origins and Media of Dissemination*. Bowling Green, Ohio: Bowling Green University Popular Press, 1979.

Davidson, Levette J., and Forester Blake, comps. *Rocky Mountain Tales*. Norman: University of Oklahoma Press, 1947.

Davidson, Levette J., and Prudence Bostwick, comps. *The Literature of the Rocky Mountain West, 1803–1903*. Caldwell, Idaho: Caxton Printers, 1939.

Harris, George Washington. *Sut Lovingood's Yarns*. Edited by M. Thomas Inge. New Haven: College and University Press, 1966.

Holbrook, Stewart Hall, ed. *Promised Land: A Collection of Northwest Writing*. New York: McGraw-Hill, 1945.

Major, Mabel, and Rebecca W. Smith, eds. *The Southwest in Literature: An Anthology for High Schools*. New York: Macmillan, 1929.

Marabale, Mary H., and Elaine Boylan, eds. *A Handbook of Oklahoma Writers*. Norman: University of Oklahoma Press, 1939.

Meine, Franklin J., ed. *Tall Tales of the Southwest: An Anthology of Southern and Southwestern Humor, 1830–1860*. 3rd ed. New York: Alfred A. Knopf, 1946.

Parker, Benjamin S., ed. *Poets and Poetry of Indiana*. New York: Silver, Burdett, 1900.

Pearce, Thomas M., and A. P. Thomason, comps. *Southwesterners Write*. Albuquerque: University of New Mexico Press, 1947.

Simpson, Claude M., ed. *The Local Colorists: American Short Stories, 1857–1900*. New York: Harper and Row, 1960.

Taft, Kendall B., ed. *Minor Knickerbockers: Representative Selections, with Introduction, Bibliography, and Notes*. New York: American Book, 1947.

Turner, Arlin, ed. *Southern Stories*. 2nd ed. New York: Holt, Rinehart and Winston, 1965.

Warfel, Harry R., and G. Harrison Orians, eds. *American Local-Color Stories*. New York: American Book, 1941. Reprint. New York: Cooper Square, 1970.

Warren, Robert Penn, ed. *A Southern Harvest: Short Stories by Southern Writers*. Boston: Houghton Mifflin, 1937.

Periodicals

Journal of Popular Culture. Bowling Green, Ohio, 1967–.
Journal of Regional Cultures. Bowling Green, Ohio, 1981–.
Studies in Popular Culture. Tallahassee, Fla., 1978–.

Science

ELIZABETH BARNABY KEENEY

The nature and power of science as a cultural force in modern America is profound. Coexistence with the payoffs and fallouts from modern science—the space race, nuclear weaponry and power, the miracles and dilemmas of genetics, and a host of other developments—has bred a culture in which science is pervasive in content, style, and imagery. This chapter will explore some of the routes by which science came to play an important role in modern culture, examine the place it occupies, and assess the current place of science.

Several themes are of sufficient importance to be laid out from the start. The most obvious revolves around the transmission of science into popular culture. How do lay people get their scientific knowledge? Who generates it? Who receives it? Why? What happens to it and to them in the process? What is the perceived importance or meaning of science as popular culture? The second broad theme focuses on the popular image of science and the scientist. What is the perceived importance of science as an intellectual pursuit? How is it seen as relating to other areas of knowledge, especially religion? What is the image of science and the scientist? What is the perceived impact of science and scientists on society? These two themes—transmission and image—will be traced over the course of American history with the aim of steering the reader to the relevant questions, figures, and literature.

HISTORIC OUTLINE

As Europeans first began to settle in the New World, one of the tasks they turned to was the exploration of the natural resources of their new home. Their interest was driven in large part by the need to survive, which was obviously linked to the environment. Curiosity also played a major part, as the New World was populated and covered with unfamiliar plants, animals, and geological productions that mystified and delighted not only the settlers, but also those Europeans lucky enough to be the recipients of shipments of specimens and accounts. Religious interest—spawned by the widespread belief that by studying nature one could find evidence of the existence and character of its designer and creator—also proved to be an important motivation. The intellectual elite—ministers, physicians, lawyers, and other scholars—maintained a strong interest in science. As cities emerged in the clearings and on the hillsides, so too did the trappings of learned culture that science needs to thrive—learned societies, libraries, schools, and the like. European naturalists encouraged those colonists they knew to be interested in natural history by arranging for shipments of specimens, providing books, supplies, equipment, and ensuring the publication of findings. This encouragement evolved into an informal network, the "natural history circle," which consisted of naturalists up and down the East Coast and in Europe. Many colonists corresponded less formally about natural history. Still others sent astronomical observations and descriptions of native American life. Twenty-five colonists were rewarded for their contributions by election to the Royal Society of London. Accounts of the New World written by colonists—for example, Thomas Jefferson's *Notes on Virginia*—which included careful descriptions of natural history, were popular reading in America and in Europe.

More accessible writings—almanacs and newspapers, for example—were far more important to the spread of scientific culture in the colonies than were these longer narratives. Almanacs sprinkled comments on astronomy, medicine, and natural history among the agricultural and meteorological advice that formed their cores. The new heliocentric astronomy, for example, found its way into American culture via this vehicle. Newspaper science was even more diverse, as were popular lectures, providing both education and entertainment. Toward the end of the colonial period, attempts began at the publication of magazines with varying degrees of interest in science, but financial problems meant that few lasted long.

For those seriously interested in science, the late colonial period saw the emergence of "American" rather than "colonial" learned and scientific institutions. Learned colonists banded together to share their interests and encourage each other first and most successfully in Philadelphia in Benjamin Franklin's Junto (1727), and slowly in other cities as well. In 1769 the Junto merged with Franklin's American Philosophical Society (1744) to become the American Philosophical Society Held at Philadelphia for Promoting Useful Knowledge, which remains one of the nation's leading learned societies today. Colonial libraries—those of the American Philosophical Society, the young colleges, and the library companies like the Redwood

Library at Newport, Rhode Island—began to develop collections that included scientific tracts. At the colonial colleges, where young men were trained for the ministry and other learned callings, science played a small but significant role in the curriculum as a piece of learned culture that was important to a full understanding of God's natural creations. As it became a reality that, in the words of Benjamin Franklin in 1743, "the first drudgery of settling new colonies which confines the attention of people to mere necessaries is now pretty well over; and there are men in every province in circumstances that set them at ease, and afford them the leisure to cultivate the finer arts and improve the common stock of knowledge," the institutions of science and the interest and support needed to sustain them emerged.[1]

Despite this development, however, science still remained primarily an activity or interest of the elite of society on the eve of the Revolution. Newspaper science and popular lectures aside, few Americans had the luxury of interest in science for its own sake. In the colonial upper class, men, and occasionally women, as Joan Hoff Wilson has observed, could pursue science, but most colonists, male or female, were occupied with more immediate concerns.[2]

In the wake of the Revolution, science took a back seat to the creation of a new nation in the public mind. Not all Americans saw science as a positive piece of the new nation. Young William Cullen Bryant reflected a sentiment popular among his elders in his 1809 poem "The Embargo" when he chastised President Thomas Jefferson for his scientific interests:

> Go, wretch, resign the presidential chair,
> Disclose thy secret measures, fowl or fair.
> Go, search with curious eye, for horned frogs,
> Mid the wild wastes of Louisianian bogs;
> Or, where Ohio rolls his turbid stream,
> Dig for huge bones, thy glory and thy theme.[3]

The British support that had been so important was no more, and no American structure was yet in place. The challenge, in the words of Franklin in 1785, was to make a reality of "the favourable influence that Freedom has upon the growth of useful Sciences and Arts." Science was shaped by nationalism and at the same time became a tool of nationalism. On the one hand, the promise of the utility of science and the potential national gain associated with scientific advance served to promote science. On the other, these same motivations dictated specific sorts of science and scientific culture over others. Geographic and observational sciences, most especially botany, zoology, and geology, which held dual promises of utility and illustration of the Creator's hand, thrived. Theoretical science, for example chemistry and physics, did less well.

The early nineteenth century saw the emergence of a new American science both in terms of its intellectual structure and its social structure. Emphasis on Scottish common-sense realism and adherence to an approach to science promoted long before by Francis Bacon that stressed fact gathering and observation produced a peculiarly American science, which was perceived as the handmaiden of religion. Nascent professionals and amateurs alike took interest in geology or botany because it not only would potentially yield practical knowledge that would better the nation, but also because it would lend an understanding of God. Discussions about the relationship of science and religion centered not over conflicts but rather over reconciliation. Scientists and theologians were more likely to argue that because one Creator was behind both revealed theology (based on the Bible) and natural theology (based on God's creations and works in the natural world) any conflicts between science and religion must be with errors of interpretation, than they were to assert that their field was correct to the exclusion of the other or that the two spheres were unrelated.

Among the institutions of the new nation were many that supported education and entertainment in a variety of fields, including science. The antebellum period saw gains in formal education of all sorts from primary schools through colleges, and science came out a winner at all levels. Children's readers were filled with essays on science and on natural theology, the academy curricula for both male and female students included heavy doses of science, and the antebellum college increasingly added courses in natural history and natural philosophy (physical sciences), while keeping classes in natural theology, all during a period when enrollment at each level was up. In the 1820s public lecturing became organized into the lyceum movement, which sponsored lecture series in towns across the country on a range of topics, many of them scientific. By the 1840s, Boston's Lowell Institute could attract audiences of 2,000 when a popular lecturer like Yale professor Benjamin Silliman held forth on science. Antebellum America was abuzz with reform movements and self-improvement schemes, and the promoters of science, not surprisingly, cast their pastime in this light. Scientific culture was woven into a larger mesh of piety, industriousness, and socially acceptable behavior. While institutions certainly encouraged this, they were not alone. Scientific textbooks, especially those that could be used equally well at home for self-instruction, became best sellers, and other publications followed suit. With a popular text such as Mrs. Almira Hart Lincoln Phelps's *Familiar Lectures on Botany* or *Botany for Beginners,* both best sellers, and a local field guide in hand, many antebellum Americans pursued science on their own as a valued pastime. This interest—both institutional and individual—in self-improvement led to a boom in publishing and shaped the nature of what was published.

The antebellum period saw the first long-lived American periodicals, including the first dedicated to science, the *Medical Repository* (1797), which covered both medicine and science, and Benjamin Silliman's *Amer-*

ican Journal of Science (1818). The *American Journal of Science,* known as Silliman's journal for its editor, never had a particularly big circulation even by nineteenth-century standards, but its impact on amateurs and professionals alike was nonetheless great. Throughout the century, it served to keep those interested in science abreast of the latest news and developments, though by late century it had begun to specialize in geology and was joined by a host of other periodicals. Some, like the *American Naturalist* (1867) and the *Scientific American* (1845), which began as a technical journal, focused on one area of science. Others, like the *Popular Science Monthly* (1872) (now *Popular Science*) and *Popular Astronomy* (1893), targeted lay people, while still others, like the *Botanical Gazette* (1875), targeted professionals.

Many of the new periodicals were organs of the new scientific societies, which increased exponentially as the century progressed. In towns and cities across the new nation the scientifically literate and curious banded together. Joining the ranks of general learned and scientific societies were specialized clubs—the Torrey Botanical Club and the Nuttall Ornithological Club to name but two—as well as, increasingly, societies that catered only to professionals—the Botanical Society of America, for example. Often one of the activities of a society was to publish a magazine—for example, the Torrey Botanical Club's *Bulletin* (1870). *Science* (1883) emerged as the organ of the American Association for the Advancement of Science and today remains the nation's most important scientific periodical.

Popular periodicals of a more general nature also included science, and indeed found it to be a topic that appealed to readers. Relatively intellectual periodicals like the *North American Review* (1815), *Southern Literary Messenger* (1834), *Harper's Magazine* (1850), or the *Atlantic Monthly* (1857) found scientific coverage to be well worth the space in terms of reader interest. Women's magazines—for example, *Godey's Lady's Book* (1830)—children's—for example, the *Youth's Companion* (1827) and *Merry's Museum and Parley's Magazine* (1842)—farmers'—for example, the *Country Gentleman* (1853)—all filled their pages with science. At the turn of the century, nature magazines sponsored by institutions gained importance. *National Geographic* (1888) emerged as a way for enthusiasts to support exploration—scientific and general—from their armchairs. *Audubon Magazine* (1899) gave them a way to support preservation. Museum publications like *Natural History* (1900) and, more recently, *Smithsonian* (1970/71) gave them a way to support research and education.

Museums, botanical gardens, zoological parks, and observatories all walked the line between education and entertainment as well. Beginning as a chance to display the wonders of God's handiwork as found in the objects of creation, they soon became not merely places for research and self-improvement, but places for entertainment as well. In part this was the nation's collecting mania on a grand scale. Children were exhorted to begin their own "museums" in books like Jacob Abbott's *Rollo's Museum,* and adults to support more formal institutions financially. Colleges, cities, private groups, and eventually the federal government as guardian of the bequest of James Smithson, a British enthusiast, all became the keepers of an array of scientific institutions that combined education and entertainment. From these sprung yet more periodicals, books, lecture series, expeditions, and, in more recent times, television shows and motion pictures.

The interest in nature spawned here gave rise to a literary genre of popular nature writing, which followed from the early accounts of colonists like Jefferson through the transcendentalists, most notably Henry David Thoreau and Ralph Waldo Emerson. Later in the century, more realistic and less romantic writers, including John Muir and John Burroughs, became popular. In the twentieth century, Aldo Leopold, Rachel Carson, and a host of modern writers on nature, of whom Lewis Thomas and Annie Dillard are but two, carried on the tradition.

Over time science became increasingly professionalized, and the directions in which professionals chose to push science were not always ones that sat well with the public. With the coming of Darwinian evolution and the revolution in physics, increasingly science became both the threat and the promise it is in modern America. Thermodynamics, which many American intellectuals felt implied decay, not progress, in the natural world and human society, and organic evolution, which heated already brewing controversies that remain with us yet today about the relationship of science and religion, cast an increasing shadow over science and the scientist.

The relationship between science and religion in American thought is immensely complex. On the one hand, religion and science provide a motivation for studying science, as the two can be, and often have been, seen to be talking about one and the same material, and hence each can enhance the other. Well into the nineteenth century scientific leaders and lay people alike saw natural theology—the study of God through his creation and actions in the natural world rather than through revelation—as one of the strongest reasons to pursue science. Conflicts between science and religion must be due to errors in interpretation, as one great author lay behind both the book of nature and the Bible. The American religious response to scientific theories in the nineteenth century thus was in large part determined by the role they left, implicitly or explicitly, for God in creating and governing the world. In the case of organic evolution, the responses ranged from complete acceptance of Darwinian evolution, to acceptance of evolution but not of natural selection, to rejection on the grounds of Biblical literalism. By late century, what had been a comfortable relation between science and religion was strained in some quarters, though certainly not all.

In the early twentieth century, conservative Christians began to worry about a variety of challenges to Biblical literalism, including the teaching of evolutionary theory, especially the notion that humans have evolved, in the public schools. Legislative attempts to ban the teaching of evolution ensued, and the Scopes trial—the so-called monkey trial—in Dayton, Tennessee, in 1925 became a major media event and brought the movement to the public eye. In the wake of the creationist victory in Dayton, textbook publishers softened or removed discussions of evolution from high school biology texts, and the issue quieted down until the early sixties, when a National Science Foundation funded textbook project—the Biological Sciences Curriculum Study—reintroduced evolution forcefully. The past twenty-five years have seen repeated attempts by creationists either to ban the teaching of evolution or to present it alongside the Biblical account of creation.

Through the works of one of Darwin's chief popularizers, Herbert Spencer, Americans became familiar with a dark side of evolution, competition and struggle. Spencer, whose essays were widely read in both collected volumes and in the *Popular Science Monthly,* adapted and modified Darwin's ideas to discuss human society. His followers, so-called Social Darwinists, believed that competition and survival of the fittest were not merely phenomena of nature but of human society as well. Literary naturalists—most especially Jack London—reflected the horror of this realization in their fiction, while social theorists used it to justify reform schemes that equated poverty and illness with "unfitness," and hence unworthiness to survive. This reached its nadir in America in the eugenics movement, which sought to influence the human gene pool, and hence society, by immigration quotas and forced sterilization of groups perceived as "unfit" because of ethnicity, social class, or alleged "feeble-mindedness" or "criminal character," and through attempts to encourage the reproduction of the "fit." Changes in scientific understanding of heredity and the horrors of World War II brought these sorts of attempts largely to an end.

Despite this, the early twentieth century saw the high point of the public image of science and scientists in which scientists were portrayed as heroes and science as the key to all social reform. Throughout the Progressive era this positive image of science found embodiment in everything from food and drug legislation and workplace reforms to programs to help mothers and infants. Sinclair Lewis's *Arrowsmith* (1925) and Upton Sinclair's *The Jungle* (1906) stand as pillars of this imagery.

As the war era loomed, science was seen as the nation's best tool not only to win war but perhaps to prevent it. In the wake of World War II, however, such optimism was challenged by the growing realization that science could at once create and destroy. Concerns about nuclear weaponry and power, about genetic engineering, and about the environment all led to major debates about the nature and value of science. Even the space program, which stood as a symbol of what science could accomplish, has gone sour in the wake of the Challenger tragedy and the connection with the Strategic Defense Initiative (Star Wars).

The means by which Americans learn about science have changed dramatically. Books and periodicals are still chief agents. Stephen Jay Gould has joined the ranks of Loren Eisley, Isaac Asimov, Carl Sagan, and the host of other post-World War II writers whose scientific works have captured a popular audience. Science magazines have multiplied, and the standards—*Scientific American* and *National Geographic*—have been joined by a series of new journals. *Sky and Telescope* (1941), *Environment* (1959), and many other specialized popular periodicals emerged in mid-century. *Smithsonian* (which is a general magazine with a high science content) ushered in the seventies, a decade that saw a number of new science periodicals, most notably *Omni* (1978). The trend appeared to be continuing in the eighties, when *Discover* (1980) began publication, but the mid-eighties saw a number of science magazines die, perhaps because of waning interest but more probably because of competition not only among the many periodicals but from other media as well.

Print media are no longer the only show, or perhaps even the dominant show, in town in the eighties. From its earliest days television attempted to combine education and entertainment with "Mr. Wizard" and other science shows. "National Geographic" specials began running in 1965, and the seventies and eighties have seen a dramatic increase in both the quantity and quality of science shows. "NOVA" and other series and specials too numerous to list cater to all ages. "Newton's Apple" and "3–2–1 Contact" have brought children's science television a long way from the early days of "Mr. Wizard."

Increasingly in the postwar era, mass media have played a major role in determining the public's reaction to science. Breaking news on science and its effects is often presented as either miraculous—as is often the case with scientific breakthroughs that affect medicine—or disastrous—for example, the accident at Three Mile Island. Often, though, the situation is more complicated, with the potential of both great benefit and significant threat, as in the case of pesticides that can both improve crop production and cause environmental harm. Science and its byproducts have become neither savior nor demon but both, a Dr. Jekyll and Mr. Hyde in the public imagination.

REFERENCE WORKS

The general neglect of popular science is nowhere felt so clearly as in the dearth of reference works specifically aimed at the phenomenon. The most practical approach is to begin with the many works that aim at science generally and to winnow out popular works and studies of science and popular culture from among the mass of literature.

Finding one's way around the many bibliographies, encyclopedias, and other reference works on science is facilitated by Ching-Chih Chen's *Scientific and Technical Information Sources,* which is an annotated guide. Older primary and secondary sources on natural history can be located through

Max Meisel's *A Bibliography of American Natural History: The Pioneer Century, 1769–1865*. The *McGraw-Hill Encyclopedia of Science and Technology* and *The Harper Encyclopedia of Science*, edited by James R. Newman, provide good introductions to many subjects, as does the *Encyclopaedia Britannica*. The *McGraw-Hill Dictionary of Scientific and Technical Terms* and *The Penguin Dictionary of Science* are useful tools for deciphering specialized terminology.

Several guides to the historical sources are useful. The journal *Isis* publishes an annual critical bibliography of the history of science that includes works on science in American culture. Two cumulations of these bibliographies—Magda Whitrow's *Isis Cumulative Bibliography*, which covers 1913–65, and John Neu's *Isis Cumulative Bibliography, 1966–1975*—include detailed subject breakdowns by area of science, culture, and historical period. Hamilton Craven's "Science, Technology, and Medicine" and Marc Rothenberg's *The History of Science and Technology in the United States: A Critical and Selective Bibliography* both offer excellent guides to the literature on American science. The essays in Sally Gregory Kohlstedt and Margaret W. Rossiter's *Historical Writing on American Science: Perspectives and Prospects* offer critical appraisal of a number of fields and topics of interest, although none of the essays deals directly with science and popular culture.

Biographical studies of scientists abound. Living scientists are described briefly in *American Men and Women of Science*. Clark Elliott's *Biographical Dictionary of American Science: The Seventeenth Through the Nineteenth Centuries* provides a short sketch and bibliography for all but the most obscure. The most prominent deceased scientists are included in the *Dictionary of Scientific Biography*. The *Isis Cumulative Bibliographies* include biographical volumes.

RESEARCH COLLECTIONS

Many libraries in the United States have fine collections of popular science holdings. The Library of Congress and major public libraries are particularly apt to have popular—as opposed to academic—works. University and college libraries vary considerably in their approach to collecting popular works, though those with education schools often have very good collections. Those interested in the pre-Civil War period will find that since the lines between popular and scholarly science had not yet been firmly drawn, any major science collection with historic holdings is apt to be of interest. The best academic libraries in this regard are generally found at institutions with programs in the history of science. Those specifically interested in areas that touch on medicine should not overlook the National Library of Medicine in Bethesda, Maryland. Those interested in natural history will find valuable libraries at many museums, most notably the Academy of Natural Sciences in Philadelphia.

Those interested in specific scientists may find their papers and correspondence of interest. The location of collections can be found in the biographical sketches in Clark Elliott's *Biographical Dictionary of American Science* and the *Dictionary of Scientific Biography*. Pre-twentieth-century collections can be especially revealing about popular science as many amateurs corresponded with national luminaries. The Library of Congress and the American Philosophical Society in Philadelphia each hold extensive collections, but state historical societies, colleges, and universities also have important collections. Those specifically interested in women will find the holdings of the Schlesinger Library on the History of Women at Harvard University immensely valuable.

HISTORY AND CRITICISM

The past twenty-five years have seen a revolution in the historical study of science that has included a growing realization that science is both culturally bound and part of popular culture. The result is growing literatures on American science and science in American culture, both of which deserve our attention here. American historians have generally devoted little interest to science, even in their social and intellectual histories, but there are exceptions, and recent works suggest that the situation is improving. Merle Curti's *The Growth of American Thought* speaks eloquently about science as both intellectual and popular culture. Perry Miller's *The Life of the Mind in America: From the Revolution to the Civil War,* and unfinished posthumous work, provides an intriguing outline. Similarly, historians of American science have been more concerned with the scientific community and its work than with popular culture. George Daniels's *Science in American Society: A Social History,* though problematic, provides an introduction. The essays in Nathan and Ida Reingold's *The Sciences in the American Context: New Perspectives* explore a number of areas of science from different perspectives. Reingold's two volumes of documentary history—the second co-edited with Ida Reingold—provide insights to both professional and amateur scientists, but mostly the former.

More focused, chronological studies from both disciplines offer more on science in popular culture. Louis B. Wright's chapter on "Scientific Interest and Observation," in his *The Cultural Life of the American Colonies,* remains a classic. Brooke Hindle's *The Pursuit of Science in Revolutionary America* and the volume of essays from *Isis* he edited, *Early American Science,* cover both popular and professional science in the colonial era. Older, but still valuable and lively, is Dirk Struik's *Yankee Science in the Making.* Antebellum America has received major attention from historians of American science. John C. Greene's *American Science in the Age of Jefferson* joins George Daniels's *American Science in the Age of Jackson* to survey scientific developments. Greene's essay "Popular Science in the Age of Jefferson" (reprinted in Hindle, *Early American Science*) remains, with Donald Zochert's essays "Science and the

Common Man in Ante-bellum America" (reprinted in Reingold, *Science in America Since 1820*) and "The Natural History of an American Pioneer: A Case Study," as well as Walter Hendrickson's "Science and Culture in the American Middle West" (also reprinted in Reingold), the most explicit treatment of popular science. Howard Miller's *Dollars for Research* and A. Hunter Dupree's *Science in the Federal Government* offer insight into why Americans chose to fund science in the nineteenth century.

Robert Bruce's *The Launching of Modern American Science, 1846–1876* carries us through the Civil War in Pulitzer Prize-winning style. Paul Carter's *The Spiritual Crisis of the Gilded Age* provides a sense of American thought in the era. Cynthia Russett's *Darwin in America* and Paul Boller, Jr.'s *American Thought in Transition,* while topical, offer many insights into the relationship of science and social thought in this period, as does the more diverse collection of essays by Charles Rosenberg, *No Other Gods: On Science and American Social Thought.* Douglas Sloan's "Science in New York City" explores the place of science in one American city, while Oleson and Brown present essays on a variety of places and disciplines in *The Pursuit of Knowledge in the Early American Republic: American Scientific and Learned Societies from Colonial Times to the Civil War.*

Samuel Hays's *Conservation and the Social Gospel of Efficiency* illuminates the Progressives' concern with science. Ronald Tobey's *The American Ideology of National Science, 1919–1930* and his *Saving the Prairies: The Life Cycle of the Founding School of American Plant Ecology, 1895–1955* explore the interfaces of science and society. As even the rather narrow focus of these two works suggests, for other aspects of the twentieth century one is best off exploring the topical histories. Everett Mendelsohn's "Science in America: The Twentieth Century," though somewhat dated, provides an introduction to the era.

Daniel J. Kevles's *The Physicists,* which focuses on the emergence of a profession in America, provides a fine introduction and bibliography. One area of physical science where amateurs have and do participate is astronomy. Marc Rothenberg's "Organization and Control: Professionals and Amateurs in American Astronomy, 1899–1918" explores one aspect of this participation; Russell McCormmach's "Ormsby MacKnight Mitchell's *Sidereal Messenger,* 1846–48" explores another. Hyman Kuritz's "The Popularization of Science in Nineteenth-Century America" emphasizes physics, as does Linda Kerber's "Science in the Early Republic."

Natural history has had many chroniclers. Max Meisel's *Bibliography of American Natural History* offers a useful introduction and guide to sources. Joseph Kastner's general *A Species of Eternity* and his history of birdwatching, *A World of Watchers,* nicely blend the professional and amateur interests. Smallwood and Smallwood, *Natural History and the American Mind,* and Huth, *Nature and the American,* remain classics and are now complemented by Charlotte Porter's *The Eagles Nest: Natural History and American Ideas,*

1812–1842. Clive Bush's *The Dream of Reason* is a recent exploration of the cultural meaning of nature in America. Donald Worster's *Nature's Economy: A History of Ecological Ideas* explores the transformation of interest in nature into interest in the environment. Lynn Barber's *The Heyday of Natural History, 1820–1870* focuses heavily on Great Britain but does provide insight into America as well, while Wayne Hanley's *Natural History in America* provides biographical sketches of a handful of prominent figures. Peter Schmitt's *Back to Nature* provides an insightful look into why turn-of-the-century Americans grew so interested in the natural world.

Emanuel Rudolph's essays on amateur botany and botany education provide glimpses into one popular field. Marianne Ainley's "The Contribution of the Amateur to North American Ornithology" explores a field in which amateurs are still heavily involved. John Warner's " 'Exploring the Inner Labyrinths of Creation' " details popular microscopy in turn-of-the-century America.

It is at least arguable that no area of science has had more impact on popular culture than organic evolution, and historians have approached the topic from a number of angles. R. J. Wilson's *Darwinism and the American Intellectual* and George Daniels's *Darwinism Comes to America* both collect primary documents, including reviews, responses, and reflections. Ronald Numbers's essay "Science and Religion" in the Kohlstedt and Rossiter volume is a good introduction to both the broad intellectual response and the religious dimensions. Thomas Glick's *The Comparative Reception of Darwinism* includes valuable essays by Edward Pfeifer and Michele Aldrich on the United States. Stow Persons's *Evolutionary Thought in America* and Paul Boller's *American Thought in Transition* join Cynthia Russett's volume mentioned above to cover many aspects of evolutionary thought in America. William Coleman's essay on evolutionary themes in Frederick Jackson Turner's "frontier thesis" and Richard Hofstadter's classic *Social Darwinism in American Thought* explore some of the ways in which American intellectuals used evolutionary thought in nonbiological arenas. The reflection of biological thought in social theory predates Darwinism, as William Stanton's *The Leopard's Spots: Scientific Attitudes Towards Race in America, 1815–1859* amply demonstrates. Daniel Kevles's *In the Name of Eugenics* talks about the use and misuse of understandings of human heredity in America and Great Britain, while Stephen J. Gould's *The Mismeasure of Man* specifically outlines problems with early attempts to quantify fitness, especially intelligence. Dorothy Nelkin's *The Creation Controversy: Science or Scripture in the Schools,* Edward Larson's *Trial and Error,* and Ronald Numbers's "The Creationists" all discuss the debates between evolutionists and creationists in the twentieth century.

The interest in gardens, zoos, and museums spawned by natural history is now being documented. Charles Sellers's *Mr. Peale's Museum* presents a lively account of one of America's first natural history museums. Neil Harris's *Humbug: The Art of P. T. Barnum* and John Richards Betts's "P. T. Barnum and the Popularization of Natural History" recount one man's very successful attempt to blend entertainment and education. George Brown Goode's *The Smithsonian Institution, 1846–1896* and Paul Oehser's *Sons of Science: The Story of the Smithsonian Institution and Its Leaders* are old but invaluable. Geoffrey Hellman provides a more modern account in *The Smithsonian: Octopus on the Mall*. William Deiss's "Spencer F. Baird and His Collectors," Phillip Kopper's *The National Museum of Natural History*, and Curtis Hinsley's *Savages and Scientists: The Smithsonian Institution and the Development of American Anthropology, 1846–1910* provide more focused accounts. Philip J. Pauly's "The World and All That Is in It: The National Geographic Society, 1888–1918" and Nancy Lurie's *A Special Style: The Milwaukee Public Museum, 1882–1982* describe two other institutions. Ann Leighton's volumes on gardens and Jeffery Stott's "The Historical Origins of the Zoological Park in American Thought" are among the only historical Treatments of these forms of entertainment and education.

Well into the nineteenth century, learned and scientific societies served as an interface between popular culture and academic science. The standard source on American scientific societies is Ralph Bates's *Scientific Societies in the United States*, which, while somewhat dated, remains the only survey. Max Meisel's *Bibliography* lists many of the smaller societies, as well as the more major ones, and provides bibliographical material. Douglas Sloan's "Science in New York City, 1867–1907" provides a good account of the cultural meaning and import of scientific societies in one time and place. Many individual societies have been the subject of study. Raymond Stearns's *Science in the British Colonies of North America* focuses on the role of the Royal Society of London. The American Association for the Advancement of Science, modern America's most important scientific society, is the subject of Sally Gregory Kohlstedt's *The Formation of the American Scientific Community*. Alexandra Oleson and Sanborn Brown's *The Pursuit of Knowledge in the Early American Republic* and Alexandra Oleson and John Voss's *The Organization of Knowledge in Modern America, 1860–1920* both contain many useful articles on societies. Walter Hendrickson's *The Arkites, and Other Pioneer Natural History Organizations of Cleveland* details both the learned and the social activities of a Cleveland society. Sally Gregory Kohlstedt's "The Nineteenth-Century Amateur Tradition: The Case of the Boston Society of Natural History" discusses the changing role of amateurs as science became increasingly professionalized.

Schools are an immensely important vehicle for the dissemination of popular science. Ruth Elson's *Guardians of Tradition* explores the content of nineteenth-century textbooks. Emanuel Rudolph's "The Introduction of the Natural System of Classification of Plants to Nineteenth Century American Students" examines the importance of one idea. Stanley Guralnick's *Science in the Antebellum America Colleges* explores how and why science made its way into higher education.

In the days before mass communication, public lecturing on science was a popular form of entertainment and edification. Carl Bode's *The American Lyceum: Town Meeting of the Mind* chronicles the popular lecture movement of the nineteenth century. Margaret Rossiter's "Benjamin Silliman and the Lowell Institute" and Edward Weeks's *The Lowells and Their Institute* discuss the most important of the sponsors of public lectures.

The popular magazine still awaits a history. Frank Luther Mott's *A History of American Magazines* is an invaluable tool, despite being dated and sometimes inaccurate, because it has not been surpassed. Donald Beaver's "Altruism, Patriotism and Science: Scientific Journals in the Early Republic" and Mathew D. Whalen and Mary F. Tobin's "Periodicals and the Popularization of Science in America, 1860–1910" are two of the few studies of scientific periodicals specifically. Two popular periodicals have been the subject of individual studies. The *Popular Science Monthly* and its editor are the subject of William E. Leverette, Jr.'s "E. C. Youmans' Crusade for Scientific Autonomy and Respectability." Russell McCormmach's "Ormsby MacKnight Mitchell's *Sidereal Messenger,* 1846–48" examines a short-lived but important popular astronomy magazine. Dorothy Nelkin examines contemporary science journalism in *Selling Science: How the Press Covers Science and Technology.* Thomas Maugh's "The Media: The Image of the Scientist Is Bad" examines the content of reporting, rather than the format.

A number of specific issues have caught the media's attention over the years. The relationship of science and religion has in recent years galvanized around controversies surrounding the teaching of evolution as described above, but the background and setting for that debate are too often overlooked. Wendell Glick's "Bishop Paley in America" recounts the teaching of natural theology in early America. Theodore Bozeman's *Protestants in an Age of Science* and Herbert Hovenkamp's *Science and Religion in America, 1800–1860* both explore the interaction of Protestant theology and Baconian science. Ronald Numbers's *Creation by Natural Law* explores the religious influence on and reaction to one scientific theory, Laplace's "nebular hypothesis." Herbert Leventhal's *In the Shadow of the Enlightenment: Occultism and Renaissance Science in Eighteenth-Century America* and Laurence Moore's *In Search of White Crows: Spiritualism, Parapsychology, and American Culture* examine two aspects of the relationship of pseudo-science and religion.

Other aspects of science have also attracted much public attention. In modern America concern about the real or potential perils of science has led to a situation where potential benefits must be weighed against possible risk. Nuclear power and weaponry, developments in genetics, and environmental concerns are but three of the best documented. Paul Boyer's *By the Bomb's Early Light: American Thought and Culture at the Dawn of the Atomic Age* surveys the popular response to the promise and the threat of nuclear weaponry. Clifford Grobstein's *A Double Image of the Double Helix: The Recombinant-DNA Debate* and John Richards's *Recombinant DNA: Science, Ethics, and Politics* chronicle public and professional response to advances in genetics. Rachel Carson's *Silent Spring* touched off public concern about the environment that had been smoldering beneath the surface. James Whorton's *Before Silent Spring* and Thomas Dunlap's *DDT* recount the background to Carson's concerns. Frank Graham's *Since Silent Spring* describes the aftermath.

Many of the best entryways to popular science are biographies of both prominent and lesser-known scientists. Works on prominent scientists are so numerous that only a few of the best can be listed here. The Berkeleys' biography of naturalist John Bartram provides a glimpse of colonial scientific culture. A. Hunter Dupree's life of botanist Asa Gray and Edward Lurie's of zoologist Louis Agassiz illustrate a fascinating contrast in scientific style and reaction to Darwinism. Tamara Haygood's biography of botanist Henry William Ravenel locates science in its southern context, while David Livingstone's biography of Nathaniel Southgate Shaler illustrates how those on the border of science and culture translated science to the broader world in the late nineteenth century. Kenneth Manning has eloquently described the life of a black biologist, Ernest Just, in *Black Apollo of Science*. The impact of science on women's lives in nineteenth-century America is explored in Deborah Jean Warner's biography of Graceanna Lewis.

Other aspects of women's interaction with science have recently begun to receive attention from historians. Margaret Rossiter's *Women Scientists in America: Struggles and Strategies to 1940* discusses the pursuit of science by women and includes an extensive bibliography. Patricia Siegel and Kay Finley's *Women in the Scientific Search* provides further bibliographic help. Joan Hoff Wilson's "Dancing Dogs" makes a case that colonial women were surprisingly involved in science. Deborah Jean Warner describes the entry of science into the female academy curriculum in "Science Education for Young Women in Ante-bellum America." Emanuel Rudolph has explored the special relationship of women and botany, especially the role of Almira Hart Lincoln Phelps, in a series of articles. Laura Shapiro examines the impact of modern nutrition on female nonscientists in *Perfection Salad: Women and Cooking at the Turn of the Century*.

Finally, in late 1987, the role of science in American popular culture, long treated in the fragmentary fashion suggested above, was the subject of a book: John C. Burnham's *How Superstition Won and Science Lost: Popularizing Science and Health in the United States*. In it Burnham explores how popular science diverged from professional science to the detriment of public understanding. Superstition, Burnham argues, is alive and well in the public mind, having beaten out scientific enlightenment, in large part because of the nature of popularization. The volume offers a very rich plate of ideas and is well documented. Those interested in science as popular culture in America would do well to begin here.

ANTHOLOGIES AND REPRINTS

Few collections of either primary or secondary works have appeared, but those that have are valuable. George Daniels's *Darwinism Comes to America* and Robert Wilson's *Darwinism and the American Intellectual: A Book of Readings* both contain reviews and reflections. They present startlingly different focuses that remind the reader how much more we have to learn about the reception of Darwinism. Two collections of articles previously printed in *Isis* are also of special interest: Nathan Reingold's *Science in America Since 1820* and Brooke Hindle's *Early American Science*.

NOTES

1. Quoted in Brooke Hindle, *The Pursuit of Science in Revolutionary America* (New York: W. W. Norton, 1974), p. 1.
2. Joan Hoff Wilson, "Dancing Dogs of the Colonial Period: Women Scientists," *Early American Literature,* 7 (1973), 225.
3. William Cullen Bryant, *The Embargo* (Gainesville, Fla.: Scholar's Facsimiles and Reprints, 1955), p. 40 (facsimile of the 1808 and 1809 editions).

BIBLIOGRAPHY

Books and Articles

AAAS Science Book List: A Selected and Annotated List of Science and Mathematics Books for Secondary School Students, College Undergraduates and Nonspecialists. 3rd ed. Washington, D.C.: AAAS, 1970.

AAAS Science Book List Supplement. Edited by Katheryn Wolff and Jill Story. Washington, D.C.: AAAS, 1978.

AAAS Science Film Catalog. Compiled by Ann Seltz-Petrash and Katheryn Wolff. New York: R. R. Bowker and AAAS, 1975.

Abbott, Jacob. *Rollo's Museum.* Boston: Weeks, Jordon, 1839.

Ainley, Marianne Gostonyi. "The Contribution of the Amateur to North American Ornithology: A Historical Perspective." *The Living Bird,* 18 (1979), 161–77.

Aldrich, Michele L. "United States Bibliographic Essay." In *The Comparative Reception of Darwinism.* Edited by Thomas F. Glick. Austin: University of Texas Press, 1972.

American Men and Women of Science. Edited by Jaques Cattell. 15th ed. 15 vols. New York: R. R. Bowker, 1982.

Ash, Lee. *Subject Collections: A Guide to Special Book Collections and Subject Emphasis as Reported by University, College, Public and Special Libraries and Museums in the United States and Canada.* 6th ed. New York: R. R. Bowker, 1985.

Asimov, Isaac. *Asimov's Biographical Encyclopedia of Science and Technology*. 2nd rev. ed. Garden City, N.Y.: Doubleday, 1982.

———. *Asimov's New Guide to Science*. New York: Basic Books, 1984.

Barber, Lynn. *The Heyday of Natural History, 1820–1870*. Garden City, N.Y.: Doubleday, 1980.

Basalla, George. "Pop Science: The Depiction of Science in Popular Culture." In *Science and Its Public: The Changing Relationship*. Edited by Gerald Holton and William A. Blanpied. Dordrecht, Holland: Reidel, 1976.

Bates, Ralph S. *Scientific Societies in the United States*. New York: Technology Press, 1958. 3rd ed. Cambridge, Mass.: MIT Press, 1965.

Beaver, Donald deB. "Altruism, Patriotism and Science: Scientific Journals in the Early Republic." *American Studies*, 12 (1971), 5–19.

———. *The American Scientific Community, 1800–1860: A Statistical-Historical Study*. New York: Arno Press, 1980.

Bender, Thomas. "Science and the Culture of American Communities: The Nineteenth Century." *History of Education Quarterly*, 16 (1976), 63–77.

Berkeley, Edmund, and Dorothy Smith Berkeley. *The Life and Travels of John Bartram: From Lake Ontario to the River St. John*. Tallahassee: University Presses of Florida, 1982.

Besterman, Theodore. *Biological Sciences: A Bibliography of Bibliographies*. Totowa, N.J.: Rowman and Littlefield, 1971.

———. *Physical Sciences: A Bibliography of Bibliographies*. Totowa, N.J.: Rowman and Littlefield, 1971.

Betts, John Richards. "P. T. Barnum and the Popularization of Natural History." *Journal of the History of Ideas*, 20 (1959), 353–68.

Black, George W., Jr. *American Science and Technology: A Bicentennial Bibliography*. Carbondale and Edwardsville: Southern Illinois University Press, 1979.

Bode, Carl. *The American Lyceum: Town Meeting of the Mind*. New York: Oxford University Press, 1956.

Boller, Paul, Jr. *American Thought in Transition: The Impact of Evolutionary Naturalism, 1865–1900*. Chicago: Rand McNally, 1969.

Boyer, Paul S. *By the Bomb's Early Light: American Thought and Culture at the Dawn of the Atomic Age*. New York: Pantheon, 1985.

Bozeman, Theodore Dwight. *Protestants in an Age of Science: The Baconian Ideal and Antebellum American Religious Thought*. Chapel Hill: University of North Carolina Press, 1977.

Bronowski, Jacob. *The Ascent of Man*. Boston: Little, Brown, 1973.

Bruce, Robert. *The Launching of Modern American Science, 1846–1876*. New York: Alfred A. Knopf, 1987.

Bryant, William Cullen. *The Embargo*. Facsimile of 1808 and 1809 editions, with introduction and notes by Thomas O. Mabbott. Gainesville, Fla.: Scholar's Facsimiles and Reprints, 1955.

Buckman, Thomas R., ed. *Bibliography and Natural History*. Lawrence: University of Kansas, 1966.

Burnham, John C. *How Superstition Won and Science Lost: Popularizing Science and Health in the United States*. New Brunswick, N.J.: Rutgers University Press, 1987.

Bush, Clive. *The Dream of Reason: American Conciousness and Cultural Achievement from Independence to the Civil War*. London: Edward Arnold, 1977.

Carson, Rachel. *Silent Spring*. Boston: Houghton Mifflin, 1962.

Carter, Paul A. "Science and the Common Man." *American Scholar*, 45 (1975–76), 778–94.

————. *The Spiritual Crisis of the Gilded Age*. DeKalb: Northern Illinois University Press, 1971.

Catalog of Motion Pictures and Filmstrips for Rent and Sale by the National Audiovisual Center, 1969. Supplements, 1971– . Washington, D.C.: National Audiovisual Center, 1971.

Chen, Ching-Chih. *Scientific and Technical Information Sources*. Cambridge, Mass.: MIT Press, 1987.

Clapp, Jane, ed. *Museum Publications*. 2 vols. Metuchen, N.J.: Scarecrow Press, 1962.

Coleman, William. "Science and Symbol in the Turner Frontier Hypothesis." *American Historical Review*, 72 (1966), 22–49.

Cravens, Hamilton. "Science, Technology, and Medicine." In *American Studies: An Annotated Bibliography*. Edited by J. Salzman. Cambridge, England: Cambridge University Press, 1988.

Curti, Merle. *The Growth of American Thought*. 3rd ed. New Brunswick, N.J.: Transition Books, 1982.

Daniels, George H. *American Science in the Age of Jackson*. New York: Columbia University Press, 1968.

————. *Darwinism Comes to America*. New York: Blaisdell, 1968.

————. *Nineteenth-Century American Science: A Reappraisal*. Evanston, Ill.: Northwestern University Press, 1972.

————. *Science in American Society: A Social History*. New York: Alfred A. Knopf, 1971.

Deiss, William A. "Spencer F. Baird and His Collectors." *Journal of the Society for the Bibliography of Natural History*, 9 (1980), 635–45.

de Ropp, Robert S. *The New Prometheans: Creative and Destructive Forces in Modern Science*. New York: Dell, 1973.

de Tocqueville, Alexis. *Democracy in America*. Edited by Henry Reeve, Francis Bowen, and Philips Bradley. New York: Alfred A. Knopf, 1966.

De Young, Greg. "Postage Stamps and the Popular Iconography of Science." *Journal of American Culture*, 9 (Summer 1986), 1–13.

Dictionary of Scientific Biography. 16 vols. New York: Scribner's, 1970–80.

Dillard, Annie. *Pilgrim at Tinker's Creek*. New York: Harper's Magazine Press, 1974.

Documentary Film Classics Produced by the United States Government. Washington, D.C.: National Audio Visual Center, 1980.

Dunlap, Thomas R. *DDT: Scientists, Citizens, and Public Policy*. Princeton, N.J.: Princeton University Press, 1981.

Dupree, A. Hunter. *Asa Gray, 1810–1888*. New York: Atheneum, 1968.

————. *Science in the Federal Government: A History of Policies and Activities to 1940*. Cambridge, Mass.: Belknap Press of Harvard University Press, 1957.

Eiseley, Loren. *Darwin's Century: Evolution and the Men Who Discovered It*. Garden City, N.Y.: Doubleday, 1958.

————. *The Firmament of Time*. New York: Atheneum, 1962.

————. *The Immense Journey*. New York: Random House, 1957.

————. *The Unexpected Universe*. New York: Harcourt Brace Jovanovich, 1969.

Elliot, Clark A. *Biographical Dictionary of American Science: The Seventeenth Through the Nineteenth Centuries*. Westport, Conn.: Greenwood Press, 1979.

Elson, Ruth Miller. *Guardians of Tradition: American Textbooks of the Nineteenth Century*. Lincoln: University of Nebraska Press, 1964.

Encyclopaedia Britannica. 15th ed. Chicago: Encyclopaedia Britannica, 1972.

Etzioni, Amitai, and Clyde Nunn. "The Public Appreciation of Science in Contemporary America." In *Science and Its Public: The Changing Relationship*. Edited by Gerald Holton and William A. Blanpied. Dordrecht, Holland: Reidel, 1976.

Ewan, Joseph. *Rocky Mountain Naturalists*. Denver: University of Denver Press, 1950.

Foerster, Norman. *Nature in American Literature: Studies in the Modern View of Nature*. New York: Russell and Russell, 1958.

Gardner, Martin. *Fads and Fallacies in the Name of Science*. New York: Dover, 1957.

Geiser, Samuel Wood. *Naturalists on the Frontier*. Dallas: Southern Methodist University Press, 1937.

Glass, Bentley. "The Scientist in Contemporary Fiction." *Scientific Monthly*, 85 (1957), 288–93.

Glick, Thomas F., ed. *The Comparative Reception of Darwinism*. Austin: University of Texas Press, 1972.

Glick, Wendell. "Bishop Paley in America." *New England Quarterly*, 27 (1954), 347–54.

Goetzman, William H. *Exploration and Empire: The Explorer and the Scientist in the Winning of the American West*. New York: W. W. Norton, 1966.

Goode, George B. *The Smithsonian Institution, 1846–1896: The History of Its First Half Century*. Washington, D.C.: Smithsonian Institution, 1897.

Gould, Stephen Jay. *Ever Since Darwin: Reflections in Natural History*. New York: W. W. Norton, 1979.

————. *The Flamingo's Smile: Reflections in Natural History*. New York: W. W. Norton, 1985.

————. *Hen's Teeth and Horse's Toes*. New York: W. W. Norton, 1983.

————. *The Mismeasure of Man*. New York: W. W. Norton, 1981.

————. *The Panda's Thumb: More Reflections in Natural History*. New York: W. W. Norton, 1983.

Graham, Frank. *Since Silent Spring*. Boston: Houghton Mifflin, 1970.

Green, Harvey. "Popular Science and Political Thought Converge: Colonial Survival Becomes Colonial Revival, 1830–1910." *Journal of American Culture*, 6 (Fall 1983), 3–24.

Greene, John C. *American Science in the Age of Jefferson*. Ames: Iowa State University Press, 1984.

Greene, Mott T. *Geology in the Nineteenth Century: Changing Views of a Changing World*. Ithaca, N.Y.: Cornell University Press, 1982.

Grobstein, Clifford. *A Double Image of the Double Helix: The Recombinant-DNA Debate*. San Francisco: Freeman, 1979.

Grogan, Denis J. *Science and Technology: An Introduction to the Literature*. Hamden, Conn.: Archon Books, 1970.

Guralnick, Stanley M. *Science and the AnteBellum American Colleges*. Memoirs, Vol. 109. Philadelphia: American Philosophical Society, 1975.

Handlin, Oscar. "Science and Technology in Popular Culture: A Study of Cohesive and Disjunctive Forces." *Daedalus*, 94 (Winter 1965), 156–70. Reprinted in *Science and Culture*. Edited by Gerald Holton. Boston: Houghton Mifflin, 1965.

Hanley, Wayne. *Natural History in America: From Mark Catsby to Rachel Carson*. New York: Quadrangle/New York Times Books, 1977.

Harris, Neil. *Humbug: The Art of P. T. Barnum*. New York: Little, Brown, 1973.

Haygood, Tamara Miner. *Henry William Ravenel, 1814–1887: South Carolina Scientist in the Civil War Era*. Tuscaloosa: University of Alabama Press, 1987.

Hays, Samuel P. *Conservation and the Gospel of Efficiency: The Progressive Conservation Movement, 1890–1920*. Cambridge, Mass.: Harvard University Press, 1959.

Hellman, Geoffrey. *The Smithsonian: Octopus on the Mall*. Philadelphia: J. B. Lippincott, 1967.

Hendrickson, Walter. *The Arkites, and Other Pioneer Natural History Organizations of Cleveland*. Makers of Cleveland series, No. 1. Cleveland: Press of Western Reserve University, 1962.

Herbert, Don. *Mr. Wizard's Science Secrets*. 2nd ed. New York: Hawthorn Books, 1973.

Herbert, Don, and Hy Ruchlis. *Mr. Wizard's Science Activities*. New York: Book-Lab, 1973.

Hindle, Brooke. *The Pursuit of Science in Revolutionary America*. 1956. Reprint. New York: W. W. Norton, 1974.

———, ed. *Early American Science*. New York: Science History Publications, 1976.

Hinsley, Curtis J. *Savages and Scientists: The Smithsonian Institution and the Development of American Anthropology, 1846–1910*. Washington, D.C.: Smithsonian Institution Press, 1980.

Hofstadter, Richard. *Social Darwinism in American Thought*. Rev. ed. Boston: Beacon Press, 1955.

Holton, Gerald. "Modern Science and the Intellectual Tradition." *Science*, 131 (1960), 1187–93.

Holton, Gerald, and William A. Blanpied. *Science and Its Public: The Changing Relationship*. Dordrecht, Holland: Reidel, 1976.

Hovenkamp, Herbert. *Science and Religion in America, 1800–1860*. Philadelphia: University of Pennsylvania Press, 1978.

Huth, Hans. *Nature and the American: Three Centuries of Changing Attitudes*. Berkeley: University of California Press, 1957.

Jaffe, Bernard. *Men of Science in America*. New York: Simon and Schuster, 1944.

Jenkins, Frances B. *Science Reference Sources*. 5th ed. Cambridge, Mass.: MIT Press, 1969.

Johnson Thomas C., Jr. *Scientific Interests in the Old South*. New York: Appleton-Century, 1936.

Judson, Horace F. *The Eighth Day of Creation: Makers of the Revolution in Biology*. New York: Simon and Schuster, 1979.

Kastner, Joseph. *A Species of Eternity*. New York: Alfred A. Knopf, 1977.

———. *A World of Watchers*. New York: Alfred A. Knopf, 1986.

Kerber, Linda K. "Science in the Early Republic: The Society for the Study of Natural Philosophy." *William and Mary Quarterly,* 29 (1972), 263–80.

Kevles, Daniel J. *In the Name of Eugenics: Genetics and the Uses of Human Heredity.* New York: Alfred A. Knopf, 1985.

———. *The Physicists: The History of a Scientific Community in Modern America.* New York: Alfred A. Knopf, 1978.

Kohlstedt, Sally Gregory. *The Formation of the American Scientific Community: The American Association for the Advancement of Science, 1848–60.* Urbana: University of Illinois Press, 1976.

———. "The Nineteenth-Century Amateur Tradition: The Case of the Boston Society of Natural History." In *Science and Its Public: The Changing Relationship.* Edited by Gerald Holton and William A. Blanpied. Dordrecht, Holland: Reidel, 1976.

Kohlstedt, Sally Gregory, and Margaret W. Rossiter. *Historical Writing on American Science: Perspectives and Prospects.* Baltimore: Johns Hopkins University Press, 1986.

Kopper, Philip. *The National Museum of Natural History.* New York: Harry N. Abrams, 1982.

Kranz, Stewart. *Science and Technology in the Arts.* New York: Van Nostrand Reinhold, 1974.

Kuritz, Hyman. "The Popularization of Science in Nineteenth-Century America." *History of Education Quarterly,* 21 (1981), 259–74.

La Follette, Marcel Chotkoski. *The Citizen and Science: Almanac and Annotated Bibliography.* Bloomington, Ind.: Poynter Center on American Institutions, 1977.

Larson, Edward J. *Trial and Error: The American Controversy over Creation and Evolution.* New York: Oxford University Press, 1985.

Lasworth, Earl James. *Reference Sources in Science and Technology.* Metuchen, N.J.: Scarecrow Press, 1972.

Leighton, Ann. *American Gardens in the Eighteenth Century: "For Use or for Delight."* Amherst: University of Massachusetts Press, 1986.

———. *American Gardens of the Nineteenth Century: "For Comfort and Affluence."* Amherst: University of Massachusetts Press, 1987.

———. *Early American Gardens: "For Meat or Medicine."* Amherst: University of Massachusetts Press, 1986.

Leventhal, Herbert. *In the Shadow of the Enlightenment: Occultism and Renaissance Science in Eighteenth-Century America.* New York: New York University Press, 1976.

Leverette, William E., Jr. "E. C. Youmans' Crusade for Scientific Autonomy and Respectability." *American Quarterly,* 17 (1965), 12–32.

Lewis, Sinclair. *Arrowsmith.* New York: Harcourt Brace, 1925.

Livingstone, David N. *Nathaniel Southgate Shaler and the Culture of American Science.* Tuscaloosa: University of Alabama Press, 1987.

London, Jack. *Martin Eden.* New York: Macmillan, 1909.

Lurie, Edward. *Louis Agassiz: A Life in Science.* Chicago: University of Chicago Press, 1960.

Lurie, Nancy Oestereich. *A Special Style: The Milwaukee Public Museum, 1882–1982.* Milwaukee: Milwaukee Public Museum, 1984.

McCormmach, Russell. "Ormsby MacKnight Mitchell's *Sidereal Messenger*, 1846–48." *Proceedings of the American Philosophical Society*, 110 (1960), 35–47.

McGraw-Hill Dictionary of Scientific and Technical Terms. New York: McGraw-Hill, 1984.

McGraw-Hill Encyclopedia of Science and Technology. 6th ed. 20 vols. New York: McGraw-Hill, 1987.

McGraw-Hill Modern Scientists and Engineers. 3 vols. New York: McGraw-Hill, 1980.

Malinowsky, H. Robert. *Science and Engineering Literature: A Guide to Reference Sources.* 3rd ed. Littleton, Colo.: Libraries Unlimited, 1980.

Manning, Kenneth. *Black Apollo of Science: The Life of Ernest Everett Just.* New York: Oxford University Press, 1983.

Maugh, Thomas H., II. "The Media: The Image of the Scientist Is Bad." *Science,* 200 (April 7, 1978), 37.

Meisel, Max. *A Bibliography of American Natural History: The Pioneer Century, 1769–1865.* 3 vols. 1924. Facsimile reprint. New York: Hafner Publishing, 1967.

Mendelsohn, Everett. "Science in America: The Twentieth Century." In *Paths of American Thought.* Edited by A. M. Schlesinger, Jr., and M. White. Boston: Houghton Mifflin, 1963.

Miller, Howard S. *Dollars for Research: Science and Its Patrons in Nineteenth-Century America.* Seattle: University of Washington Press, 1970.

Miller, Perry. *The Life of the Mind in America: From the Revolution to the Civil War.* New York: Harcourt Brace and World, 1965.

Moore, Laurence. *In Search of White Crows: Spiritualism, Parapsychology, and American Culture.* New York: Oxford University Press, 1977.

Mott, Frank Luther. *A History of American Magazines.* 5 vols. Cambridge, Mass.: Harvard University Press, 1938–68.

National Geographic Index, 1888–1946; 1947–1983. 2 vols. Washington, D.C.: National Geographic Society, 1984.

Nelkin, Dorothy. *The Creation Controversy: Science or Scripture in the Schools.* New York: W. W. Norton, 1982.

———. *Science Textbook Controversies and the Politics of Equal Time.* Cambridge, Mass.: MIT Press, 1977.

———. *Selling Science: How the Press Covers Science and Technology.* New York: Freeman, 1987.

Neu, John, ed. *Isis Cumulative Bibliography, 1966–1975.* 2 vols. London: Mansell, 1980.

Newman, James R., ed. *The Harper Encyclopedia of Science.* Rev. ed. New York: Harper and Row, 1967.

NOVA Science Adventures on Television: A Series of Reading Lists. Boston: Boston Public Library, 1974.

Numbers, Ronald L. *Creation by Natural Law: Laplace's Nebular Hypothesis in America.* Seattle: University of Washington Press, 1977.

———. "The Creationists." In *God and Nature: Historical Essays on the Encounter Between Christianity and Science.* Edited by David C. Lindberg and Ronald L. Numbers. Berkeley: University of California Press, 1986.

Oehser, Paul H. *Sons of Science: The Story of the Smithsonian Institution and Its Leaders.* New York: Schuman, 1949.

Oleson, Alexandra, and Sanborn C. Brown, eds. *The Pursuit of Knowledge in the*

Early American Republic: American Scientific and Learned Societies from Colonial Times to the Civil War. Baltimore: Johns Hopkins University Press, 1976.

Oleson, Alexandra, and John Voss, eds. *The Organization of Knowledge in Modern America, 1860–1920*. Baltimore: Johns Hopkins University Press, 1979.

Pauly, Philip J. "The World and All That Is in It: The National Geographic Society, 1888–1918." *American Quarterly*, 31 (1979), 517–32.

The Penguin Dictionary of Science. New York: Schocken Books, 1972.

Persons, Stow, ed. *Evolutionary Thought in America*. New Haven: Yale University Press, 1950. Reprint. New York: Archon Books, 1968.

Pfeifer, Edward J. "United States." In *The Comparative Reception of Darwinism*. Edited by Thomas F. Glick. Austin: University of Texas Press, 1972.

[Phelps,] Almira Hart Lincoln. *Botany for Beginners*. Hartford: F. J. Huntington, 1833.

———. *Familiar Lectures on Botany*. Hartford: H. and F. J. Huntington, 1829.

Porter, Charlotte. *The Eagles Nest: Natural History and American Ideas, 1812–1842*. University: University of Alabama Press, 1986.

Pure and Applied Science Books, 1876–1982. New York: R. R. Bowker, 1982.

Reingold, Nathan, ed. *Science in America Since 1820*. New York: Science History, 1976.

———, ed. *Science in Nineteenth-Century America: A Documentary History*. New York: Hill and Wang, 1964.

———, ed. *The Sciences in the American Context: New Perspectives*. Washington, D.C.: Smithsonian Institution Press, 1979.

Reingold, Nathan, and Ida H. Reingold, eds. *Science in America: A Documentary History, 1900–1939*. Chicago: University of Chicago Press, 1981.

Richards, John, ed. *Recombinant DNA: Science, Ethics, and Politics*. New York: Academic Press, 1978.

Rosenberg, Charles E. *No Other Gods: On Science and American Social Thought*. Baltimore: Johns Hopkins University Press, 1976.

Rossiter, Margaret W. "Benjamin Silliman and the Lowell Institute: The Popularization of Science in Nineteenth-Century America." *New England Quarterly*, 44 (December 1971), 602–26.

———. *Women Scientists in America: Struggles and Strategies to 1940*. Baltimore: Johns Hopkins University Press, 1982.

Rothenberg, Marc. *The History of Science and Technology in the United States: A Critical and Selective Bibliography*. New York: Garland, 1982.

———. "Organization and Control: Professionals and Amateurs in American Astronomy, 1899–1918." *Social Studies of Science*, 11 (1918), 305–25.

Rudolph, Emanuel D. "Almira Hart Lincoln Phelps (1793–1884) and the Spread of Botany in Nineteenth Century America," *American Journal of Botany*, 71 (1984), 1161–67.

———. "Botany in American and British Chapbooks Before 1860." *Plant Science Bulletin*, 19 (1973), 34–36.

———. "How It Developed That Botany Was the Science Thought Most Suitable for Victorian Young Ladies." *Children's Literature*, 2 (1973), 92–97.

———. "The Introduction of the Natural System of Classification of Plants to Nineteenth Century American Students." *Archives of Natural History*, 10 (1982), 461–68.

————. "Women in Nineteenth Century American Botany: A Generally Unrecognized Constituency." *American Journal of Botany,* 69 (1982), 1346–55.

Russett, Cynthia E. *Darwin in America: The Intellectual Response, 1865–1912.* San Francisco: Freeman, 1976.

Sagan, Carl. *Broca's Brain: Reflections on the Romance of Science.* New York: Random House, 1979.

————. *Cosmos.* New York: Random House, 1980.

————. *The Dragons of Eden: Speculations on the Evolution of Human Intelligence.* New York: Random House, 1977.

Schmitt, Peter J. *Back to Nature: The Arcadian Myth in Urban America.* New York: Oxford University Press, 1969.

Science Year: The World Book Science Annual. Chicago: Field Enterprises Educational, 1965–.

Sellers, Charles Coleman. *Mr. Peale's Museum: Charles Wilson Peale and the First Popular Museum of Natural History and Art.* New York: W. W. Norton, 1980.

Shapiro, Laura. *Perfection Salad: Women and Cooking at the Turn of the Century.* New York: Holt, 1986.

Shinn, Terry, and Richard Whitley, eds. *Expository Science: Forms and Functions of Popularisation.* Dordrecht, Holland: Reidel, 1985.

Shurter, Robert L. *The Utopian Novel in America, 1865–1900.* New York: AMS Press, 1973.

Siegel, P. J., and Kay T. Finley. *Women in the Scientific Search: An American Biobibliography, 1724–1979.* Metuchen, N.J: Scarecrow Press, 1985.

Sill, William B., ed. *The New Popular Science Encyclopedia of the Sciences.* Rev. ed. New York: Grosset and Dunlap, 1968.

Sinclair, Upton. *The Jungle.* New York: Doubleday, Page, 1906.

Sloan, Douglas. "Science in New York City, 1867–1907." *Isis,* 71 (1980), 35–76.

Smallwood, William Martin, and Mabel Sarah Coon Smallwood. *Natural History and the American Mind.* New York: Columbia University Press, 1941.

Smithsonian Scientific Series. 12 vols. New York: Smithsonian Institution Press, 1943.

Smithsonian Year: Programs and Activities. Washington, D.C.: Smithsonian Institution Press, 1971–. Annual.

Stanton, William. *The Leopard's Spots: Scientific Attitudes Towards Race in America, 1815–1859.* Chicago: University of Chicago Press, 1960.

Stearns, Raymond P. *Science in the British Colonies of America.* Urbana: University of Illinois, 1970.

Stern, Madeleine. *Heads and Headlines: The Phrenological Fowlers.* Norman: University of Oklahoma Press, 1971.

Stoehr, Taylor. *Hawthorne's Mad Scientists: Pseudoscience and Social Science in Nineteenth-Century Life and Letters.* Hamden, Conn.: Archon Books, 1978.

Stott, Jeffery R. "The Historical Origins of the Zoological Park in American Thought." *Environmental Review,* 5 (1981), 52–65.

Struik, Dirk J. *Yankee Science in the Making.* Rev. ed. New York: Viking Press, 1974.

Subramanan, K. *Scientific and Technical Information Resources.* New York: Marcel Dekker, 1981.

Thomas, Lewis. *The Lives of a Cell: Notes of a Biology Watcher.* New York: Viking Press, 1974.

――――. *The Medusa and the Snail: More Notes of a Biology Watcher.* New York: Viking Press, 1979.

Thoreau, Henry D. *The Journal of Henry D. Thoreau.* Edited by Bradford Torrey and Francis H. Allen. Rev. ed. in 2 vols. New York: Dover, 1962.

Thornton, John L., and R. I. Tully, Jr. *Scientific Books, Libraries, and Collectors: A Study of Bibliography and the Book Trade in Relation to Science.* Rev. ed. London: Library Association, 1962.

Tobey, Ronald C. *The American Ideology of National Science, 1919–1930.* Pittsburgh: University of Pittsburgh Press, 1971.

――――. *Saving the Prairies: The Life Cycle of the Founding School of American Plant Ecology, 1895–1955.* Berkeley: University of California Press, 1981.

Turner, James. *Without God, Without Creed: The Origins of Unbelief in America.* Baltimore: Johns Hopkins University Press, 1985.

Van Nostrand's Scientific Encyclopedia. 6th ed. New York: Van Nostrand Reinhold, 1983.

Van Tassel, David, and Michael G. Hall, eds. *Science and Society in the United States.* Homewood, Ill.: Dorsey, 1966.

Walcutt, Charles C. *American Literary Naturalism: A Divided Stream.* Minneapolis: University of Minnesota Press, 1956.

Warner, Deborah Jean. *Graceanna Lewis: Scientist and Humanitarian.* Washington, D.C.: Smithsonian Institution Press, 1979.

――――. "Science Education for Women in Ante-bellum America." *Isis,* 69 (1978), 58–67.

Warner, John Harley. " 'Exploring the Inner Labyrinths of Creation': Popular Microscopy in Nineteenth-Century America." *Journal of the History of Medicine and Allied Sciences,* 37 (1982), 7–33.

Wasserman, Paul, ed. *Museum Media: A Biennial Directory and Index of Publications and Audio-visuals Available from United States and Canadian Institutions.* Detroit: Gale Research, 1973.

Watson, James D. *The Double Helix: A Personal Account of the Discovery of the Structure of DNA.* New York: Atheneum, 1968.

Weeks, Edward. *The Lowells and Their Institute.* Boston: Little, Brown, 1966.

Whalen, Matthew D. "Science, the Public and American Culture: A Preface to the Study of Popular Science." *Journal of American Culture,* 4 (Winter 1981), 14–26.

Whalen, Matthew D., and Mary F. Tobin. "Periodicals and the Popularization of Science in America, 1860–1910." *Journal of American Culture,* 3 (1980), 195–203.

White, Andrew D. *A History of the Warfare of Science and Theology in Christendom.* New York: Appleton, 1895.

Whitrow, Magda, ed. *ISIS Cumulative Bibliography: A Bibliography of the History of Science Formed from ISIS Critical Bibliographies 1–90, 1913–1965.* 6 vols. London: Mansell, 1971–84.

Whorton, James C. *Before Silent Spring: Pesticides and Public Health in Pre-DDT America.* Princeton, N.J.: Princeton University Press, 1974.

Wilson, Joan Hoff. "Dancing Dogs of the Colonial Period: Women Scientists." *Early American Literature,* 7 (1973), 225–35.

Wilson, Robert J., ed. *Darwinism and the American Intellectual: A Book of Readings.* Homewood, Ill.: Dorsey, 1967.

Worster, Donald. *Nature's Economy: A History of Ecological Ideas.* Cambridge, England: Cambridge University Press, 1977.

Wright, Louis B. *The Cultural Life of the American Colonies: 1605–1763.* New York: Harper and Brothers, 1957.

Young, Margaret L., and Harold C. Young, eds. *Directory of Special Libraries and Information Centers.* 5th ed. 2 vols. Detroit: Gale Research, 1979.

Zochert, Donald. "The Natural History of an American Pioneer: A Case Study." *Transactions of the Wisconsin Academy of Sciences, Arts, and Letters,* 60 (1972), 7–15.

Periodicals

American Journal of Science. New Haven, 1818–.

American Naturalist. New York and Chicago, 1867–.

American Scientist. New Haven, 1943–. Continues *Sigma Xi Quarterly.* New Haven, 1913–42.

Atlantic Monthly. New York, 1857–.

Audubon Magazine. New York, 1899–.

Botanical Gazette. Crawfordsville, Ind., and Chicago, 1875–1919.

The Country Gentleman. Philadelphia, 1853–1955.

Discover. New York, 1980–.

Environment. St. Louis and Washington, D.C., 1959–.

Godey's Lady's Book. Philadelphia, 1830–98.

Harper's Magazine. New York, 1850–.

Isis. Philadelphia and Beltsville, Md., 1913–.

Journal of the Franklin Institute. Philadelphia, 1826–.

Medical Repository. New York, 1797–1824.

Merry's Museum and Parley's Magazine. Boston, 1842–72.

National Geographic. Washington, D.C., 1888–.

Natural History. New York, 1900–.

North American Review. Boston, 1815–1940.

Omni. New York, 1978–.

Popular Astronomy. Northfield, Minn., 1893–1941.

Popular Science Monthly. New York, 1872–.

Science. Lancaster, Pa., etc., 1883–.

Science Books and Films. Washington, D.C., 1965–.

Science News. Washington, D.C., 1921–.

Scientific American. New York, 1845–.

Sky and Telescope. Cambridge, Mass., 1941–.

Smithsonian. Washington, D.C., 1970/71–.

Southern Literary Messenger. Richmond, Va., 1834–64.

Southern Quarterly Review. New Orleans, Columbia, S.C., 1842–57.

Torrey Botanical Club, Bulletin. New York, 1870–.

Youth's Companion. Boston, 1827–1929.

Self-Help Tradition and Popular Religion

ROY M. ANKER

Most historians would agree that there has long existed in American life a broad and deep penchant for hopefulness: that is, an insistent and perdurable faith in the possibility of the solitary individual doing something, with or without divine aid, to alter significantly one's own physical, social, economic, or psychic circumstances. Indeed, that impetus toward self-help, as it has come to be called, has often been cited as one of the most characteristic features of America during its long history. Evidence for such a claim abounds. In virtually every facet of its long and potent history, America's popular mythology displays figures of intrepid will and hope in hard pursuit of better lives. Brave Puritan forebears search for independence and liberty; Benjamin Franklin creates himself and Poor Richard; yeoman revolutionaries trade hoes for muskets; pioneers battle plains winters and grasshoppers; and on the tale goes in endless variety: log-cabin presidents, cowboy saviors, self-made financiers, religious healers, mystic gurus from the East, and on and on. The theme improvises form upon form for the conveying of its story of hope: folktale, sermon, dime novel, advice book, television serial, advertisement, televangelism, film, and pop song.

Message after message in all these endlessly varied genres pours into, pervades, and supports that vast reservoir of desire and aspiration known as the American Dream—the elusive, nebulous ideal that has beckoned and shaped the hopes and devotion of a nation of immigrants and generations of offspring. There is in American culture, then, a strange hankering for the new and better, bred seemingly into American bones and spirits; there is, as novelist F. Scott Fitzgerald distilled and celebrated in the tragic hero of *The Great Gatsby,* "an extraordinary gift for hope, a romantic readiness" that concedes no limit to what the human spirit can accomplish. This possibility of self-help in a free land has provided ideological and spiritual fuel that has fired the engines of both capitalistic expansion and social and economic equality wherein any can rise by bootstraps in a land of opportunity. Clearly, the idea of individual betterment by individual effort has had a long, energetic, prolific, and, depending to whom one listens, problematic life in American culture.

As the title of this chapter suggests, the self-help tradition in America is often yoked with various currents in American popular religion. That joining to some extent results from the fact that the ideals and goals of self-help have often been revered and pursued with a fervor and purity that resembles religious devotion. To an even greater extent, this historical perspective stems from historians' surmises about the causal relationship between varied religious movements, differing from one another as much as Puritanism and Christian Science, and the traits, values and dreams of the self-help ethos. In short, prominent versions and proponents of the dreams, strategies, and regimens of self-help seem to have arisen from within American religions, most especially mainstream Christianity. Regardless of what thereafter happened to these visions and leaders, a consensus among historians suggests that they did emerge from deep within the bosom, as we might call it, of American Protestant Christianity. The narrative that follows seeks to describe and amend traditional notions of the interplay of popular religious ideas and practices and their consequences in the multitude of self-help aspirations and strategies that have flourished in American culture.

HISTORIC OUTLINE

The aspiration toward self-betterment does not, of course, arrive new and full-blown in America with the landing of the Pilgrims or the popularity of Horatio Alger's Ragged Dick juvenile novels. As with any human propensity that for awhile attains prominence in a given culture, the seeming universality of human nature dictates that other societies in other times and places exhibited, to a lesser degree, similar traits and longings. In all communities, from antiquity to the present, can be found histories and tales of celebrated individuals who, by their own efforts or with divine aid, counter adverse circumstances to better their material and psychic well-being.

By definition, all literature, whether oral or written, has implicit didactic or inspirational elements that bid the listener-reader to emulate the superior qualities of the hero. Those modern books that proclaim their how-to intentions only make this didactic function in literary history fully explicit. The Mesopotamian Epic of Gilgamesh (2000 B.C.), for example, heralds the strength, courage, and fortitude of its hero in overcoming vindictive passion to slay monsters and to build city walls that insure the safety of his native people. So, too, the adulation of the wit and guile of Odysseus played a formative role in creating respect for rational ingenuity and control in what came to be classical culture, with its Platonic and Aristotelian confidence that truth and inner tranquility might be attained through the exercise of reason. This central Greek emphasis later formed the basis for a vigorous minority tradition in Christianity. As early as the fourth century A.D.—a theological watershed for historic Christendom—Pelagius, a classically learned English scholar, stressed the potential of each individual to arrive at truth through rational discernment and to achieve salvation through good works, thereby disputing Augustine's insistence on faith and righteousness as the exclusive and irresistible gifts of divine grace. Similarly, the European Renaissance of the fifteenth century retrieved Hellenic ideals of reason and balance. A century later the Protestant Reformation's heirs of Augustine contended with Jacob Arminius, another proponent of the individual's rational and ethical resolution as sufficient paths to God and Heaven.

Historical Understandings of Puritan Influence

The origins, development, and persistence of the multiple strands of the self-help ethos are not easy phenomena to delineate. The impulse toward self-help has been around a long time and is an integral part of human personality and culture. In America vigorous strains of it have been around from the beginnings of European settlement, their exact shapes depending on which historians one reads. And their influence has been great, encompassing models of character and value that range from entrepreneurial frontier individualism to contemporary therapeutic quests for healthy bodies and psyches. As such a diverse and long lineage would suggest, past and present self-help ideologies have no common seminal idea or generative figure but vary in origin and emphasis in different historical periods—a fact that can hardly be overstated. In other words, the numerous permutations of the self-help theme in the flux of American experience stem from diverse and often contradictory strains of popular and elite, religious and secular, esoteric and conventional influence. After all, in this tangled knot of influence and expression are found such contrasting spirits as Benjamin Franklin and Ralph Waldo Trine, Andrew Carnegie and Mary Baker Eddy, and William James and Norman Vincent Peale. When all is said and done, however, for better or for worse, the self-help heritage perhaps offers one of those unifying modes of thought and feeling that knits together the religious, social, and ethnic pluralism of a change-ridden national history.

Most modern American historical writing, beginning in the late nineteenth century, has argued that the self-help ideal of individual effort and improvement originated in New England Puritan culture. Many of these modern historians, themselves politically liberal, reacted strongly to supposed Puritan political repression and economic individualism. Using an economic interpretive filter first set forth by historian Charles Beard in his work on the American constitution, James Truslow Adams and Vernon Parrington argued that the primary motivation of the lay Puritan in coming to the New World was economic and political—the opportunity to do what one wished for oneself; religion was a secondary consideration at best. Parrington celebrated the triumph of American "democratic liberalism" over Puritanism's clerical tyranny and capitalistic fervor.[1] Intellectually as well as politically, the American Puritans feared "the free spaces of thought," living in a "narrow and cold . . . prison" of intolerant "absolutist dogma."[2] For Adams, Parrington, and many other like-minded historians, generally known as the progressive school, religious ideas assumed value only insofar as they fostered, most often inadvertently, a progressive political liberalism. In the 1920s and 1930s, this skepticism found an indomitable popularizer in gadfly journalist H. L. Mencken, whose syndicated columns lampooned Puritan intelligence, charity, sexuality, and piety. The combination of a pronounced interpretive "climate of opinion" or ideological cast among professional historians and a talented popularizer fairly well entrenched the still dominant popular biases and caricatures of Puritan New England.

Many of these historians took at least some of their inspiration from the work of German social analyst Max Weber, one of the brilliant early founders of modern sociology. In what is probably the most provocative piece of historical sociology ever written, *The Protestant Ethic and the Spirit of Capitalism* (1904–5; translated into English in 1930), Weber speculated that the practical rational and organizational processes necessary for the emergence of modern industrial capitalism were dramatically furthered by a single central facet of Puritan theology. According to Weber, the Calvinistic doctrine of predestination imposed enormous psychological anxiety upon the believer. Uncertain of one's eternal fate, the believer sought desperately for earthly signs of God's election. The very urgency of the search impelled the seeker to interpret any good occurrence, especially material prosperity, as an indication of divine favor. With the prospect of vindicating one's salvation as an impetus, the Puritans threw themselves into this-worldly activity with the specific purpose of attaining wealth. This religious mindset created a whole new psychological ethos that fostered a new efficiency in the marketplace; after all, to put the matter bluntly, the stakes were high— a life of grim uncertainty or sweet repose. Such, more or less, is Weber's theory, and by and large, the effect of it has been to further the notion of the Puritan as intellectually timid and economically resolute or, put more bluntly, plain greedy. Moved by a powerful idea, predestination, Weber's Puritans initiated the modern world of individualistic economic pursuit. The traits supposedly inculcated by the Puritan ethos—frugality, hard work, tidiness, punctuality, busyness, and the like—would later be commonly identified by Benjamin Franklin, Horatio Alger, Andrew Carnegie, and others as the surest means to personal success and wealth.

The Puritan Social Ethos

The above portrait of Puritanism has persisted in spite of four decades of revision by modern American historians. Beginning with the different estimates of the Puritans by Harvard intellectual historians Samuel Eliot Morrison and Perry Miller and since by countless others, a substantially different picture of Puritan thought, psychology, and society has gradually emerged. Of greater importance still for clarifying the history of the self-help ethos in America have been the accomplishments of the new social history, which has greatly expanded our understanding of the role of religion and its prominence in Puritan society. Because of its focus and the questions it asks, social history has demonstrated that the much-vaunted Puritan piety was also and perhaps foremost a social piety, both ideologically and practically. The gist of that scholarship indicates that motive forces of self-concern and heedless individualism were discouraged as impediments to the Puritan social and economic ideal.

On the question of Puritan social piety, in an important summary article, one pair of scholars, T. H. Breen and Stephen Foster, have gone so far as to claim that American Puritanism's "greatest achievement" came in its "most startling accomplishment, fifty years of relative social peace."[3] And this came, as they point out, during a period of general turmoil and strife in England and Europe. In accounting for this phenomenon, Breen and Foster point to a series of factors, not the least of which was the social vision promulgated by Puritan leaders. A glimpse of that vision comes in one of the most famous sermons in American history, "A Model of Christian Charity," preached before landfall upon the flagship *Arabella* by John Winthrop, the lawyer who led the large 1630 migration to Boston and who served as the elected governor of the colony for most of the twenty remaining years of his life. Winthrop besought the migrants to be "knit together in the bond of love" and "brotherly affection," to live together "in all meekness, gentleness, patience, and liberality." While New England was to retain a medieval hierarchal class structure, as was the norm for the time, it was nonetheless to be fully informed by cooperation, interdependence, and charity so that the "rich and mighty" would not "eat up the poor," as was increasingly not the case in England. Rather, as a holy enterprise, they should all willingly "abridge ourselves of our superfluities, for supply of others' necessities." Only by such a witness of love could New England become, in Winthrop's most famous phrase, "a city upon a hill" by which the rest of the world might detect the worth of the Puritan experiment and the presence of divine care in the world. While the Puritan errand was primarily religious in establishing "a community dedicated to the fulfillment of God's will," their religious vision contained as an integral and crucial part "a model for society as a whole, not just for the religious institutions within society."[4]

In recent years the social historians have published a sufficient number of accounts of small inland New England villages to suggest strongly that Winthrop's vision, spoken as it was by an elite leader, actually filtered down to a local lay level. As Breen and Foster comment, a "strong sense of communal responsibility . . . influenced the character of . . . the Bay Colony. It was incumbent upon all men to work out their disputes as peacefully as possible, thinking always of their greater obligation to the commonwealth as a whole and ultimately to God himself."[5] So successful in following such principles was the small inland subsistence farming village that Kenneth Lockridge has described it, perhaps somewhat extravagantly, as a "Christian Utopian Closed Corporate Community."[6] While by no means all New England towns shared the harmony and stability of the small farm town, the social vision that animated them was "common to the founders of nearly all the towns in the first waves of New England settlers" and, as such, initiated "the mainstream of a wide and enduring New England tradition" that would be felt through the nineteenth century.[7]

The drive that fueled whatever degree of social accomplishment the Puritans pulled off came no doubt from the very Puritanism of the Puritans, so the speak. Puritanism was, to be sure, theologically "precise and fervent" intellectually.[8] It also entailed a vigorous and deep religious commitment. They were beset by a particular disposition or temperament, a complexion of spirit, which made them decidedly this-worldly, intensely earnest, and energetically reverent of God, the church, morality, and humanity—all traits in "the Augustinian Strain of Piety" that Perry Miller called the hallmark of the Puritan spirit. Most who came in the early years were this sort of Puritan, as Breen and Foster note in "Moving to the New World." Contrary to economic interpretations of Puritan incentives for migration, their desire and motives seem to have been primarily religious, and once in New England "they imbued their society with a deeply spiritual significance."[9] The broad currents of Puritanism, as perhaps best articulated in Winthrop's sermon, supplied the first generations with a significant ideological common ground—what today we might call a myth—"meaning for their present, a mission for their future, and, what was more, and perhaps most of all, a synthetic but compelling past" of spiritual heroism that would nourish them amid later travail and trouble.[10] These assorted English villagers lived, then, with a strong sense of destiny that furnished not only meaning and inspiration but a full panoply of responsibilities to the future. The Puritan cosmogony saw daily life infused with and as a vehicle for the divine will, a notion which in its social and ethical application encouraged the practice of charity. Life was a spiritual and ethical laboratory and drama.

The Puritans brought with them a particular social inheritance that helps explain the kind of social order they hoped to create, that is, what historians have come to call "localism," by which they mean centuries-old habits and customs of English village life. Kenneth Lockridge defines this as a "peasant ethos" that has almost universally, quite apart from cultural differences, venerated utopian ideals of a cooperative village life of security, stability, interdependence, and harmony.[11] The disruption of these economic and "social folkways" in early seventeenth-century England threatened and angered Puritans like John Winthrop and other such diverse folk as Thomas More and Captain John Smith. The spread of a new individualism in England under the aegis of kingly power, a burgeoning capitalism, and Renaissance self-confidence distressed traditionalists who revered customary social and political mores. With this affection for localism in mind, it is easy to understand how leaders and villagers alike wished to freshen the traditions of English localism with a compatible Christian social ethic and a sort of spiritual ultimacy. The consequence was a cohesive and generous spirit of mutuality and cooperation. For historian Kenneth Lockridge, Puritanism "actually perfected and sanctified the ideal of the peasant past" with "a coherent social vision" whose hallmarks were "love, forbearance, cooperation, and peace."[12]

The Puritans of the New World were helped by relative good fortune once they arrived. For one, they were generally of the same economic stratum, a condition very different from the contentious exercise of privilege and extravagance then current in England.[13] In addition, land was good and plentiful, and with hard work they were able to achieve a steady and modest prosperity. A preponderance of nuclear families provided social and emotional stability in a strange place.[14] Furthermore, the leaders were disposed to share power and responsibility to an extent undreamed of in England.[15] And during the early decades villages were laid out in a pattern that encouraged familiarity and cooperation.

In addition to the inland subsistence farming communities described above, there was an urbanized coastal region, towns like Boston and Salem, and a zone of highly commercialized agriculture, as in the Connecticut River Valley.[16] From the beginning centrally located and more commercial, Boston only briefly, if ever, shared in the sort of cohesive social vision of the agricultural towns. By the time of Winthrop's death in 1649, barely two decades after settlement, Boston citizens, churched and unchurched alike, were "generally failing in their duty to community, seeking their own aggrandizement in the rich opportunities afforded by land, commerce, crafts, and speculations, to the detriment of the community."[17] Other towns, like Springfield, founded on the frontier for commercial exploitation by William Pynchon, differed still more radically from the cooperative farming village, looking mostly like a modern-day company town. And for still other towns along the Connecticut River records conflict, depending on what social historian is reading the data. Where one has seen harmony akin to Massachusetts, another has detected strife and acrimony from the start, often involving clerical domination. And on and on the list might go, as studies of local communities have come forth. It is fair to say, however, that most communities started with similar high visions. More difficult interpretive questions intrude when scholars question to what extent those visions were realized and how soon and why they began to loose their cogency, and those questions do indeed occasion a whole host of diverse and fascinating responses.

The Case of Cotton Mather: Grace, Gratitude, and Morality

With its roots in England and before that in the European Reformation, Puritanism's visions of religion and culture had imbibed the Calvinistic spiritual dialectic between man's radical fallenness and God's gift of grace and salvation. The result was an acute consciousness of the moral insufficiency of natural man. This sense of unworthiness led to a rigoristic ethic in pursuit of sanctification—the acquisition of godliness, which was a long process of righting the self in fulfilling the promise and reality of grace, of making oneself Christlike or fit for God. This intense religious disposition no doubt found its fruition in John Bunyan's *The Pilgrim's Progress* (1678), an immensely popular tale of worldly temptation, spiritual struggle, and redemption—a fictional how-to rendering of the earthly sojourner's path to salvation. The same impulse for offering practical help and inspiration appeared in Englishman Lewis Bayly's *The Practice of Piety* (1612), which offered advice, in its twenty editions, on the route to godliness, and in Englishman Joseph Alleine's *The Sure Guide to Heaven* (1672), which sold 50,000 copies in the colonies.

The most controversial and perhaps influential American expression of the tension between worldly activity and the morality of salvation came in the life work of famous Puritan divine Cotton Mather (1663–1728). In *The Christian at His Calling* (1701), the author stressed a two-faceted vocation for the believer. The first, or general, calling entailed conversion and allegiance to Jesus Christ. The second stressed worldly vocation, wherein the Christian engaged in practical employment for the benefit of society. Whatever task the Christian undertook was not primarily for personal gain but for the good of his fellows. The importance of Mather's formulation was that it not only emphasized the obligation of gainful activity but it served also as a justification for secular pursuits. The duty of an energetic vocation in the business of supplying others and oneself with necessities and goods repudiated any lingering tendency toward quietism or monastic withdrawal.

The impulse behind Mather's worldly activism is made clearer in *Bonifacius: An Essay upon the Good,* which the prolific Mather published in 1710. Facing an increasingly secular and seemingly decadent Boston, Mather set forth in *Bonifacius* an assortment of recommendations to the godly for restoring piety and morality. While many critics, including Perry Miller, have seen this work as representative of a decline of the Puritan moral vision into legalism and nosiness, it is equally plausible, as David Levin has suggested, to see it as a latter-day "natural extension of the kind of impulse that led Puritans to establish the New England colonies in the first place," that is, the expansion of "God's work in the world."[18] Mather again urges vocational responsibility but emphatically does not urge a heedless pursuit of wealth. Moreover, his concern is to impede the self-centered neglect of societal well-being. He finds greed and business trickery to be "abominations" in the sight of God. A like degree of passion and inventiveness should be put to the service of the community and the God whose love bids that service. Mather attempted to imbue all human activity with a rigorous and ordered focus —devotion to God and labor for community well-being. For the New World Puritans, Mather among them, the wellspring and hallmark of work was the divine love conveyed in Grace. In receipt and gratitude of this gift came the impulse to work. Puritan religious psychology postulated that the convert would "rejoice in love, and celebrate with godly works," and in such, "the real motive to work develops."[19] "Society is the ground on which the Saints parade their obedience, and the force that energizes their performance is godly love engendered by the apprehension of *agape* redeeming and regenerating them."[20] Such an informing vision would long linger in American culture to sustain a deep ambivalence about the purposes of individual labor for the self and riches.

Benjamin Franklin and the Work Ethic

Few figures in American history have carried so much mythic weight, so many dimensions and overtones, as Benjamin Franklin —diplomat, politician, businessman, scientist, philosopher, inventor, public servant, author, and, in all these accomplishments, self-made man par excellence. Indeed, the conjunction of these many feats put Franklin in a unique category in the American past, a special niche occupied by Franklin alone. While no remotely precise sales figures are available, the consistent production over the centuries of Franklin's *Poor Richard's Almanack, The Way to Wealth,* and the *Autobiography* very probably make him the best-selling author in American history (if this is not true for all genres, it surely applies to the sales of nonfiction). And if Franklin's publishing success has been dwarfed by the prolific sales of contemporary romance writer Barbara Cartland or, to cite a later-day self-help proponent, Norman Vincent Peale, no other popular author has paralleled Franklin's lasting enormous influence upon American culture.

The mainspring and core of that perduring message has been Franklin's counsel of self-help, and in that advice, perhaps even more than in his famed discovery of electricity, Franklin made a still unmatched impact on the American future. Abraham Lincoln, Horatio Alger, and Jay Gatsby surely follow in Franklin's wake in the popular imagination, but even as each is variously indebted to the tradition to which Franklin gave so much impetus, none goes beyond Franklin's role in promulgating the lure and influence of a philosophy of self-help as an abiding referent in American self-understanding. In his life as in his preachments, Franklin epitomized the self-made man. Franklin's philosophy and self-portrait together initiate, in the words of John Cawelti, the vocational pattern that gave rise to "a new hero" who would come to be the "model," the very "archetypal" definition of personal success in America. This "new ideal of human excellence and virtue" would entail, as it inevitably must, "a correspondingly new concept of the social order."[21] This new vision of things social and personal entails a self-help ethic of prudential morality that has had vast consequences for American social harmony. It is in Franklin's work, especially the *Autobiography* and *The Way to Wealth,* that we find full-blown a new sort of American vision, one that contrasts sharply with the Puritan ideal and tradition.

Born in Boston in 1709 to Calvinist parents, one of seventeen children, Franklin was apprenticed at age twelve to his printer-journalist older brother James. A spat with James prompted him to run off to Philadelphia, which was then the second largest city in the colonies. His description in the *Autobiography* of his raggle-taggle first entry into Philadelphia and his encounter with the woman he would eventually marry has become one of the more famous vignettes in American literature. For a couple of years, Franklin foundered professionally, even trying England for a time. After these failed beginnings, Franklin settled down to the discipline and service that would make him world-famous as the archetypal American. By age twenty-two, he had launched his own printing business and, more important, *Poor Richard's Almanacks,* which continued for nearly two decades, eventually averaging 10,000 copies a year. After business success came service: as postmaster general, engineer of innumerable civic improvements, signer of the Declaration of Independence, ambassador to France during the Revolution, and a framer of the Constitution. His funeral would draw 20,000 mourners, a fact which by itself offers ample testimony to the notoriety Franklin's life and public career had attracted.

The *Autobiography* gives Franklin's version of his life, a moving and mythic story told, as Kenneth Silverman comments, "from the point of view of his own legend."[22] The poor and footloose lad makes good in terms that would become normative in the American future: he won the girl who had mocked him, served his country well, and became wealthy—all on his own. Estimates of his personal wealth at the time of his death valued his estate at a half million colonial dollars. By any standard, it was an extraordinary life, the very prototype for the rags-to-riches mobility. To be sure,

Franklin did not grow up in the rags of poverty—the shopkeeper's plain cloth measure of authentic fame he reached, devoting his energy first to his own pecuniary betterment and, that once attained, to the welfare of his region and his would-be nation. The full measure of Franklin's influence, even in a fluid and mobile society, can hardly be underestimated.

The crucial domain of that popular influence upon self-help lies in Franklin's ethical vision and counsel, especially in his advocacy of a prudential ethic that makes the getting of wealth and worldly status morality's chief end. Certainly this strain seems to characterize most of the maxims contained in *Poor Richard's Almanack,* or at least those aphorisms that have been passed on orally for many generations and are now a part of America's folk wisdom. While most of the almanac's maxims were not original with Franklin, he was directly responsible for most of its early contents, borrowing freely from many ancient and modern sources and improvising much material himself. As time went on, Franklin devoted himself to other interests and delegated the task of composition while retaining final editorial control.

One of many almanacs and self-help guides in the colonies, *Poor Richard* contained information and advice on a whole range of matters, from choosing a mate and excess drinking to matters of astrological and zoological curiosity. The most consistent concern, however, a preoccupation shared by Franklin and his public, was the goal of getting rich. Throughout the twenty-five years of publication, Poor Richard Saunders, the narrator, counseled a careful and calculated management of all of one's resources, both tangible and intangible. Time, energy, money, and friendship are hoarded and cautiously directed toward the goal of raising one's status economically and socially. From the perspective of this self-interested prudence, as it is often called, certain sorts of behavior could be advocated quite apart from their intrinsic moral worth and were subsequently justified according to their effectiveness in attaining personal security—in other words, how well they worked. The most famous of these maxims was the advice that "honesty is the best policy." Here honesty is wise because dishonesty is likely to bring more trouble than ease; disadvantages for the self outweigh advantages if dishonesty is discovered. Similarly, pride is condemned not because it is intrinsically wrong but because it leads to personal bad fortune in the loss of friends and diversion from necessary tasks. In short, it is not useful for building up material well-being, and its expression often pushes on into superfluities and thus into debt.

In marked contrast to Puritan motives for labor and riches, Franklin's counsel on wealth paid little heed to the social consequences of individual wealth-getting. A narrow and relentless concern with one's own estate in life is reiterated throughout. Occasional cautions about wealth warn not about wealth itself but about its excesses that might injure the self, such as food and drink, and lead to the loss of wealth. Such entreaties, though, are far outnumbered by admonitions on how to prosper. About wealth itself,

Poor Richard's advice tells the wealthy to keep their wealth against the lures of finery or even excess charity. "Get what you can, and what you get hold . . . " is not a doctrine to encourage lavishness in anything save work and hoarding. Indeed, "if you would have a faithful servant, and one that you like, serve yourself," says Poor Richard. Such a notion does not further social trust generally, let alone between servants and masters. The very artfulness of these mottoes, their wit and pithiness, goes a long way toward justifying their morality.

That Franklin's audience took this all very seriously is well indicated by the fact that in 1758, when Franklin chose to end the *Almanacks,* he did so with a collection of Poor Richard's previous twenty-some years of guidance on wealth-getting. "The Advice of Father Abraham" or, in its later pamphlet title, "The Way to Wealth," became a best-selling work in the colonies and abroad. Its many aphorisms have lived on to the present, although their users often do not know their origin. In this last edition, Poor Richard hears an old man, Father Abraham, lecturing a group of people. The entire lecture consists of quotations on wealth from the previous *Almanacks.* The most notable feature of the rendition of Poor Richard given by Father Abraham is his lecture's climactic reference to the relationship between Providence and wealth. In this concluding, and seemingly obligatory, nod to piety, gratitude, and humility, Father Abraham warns against depending "too much" on "Industry, and Frugality, and Prudence." We are told that "the blessing of Heaven" is also necessary. In the total context of *Poor Richard,* piety and humility are now seen as requisites to wealth and not as worthy ends in themselves. And if wealth is a blessing for piety, the poor and humble should not be scorned, for they too may possess virtue in the making, even as "Job suffered, and was afterwards prosperous." In any case, human worth and virtue are assessed and valued only in their relation to present or future wealth. All in all, it is very difficult to see *Poor Richard's Almanacks,* and especially their distillation in *The Way to Wealth,* in any other light than an unremitting advocacy of the individual pursuit of wealth by means that are selfishly prudential, if not altogether expedient.

Some critics would temper this interpretation of Franklin's meaning by arguing that his advice on money-making came from a sophisticated view of human nature and that his work ethic was expressly and sensibly geared to the harsh realities of a frontier society. On the frontier, the primary question could not be purity of motivation or social altruism but more immediate, and probably higher, matter of plain physical survival and modest material improvement, ends which in themselves can hardly be labeled excessive or greedy. Furthermore, the critic needs to be careful, as Louis Wright has reminded us, not to see in the colonial period the same sort of use of *Poor Richard* and the *Autobiography* that became prevalent in the Gilded Age—that is, the easy justification for a rather heartless work ethic.[23] If Franklin's ethic of labor and prudence seemed to emphasize the practical routes to economic well-being, such a model was well and, one might say, humanely suited to quite specific and pressing social exigencies. After all, diligence and frugality were minimal preconditions of personal and, by extension, civic virtue. Thus, as Charles Sanford has commented, it is easy to see how the whole of Franklin's "moral vision was colored by the presence of the frontier."[24] The widespread modest prosperity and contentment of a nation of farmers would work against the inequality and opulence of a corrupt European social order, which bothered Franklin greatly.[25]

This same sort of discussion over the meaning and intention in the *Almanack* is only amplified in interpretations of the *Autobiography*. Cawelti, for example, finds an enormous difference between *Poor Richard* and the *Autobiography*. If the former was read as a primer on wealth-getting, the memoir "presented a broad and humane ideal of self improvement" which assumed "responsibility towards one's fellow man."[26] This is indeed a generous reading of Franklin's intention, but the historian of culture not only asks what the *Autobiography* means but how it has been read through the centuries. And here there seems to be sufficient divergence between the gist of academic interpretations and popular impressions that the former often attempt to exonerate Franklin by suggesting that the common reader usually has missed its humanity, humor, and self-satire.

It is clear that in the *Autobiography* Franklin wishes again to inculcate certain values. The method changes here from aphorism to didactic drama that features certain elements of his successful career. Instead of pithy advice on how to become financially prosperous, the reader receives a narrative in which the narrator, in complex ways, is the hero of his own tale; instead of maxims, the reader is given from Franklin's own life dramatized illustrations of like truths: his first ragged entrance into Philadelphia and the encounter with his future wife, Philadelphia; his tale of initial success as a printer in Philadelphia; and his attempt to construct an "Art of Virtue" as a pathway to moral perfection. For better or worse, because of their unusual vividness of description or intellectual novelty, these instances have stood out in Franklin's account with the effect of obscuring or overshadowing most other parts of the *Autobiography*. The entrance to Philadelphia and later marriage offers proof, so to speak, of the efficacy of the journey toward wealth that is the goal of the first half of the *Autobiography*. Throughout, Franklin's commentary again emphasizes the prudential nature of virtue: the accomplishment of wisdom and service are simultaneous with the accomplishment of wealth; virtue leads to wealth. "It was . . . everyone's interest to be virtuous who wished to be happy in this world," material possession being a part of wealth and happiness. Franklin also concludes that "no qualities were so likely to make a poor man's future as those of probity and integrity." Within such a scheme of virtue, as critics of Franklin have been quick to point out, virtue becomes both instrumental and utilitarian.

Franklin's life and writing constitute a major shift in the motive and the shape of worldly activity. While Franklin has often been identified as a kind of enlightened or secularized Puritan, the Puritan approach to labor and service differs radically enough from Franklin's utilitarian ethic to call that now traditional judgment, first ventured by German sociologist Max Weber, into serious question. Intellectual historian Norman Fiering has identified the origins of Franklin's moral theory with seventeenth-century adaptations of Aristotelian moral tradition, a heritage that stressed the acquisition of moral behavior through practice and habit. This perspective stood apart from two other prominent traditions in the West: the Platonic, which stressed virtue as the product of right knowledge, and the Judeo-Christian, which emphasized conversion of man's inmost moral disposition. Throughout his examination, Fiering is careful to indicate the "profound division between Franklin's thinking and that of the Puritans."[27] Once the intellectual sources of Franklin's thought are investigated—from Plutarch to Locke—it becomes amply clear that his moral theory derived "from a particular and rather mechanistic eighteenth-century form of the Aristotelian tradition" and "was antithetical to any meaningful idea of Puritanism." With an approach that was "essentially neo-pagan," Franklin "placed almost exclusive emphasis on slow, incremental modification of external behavior," much in the manner of today's psychological behavioralism.[28]

The Puritan vision, on the other hand, contended that any virtue worth having emanated from a "divine infusion" that effected "a decisive change of heart resulting in a reorientation of the appetites or affections."[29] The practice of real virtue, then, could only be "infused rather than acquired."[30] The primary mode of Puritan moral psychology—what Fiering calls "scrupulosity" or "that intense self-examination" for "purity of intention"—is entirely missing from Franklin's moral reflection.[31] Also unlike the Puritans, Franklin would tolerate some prudential hypocrisy as long as its effects were either personally or socially benign. Fiering even doubts the Puritan character of the famous thirteen virtues. The whole of the "Art of Virtue" can be attributed to a tradition, especially Greco-Roman, other than Puritan. When seemingly Puritan virtues do appear, such as frugality and industry, their inclusion results not from religious inhibitions but from their instrumental role as supports of economic and social order.

Achievement, Wealth, Morality and a New Nation

The Franklinian blessing to economic acquisition became in effect normative for the whole of the culture, but other assorted figures in eighteenth-century and early nineteenth-century America wished to sound a note of caution. For one, a less prominent Enlightenment influence from America's patrician sector hoped for a different understanding of the nature of opportunity in an expanding nation. A part of Thomas Jefferson's democratic ideal rested on a broad faith in the potential of small sociopolitical bodies to inspire and to improve their membership. Self-help was here fostered to encourage the development of the whole person, intellectual and moral, and not just his money- or status-making skills. It is safe to say that Jefferson, while insisting on the formal separation of church and state, nonetheless wished to invest the state with functions of inculcating virtue in a manner comparable to a surrogate church. The expanded and learned notion of self-help Jefferson wished to instill effected no constraint on the populace as it and its self-help advocates rushed headlong to embrace the seemingly limitless range of economic possibility.

From a lingering Puritan ambivalence toward wealth through the first half of the nineteenth century came a far greater dissent from a host of popular cultural expressions. The famous " eclectic readers" (1836–57) of William Holmes McGuffey brought the self-help ethos to generations of juvenile readers, urging at once the values of Christian love. In "Lectures to Young Men" (1844), the famous pulpiteer Henry Ward Beecher counseled that the honest effort leading to wealth was a gift and glory of God that was too easily subverted by greed and uncharitableness. Popular novelist and essayist T. S. Arthur advised in numerous books that the way to success was through hard work that always carried service to others as a primary goal. And far from the image of Horatio Alger as a sponsor of an up-by-the-bootstraps mythos, Alger's many heroes are most always lost orphans with good blood, a lot of luck, modest ambitions, and kindly intentions. In approximately one hundred Alger novels, the greedy, exploitative, and selfishly wealthy or ambitious persons often come upon bad fortune for their kindness.

During the later part of the century, which was the height of the industrial revolution, the prominent churchman Lyman Abbott, in *How to Succeed* (1882), echoed the attitudes of most Protestant clergy in urging economic success within a proper view of the obligations of stewardship and warnings about greed. It was good to get ahead and use one's full potential, but avarice threatened always to obliterate the import of whatever virtues were exercised in the process of wealth-getting. Success was for an end beyond itself.

The late nineteenth-century caution expressed by Alger, Abbott, and others was partly countered, however, in the enormously successful lecture-pamphlet "Acres of Diamonds" by Baptist minister Russell Conwell, the founder of Temple University. Conwell argued that it was the Christian's duty to acquire wealth, for its accumulation developed character and its possession brought the power to do good. The printed version of the lecture had wide circulation, in addition to the fact that Conwell delivered it some 6,000 times throughout his meteoric career. It could be argued that what most of Conwell's audiences heard and read was a validation of the sort of opulence suggested by the title. In hindsight, Conwell's lecture seems to have served as the perfect creed for an era known as the Gilded Age.

The ambivalence in the self-help tradition initiated by Mather and repeated in substance by Beecher, Abbott, and others until the beginning of the twentieth century stressed the primacy of certain virtues of hard work and responsibility as the way toward the improvement of one's character and acquisition of success. The resources for achievement lay in the makeup of every man, and the attainment of prestige or wealth, seen as a Christian duty in glorifying God and helping neighbor, depended on the individual's fortitude and resolution. Such an ethic is understandable and perhaps appropriate in the open mercantile society of early nationhood on a rich and undeveloped continent.

While the average person, church member or not, was encouraged by manifold religious and secular sources to pursue economically and socially gainful purposes, each was almost as often cautioned against the invidious and subtle temptation of greed wherein the vision of God and social concern was displayed at enormous cost to the individual and society. Thus, there exists an almost constant attitude of ambivalence toward the improvement of the individual's material circumstance, and seldom did any self-made man justify wealth in terms of selfish economic gain of the fair spoils of the victor in a competitive marketplace. Andrew Carnegie's famous Social Darwinist essay, "Gospel of Wealth," in the *North American Review* (1889) stands out as an atypical expression of the business and self-help mentality up to and including Carnegie's own time. Because of greatly changing social and economic conditions, Carnegie's tract sounds the death knell in America for an energetic individualism based on the aspirant's potential for diligence, prudence, and perseverance.

The Mind-Cure Tradition

In mid-century America, the history of self-help and religion begins in that movement known as variously as "mind-cure" or New Thought to assume a markedly different character and perhaps an even more significant role in American history. The birth and growth of the movement is observable through several different stages: the introduction into America of the scientific oddity known as mesmerism or, as it is called today, hypnosis; the life of an innovative and inquisitive New England clockmaker named Phineas P. Quimby, the fathering genius of the New Thought movement; its numerous latter-day offshoots that still partake of its spirit; and possibly, depending upon the way one reads a shadowy historical record, Mary Baker Eddy's Christian Science. It is an unexpected turn in American religious history and one that today plays a major, if not dominant role in American religion. Its American founder, P. P. Quimby, published only a few articles during his life that in no way account for the seminal and decisive role he plays in the history of American religious life. Rather, his import is felt through the writing and institutional development done by those he treated in his many years of healing practice, notably Mary Baker Eddy. Without Quimby—this modest and comparatively obscure physician of the mind from Maine—the texture of much popular modern self-understanding would be notably different. His influence is readily and daily observable in a myriad of present-day quasi-Christian, intention-shaping, and attitude-inspiring books and assorted electronic media. In a thoroughly secular realm, Quimby's influence is no less prominent in preparing a receptive ground for the theories and methods of modern psychotherapeutic practice.

An adequate appreciation of Quimby's life and findings and his mostly unrecognized influence is necessary to understand fully most modern self-help philosophies. His life, in particular, bears notice because in many ways it anticipates the character of his audience and influence. Quimby's career and thought began with an accidental self-cure. Apparently doomed by tuberculosis in his early thirties, Quimby attempted to repeat the experience of a friend for whom horseback riding had been curative. Unable to ride because of his weak state, Quimby opted instead for carriage trips. On one such excursion, Quimby's horse balked, and the invalid was forced to run it up a long hill. Soon invigorated by this effort, he drove the beast furiously homeward, arriving there in possession of his old health. The incident planted an intellectual seed in Quimby that was to begin blossoming some years later when he attended a lecture and demonstration by a traveling mesmerist (hordes of whom were then roaming the countryside cashing in on the national curiosity about hypnosis, which was first introduced to America in 1836). Quimby read all he could on the topic and started testing its capability with volunteers. One willing subject, Lucius Burkmar, exhibited unusual clairvoyant powers in the diagnosis of disease and the prescription of remedies.

Eventually, Quimby put together the import of the carriage ride years before and the apparent healing successes obtained through the use of Burkmar. While he still accepted the trance-induced clairvoyant diagnoses of Burkmar, Quimby soon realized that many of Burkmar's patently ridiculous prescriptions could have no causal connection with the cures produced. They were, in effect, placebos in which the patient nonetheless had trusted. Healing was accomplished by the patient's faith in the medicine, not by the medicine itself. From this recognition, it was but a step to the conclusion that the operative and efficacious principles herein were the suggestion of healing at a subconscious level and the confidence of the patient in the remedy prescribed. The disease, then, could be judged to be purely mental or psychological—the product of the patient's mistaken perception of self and reality. Supposing this to be the case, the route to cure was simply a matter of changing the disturbed mental condition or wrong beliefs of the patient, of reshaping the attitudes and the faith of the ill.

Those ideas would always form the base of Quimby's healing theory and practice, although he came to redirect two of its important elements. First, after some years of practice, Quimby became sufficiently knowledgeable and confident about the psychological bases underlying his treatment procedure to discard his previous use of hypnotism as a diagnostic and therapeutic tool. The same diagnostic and therapeutic fruit could be gained, he concluded, through the conscious mind's clairvoyant receptivity to the patient's mood and malady and by explanation and mental suggestion through conversation; these are principles which, in diluted form, constitute important elements in modern psychotherapy.

A second alteration in Quimby's thinking would have great consequence for the history of New Thought and Christian Science as well as for American religious life. Quimby's early experiments with hypnosis and healing arose from a wholly practical and personal incentive—specifically, the matter of getting well. As in the reigning medical practice of the day, Quimby was justly concerned with mundane matters of cause and effect. To an uncertain extent and for obscure reasons—mysteries that plague historians to this day—Quimby gradually moved to spiritualize his previously purely mundane mental cure. He came to believe that he had discovered the healing principle in the miracles of Jesus in the New Testament. This insight involved a re-envisioning of the makeup of the human person, especially in recognizing the existence in each individual of an unconscious, which was deemed by Quimby to be a divine element partaking of the very substance of God. It was this agent or portion of the self—a repository of divine receptivity that was much cultivated by Quimby—that allowed Quimby to penetrate other minds to treat and diagnose wrong belief that denies the primacy of spirit in the attainment of health. That this radically new method of treating bodily ills was effective there was little doubt in Quimby's mind or the minds of many of his contemporaries. It has been estimated that from his Portland office Quimby treated 12,000 patients in seven years. Two of his most devoted followers were the daughters of the respected United Supreme Court Justice Ashur Ware.

The Career of Mary Baker Eddy

Surely the most controversial, if not also the most famous, of all self-help figures who have kinship with Phineas P. Quimby was Mary Baker Eddy, the founder and still-ruling spirit of the Church of Christ, Scientist (or as it is better known, Christian Science), which joins Mormonism as one of the two purely indigenous American religions. Of the multitude of new sects and cults that flourished in the Gilded Age, only Christian Science

went on to become a formal churchly body possessed of a governing ec-
clesiastical structure, a well-defined doctrinal core, and a devotional system
of weekly services and evangelical outreach. The church prohibits publication of membership figures, but recent scholars have estimated that its
worldwide membership, mostly located in the United States, has grown
since its beginnings in 1879 to one-third of a million members in over 3,000
local congregations.

On February 1, 1866, the occasional semi-invalid, would-be poetess, and
dabbler in occult healing, the then Mrs. Mary Baker Patterson (1821–1910),
was injured when she slipped and fell on the ice in Lynn, Massachusetts.
In her later recollections, she declared that she was miraculously healed
from paralysis and probable death while reading the Bible three days after
the accident. The notes of her attending physician mentioned neither the
supposed seriousness of the injury nor an immediate restoration of health.
Furthermore, in a letter in mid-February to Julius Dresser, later a founder
of New Thought, Mrs. Patterson makes no reference to a sudden cure and
acknowledges the persistence of her back affliction and asks for physical
healing from the man who was likely a successor to Quimby. Without new
historical evidence, the controversy over Mrs. Eddy's illness and healing is
not likely to dissipate.

Unfortunately, this same historical ambiguity surrounds Mrs. Eddy's
personality and several crucial events in her life, including the origin and
partial authorship of some of her seminal ideas and writings. On the question
of literary origins, debate has raged for decades over whether Eddy stole
from Quimby or Quimby from Eddy, and again no resolution of the dispute
seems likely on the basis of present evidence. Mrs. Eddy first had contact
with Quimby, then a well-known mesmeric healer, in 1862, four years
before her famous fall, when she sought his aid for a chronic spinal disorder
and nervous exhaustion. She experienced immediate relief and subsequently
became a friend of Quimby and his advocate in the press, although she was
later to discount his influence on the fully developed system of Christian
Science. During her friendship with Quimby, she did have access to numerous unpublished writings of Quimby, now known as the "Quimby
Manuscripts." Since the present copies are imprecisely dated in various
handwritings, and possibly the work of some of Quimby's patients, it is
difficult to tell when and from whom the sometimes contradictory and
fragmentary thoughts actually originated.

Apart from the seemingly irresolvable questions of intellectual indebtedness, it is important to note what Quimby did do for Mrs. Mary Baker
Eddy. For some years before encountering Quimby, the frequently bed-
ridden Mrs. Eddy had pursued relief and dabbled in spiritualism, mesmerism, and various healing theories. During the Gilded Age, these theories
were part of a national craze and offered frequent and lively topics of conversation in both taverns and drawing rooms. Her experience with Quimby

convinced Mrs. Eddy of the reality of mental healing, and forever after she devoted herself to the genesis and strategies of healing. Quimby also gave Mrs. Eddy an initial step-by-step method with which to go about treating patients, although she was later to discard and indict certain of Quimby's methods, such as the use of manipulation of the head, which is reminiscent of the laying-on of hands.

Defenders of Christian Science have contended that the founder's teachings, which are to this day the exclusive theological core and rule for the Scientist, go far beyond Quimby's thought. Furthermore, they contend that Christian Science bears no resemblance to New Thought and was the happy result of the healing method and reality encountered by Mrs. Eddy in the aftermath of her fall in Lynn in 1866. Christian Science's supposed dependence on Quimby, it is argued, results from subsequent interpreters of Quimby, largely Warren Felt Evans and Julius and Annette Dresser, who unjustly read back into Quimby many of the concepts discovered by Mary Eddy. For the Scientist, Quimby was a mesmeric mind-curist who was entirely devoid of any religious framework for his theory and practice. His work was only subsequently spiritualized and "scientized" by disciples who concealed his fundamental reliance on the suggestion techniques of hypnotism. Again, the confusion of dating and authorship surrounding Phineas Quimby's manuscripts affords little help in clarifying the matter.

The best-selling book that provoked this welter of long, intense debate is Mrs. Eddy's *Science and Health* (1875). The work underwent numerous revisions—sixteen editions in all during her lifetime—each further clarifying and changing certain emphases. With regard to the book's real impact, sales figures of *Science and Health,* which are said to be in the millions, are deceptive because Christian Scientists were required to purchase each new edition, which averaged one every two years between the first edition in 1875 and Mrs. Eddy's death in 1910. From the beginning, however, despite these incidental alterations, the unique religious vision of *Science and Health* remained the same. Its most famous and controversial theological statement, on which its practice of healing rests, ventures a step beyond the idealism of transcendentalism and denies altogether the reality of matter. The physical world of the ills of mortality seen in sin, disease, and death is an error or illusion of humankind's mortal mind. Mrs. Eddy reasons to this conclusion from the premise that an all-good and wholly spiritual God could not create entities of matter and evil that contradict its essential nature.

Human consciousness, then, is only the manifestation of an entirely benign and spiritual Divine Mind. The more the individual apprehends the purely spiritual nature of his own being and his likeness to God, the more he is able to vitiate the effects of false belief in materiality and its woe-ridden by-products. Insofar as this goal is attained, the devotee becomes less susceptible to the sin and illness that result from belief in materiality. Healing occurs when the mind turns from its acceptance of the sway of material belief and is released to the pure contemplation of the love of God. Probably the largest intellectual problem with Christian Science—one often pointed out by its orthodox Christian critics—pertains to how the mortal mind, whose product is evil, however illusory, ever comes into existence if all reality is the spiritual manifestation of a good and completely spiritual deity. Defenders readily acknowledge the problem and let it rest as an enigma, suggesting that the truth of Christian Science can only be grasped from within its belief system, wherein exists a beautiful logic to its assertions.

The importance of Christian Science for an understanding of self-help and religion lies in its notion that adversity proceeds from wrong belief and attitudinal disorientation. Christian Scientists avow that their emphasis on spiritual struggle in discarding illusion and material trust distinguishes it from the facile optimism of New Thought and positive thinking. There is a prominent strain, however, that regards first health and then economic success, or "supply" as it is called by Scientists, to be reliable evidence of proper belief and God's favor. Indeed, Mrs. Eddy and her followers have stressed that the proof of their belief lies in the empirically observable effect of healing and improved health, which is but a step from economic reassurance. In any case, later disciples of both Quimby and Eddy were less cautious in ascribing wealth as well as health to newfound trust in the power of the mind and attitude to enhance spiritual, physical, and material well-being.

For a multitude of reasons involving cultural susceptibility and readiness, Mrs. Eddy's Christian Science made a tremendous impact on late nineteenth-century American society. The woman who at age fifty was penniless and working on a book no one would wish to publish would retire three decades later as the spiritual and political head of a sizable, well-established, and accepted, if not quite respected, church body. But there, in the transition from controversial sect to respectable denomination, Mrs. Eddy's influence in American culture ceases to grow, although it does not end altogether. The history of an energetic, radical religious movement pioneered by a magnetic leader begins to assume the characteristics of institutional denominationalism. The authoritarian character of Mrs. Eddy's writing and self-understanding explicitly held that her particular interpretation of the Bible and statement of doctrines were handed down by God and were therefore definitive and final. Any attempt by a Christian Scientist to rephrase or add to the substance of belief delineated in *Science and Health* was to be prohibited. This ultraconservative theological rigidity led, during Eddy's life, to the expulsion of prominent Christian Scientists and, after the founder's death, to the absolute central control of the church and the writings of all members by an executive board.

This same tenor is still evident today in the fact that while Christian Science worship services have largely copied mainline liturgy, they have supplanted the sermon with readings from *Science and Health*. Any further words of interpretation on matters of which Mrs. Eddy once spoke could only prove superfluous and risk inadvertent distortion. Christian Science initially produced a major ideological formulation on the dominance of spirit in humanity and provided strategies for self-cure. Given its prohibition against any reexpression by anyone of Mrs. Eddy's theology, and given orthodoxy's traditional suspicion of Christian Science's unconventional metaphysics, its persisting influence is open to question. This conclusion is supported by the failure of the denomination to sustain its dramatic early growth. Since the death of Mrs. Eddy, membership increases have paralleled population growth. The observer must look to the movement known as New Thought—the other offspring of Phineas Quimby—to detect the route by which American culture became beguiled by the notion of self-help through religion.

To be sure, Mary Baker Eddy was not the only person healed by Phineas Quimby in his Portland housefront office. In 1863, the year after Quimby healed the founder of Christian Science, he successfully treated for nervous collapse Warren Felt Evans, who had just left the Methodist ministry for the Swedenborgian Church of the New Jerusalem. Six years later, and six years before Eddy's *Science and Health*, Evans published *The Mental Cure: Illustrating the Influence of the Mind on the Body, Both in Health and Disease, and the Psychological Method of Treatment* (1869). While it was not a best seller, *The Mental Cure* enjoyed steady attention, going through seven editions in sixteen years. Evans's second book, *Mental Medicine* (1873), is known to have gone through fifteen editions in its first twelve years, indicating persistent interest in Evans's thought.

Evans was religious throughout his life, and when he met Quimby he was enamored with esoteric Swedish physicist-philosopher Emmanuel Swedenborg. Evans recognized in Quimby the use of the same principles by which Jesus healed and—still further—the logical and practical extension of philosophical idealism. Evans's fourth book, *The Divine Law of Cure*, is devoted to demonstrating the extent to which some of the best philosophic minds of Europe and America—for example, Hegel, Berkeley, Fichte, Coleridge, and Edwards—prepared a theoretical base for mental healing. By his fifth book, *The Primitive Mind Cure: The Nature and Power of Faith, or Elementary Lessons in Christian Philosophy and Transcendental Medicine* (1885), which went through five editions in one year, Evans had expanded his range of intellectual support to include Oriental thought, in which there was beginning to be considerable American curiosity. And in his last book, *Esoteric Christianity and Mental Therapeutics* (1886), Evans was even more characteristically like New Thought in his trust in a kind of philosophic universalism wherein ancient and modern creeds bear significant portions of fundamental truth. Like Evans, many subsequent and less prominent New Thought writers would seek intellectual support in transcendentalism and Ralph Waldo Emerson, who chose to ignore both Christian Science and New Thought.

Throughout his six books, Evans reiterates basic conclusions from Quimby and shares many views with Mary Baker Eddy. There is always the insistence on the dominance of spirit or mind over matter. Unlike Eddy, Evans does not see matter as necessarily illusory, allowing rather that it does exist independently of human consciousness. Disease is the failure to recognize the ultimacy of the spirit and the presence of Christ or God in every person, a potentiality made manifest through Jesus of Nazareth. The route to health is through dispelling the idea or conviction of the sway of disease, which results from partial recognition of a kindly and loving God that forms the true self, residing primarily in the subconscious portions of the mind. The sufferer is in need of affirmation and hopeful thinking, which is the medium of all cures and a method to be used by later New Thoughtists and Norman Vincent Peale. Wrong or pessimistic thinking brings bodily ills.

New Thought gradually gathered momentum from the enthusiasm of other Quimby followers and of dissidents and exiles from Christian Science. Among the other famous patients of Quimby was Julius Dresser, who first visited Quimby in 1860 and was healed. While there, he met fellow-patient Annetta Seabury, whom he married in 1863. Dresser decided to discard his ambition to become a Baptist minister; he entered journalism, moved west, and returned to Boston in 1883, where he and his wife set up a mental practice according to Quimby. While they published little of their own, they did attract attention by accusing Mary Baker Eddy of pirating from the manuscript of Phineas Quimby, a controversy that has yet to be successfully resolved. The son of Annetta and Julius Dresser, Horatio, became the chief and most respected chronicler of New Thought, having studied with William James at Harvard, where he won the Ph.D. in philosophy.

The middle-aged Ursula Gestefeld cured herself after reading *Science and Health*. A zealous supporter thereafter of Mrs. Eddy, she went so far as to write an adulatory book on Mrs. Eddy and Christian Science entitled *Ursula N. Gestefeld's Statement of Christian Science* (1888). For her efforts she was driven out of the church by Mrs. Eddy. She subsequently started her own periodical, the *Exodus,* which soon had a club of devoted followers.

Emma Curtis Hopkins similarly became a devoted follower of New Thought after being driven from Christian Science in a series of disputes with Mrs. Eddy. A powerful speaker, she soon attracted a large following, an organization bearing her name, and a theological seminary in Chicago. Such people as the Dressers, Ursula Gestefeld, Emma Hopkins, and numerous others, often with their own following, books, and periodicals, joined together in 1914 to form the International New Thought Alliance, which did much to spur the notions of New Thought. One such member of the New Thought movement was the prestigious Boston Metaphysical

Club, which met for the first time in 1895. All these diverse people, whose exact number is impossible to gauge, shared in the general hopes and tenets of mental healing as spelled out by Quimby and Evans. The sole point of division was perhaps how much they individually wished to "theologize" notions of incarnation, sin, and the existence of matter. In any case, differences were not sufficiently acute to cause acrimony or schism.

New Thought received a new level of public attention and a controversial new theme in 1897, with its first authentic best seller, *In Tune with the Infinite: Fullness of Peace, Power, and Plenty,* by Ralph Waldo Trine. The book contained straightforward explanations of the main precepts of New Thought. Its acceptance by a largely orthodox reading public resulted in part from the fact that Trine, a skilled stylist and expositor, tended to blur some of the key differences between conservative Christianity and New Thought, and when choices in phraseology came, Trine tended to use the language of traditional belief. As a whole, *In Tune with the Infinite* sought to emphasize the closeness of conventional Christian thinking and New Thought. Most readers saw in it the noble inspiration of established wisdom rather than the influence of esoteric philosophy or any particular healing cult. What readers encountered in Trine's book was an explicit presentation of a latent strain in New Thought and Christian Science—that is, the promise of prosperity and economic plenty as the inevitable result of being in tune with the Infinite.

Whether this new conspicuous element accounted for Trine's success is impossible to tell. Spiritual tranquility and physical well-being had been a part of Quimby's pioneering views and were expounded by his disciples. Here, the hope of wealth and personal power began to equal, if not surpass, the expectations of health and psychic repose. A little over a decade before, Warren Felt Evans had expounded on "the power of faith" to heal in the Primitive Mind Cure. But until Trine's book, the emphasis on "supply," as Mary Baker Eddy called it, had been largely subordinated to the individual's ability to influence his own person—the mind and the body. Trine's work extended control of the self outward to suggest a causal connection between spiritual attitude and financial reward and success.

If most readers were not aware of the New Thought they were getting in Trine's book, the same can be said for the wisdom and the service offered by New Thought's only enduring and widely recognized organization, the Unity School of Christianity, founded in Kansas City by Emma Hopkins's disciples Charles and Myrtle Filmore. In 1887, the Filmores had been in ill health when they heard Dr. E. B. Weeks lecture on Hopkins's doctrines. For the first time, Myrtle Filmore saw herself as a child of God over whom sickness had no power. So began a healing that took some two years, but healed she was. Impressed friends, as well as her initially skeptical husband Charles, began to inquire into the causes of Myrtle's healing. Eventually convinced, Charles began publication of a magazine called *Modern Thought* in 1890. In the same year the Society of the Silent Help was announced in its pages. This organization grew out of weekly prayer meetings by the Fillmores and their friends, wherein they would specifically pray for the suffering, troubled, and needy, using the New Thought healing concept known as "absent treatment" or thought transference. The group grew quickly, becoming known simply as Silent Unity, and requests for prayers flooded the magazine's offices. Today, this service is offered around the clock, and 150 people are employed to handle over half a million requests annually. So successful have been its methods that they are now imitated by evangelist Oral Roberts and possibility-thinking television preacher Robert Schuller.

Eschewing the opportunity to become a church, Silent Unity became Unity School of Christianity, devoted to the soft-sell promulgation of its New Thought Christianity through books, pamphlets, and media advertising and to the daily practice of healing and aid first initiated by Silent Unity. Unity published *Wee Wisdom,* begun in 1893, which became the longest-running children's magazine in America, with a circulation of around a quarter of a million readers. Begun in 1924, *Daily Word,* a monthly inspirational booklet for adults, reached a peak circulation of 180,000. In addition, there were *Weekly Unity* (1909), a mixture of newsletter and magazine; *Progress* (1924), which addressed adolescents; and *Good Business* (1924), advocating the proposition that Christian ethics is good business practice. The message of Unity finds its way into even more homes through television and radio advertising that features inspirational talks by prominent Hollywood celebrities.

While it is not a formal church, Unity has found it necessary to authorize leaders and ministers for the local Unity centers that have sprung up across the country. Unity's publishing enterprise and its extensive headquarters-campus in suburban Kansas City is supported mostly by small contributions from donors. The organization is run by the children and grandchildren of the founders. While its rhetoric sounds like orthodox Christianity, it remains very much a descendant of New Thought in its emphasis on the partial divinity or Christliness of each person, the possibility of healing through the recognition of that Christly potential, and the ready supply of material blessing.

The Coming of Positive Thinking

One of the best known of all avowed New Thought figures in the twentieth century, amounting to national celebrity status, was Emmet Fox, a best-selling author and a noted preacher who regularly preached to thousands in New York's Hippodrome and in Carnegie Hall. In 1930, in order to carry on the work started in his native England, Fox came to America, where he found an enthusiastic following. The titles of his popular books

amply illustrate his connection to New Thought, of which he was an or-
dained minister in the Church of Divine Science. *Power Through Constructive
Thinking* (1932), *Make Your Life Worthwhile* (1942), and *Find and Use Your
Inner Power* (1940) announce the divine potentiality of each individual, which
is unleashed through affirmative prayer that eliminates pessimism and fear,
the sources of psychic stress, illness, and failure. Realizing God and the
reality of divine love and assuming a new mentality yielded tangible evi-
dences of its truth and efficacy in increased health and prosperity.

Fox's prominence was soon upstaged from an unexpected and surprising
source. From dour Dutch Calvinism and America's oldest denomination—
the small Reformed Church in America—came the message of ex-Methodist
Norman Vincent Peale, whose best-selling books and frequent radio and
television appearances have made his name and his "positive-thinking"
credo household words. Peale admits to having been influenced deeply by
New Thought during a crisis of relevance early in his ministry. The insights
learned then proved useful when Peale assumed the pulpit in the 1940s of
New York City's prestigious Marble Collegiate Church, where he encountered much psychic dis-ease among the well-to-do.

Along with psychiatrist Smiley Blanton, a future co-author, Peale established an extensive psychological counseling service in his new parish. His
main work, though, has been his books, whose titles once again show
obvious connections with New Thought. *A Guide to Confident Living* (1948)
was on the best-seller list for two years, selling over 600,000 copies, and
The Power of Positive Thinking (1952) sold 2.5 million copies in four straight
years near the very top of best-seller lists. Now in its thirty-fifth volume,
the magazine *Guideposts: A Practical Guide to Successful Living,* edited and
published by Peale, has a circulation of over one million readers. It is
estimated that in 1957 Peale reached a weekly audience of thirty million
people through an extensively syndicated newspaper column, a radio program reaching one million homes, a television show on more than one
hundred stations, a column in *Look,* and the monthly *Guideposts.*

Peale, in effect, borrows many of his major ideas and methods from New
Thought, although he is careful to deemphasize theologically questionable
matters, such as the presence of Christ in each person and the stature of
Jesus. Nonetheless, Peale has retained emphasis on the impact of attitude
or confidence on self-perception, social acceptance, and worldly success.
Peale has further stressed the tangible evidence or fruits of changed thinking
as witness to the efficacy of his theories. His literary method is largely
comprised of strategies to accomplish these ideological ends. While previous
New Thought writers have largely written straight and sometimes detailed
exposition of their ideals, Peale's books are aphoristic and anecdotal, with
patterns of statement and exemplum, ad infinitum.

The decades of Peale's success saw a popular ecumenical consensus about
his goals of inner confidence and hope, if not his exact methods and in-

spiration. Boston Rabbi Joshua Loth Liebman's *Peace of Mind* (1964) stayed near the top of the best-seller list for three years, eventually selling well over one million copies. Liebman combined modern depth psychology with Judaism in a guide to overcoming self-hatred, disabling guilt, and social maladjustment. The liberal Protestant preacher of Riverside Church in New York City, Henry Emerson Fosdick, in *On Being a Real Person* (1943) and other books, again melded psychology with religion. A positive faith was necessary to overcome pessimism, lethargy, and loneliness. By cultivating one's resources, the person could engage in, as the title of another of Fosdick's popular books puts it, *Adventurous Religion* (1926).

In contrast to Liebman's and Fosdick's trust in the new psychology, Roman Catholic Fulton Sheen counseled a return to orthodox and mildly ascetic Christianity in his best-selling *Peace of Soul* (1949) and *Life Is Worth Living* (1953). Self-control and repose proceeded from bringing one's anxiety and self-seeking to God. Conservative evangelical Protestantism found a spokesman in revivalist preacher Billy Graham with his *Peace of God* (1953). Like Sheen, Graham's solutions to psychic distress ignored the new psychologies and partook of the well-established Protestant tradition of pietism. Graham repeated the same counsel more than two decades later in his best-selling manual *How to Be Born Again* (1977).

The fundamentalism in which Graham has his roots had long featured its own tradition of religion as a path to the solution of one's ethical, spiritual, and physical ills. Revivalists' pleas have always manifested, at least implicitly, an appeal to self-interest insofar as the sinner was urged to accept God's grace and avoid the fires of hell. The more extreme healing sects have in addition emphasized faith as the route to emotional and physical well-being. A former revivalist and now a television personality and president of Oral Roberts University in Tulsa, Oklahoma, Oral Roberts began his ministry on such a platform. Roberts's convictions have in the last decade led him to construct a large teaching hospital based on the integration of physical and spiritual healing. In the summer of 1987 Roberts's efforts to raise money for the debt-plagued hospital won him dubious notoriety with the claim that God would "take him home" if his ministry did not receive enough donations.

The best known of recent faith healers was revivalist-television personality Kathryn Kuhlman, who died in 1976. A similar strain appears in the faith-to-riches ministry of the Reverend Frederick J. Eicherenkoetter II— or "Rev. Ike," as he is better known—a black evangelist who promises prosperity in return for faith in God and economic generosity to the preacher's cause. These all follow in the tradition of the controversial faith healer Aimee Semple McPherson, for some a female Elmer Gantry, whose public career was plagued by scandal.

Perhaps the most recent and well known of the active self-help preaching demonstrates the persistence of the New Thought–Peale tradition. Peale's mantle has seemingly passed to a younger disciple, Robert H. Schuller, a native of rural Iowa and also a son of the Dutch Reformed Church. Schuller began his controversial ministry atop a drive-in theater refreshment stand in Garden Grove, California, a suburban community near Disneyland. Schuller, too, has written many books on "possibility thinking," his own modification of Peale's famous credo. He is best known, however, for weekly telecasts from his impressive Burgee-Johnson Crystal Cathedral drive-in church. The services and sermons are, in effect, dramatizations of the literary method pioneered by Peale and the strain of thought alive in America for over one hundred years. Its persistence and vitality are amply indicated by Schuller's meteoric success; his weekly program, "The Hour of Power," is now broadcast nationwide.

The tradition of New Thought, Christian Science, and the popularity of "positive thinking" presents, in effect, a second and influential self-help tradition in America that emphasizes the instrumental utility of religious belief. Faith in the acquisition of a new, affirmative frame of mind becomes a means of mending one's psychic or physical ills. In the older Puritan-endorsed self-help philosophy, the individual sought justification of the success-getting strategies and goals by assessing the extent to which those methods and ends conformed to Christian principles of fairness, charity, and stewardship. The New Thought tradition inverted this older perspective by making the curative and endowing powers of God the vehicle to success and well-being. Right attitudes or affirmative prayer becomes the means by which the individual acquires the traits and attitudes necessary for becoming a success. Moral questions about the appropriateness of affluence or means of acquisition receive little or no attention. In a kind of mental behavioralism, the individual, through autosuggestion, produces an attitude and expectation of success that will yield the reality. The results validate faith and constitute an empirical test of the truth and efficacy of religion.

REFERENCE WORKS

The inquiry into the theme of self-help and its interaction with American religious thought has not yet progressed sufficiently to yield bibliographies or checklists specifically devoted to cataloging primary or secondary materials. For a listing of primary sources on a given topic, the best scholars can do is to consult the notes and bibliographical essays supplied in a number of secondary books on a particular interest. Fortunately, some very good, but by no means definitive, bibliographies do exist in such works.

In the general history of self-help in America, Irvin G. Wyllie supplies an erratically useful "Note on Sources" at the end of *The Self-Made Man in America: The Myth of Rags to Riches*. Wyllie's bibliographic comment, as in the case of the text itself, is primarily useful for establishing a checklist of significant authors of both primary and secondary sources, rather than for the beginnings of any comprehensive listing of works by those authors. A somewhat better bibliographical article is contained in John G. Cawelti's *Apostles of the Self-Made Man*. It is more complete, analytic, and discerning insofar as Cawelti, an eminent scholar and interpreter of American popular culture, attempts to discuss problems of bibliographical detective work. As in Wyllie's work, the very nature of the broad historical survey that Cawelti undertakes limits the extent to which he can establish or provide exhaustive listings. Much to its credit, it does evaluate existing books on particular figures and subjects.

Still another survey on self-help and success is Richard Weiss's *The American Myth of Success: From Horatio Alger to Norman Vincent Peale,* which contains a very good selective bibliography, especially enumerating the more influential writers of the early New Thought movement as they affected psychological and religious thought. The extensive notes offer a resource for contemporaneous comment from a wide range of sources. The most complete listing and discussion of primary and secondary sources for self-help appears in the extensive notes to Richard M. Huber's *The American Idea of Success*. The thorough research and comprehensive intent of Huber's work as a whole account for its greater usefulness.

Of use generally to students of American religious history, although now somewhat dated, is Nelson R. Burr's two-volume *A Critical Bibliography of Religion in America*. This lengthy bibliographic discussion offers the reliable and efficient starting place for any inquiry into religious institutional history as well as into the relations between society and religion. More recent than Burr's work is the selective bibliography that cites some 600 titles in thirty-two areas of interest, supplied by Sydney E. Ahlstrom in *A Religious History of the American People,* winner of a National Book Award for 1972. New books in American religious history published are regularly reviewed in the quarterly journal *Church History* and in a newer periodical, *Religious Studies Review*. Pertinent articles and historical essays appearing in periodicals are listed in the quarterly bibliography of recent historical articles in American journals by *The Journal of American History,* formerly known as *The Mississippi Valley Historical Review*. Several periodicals stand out for their excellent analysis of issues dealing with religion and culture. For New England, there is the *New England Quarterly,* while early American culture as a whole receives close attention in the *William and Mary Quarterly*. The best journal to deal with the full range of American culture is *American Quarterly*. All the above contain useful reviews of new books and on occasion historiographic essays.

A good introduction to the controversial Weber thesis—a key focus in almost any discussion on the relation between individualism and religion— appears in Burr's "Religion and Capitalism," in Volume 2 of *A Critical Bibliography of Religion in America*. A discussion of sources for the "Gospel of Wealth," which is for some a latter-day manifestation of the Weberian thesis, is also found in Burr. Of additional usefulness for background and for suggestions for further reading on this topic is Robert W. Green's casebook, *Protestantism and Capitalism: The Weber Thesis and Its Critics*.

An objective and thorough history, much less a satisfactory bibliography, of Christian Science is presently not possible because the directors of the Church of Christ, Scientist prohibit free access to the archives of the Mother Church in Boston. Scholars of Christian Science suggest that there is in the collection of the Boston headquarters an enormous quantity of unpublished material by and about Mrs. Eddy and subsequent church leaders. Because of the numerous and seemingly inevitable opposing views of Mrs. Eddy and her movement, the objective scholar will be impatient until free access to this archival material is permitted. Modern editions of Mrs. Eddy's writings have been issued by the Christian Science Publishing Society. Early editions of Mrs. Eddy's *Science and Health* (1875), which the author revised significantly, are rare, but Edwin F. Dakin lists locations for these in the partly annotated bibliography to *Mrs. Eddy: The Biography of a Virginal Mind*. Dakin also mentions libraries that have complete or nearly complete holdings of various Christian Science periodicals. The most complete bibliography of works about Christian Science members, admirers, and critics is found in Charles S. Braden's *Christian Science Today: Power, Policy, Practice*, a list of some 280 titles and theological refutations to testimonial confessions, inspirational guides, and some thirteen pro-Scientist novels. The fullest listing of Mrs. Eddy's unpublished writing is in the notes to Robert Peel's three-volume biography, *Mary Baker Eddy: The Years of Discovery*, *Mary Baker Eddy: The Years of Trial*, and *Mary Baker Eddy: The Years of Triumph*. For materials on the New Thought movement, Charles S. Braden is again the most exhaustive bibliographer. His *Spirits in Rebellion: The Rise and Development of New Thought* contains nearly 600 items of primary material itemized in ten general categories. Included in the listings are approximately one hundred New Thought periodicals, about twenty of which survive into the present. Braden also mentions the locations for access to the original Quimby manuscripts. The original handwritten copies are in the Library of Congress. Photocopies are available at the Bridwell Library of Southern Methodist University and the library of the Pacific School of Religion, Berkeley, California. The greatest part of the Quimby writings is also available in *The Quimby Manuscripts*, edited by Horatio W. Dresser. For materials on the historical and religious context into which both Christian Science and New Thought came, see Paul A. Carter's extensive listing of contemporary religious documents in *The Spiritual Crisis of the Gilded Age*. The selective bibliography and notes to Richard Weiss's *The American Myth of Success* are useful for establishing the specific appeal of New Thought in its historical setting.

Since the primary means of communication of various self-help ideas has been the printed word, in both inspirational and fictional genres, bibliographies detailing such materials and their popularity are especially useful, if only to provide a listing of those authors who had extraordinary influence among the many who wrote. The most accessible of such general guides are Frank Luther Mott's *Golden Multitudes,* Alice Payne Hackett and James Henry's *Eighty Years of Best-Sellers, 1895–1975,* James D. Hart's *The Popular Book: A History of America's Literary Taste,* and Louis Schneider and Sanford M. Dornbusch's *Popular Religion: Inspiration Books in America.*

In addition to larger questions on the relation of literature and religion, specific best-selling novels featuring the interplay of religion and society throughout American history are discussed in Burr's *A Critical Bibliography.* A more detailed discussion and listing can be found in an unpublished doctoral dissertation by Ralph Allison Carey, "Best-Selling Religion: A History of Popular Religious Thought in America as Reflected in Religious Best-Sellers, 1850–1960."

Unpublished dissertation studies of fiction in the late nineteenth century— the heyday of religious fiction and a watershed for notions of self-help and religion—are comprehensive in intent. See Elmer F. Suderman's "Religion and the American Novel, 1870–1900" and, for a narrower focus, important for the Understanding of the crisis of religious epistemology that struck the Gilded Age, Roy M. Anker's "Doubt and Faith in Late Nineteenth-Century American Fiction." A general survey and discussion of more recent religious self-help literature, most of it nonfiction, appears in Donald B. Meyer's *The Positive Thinkers: A Study of the American Quest for Health, Wealth, and Personal Power from Mary Baker Eddy to Norman Vincent Peale.*

A superb and thorough bibliographical discussion of primary and secondary sources on the Pentecostal and charismatic healing movements is found in David Edwin Harrell, Jr.'s *All Things Are Possible: The Healing and Charismatic Revivals in Modern America.* His survey satisfactorily delves into almost all related areas, from history to tongue-speaking and critical estimates.

RESEARCH COLLECTIONS

Research collections of either secular or religious self-help literature are almost nonexistent. Because of its great popularity in its day, much of the literature discussed in this essay can be found in major public or university libraries as well as in bookstores that specialize in old and used books. Even though he has been located at a rural midwestern college, this author has had little difficulty in obtaining all necessary materials for this study through interlibrary loan services.

Bridwell Library of Southern Methodist University has established a New Thought collection, collecting books, pamphlets, periodicals, personalia, archives, and miscellaneous documents of people and organizations associated with the New Thought Alliance.

Materials on Christian Science—periodicals and unpublished primary source materials—are located at the Mother Church in Boston. While it is generally believed that the collection of unpublished documents is extensive, there is a sizable and important portion of the holdings to which the public is not permitted access, as many scholars have complained. In the past, access has been granted in proportion to the scholar's likely fealty to Christian Science.

Since many of the recent declaimers of self-help have been prominent churchmen, full collections of their writings and electronically recorded messages are retained in the archives and libraries of the congregations served. Hence, Norman Vincent Peale's numerous books and a full run of his magazine, *Guideposts*, can be found at Marble Collegiate Church in New York City. Similarly, the Robert H. Schuller Televangelism Association, which produces Schuller's weekly "Hour of Power," retains tapes of all broadcasts and regularly prints in pamphlet form Schuller's sermons. Free access is permitted at the association's offices on the campus of Garden Grove Community Church, Garden Grove, California.

The Billy Graham Center at Wheaton College in Wheaton, Illinois, houses the Center for the Study of American Evangelicals, which houses research collections of primary materials for the study of all phases of American fundamentalism and evangelicalism. Oral Roberts University in Tulsa, Oklahoma, holds a significant collection of Pentecostal material. The problems of research in the area are acute because revivalist traditions usually thrived on the spoken word and evangelists often did not bother to retain notes or printed texts of their work. Often the best resources for information about revivalist events and traditions are participants or observers of the events and personalities.

HISTORY AND CRITICISM

For its supposed prominence and influence in American culture, few books dealing specifically with self-help ideologies have been written, and an adequate comprehensive history of self-help in relation to American religion and its environing culture is still to be completed. Needless to say, a plethora of interpretive books on innumerable facets and overall meanings of American religion have appeared in recent decades. While these studies lie outside the purview of this essay, any full view of self-help in American culture must at some time or another consult them.

Given the persistence of self-help literature, the study of this phenomenon as an index to American culture is a recent development, as are most studies of American popular culture. The first published study to appear was Irvin G. Wyllie's *The Self-Made Man in America: The Myth of Rags to Riches*. As first studies tend to be, Wyllie's is useful, but it has been largely superseded by subsequent authors. The book is organized in chapters centered on particular values and motifs of self-help literature, and consequently there is little sense of chronological development or of the distinctions between one writer and another. Furthermore, Wyllie gives only scant attention to the pre-nineteenth-century expressions of self-help aspiration. He concludes that the literature as a whole glorified poverty, rural childhood, and reliability. Protestant Christianity is seen to be a major proponent of the rightness of success, and it raises only incidental objections about greed and selfishness and the dismissal of the stewardship ideal.

In contrast to the other books under discussion here, Wyllie provides a useful chapter in criticism of self-help, depending on recent sociological studies of the truth of the rags-to-riches mythology. Wyllie seems to expect the imminent demise of the cruel joke that was the self-help credo. His hopes were foiled by the publication of the pastoral encouragements of Norman Vincent Peale and a host of others.

A far better book is John Cawelti's *Apostles of the Self-Made Man,* insofar as it carefully chronicles distinctions and changes in America's understanding of success and the route to it. Cawelti treats Franklin's ideal of economic success as an incentive to virtue and Jefferson's view of self-government as a means to practical and moral self-improvement. Literature throughout the nineteenth century reveals conflict between the ideal of holistic self-improvement and mere economic acquisition, although the moral emphasis becomes a subsidiary strain by the close of the century. The last remnant of the holistic ideal of self-culture appears in the popularized spiritual saga of Abraham Lincoln and in Emerson's belief in the infinite potential of the whole man, which is brought to fulfillment by communion with the over-soul. Cawelti offers a healthy corrective to present images of Horatio Alger as a mindless proselytizer of the rags-to-riches idea. Rather, the Alger novels stress the importance of luck in success in relation to modest ambitions and a spirit of helplessness.

Materialistic renderings of the self-help ethos appear in the Gilded Age best-selling novels of Mrs. E.D.E.N. Southworth and minister E. P. Roe, whose fiction is too briefly treated for the kinds of conclusions Cawelti makes about Roe's changing views of American society. Mark Twain, William Dean Howells, and Henry James are examined for their critiques of corruption, injustice, and the barrenness of America's vision of easy wealth. These minority voices of protest were drowned out by an image of success rephrased to meet the needs of a new corporate economic order. The new apologists of success fully dispensed with lingering moral notions about the religious usefulness and meaning of work and embraced competition and the reward of wealth as the sole ends of individual effort. Business acumen and personal power became the new means to wealth. Twentieth-century positive-thinking success literature exhibits a confusion of ends between inner tranquility and material wealth and a confusion about which is the means to the other. In the closing pages, Cawelti examines the attitudes toward success of Theodore Dreiser, F. Scott Fitzgerald, Robert Penn Warren, and John Dewey, all of whom would argue for a return to older and more holistic virtues of success.

In *The American Myth of Success: From Horatio Alger to Norman Vincent Peale,* Richard Weiss inevitably retraces some of the ground covered by Wyllie and Cawelti. To their work he extends two necessary correctives. First, Weiss's survey finds a greater prominence of critical and cautionary advice against greed in self-help books from McGuffey to Horatio Alger, E. P. Roe, and New Thought. Second, Weiss also gives due prominence to the considerable and neglected influence of New Thought, although he overstates its connection with transcendentalism. He also correctly stresses the significance of New Thought's pragmatic and utilitarian tests for the truth of religious belief and its connections with the emergence of psychotherapy.

The latest, fullest, and in some ways, best survey of the interplay between religion and self-help is in *The American Idea of Success* by Richard M. Huber. Like Weiss, Huber extensively details the ambivalence toward material success that has characterized almost all self-help literature. He convincingly disputes Cawelti's assertion of the prominence of Social Darwinist justifications for competition and success. In tracing the secular and religious rationales for self-help, Huber is particularly perceptive in dealing with the ambiguities of success in the larger context of America's visions of itself as a special and chosen nation of opportunity. He also exhibits an acute sympathy toward the social and economic complexities in which America, from Puritanism to Peale, attempted to work out its own peculiar sense of destiny. More than any other chronicler of our theme, Huber bothers to delve briefly and helpfully into the biographies of the self-help counselors.

Differing markedly from the dispassionate scholarly work of Wyllie, Cawelti, Weiss, and Huber is Donald Meyer's *The Positive Thinkers: A Study of the American Quest of Health, Wealth, and Personal Power from Mary Baker Eddy to Norman Vincent Peale.* The tone of Meyer's work tends toward the judgmental and the glib in his characterization of self-help among the asserted popularizers from New Thought to the present. The virtue of *The Positive Thinkers* lies in the diagnosis of the social and psychological temper of the Gilded Age and the modern age that made the new theologies and psychologies ready answers to widespread religious and moral malaise. As such, Meyer explores changing sex roles amid new feminine leisure, the anxiety wrought in the business world by an amoral code, the loss of relevance and creativity in mainline Protestantism, and the appeal of psychotherapeutic remedies to problems of guilt.

A straightforward and careful scholarly survey of the twentieth-century best-selling religious self-help guides is found in *Popular Religion: Inspirational Books in America* by sociologists Louis Schneider and Sanford M. Dornbusch. Through systematic and painstaking content analysis, the authors scrutinize the work of Fox, Fosdick, Peale, Liebman, and others for their treatments of salvation, guilt, health, and piety, to name a few. Of particular merit is the authors' careful labeling of themes and trends with the precise language and clarity of the formal sociological study of religion, an element that is often unfortunately missing in studies of religion and self-help.

A useful general analysis of the origins and theological views of religious groups is provided by F. E. Mayer's *Religious Bodies of America*. The fullest running history of American religion is Sydney E. Ahlstrom's *A Religious History of the American People*. Especially useful is his survey of New Thought and mid-twentieth-century religious groups (chapters 60 and 61). Peter Williams's *Popular Religion in America: Symbolic Change and the Modernization Process in Historical Perspective* is, as its title suggests, a heavily sociological analysis of the role of popular religious groups in American Life. Other recent and more detailed introductory surveys of the growth and theological content of the various groups following the general tradition of Phineas Quimby are the sympathetic treatments of J. Stillson Judah in *The History and Philosophy of the Metaphysical Movements in America* and Charles S. Braden's *These Also Believe: A Study of Modern American Religious Cults and Minority Religious Movements*. Both books treat such movements as Theosophy, Divine Science, and the Unity School of Christianity. A somewhat older volume, *Modern Religious Cults and Movements* by Gaius Glenn Atkins, retains its usefulness for its perceptive summary of contemporary religious problems. The role in Christian Science and New Thought of hypnosis or, as it was then called, mesmerism is traced by Robert C. Fuller in *Mesmerism and the American Cure of Souls*. Among a number of hostile conservative Protestant critical works on the doctrinal aberrations of Christian Science and New Thought, the most theologically mature is Anthony A. Hoekema's *The Four Major Cults: Christian Science, Jehovah's Witnesses, Mormonism, and Seventh-Day Adventism*.

As noted in the historic outline above, almost all the literature on Mary Baker Eddy and Christian Science is marred by partisan attitudes, ranging from hagiolatry to debunkery, with little in between. Needless to say, it is difficult for the disinterested observer to arrive at something close to an objective or balanced view of Mrs. Eddy and her movement. The adulatory strain is evidenced in the official biography by Sybil Wilbur, *The Life of Mary Baker Eddy*, which was first published in 1907 as a revision of articles that appeared in *Human Life* magazine. It is now published by the Christian Science Publishing Society.

An antagonistic biography, *The Life of Mary Baker Eddy and the History of Christian Science* by Georgine Milmine, appeared shortly thereafter, following a first draft in the muckraking *McClure's Magazine*. So hostile was the Christian Science reaction to the book, which pandered to the reader's worst suspicions, that the copyright was later purchased and the plates destroyed by a friend of Christian Science. The book has since been reissued by Baker Book House in Grand Rapids. Such has been the pattern, however, that has surrounded books published about Mrs. Eddy and Christian Science. Whether in press commentary or in books, critical accounts of Mrs. Eddy or Christian Science have been met with resolute resistance by the board of directors and the Publishing Society of Christian Science, an intransigence that has prevailed since the death of Mrs. Eddy.

Edwin F. Dakin's well-documented, convincing, and unnecessarily caustic study, *Mrs. Eddy: The Biography of a Virginal Mind*, sees Mrs. Eddy as beset by a hysterical paranoia throughout her life. The Christian Science leadership sought to prevent publication by intimidating the publisher, Charles Scribner and Son, and after failing there, they mounted a national campaign to obstruct sales of the book. The Christian Science Church has also voiced its official disapproval of the comprehensive biography *Mary Baker Eddy: The Truth and the Tradition*, by two eminent and still-respected former Christian Scientists, Ernest Sutherland Bates and John Valentine Dittemore. The same is true for Hugh A. Studdert-Kennedy's appreciative *Mrs. Eddy: Her Life, Her Work, Her Place in History*.

As a whole, these books extend fair and sympathetic treatment to Mrs. Eddy, attempting to do justice to her sincerity, originality, and leadership, while not losing sight of her quite human failings of rigidity, defensiveness, and pride. Books that have won approval by the church are Lyman Powell's *Mary Baker Eddy: A Life-Size Portrait* and Norman Beaseley's *The Cross and the Crown*. While he is not a Christian Scientist, Beaseley's several books on Christian Science are nonetheless so sentimentally adulatory that they are barely sufferable even for the religiously sympathetic reader.

Surely the best work thus far for its sheer wealth of material, much of it previously unpublished, and for its admirable efforts at objectivity is Robert Peel's three-volume biography: *Mary Baker Eddy: The Years of Discovery, Mary Baker Eddy: The Years of Trial*, and *Mary Baker Eddy: The Years of Triumph*. An open apologist for Christian Science, Peel attempts, perhaps too facilely, to ignore or explain away many of the critiques of Mrs. Eddy. The book would have been better if Peel had directly confronted and dealt with the critics instead of relegating their comments to the notes.

Stephen Gottschalk's *The Emergence of Christian Science in American Religious Life* stands beside Peel's work as an admirable effort to deal fairly and objectively with Mrs. Eddy and her movement. Gottschalk's full and sympathetic treatment contains a perceptive analysis of the several Victorian religious crises that made Protestant America receptive to the particular appeal of Christian Science. Gottschalk argues that in the face of the new scientism, Darwinism especially, and Biblical criticism, Christian Science provided in its healing theories the possibility of an empirically verifiable criterion for the truth of religion. Another virtue of Gottschalk's work is his excellent, and probably best available, explication of Mrs. Eddy's sometimes elusive thought. The sometimes controversial history of Christian Science since the death of Mrs. Eddy in 1910 is covered in Charles S. Braden's *Christian Science Today: Power, Policy, Practice*. Braden straightforwardly chronicles the various disputes over orthodox Christian Science that have led to the exclusion of members and the banning of books. A current analysis of Christian Science in relation to mainline Protestantism and the issue of healing is Gottschalk's "Christian Science Today: Resuming the Dialogue."

The opening chapters of Robert Peel's *Christian Science: Its Encounter with American Culture* also attempt to convey the tone of pre-Civil War religious experimentation, especially in transcendentalism, that eventually made the nation receptive to Christian Science. The remainder of the book deals with Mrs. Eddy's occasional relationship with transcendentalist Bronson Alcott. The influence of Oriental thought on transcendentalism and the cultural climate in which Christian Science and New Thought flourished is Carl T. Jackson's *The Oriental Religions and American Thought: Nineteenth-Century Explorations*. Henry W. Steiger's *Christian Science and Philosophy* does not deal with the intellectual background of Christian Science but rather is an after-the-fact attempt at philosophical justification for Christian Science. "The Occult Connection? Mormonism, Christian Science, and Spiritualism" by Laurence R. Moore examines the grounds for mainline suspicions of insurgent religious groups. A more extended treatment by Moore of the origins, appeal, and influence of Christian Science within American religious heterogeneity is "Christian Science and American Popular Religion" in Moore's *Religious Outsiders and the Making of Americans*.

The most thorough history that is devoted exclusively to New Thought is Charles S. Braden's *Spirits in Rebellion: The Rise and Development of New Thought*. Braden's work is comprehensive in describing Quimby's work and the intellectual genealogies of his followers. In addition to a systematic survey of New Thought theology, Braden provides a complete treatment of the various New Thought churches and organizations in this country and abroad. Gail Thain Parker's *Mind Cure in New England: From the Civil War to World War I* offers a sympathetic, if somewhat impressionistic, interpretation of various New Thought figures and tendencies: increased religious doubt, more leisure, and suspicion of orthodox medicine give rise to a quest for psychic fulfillment that is otherwise not available in a listless orthodoxy, a repressed feminism, and a frantic work ethic. A flawed book, *Mind Cure* suffers from a lack of systematic discussion and close textual reading, which makes it elliptical and obscure.

A paucity of secondary material exists on the Pentecostal and charismatic healing revivals in this century. A useful, sympathetic overview of the healing tradition in the history of Christianity is Morton T. Kelsey's *Healing and Christianity*. A brief history of Pentecostalism and its doctrinal departures from historical creedalism is found in Fredrick Dale Bruner's *A Theology*

of the Holy Spirit: The Pentecostal Experience and the New Testament Witness.
A useful anthology of divergent views among charismatics, *The Charismatic
Movement,* is edited by Michael P. Hamilton. *Modern Revivalism: From
Charles Grandison Finney to Billy Graham* by William G. McLoughlin gives
a scholarly treatment of the subject. Dealing specifically with Pentecostal
and charismatic healing is David Edwin Harrell, Jr.'s *All Things Are Possible:
The Healing and Charismatic Revivals in Modern America.* Harrell treats such
popular figures as Aimee Semple McPherson, Oral Roberts, and Kathryn
Kuhlman. A less objective, though still informative, work is James Morris's
The Preachers, which includes studies of the backgrounds and messages of
faith healers Oral Roberts, Kathryn Kuhlman, and Reverend Ike as well as
a number of politically reactionary evangelical preachers. Robert Schuller
has received careful attention in Dennis Voskuil's *Mountains into Goldmines:
Robert Schuller and the Gospel of Success.*

An indispensable guide to the seemingly perennial American conflict between individualistic impulses and social commitment is the best-selling
Habits of the Heart: Individualism and Commitment in American Life by sociologists Robert N. Bellah, Richard Madsen, William M. Sullivan, Ann
Swidler, and Steven M. Tipton. A critique of mid-century forms of psychological self-exaltation is found in Christopher Lasch's best-selling *The
Culture of Narcissism: American Life in an Age of Diminishing Expectations,*
which dissects the origins and complexion of the new psychotherapeutic
and entertainment industries. The role of psychology in contemporary
America is the focus of *The Psychological Society: A Critical Analysis of Psychiatry, Psychotheraphy, Psychoanalysis, and the Psychological Revolution* by
Martin L. Gross. The religious dimensions of modern psychotherapy are
explored in *Psychology as Religion: The Cult of Self-Worship* by Paul Vitz.
And finally, Peter Clecak's *America's Quest for the Ideal Self* attempts to
situate that quest within the cultural history of the 1960s and 1970s.

NOTES

1. James Truslow Adams, *The Founding of New England* (Boston: N.p., 1921),
pp. 121–22; Vernon L. Parrington, *Main Currents in American Thought: The Colonial
Mind, 1620–1800* (New York: Harcourt, 1927), p. 13.

2. Parrington, pp. 12, 13.

3. T. H. Breen and Stephen Foster, "The Puritans' Greatest Achievement: Social
Cohesion in Seventeenth-Century Massachusetts," *Journal of American History,* 60
(1973), 5.

4. Benjamin W. Labaree, *Colonial Massachusetts: A History* (Millwood, NY: KTO
Press, 1979), pp. 40, 72.

5. Breen and Foster, p. 12

6. Kenneth A. Lockridge, *A New England Town: The First Hundred Years, Dedham, Massachusetts, 1636–1736* (New York: W. W. Norton, 1970), p. 16.

7. Ibid., p. 7.

8. Martin E. Marty, *Pilgrims in Their Own Land: 500 Years of Religion in America* (Boston: Little, Brown, 1984), p. 63.

9. Virginia DeJohn Anderson, "Migrants and Motives: Religion and the Settlement of New England, 1630–1640," *New England Quarterly*, 58 (1985), 382.

10. Breen and Foster, p. 10.

11. Lockridge, p. 16.

12. Ibid., pp. 4, 13.

13. Anderson, pp. 366–67.

14. Ibid., pp. 348–49.

15. Sumner Chilton Powell, *Puritan Village: The Formation of a New England Town* (Middletown, Conn.: Wesleyan University Press, 1963), p. 100.

16. Stephen Innes, *Labor in a New Land: Economy and Society in Seventeenth-Century Springfield* (Princeton, N.J.: Princeton University Press, 1983), p. xvi.

17. Darrett B. Rutman, *Winthrop's Boston: A Portrait of a Puritan Town* (Chapel Hill: Institute of Early American History and Culture by the University of North Carolina Press, 1965), p. 243.

18. David Levin, "Introduction." in Cotton Mather, *Bonifacius: An Essay on the Good* (Boston: Harvard University Press, 1966), p. xv.

19. Charles Cohen, *God's Caress: The Psychology of Puritan Religious Experience* (New York: Oxford University Press, 1986), p. 119.

20. Ibid., p. 130.

21. John G. Cawelti, *Apostles of the Self-Made Man* (Chicago: University of Chicago Press, 1965), pp. 9, 12.

22. Kenneth Silverman, "Introduction" in Benjamin Franklin, *The Autobiography and Other Writings* (New York: Penguin Books, 1987), p. ix.

23. Louis B. Wright, "Franklin's Legacy to the Gilded Age," *Virginia Quarterly Review*, 22 (1946), 268–79.

24. Charles Sanford, *Benjamin Franklin and the American Character* (Boston: Heath, 1955), p. 68.

25. Cawelti, pp. 15–16.

26. Ibid., p. 16.

27. Norman S. Fiering, "Benjamin Franklin and the Way to Virtue," *American Quarterly*, 30 (1978), 202.

28. Ibid., pp. 206, 223.

29. Ibid., pp. 221, 222.

30. Ibid., p. 205.

31. Ibid., p. 207.

BIBLIOGRAPHY

Books and Articles

Adams, James Truslow. *The Founding of New England*. Boston: N.p., 1921.

Ahlstrom, Sydney E. *A Religious History of the American People*. New Haven: Yale University Press, 1972.

Albanese, Catherine L. *America, Religions and Religion*. Belmont, Calif.: Wadsworth, 1981.

Allen, David Grayson. "Both Englands." In *Seventeenth-Century New England*. Edited by David D. Hall and David Grayson Allen. Boston: Colonial Society of Massachusetts, 1984, pp. 55–82.

———. *In English Ways: The Movement of Societies and the Transferal of English Local Law and Custom to Massachusetts Bay in the Seventeenth Century*. Chapel Hill: University of North Carolina Press, 1981.

Anderson, Virginia DeJohn. "Migrants and Motives: Religion and the Settlement of New England, 1630–1640." *New England Quarterly*, 58 (1985), 339–83.

Anker, Roy M. "Doubt and Faith in Late Nineteenth-Century American Fiction." Ph.D. dissertation, Michigan State University, 1973.

Atkins, Gaius Glenn. *Modern Religious Cults and Movements*. New York: Revell, 1923.

Baltzell, E. Digby. *Puritan Boston and Quaker Philadelphia: Two Protestant Ethics and the Spirit of Class Authority and Leadership*. Boston: Beacon Press, 1979.

Banta, Martha. *Failure and Success in America: A Literary Debate*. Princeton, N.J.: Princeton University Press, 1978.

Barkun, Michael. *The Crucible of the Spirit: The Burned-Over District of New York in the 1840s*. Syracuse: Syracuse University Press, 1986.

Bates, Ernest Sutherland, and John Valentine Dittemore. *Mary Baker Eddy: The Truth and the Tradition*. New York: Alfred A. Knopf, 1932.

Baym, Nina. *Novels, Readers, and Reviewers: Responses to Fiction in Antebellum America*. Ithaca, N.Y.: Cornell University Press, 1984.

———. *Woman's Fiction: A Guide to Novels by and About Women in America 1820–1870*. Ithaca, N.Y.: Cornell University Press, 1978.

Beard, Charles. *An Economic Interpretation of the Constitution of the United States*. New York: Macmillan, 1913.

Beasley, Norman. *The Continuing Spirit*. New York: Duell, Sloan and Pearce, 1958.

———. *The Cross and the Crown: The History of Christian Science*. New York: Duell, Sloan and Pearce; Little, Brown, 1952.

———. *Mary Baker Eddy*. New York: Duell, Sloan and Pearce, 1963.

Bednarowski, Mary Farrell. *American Religion: A Cultural Perspective*. Englewood Cliffs, N.J.: Prentice-Hall, 1980.

Bellah, Robert N. *The Broken Covenant: American Civil Religion in a Time of Trial*. New York: Seabury, 1975.

Bellah, Robert N., et al. *Habits of the Heart: Individualism and Commitment in American Life*. Berkeley: University of California Press, 1985.

Bellman, Anita Clair, and Michael Fellman. *Making Sense of Self: Medical Advice Literature in Late Nineteenth-Century America*. Philadelphia: University of Pennsylvania Press, 1981.

Bercovitch, Sacvan. "The Puritan Vision of the New World." *Columbia Literary History of the United States*. Edited by Emory Elliott. New York: Columbia University Press, 1988.

Bernhard, Virginia. "Cotton Mather and the Doing of Good: A Puritan Gospel of Wealth." *New England Quarterly*, 49 (1976), 225–41.

Bier, Jesse. "Weberism, Franklin, and Transcendental Style." *New England Quarterly*, 43 (1970), 179–92.

Bonomi, Patricia U. *Under the Cope of Heaven: Religion, Society and Politics in Colonial America*. New York: Oxford University Press, 1986.

Braden, Charles S. *Christian Science Today: Power, Policy, Practice.* Dallas: Southern Methodist University Press, 1963.

————. *Spirits in Rebellion: The Rise and Development of New Thought.* Dallas: Southern Methodist University Press, 1958.

————. *These Also Believe: A Study of Modern American Religious Cults and Minority Religious Movements.* New York: Macmillan, 1949.

Breen, T. H. *Puritans and Adventurers: Change and Persistence in Early America.* New York: Oxford University Press, 1980.

Breen, T. H., and Stephen Foster. "Moving to the New World: The Character of Early Massachusetts Migration." *William and Mary Quarterly,* 3rd ser. 30 (1973), 189–222.

————. "The Puritans' Greatest Achievement: Social Cohesion in Seventeenth-Century Massachusetts." *Journal of American History,* 60 (1973), 5–22.

————. *Tobacco Culture: The Mentality of the Great Tidewater Planters on the Eve of the Revolution.* Princeton, N.J.: Princeton University Press, 1985.

Breitweiser, Mitchell Robert. *Cotton Mather and Benjamin Franklin: The Price Representative Personality.* Cambridge, England: Cambridge University Press, 1984.

Bridenbaugh, Carl. *Early Americans.* New York: Oxford University Press, 1981.

Bromberg, Walter. *From Shaman to Psychotherapist: A History of the Treatment of Mental Illness.* Chicago: Regnery, 1975.

Bruner, Frederick Dale. *A Theology of the Holy Spirit: The Pentecostal Experience and the New Testament Witness.* Grand Rapids, Mich.: Eerdmans, 1970.

Burr, Nelson R., in collaboration with James Ward Smith and A. Leland Jamison. *A Critical Bibliography of Religion in America.* 2 vols. Princeton, N.J.: Princeton University Press, 1971.

Bushman, Richard. *From Puritan to Yankee: Character and the Social Order in Connecticut, 1690–1765.* Cambridge, Mass.: Harvard University Press, 1967.

Buxbaum, Melvin H. *Benjamin Franklin and the Zealous Presbyterians.* University Park: Pennsylvania State University Press, 1975.

————. "Introduction." In *Critical Essays on Benjamin Franklin.* Edited by Melvin H. Buxbaum. Boston: G. K. Hall, 1987.

Caldwell, Patricia. *The Puritan Conversion Narrative: The Beginnings of American Expression.* Cambridge, England: Cambridge University Press, 1983.

Carey, Ralph Allison. "Best-Selling Religion: A History of Popular Religious Thought in America as Reflected in Religious Best-Sellers, 1850–1960." Ph.D. dissertation, Michigan State University, 1971.

Carter, Paul A. *The Spiritual Crisis of the Gilded Age.* DeKalb: Northern Illinois University Press, 1971.

Cawelti, John G. *Apostles of the Self-Made Man.* Chicago: University of Chicago Press, 1965.

Clebsch, William A. *From Sacred to Profane America: The Role of Religion in American History.* New York: Harper, 1968.

Clecak, Peter. *America's Quest for the Ideal Self: Dissent and Fulfillment in the 60s and 70s.* New York: Oxford University Press, 1983.

Cohen, Charles. *God's Caress: The Psychology of Puritan Religious Experience.* New York: Oxford University Press, 1986.

Cott, Nancy F. *The Bonds of Womanhood: "Woman's Sphere" in New England, 1780–1835.* New Haven: Yale University Press, 1977.

Coulson, William R. *Groups, Gimmicks, and Instant Gurus: An Examination of Encounnter Groups and Their Distortions.* New York: Harper, 1972.

Cousins, Norman. *Anatomy of an Illness as Perceived by the Patient: Reflections on Healing and Regeneration.* New York: W. W. Norton, 1979.

Dakin, Edwin Franden. *Mrs. Eddy: The Biography of a Virginal Mind.* New York: Scribner's, 1929.

Dawson, Hugh J. "Fathers and Sons: Franklin's 'Memoirs' as Myth and Metaphor." In *Critical Essays on Benjamin Franklin.* Edited by Melvin H. Buxbaum. Boston: G. K. Hall, 1987.

Demos, John. *A Little Commonwealth: Family Life in Plymouth Colony.* New York: Oxford University Press, 1970.

de Tocqueville, Alexis. *Democracy in America.* Edited by J. P. Mayer and Max Lerner. New York: Harper, 1966.

Diggins, John Patrick. *The Lost Soul of American Politics: Virtue, Self-Interest, and the Foundations of Liberalism.* New York: Basic Books, 1984.

Douglas, Ann. *The Feminization of American Culture.* New York: Alfred A. Knopf, 1977.

Dresser, Horatio W. *A History of the New Thought Movement.* New York: Crowell, 1919.

———, ed. *The Quimby Manuscripts.* New York: Crowell, 1921.

Eckhardt, A. Roy. *The Surge of Piety in America.* New York: Association Press, 1958.

Ellwood, Robert S. *Alternative Altars: Unconventional and Eastern Spirituality in America.* Chicago: University of Chicago Press, 1979.

Elson, Ruth Miller. *Myths and Mores in American Best Sellers, 1865–1965.* New York: Garland, 1985.

Fiering, Norman S. "Benjamin Franklin and the Way to Virtue." *American Quarterly,* 30 (1978), 199–223.

Foster, Stephen. "The Godly in Transit: English Popular Protestantism and the Creation of a Puritan Establishment in America." In *Seventeenth-Century New England.* Edited by David D. Hall and David Grayson Allen. Boston: Colonial Society of Massachusetts, 1984, pp. 185–238.

———. *Their Solitary Way: The Puritan Social Ethic in the First Century of Settlement in New England.* New Haven: Yale University Press, 1971.

Fox, Richard W., and T. J. Jackson Lears, eds. *The Culture of Consumption.* New York: Pantheon, 1983.

Frady, Marshall. *Billy Graham: A Parable of American Righteousness.* Boston: Little, Brown, 1979.

Fuller, Robert C. *Americans and the Unconscious.* New York: Oxford University Press, 1986.

———. *Mesmerism and the American Cure of Souls.* Philadelphia: University of Pennsylvania Press, 1982.

Gans, Herbert J. *Popular Culture and High Culture: An Analysis and Evaluation of Taste.* New York: Basic Books, 1974.

Giddens, Anthony. "Introduction." In Max Weber, *The Protestant Ethic and the Spirit of Capitalism.* Translated by Talcott Parsons. New York: Scribner's, 1976.

Gilbert, James B. "Popular Culture." *American Quarterly,* 35 (1983), 141–54.

Gottschalk, Stephen. "Christian Science Today: Resuming the Dialogue." *The Christian Century,* 103 (1986), 1146–48.

———. *The Emergence of Christian Science in American Religious Life.* Berkeley: University of California Press, 1973.

Green, Harvey. *Fit for America: Health, Fitness, Sport, and American Society.* New York: Pantheon, 1986.

Green, Robert W., ed. *Protestantism and Capitalism: The Weber Thesis and Its Critics.* Boston: Heath, 1959.

Greven, Philip J., Jr. *Four Generations: Population, Land, and Family in Colonial Andover, Massachusetts.* Ithaca, N.Y.: Cornell University Press, 1970.

Griswold, A. Whitney. "The American Gospel of Success." Ph.D. dissertation, Yale University, 1934.

———. "Three Puritans on Prosperity." *New England Quarterly,* 7 (1934), 475–93.

Gross, Martin L. *The Psychological Society: A Critical Analysis of Psychiatry, Psychotherapy, Psychoanalysis, and the Psychological Revolution.* New York: Random House, 1978.

Guthrie, Shirley C., Jr. "The Narcissism of American Piety: The Disease and the Cure." *Journal of Pastoral Care,* 31 (1977), 220–29.

Hackett, Alice Payne, and James Henry. *80 Years of Best Sellers, 1895–1975.* New York: R. R. Bowker, 1977.

Hall, David D. "Toward a History of Popular Religion in New England." *William and Mary Quarterly,* 3rd ser. 41 (1984), 49–55.

———. "A World of Wonders: The Mentality of the Supernatural in Seventeenth-Century New England." In *Seventeenth-Century New England.* Edited by David D. Hall and David Grayson Allen. Boston: Colonial Society of Massachusetts, 1984, pp. 239–74.

Halttunen, Karen. *Confidence Men and Painted Women: A Study of Middle-Class Culture in America, 1830–1870.* New Haven: Yale University Press, 1982.

Hambrick-Stowe, Charles E. *The Practice of Piety: Puritan Devotional Disciplines in Seventeenth-Century New England.* Chapel Hill: University of North Carolina Press for the Institute of Early American History and Culture, 1982.

Hamilton, Michael P., ed. *The Charismatic Movement.* Grand Rapids, Mich.: Eerdmans, 1975.

Harrell, David Edwin, Jr. *All Things Are Possible: The Healing and Charismatic Revivals in Modern America.* Bloomington: Indiana University Press, 1975.

Hart, James D. *The Popular Book: A History of America's Literary Taste.* New York: Oxford University Press, 1950.

Herberg, Will. *Protestant, Catholic, Jew: An Essay in American Religious Sociology.* Rev. ed. New York: Anchor, 1960.

Hoekema, Anthony A. *The Four Major Cults: Christian Science, Jehovah's Witnesses, Mormonism, and Seventh-Day Adventism.* Grand Rapids, Mich.: Eerdmans, 1963.

Hofstadter, Richard. *The Progressive Historians: Turner, Beard, Parrington.* New York: Alfred A. Knopf, 1968.

Huber, Richard M. *The American Idea of Success.* New York: McGraw-Hill, 1971.

Innes, Stephen. *Labor in a New Land: Economy and Society in Seventeenth-Century Springfield.* Princeton, N.J.: Princeton University Press, 1983.

Jackson, Carl T. *The Oriental Religions and American Thought: Nineteenth-Century Explorations.* Westport, Conn.: Greenwood Press, 1981.

Johnson, Paul. *A History of Christianity.* New York: Atheneum, 1977.

Judah, J. Stillson. *The History and Philosophy of the Metaphysical Movements in America.* Philadelphia: Westminster, 1967.

Kelsey, Morton T. *Healing and Christianity: In Ancient Thought and Modern Times.* New York: Harper, 1973.

Labaree, Benjamin W. *Colonial Massachusetts: A History.* Millwood, N.Y.: KTO Press, 1979.

Larkin, Jack. "The View from New England: Notes on Everyday Life in Rural America to 1850." *American Quarterly,* 34 (1982), 244–61.

Larson, David. "Franklin on the Nature of Man and the Possibility of Virtue." *Early American Literature,* 10 (1975), 111–20.

Lasch, Christopher. *The Culture of Narcissism: American Life in an Age of Diminishing Expectations.* New York: W. W. Norton, 1979.

Lazerow, Jama. "Religion and Labor Reform in Antebellum America: The World of William Field Young." *American Quarterly,* 38 (1986), 265–86.

Lears, T. J. Jackson. *No Place of Grace: Antimodernism and the Transformation of American Culture, 1880–1920.* New York: Pantheon, 1983.

Levin, David. "Introduction." In *Bonifacius: An Essay on the Good,* by Cotton Mather. Boston: Harvard University Press, 1966.

Lockridge, Kenneth A. *A New England Town: The First Hundred Years, Dedham, Massachusetts, 1636–1736.* New York: W. W. Norton, 1970.

———. *Settlement and Unsettlement in Early America: The Crisis of Political Legitimacy Before the Revolution.* Cambridge, England: Cambridge University Press, 1981.

Long, Elizabeth. *The American Dream and the Popular Novel.* London: Routledge and Kegan Paul, 1985.

Lucas, Paul R. *Valley of Discord: Church and Society Along the Connecticut River, 1636–1725.* Hanover, N.H.: University Press of New England, 1976.

Lynn, Kenneth S. *The Dream of Success: A Study of the Modern American Imagination.* Boston: Little, Brown, 1955.

McConnell, Donald. *Economic Virtues in the United States: A History and Interpretation.* New York: Arno, 1973.

McCoy, Drew R. "Benjamin Franklin's Vision of a Republican Political Economy for America." *William and Mary Quarterly,* 3rd ser. 35 (1978), 605–28.

McDannell, Colleen. *The Christian Home in Victorian America, 1840–1920.* Bloomington: Indiana University Press, 1986.

Macleod, David I. *Building Character in the American Boy: The Boy Scouts, YMCA, and Their Forerunners, 1870–1920.* Madison: University of Wisconsin Press, 1983.

McLoughlin, William G. *Modern Revivalism: From Charles Grandison Finney to Billy Graham.* New York: Ronald Press, 1959.

Marchand, Roland. *Advertising the American Dream: Making Way for Modernity.* Berkeley: University of California Press, 1985.

Marty, Martin E. *Modern American Religion.* Vol. 1: *The Irony of It All: 1893–1919.* Chicago: University of Chicago Press, 1987.

———. *The New Shape of American Religion.* New York: Harper, 1959.

————. *Pilgrims in Their Own Land: 500 Years of Religion in America.* Boston: Little, Brown, 1984.

Mather, Cotton. *Bonifacius: An Essay upon the Good.* Edited by David Levin. Cambridge, Mass.: Harvard University Press, 1966.

Matthews, Glenna. *"Just a Housewife" : The Rise and Fall of Domesticity in America.* New York: Oxford University Press, 1987.

May, Henry F. *The Enlightenment in America.* New York: Oxford University Press, 1976.

————. "Philip Greven and the History of Temperament." In *Ideas, Faiths, and Feelings: Essays on American Intellectual and Religious History 1952–82.* New York: Oxford University Press, 1983.

————. "The Recovery of American Religious History." In *Ideas, Faiths, and Feelings: Essays on American Intellectual and Religious History 1952–82.* New York: Oxford University Press, 1983.

Mayer, F. E. *The Religious Bodies of America.* St. Louis: Concordia, 1961.

Meyer, Donald B. *The Positive Thinkers: A Study of the American Quest for Health, Wealth, and Personal Power from Mary Baker Eddy to Norman Vincent Peale.* Garden City, N.Y.: Doubleday, 1965.

Meyer, Donald H. "Franklin's Religion." In *Critical Essays on Benjamin Franklin.* Edited by Melvin H. Buxbaum. Boston: G. K. Hall, 1987.

Miles, Richard D. "The American Image of Benjamin Franklin." *American Quarterly,* 9 (1957), 117–43.

Miller, Perry. *The New England Mind: From Colony to Province.* Boston: Harvard University Press, 1953.

————. *The New England Mind: The Seventeenth Century.* Boston: Beacon, 1961.

Milmine, Georgine. *The Life of Mary Baker Eddy and the History of Christian Science.* 2nd ed. Grand Rapids, Mich.: Baker Book House, 1971.

Mitchell, Robert M. *Calvin's and the Puritan's View of the Protestant Ethic.* Washington, D.C.: University Press of America, 1979.

Moore, Laurence R. *In Search of White Crows: Spiritualism, Parapsychology, and American Culture.* New York: Oxford University Press, 1977.

————. "The Occult Connection? Mormonism, Christian Science, and Spiritualism." In *The Occult in America: New Historical Perspectives.* Edited by Howard Kerr and Charles L. Crow. Urbana: University of Illinois Press, 1986.

————. *Religious Outsiders and the Making of Americans.* New York: Oxford University Press, 1986.

Morris, James. *The Preachers.* New York: St. Martin's Press, 1973.

Morrison, Samuel Eliot. *Builders of the Bay Colony.* Boston: N.p., 1930.

Morton, Marian J. *The Terrors of Ideological Politics: Liberal Historians in a Conservative Mood.* Cleveland: Press of Case Western Reserve University, 1972.

Moseley, James G. *A Cultural History of Religion in America.* Westport, Conn.: Greenwood Press, 1981.

Mott, Frank Luther. *Golden Multitudes: The Story of Best Sellers in the United States.* New York: Macmillan, 1947.

Mott, Tracy, and George W. Zinke. "Benjamin Franklin's Economic Thought: A Twentieth Century Appraisal." In *Critical Essays on Benjamin Franklin.* Edited by Melvin H. Buxbaum. Boston: G. K. Hall, 1987.

Myers, David. *The Inflated Self: Human Ills and the Biblical Call to Hope.* New York: Seabury, 1980.

Myers, Gerald E. *William James: His Life and Thought.* New Haven: Yale University Press, 1986.

Nash, Gary. *Class and Society in Early America.* Englewood Cliffs, N.J.: Prentice-Hall, 1970.

Niebuhr, H. Richard. *Christ and Culture.* New York: Harper, 1951.

———. *The Kingdom of God in America.* New York: Harper, 1937.

———. *The Social Sources of Denominationalism.* Cleveland: World, 1957.

Noll, Mark A., et al. *Eerdmans' Handbook to Christianity in America.* Grand Rapids, Mich:. Eerdmans, 1983.

Noll, Mark A., Nathan O. Hatch, and George M. Marsden. *The Search for Christian America.* Grand Rapids, Mich: Eerdmans, 1983.

Norton, Mary Beth. "The Evolution of White Women's Experience in Early America." *American Historical Review,* 89 (1984), 593–619.

Parker, Gail Thain. *Mind Cure in New England: From the Civil War to World War I.* Hanover, N.H.: University Press of New England, 1973.

Parrington, Vernon L. *Main Currents in American Thought: The Colonial Mind, 1620–1800.* New York: Harcourt, 1927.

Peel, Robert. *Christian Science: Its Encounter with American Culture.* New York: Holt, 1958.

———. *Mary Baker Eddy: The Years of Discovery.* New York: Holt, 1966.

———. *Mary Baker Eddy: The Years of Trial.* New York: Holt, 1971.

———. *Mary Baker Eddy: The Years of Triumph.* New York: Holt, 1977.

Powell, Lyman. *Mary Baker Eddy: A Life-Size Portrait.* Boston: Christian Science Publishing Society, 1930.

Powell, Sumner Chilton. *Puritan Village: The Formation of a New England Town.* Middletown, Conn.: Wesleyan University Press, 1963.

Reay, Barry. "Popular Religion." In *Popular Culture in Seventeenth-Century England.* Edited by Barry Reay. London: Croom Helm, 1985.

Rieff, Philip. *The Triumph of the Therapeutic: Uses of Faith After Freud.* New York: Harper, 1966.

Rischin, Moses, ed. *The American Gospel of Success: Individualism and Beyond.* Chicago: Quadrangle, 1965.

Rosen, R. D. *Psychobabble: Fast Talk and Quick Cure in the Era of Feeling.* New York: Atheneum, 1977.

Rutman, Darrett B. *Winthrop's Boston: A Portrait of a Puritan Town.* Chapel Hill: Institute of Early American History and Culture by University of North Carolina Press, 1965.

Salzman, Jack, ed. *American Studies: An Annotated Bibliography.* 3 vols. New York: Cambridge University Press, 1986.

Sanford, Charles. *Benjamin Franklin and the American Character.* Boston: Heath, 1955.

Schneider, Louis, and Sanford M. Dornbusch. *Popular Religion: Inspiration Books in America.* Chicago: University of Chicago Press, 1958.

Selement, George. *Keepers of the Vineyard: The Puritan Ministry and Collective Culture in Colonial New England.* New York: University Press of America, 1984.

———. "The Meeting of Elite and Popular Minds at Cambridge, New England, 1963–45." *William and Mary Quarterly,* 3rd ser. 41 (1984), 32–48.

Shi, David E. *The Simple Life: Plain Living and High Thinking in American Culture.* New York: Oxford University Press, 1985.

Silverman, Kenneth. "From Cotton Mather to Benjamin Franklin." In *Columbia Literary History of the United States*. Edited by Emory Elliot. New York: Columbia University Press, 1988.

———. "Introduction." In *The Autobiography and Other Writings,* by Benjamin Franklin. New York: Penguin Books, 1987.

Skotheim, Robert Allen. *American Intellectual Histories and Historians*. Princeton, N.J.: Princeton University Press, 1966.

Smith, James Ward, and A. Leland Jamison, eds. *The Shaping of American Religion*. Princeton, N.J.: Princeton University Press, 1961.

Steiger, Henry W. *Christian Science and Philosophy*. New York: Philosophical Library, 1948.

Stout, Harry S. *The New England Soul: Preaching and Religious Culture in Colonial New England*. New York: Oxford University Press, 1986.

Studdert-Kennedy, Hugh A. *Mrs. Eddy: Her Life, Her Work, Her Place in History*. San Francisco: Farallon Press, 1947.

Suderman, Elmer F. "Religion and the American Novel, 1870–1900." Ph.D. dissertation, University of Kansas, 1961.

Sussman, Warren I. *Culture as History: The Transformation of American Society in the Twentieth Century*. New York: Pantheon, 1984.

Turner, James. *Without God, Without Creed: The Origins of Unbelief in American Culture*. Baltimore: Johns Hopkins University Press, 1985.

Vance, Norman. *The Sinews of the Spirit: The Ideal of Christian Manliness in Victorian Literature and Religious Thought*. Cambridge, England: Cambridge University Press, 1985.

Vidich, Arthur J., and Stanford M. Lyman. *American Sociology: Worldly Rejections of Religion and Their Directions*. New Haven: Yale University Press, 1985.

Vitz, Paul. *Psychology as Religion: The Cult of Self-Worship*. Grand Rapids, Mich.: Eerdmans, 1979.

Voskuil, Dennis. *Mountains into Goldmines: Robert Schuller and the Gospel of Success*. Grand Rapids, Mich.: Eerdmans, 1983.

Walzer, Michael. *The Revolution of the Saints: A Study in the Origins of Radical Politics*. Cambridge, Mass.: Harvard University Press, 1965.

Weber, Max. *The Protestant Ethic and the Spirit of Capitalism*. Translated by Talcott Parsons. New York: Scribner's, 1958.

Weintraub, Karl J. "The Puritan Ethic and Benjamin Franklin." *Journal of Religion,* 56 (1976), 223–37.

Weiss, Richard. *The American Myth of Success: From Horatio Alger to Norman Vincent Peale*. New York: Basic Books, 1969.

Welter, Barbara. *Dimity Convictions: The American Woman in the Nineteenth Century*. Athens: Ohio University Press, 1976.

Whalen, William J. *Faiths for the Few: A Study of Minority Religions*. Milwaukee: Bruce, 1963.

Wilbur, Sybil. *The Life of Mary Baker Eddy*. Boston: Christian Science Publishing Society, 1913.

Williams, Peter. *Popular Religion in America: Symbolic Change and the Modernization Process in Historical Perspective*. Englewood Cliffs, N.J.: Prentice-Hall, 1980.

Wise, Gene. *American Historical Explanations: A Strategy for Grounded Inquiry*. 2nd ed. Minneapolis: University of Minnesota Press, 1980.

Wright, Louis B. *The Cultural Life of the American Colonies, 1607–1793.* New York: Harper, 1957.

———. "Franklin's Legacy to the Gilded Age." *Virginia Quarterly Review,* 22 (1946), 268–79.

———. *New Interpretations of American Colonial History.* Washington, D.C.: American Historical Association, 1960.

Wyllie, Irvin G. *The Self-Made Man in America: The Myth of Rags to Riches.* New York: Free Press, 1954.

Zuckerman, Michael. *Peaceable Kingdoms: New England Towns in the Eighteenth Century.* New York: Alfred A. Knopf, 1970.

———. "The Social Context of Democracy in Massachusetts." *William and Mary Quarterly,* 3rd ser. 25 (1968), 523–44.

Zweig, Paul. *The Heresy of Self-Love: A Study of Subversive Individualism.* Princeton, N.J.: Princeton University Press, 1980.

Zweig, Stefan. *Mental Healers: Franz Anton Mesmer, Mary Baker Eddy, Sigmund Freud.* New York: Frederick Ungar, 1962.

Periodicals

American Quarterly. Baltimore, 1948–.

Church History. Wallingford, Pa., 1931–.

Journal of American History. Montpelier, Vt., 1914–.

New England Quarterly. Boston, 1927–.

Religious Studies Review. Macon, Ga., 1974–.

William and Mary Quarterly. Richmond, Va., 1943–.

Sports

ROBERT J. HIGGS

What is sport? The truth is that no one knows, and the challenge to define it, or at least to describe its characteristics, has engaged the attention of some of the best scholars of our time, always with beneficial results but never with answers that satisfy completely. Johan Huizinga in *Homo Ludens,* a book that is *sine qua non* on any aspect of the subject of sport, says, "In our heart of hearts we know that none of our pronouncements is absolutely conclusive."[1] Like Tennyson's flower in the crannied wall, we know that sport *is,* but we do not know with certainty what it is. Nevertheless, we are compelled to seek understanding of anything that so engages the interest of mankind as sport or play. In fact, play has become so important that it can no longer be left exclusively to the players. The influence of games on societies, from the bloody Roman spectacles to the staged demonstrations of the modern Olympiad and the Super Bowl, is simply staggering. Sport, as one observer has claimed, is the new opiate of the masses, as it has probably always been, though never so freely administered as in the modern world.

" 'Sport', 'athletics', 'games', and 'play'," says Paul Weiss, "have in common the idea of being cut off from the workaday world."[2] Here he is in agreement with Huizinga as he is with Roger Caillois, who claims that play is free, separate, uncertain, unproductive, and governed by both rules and make-believe.[3] "Sport," as Weiss reminds us, means "to disport," "that is, to divert and amuse." Hence sport is that aspect of culture by which men divert themselves from labor as opposed to work. This important distinction is well made by Hannah Arendt in *The Human Condition* in her discussion of the difference between *animal laborans,* laboring animal, and *homo faber,* man the maker or artist, which is succinctly implied in the phrase "the work of our hands and the labor of our body."[4] Today it is essential to realize that in professional sports the athlete is quite often player, laborer, and artist, one who laboriously sculpts a life of meaning out of his or her physical nature. Though lines between different activities frequently become blurred, I consider sport as "unnecessary" action in the sense that it is not *required* for survival as are forms of labor, such as farming. I also regard sport as an activity that requires the expenditure of a substantial amount of physical energy, more than that needed to play a game of bridge or checkers, though these too are certainly forms of play and diversions from labor.

HISTORIC OUTLINE

"What is play? What is serious?" Huizinga asks. The Puritans would have had far less difficulty in answering these questions than we would today. For them, any effort not devoted to the good of the colony was to be eschewed, and games did not seem to lend themselves to the general welfare. In 1621 Governor William Bradford rebuked the young men he found "in ye streete at play, openly; some pitching ye barr and some at stooleball, and such like sports." There should not be, in the governor's view, any "gameing or revelling in ye streets," nor, if we are to judge from the incident of the maypole of Merry Mount, any reveling in the country either.

Though there is debate as to the degree of hostility the Puritans held toward games, it seems safe to say that they were not exactly sports fans.[5] In 1647, for instance, a court order was issued against shuffleboard in Massachusetts Bay, and in 1650 the same injunction was extended against "bowling or any other play or games in or about houses of common entertainment."[6] In 1693 in eastern Connecticut a man "was fined twelve shillings and sentenced to six hours in the stocks for playing ball on the Sabbath. . . . Apparently, either he was playing alone or his teammates were let go with a warning, since he was the only man convicted."[7] The Puritan attitude toward fun and games in the view of many is perhaps best illustrated in Macaulay's remark that bear-baiting was stopped not because it gave pain to the bear but because it provided pleasure to the spectators.

The "Detestation of Idleness" was not confined to New England. In Virginia in 1619 "the assembly decreed that any person found idle should be bound over to compulsory work; it prohibited gaming at dice or cards, strictly regulated drinking, provided penalties for excess in apparel and rigidly enforced Sabbath observance."[8] Interdictions against racing within the city limits of New Amsterdam were issued in 1657, and two years later Governor Peter Stuyvesant proclaimed a day of fast on which would be forbidden "all exercise and games of tennis, ball-playing, hunting, fishing, plowing, and sowing, and moreover all unlawful practices such as dice and drunkenness.'"[9] Restrictions of activities in some form on Sunday could be found wherever the new American civilization was extended on the frontier.

As John A. Krout, Foster Rhea Dulles, and others have pointed out, the theocracy did not represent all of New England, and the narrow sanctions of the ruling class had in the long run little chance of being obeyed. The human propensity to play could not be stilled. Sport grew not only in New England but all along the frontier. Hunting and fishing flourished, frequently as a means for gaining food, but also as a form of diversion. Forests and rivers seemed to contain an endless supply of game and fish, and many availed themselves of the abundance: "Even Cotton Mather fished. Samuel Sewall tells of the time when the stern old Puritan went out with line and tackle and fell into the water at Spy Pond, 'the boat being ticklish.' "[10] For those who have read Mather's prose, this is a pleasing image indeed.

The growth of recreation, even during the latter part of the seventeenth century, can be inferred from the journal of Sarah Kembell Knight, who wrote of her travels through Connecticut in 1704:

Their diversions in this part of the country are on lecture days and training days mostly: on the former there is riding from town to town . . . and on training days the youth divert themselves by shooting at the targets, as they call it (but it very much resembles a pillory). When he that hits nearest the white has some yards of red ribbon presented to him, which being tied to his hattband, he is led away in triumph, with great applause, as the winners of the Olympiak Games.[11]

At the beginning of the nineteenth century there was a wide diversity of amusements in the North, at least as reported by President Timothy Dwight of Yale:

The principal amusements of the inhabitants are visiting, dancing, music, conversation, walking, riding, sailing, shooting at a mark, draughts, chess, and unhappily, in some of the larger towns, cards and dramatic exhibitions. . . . Our countrymen also fish and hunt. Journeys taken for pleasure are very numerous, and are a very favorite object. Boys and young men play at foot-ball, cricket, quoits, and at many other sports of an athletic cast, and in the winter are peculiarly fond of skating. Riding in a sleigh, or sledge, is also a favorite diversion in New England.[12]

Ninepins, skittles, and bowls were common at inns in the North for the convenience of the guests,[13] while in the South shooting matches were preferred, with "beef shooting" being one of the favorite forms.[14]

The sports that seemed to attract the most attention in the South, however, were cockfighting and horseracing. According to Hugh Jones in 1724, "The common planters don't much admire labour or any other manly exercise except Horse racing, nor diversion, except Cock-Fighting, in which some greatly delight." In tones suggestive of William Byrd, he adds, "This

Way of Living and the Heat of the Summer make some very lazy, who are then said to be Climate-struck."[15]

While the foreign traveler, especially the English, as Henry Adams notes,

charged the Virginians with fondness for horse-racing and cock-fighting, betting and drinking, . . . the popular habit which most shocked them, and with which books of travel filled pages of description was the so-called rough and tumble fight. The practice was not one on which authors seemed likely to dwell; yet foreigners like Weld, and Americans like Judge Longstreet in 'Georgia Scenes' united to give it a sort of grotesque dignity like that of the bull-fight, and under their treatment it became interesting as a popular habit.[16]

The rough and tumble, Adams argues, did not originate in Virginia, but came to America from England, as did, according to Jennie Holliman, most American sports, excepting those practices learned from the Indians, such as methods of hunting and trapping deer and bear, the use of bows and arrows, fishing at night with lights on canoes, lacrosse, and even rolling the hoop. Still, the predominant influence was from abroad. The gun itself is a good example. "Up to 1830," says Holliman, "a few fine guns had been made in America, but they did not sell to an advantage simply because they were not imported." The same was true for fishing equipment, twine, tackles, hooks, flies, and rods, which came from Holland as well as England. Sleighs also came from Holland, while bridles, harnesses, and saddles came from England.[17]

The history of horseracing has to a large extent been the history of selective breeding, of which Diomed and Messenger provide excellent examples. Diomed was brought to Virginia in 1789 and came to be held in such esteem that his death in 1808 caused almost as much mourning as that for Washington in 1799.[18] Messenger, bred by the Earl of Grosvenor on his Yorkshire farm, was brought to America a few years after the Revolution by Thomas Berger of Pennsylvania. Prized as a stud, Messenger was the sire of a long line of racing immortals, including American Eclipse, who defeated Sir Henry of Virginia at the Union course on Long Island in 1823, the first intersectional race that illustrated once and for all the popular appeal of the sport. Another offspring of Messenger was Hambletonian, the horse that turned harness racing into a national mania: "In the 1850's, the nation worshipped Hambletonian. It bought commemorative plates on which his likeness was inscribed. Children talked about him as if he were human."[19] Spurred on by the creation of jockey clubs, the establishment of race courses, and the support of the aristocracy, horseracing became America's first organized sport and has remained unquestionably one of its most popular.

The wide interest in the turf helped to bring about the rise of sporting literature in the three decades before the Civil War. The first sporting magazine in America was the *American Turf Register,* published in Baltimore in 1829 by John Stuart Skinner. Ten years later Skinner sold the *Register* to William Trotter Porter, who had already begun his own weekly sporting publication called *Spirit of the Times,* one of the most famous of all American publications and a reservoir of the history of American popular culture from 1831 to 1861. Prominent among contributors to this magazine were Thomas B. Thorpe, who inaugurated the "Big Bear school of humor," and the Englishman Henry William Herbert, who wrote under the pen name "Frank Forester" and who introduced "something of the English point of view of sport for sport's sake."[20]

Baseball, like horseracing, has its roots in the nineteenth century and, also like horseracing, owes more perhaps to the English than we are inclined to admit. The myth that Abner Doubleday invented baseball is totally without foundation. According to Wells Twombly, "The rules of baseball attributed to Doubleday in 1839 were identical to those in a rule book for the English game of rounders published in London in 1827."[21] In America rounders became known as "town ball" and was played at Harvard as early as 1829. In *The Book of Sport* (1827) Robert Carver related that many Britons, like the Americans, were calling the game by a new name, "base ball," and that it was "becoming a distinct threat to cricket."[22] Both the game and the new name caught on quickly in America, and by the 1850s the *Spirit of the Times* was calling it "The National Game."[23] By the 1880s daily attendance at the games was some 60,000. It had become "far and away the leading spectator sport."[24]

As Foster Rhea Dulles has observed, the role of colleges in the rise of sports in the decades after the Civil War was not one of leadership. The only sport that undergraduates developed was football, and again the English influence is incontrovertible. Basketball, in fact, is the only popular American ball game whose origins are not English, being invented by James A. Naismith in Springfield, Massachusetts, in 1891. American football evolved from soccer to rugby to "American" rugby and finally to the game we know today. While the basic forms derived from England, the Americans had long demonstrated a fondness for games of mayhem. Harvard, for example, "had a festival in the early 1800's which qualified vaguely as football. It was called Bloody Monday, but the upperclassmen mostly kicked the freshmen and only occasionally the ball."[25] Though it was essentially soccer instead of rugby, what is called the first intercollegiate football game took place in 1869 between Princeton and Rutgers at New Brunswick. Rutgers won, no thanks to the player who, becoming confused and endearing himself to all future generations, kicked the ball through the opposing Princeton's goal. The first contest was played before a small crowd, but approximately twenty years later Princeton played Yale before a crowd of almost 40,000.[26] Thus long before the turn of the century football was well established as a mass spectator sport.

The one overriding fact concerning sport in America is its phenomenal growth. From William Bradford's injunction against games on Christmas Day in 1621 to Super Sunday of any year there has been a complete reversal of attitudes. Why did such changes occur? No one seems to be able to offer any conclusive answers except the human love of sport and the need for heroes. One thing is undeniable, however, and that is the argument that the widespread growth of sport was brought about in part by the revolution in technology in the decades after the Civil War. Says John R. Betts, "Antebellum sport had capitalized on the development of the steamboat, the railroad, the telegraph, and the penny press, and in succeeding decades the role of technology in the rise of sport proved even more significant."[27]

Of major importance in the promotion of sports has been the press, a major product of technology. Following the lead of the *Spirit of the Times*, new periodicals drawing attention to sport began to appear after the war. Among these were *Baseball Magazine, Golfer's Magazine, Yachting*, and the *Saturday Evening Post*. Newspapers from coast to coast began to devote more and more space to sports, until finally they had a section of their own. According to Betts, "Frank Luther Mott designated the years 1892–1914 as a period in newspaper history when sporting news underwent remarkable development, being segregated on special pages, with special makeup pictures, and news writing style."[28] Books, too, continued to arouse interest, especially among the younger generation. Among the many writers bringing dreams of fair play and heroism to millions of American youth were Gilbert Patten (Burt L. Standish), Henry Barbour, Zane Grey, and Edward Stratemeyer.[29] The champion producer of all in this group of juvenile writers was Gilbert Patten, who wrote a Frank Merriwell story once a week for nearly twenty years and had only one nervous breakdown. Estimates of the sales of Merriwell novels run as high as 500 million copies.[30]

The press helped bring together heroes and hero worshippers, but other developments also played crucial roles in the expansion of sports. It would be hard, for example, to overestimate the importance of the railroad and the telegraph in the spread of games. Because of the growing rail network, the Cincinnati Red Stockings could travel from Maine to California, and John L. Sullivan could go on a grand tour of athletic clubs, opera houses, and theaters. Revolution in mass transit meant mass audiences, and for those who could not come to the games, the telegraph provided instant news of results. The Atlantic cable, electrification, radio, and television all influenced sport in profound ways that are still only vaguely understood. Because of technology the city of New Orleans could build in 1974 a bronze-topped stadium with a gigantic screen for instant replays at a total cost of over $285 million. As Wells Twombly asks, "Was this only the beginning . . . or was it the end?"

REFERENCE WORKS

A basic reference work that librarians will find indispensable and researchers in sport very helpful is *Biography Index*, a multi-volume cumulative index of biographical material in books and magazines dating from 1946 to the present. In the area of sport almost one hundred categories and associated fields are listed, and further distinction is made between adult and juvenile items. Literally hundreds and perhaps thousands of biographies and auto-biographies have been written on American sports figures. Most of the autobiographies are co-authored and seem to follow the same general pattern, describing the hero's or heroine's childhood, early promises and disappointments, and the subsequent rise to fame and success. Joseph Campbell's theory of the monomyth is no doubt confirmed in every issue. For facts and bibliographic information on players, managers, officials, coaches, and even executives and administrators, the source to consult is *Biographical Dictionary of American Sports,* edited by David L. Porter, with separate volumes on football, baseball, indoor sports, and outdoor sports.

The need for basic information in any research is unending, and in sport the best source is Frank G. Menke's *The Encyclopedia of Sport.* The sixth edition of this work is over 1,000 pages long and contains a listing of records in both amateur and professional sports as well as attendance figures, all-American teams, money won on horse and dog racing, and other data. *Webster's Sports Dictionary* is well designed to serve another recurring need, that for a quick explanation of the many terms that saturate the world of sports. Other helpful features of the dictionary are diagrams of courts and fields (with measurements) and action illustrations, as well as referee signals and methods of keeping score. *The Oxford Companion to World Sport and Games,* edited by John Arlott, also contains such information in even more detail. For books and articles on the issues of sports see *Sports: A Reference Guide* by Robert J. Higgs.

RESEARCH COLLECTIONS

The booming popularity of sport and the quiet dedication of librarians, scholars, and sports enthusiasts have led to a number of fine collections of sporting materials in libraries in various parts of the country. One of the most comprehensive is that of the Citizens Savings Athletic Foundation in Los Angeles. The foundation maintains both a sports museum, which contains perhaps the most complete collection in the world of Olympic games awards and memorabilia, and a sports library, which is especially strong on Olympic games publications. It has a large number of sports films, available on a loan basis, and thousands of sports photographs, files of sports magazines, and souvenir programs dating back many years. The foundation has also instituted Halls of Fame, excepting baseball, in various sports. The sites of these institutions, many of which house libraries as well as museums, can be obtained by writing the foundation.

One of the most extensive collections on sporting materials of all kinds is in the Applied Life Studies Library at the University of Illinois at Champaign-Urbana. The library's card catalog of approximately 51,000 entries was published by G. K. Hall and Company in 1976. Fields included in this impressive listing are sports medicine, recreation materials, theories of play, health and safety, and dance, to mention only a few. The Chicago Historical Society has a general collection of about 2,000 volumes concerned primarily with team sports in the areas of biography, history, and statistics. For additional information on the collection, see appendix 2 in *Sports: A Reference Guide* by Higgs.

HISTORY AND CRITICISM

A study of the history of sport tells us what role sport has actually played in our lives; a study of the issues reveals what roles sport *should* play. Among these many issues are the questions of emphasis, mind/body relationship, professionalism and amateurism, religion, racism, women in sports, language, drugs, and aggression. Before the interested scholar begins study in these or other aspects of sports, however, he or she needs some knowledge of what has already occurred on the American sporting scene, and the few books already referred to are indispensable in this regard.

The basic book to start with is John A. Krout's *Annals of American Sport*, the first full-length study of the subject. The influence of Krout is acknowledged in one way or another by the authors of other important histories, including Jennie Holliman in *American Sports (1785–1835)*, Foster Rhea Dulles in *America Learns to Play*, and John R. Betts in his invaluable *America's Sporting Heritage, 1850–1950*. Betts's book grew out of his 1951 dissertation at Columbia University and is without question the most comprehensive work ever done in the history of American sport. It is a mine of information, and the extensive references are probably the most exhaustive ever published on the popular aspects of sport. An excellent bibliography of sources through the 1850s is Robert W. Henderson's *Early American Sport*, and a good general bibliography can be found in the appendix to Robert Boyle's *Sport: Mirror of American Life*.

Another section of Boyle's book worthy of notice is the chapter on Frank Merriwell entitled "The Unreal Ideal." Merriwell's influence as a hero has been pervasive, and another, more detailed look at this phenomenon can be found in Patten's autobiography, *Frank Merriwell's "Father."* Another work that sheds a great deal of light on juvenile sports literature is Robert Cantwell's article on Ralph Henry Barbour and William Heyliger, called "A Sneering Laugh with the Bases Loaded," in *Sports Illustrated*. One oversight in almost all bibliographies is the omission of certain sections in Henry Adams's *History of the United States During the Jefferson and Madison Administrations*, especially chapters 1–6. Not only does Adams offer humorous and penetrating insights of his own, but he summarizes effectively the opinions of a number of foreign travelers commenting upon American culture.

Among several texts suitable for classroom use in sports history are *American Sports: From the Age of Folk Games to the Age of Spectators* by Benjamin G. Rader, *Saga of American Sport* by John A. Lucas and Ronald A. Smith, *Sport and American Mentality, 1880–1940* by Donald J. Mrozek, *Sports in Modern America* by William J. Baker and John M. Carroll, and *Sports in America: New Historical Perspectives,* edited by Donald Spivey. A number of model studies deal with sport in a specific locale, such as *The Rise of Sports in New Orleans, 1850–1900* by Dale A. Somers and *A Sporting Time: New York City and the Rise of Modern Athletics, 1820–70* by Melvin L. Adelman. These should also be considered as sources for texts when planning courses.

A student of American sport will frequently find it desirable to know something of attitudes toward sport in other times and places, especially ancient Greece and Rome and nineteenth-century England. E. Norman Gardiner's *Athletics of the Ancient World* is a seminal work on sport in classical times and still of great worth, especially if supplemented by such works as *The Olympic Games: The First Thousand Years,* by M. I. Finley and H. W. Plecket, an impressive work that challenges many of the traditional assumptions on ancient sports. David Young, in turn, in *The Olympic Myth of Greek Amateur Athletics,* takes Plecket and others to task for imposing, in Young's view, nineteenth-century attitudes toward amateurism on ancient sports where, he says, the idea did not exist. A valuable bibliography is Rachel Sargent Robinson's *Sources for the History of Greek Athletics,* which should be supplemented by Thomas F. Scanlon's *Greek and Roman Athletics: A Bibliography,* which includes works from 1573 to 1983. For a background on English sport, an indispensable book is Joseph Strutt's *The Sports and Pastimes of the People of England.* A good treatment of sport during the later Victorian period, especially as dealt with in the literature of the period, is Bruce Haley's *The Healthy Body and Victorian Culture.* On the relationship between sports and education, the work to turn to is *Athleticism in the Victorian and Edwardian Public Schools* by J. A. Mangan.

An excellent text which traces sports from ancient times to the present is *Sports in the Western World* by William J. Baker. Several observers have noted disturbing parallels between the excesses of ancient and modern sports, most notably, perhaps, Arnold Toynbee in *The Breakdown of Civilizations,* Volume 4, *A Study of History.*

American literature is a vast reservoir of popular culture. William T. Porter's journal *Spirit of the Times: A Chronicle of the Turf, Agriculture, Field Sports, Literature and Stage,* which was published from 1830 to 1861, is itself a mine of sporting stories in the nineteenth century. Sports, that is, athletics in contrast to sport, hunting, and fishing, did not become prominent in fiction until the second decade of this century; the writer who introduced the subject to the American public on a broad scale was Ring Lardner with his stories of bushers. Since Lardner, virtually every major writer and playwright has dealt in some way with the theme of sports. As in history, there are several anthologies, among them *Literature of Sport,* edited by Tom Dodge, *Sport Inside Out,* edited by David L. Vanderwerken and Spencer K. Wertz, and *The Sporting Spirit: Athletes in Literature and Life,* edited by Robert J. Higgs and Neil D. Isaacs. *American Sport Culture: The Humanistic Dimensions,* edited by Wiley Lee Umphlett, is especially suitable for an interdisciplinary approach, as is *Sport Inside Out.*

With the rise in popularity of sports literature, there have also appeared a number of critical studies. The first, *The Sporting Myth and the American Experience,* was by Wiley Lee Umphlett, who shows that much American fiction from the early romances to recent neo-romanticism makes use of sports figures to give form and meaning to the American experience. *Laurel and Thorn* by Robert J. Higgs examines the types of athletes in American literature as representatives of the balance between body and mind. In *Playful Fiction and Fictional Players,* Neil D. Berman provides an in-depth study of five novels—*Fat City, North Dallas Forty, End Zone, One on One,* and *Universal Baseball Association*—and argues that in order to become a transforming reality in the indoor world, play must be internalized. Christian K. Messenger in *Sport and the Spirit of Play in American Fiction* looks at American literature from Hawthorne to Faulkner in terms of play modes identified by Roger Caillois in *Man, Play and Games*—*Agon* (competition), *Alea* (chance), *Mimicry* (imitation), and *Ilinx* (irrational whirling)—and concludes that Faulkner's "work with play images is the most complete for he could create in all the play modes." Michael Oriard[31] in *Dreaming of Heroes: American Sports Fiction, 1868–1980* treats sports fiction in terms of country and. city, youth and age, history and myth, all of which figure prominently in Bernard Malamud's *The Natural,* which Oriard examines at length, relating events in the novel to events in American life as well as to ancient myths. Since a number of colleges now offer courses on literature and the history of sports, there is even a published collection of syllabi entitled *Sport History: Selected Reading Lists and Course Outlines from American Colleges and Universities,* edited by Douglas A. Noverr and Lawrence E. Ziewacz.

Other disciplines have not neglected the study of sports as seen in such texts as *Philosophic Inquiry in Sport,* edited by William J. Morgan and Klaus V. Meier, and *Studies in the Sociology of Sport,* edited by Aiden O. Dunleavy, Andrew W. Miracle, and C. Roger Rees. A highly acclaimed book on politics is *Sport and Political Ideology* by John M. Hoberman, who seeks to examine why political ideologies such as Marxism and Nazism demonstrate distinctive views of sports. Since there have been so many celebrated abuses in sports, it is not surprising that many recent books and articles deal with the ethics of sports. Among the best of these is *Sports and Social Values* by Robert L. Simon, who believes that competition can be beneficial to all participants if conceived and applied as a mutual quest for excellence as opposed to an egotistical quest for superiority. A contrary view is that of

Bruce C. Ogilive and Thomas A. Tutko, as is suggested by the title of their article, "Sports: If You Want to Build Character, Try Something Else."

Whether or not sports can build character is debatable, but there is no debating the emerging alliance between sport and religion. In *Sociology of Sport* Harry Edwards has pointed out numerous parallels between sport and religion, and some, such as Charles Prebish, cited in an article by N. Scott Vance, have gone so far as to call sports a new religion. The kinship between sports and religion is as old as the beginning of the Olympics, and in America was remarked most notably at the turn of the century by Thorstein Veblen who, in *Theory of the Leisure Class* saw sports and religion as two of the four occupations of the leisure class and predatory culture, the other two being government and warfare. Veblen's argument is a compelling one and, as far as I know, has never been successfully refuted. Sports and religion was the subject of a three-part series in *Sports Illustrated* in 1977 by Frank Deford, who coined the term *sportianity* and examined the growing phenomenon with the perceptive eye of the reporter. Michael Novak's highly readable *The Joy of Sports* is not only a ringing defense of sports but an argument that sports inevitably spring from a religious commitment, regardless of the form that commitment may take.

To what extent sport and religion are allied or ought to be is open to question, but that sports generate and reflect social and cultural attitudes and hence values there seems to be little doubt. The commercialism that helped to bring about the proliferation of sports has, ironically, precipitated a widespread criticism of the athletic establishment. At least by the 1920s, and probably much earlier, observers were questioning the commercialism of mass sports, and by the 1960s and 1970s the concern had grown to a type of outrage, as seen in such works as Paul Hoch's *Rip Off the Big Game: The Exploitation of Sports by the Power Elite* and Jack Scott's *The Athletic Revolution*. Athletes, too, jumped on the bandwagon. Dave Meggyesy in *Out of Their League* and Gary Shaw in *Meat on the Hoof* voiced trenchant criticism over the way athletes were being exploited for materialistic ends. While football was the sport generally singled out for attack, baseball has not been completely immune. Even such a devoted fan as Roger Angell in *Five Seasons: A Baseball Companion* has registered regret over promotional practices that tend to rob the game of its traditional appeal. *Jock Culture, USA* by Neil D. Isaacs and *Sportsworld: An American Dreamland* by Robert Lipsyte not only examine the exploitation of the athlete but also question the pervasiveness of sports in our society and warn against the dangers as far as values, institutions, and modes of thought are concerned.

The purpose of some books is not so much to criticize the current sports establishment as to point to new directions in mind/body relationships. Two engaging works published in the Esalen-Viking series are Michael Murphy's *Golf in the Kingdom* and George Leonard's *The Ultimate Athlete*.

Both examine the concept of the "inner body." Leonard's book contains an appendix listing seven new games for the "Sports Adventurers." In *The Psychic Side of Sports* Michael Murphy and Rhea A. White present numerous stories from "the spiritual underground of sports." Well documented, it contains a bibliography of 538 items identified in ten categories of psychic phenomena in sports. As valuable as the book is, the implied parallel between the spirit in religion and the spirit in sport may be askew. The psychic and the sacred are not exactly synonymous.

Both Leonard and Murphy reflect a strong element of Eastern influence, and the classic work on the Oriental approach to sport, indeed the precursor of many others, is Eugene Herrigel's *Zen in the Art of Archery,* which is generally praised but which comes under attack by Arthur Koestler in *The Lotus and the Robot.* In the Zen mastery of archery Koestler finds not the spirit of the Buddha but the basic principles of modern behaviorism. Whether science or religion (or both) is a work in the Zen way, the impact it has had upon American culture in recent years has been immeasurable, not only upon Americans sitting still and meditating but upon those in action, and not just in aikido. The principles, the theory goes, apply to any undertaking, hence a spate of books and articles in which Eastern methods are applied to Western sports, for example, Fred Rohe's *Zen of Running.* A good discussion of the marriage of East and West is "Sport Is Western Yoga" in *Powers of Mind* by Adam Smith. Another work influenced by Zen, as well as by Shinto and Confucianism, which serves as a guide for businessmen as well as athletes is *A Book of Five Rings* by Miyamoto Musashi (1584–1645), Japanese "sword-saint." An ancient classic, it has become a modern best seller, heading every martial arts bibliography. It has been called "Japan's answer to the Harvard MBA." To some, an element of sophistry appears in the ease with which ancient Oriental formulas for strength and wisdom are put to the service of profit. Concentration is concentration, but a difference in the goals of activities must be considered. Self-defense and self-knowledge, the goals of Oriental martial systems, do not in the long run automatically equate with financial success.

A recurring theme in the plethora of books critical of modern sports has been the status of the black athlete. Notable works on this subject are Harry Edwards's *The Revolt of the Black Athlete,* Jack Olsen's *The Black Athlete: A Shameful Story,* and *Baseball's Great Experiment: Jackie Robinson and His Legacy* by Jules Tygiel. Since much of the controversy over the black athlete has centered not only around forms of exploitation but also on arguments of racial superiority, the researcher should not overlook John Lardner's *White Hopes and Other Tigers,* Martin Kane's *Sports Illustrated* article, "An Assessment of 'Black is Best,' " Harry Edwards's rebuttal in "The Myth of the Racially Superior Athlete," and the *Time* article, "The Black Dominance." Also instructive in putting the black athlete in perspective is David

K. Wiggins's article, "Clio and the Black Athlete in America: Myths, Heroes, and Realities."

The role of women in sports is also a frequently debated issue supposedly settled by the passage of Title IX of the Education Amendments Act of 1972, which stipulated the withholding of federal funds for those who discriminate on the basis of sex in school programs, including physical education and athletics. Conceivably, this act in and of itself could revolutionize athletics in the schools, but that is not likely to happen without a wider understanding of the role and possibilities of women in sport. Important works in this area are those by Pearl Berlin et al., *The American Woman in Sports*, Eleanor Metheny, *Connotations of Movement in Sport and Dance*, Donna Mae Miller and Katherine R. E. Russell, *Sport: A Contemporary View*, and J. A. Mangan and Roberta J. Park, *From 'Fair Sex' to Feminism*. A number of anthologies contain sections on the subject and/or extensive references and bibliographies. Among these are *Sport in the Sociocultural Process*, edited by Marie M. Hart. Perhaps the most comprehensive reference work, edited by Mary L. Remley, is *Women in Sport: A Guide to Information Sources*.

The student of popular culture and especially the teacher of English will more than likely be interested in the relationship between sports and language, since the abuse of language, especially superlatives, is a daily occurrence. Again, on this subject, as on many others, a good place to start is with John R. Betts in the section entitled "Lingo, Lexicon, and Language" in *America's Sporting Heritage, 1850–1950*. Helpful sources are referred to in his notes. A good article on sports and mass communications is "Sportuguese: A Study of Sports Page Communication," which is included in one of the best anthologies on the sociological aspects of sports, *Sports, Culture and Society*, edited by John W. Loy, Jr., and Gerald S. Kenyon. Also included in this work is an article on sport in mass society from a seminal book on mass media and popular culture, Reuel Denney's *The Astonished Muse*. There are several how-to books by sports writers; the best of these is *The Red Smith Reader*.

Stirred by the endless use of such terms in sports pages as "scalp," "throttle," "blast," etc., the controversy on the aggressive nature of sport shows no sign of abating. Again the matter of definitions is crucial. What is aggression? A wide range of answers can be found in the following works: *Aggression: A Social Psychological Analysis* by Leonard Berkowitz, *On Aggression* by Konrad Lorenz, and *Sports Violence*, edited by Jeffrey Goldstein. *Sports in America* by James Michener has a good discussion of violence as it relates to competition. Michener also has an informative section on women in sports.

On the matter of aggression, the central unsolved question seems to be: Do sports enhance aggression or relieve it? This is a difficult question but a compelling one in a world where violence in sports is part of our daily scene. Don Atyeo is convinced, as he shows in *Violence in Sports,* with its sickening accounts of cruelty in competition, that the catharsis or safety valve theory of aggression is wrong. The inherent violence in several sports creates more combative attitudes in spectators. Allen Guttman in *Sports Spectators* is skeptical of the theory but also points to instances where sports seem to have had a civilizing effect. On the subject of spectators, the student of popular culture will not want to overlook *Fans!* by Michael Roberts, a sobering book but often a funny one, as seen in one chapter title, "Jesus Christ (Pro Football) Superstar."

Considering the ubiquitous nature of sports in American society and the increasing awareness of their significance by scholars in various disciplines, one is probably safe in predicting that within a few years the study of sport as an aspect of popular culture will be as commonplace in the universities as the study of languages is now. Already there are journals in practically every discipline in the humanities devoted to the study of sports, for example, *Aethlon: The Journal of Sports Literature* (formerly *Arete*), and they continue to receive their share of attention in the field of popular culture, the Spring 1983 issue of the *Journal of Popular Culture,* "Sports in America," edited by David A. Jones and Leverett T. Smith, Jr., being devoted to them. Whether or not sports remain an area of intensive investigation in the universities, there is little doubt that they will continue to influence our lives in both obvious and subtle ways, for one thing is certain—man will play. He may even cease to go to war, but he will never cease to play as long as there is time called leisure after labor is done.

NOTES

1. Johan Huizinga, *Homo Ludens: A Study of the Play Element in Culture* (Boston: Beacon, 1960), p. 212.

2. Paul Weiss, *Sport: A Philosophic Inquiry* (Carbondale: Southern Illinois University Press, 1969), p. 134.

3. Roger Caillois, *Man, Play, and Games,* trans. Meyer Barash (New York: Free Press, 1961), pp. 9–10.

4. Hannah Arendt, *The Human Condition* (Chicago: University of Chicago Press, 1958), p. 85.

5. See, for example, Nancy Struna, "Puritans and Sport: The Irretrievable Tide of Change," *Journal of Sport History,* 4 (Spring 1977), 1–21, and Peter Wagner, "Puritan Attitudes Towards Physical Education in Seventeenth Century New England," *Journal of Sport History,* 3 (Summer 1976), 139–51.

6. Herbert Manchester, *Four Centuries of American Sport, 1490–1890* (1931; rpt. New York: Benjamin Blom, 1968), p. 16

7. Wells Twombly, *200 Years of Sport in America* (New York: McGraw-Hill, 1976), p. 18

8. Foster Rhea Dulles, *America Learns to Play: A History of Popular Recreation, 1607–1940* (New York: Appleton-Century), 1940, p. 5.

9. Manchester, p. 17.

10. Dulles, p. 25.

11. Sarah Kemball Knight, *Private Journal* (Albany, 1865), pp. 52–53. Quoted in Dulles, p. 29.

12. Quoted in Henry Adams, "The United States in 1800," in *Henry Adams: The Education of Henry Adams and Other Selected Writings,* ed. Edward N. Saveth (New York: Washington Square Press), pp. 72–73.

13. Jennie Holliman, *American Sports (1785–1835)* (1931; rpt. Philadelphia: Porcupine Press, 1975), p. 81.

14. Ibid., p. 23.

15. Quoted in Dulles, p. 35.

16. Adams, p. 74.

17. Holliman, pp. 6–7.

18. Ibid., p. 108.

19. Twombly, p. 30.

20. Manchester, p. 77.

21. Twombly, p. 43.

22. Ibid., p. 46.

23. Manchester, p. 127.

24. Dulles, pp. 223–24.

25. Ivan N. Kaye, *Good Clean Violence: A History of College Football* (Philadelphia: J. B. Lippincott, 1973), p. 17.

26. Dulles, p. 198.

27. John R. Betts, *America's Sporting Heritage, 1850–1950* (Reading, Mass.: Addison-Wesley, 1974), p. 69.

28. Ibid., p. 68.

29. Ibid., p. 237.

30. Gilbert Patten (Burt L. Standish), *Frank Merriwell's "Father" : An Autobiography* (Norman: University of Oklahoma Press, 1964), p. 181.

31. Christian Karl Messenger, *Sport and the Spirit of Play in American Fiction* (New York: Columbia University Press, 1981), p. 313.

BIBLIOGRAPHY

Books and Articles

Adams, Henry. *Henry Adams: The Education of Henry Adams and Other Selected Writings.* Edited by Edward N. Saveth. New York: Washington Square Press, 1963.

Adelman, Melvin L. *A Sporting Time: New York City and the Rise of Modern Athletics, 1820–70.* Urbana: University of Illinois Press, 1986.

Angell, Roger. *Five Seasons: A Baseball Companion.* New York: Simon and Schuster, 1977.

Arendt, Hannah. *The Human Condition.* Chicago: University of Chicago Press, 1958.

Arlott, John, ed. *The Oxford Companion to World Sports and Games*. London: Oxford University Press, 1975.

Atyeo, Don. *Violence in Sports*. New York: Van Nostrand Reinhold, 1979.

Baker, William J. *Sports in the Western World*. Totowa, N.J.: Rowan and Littlefield, 1987.

Baker, William J., and John M. Carroll. *Sports in Modern America*. St. Louis: River City, 1981. Rev ed. Urbana: University of Illinois Press, 1988.

Berkowitz, Leonard. *Aggression: A Social Psychological Analysis*. New York: Mc-Graw-Hill, 1962.

Berlin, Pearl, et al. *The American Woman in Sports*. Reading, Mass.: Addison-Wesley, 1974.

Berman, Neil D. *Playful Fiction & Fictional Players: Games, Sport, & Survival in Contemporary Fiction*. Port Washington, N.Y.: Kennikat Press, 1980.

Betts, John R. *America's Sporting Heritage, 1850–1950*. Reading, Mass.: Addison-Wesley, 1974.

Biography Index. New York: H. W. Wilson, 1946–.

"The Black Dominance." *Time*, 109 (May 9, 1977), 57–60.

Boyle, Robert. *Sport: Mirror of American Life*. Boston: Little, Brown, 1963.

Caillois, Roger. *Man, Play, and Games*. Translated by Meyer Barash. New York: Free Press, 1961.

Cantwell, Robert. "A Sneering Laugh with the Bases Loaded." *Sports Illustrated*, 16 (April 23, 1962), 68–76.

Crepeau, Richard. *Baseball: America's Diamond Mind*. Gainesville: University Press of Florida, 1980.

Deford, Frank. "Religion in Sport." *Sports Illustrated*, 44 (April 19, 1976), 88–102; see also "Endorsing Jesus," 44 (April 26, 1976), 54–69; and "Reaching for the Stars," 44 (May 3, 1976), 42–60.

Denney, Reuel. *The Astonished Muse*. Chicago: University of Chicago Press, 1975.

Dictionary Catalog of Applied Life Studies Library. Boston: G. K. Hall, 1977.

Dodge, Tom, ed. *Literature of Sport*. Lexington, Mass.: D. C. Heath, 1980.

Dollard, John, et al. *Frustration and Aggression*. New Haven: Yale University Press, 1974.

Dulles, Foster Rhea. *America Learns to Play: A History of Popular Recreation, 1607–1940*. New York: Appleton-Century, 1940.

Dunleavy, Aidan O., Andrew W. Miracle, and C. Roger Rees. *Studies in the Sociology of Sport*. Fort Worth: Texas Christian University Press, 1982.

Edwards Harry. "The Myth of the Racially Superior Athlete." *Black Scholar*, 3 (1971), 16–28.

———. *The Revolt of the Black Athlete*. New York: Free Press, 1969.

———. *Sociology of Sport*. Homewood, Ill.: Dorsey Press, 1973.

Finley, M. I., and H. W. Plecket. *The Olympic Games: The First Thousand Years*. New York: Viking, 1976.

Gardiner, E. Norman. *Athletics of the Ancient World*. London: Oxford University Press, 1930.

Gerber, Ellen W., et al., eds. *The American Woman in Sport*. Reading, Mass.: Addison-Wesley, 1974.

Goldstein, Jeffrey H., ed. *Sports Violence*. New York: Springer-Verlag, 1983.

Guttman, Allen. *From Ritual to Record: The Nature of Modern Sports*. New York: Columbia University Press, 1978.

———. *Sports Spectators*. New York: Columbia University Press, 1986.

Haley, Bruce. *The Healthy Body and Victorian Culture*. Cambridge, Mass.: Harvard University Press, 1978.

Hart, Marie M., ed. *Sport in the Socio-cultural Process*. Dubuque, Iowa: William C. Brown, 1972.

Henderson, Robert W. *Early American Sport*. New York: Grolier Club, 1937. Reprint. Cranbury, N.J.: Associated University Presses, 1977.

Herrigel, Eugen. *Zen in the Art of Archery*. Translated by R. F. C. Hull. 1953. Reprint. New York: Pantheon, 1971.

Higgs, Robert J. *Laurel and Thorn: The Athlete in American Literature*. Lexington: University Press of Kentucky, 1981.

———. *Sports: A Reference Guide*. Westport, Conn.: Greenwood Press, 1982.

Higgs, Robert J., and Neil D. Isaacs, eds. *The Sporting Spirit: Athletes in Literature and Life*. New York: Harcourt Brace Jovanovich, 1977.

Hoberman, John M. *Sport and Political Ideology*. Austin: University of Texas Press, 1986.

Hoch, Paul. *Rip Off the Big Game: The Exploitation of Sports by the Power Elite*. New York: Doubleday, 1972.

Holliman, Jennie. *American Sports (1785–1835)*. 1931. Reprint. Philadelphia: Porcupine Press, 1975.

Huizinga, Johan. *Homo Ludens: A Study of the Play Element in Culture*. Boston: Beacon Press, 1960.

Isaacs, Neil D. *All the Moves: A History of U.S. College Basketball*. Philadelphia: J. B. Lippincott, 1975.

———. *Jock Culture, USA*. New York: W. W. Norton, 1978.

Jones, David A., and Leverett T. Smith, Jr., eds. "Sports in America." *Journal of Popular Culture*, 16 (Spring 1983), 1–102. Special issue.

Kane, Martin. "An Assessment of 'Black Is Best.' " *Sports Illustrated*, 34 (January 18, 1971), 72–76.

Kaye, Ivan N. *Good Clean Violence: A History of College Football*. Philadelphia: J. B. Lippincott, 1973.

Koestler, Arthur. *The Lotus and the Robot*. New York: Macmillan, 1961.

Krout, John A. *Annals of American Sport*. Pageant of America series, Vol. 15. New Haven: Yale University Press, 1929.

Lardner, John. *White Hopes and Other Tigers*. Philadelphia: J. B. Lippincott, 1956.

Lardner, Ring. *The Portable Ring Lardner*. Edited by Maxwell Geismer. New York: Scribner's, 1963.

Leonard, George. *The Ultimate Athlete*. New York: Viking, 1974.

Lipsyte, Robert. *Sportsworld: An American Dreamland*. New York: Quadrangle, 1975.

Lorenz, Konrad. *On Aggression*. New York: Harcourt, Brace and World, 1966.

Loy, John W., and Gerald S. Kenyon, eds. *Sports, Culture and Society*. London: Macmillan, 1969.

Lucas, John A., and Ronald A. Smith. *Saga of American Sport*. Philadelphia: Lea and Febiger, 1978.

Manchester, Herbert. *Four Centuries of American Sport, 1490–1890*. 1931. Reprint. New York: Benjamin Blom, 1968.

Mangan, J. A. *Athleticism in the Victorian and Edwardian Public Schools: The Emergence and Consolidation of Educational Psychology*. Cambridge, England: Cambridge University Press, 1981.

Mangan, J. A., and Roberta Park, eds. *From Fair Sex to Feminism: Sport and the Socialization of Women in the Industrial and Post-Industrial Eras*. Totowa, N.J.: Frank Cass, 1987.

Meggyesy, Dave. *Out of Their League*. Berkeley, Calif.: Ramparts Press, 1970.

Menke, Frank G. *The Encyclopedia of Sport*. 6th ed. Cranbury, N.J.: A. S. Barnes, 1978.

Messenger, Christian Karl. *Sport and the Spirit of Play in American Fiction*. New York: Columbia University Press, 1981.

Metheny, Eleanor. *Connotations of Movement in Sport and Dance*. Dubuque, Iowa: William C. Brown, 1965.

Michener, James. *Sports in America*. New York: Random House, 1977.

Miller, Donna Mae, and Katherine R. E. Russell. *Sport: A Contemporary View*. Philadelphia: Lea and Febiger, 1971.

Morgan, William J., and Klaus V. Meier, eds. *Philosophic Inquiry in Sport*. Champaign, Ill.: Human Kinetic Publishers, 1988.

Mrozek, Donald J. *Sport and American Mentality, 1880–1940*. Knoxville: University of Tennessee Press, 1983.

Murphy, Michael. *Golf in the Kingdom*. New York: Viking, 1972.

Murphy, Michael, and Rhea A. White. *The Psychic Side of Sports*. Reading, Mass.: Addison-Wesley, 1978.

Musashi, Miyamato. *A Book of Five Rings: The Classic Guide to Strategy*. Translated by Victor Harris. New York: Overlook Press, 1974.

Novak, Michael. *The Joy of Sports*. New York: Basic Books, 1976.

Noverr, Douglas A., and Lawrence E. Ziewacz, eds. *Sport History: Selected Reading Lists and Course Outlines from American Colleges and Universities*. New York: Markus Wiener, 1987.

Ogilive, Bruce C., and Thomas A. Tutko. "Sports: If You Want to Build Character, Try Something Else." *Psychology Today*, 5 (October 1971), 61–63.

Olsen, Jack. *The Black Athlete: A Shameful Story*. New York: Time-Life Books, 1968.

Oriard, Michael. *Dreaming of Heroes: American Sports Fiction, 1868–1980*. Chicago: Nelson Hall, 1982.

Patten, Gilbert (Burt L. Standish). *Frank Merriwell's "Father" : An Autobiography*. Norman: University of Oklahoma Press, 1964.

Porter, David L. *Biographical Dictionary of American Sports*. 4 vols. (Baseball, Football, Indoor Sports, and Outdoor Sports). Westport, Conn.: Greenwood Press, 1987–88.

Rader, Benjamin G. *American Sports: From the Age of Folk Games to the Age of Spectators*. Englewood Cliffs, N.J.: Prentice-Hall, 1983.

Rahner, Hugo. *Man at Play*. New York: Herder and Herder, 1972.

Remley, Mary L., ed. *Women in Sport: A Guide to Information Sources*. Detroit: Gale Research, 1980.

Roberts, Michael. *Fans! How We Go Crazy over Sports*. Washington, D.C.: New Republic Book Co., 1976.

Robinson, Rachel S. *Sources for the History of Greek Athletics*. Cincinnati: University of Cincinnati Press, 1955.

Rohe, Fred. *Zen of Running*. New York: Random House, 1975.

Sage, George H., ed. *Sport and American Society: Selected Readings*. Reading, Mass.: Addison-Wesley, 1970.

Scanlon, Thomas F. *Greek and Roman Athletics: A Bibliography*. Chicago: Ares, 1984.

Scott, Jack. *The Athletic Revolution*. New York: Free Press, 1971.

Shaw, Gary. *Meat on the Hoof*. New York: Dell, 1973.

Simon, Robert L. *Sports and Social Values*. Englewood Cliffs, N.J.: Prentice-Hall, 1985.

Slusher, Howard S. *Man, Sport, and Existence: A Critical Analysis*. Philadelphia: Lea and Febiger, 1967.

Smith, Adam. *Power of Mind*. New York: Ballantine, 1975.

Smith, Red. *The Red Smith Reader*. New York: Vintage, 1975.

Somers, Dale A. *The Rise of Sports in New Orleans, 1850–1900*. Baton Rouge: Louisiana State University Press, 1972.

Spivey, Donald. *Sports in America: New Historical Perspectives*. Westport, Conn.: Greenwood Press, 1985.

Struna, Nancy. "Puritans and Sport: The Irretrievable Tide of Change." *Journal of Sport History,* 4 (Spring 1977), 1–21.

Strutt, Joseph. *The Sports and Pastimes of the People of England*. 1833. Reprint. New York: A. M. Kelley, 1970.

Toynbee, Arnold. *The Breakdown of Civilizations*. Vol. 4, *A Study of History*. New York: Oxford University Press, 1939.

Twombly, Wells. *200 Years of Sport in America*. New York: McGraw-Hill, 1976.

Tygiel, Jules. *Baseball's Great Experiment: Jackie Robinson and His Legacy*. New York: Vintage, 1984.

Umphlett, Wiley Lee, ed. *American Sport Culture: The Humanistic Dimensions*. Lewisburg, Penn.: Bucknell University Press, 1983.

——, ed. *Mythmakers of the American Dream: The Nostalgic Vision in Popular Culture*. Lewisburg, Penn.: Bucknell University Press, 1983.

——, ed. *The Sporting Myth and the American Experience*. Lewisburg, Penn.: Bucknell University Press, 1975.

Vance, N. Scott. "Sport Is a Religion in America Controversial Professor [Charles S. Prebish] Argues." *Chronicle of Higher Education* (May 16, 1984), 25–27.

Vanderwerken, David L., and Spencer K. Wertz, eds. *Sport Inside Out*. Fort Worth: Texas Christian University Press, 1985.

Veblen, Thorstein. *Theory of the Leisure Class*. 1899. Reprint. New York: Macmillan, 1953.

Voigt, David Q. *American Baseball*. 3 vols. University Park: Pennsylvania State University Press, 1983.

Wagner, Peter. "Puritan Attitudes Towards Physical Education in Seventeenth Century New England." *Journal of Sport History,* 3 (Summer 1976), 139–51.

Webster's Sports Dictionary. Springfield, Mass.: G. and C. Merriam, 1976.

Weiss, Paul. *Sport: A Philosophic Inquiry*. Carbondale: Southern Illinois University Press, 1969.

Wiggins, David K. "Clio and the Black Athlete in America: Myths, Heroes, and Realities." *Quest,* 32 (1980), 217–25.

Young, David C. *The Olympic Myth of Greek Amateur Athletics*. Chicago: Ares, 1984.

Periodicals

Aethlon: The Journal of Sports Literature. Johnson City, Tenn., 1983–.
The International Journal of the History of Sport. London, 1983–.
Journal of Sport History. University Park, Pa., 1973–.
Journal of the Philosophy of Sport. Champaign, Ill., 1973–.

Stage Entertainment

DON B. WILMETH

HISTORIC OUTLINE

Other than the occasional staged variety show, the lone stand-up comic attempting to eke out a living in the few surviving nightclubs or cabarets, or the spectacular revues of Las Vegas, popular live stage entertainment appealing to a large mass of Americans is a phenomenon of the past, replaced today by spectator sports, mass media, and rock concerts. In 1932, when the movies took over the Palace Theatre in New York, vaudeville symbolically died, although its slow death began in the 1890s as the motion picture slowly assimilated vaudeville and then replaced it as a more efficient and inexpensive medium. When the Minsky brothers introduced full-fledged strippers into their burlesque empire in the 1930s, burlesque as a unique and significant form of stage entertainment began its slow death. As Charles West, manager of his wife/stripper Evelyn "$50,000 Treasure Chest" West, recently commented as he observed the death of St. Louis's last burlesque house, burlesque's American decline began when taped music replaced bands, elaborate settings were eliminated, and comedians were canned. The decline, of course, began earlier, but he was correct when he added, "All that was left were the strippers." Each major American form of stage entertainment underwent a similar demise or merged into newer forms and vanished.

In the nineteenth century, however, the climate was right for live entertainment to prosper. Prior to the late eighteenth century, it was not possible for popular stage entertainments to appeal to large audiences, for it was necessary that there be a more concentrated society and the incorporation of the majority of the population into that society in order to foster popular entertainment. In this country, with the rise of technology and the rapid expansion of the frontier during the nineteenth century, Americans found increased time for leisure activities and developed a hunger for entertainment to fill what was for many a dreary and difficult existence. As cities grew and Americans were concentrated into cohesive urban or near-urban units with common social, economic, and cultural characteristics, a huge market for entertainment was created.

Although often similar in structure and form to the more legitimate, mainstream theatrical forms, popular stage entertainment offered the ordinary man a vital and appealing alternative theater that satisfied his needs and desires. Professional showmen quickly perceived what would be accepted and consciously attempted to appeal to the majority, creating entertainment that was neither complex nor profound but readily comprehended, thus popular in the sense that the majority of people liked and approved it, with few deviations from its standards and conventions. Hundreds of professional troupes and individual performers emerged during the mid-nineteenth century to provide a variety of entertainment forms, some new, some adaptations of earlier forms, but all aimed at a new audience seeking amusement. Urban centers developed theaters and "palaces" of entertainment; rural America depended upon the traveling troupe, be it a circus; a Wild West show; a repertoire company playing town halls, an opera house, or even a tent; Lyceum and Chautauqua troupes performing under the guise of religion or culture; and variety companies of all sorts and descriptions.

Dime Museums and Medicine Shows

Prior to the American Revolution, strolling exhibitors of curiosities operated in the colonies along with numerous other mountebanks and itinerant entertainers. They presented crude and disorganized entertainments—animals, freaks, mechanical and scientific oddities, wax figures, peep shows, and the like. By the beginning of the nineteenth century showmen had begun to organize such exhibits into "museums" or "cabinets of curiosities," with little competition from legitimate or serious museums. By mid-century the dime museum was established as a major form of American entertainment, and the first formidable American showman emerged, Phineas T. Barnum, entrepreneur of the American Museum in New York, beginning in 1841.

Barnum's museum established the ultimate pattern for the museum rage, with exhibits of every sort and a so-called lecture room where visitors witnessed extra "edifying" attractions running the gamut from jugglers and dioramas to comics, musicians, and popular theater fare, such as *The Drunkard*. The museums, operating under the thin veneer of culture and learning, soon spread to every medium-sized city in America and survived as a uniquely American institution until World War I. The dime museum filled an important void; unsophisticated Americans and recent immigrants could find here cheap and comprehensible entertainment that was acceptable on moral and religious grounds.

Like the itinerant pre-revolutionary mountebank, the roving, performing quack selling his tonics and elixirs evolved into a major form of American entertainment, the medicine show, which, with the phenomenal growth of the American patent medicine industry in the nineteenth century, became a major business. Before the turn of the nineteenth century, the traveling medicine show, with its pitchman and frequent humbug Indian spectaculars, was a flourishing form of entertainment, borrowing everything that was taking place in the American theater and adapting it to its own needs.

The Minstrel Show

Of the major forms of stage entertainment, the first unique American show business form was the minstrel show, which, beginning in the 1840s, literally swept the nation, producing in time a tremendous impact on subsequent forms, in particular vaudeville and burlesque. Using what they claimed were credible black dialects, songs, dances, and jokes, white showmen in blackface created extremely popular and entertaining shows while at the same time perpetuating negative stereotypes of blacks that endured in American popular thought long after the show had vanished. The popularity of the black native character dates from about 1828 when Thomas D. Rice created his "Jim Crow" song and dance routine. Evolving out of the "Ethiopian delineators" of the 1820s, the name for blackfaced white entertainers, four performers calling themselves the Virginia Minstrels, organized by Dan Emmett, developed the first full-length example of the new entertainment in 1843; soon a flood of competitors followed. In 1846 E. P. Christy gave the minstrel show its distinctive three-part structure: repartee between the master of ceremonies, or interlocutor, and the endmen (Bruder Tambo and Bruder Bones) sitting on either end of a semicircular arrangement of the company, followed by the "olio" or the variety section, and culminating with a one-act skit.

Minstrelsy was the first major stage entertainment to avoid the elitist reputation of legitimate drama and commit itself to the new common-man audience. It was immediate, unpretentious, and devoted to fun, the emotional outlet that its urban patrons needed so desperately. Its use of music and comedy created its greatest appeal and most lasting influence. With its endmen and interlocutor the audience was engulfed with an endless string of puns, malapropisms, riddles, and jokes, delivered as rapid-fire exchanges and carried over into the later urban humor of vaudeville, burlesque, and even radio, motion pictures, and television.

After the Civil War, the minstrel show expanded in diversity and scope, incorporating elements from newer forms of entertainment, reaching its peak in 1870. Although the changes prolonged its life for a short time, its uniqueness was destroyed. By 1896 only ten companies remained, and the minstrel show was no longer America's major stage entertainment; its new replacement was vaudeville.

Vaudeville

Like the minstrel show, American vaudeville was largely indigenous, the product of American saloon owners' efforts to attract eager and free-spending drinkers by enticing them with free shows. Early variety shows included risqué girlie shows, and their reputation soon became blighted. By the 1890s the older variety had been renamed vaudeville, capitalizing on the more elegant sound of the French word for light pastoral plays with musical interludes but having nothing in common with its French namesake. Instead, vaudeville developed its own brand of a highly organized, nationwide big business. Vaudeville became, after the early efforts of Tony Pastor (1837–1908), a symbol of Americanism; its performer, according to Robert Toll, the constant symbol of individual liberty and pioneer endeavor.

Modern vaudeville's heyday lasted a scant fifty years or so, from the 1880s to the early 1930s, but during its time Americans of all classes were amused and found relief from the relatively new industrial complex. Huge circuits of vaudeville theaters, led by such magnates as E. F. Albee, B. F. Keith, Marcus Loew, Martin Beck, F. F. Proctor, and Alexander Pantages, were in constant competition and, as rivalries blossomed, vaudeville flourished. The Keith-Albee combine, the most prestigious of them all, developed a formula catering to family audiences with continuous shows in luxurious vaudeville palaces. To protect their interests, managements formed conglomerates; performers quickly retaliated by founding the White Rats, modeled on the British music hall performers' union, the Water Rats, but with little success.

Although vaudeville appeared to its audiences as an unstructured collection of dissimilar acts, it was actually a meticulously planned and executed balance of "turns" designed to control the audiences' responses and interest, while enhancing the appeal of each act and providing a smorgasbord of the best available entertainment—magicians, vocalists, jugglers, comics, animal acts, skits, and even recitations and guest appearances by celebrities of the day. In 1913, the international star Sarah Bernhardt opened at the Palace in New York City and collected $7,000 for her talents. Because of its tremendous popularity, vaudeville helped to dictate morals and attitudes, whether consciously or not. Ethnic humor, for example, was a powerful force and, although immigrants were aided in their assimilation into the American populace by ethnic comics, their jokes helped to sustain the sterotyped misunderstandings and mythologies that still permeate American culture.

Burlesque

By the turn of the century of new form of stage entertainment had begun to assert its own unique brand of amusement: burlesque. The origins of burlesque are complex and confusing. Its components can be traced to numerous forms: English and American literary burlesque and parody, the circus, the knockabout farces of the medicine show and dime museums, the farces of such popular theater writers as Edward Harrigan and Charles Hoyt, the sketches of the minstrel show, concert saloons and beer gardens, Western honky-tonks, and even the stage Yankee. It is, however, misleading to attach the American form of burlesque to the older and more reputable forms, for American burlesque was clearly rooted in native soil. Historians usually date its true beginnings to the 1860s when a troupe of stranded ballet dancers in 1866 were incorporated into a musical extravaganza called *The Black Crook* at Niblo's Gardens in New York, followed in 1869 by Lydia Thompson and her "British Blondes" appearing in burlesques that emphasized feminine charms more than parody, the previous thrust of burlesque. As significant as these events were, they were less important than the influence of the honky-tonk, half beer hall and half brothel, with its variety entertainments of the most vulgar sort. The audiences were unsophisticated, and the atmosphere was similar to that of the early English music hall—rough and convivial. The first burlesque impresario, M. B. Leavitt, who began his career in 1870, combined the atmosphere of the honky-tonk with the structure of the minstrel show, took it out of the saloon, and put it into theaters. Soon burlesque assumed its standard form: variety acts and "bits" mingled with musical numbers, featuring beautiful women and bawdy humor. By the turn of the century the comedian was the center of the performance, despite the slow but constant increase of interest in the sensuous presence of the female form, made more prominent beginning with Little Egypt's "cooch dancing" in 1904 at the Columbia Exposition in St. Louis. The comic retained his central position, however, until the advent of the striptease in the early 1930s.

The "golden age" of burlesque began in 1905 with the organization of the Columbia circuit or wheel and began to change in the 1920s when the new Mutual Burlesque Association added greater permissiveness. With an increase in its sexual overtones, burlesque came to appeal primarily to male audiences, reaching the height of its popularity just prior to World War I. As erotic stimulation replaced bawdy humor, burlesque audiences became jaded and bored; burlesque fell on bad days. Without its basically cheerful humor, never bitter or moralistic, burlesque, like the minstrel show before it, lost its identity and its uniqueness.

Popular Theater

From the earliest days of the American theater, popular fare dominated much of the best of native production, beginning with the stage Yankee, Jonathan, in Royall Tyler's *The Contrast* (1787). As more common people found their way into theaters, the popularization of drama became a necessity. Native actors gained prominence in plays with native themes and types: *James Hackett* as the Yankee with his common sense and rustic manners; Joseph Jefferson III, as Rip Van Winkle, providing the audience a momentary escape into a world of fantasy and freedom; Frank Mayo as the idealized American hero Davy Crockett; Frank Chanfrau as the Irish volunteer fireman from the Bowery, "Mose the Fire Bhoy." By the late nineteenth century, some versions of all the most popular plays began to reach small-town America. The earlier stock resident company gave way to "combination" traveling companies. During the last thirty years of the century, with the increase of railroad mileage after the Civil War, previously inaccessible towns became important and profitable stops for touring companies. Nearly every village and hamlet began to construct a local "opera house" to accommodate traveling entertainments, creating a vast theatrical network known as "the road." If an "opera house" or "academy of music" was unavailable, traveling shows turned to existing courthouses, schools, town halls, churches, or other large halls.

The most enduring form of theater that appealed to the common people and reflected their desires, needs, and tastes was the melodrama, which dominated the popular stage during its heyday, 1850–1920. Although much of the popular fare, called *10–20–30 melodrama* after its admission prices, was poorly written, its formula was such that it could accommodate any setting, time, or character, and the simplistic dramatis personae were immediately identifiable to the audience. To a public that found its traditional values exalted, melodrama was more real than reality. Although melodrama rarely dealt with social issues or problems several of the more prominent examples were significant exceptions: *Uncle Tom's Cabin,* ostensibly against slavery but popular because of its emotionally moving, melodramatic scenes and its spectacle, gave rise to dozens of touring companies called Tommers or Tom shows which toured the nation well into the twentieth century; *Ten Nights in a Barroom* and *The Drunkard,,* temperance plays, created patronage for the theater from people who had condemned it as immoral.

The thirst for a nostalgic look at the American past and a reminder of simpler, nobler times, as well as the need for the reinforcement of stable values that were rapidly changing, gave melodrama writers fertile ground for creation, from Denman Thompson's 1876 study of rural America, *The Old Homestead,* to William F. Cody's mythic creations of genuine western heroes in both drama and Wild West shows, to Civil War dramas that ignored the broad issues and the causes of the suffering and the divisiveness in the 1880s.

In time, small towns were invaded by too many touring companies, each doing much the same thing. During the season of 1900, 340 theatrical companies were touring; by 1920 the number had dwindled to less than 50. As the new century began, a trend developed toward outdoor entertainment, and tent show repertoire became very much a part of the movement. As repertoire companies found themselves squeezed out of many opera houses, in part because of the control of established houses by theatrical trusts, they looked toward more remote areas where one-night-stand companies never appeared, and where, as William Lawrence Slout points out, audiences could not compare entertainment values and obscurity was a protection against tightened copyright enforcement. The solution for many was the canvas pavilion used by the circus as well as medicine shows and other forms of variety entertainment. Ironically, the movement was encouraged by cultural and religious organizations, first the Millerites in 1842 and the most popular of the movements, the Chautauqua, during the first quarter of the twentieth century. Between 1900 and 1910 there were well over one hundred repertoire companies under canvas. By the summer of 1921, faced with a recession, the golden years of the tent repertoire ended.

Emerging from the tent tradition was one of the last native stock characters, Toby, a redheaded, freckle-faced, rustic country boy who became a nightly fixture and feature attraction with many tent rep companies. As tent show dramas lost relevance for rural audiences and Toby became so exaggerated as to lose identity with them, a final chapter in American popular theater fell into decline. While it lasted, however, American drama truly belonged to the people. The combined yearly attendance at tent shows exceeded that of the New York theater, despite the makeshift, shabby quality of the performances.

Popular stage entertainments, including popular theater, were ultimately assimilated into those new media of mass communication, radio and the motion picture. Popular theater in film form could certainly be brought into America's heartland more inexpensively than the "real" thing, and with a minimum of effort. With the loss of personal contact between patron and performer, Americans would never again be able to shape and mold drama in their own image. In general, then, modern technology and its new techniques for duplicating and multiplying materials, along with more efficient methods of production and distribution, quickly spread popular culture in this century, while at the same time replacing the need for live professional entertainment aimed at a large popular audience.

HISTORY AND CRITICISM

The student and scholar of American popular culture has too frequently assumed that live amusements created by professional showmen for profit and aimed at broad, relatively unsophisticated audiences were unworthy of serious attention—if noted at all. The reasons for this oversight can be traced to the anticommercial bias with which too many scholars have looked at popular entertainment, the apparent unimportance of such areas for investigation, and even the lack of a strong literary base for most popular entertainment forms, for indeed most of these forms depend more significantly on the performer and the audience than on a written text. There are legitimate difficulties in investigating popular stage entertainments; throughout history popular forms have appeared, merged, mutated, disappeared, and, in some cases, reappeared in new guises, all the while virtually ignored by scholars and historians, until very recently.

Although many of the better sources on stage entertainment are what one might call "good bad" books—chatty autobiographies and memoirs, undocumented histories, and the like—the attention paid to popular entertainment has changed drastically in recent years. No longer are forms like vaudeville, burlesque, and popular theater considered insignificant because they are not abstruse, profound, or complicated. Beyond their primary function, to entertain, as important as that is, social scientists and humanists are discovering other values, the reflection and expression of aesthetic and other needs of a large population base, as well as the creation of effective satire or politically motivated comment. Indications of the broader importance can be seen, for example, in American minstrelsy, which spoke for and to huge numbers of common Americans in the nineteenth century and during its heyday provided unique insights into the thoughts, feelings, needs, and desires of the common people who shaped the show in their own image, or in vaudeville, which also spoke to a new audience and if taken seriously, as something more than an idle form of mass amusement, can be seen as a manifestation of psychic and social forces at work in American history.

Underscoring the newfound significance of popular entertainment as a legitimate area of study is the attention paid the subject by scholarly journals and organizations. The Center for the Study of Popular Culture at Bowling Green University publishes significant books under the aegis of the Bowling Green University Popular Press and issues the important *Journal of Popular Culture* and *Journal of American Culture,* both, periodically, with articles on stage entertainments. In the 1970s several important journals devoted special issues to the subject of popular stage entertainment: "People's Theatre" in *Theatre Quarterly,* 1971 (published in London; a new series now appears as *New Theatre Quarterly*); *The Drama Review,* the single best source for essays dealing with the influence of popular entertainment on the avant garde, as well as other relevant topics, published an issue in 1974 devoted to "popular entertainments," including an excellent introduction to the subject by Brooks McNamara that lays out a sensible categorization of forms; in 1975 the *Educational Theatre Journal* (now *Theatre Journal*) published an issue on popular theater with a number of excellent essays; and *Theatre Studies* in a double issue (1977–79) offered a number titled "The Popular North American Theatre: Provincial Stages in the Nineteenth Century." Other journals have begun to feature frequent essays on stage entertainment, most notably *Theatre History Studies* and *Nineteenth Century Theatre* (formerly *Nineteenth Century Theatre Research*), the latter clearly stating in 1987 an editorial policy to include articles on forms other than legitimate theater.

The 1970s also witnessed a number of conferences on popular performance, most notably the Conference on the History of American Popular Entertainment in 1977, cosponsored by the American Society for Theatre Research and the Theatre Library, the proceedings of which were published in 1979, edited by Myron Matlaw. In October 1987 an international conference on "Popular Entertainment as a Reflection of National Identity" was held in New York City, cosponsored by the same organizations plus the Society of Dance History Scholars and the International Federation for Theatre Research.

These various activities and journal issues have resulted in the legitimization of the study of popular entertainment. Scholarship in the area is now commonplace, both in publication and graduate research. What was once considered inappropriate for serious study is now encouraged and promoted, adding immeasurably to the general field of American popular culture.

Despite the mediocre nature of much of the literature on stage entertainments, a tremendous amount has been written. The time coverage of a majority of the sources discussed here is limited to the period from the emergence of a huge market for entertainment in the late eighteenth century (paralleling the appearance of a predominantly middle-class civilization in the Western world, which in turn drastically changed the cultural pattern) to the emergence early in the twentieth century of the motion picture, other than works on the stand-up comic. The focus throughout will be on the best sources available (both recent and standard works in the field). The categories used are, at best, often artificial divisions because of the overlapping nature of the forms.

REFERENCE WORKS

The two most comprehensive bibliographical sources covering all major forms are Don B. Wilmeth's *American and English Popular Entertainment* (1980) and *Variety Entertainment and Outdoor Amusements* (1982). Combined, these two resources list most major sources through 1981. This chapter attempts to bring these lists up through early 1987. More detailed updates can be found in the annual bibliographical issue of *Prospects,* the first (1987) covering 1984 publications. Two additional recent assessments of sources on American drama (and, in a larger sense, theater) are worth noting: Charles A. Carpenter's "American Drama: A Bibliographical Essay" (1983) and Joyce Flynn's "Melting Plots: Patterns of Racial and Ethnic Amalgamation in American Drama Before Eugene O'Neill" (1986).

The importance of the performer has been illustrated in another recommended bibliography, Stephen M. Archer's *American Actors and Actresses*
(1983), and to a lesser degree in George B. Bryan's *Stage Lives* (1985). A
useful guide to general sources on the period under scrutiny in this chapter
is Don B. Wilmeth's *The American Stage to World War I*. The special language
of vaudeville, burlesque, Toby shows, and other forms of stage entertainment is given extensive attention in Wilmeth's *The Language of American
Popular Entertainment*. Excellent examples of comic material used in all forms
of variety entertainment, from the medicine show to vaudeville and burlesque, can be found in *American Popular Entertainments,* edited by Brooks
McNamara.

Few attempts have been made to produce a comprehensive history of
popular entertainments. My book *Variety Entertainment and Outdoor Amusements,* mentioned above, includes a potted history of all major forms with
very selective coverage. Two earlier sources are still useful. Samuel
McKechnie's *Popular Entertainments Through the Ages,* although originally
published in 1931, still offers a good introduction to major forms, although
the focus is European and the coverage is most useful for background and
roots of American entertainment. Robert C. Toll's *On with the Show* is the
only real attempt to chronicle American forms of entertainment and is
generally a good introduction to major American forms, including an excellent bibliographical essay and a comparative chronology showing the
parallel between the evolution of American society and American show
business. Though not a true history, *American Popular Entertainment,* edited
by Myron Matlaw, provides twenty-six excellent essays on all aspects of
stage entertainments. Joseph and June Bundy Csida's *American Entertainment:
A Unique History of Popular Show Business* attempts to fashion a history of
American popular entertainments from the files of *Billboard.* The art critic
and social historian Russell Lynes has provided a useful survey of the public
arts and their audience from the turn of the century to 1950 in *The Lively
Audience.* Though uneven, a book of interest investigating one important
aspect of popular theater is Bruce McConachie and Daniel Friedman's *Theatre for Working-Class Audiences in the United States, 1830–1980.* Finally, Martin Gottfried's *In Person,* though designed as a coffee-table book, focuses
on great entertainers in most variety forms, including vaudeville, burlesque,
and the nightclub circuit. More limited in scope but similar in focus is
Stanley Green's *The Great Clowns of Broadway* (Fanny Brice, Jimmy Durante, Ed Wynn, Bert Lahr, W. C. Fields, Joe Cook, Beatrice Lillie, Bobby
Clark, Willie Howard, and Victor Moore). Much of the history of popular
stage entertainment is being written in scholarly journals, in particular those
mentioned above. To these titles should be added some of the more historically important serials: *Billboard, New York Clipper, New York Mirror,
Spirit of the Times,* and *The Theatre* or *The Theatre Magazine.*

There is not room here to include coverage of the many studies of popular culture relevant to stage entertainments, though a large number can be found in my two book-length guides discussed above. A few, however, deserve inclusion here. Gilbert Seldes's *The 7 Lively Arts* was the first attempt by an American to justify and defend popular entertainments and as such is still stimulating. The works of Constance Rourke (*American Humor* and *The Roots of American Culture*) are still important, basic analyses of American comic stereotypes in the nineteenth century. Foster Rhea Dulles's *America Learns to Play* remains a good general study of early American popular entertainment, and Russel Nye's *The Unembarrassed Muse* is an excellent introduction to the popular arts, including a useful section on popular theater.

American stage entertainments depend a great deal on general histories for investigation. Although it is necessary to exclude most of these here, two are essential for the student of popular entertainment: G. C. D. Odell's *Annals of the New York Stage* and T. Allston Brown's three-volume *History of the New York Stage*. Odell remains the standard history through the 1893–94 season and is written with charm, accuracy, and impressive scholarship; Brown, a theatrical agent and historian, was a devotee of popular entertainment, and his work contains histories of over 400 New York theaters, opera houses, music halls, circuses, and other places of entertainment. Brooks Atkinson's *Broadway* is a more up-to-date overview of New York entertainment from 1900 to 1974. Edward Bennett Marks's *They All Had Glamour,* although not limited to popular entertainment, is an amusing source for lesser-known theater and musical artists and contains a good glossary, "Old-Time Colloquialisms." Allen Churchill, the author of numerous theater studies, offers a survey of Broadway from 1900 to 1919 in *The Great White Way* and during the revue era and the birth of the modern American musical in *The Theatrical Twenties.* Langston Hughes and Milton Meltzer produced a useful survey of the black performer in American entertainment in their *Black Magic,* although much of their coverage has been superseded in Henry T. Sampson's *Blacks in Blackface.* Joseph Boskin's recent *Sambo: The Rise & Demise of an American Jester* provides a perceptive analysis of the stereotypical image of the black male in all levels of popular culture, including many entertainment forms, in particular the circus and the minstrel show. *A Book About the Theater* gives an interesting perspective on popular entertainments by an important early American theater historian, Brander Matthews, as do George Jean Nathan's *Encyclopaedia of the Theatre* and Laurence Hutton's *Curiosities of the American Stage.* In *America Takes the Stage,* Richard Moody traces the development of romanticism in American drama and theater from 1750 to 1900 and deals prominently with the stage Yankee and Negro minstrelsy. Brooks McNamara has written numerous essays of a general nature that are extremely valuable, among them "Popular Scenography," a survey of the architecture and design of traditional popular entertainment, and "Scavengers of the Amusement World," in which he

shows the indebtedness of early cinema to vaudeville and other stage entertainments. An excellent period source is John Jennings's *Theatrical and
Circus Life,* a compendium of popular forms.

The most recent survey of the American stage, Mary C. Henderson's
Theater in America, provides a wonderful overview as well as stunning
illustrations, a time chart showing key theatrical events and personages,
and a very good basic bibliography recommended as a supplement to this
limited guide.

Dime Museums and Medicine Shows

Two significant areas of popular stage entertainment that have received
surprisingly scant coverage are dime museums and medicine shows. Indeed,
little attention has been given the theatrical format of these two American
institutions, although both had long and fascinating histories. The medicine
show belongs to a tradition of mountebanks, charlatans, and quack doctors
selling tonics and elixirs, mixed with attention-getting free entertainment
that dates back to the Middle Ages. The dime museum, from the Civil War
to World War I, provided a variety of entertainment to working-class audiences in virtually every city and town in the United States.

A reasonably good, though not always accurate, survey of early itinerant
performers is Richardson Wright's *Hawkers and Walkers in Early America.*
Only one major full-length study can be included on the American medicine
show, Brooks McNamara's *Step Right Up: An Illustrated History of the American Medicine Show,* which is not only the sole documented history of the
phenomenon but an excellent reference for additional sources on patent
medicine and related topics, examples of medicine show skits, and a glossary
of pitchmen's terms. In addition, McNamara has published a number of
valuable essays. The earlier ones were largely incorporated into his book;
however, more recent articles are valuable supplements to the work, most
specifically "Talking" (1987), on the career of Doc Fred Foster Bloodgood,
a med show pitchman, and "The Medicine Show Log" (1984), on the
problems involved in reconstructing a traditional medicine show for the
Smithsonian's Summer 1979 Folklife Festival. Also useful, if obtainable, is
the souvenir program for a similar effort at the American Place Theatre in
New York in 1983. This source, edited by C. Lee Jenner, contains essays
and an excellent bibliography (including film and records). Graydon Freeman's *The Medicine Showman,* Thomas Kelley's *The Fabulous Kelley,* and
Malcolm Webber's fictionalized reminiscences, *Medicine Show,* are earlier
but less effective attempts to record aspects of the medicine show. In Mae
Noell's "Some Memories of a Medicine Show Performer," a medicine show
artist recalls the best-loved "bits" and life on the rural circuits and provides
some additional insights into this American institution. McNamara, however, remains the definitive source. Background on American patent med-

icines and their relationship to the medicine show are treated in depth by James Young in *The Toadstool Millionaires* and *The Medical Messiahs*.

The dime museum has received even less attention and, again, the major source to date is by Brooks McNamara, "A Congress of Wonders': The Rise and Fall of the Dime Museum," an excellent survey of the origin and development of this uniquely American brand of popular entertainment. The name most closely associated with the dime museum tradition is Phineas T. Barnum. Although the tendency is to lump him into the American circus tradition, where he indeed did make some contributions, Barnum's major involvement was with his New York museum, where he displayed some 600,000 items plus live entertainment. John Betts's "P. T. Barnum and the Popularization of Natural History" offers a good critical perspective on Barnum's museum, although the definitive and only documented study of Barnum's career is Neil Harris's *Humbug: The Art of P. T. Barnum,* an excellent analysis of Barnum's contributions in their social, economic, entertainment, and intellectual contexts. Less useful are the two other major standard biographies of Barnum: M. R. Werner's *Barnum* and Irving Wallace's *The Fabulous Showman,* the latter containing an extensive bibliography. Alice Desmond's *Barnum Presents General Tom Thumb* is a pleasant biography of Barnum's famous attraction, Charles Stratton. Barnum himself authored numerous books and, although their total credibility should be questioned, they are still important sources. His *Humbugs of the World* (1865) and *Struggles and Triumphs* (1869) have both been reprinted frequently.

A. H. Saxon, currently completing what promises to be the definitive biography of Barnum for Columbia University Press, has edited selected letters of Barnum, with superb notes and an informative introduction. W. Porter Ware and Thaddeus C. Lockard have authored what must be considered the definitive story of the American tour of the Swedish Nightingale under Barnum's aegis in *P. T. Barnum Presents Jenny Lind.* A wonderful recent book that explores the variety of human oddities frequently displayed in dime museums is Ricky Jay's *Learned Pigs and Fireproof Women.* Additional sources on human oddities and freaks can be found in the chapter on the circus and outdoor entertainment in this handbook.

Variety Forms: Minstrelsy, Vaudeville, and Burlesque

Variety can include all entertainment that depends on a compartmented structure; the three most prominent American examples, minstrel shows, vaudeville, and burlesque, dominated American popular stage entertainment during their heydays. Each grew out of earlier saloon and variety structures and collectively demonstrate the type of mutation that occurred in American popular entertainment.

In-depth study of American variety entertainment still depends a great deal on periodicals of the time and special collections. Of the numerous newspapers of the period, the most valuable are *Billboard* (beginning in 1894), the New York *Clipper*(1900–1918), *Variety* (especially 1905 to 1937), and the New York *Mirror* (1879–1922). Some of the more extensive collections on variety forms are located in well-known libraries: the Library of Congress, the Harvard Theatre Collection, the Hoblitzelle Theatre Arts Library of the University of Texas at Austin, the Library of the Performing Arts at Lincoln Center, and the Boston Public Library. Good minstrel materials are to be found in the Harris Collection, Brown University, and the Buffalo and Erie County Library. Other collections, noted in William C. Young's *American Theatrical Arts,* contain useful holdings of playlets, joke books, sheet music, song books, and similar primary materials.

Robert Toll's *Blacking Up* is the most comprehensive history and analysis of the minstrel show. Toll portrays minstrelsy as an institution that represents an important reflection of American attitudes; he also provides a superb bibliography of primary and secondary sources. A variant point of view is presented by William F. Stowe and David Grimsted in their essay, "White-Black Humor," and Joseph Boskin in *Sambo* explores all major interpretations of the minstrel show's appeal. Other, older, sources on the meaning of minstrelsy can be found in my *Variety Entertainment and Outdoor Amusements* (Chapter 7). Carl Wittke's *Tambo and Bones,* though dated, is still a good basic history and explanation of minstrelsy form. Dailey Paskman's *"Gentlemen, Be Seated!"* (originally published in 1928) has been revised recently by Paskman and updated to include recent offshoots of minstrelsy. It remains, however, a romanticized history but with good examples of music, sample minstrel routines, and good illustrations. For a how-to book, Jack Haverly's *Negro Minstrels: A Complete Guide* is an interesting outline by a successful minstrel manager. Edward Rice's *Monarchs of Minstrelsy* supplies biographical sketches of minstrel specialists, an index of minstrels, and a list of minstrel organizations up to 1911. Richard Moody's "Negro Minstrelsy" provides a good appraisal of minstrelsy largely as a romantic invention of northern whites.

The career of the first blackface comedian, T. D. Rice, is effectively summarized by Molly Ramshaw in "Jump, Jim Crow! A Biographical Sketch of Thomas D. Rice" Hans Nathan's *Dan Emmett and the Rise of Early Negro Minstrelsy* chronicles the life of this minstrel specialist and the early period of minstrelsy from the point of view of a musicologist. Tom Fletcher's *100 Years of the Negro in Show Business* places minstrelsy, with a focus on individuals, in the context of black performers over a one hundred year period. The tremendous impact of minstrelsy in Great Britain is adequately told by Harry Reynolds in *Minstrel Memories,* covering the period 1836 to 1927. Two good specialized essays are Marian Winter's "Juba and American Minstrelsy" and Jules Zanger's "The Minstrel Show as Theater of Misrule." Two dissertations on minstrelsy and songsters—Frank Davidson's "The

Rise, Development, Decline, and Influence of the American Minstrel Show"
and Cecil L. Patterson's "A Different Drummer"—add scholarly credibility
to the topic.

The definitive history of early variety has yet to be written, although the
standard works on vaudeville and one recent study, Parker Zellers's *Tony
Pastor: Dean of the Vaudeville Stage,* include some coverage of the early years.
Zellers's essay, "The Cradle of Variety: The Concert Saloon," also sheds
light on early variety. Myron Matlaw's essay on Pastor's early years, beginning in 1846, is a useful complement to Zellers. Lloyd Morris in his
chatty book *Incredible New York* discusses the atmosphere, reputation, and
dangers of various concert saloons; Clair Willson, in *Mimes and Miners,*
gives a good sense of variety in the West; and Eugene Bristow's scholarly
study of variety in Memphis during the late nineteenth century ("Look Out
for Saturday Night") provides good social insights.

Of the general histories of vaudeville during its peak period, John
DiMeglio's *Vaudeville U.S.A.* is the best documented and furnishes the
most extensive notes and bibliography. Several older histories should still
be considered essential: Abel Green and Joe Laurie's *Show Biz from Vaude
to Video,* Joseph Laurie's *Vaudeville: From the Honky-Tonks to the Palace,* and
Douglas Gilbert's *American Vaudeville: Its Life and Times.* Of more recent
investigations, Albert McLean's *American Vaudeville as Ritual* represents the
most thorough job of analyzing vaudeville in its social-historical framework
and delving below the surface for greater significance. His more recent
article, "U.S. Vaudeville and the Urban Comics," is a natural extension of
his book. Paul Distler's dissertation, "The Rise and Fall of the Racial Comics
in American Vaudeville," and essay, "Exit the Racial Comics," are excellent
scholarly studies of racial comedy in vaudeville.

A large number of active participants in vaudeville left autobiographies
or memoirs. The following early ones are especially informative: M. B.
Leavitt's *Fifty Years in Theatrical Management,* Robert Grau's two volumes
of memoirs, *The Business Man in the Amusement World* and *Fifty Years of
Observation of Music and the Drama,* and Brett Page's insider's view of vaudeville, *Writing for Vaudeville.* Eugene Elliott's study, *A History of Variety-
Vaudeville in Seattle,* though brief, offers a good look at that northwestern
vaudeville capital. William Marston and John H. Fellers's *F. F. Proctor,
Vaudeville Pioneer* and Felix Isman's *Weber and Fields* are among the better
biographies of vaudeville luminaries. Bernard Sobel's *A Pictorial History of
Vaudeville,* recommended for its illustrations, though directed at a popular
audience, is still an accurate and informative guide. Caroline Caffin's *Vaudeville* is a good source of critical essays on vaudeville as seen by a member
of the audience. The efforts to create a union for vaudevillians are detailed
by George Golden, one of its major organizers, in *My Lady Vaudeville and
Her White Rats.*

Most recent vaudeville studies are offshoots of the nostalgia craze and vary greatly in content and value. Charles and Louise Samuels's *Once upon a Stage* is an informal and undocumented history and in no way supersedes earlier histories; Bill Smith's *The Vaudevillians* is a sad and wistful look at daily life on the vaudeville circuit via interviews with thirty-one former headliners (and includes a brief glossary of vaudeville terms); and Marcia Keegan's *We Can Still Hear Them Clapping* is a photographic essay, with limited text, recording the impressions and reminiscences of former vaudevillians still living in the Times Square district. A fair account of the final chapter in vaudeville's history is Marian Spitzer's *The Palace,* which covers this pinnacle in vaudeville from its opening in 1913.

A few more recent publications deserve special attention. Probably the best book on vaudeville of the past decade is Shirley Staples's *Male-Female Comedy Teams in American Vaudeville, 1865–1932.* Among other things, Staples's dissertation is a very good history of vaudeville; it is a great deal more than this, however. One of the major sections analyzes the comedy of Burns and Allen, far more successfully it should be noted than the recent *Say Goodnight, Gracie!* by Cheryl Blythe and Susan Sackett. Another recent scholarly study of peripheral interest to variety/vaudeville is Stephen Burge Johnson's *The Roof Gardens of Broadway Theatres, 1883–1942.* The phenomenon of black vaudeville, in particular the entertainment seen at Harlem's Apollo Theatre from the 1930s to the 1970s, is covered extensively in Jack Schiffman's *Harlem Heydey.* Though far from exhaustive, Anthony Slide's *The Vaudevillians* provides brief biographical sketches of most major performers from vaudeville's heyday. Finally, a most useful collection of some seventy-five essays written during the existence of vaudeville, creating a kind of history of the subject, is *American Vaudeville as Seen by Its Contemporaries,* edited by Charles W. Stein.

Stage magic was a prominent feature of vaudeville and developed into a form of popular stage entertainment in its own right. Since magic is covered elsewhere in this handbook, the extensive literature on the subject will not be discussed here, other than to mention in passing a few major sources. Certainly the subject of the early history of magic can be explored rather thoroughly by using as a guide Raymond Toole-Stott's two-volume *A Bibliography of English Conjuring, 1581–1876* even though the focus is British. A more recent, basic reference, including chapters on histories of magic and biographies and autobiographies of magicians, as well several useful appendixes, is Earle J. Coleman's *Magic.* The standard history remains the late Milbourne Christopher's *The Illustrated History of Magic;* the most recent, although the emphasis is on the career of the magician Blackstone, is Harry Blackstone, Jr.'s *The Blackstone Book of Magic & Illusion.* Consult the chapter on magic for additional sources or Chapter 11 in my *Variety Entertainment and Outdoor Amusements.*

Burlesque has received even less scholarly treatment than other forms of variety and is invariably admixed with the striptease show, which actually spelled the demise of true American burlesque. American burlesque, not to be confused with the literary tradition effectively dissected by V. C. Clinton-Baddeley in *The Burlesque Tradition in the English Theatre After 1600,* has only one fairly comprehensive history, Irving Zeidman's *The American Burlesque Show,* and the latter, terribly biased in an almost puritanical way, fails to document his investigation. The single best scholarly source, therefore, on the origin and content of burlesque up to the 1930s is Ralph Allen's "Our Native Theatre: Honky-Tonk, Minstrel Shows, Burlesque." The standard sources, generally weak on historical fact and the separation of striptease from true burlesque, are Ann Corio's *This Was Burlesque* and Bernard Sobel's *Burleycue* and *A Pictorical History of Burlesque.* The latter contains an informative text along with excellent photographs. Also useful is Trish Sandberg's "An Interview with Steve Mills," a superb old-time burlesque comic, and Mills's version of one of his "bits," " 'An Artist's Studio': A Comic Scene from Burlesque." Although a fanciful account of burlesque in the 1920s, Rowland Barber's *The Night They Raided Minsky's* provides a sense of the transition from true burlesque to striptease. The Minsky era has been discussed in a scholarly essay by William Green and in a recent, and disappointing, account by Morton Minsky and Milt Machlin titled *Minsky's Burlesque.*

The subject of striptease is no longer limited to latter-day burlesque but more appropriately belongs today to the world of carnivals, fairs, strip clubs, and striptease cabarets. Nevertheless, as an offshoot of burlesque it deserves inclusion, and, surprisingly, the subject has begun to stimulate intriguing sociological and psychological investigations. Few of the numerous memoirs of strippers are worthy of consideration, although two stand apart from the others: Gypsy Rose Lee's memoirs are coherent and offer good backstage atmosphere; Georgia Sothern's *Georgia: My Life in Burlesque* is the best of its ilk—witty, entertaining, and provocative. Gypsy's career after retiring from burlesque has recently been told by her son Erik Lee Preminger in *Gypsy and Me,* a chatty but enlightening account. Striptease also lacks a comprehensive history, although Richard Wortley's *A Pictorial History of Striptease* makes a somewhat feeble effort. Susan Meiselas's *Carnival Strippers* is a more forthright and honest pictorial essay on the stripper, as is Roswell Angier's *A Kind of Life,* which combines pictorial and textual insights into the life of strippers in Boston's "Combat Zone." Investigations into strippers' morality and the sociological/psychological implications of their profession have been undertaken with varying degrees of success by Bernard Lipnitski, "God Save the Queen," James Skipper, Jr. and Charles McCaghy, " Stripteasers," and Marilyn Salutin, "Stripper Morality." Striptease-dominated burlesque and strip joints minus burlesque entertainment are discussed in my *Variety Entertainment and Outdoor Amusements,* with a number of good sources included on nightclub strippers and contemporary sex shows. The most recent full-length study of such entertainment in New York City after the death of burlesque, a gritty and realistic account, is Josh Alan Friedman's *Tales of Times Square,* based largely on interviews and firsthand observation.

Popular Theater

Popular theater encompasses the largest body of sources of any form of stage entertainments, primarily because of its scripted nature and its overlap with mainstream theater forms. Virtually all American theater histories deal with various aspects of popular theater, such as nineteenth-century melodrama, Tom shows, Toby and Suzy shows, hippodrama, tent theater and touring troupes, mining camp theater, and other topics that use mainstream theater structures and techniques. This chapter covers only major sources; additional relevant material can be found in Don B. Wilmeth's guide to the American stage to World War I. A familiarity with the journal *Nineteenth Century Theatre* is a must in this area of study, as are the major theater collections and periodicals of the period.

An excellent overview of popular theater is included in Robert C. Toll's *On With the Show,* along with a good selective bibliography. Toll is especially effective in his analysis of the native themes and characters dealt with in American drama. A recent source that analyzes the period of popular theater's greatest thrust, Brenda Murphy's *American Realism and American Drama, 1880–1940,* includes an excellent up-to-date bibliography as well. Also recommended for coverage of part of this era is C. W. E. Bigsby's *A Critical Introduction to Twentieth-Century American Drama. Volume 1: 1900–1940.* A. H. Quinn's *A History of the American Drama from the Beginning to the Present Day* is still a useful survey of specific plays and playwrights (anthologies of American drama are excluded from this selective survey but should be consulted as well), although a series by Walter J. Meserve, still in progress, will no doubt supersede Quinn's dated work. Studies of specific plays and popular theater genres are simply too extensive, thus most must be excluded in this selective overview.

Essays on specific performers of the popular theater can be found in William C. Young's *Famous Actors and Actresses on the American Stage,* a disappointing but nonetheless useful collection by or about 225 performers. Less comprehensive but still recommended is Donald Mullin's *Victorian Actors and Actresses in Review.* Of the more recently published serious studies of popular performers, the following are worth investigation: James C. Burge's *Lines of Business,* Albert Auster's *Actresses and Suffragists,* Claudia D. Johnson's *American Actress: Perspective on the Nineteenth Century,* and especially Benjamin McArthur's *Actors and American Culture, 1880–1920,* a fitting complement to Garff Wilson's earlier *A History of American Acting.*

It should be noted that many of the more useful scholarly studies on subjects relating to popular theater have been published in recent years by

Greenwood Press and UMI Research Press (many revised doctoral dissertations). In addition to sources already discussed, one of UMI's most useful books in this area is John W. Frick's *New York's First Theatrical Center: The Rialto at Union Square.*

For drama, the most important developments in the late nineteenth century took place in small-town America, where versions of most of the popular plays of the day were presented. Basic formulas evolved that virtually guaranteed success. Identifiable, native American characters figure prominently in the evolution of popular theater. Other than general studies already noted, Francis Hodge's *Yankee Theatre,* Richard Moody's essays, "Uncle Tom, the Theater, and Mrs. Stowe" and, with A. M. Drummond, "The Hit of the Century: *Uncle Tom's Cabin,"* Moody's *Ned Harrigan,* Harry Birdoff's *The World's Greatest Hit,* and Willis Turner's "City Low-Life on the American Stage to 1900" are especially recommended. Hodge's book is the definitive history of the stage Yankee type during its peak period, and Birdoff is a study of "Tommers" and derivatives from the original *Uncle Tom's Cabin.* Though not limited to the stage version, Thomas F. Gossett's *Uncle Tom's Cabin and American Culture* is an excellent examination of this phenomenon with two major chapters on theatrical versions. Richard Dorson has written an excellent essay entitled "Mose the Far-Famed and World Renowned."

The story of the "trouper" and the evolution of traveling companies, culminating in repertoire tent shows, is effectively and comprehensively told in William Slout's *Theatre in a Tent,* also an excellent source on operational practices. An excellent introduction to the entertainment business in small-town America, although one of those "good bad" books, is Harlowe Hoyt's *Town Hall Tonight.* Philip Lewis's *Trouping: How the Show Came to Town* is a pleasant but unreliable history of the same subject. A less successful study of the tent show is Marian McKennon's book, *Tent Show.* A more scholarly analysis of touring systems, specifically in California from 1849 to 1859, is Douglas McDermott's fine essay, "Touring Patterns on California's Theatrical Frontier, 1849–1859." "The Jefferson Company, 1830–1845" by Arthur W. Bloom, stimulated by some of McDermott's later work on frontier theater, provides a good, detailed case study of touring in the mid-nineteenth century; and *Theatrical Touring and Founding in North America,* edited by L. W. Conolly, which concludes with a superb bibliographical essay of relevant sources, is a collection of numerous germane contributions.

Much of the atmosphere and climate for popular theater is reflected in early western theater and amusements in the mining frontiers of Arizona, Oregon, California, and Nevada. This aspect is well covered in studies by Robert Ericson, "Touring Entertainment in Nevada During the Peak Years of the Mining Boom"; Alice Ernst, *Trouping in the Oregon Country;* Joseph Gaer, *Theater of the Gold Rush Decade in San Francisco;* Edmond Gagey, *The*

San Francisco Stage; Constance Rourke, *Troupers of the Gold Coast;* George MacMinn, *The Theater of the Golden Age in California;* and Margaret Watson, *Silver Theatre.* The importance of the frontier opera house during the last third of the nineteenth century is explored by Ronald Davis in "Sopranos and Six Guns." Popular theater in New York is revealed with scholarly exactitude in Marvin Felheim's study of the playwright-manager Augustin Daly and Lise Leone-Marker's book on the director-playwright David Belasco. *Plays by Augustin Daly,* edited by Wilmeth and Cullen, provides a potted history of Daly's career and the theater of his day in its lengthy introduction. This volume is part of a series on nineteenth-century British and American plays with useful introductions, notes, and illustrations. Cullen and Wilmeth have also edited *Plays by William Hooker Gillette* which, along with Doris Cook's small book on Gillette, provides the most accessible assessment of this popular actor-playwright, author of a number of popular melodramas. Cody's involvement in melodrama is touched upon in Don Russell's *The Wild West* and summarized by William Coleman, "Buffalo Bill on Stage," and Jay Monaghan, "The Stage Career of Buffalo Bill." The importance and influence of a strictly American institution, the Chautauqua, which included popular entertainment and theater under the guise of culture and religion, is dealt with in detail in Theodore Morrison's history of Chautauqua, Charles F. Horner's *Strike the Tents,* Marian Scott's *Chautauqua Caravan,* and Harry P. Harrison's *Culture Under Canvas,* the latter a recounting of the traveling tent shows by the manager of the Redpath Chautauqua.

The American showboat, which included not only floating theaters but circus and medicine showboats, has been most fully explored by Philip Graham in *Showboats,* although George Ford's *These Were Actors* is an interesting, if fanciful, account of one of the earliest showboat families and should be consulted as well.

Of all dramatic formulas, the melodrama was the most enduring in American popular culture. A penetrating analysis of the cultural milieu in which melodrama developed and thrived is David Grimsted's *Melodrama Unveiled,* a well-documented scholarly work that includes chapters on critics, audiences, stages, and plays, and offers an excellent bibliographical essay on sources. Frank Rahill's *The World of Melodrama* is also an important treatment of the genre, although less perceptive than Grimsted. A most perceptive, recent essay on American melodrama introduces Daniel C. Gerould's edited volume of selected plays of the genre. The home of melodrama in New York during the nineteenth century, the Bowery Theatre, is given detailed treatment in Alvin Harlow's *Old Bowery Days* and Theodore Shank's "Theatre for the Majority," based in part on his 1956 Stanford dissertation. More recently, Rosemarie Bank has undertaken a series of essays on the Bowery, the most recent of which deals with the phenomenon of the long run at this house. There is a close relationship between English and American melodrama; consequently a number of good English sources are recommended, especially Michael Booth, *English Melodrama;* Maurice Disher, *Melodrama: Plots That Thrilled;* Ernest Reynolds, *Early Victorian Drama, 1830–1870;* and George Rowell, *The Victorian Theatre.*

The stock character Toby has been the subject of several scholarly investigations, in particular those of Larry Clark, "Toby Shows"; Sherwood Snyder, "The Toby Shows"; and Jere C. Mickel, "The Genesis of Toby" and *Footlights on the Prairie.* Neil E. Schaffner and Vance Johnson's *The Fabulous Toby and Me,* the story of Neil Schaffner, the last of the well-known tent repertoire showmen, is an entertaining and sometimes revealing look at the tag end of an American tradition. The career of another famous Toby popular during the first quarter of this century has been told by Clifford Ashby and Suzanne DePauw May in *Trouping Through Texas: Harley Sadler and His Tent Show.*

Stand-up Comics

A form of stage entertainment that has received scant serious attention is the stand-up comic, although beginning with Trevor Griffith's successful Broadway play *Comedians* during the 1976–77 seasons, and more recently in the 1980s with award-winning appearances on Broadway by Lily Tomlin and Jackie Mason in one-person shows that are essentially extensions of stand-up routines, new attention has been given to this unique performance form. The roots of the American stand-up comic date back to the early talking clown of the American circus, basically a stand-up comic. The most famous of the early clowns was Dan Rice, whose life and times have been written most effectively by John Kunzog (*The One-Horse Show*) and Maria Brown (*The Life of Dan Rice*). An excellent survey of the history of clowns, not limited to the stand-up comic, is John Towsen's *Clowns,* which is highly recommended. Other sources on clowns are discussed in the chapter on the circus and outdoor entertainment.

Few general studies deal exclusively with the stand-up comic, although Phil Berger's *The Last Laugh* is a reasonably successful study of the lives, gags, and routines of the major contemporary stand-up comics. William Cahn's *The Laugh Makers* (and the revised version, *A Pictorial History of the Great Comedians*) is one of the better contemporary sources on stand-up comics, although short on analytical text. *Joe Franklin's Encyclopedia of Comedians* is a useful compendium of biographical sketches of most major comedians from the turn of the century through the 1970s, while Linda Martin and Kerry Segrave's *Women in Comedy* offers more detailed biographies and analyses of major female comedians for much the same period, including such stand-up comics as Totie Fields, Phyllis Diller, Lily Tomlin, Joan Rivers, and Whoopi Goldberg. Abel Green and Joe Laurie's *Show Biz from Vaude to Video* sums up seven great eras of show business up to 1951 and includes selected emphasis on the place of the stand-up comic. Martin Gottfried's *In Person,* discussed elsewhere in this chapter, should also be consulted.

Of specific works by or about individual stand-up comics, most are so chatty and informal as to be almost useless. The writings of Joey Adams, especially his *Encyclopedia of Humor, From Gags to Riches,* and *The Borscht Belt,* are exceptions, as are the writings of Steve Allen, especially *The Funny Men,* a better than average literary effort; Art Cohn's *The Joker Is Wild* is a fair biography of Joe E. Lewis. Lenny Bruce, the subject of great attention as a controversial and revolutionary stand-up comic, has been given good treatment in such sources as Albert Goldman's biography, *Ladies and Gentlemen, Lenny Bruce!,* John Cohen's *The Essential Lenny Bruce,* and *The Almost Unpublished Lenny Bruce,* gathered from the private collection of Kitty Bruce.

The traditional venues of the stand-up comic—the nightclub and the cabaret, terms used almost interchangeably in this country—have received scant attention, although a handful of good sources are available, most recently a scholarly study of New York nightlife, with major emphasis on the cabaret and nightclub tradition, Lewis A. Erenberg's *Steppin' Out.* Though dated, three other books on the nightclub deserve mention: Stanley Walker's *The Night Club Era;* Jimmy Durante and Jack Kofoed's *Night Clubs* (especially Kofoed's early section on the beginning of nightclubs); and Robert Sylvester's *No Cover Charge.* The standard historical survey and analytical account in English of the more traditional cabaret from its Parisian beginnings to its more recent manifestations in London and the United States is Lisa Appignanesi's *The Cabaret.* Two relatively recent sources focus on the black entertainer's association with nightclubs: Jim Haskins's *The Cotton Club* provides vivid portraits of black entertainers associated with this famous club of the 1930s and 1940s, and *Bricktop,* by Bricktop (the late Ada Smith who died in 1984) and Haskins, is a wonderful autobiography of the black entertainer and nightclub owner known as queen of the nightclubs.

BIBLIOGRAPHY

Books and Articles

Reference and General Sources

Archer, Stephen M. *American Actors and Actresses: A Guide to Information Sources.* Detroit: Gale Research, 1983.
Atkinson, Brooks. *Broadway.* Rev. ed. New York: Macmillan, 1974.
Boskin, Joseph. *Sambo: The Rise and Demise of an American Jester.* New York: Oxford University Press, 1986.

Brown, T. Allston. *History of the New York Stage.* 3 vols. 1903. Reprint. New York: Benjamin Blom, 1963.

Bryan, George B. *Stage Lives: A Bibliography and Index to Theatrical Biographies in English.* Westport, Conn.: Greenwood Press, 1985.

Carpenter, Charles A. "American Drama: A Bibliographical Essay." *American Studies International,* 21 (October 1983), 3–52.

Churchill, Allen. *The Great White Way.* New York: E. P. Dutton, 1962.

———. *The Theatrical Twenties.* New York: McGraw-Hill, 1975.

Csida, Joseph, and June Bundy Csida. *American Entertainment: A Unique History of Popular Show Business.* New York: Billboard/Watson-Guptill, 1978.

Dulles, Foster Rhea. *America Learns to Play: A History of Popular Recreation, 1607–1940.* New York: Appleton-Century, 1940.

Flynn, Joyce. "Melting Plots: Patterns of Racial and Ethnic Amalgamation in American Drama Before Eugene O'Neill." *American Quarterly,* 38 (Bibliography 1986), 417–38.

Gottfried, Martin. *In Person: The Great Entertainers.* New York: Harry N. Abrams, 1985.

Green, Stanley. *The Great Clowns of Broadway.* New York: Oxford University Press, 1984.

Henderson, Mary C. *Theater in America: 200 Years of Plays, Players, and Productions.* New York: Harry N. Abrams, 1986.

Hughes, Langston, and Milton Meltzer. *Black Magic: A Pictorial History of the Negro in American Entertainment.* Englewood Cliffs, N.J.: Prentice-Hall, 1967.

Hutton, Laurence. *Curiosities of the American Stage.* New York: Harper and Brothers, 1891.

Jennings, John T. *Theatrical and Circus Life: or, Secrets of the Stage, Green-Room and Sawdust Arena.* St. Louis: Herbert and Cole, 1882.

Lynes, Russell. *The Lively Audience: A Social History of the Visual and Performing Arts in America 1890–1950.* New York: Harper and Row, 1985.

McConachie, Bruce A., and Daniel Friedman. *Theatre for Working-Class Audiences in the United States, 1830–1980.* Westport, Conn.: Greenwood Press, 1985.

McKechnie, Samuel. *Popular Entertainments Through the Ages.* 1931. Reprint. New York: Benjamin Blom, 1969.

McNamara, Brooks. "Popular Scenography." *The Drama Review,* 18 (March 1974); 16–25.

———. "Scavengers of the Amusement World: Popular Entertainment and the Birth of the Movies." In *American Pastimes.* Brockton, Mass.: Brockton Art Center, 1976.

———, ed. *American Popular Entertainments: A Collection of Jokes, Monologues & Comedy Routines.* New York: Performing Arts Journal Publications, 1983.

Marks, Edward Bennett. *They All Had Glamour.* New York: Messner, 1944.

Matlaw, Myron, ed. *American Popular Entertainment.* Westport, Conn.: Greenwood Press, 1979.

Matthews, Brander. *A Book About the Theater.* New York: Scribner's, 1916.

Moody, Richard. *America Takes the Stage.* Bloomington: Indiana University Press, 1955.

Nathan, George Jean. *Encyclopaedia of the Theatre.* New York: Alfred A. Knopf, 1940.

Nye, Russel B. *The Unembarrassed Muse: The Popular Arts in America*. New York: Dial, 1970.

Odell, G.C.D. *Annals of the New York Stage*. 15 vols. New York: Columbia University Press, 1927–49.

"People's Theatre." *Theatre Quarterly*, 1 (October–December 1971). Special issue.

"Popular Entertainments." *The Drama Review*, 18 (March 1974). Special issue.

"The Popular North American Theatre: Provincial Stages in the Nineteenth Century." *Theatre Studies*, no. 24/25 (1977/78–1978/79). Special issue.

"Popular Theatre." *Educational Theatre Journal*, 27 (October 1975). Special issue.

Rourke, Constance. *American Humour: A Study of the National Character*. New York: Harcourt, Brace, 1931.

———. *The Roots of American Culture*. New York: Harcourt, Brace, 1942.

Sampson, Henry T. *Blacks in Blackface: A Source Book on Early Black Musical Shows*. Metuchen, N.J.: Scarecrow Press, 1980.

Seldes, Gilbert. *The 7 Lively Arts*. Rev. ed. New York: Sagamore Press, 1957.

Toll, Robert C. *On with the Show*. New York: Oxford University Press, 1976.

Wilmeth, Don B. *The American Stage to World War I: A Guide to Information Sources*. Detroit: Gale Research, 1978.

———. *American and English Popular Entertainment: A Guide to Information Sources*. Detroit: Gale Research, 1980.

———. *The Language of American Popular Entertainment: A Glossary of Argot, Slang and Terminology*. Westport, Conn.: Greenwood Press, 1981.

———. *Variety Entertainment and Outdoor Amusements*. Westport, Conn.: Greenwood Press, 1982.

Dime Museums and Medicine Shows

Barnum, Phineas T. *The Humbugs of the World*. 1865. Reprint. Detroit: Gale Research, 1970.

———. *Struggles and Triumphs; or, The Life of P. T. Barnum*. 1869. Reprint. New York: New York Times/Arno Press, 1970.

Betts, John R. "P. T. Barnum and the Popularization of Natural History." *Journal of the History of Ideas*, 20 (1959), 353–68.

Desmond, Alice C. *Barnum Presents General Tom Thumb*. New York: Macmillan, 1954.

Freeman, Graydon Laverne. *The Medicine Showman*. Watkins Glen, N.Y.: Century House, 1957.

Harris, Neil. *Humbug: The Art of P. T. Barnum*. Boston: Little, Brown, 1973.

Jay, Ricky. *Learned Pigs & Fireproof Women: Unique, Eccentric and Amazing Entertainers*. New York: Villard Books, 1987.

Jenner, C. Lee, ed. *The Vi-Ton-Ka Medicine Show*. New York: American Place Theatre, 1983.

Kelley, Thomas. *The Fabulous Kelley: He Was King of the Medicine Men*. New York: Pocket Books, 1968.

McNamara, Brooks. " 'A Congress of Wonders': The Rise and Fall of the Dime Museum." *Emerson Society Quarterly*, 20 (1974), 216–32.

———. "The Indiana Medicine Show." *Educational Theatre Journal*, 23 (1971), 431–45.

————. "The Medicine Show Log: Reconstructing a Traditional American Entertainment." *The Drama Review,* 28 (Fall 1984), 74–97.

————. "Talking." *The Drama Review,* 31 (Summer 1987), 39–56.

———— "Medicine Shows: American Vaudeville in the Marketplace." *Theatre Quarterly,* 4 (1974), 19–30.

————. *Step Right Up: An illustrated History of the American Medicine Show.* Garden City, N.Y.: Doubleday, 1976.

Noell, Mae. "Some Memories of a Medicine Show Performer." *Theatre Quarterly,* 4 (May-July 1974), 25–30.

Saxon, A. H., ed. *Selected Letters of P. T. Barnum.* New York: Columbia University Press, 1983.

Wallace, Irving. *The Fabulous Showman.* New York: Alfred A. Knopf, 1959.

Ware, W. Porter, and Thaddeus C. Lockard, Jr. *P. T. Barnum Presents Jenny Lind: The American Tour of the Swedish Nightingale.* Baton Rouge: Louisiana State University Press, 1980.

Webber, Malcolm. *Medicine Show.* Caldwell, Idaho: Caxton Printers, 1941.

Werner, M. R. *Barnum.* New York: Harcourt, Brace, 1923.

Wright, Richardson. *Hawkers and Walkers in Early America.* 1927. Reprint. New York: Frederick Ungar, 1965.

Young, James Harvey. *The Medical Messiahs.* Princeton, N.J.: Princeton University Press, 1967.

————. *The Toadstool Millionaires.* Princeton, N.J.: Princeton University Press, 1961.

Variety Forms: Minstrelsy, Vaudeville, and Burlesque

Allen, Ralph G. "Our Native Theatre: Honky-Tonk, Minstrel Shows, Burlesque." In *The American Theatre: A Sum of Its Parts.* Edited by Henry B. Williams. New York: Samuel French, 1971.

Angier, Roswell. *A Kind of Life: Conversations in the Combat Zone.* Boston: Addison House, 1976.

Barber, Rowland. *The Night They Raided Minsky's.* New York: Simon and Schuster, 1960.

Blackstone, Harry, Jr. *The Blackstone Book of Magic and Illusion.* With Charles and Regina Reynolds. New York: Newmarket Press, 1985.

Blythe, Cheryl, and Susan Sackett. *Say Goodnight, Gracie!* New York: E. P. Dutton, 1986.

Boskin, Joseph. *Sambo: The Rise & Demise of an American Jester.* New York: Oxford University Press, 1986.

Bristow, Eugene. "Look Out for Saturday Night: A Social History of Professional Variety Theatre in Memphis, Tennessee, 1859–1880." Ph.D. dissertation, State University of Iowa, 1956.

Caffin, Caroline. *Vaudeville.* New York: Michell Kemerley, 1914.

Christopher, Milbourne. *Houdini: The Untold Story.* New York: Thomas Y. Crowell, 1969.

————. *The Illustrated History of Magic.* New York: Thomas Y. Crowell, 1973.

Claflin, Edward, and Jeff Sheridan. *Street Magic: An Illustrated History of Wandering Magicians and their Conjuring Arts.* Garden City, N.Y.: Doubleday, 1977.

Clark, Hyla M. *The World's Greatest Magic*. New York: Tree Communications Edition (Crown Publishers), 1976.

Clinton-Baddeley, V.ˆC. *The Burlesque Tradition in the English Theatre After 1600*. London: Methuen, 1952.

Corio, Ann, with Joe DiMona. *This Was Burlesque*. New York: Grosset and Dunlap, 1968.

Davidson, Frank C. "The Rise, Development, Decline, and Influence of the American Minstrel Show." Ph.D. dissertation, New York University, 1952.

DiMeglio, John E. *Vaudeville U.S.A.*. Bowling Green, Ohio: Bowling Green University Popular Press, 1973.

Distler, Paul A. "Exit the Racial Comics." *Educational Theatre Journal*, 18 (1966):247–54.

———. "The Rise and Fall of the Racial Comics in American Vaudeville." Ph.D. dissertation, Tulane University, 1963.

Elliott, Eugene C. *A History of Variety-Vaudeville in Seattle*. Seattle: University of Washington Press, 1944.

Fletcher, Tom. *100 Years of the Negro in Show Business*. New York: Burdge and Co., 1934.

Friedman, Josh Alan. *Tales of Times Square*. New York: Delacorte Press, 1986.

Gilbert, Douglas. *American Vaudeville: Its Life and Times*. 1940. Reprint. New York: Dover, 1968.

Golden, George Fuller. *My Lady Vaudeville and Her White Rats*. New York: Broadway Publishing Co., 1909.

Grau, Robert. *The Business Man in the Amusement World*. New York: Broadway Publishing Co., 1910.

———. *Fifty Years of Observation of Music and the Drama*. New York: Broadway Publishing Co., 1909.

Green, Abel, and Joe Laurie, Jr. *Show Biz from Vaude to Video*. Garden City, N.Y.: Permabooks, 1953.

Green, William. "The Audiences of the American Burlesque Show of the Minsky Era (ca. 1920–40)." In *Das Theater und Sein Publikum*. Vienna: Verlag der Osterreichischen Akadimie der Wissenschaften, 1977.

Haverly, Jack. *Negro Minstrels: A Complete Guide*. Chicago: Frederick J. Drake, 1902.

Isman, Felix. *Weber and Fields: Their Tribulations, Triumphs, and Their Associates*. New York: Boni and Liveright, 1924.

Johnson, Stephen Burge. *The Roof Gardens of Broadway Theatres, 1883–1942*. Ann Arbor, Mich.: UMI Research Press, 1985.

Keegan, Marcia. *We Can Still Hear Them Clapping*. New York: Avon Books, 1975.

Laurie, Joseph. *Vaudeville: From the Honky-Tonks to the Palace*. 1953. Reprint. Port Washington, N.Y.: Kennikat Press, 1972.

Leavitt, M. B. *Fifty Years in Theatrical Management, 1859–1909*. New York: Broadway Publishing Co., 1912.

Lee, Gypsy Rose. *Gypsy: A Memoir*. New York: Harper and Brothers, 1957.

Lipnitski, Bernard. "God Save the Queen." *Esquire*, 72 (Augus 1969), 104–7.

McLean, Albert F., Jr. *American Vaudeville as Ritual*. Lexington: University of Kentucky, 1965.

———. "U.S. Vaudeville and the Urban Comics." *Theatre Quarterly*, 1 (October–December 1971), 50–57.

Marston, William, and John H. Fellers. *F. F. Proctor, Vaudeville Pioneer*. New York: Richard R. Smith, 1943.

Matlaw, Myron. "Tony the Trouper: Pastor's Early Years." *Theatre Annual*, 24 (1968), 70–90.

Meiselas, Susan. *Carnival Strippers*. New York: Farrar, Straus and Giroux, 1976.

Mills, Steve. " 'An Artist's Studio': A Comic Scene from Burlesque." *Educational Theatre Journal*, 27 (October 1975), 342–44.

Minsky, Morton, and Milt Machlin. *Minsky's Burlesque: A Fast and Funny Look at America's Bawdiest Era*. New York: Arbor House, 1986.

Moody, Richard. "Negro Minstrelsy." *Quarterly Journal of Speech*, 30 (October 1944), 321–28.

Morris, Lloyd. *Incredible New York*. New York: Random House, 1957.

Nathan, Hans. *Dan Emmett and the Rise of Early Negro Minstrelsy*. Norman: University of Oklahoma Press, 1962.

Page, Brett. *Writing for Vaudeville*. Springfield, Mass.: Home Correspondence School, 1915.

Paskman, Dailey. *"Gentlemen, Be Seated!" A Parade of the Old-Time Minstrels*. Rev. ed. New York: Clarkson N. Potter, 1976.

Patterson, Cecil L. "A Different Drummer: The Image of the Negro in Nineteenth Century Popular Song Books." Ph.D. dissertation, University of Pennsylvania, 1961.

Preminger, Erik Lee. *Gypsy & Me: At Home and on the Road with Gypsy Rose Lee*. Boston: Little, Brown, 1984.

Ramshaw, Molly Niederlander. "Jump, Jim Crow! A Bibliograhical Sketch of Thomas D. Rice." *Theatre Annual*, 17 (1960), 36–47.

Reynolds, Harry. *Minstrel Memories: The Story of Burnt Cork Minstrelsy in Great Britain from 1836–1927*. London: Alston Rivers, 1928.

Rice, Edward LeRoy. *Monarchs of Minstrelsy, from "Daddy" Rice to Date*. New York: Kenny Publishing Co., 1911.

Salutin, Marilyn. "Stripper Morality." *Transaction*, 8 (June 1971), 12–22.

Samuels, Charles, and Louise Samuels. *Once upon a Stage: The Merry World of Vaudeville*. New York: Dodd, Mead, 1974.

Sandberg, Trish. "An Interview with Steve Mills." *Educational Theatre Journal*, 27 (October 1975), 331–41.

Schaffner, Neil E., and Vance Johnson. *The Fabulous Toby and Me*. Englewood Cliffs, N.J.: Prentice-Hall, 1968.

Schiffman, Jack. *Harlem Heyday: A Pictorial History of Modern Black Show Business and the Apollo Theatre*. Buffalo, N.Y.: Prometheus Books, 1984.

Skipper, James K., Jr., and Charles H. McCaghy. "Lesbian Behavior as an Adaptation to the Occupation of Stripping." *Social Problems*, 17 (Fall 1969), 262–70.

———. "Stripteasers: The Anatomy and Career Contingencies of a Deviant Occupation." *Social Problems*, 17 (Winter 1970), 391–405.

Slide, Anthony. *The Vaudevillians: A Dictionary of Vaudeville Performers*. New York: Arlington House, 1981.

Smith, Bill. *The Vaudevillians*. New York: Macmillan, 1976.

Sobel, Bernard. *Burleyque: An Underground History of Burlesque Days*. New York: Farrar and Rinehart, 1931.

————. *A Pictorial History of Burlesque.* New York: G. P. Putnam's Sons, 1956.

————. *A Pictorial History of Vaudeville.* New York: Citadel Press, 1961.

Sothern, Georgia. *Georgia: My Life in Burlesque.* New York: Signet Books, 1972.

Spitzer, Marian. *The Palace.* New York: Atheneum, 1969.

Staples, Shirley. *Male-Female Comedy Teams in American Vaudeville, 1865–1932.* Ann Arbor, Mich.: UMI Research Press, 1984.

Stein, Charles W., ed. *American Vaudeville as Seen by Its Contemporaries.* New York: Alfred A. Knopf, 1984.

Stowe, William F., and David Grimsted. "White-Black Humor." *Journal of Ethnic Studies,* 2 (Summer 1975), 78–96.

Toll, Robert C. *Blacking Up: The Minstrel Show in Nineteenth Century America.* New York: Oxford University Press, 1974.

Toole-Stott, Raymond. *A Bibliography of English Conjuring, 1581–1876.* 2 vols. Derby, England: Harpur and Sons, 1976–78.

Willson, Clair. *Mimes and Miners: Theater in Tombstone.* Tucson: University of Arizona Press, 1935.

Winter, Marian Hannah. "Juba and American Minstrelsy." *Dance Index,* 6 (1947), 28–47.

Wittke, Carl. *Tambo and Bones. A History of the Minstrel Stage.* 1930. Reprint. Westport, Conn.: Greenwood Press, 1968.

Wortley, Richard. *A Pictorial History of Striptease: 100 Years of Undressing to Music.* Secaucus, N.J.: Chartwell Books, 1976.

Young, William C. *American Theatrical Arts: A Guide to Manuscripts and Special Collections in the United States and Canada.* Chicago: American Library Association, 1971.

Zanger, Jules. "The Minstrel Show as Theatre of Misrule." *Quarterly Journal of Speech,* 60 (February 1974), 33–38.

Zeidman, Irving. *The American Burlesque Show.* New York: Hawthorn Books, 1967.

Zellers, Parker. "The Cradle of Variety: The Concert Saloon." *Educational Theatre Journal,* 20 (December 1968), 578–85.

————. *Tony Pastor: Dean of the Vaudeville Stage.* Ypsilanti: Eastern Michigan University Press, 1971.

Popular Theater

Ashby, Clifford, and Suzanne DePauw May. *Trouping Through Texas: Harley Sadler and His Tent Show.* Bowling Green, Ohio: Bowling Green University Popular Press, 1982.

Auster, Albert. *Actresses and Suffragists: Women in the American Theatre 1890–1920.* New York: Praeger, 1984.

Bank, Rosemarie K. "Antedating the Long Run: A Prolegomenon." *Nineteenth Century Theatre Research,* 13 (Summer 1985), 33–36.

Bigsby, C.W.E. *A Critical Introduction to Twentieth-Century American Drama. Volume 1: 1900–1940.* Cambridge and London: Cambridge University Press, 1982.

Birdoff, Harry. *The World's Greatest Hit—Uncle Tom's Cabin.* New York: S. F. Vanni, 1947.

Bloom, Arthur W. "The Jefferson Company, 1830–1845." *Theatre Survey,* 27 (May and November 1986), 89–153.

Booth, Michael R. *English Melodrama.* London: Jenkins, 1965.

Burge, James C. *Lines of Business: Casting Practice and Policy in the American Theatre, 1752–1899.* New York: Peter Lang, 1986.

Clark, Larry Dale. "Toby Shows: A Form of American Popular Theatre." Ph.D. dissertation, University of Illinois, 1963.

Coleman, William S. E. "Buffalo Bill on Stage." *Players, Magazine of American Theatre,* 47 (December-January), 80–91.

Conolly, L. W., ed. *Theatrical Touring and Founding in North America.* Westport, Conn.: Greenwood Press, 1982.

Cook, Doris E. *Sherlock Holmes and Much More.* Hartford: Connecticut Historical Society, 1970.

Cullen, Rosemary, and Don B. Wilmeth, eds. *Plays by William Hooker Gillette.* New York: Cambridge University Press, 1983.

Davis, Ronald L. "Sopranos and Six Guns: The Frontier Opera House as a Cultural Symbol." *The American West,* 7 (November 1970), 10–17.

Disher, Maurice Willson. *Melodrama: Plots That Thrilled.* London: Rockliff, 1954.

Dorson, Richard M. "Mose the Far-Famed and World Renowned." *American Literature,* 15 (November 1943), 288–300.

Ericson, Robert Edward. "Touring Entertainment in Nevada During the Peak Years of the Mining Boom." Ph.D. dissertation, University of Oregon, 1970.

Ernst, Alice Henson. *Trouping in the Oregon Country.* Portland: Oregon Historical Society, 1961.

Felheim, Marvin. *Theater of Augustin Daly.* Cambridge, Mass.: Harvard University Press, 1956.

Ford, George D. *These Were Actors.* New York: Library Publishers, 1955.

Frick, John W. *New York's First Theatrical Center: The Rialto at Union Square.* Ann Arbor: UMI Research Press, 1985.

Gaer, Joseph, ed. *Theater of the Gold Rush Decade in San Francisco.* 1935. Reprint. New York: Burt Franklin, 1970.

Gagey, Edmond M. *The San Francisco Stage.* New York: Columbia University Press, 1950.

Gerould, Daniel C., ed. *American Melodrama.* New York: Performing Arts Journal Publications, 1983.

Gossett, Thomas F. *Uncle Tom's Cabin and American Culture.* Dallas: Southern Methodist University Press, 1985.

Graham, Philip. "Showboats in the South." *Georgia Review,* 12 (Summer 1958), 174–85.

———. *Showboats: The History of an American Institution.* Austin: University of Texas Press, 1951, 1969.

Grimsted, David. *Melodrama Unveiled: American Theatre & Culture, 1800–1850.* Chicago: University of Chicago, 1968.

Harlow, Alvin F. *Old Bowery Days.* New York: Appleton, 1931.

Harrison, Harry P., as told to Karl Detzer. *Culture Under Canvas: The Story of Tent Chautauqua.* New York: Hastings House, 1958.

Hodge, Francis. *Yankee Theatre: The Image of America on Stage, 1825–1850.* Austin: University of Texas Press, 1964.

Horner, Charles F. *Strike the Tents: The Story of the Chautauqua.* Philadelphia: Dorrance and Co., 1954.

Hoyt, Harlowe. *Town Hall Tonight.* New York: Bramhall House, 1955.

Johnson, Claudia D. *American Actress: Perspective on the Nineteenth Century*. Chicago: Nelson-Hall, 1984.

Leone-Marker, Lise. *David Belasco: Naturalism in the American Theatre*. Princeton, N.J: Princeton University Press, 1975.

Lewis, Philip C. *Trouping: How the Show Came to Town*. New York: Harper and Row, 1973.

McArthur, Benjamin. *Actors and American Culture, 1880–1920*. Philadelphia: Temple University Press, 1984.

McDermott, Douglas. "Touring Patterns on California's Theatrical Frontier, 1849–1859." *Theatre Survey*, 15 (May 1974), 18–28.

McKennon, Marian. *Tent Show*. New York: Exposition Press, 1964.

MacMinn, George R. *The Theater of the Golden Age in California*. Caldwell, Idaho: Caxton Printers, 1941.

Meserve, Walter J. *An Emerging Entertainment: The Drama of the American People to 1828*. Bloomington: Indiana University Press, 1977.

———. *Heralds of Promise: The Drama of the American People in the Age of Jackson, 1829–1849*. Westport, Conn.: Greenwood Press, 1986.

Mickel, Jere C. *Footlights on the Prairie*. St. Cloud, Minn.: North Star Press, 1974.

———. "The Genesis of Toby." *Journal of American Folklore*, 80 (October-December 1967), 334–40.

Monaghan, Jay. "The Stage Career of Buffalo Bill." *Journal of the Illinois State Historical Society*, 31 (December 1938), 411–23.

Moody, Richard. *Ned Harrigan: From Corlear's Hook to Herald Square*. Chicago: Nelson-Hall, 1980.

———. "Uncle Tom, the Theater, and Mrs. Stowe." *American Heritage*, 6 (October 1955), 29–33, 102–3.

Moody, Richard, and A. M. Drummond. "The Hit of the Century: *Uncle Tom's Cabin*." *Educational Theatre Journal*, 4 (1952), 315–22.

Morrison, Theodore. *Chautauqua*. Chicago: University of Chicago Press, 1974.

Mullin, Donald, ed. *Victorian Actors and Actresses in Review*. Westport, Conn.: Greenwood Press, 1983.

Murphy, Brenda. *American Realism and American Drama, 1880–1940*. New York: Cambridge University Press, 1987.

Quinn, Arthur Hobson. *A History of the American Drama from the Beginning to the Present Day*. 2 vols. New York: Appleton-Century-Crofts, 1943.

Rahill, Frank. *The World of Melodrama*. University Park: Pennsylvania State University Press, 1967.

Reynolds, Ernest. *Early Victorian Drama, 1830–1870*. Cambridge, England: Heffer, 1936.

Rourke, Constance. *Troupers of the Gold Coast, or the Rise of Lotta Crabtree*. New York: Harcourt, Brace, 1928.

Rowell, George. *The Victorian Theatre*. 2nd ed. New York: Cambridge University Press, 1978.

Russell, Don. *The Wild West; or, A History of the Wild West Shows*. Fort Worth, Tex.: Amon Carter Museum of Western Art, 1970.

Schaffner, Neil E., with Vance Johnson. *The Fabulous Toby and Me*. Englewood Cliffs, N.J.: Prentice-Hall, 1968.

Scott, Marian. *Chautauqua Caravan*. New York: Appleton-Century, 1939.

Shank, Theodore J. "Theatre for the Majority: Its Influence on a Nineteenth-Century American Theatre" *Educational Theatre Journal,* 11 (1959), 188–89.

Slout, William Lawrence. *Theatre in a Tent: The Development of a Provincial Entertainment.* Bowling Green, Ohio: Bowling Green University Popular Press, 1972.

Snyder, Sherwood, III. "The Toby Shows." Ph.D. dissertation, University of Minnesota, 1966.

Toll, Robert C. *On with the Show.* New York: Oxford University Press, 1976.

Turner, Willis L. "City Low-Life on the American Stage to 1900." Ph.D. dissertation, University of Illinois, 1956.

Watson, Margaret. *Silver Theatre: Amusements of the Mining Frontier in Early Nevada, 1850–1864.* Glendale, Calif.: A. H. Clark, 1964.

Wilmeth, Don B., and Rosemary Cullen, eds. *Plays by Augustin Daly.* New York: Cambridge University Press, 1984.

Wilson, Garff B. *A History of American Acting.* Bloomington: Indiana University Press, 1966.

Young, William C. *Famous Actors and Actresses on the American Stage.* 2 vols. New York: R. R. Bowker, 1975.

Stand-up Comics

Adams, Joey. *Encyclopedia of Humor.* Indianapolis: Bobbs-Merrill, 1968.

———. *From Gags to Riches.* New York: Frederick Fell, 1946.

Adams, Joey, with Henry Tobia. *The Borscht Belt.* New York: Avon Books, 1967.

Allen, Steve. *The Funny Men.* New York: Simon and Schuster, 1956.

Appignanesi, Lisa. *The Cabaret.* New York: Universe Books, 1976.

Berger, Phil. *The Last Laugh: The World of Stand-up Comics.* New York: William Morrow, 1975.

Bricktop, with James Haskins. *Bricktop.* New York: Atheneum, 1983.

Brown, Maria Ward. *The Life of Dan Rice.* Long Beach, N.J.: Privately Printed, 1901.

[Bruce, Kitty]. *The Almost Unpublished Lenny Bruce.* Philadelphia: Running Press, 1984.

Cahn, William. *The Laugh Makers: A Pictorial History of American Comedians.* New York: G. P. Putnam's Sons, 1957.

———. *A Pictorial History of the Great Comedians.* New York: Grosset and Dunlap, 1970.

Cohen, John. *The Essential Lenny Bruce.* New York: Ballantine, 1967.

Cohn, Art. *The Joker Is Wild: The Story of Joe E. Lewis.* New York: Random House, 1955.

Durante, Jimmy, and Jack Kofoed. *Night Clubs.* New York: Alfred A. Knopf, 1931.

Erenberg, Lewis A. *Steppin' Out: New York Nightlife and the Transformation of American Culture, 1890–1930.* Westport, Conn.: Greenwood Press, 1981.

Franklin, Joe. *Joe Franklin's Encyclopedia of Comedians.* 1979. Reprint. New York: Bell, 1985.

Goldman, Albert. *Ladies and Gentlemen, Lenny Bruce!* New York: Random House, 1971.

Green, Abel, and Joe Laurie, Jr. *Show Biz from Vaude to Video.* Garden City, N.Y.: Permabooks, 1953.

Haskins, Jim. *The Cotton Club: A Pictorial and Social History of the Most Famous Symbol of the Jazz Era.* New York: Random House, 1977.

Kunzog, John C. *The One-Horse Show: The Life and Times of Dan Rice, Circus Jester and Philanthropist.* Jamestown, N.Y.: John C. Kunzog, 1962.

Martin, Linda, and Kerry Segrave. *Women in Comedy: The Funny Ladies from the Turn of the Century to the Present.* Secaucus, N.J.: Citadel Press, 1986.

Sylvester, Robert. *No Cover Charge: A Backward Look at the Night Clubs.* New York: Dial Press, 1956.

Towsen, John N. *Clowns.* New York: Hawthorn Books, 1976.

Walker, Stanley. *The Night Club Era.* New York: Frederick A. Stokes, 1933.

Periodicals

Billboard. Los Angeles, 1894–.

The Drama Review. New York, 1955–.

Educational Theatre Journal (now *Theatre Journal*). Cambridge, Mass., 1949–.

Journal of American Culture. Bowling Green, Ohio, 1978–.

Journal of Popular Culture. Bowling Green, Ohio, 1967–.

New York Clipper. New York, 1900–1918.

New York Mirror. New York, 1879–1922.

Nineteenth Century Theatre Research (now *Nineteenth Century Theatre*). Amherst, Mass., 1973–.

Prospects. New York, 1975–.

Spirit of the Times. New York, 1856–1902.

The Theatre or *The Theatre Magazine.* New York, 1900–1931.

Theatre History Studies. Grand Forks, N.D., 1981–.

Theatre Quarterly (now *New Theatre Quarterly*). Cambridge, England, 1971–.

Theatre Studies. Columbus, Ohio, 1955–.

Variety. New York, 1905–.

Stamp and Coin Collecting

JOHN BRYANT

In recent decades Americans have turned to leisure activities with an intensity that nearly belies the function of "rest and relaxation." Like sports, hobbies are for millions an outlet or even substitute for passion, controlled forms of mania which allow the participant to escape from or create order in a restless world. The most popular type of hobby is collecting. Our compulsion to collect, notes W. D. Newgold in the *Encyclopaedia Britannica*, probably dates back to those happy, preliterate days when man foraged for nuts and berries.[1] But today's collector does not forage in order to consume; he catalogs and displays his nuts and berries. The modes of collecting are as numerous as the objects that can be collected, and today anything that is abundant enough to be accessible yet scarce enough to be a challenge can become a "collectible." Some collect natural specimens. (We are told that Howard Hughes collected bits of himself.) Some collect rare books or art. Others collect the detritus of our industrial civilization: tinfoil, beer cans, or barbed wire. More collect antiques or dolls. But most people who collect, collect stamps or coins.

The American Philatelic Society reports that its membership now numbers 50,000 individuals. A likelier estimate of serious stamp collectors is more than double that figure, and the number of "nonprofessional" collectors—the child or adult who keeps a cigar box or tidy album of stamps—undoubtedly swells into the millions. The U.S. Postal Service claims that upward of twenty million Americans use its philatelic windows each year. The American Numismatic Association reports 34,000 members.

More impressive than these figures is the remarkable activity that philatelists and numismatists precipitate in both the business and leisure worlds. Many governments maintain philatelic agencies designed to promote collecting and coordinate the year's steady stream of colorful new issues. Coins, too, in recent decades have assumed eye-çatching designs. Collectors in both fields belong to local, national, and international associations, nearly all of which hold exhibitions ranging from modest hotel gatherings to major expositions with juried exhibits, lectures, and dealers' tables. Over 130 stamp and 26 coin groups meet regularly to examine special aspects of the hobbies. Each week over one hundred syndicated stamp or coin columns address the general reading public. Also, America's presses generate a bewildering array of books, scholarship, catalogs, and at present well over 200 specialized stamp or coin periodicals.

To touch the past, to gain mental control over a proliferating world by gathering specimens of it, or simply to research a project—these are human needs that are routinely satisfied by putting a stamp or coin in an album. Determining the social and psychological roots of the collecting phenomenon is challenging; equally fascinating are the cultural implications of the stamps and coins themselves. Overtly, both stamps and coins serve basic economic functions; covertly, they are modes of governmental propaganda. From an aesthetic perspective, they provide unique popular art forms combining miniature and medallic art, engraving, mass production, and, in some cases, the work of premiere American artists and artisans. (At various times, for instance, Americans have been able to purchase an engraved Gilbert Stuart reproduction on a stamp with a coin designed by Augustus St. Gaudens.) Finally, as social icons, stamps and coins reflect shifting American ideologies and may in guarded cases be used as evidence supplementing a scholar's historical or cultural observations.

In the past 150 years, philatelists and numismatists have published a substantial body of literature. Yet the amount of material published by our universities' cultural historians on these subjects is minute. In the process of reporting the scope and nature of philatelic and numismatic literature, assessing the scant number of publications in the area, and suggesting topics for further study, I hope to confront three problems: the phenomenon of collecting, the aesthetic merits of stamps and coins themselves, and the use of stamps and coins as reliable indicators of cultural development.

HISTORIC OUTLINE

Since postal and monetary history are academic fields in their own right and plump bibliographies exist for them elsewhere, I shall not detail the histories of the mails or money except when such details directly influence the development of the two hobbies. Generally speaking, three factors have shaped the growth of philately and numismatics: democratization, or the spreading of an elite hobby among the masses; commercialization, or the transformation of the hobby into a business; and specialization, or the creation within the hobby of special, even scholarly, modes of collecting.

Stamps

Unlike coins, which are as old as sin, postage stamps are an invention of the industrial age and imperial Britain's need for an efficient communication system. Sir Rowland Hill introduced postal reforms and adhesive postage stamps to the public in 1840. Previously, letters were ink-stamped, and the price of delivery was paid by the receiver to the courier on delivery. Numerous private delivery agencies competed in an open market. Hill instituted a government postal monopoly and essentially inverted the process of mail delivery. Now senders paid for delivery by purchasing one-cent "Penny Black" stamps, which they then affixed to their letters. The result was more revenues going directly into government coffers and broadened mail circulation. Although an American allegedly introduced the idea of prepaid postage stamps to Hill, Americans were slower to adopt the new system. The first official U.S. stamps were not printed until 1847, and the government did not gain a monopoly until 1863.

Serious stamp collecting began some twenty years after Hill's invention. In the 1840s stamps were a fad but not a hobby: a socialite in British Mauritia printed her own "Penny Blacks" to adorn party invitations, and in England something called a "stamp ball" was the rage. The less affluent fancied stamps, too, using them to decorate their walls and lapels. By the 1860s, however, the fad had clearly grown into a hobby. Used stamp transactions were a common sight in the open markets of Europe. London could boast sixty stamp dealers, and French officials, fearing that stamp markets encouraged forgeries and the corruption of youths, closed the Paris markets twice before letting hobbyists be. Philatelic literature (how-to books, catalogs, price lists, and even books on counterfeit detecting) appeared as early as 1862. In 1865, British dealer J. W. Scott set up business in New York, and his new company (still a major U.S. stamp firm) stimulated an already growing market in this country.

From the beginning philately shared in the democratic spirit of the age. Although more prominent philatelists have generally been wealthy men (John K. Tiffany, Count Ferarri, King Farouk, Franklin Delano Roosevelt), the hobby has been a relatively cheap, accessible, and convenient pastime shared (as handbook authors like to crow) by "kings and kids" alike. Even the earliest guides to the hobby proclaim philately's universal appeal. Stamps were easily packaged and mailed for trade or purchase; they were generally inexpensive and required no costly paraphernalia (such as the traditional coin cabinet). A working-class child with few resources could acquire a modest collection through trade and discovery, if not purchase. Moreover, stamp collecting was seen then as now as a form of play providing moral instruction, knowledge, and good preparation for social advancement. The publisher of Henry J. Bellars's *The Standard Guide to Postage Stamp Collecting,* for instance, argues that young collectors "have a more perfect knowledge of their studies, and, above all, obtain a quicker experience of actual life, *and the value of money.*"[2] More than a pastime for the idle rich, philately adhered to the Protestant ethic and gave youngsters a boost up the ladder of success.

To be sure, the major advances and research in the nineteenth century were made by the wealthy. The London (now Royal) Philatelic Society, founded in 1869, was followed in 1886 by the American Philatelic Association (now Society), organized by John Tiffany, a collector since 1859 and a bibliographer of philatelic literature. J. W. Scott presided over the first years of the Collectors Club of New York, founded in 1896, which listed among its members some of the nation's elite. The backbone of American philately, however, was in the middle and working classes; from 1870 to 1890 interest in the hobby was strong enough to sustain some 300 popular and scholastic periodicals in the United States.

By the turn of the century, major stamp exhibitions in Antwerp (1887) and New York (1889) established philately as an international hobby. In 1890 a third such fair in London celebrated the fiftieth anniversary of Hill's invention and introduced an important decade in the commercialization of the hobby. Until this time governmental postal issues had been predominantly portrait stamps. England had Victoria; America had Washington and Franklin. The first major step in the transformation of the hobby into a big government business occurred when authorities reckoned that prettier stamps might attract the eye and pennies of collectors. In the long run they were right, but the idea did not catch on immediately. As early as 1876 the U.S. government had, in fact, issued a series of seven "pictorial" stamps with vignettes of the signing of the Declaration of Independence, the landing of Columbus, and various "icons" such as a locomotive, steamship, and mounted courier; but these stamps did not sell well. A more notorious "experiment" in stamp marketing occurred in 1893, when N. F. Seebeck of the Hamilton Note Company of New York designed and printed a set of colorful stamps for certain Central and South American nations. Called "Seebecks," these stamps were primarily meant to be sold to collectors. The scheme failed, but in 1894 the republic of San Marino set up its philatelic agency to do precisely what Seebeck had hoped to do—create stamps not as postage but as collector's items.

At first collectors were scandalized by any government's attempt to capitalize on the hobby, but the trend toward special and commemorative stamps was irreversible, and today most government postal services actively promote stamp collecting. The frequency of special issues has grown slowly but distinctly in the United States since the printing in 1893 of our first special issues commemorating Columbus's discovery of America. By the 1920s the United States was printing only about three special issues a year. However, 1932 was a banner year for U.S. commemoratives; nineteen in all were issued. The average number of issues in the 1950s was eleven; but since the Bicentennial the figure has approached thirty a year. Government stamp sales are a significant source of income ranging in the millions of dollars. Some speculate, too, that nearly 40 percent of U.S. stamps each year (almost 1.5 billion stamps in 1974) never circulate; they are collected or bought by dealers to be sold to collectors.

The boom in philately during the 1930s and 1940s deeply penetrated various sectors of American culture. Government, entrepreneurs, educators, churches, radio, and universities promoted the hobby. During his administration Franklin Roosevelt assumed complete control over stamp issues, and his flamboyant postmaster general, James Farley, was responsible one year for a $1 million clear profit on the sale of stamps. Also at this time, philately was introduced as a teaching device in public schools. Junior-level history books, for instance, used stamps to "tell the story of America." Church-affiliated stamp clubs sprang up. Bell Telephone encouraged employees to collect, and Ivory Soap sponsored a long-running radio program for collectors. Even the University of Michigan offered a course in philately. Since World War II national and local stamp organizations have strengthened their civic-mindedness. The three major associations, the American Philatelic Society (APS), the Society of Philatelic Americans (SPA), and the American Topical Association (ATA), maintain close ties with civic and educational groups through slide shows, displays, and lecture programs.

For the most part the 1950s and early 1960s brought a continued expansion of philately's democratization and commercialization. More people were adopting the hobby, and the hobby business, in both private and government sectors, was growing. The notion that stamps make good investments has always been an important part of philately's commercial side, but it was not until the early 1950s and the advent of swift inflation that the idea began to sink in. Stamp guides, such as Henry M. Ellis's *Stamps for Fun and Profit,* indicate the trend. Temple University's Business School went so far as to offer a two-year course in philately. Since the Vietnam War, investors have turned more to stamps and coins as hedges against inflation, and Ed Reiter, coin columnist for the *New York Times,* reported that in 1980 Adelphi College offered courses in philately and numismatics to educate dealers and investors in the ways of the market.[3] Thus, the history of the commercialization of the postage stamp has moved from fad to hobby to private and government business to speculative finance. But despite the bull market of the 1980s, philatelic speculation has fallen off rapidly; stamp prices have stabilized, and sales are sluggish.

To a certain degree, a history of philately can be keyed to the emergence of new ways to collect or specialize. Just as Jaques discerns seven ages of man, there are roughly the same number of "ages" of specialization for the collector. The first age is the generalist who collects any and all stamps. The first step toward specialization is the focus on the stamps of one nation or a particular historical period. A slightly more refined third age is collecting types of stamps (airmail, revenue, postage due) or stamps with peculiar markings or arrangements such as "overprints" and "perfins" (stamps precancelled with perforated initials).

A fourth form of specialization is considered by many to be the height of traditional collecting (and, of course, madness, by the layperson). Here, a philatelist will focus on one particular stamp (usually a regular issue) and collect all of its plate, color, and press variants. Such a mode requires scholastic aptitude since the focal stamp's printing history must be meticulously researched down to the hairline cracks that appear in certain plates. (The process is comparable to literary textual analysis, only more difficult.) Growing out of the need for the analysis of variants and counterfeits was the foundation in 1940 of the Philatelic Research Laboratory of New York, which introduced various technological innovations to the hobby.

Anathema (it seems) to traditional philately is the fifth, upstart age of "topical" collecting. Here philatelists collect internationally but only along the lines of a particular subject matter depicted on the stamp. The American Topical Association, organized in 1940 and now 10,000 strong, recognizes at least 700 categories, including John F. Kennedy; space; Americana on American or non-American stamps; journalists, artists, and poets on stamps (JAPOS); women; and so on up to an amazingly self-reflexive topic, stamps with pictures of stamps on them. Topical collecting (or "thematics," as the British call it) has grown in popularity, and some traditional philatelists disparage the mode because it develops an interest in a stamp's message rather than the stamp itself or its history. Government post offices, however, have shaped their special issues to attract the topicalist. In the last two decades the U.S. postal authorities have introduced new printing methods which allow for more color and experimental groupings. (Two or four related stamps, for instance, may be printed together in a strip or block. These are called *setens,* from the French *se tenant,* and, yes, one can collect only *setens.*) At the moment, topical collecting is becoming the dominant mode of collecting.

A sixth age of philately involves those who collect postal material rather than just stamps. Of recent interest to investors and long-standing interest to postal historians are mailed (or even unused) envelopes or "covers" that bear the intricate markings of the mail service. Cover philatelists may, of course, collect material dating before the invention of the postage stamp, but such items are quite often found in museums. Slightly more accessible modern rarities include airmail covers delivered to Paris by Charles Lindbergh or to the United States via zeppelin. Covers also allow collectors to examine postmarks. Up until the turn of the century, letters were hand-cancelled, and early regional postmasters carved their own cancellation marks. Pumpkins, devils, eagles, and other elaborately designed or "fancy" cancellations can be collected, cataloged, and displayed.

The final age of the philatelist (not to be compared too closely to Jaques's "second childhood") is the most academic: postal history. Today even philatelists do not fully understand the difference between postal history and cover collecting. Since collection categories are interpreted by national and international exhibition judges, we might expect clear distinctions from these authorities, but, as a seminar at a southeast Pennsylvania stamp exposition revealed, not all judges agree. Generally speaking, a cover collection is merely a collection of covers, but a postal history collection demonstrates developments in postal history. Thus, as one seminar participant put it, the two types of collections may use precisely the same material but the difference is whether the collection is "written up" to demonstrate history or merely to describe the covers. The philatelist of the future, then, must sharpen his rhetoric.

Coins

Coin collecting presents a significantly different pattern of development. Unlike philately, which began in the industrial age as a fad, spread democratically, yet has become as much an academic pursuit as a hobby, numismatics has been from the beginning and until only recently the concern of the intellectual and social elite. Old coins have always been attractive to the antiquarian; Petrarch, for instance, was one of the first to have collected antique Roman coins. By the eighteenth century no Sun King or even his lesser luminaries could feel properly furnished without a coin cabinet. Men of substance acquired coins as they would art or rare books. Also at this time numismatics entered the university. As early as the Renaissance, gentlemen had written brief treatises on the history of coins, but by the early 1700s in Germany (still the central arena for numismatic research) scholars were beginning to use coins as historical evidence. The compulsion that drove Heinrich Schliemann a century later to dig at the layered ruins of Troy was in part the same desire that brought early scholars closer to coins. Since then numismatics has been an important handmaiden to the archeologist and historian as well as the aesthetician.

The nineteenth century brought a number of developments that shaped and redefined numismatics from the study of coins to that of money in general and medals. As Elvira E. Clain-Stefanelli remarks in her monograph, *Numismatics—An Ancient Science: A Survey of Its History,* the Napoleonic wars generated many medals which were in turn studied in weighty French tomes. In the New World, British and American governments struck medals to "honor" American Indian peace alliances. The quickly expanding and contracting economies of the world also generated more varieties of currency: paper money, bank notes, scrip, tokens, and even unofficial yet negotiable coins. The shortage of coins resulting from Andrew Jackson's refusal to recharter the Second Bank of the United States forced banks and merchants to issue fractional currency and "hard times coins" as late as 1844 in order to make change. With more of such items to collect, numismatists began to focus on material of more recent vintage and of the modern nations. By mid-century, museums as well as universities had become the principal lodgings for major collections. More people were able to see the rarities; more people could also afford modest collections of their own. Yet more scholarly research, publication, and cataloging developed during this period. Thus, numismatics was able to broaden its appeal but also rise in academic respectability.

Although American coinage can be dated back to 1616, we have records of only a few colonial coin collectors. American numismatics dates primarily from the mid-nineteenth century. Philadelphia, home of the U.S. Mint, was logically the first center of numismatic interest. As Clain-Stefanelli records, the mint's chief coiner, Adam Eckfeldt, began a collection at the mint that would become one of the United States' and the world's finest. In 1858 several Philadelphians formed the Numismatic and Antiquarian Society. Also founded that year but destined to outlive the Philadelphia organization was the scholarly American Numismatic Society (ANS). This group and the larger, more hobby-oriented American Numismatic Association (ANA), founded in Chicago in 1891, have become the country's principal numismatic organizations. During the latter half of the century, periodicals such as the *American Journal of Numismatics* (no longer published), *The Numismatist,* and other more ephemeral publications provided amateurs and newcomers with an opportunity to prepare themselves for the rigors of numismatic technique. Landmark works in U.S. numismatic scholarship appeared in these decades. Consonant with international scholarship of that age, American numismatists tended to use currency as clues to economic development rather than as archeological evidence. It has been only recently that scholars have begun to appreciate the artistic merit of America's coinage.

Although by the turn of the century numismatics was growing, it was still a gentleman-scholar's hobby horse. The democratization of the hobby was impeded by certain obvious physical problems. At the time, cumbersome coins required boxes, drawers, and cabinets for storage. Also, modern collecting was inhibited by the fact that governments (which are still conservative when it comes to coinage) rarely minted commemorative, special, or even new issues. At least three developments served to rectify these problems. First, from 1892 to 1934, the U.S. government experimented with commemorative coins, some of which were issued alongside similar commemorative stamps. Also during this period the mint, in an attempt to generate interest in collecting, made available "proof sets" of each year's new or newly dated coins. Unfortunately, the Depression and World War II slowed down the collection of such items until the 1950s. A third development was the marketing in the late 1930s of "coin books" made of cardboard pages with holes cut to fit individual coins. The convenient device gave the hobby its biggest boost. At the time, traditional numismatists laughed, but hobbyists today continue to search loose change and coin rolls for that elusive 1919 D one-cent to stick in their books.

Although numismatics preceded philately as an intellectual discipline, coin collectors of the 1930s did well by following commercial techniques that had been in vogue among stamp collectors for decades. Chatty but reliable journals such as the *Numismatic Scrapbook Magazine* provided trade and sale information. In 1942 Richard S. Yeoman (who first marketed the coin book) began publishing the *Handbook of United States Coins,* "an objective pricing guide" for dealers, and in 1946 he put out the first edition of the *Guidebook of United States Coins,* now an annual mainstay for collectors.

Since World War II the growth of the hobby can be gauged somewhat by the fact that the mint sold nearly four million proof sets in 1964 over the 50,000 sold in 1950. In recent years private mints have promoted the medallic arts, but the most important force in the hobby today is investment—the hope that coin collecting will somehow keep the wolf of inflation at bay. This, however, may destroy rather than promote the hobby, since the price of gold and silver has recently made even collector's items more valuable if melted down. Ed Reiter reports that more coins are heading toward the furnace. This reduce the number of collector's items and raise their value but also reduce the number of those who can afford to collect.[4] Thus, this century has seen numismatics develop in ways contrary to philately. Beginning as a highly specialized field, coin collecting has enjoyed an age of democratization which may be cut short by overcommercialization and speculative finance.

REFERENCE WORKS

As already stated, the principal concerns of this essay are the collecting of stamps and coins as both aesthetic objects and social icons and the collecting of stamps and coins as a phenomenon. A remarkably large body of philatelic and numismatic literature exists, but little of it deals with these issues. Most published material addresses specialized audiences for the purposes of identifying, cataloging, and pricing collector's items. Although brief histories of collecting can be found in beginner's guides and some good aesthetic and social interpretations have been published, primarily in philatelic and numismatic periodicals, much remains for the cultural historian to pull together and assess. The following is a selection of the general and more specialized reference works used by philatelists and numismatists in their own fields that are likely to be useful for the student of popular culture or cultural history.

Stamps

At the moment no complete bibliography of American philatelic literature exists, and, despite valiant efforts among philatelic librarians and bibliographers, no thorough compilation is likely to be published soon. Specialized or incomplete bibliographies do exist; however, they are hard to find. William R. Ricketts's *The Philatelic Literature Bibliography Index* is typical: a privately mimeographed author-and-subject index of international material from 1863 to 1912, complete only up to the letter K. A more useful resource is Richard H. Rosichan's *Stamps and Coins,* which includes detailed annotations for many of its 500 philatelic entries. While Rosichan seems to be an astute bibliographer, his selection is limited to works published primarily since 1959. Important early scholastic works are included only if they are still in print. Although international in scope, American works are emphasized, but there are glaring omissions (nothing, for instance, by Max Johl or August Dietz). Lists of current periodicals and libraries are incomplete. Rosichan's book is geared toward the hobbyist, but the scholar beginning to study philately should consult this resource. Found in Rosichan, for instance, are two specialized bibliographic items: Stamps Information Associates' *Collecting: United States* is a list of U.S. stamp catalogs; and James Lowe's *Bibliography of Postcard Literature* should delight all deltiologists.

One man's attempt to give some sense of order to bibliographic problems in philately is John B. Kaiser's "Bibliography: The Basis of Philatelic Research," which lists bibliographies, catalogs, and periodical indexes and is a good starting place for the researcher. Kaiser's "conspectus" of cumulative periodical indexes, for instance, is a simple but useful tool arranging a dozen periodical guides chronologically by coverage dates so that researchers can more readily locate indexes to journals of a particular era.

Published catalogs of philatelic libraries are the best substitutes for bibliographies, but they too are hard to find. John K. Tiffany's *The Philatelical Library: A Catalogue of Stamp Publications* is an excellent reference to nineteenth-century material by one of America's first collectors. The catalog lists 569 books and periodicals, nearly as many price lists and stamp catalogs, and 272 items on collecting and postal history. Supplementing Tiffany is E. D. Bacon's *Catalogue of the Philatelic Library of the Earl of Crawford, K. T.,* which is arranged by author and nation. More recent is the Johannesburg (South Africa) Public Library's *Catalogue of the Philatelic Collection,* also arranged by nation.

Catalogs of significant American collections of philatelic literature include the *Catalogue of the Philatelic Library of the Collectors Club* and *Postage Stamps: A Selective Checklist of Books on Philately in the Library of Congress.* The latter volume includes a prose paean to philately by poet-librarian Archibald MacLeish as well as a fine list of nineteenth-century handbooks, guides, and scholastic works. Lamentably, the Library of Congress has not updated this catalog even though its collection (now located in the Smithsonian) has grown since 1940 to be the best in the nation. On par with the Collectors Club and Smithsonian collections is the American Philatelic Research Library (APRL), with its catalog of nearly 8,000 books and periodicals. Finally, a convenient and still fairly reliable guide to the location of important bibliographical items can be found in John Freehafer and Helen K. Zirkle's "A Selective List of Philatelic Handbooks, with a List of Libraries in Which They May Be Found." Not to be dismissed by researchers is the annual *A Master List of Philatelic Literature* put out by the HJMR Publishing Company. It is an exhaustive price list of books and journals arranged by nation and topic.

Over the past two decades, significant bibliographic research has been carried on in the pages of the *Philatelic Literature Review*. As the journal for the American Philatelic Research Library, this quarterly supplements Kaiser's work by publishing indexes to philatelic periodicals. A guide to indexes not found in that journal is James Negus's "A List of Cumulative Indexes to Single Periodicals." The *Philatelic Literature Review* also notices about fifty new philatelic publications per issue. The definitive list of nineteenth- and twentieth-century stamp journals with title, publisher, and dates of publication is Chester Smith's print-out *American Philatelic Periodicals*. A remarkable analysis of philatelic periodical literature in the United States is George T. Turner's "Trends in United States Philatelic Literature." Turner (whose massive philatelic library is now a part of the Smithsonian's collection) provides extensive quantitative analysis of periodical output from 1860 to 1945. The study, of course, needs significant updating, but it should provide a model for similar studies of trends in other forms of philatelic literature such as beginner's guides to the hobby.

A sign of the growing importance of philatelic literature to collectors is that many guides to the hobby include selected bibliographies, some of which can be useful to the researcher if the more complete bibliographies are not available. An exhaustive and convenient guide to the present state of the hobby is *Linn's World Stamp Almanac,* put out yearly by the publishers of America's principal philatelic trade weekly, *Linn's Stamp News.* This fact book's 450-item bibliography is extensive yet went to press without the benefit of the *MLA Style Sheet.*

Nevertheless, Linn's list of over 200 current periodicals is useful. Also in the almanac are the year's philatelic news in review, histories of the U.S. Postal Service and the Bureau of Engraving and Printing, descriptions of important research collections, and various sections on how to get a stamp design accepted by the Citizen's Stamp Advisory Committee and how to start a collection or a stamp club. Here one learns, for instance, that as of

1978 no stamp had been issued on August 8 in any given year. Smaller than Linn's bibliography but covering most major works is the checklist of literature in *Scott's New Handbook for Philatelists,* an adequate introduction to philately which includes a useful list of one hundred designers of U.S. stamps. Other guides elucidate the philatelist's patois. Prominent philatelist Henry M. Konwiser, for instance, provides sometimes quirky but always reliable entries on stamp vocabulary and U.S. postal history in *The American Stamp Collector's Dictionary.* Less ambitious but still useful is R. J. Sutton and K. W. Anthony's *The Stamp Collector's Encyclopedia.*

The student of stamps and collecting necessarily requires some acquaintance with postal history. Alvin Harlow's *Old Post Bags: The Story of the Sending of a Letter in Ancient and Modern Times* is dated but reliable. More recent is Wayne E. Fuller's *The American Mail: Enlarger of the Common Life,* an excellent history of the people's conception of the post office. The author's bibliographical essay is invaluable. Carl H. Scheele's *A Short History of the Mail Service* is a readable introduction to U.S. postal history in the context of Old World systems. Histories of regional or specialized postal systems are too numerous to mention. Worthy of inclusion, however, are Kay Horowicz and Robson Lowe's *Colonial Posts in the United States of America, 1606–1783,* August Dietz's *The Postal Service of the Confederate States of America,* and Wayne E. Fuller's *RFD: The Changing Face of Rural America.*

The scholar interested in postage stamps as art objects, social icons, or historical evidence stands before a field virtually untouched by the cultural historian. The few interpretative works on these issues will be treated later. The major concern here is where the researcher can find the stamps or suitable reproductions and basic information on the design, printing, distribution, and popularity of a given stamp. More often than not a pricing catalog is the best available resource.

Given the limited circulation of philatelic literature, most publications are as rare as the stamps they describe. Yet most libraries have at least one of the stamp catalogs put out each year by the publishing firms of Harris, Scott, and Minkus. *Scott's Specialized Catalogue of United States Stamps* is the most extensive. Its numbering systems for stamp types and individual stamps are almost universally accepted. Front matter includes a commemorative stamp index, information for collectors (explaining printing process and postal history), and an "Identifier of Definitive Issues." A black-and-white photo enlargement of each stamp is complemented by details concerning design source, designer, engraver, printer, and date of issue. Useful in gauging the relative popularity of a stamp is the chart of quantities of the commemorative stamps issued. Also included are enlargements of proprietary, local, and Confederate stamps. Although "unofficial," these stamps may in fact provide icons more suggestive of American life than official issues.

Several government publications are helpful. *Postage Stamps of the United*

States (updated yearly) does not deal with anomalies or variants but does provide good photographs of each stamptype and a verbal description of its dimensions and printing history. End matter includes a table of plates used in printing commemoratives and a table of the quantities of each commemorative issued. Also found are lists of stamp designers and engravers since 1953 and of stamp topics. *The United States Official Postal Guide,* issued annually, is an important storehouse of stamp issues and postal regulations. Finally, since the person responsible for coordinating stamp issues is the third assistant postmaster general, this official's documents stored in the National Archives constitutes important firsthand information on why a stamp is issued when. See the *Preliminary Inventories of the United States Archives,* nos. 63 (1953), 82 (1955), and 114 (1959) for their location.

Book-length and monographic studies by philatelists fall into four categories: general histories of the U.S. issues; specialized studies of stamp essays, types, and variants; topical studies; and works on nonstamp philately.

Perhaps the most useful general histories are Lester G. Brookman's two-volume *Nineteenth Century Postage Stamps of the United States* and the five-volume *United States Stamps of the Twentieth Century* by Max Johl and Beverly S. King. Supplementing the latter is Sol Glass's *United States Postage Stamps, 1945–52.* Each work contains illustrations and data on the printing histories of each relevant stamp. Superb printing histories of commemoratives alone are Johl's two-volume *United States Commemoratives of the Twentieth Century* and G. C. Hahn's treatment of an important set of stamps in *United States Famous American Series of 1940.* Other works are Ralph A. Kimble, *Commemorative Postage Stamps of the United States,* and Fred Reinfeld, *Commemorative Stamps of the United States of America.*

To understand the utility of the following specialized studies, the reader may require an explanation of stamp production. The final stamp design of a particular issue is chosen from various engraved trial entries submitted by individual engravers. The rejected samples are called "essays," and in many cases they are completely different in design from the final chosen entry. Thus, fascinating evidence of what officials could have chosen as our postal icons appears in such works as Clarence Brazer's *Essays for United States Adhesive Postage Stamps* and George T. Turner's *Essays and Proofs of United States Internal Revenue Stamps.* The Smithsonian also possesses in its vault a fine collection of stamp essays. Once a stamp goes to press, various plates, inks, and papers may be used before the run is complete. "Traditional" philatelic research has delineated the types and variants of many definitive U.S. issues. The specificity of this research will not likely aid the cultural historian. However, the art historian may find value in such landmark texts as Stanley B. Ashbrook's *The Types and Plates of the United States One-cent Stamp of 1851–57* and *The United States Ten-cent Stamp of 1855–57.*

Works on "topicals" dating as far back as 1910 may be most useful to the cultural historian. The American Topical Association's bimonthly *Topical Times* is a good introduction to the various facets of this "sub-hobby." Social, cultural, or popular historians interested in such topics as women, minorities, Americana, art and artists, or such less "traditional" topics as games, toys, and sports might consult the appropriate topic handbooks published each year. APS and ATA study groups also publish their own journals ranging from the *JAPOS Bulletin* to everyone's favorite, *Let's Talk Parachutes*. (Do not assume your specialized field has not been made a stamp topic.) Relevant to the nineteenth-century specialists is the *1869 Times*, focusing entirely on the important "pictorial" series of 1869. Journals dealing with airmails may provide insights into various conceptions of the history of flight: two such periodicals are the bimonthly *Aero Philatelist Annals* and the monthly *Airpost Journal*, both edited by the American Airmail Society.

Studies of individuals or types of people who appear on stamps are numerous if not scholarly. An excellent guide, however, to all individuals who appear on stamps and which nations have printed their likenesses is Kent B. Stiles's *Postal Saints and Sinners: Who's Who on Stamps*. A general reference to portraiture is Edmund Burke Thompson's *Portraits on Our Postage Stamps*. Two dated works on minorities are Margaret N. McCluer's *Women as Presented on United States Stamps* and H. A. Fischel's provocative article, "Philatelic Portrait of the Modern Jew." This important list reveals that as of 1958 only 3 out of 117 famous Americans on our stamps were Jews. Arieh Lindenbaum's *Great Jews and Stamps* indicates some advancement in that area.

The following works on stamp portraiture are also dated and brief: J. H. van Peursem's *George Washington*, E. M. Allen's "America's Best-selling Portrait: Franklin," Emery Kelen, *Stamps Tell the Story of John F. Kennedy*, and Mary B. Lane and Elliott Perry, *The Harry F. Allen Collection of Black Jacks*. The latter is a catalog of one of America's finest philatelic specimens, the two-cent portrait of Andrew Jackson issued first in 1863. Finally, the Lincoln Society of Philately (Indianapolis) publishes a bimonthly on our sixteenth president, predictably styled *The Lincoln Log*.

Nonstamp philatelic material such as illustrated envelopes, postcards, postmarks, and cancellation slogans may serve as useful evidence. Envelopes come in various forms, official and unofficial, decorated with elaborate vignettes (called cachets) or not. *Thorp-Bartel's Catalogue of the Stamped Envelopes and Wrappers of the United States*, edited by Prescott H. Thorp, is a thorough analysis and pricing of postal envelopes. The important illustrated catalogs of Civil War postal covers are Robert Laurence's *The George Walcott Collection of Used Civil War Patriotic Covers* and Robert W. Grant's continually updated, loose-leaf *Handbook of Civil War Patriotic Envelopes and Postal History*. A revealing area of study for the cultural historian is the illustrated postcard, which dates back to the latter half of the nineteenth century. Richard Carline's *Pictures in the Post* attempts to place this phenomenon in "the history of popular art" with engaging essays on various colorful but generally European examples. Frank Staff's *The Picture Postcard and Its Origins* and Marian Klamkin's *Picture Postcards* are similar offerings, although Klamkin has sections on American cards. John M. Kaduck's illustrated price list of over 1,000 patriotic American postcards provides the student of popular culture with solid evidence of the way Americans have viewed their heroes and accomplishments from the Gilded Age on. Klamkin's book discusses British and American patriotic cards as well as the history of deltiology, or the collecting of postcards. An important early study of U.S. postmarks is Delf Norona's recently reprinted *Cyclopedia of United States Postmarks and Postal History*. The subcategory of "fancy" cancellations, or a postmaster's individualized postmark, is treated by Michel Zareski and Herman Herst, Jr., in *Fancy Cancellations on 19th Century United States Postage Stamps*. Lists of postal clichés can be found in Moe Luff's *United States Postal Slogan Cancel Catalog* and in the Smithsonian's Philatelic Collection.

Coins

In recent decades, philatelic scholarship has expanded both in size and scope, but given the age and scholastic roots of numismatics, it is no surprise that the body of numismatic literature is still larger, better indexed, and broader in intellectual range than philatelic literature, as the excellent state of numismatic bibliography indicates. The chief work in the field is Elvira E. Clain-Stefanelli's impressive volume *Select Numismatic Bibliography*. Although not "exhaustive," it is by far the researcher's best starting point. It places special emphasis on standard references and other important publications since 1885, as well as "the still used classical works of the past 200 years." Giving particular attention throughout to American references, the author's compilation lists guides, collection and exhibition catalogs, biographies of numismatists, and periodicals. Special sections such as "Art on Coinage" are also useful. Richard H. Rosichan's focus on post-1959 material in *Stamps and Coins* makes his annotated bibliography (discussed earlier in this section) of nearly 1,100 items a good supplement to Clain-Stefanelli. For an important nineteenth-century American bibliography, see Emmanuel J. Attinelli's *Numisgraphics, or a List of Catalogues, Price Lists and Various Publications of More or Less Interest to Numismatologists*.

Since 1947, the American Numismatic Society has published *Numismatic Literature*, an excellent annotated listing of numismatic periodical literature appearing in nearly all scholarly journals and many non-numismatic publications. *The Numismatist*, published by the American Numismatic Association, is a felicitous blend of scholarship and trade news. Its author-subject indexes (1939 and 1959) will lead the researcher to important material on iconography, portraiture, coin design, medals, tokens, and the growth of the hobby. The index to the first, but now defunct, coin periodical, *American Journal of Numismatics* (1866–1924), is located in volume 51 (1917).

As with philatelic literature, catalogs of numismatic literature are of vital importance. The American Numismatic Society's seven-volume *Dictionary Catalogue of the Library of the American Numismatic Society* reprints the card catalog for that society's excellent library. Included here are books, all periodicals since 1930, price list, unpublished manuscripts, and auction catalogs. Also available is the *Library Catalogue of the American Numismatic Association*. Of interest to nineteenth-century researchers is the *Catalogue of the Numismatic Books in the Library of the American Numismatic and Archaeological Society*.

A convenient introduction to the hobby and its present state is *Coin World Almanac*. Put out by the people who published *Linn's World Stamp Almanac*, this more elegantly printed tome provides similar articles on the year's numismatic news, numismatic law, and histories of gold, silver, and U.S. coins. Also found here are lists of designers, engravers, and portraits on coins and paper money. (Did you know that Martha Washington graced our one-dollar bill from 1886 to 1891?) Nearly half the book provides facts and analysis of market trends in gold and silver trading. *Cowles' Complete Encyclopedia of United States Coins,* written and illustrated by *Coin World* columnist Mort Reed, is an enjoyable and well-researched introduction to American coins, their iconography, and minting process. A fairly learned, adult-level guidebook to the hobby and science is Philip Grierson's *Numismatics*. Finally, two numismatic word books are Albert Frey's *Dictionary of Numismatic Names* and Mark Salton's *Glossary of Numismatic Terms*. For a survey of monetary history that may be necessary before embarking upon any numismatic study, one can turn to Arthur Nussbaum's *A History of the Dollar*, an authoritative study (with bibliography). For a late nineteenth-century treatment of the same topic see A. Barton Hepburn, *A History of Currency in the United States*. First published in 1903, this work is still consulted today. Specialized studies are not hard to find: two important works are Richard Cecil Todd's definitive *Confederate Finance* (with bibliography) and Irwin Unger's *The Greenback Era: A Social and Political History of American Finance, 1865–1879*.

Standard pricing catalogs are generally the most convenient means a researcher has to view coins. The most widely used is Richard S. Yeoman's *Guidebook of United States Coins*. Referred to as the "Red Book," this annual price list offers a brief introduction to American coinage and suitable photographs of colonial and official U.S. coin types. Don Taxay's *Comprehensive Catalogue and Encyclopedia of United States Coins* lists proofs and variants as well as their locations in various collections. Abe Kosoff's *An Illustrated History of United States Coins* gives glimpses of proposed coin designs as well as illustrations of definitive issues. Robert Friedberg's *Paper Money of the United States* is a good collector's guide illustrating all U.S. issues. Grover and Clarence Criswell's *Confederate and Southern States Currency* is the definitive, illustrated catalog in the field of southern numismatics.

Studies acquainting the researcher with the facts of America's official and unofficial currency are found in general histories of our coinage and works on such specialized topics as commemoratives, essays, paper money, fractional currency, medals, and tokens.

A well-researched assessment of the U.S. Mint and America's definitive issues is Don Taxay's *The United States Mint and Coinage: An Illustrated History from 1776 to the Present.* J. Earl Massey's *America's Money: The Story of Coins and Currency* relates coinage to American history in general. Brief histories by established numismatists can be found in Theodore V. Buttrey, Jr., editor, *Coinage of the Americas,* which includes articles on "Colonial Coinages" by Eric P. Newman and "Coinage of the US" by Walter Breen. An excellent history (with bibliography) is Taxay's *Money of the American Indian and Other Primitive Currencies of the Americas.* Other histories with a narrower focus are Neil Carothers's *Fractional Money: A History of the Small Coins and Fractional Paper Currency of the United States,* William H. Griffiths's *The Story of the American Bank Note Company,* and the U.S. Government Printing Office's *History of the Bureau of Engraving and Printing (1862–1962).*

Studies focusing on the influence of particular individuals on American coinage are the American Numismatic Association's monographs on Benjamin Franklin and Theodore Roosevelt as well as two works by Walter Breen: *The Secret History of the Gobrecht Coinages (1836–1840),* concerning an early chief of the U.S. Mint, and *Brasher and Bailey, Pioneer New York Coiners.* Early histories should not be overlooked. Montroville W. Dikeson's remarkable volume *The American Numismatic Manual* is a thorough and beautifully illustrated study of Indian, colonial, state, and federal currencies.

General studies of America's commemorative coinage are of particular interest to cultural historians. Don Taxay's *An Illustrated History of United States Commemorative Coins* is the definitive work. Focusing more on topics depicted on coins is Warren A. Ruby's *Commemorative Coins of the United States.* Not to be discounted is Arlie Slaubaugh's *United States Commemorative Coins: The Drama of America as Told by Our Coins.* Despite the didactic subtitle, this study of America's 157 commemorative varieties provides important historical background as well as design and engraving information on each coin.

The numismatic counterpart of the stamp "essay" is the "pattern." Specialized studies of coins in this state are crucial in understanding the evolution of American coin iconography. They are Edgar H. Adams and William H. Woodin, *United States Patterns, Trial and Experimental Pieces,* and J. Hewitt Judd and Walter Breen, *United States Patterns, Experimental, and Trial Pieces,* both of which are fully illustrated. A number of works designed to meet the needs of specialized collectors may also interest the popular art historian.

They are Roger S. Cohen and others, *American Half Cents, the "Little Half Sisters" : A Reference Book on the United States Half Cent Coined from 1793 to 1857;* William H. Sheldon and others, *Penny Whimsey;* Martin Luther Beistle, *A Register of Half Dollar Varieties and Sub-Varieties;* and Leroy C. Van Allen and A. George Mallis, *Guide to Morgan and Peace Dollars: A Complete Guide and Reference Book on United States Silver Dollars.*

Also of interest to the cultural historian and aesthetician are the icons and designs found on America's "unofficial" currency: bank notes, fractional currency, and scrip. Monographic studies on bank notes by John A. Muscalus provide a wealth of material: *Index of State Bank Notes that Illustrate Characters and Events, Index of State Bank Notes that Illustrate Washington and Franklin, Index of State Bank Notes that Illustrate Presidents, Famous Paintings Reproduced on Paper Money of State Banks, 1800–1866,* and *The Views of Towns, Cities, Falls, and Buildings Illustrated on 1800–1866 Bank Paper Money.* Matt Rothert's *A Guidebook of United States Fractional Currency* is well illustrated and has a good bibliography. For views of what happens to currency when times get tough, see Lyman H. Low's *Hard Times Tokens* and Charles V. Kappen and Ralph A. Mitchell's *Depression Scrip of the United States.*

Just as philately has expanded to include the collection of nonstamp material, numismatics has, for over a century, embraced the medallic arts. Indeed, the design, iconography, and striking of American medals are as important to the scholar as coins themselves. General surveys of the field include Charles W. Betts, *American Colonial History Illustrated by Contemporary Medals;* Joseph F. Loubat, *The Medallic History of the United States of America, 1776–1876;* Clifford Mishler, *United States and Canadian Commemorative Medals and Tokens;* and Georgia S. Chamberlain, *American Medals and Medalists.* An indispensable resource is Leonard Forrer's *Biographical Dictionary of Medalists.* See also Richard D. Kenney, *Early American Medalists and Die-Sinkers.* Studies of special types of medals include Gilbert Grosvenor and others, *Insignia and Decorations of the United States Armed Forces,* Evans E. Kerrigan, *American War Medals and Decorations,* and Jennings Hood and Charles J. Young, *American Orders and Societies and Their Decorations.* An important branch of American numismatics and one of special interest to American scholars in general is the Indian peace medals. A study of Britain's medals is Melvill Allan Jamieson's *Medals Awarded to North American Indian Chiefs, 1714–1922.* Less tame are the U.S. government medals given to Indians as illustrated in a well-researched volume, Bauman L. Belden's *Indian Peace Medals Issued in the United States, 1789–1889.* Studies of medals struck in honor of individuals or groups include the following: Elston G. Bradfield, "Benjamin Franklin: A Numismatic Summary"; William S. Baker, *Medallic Portraits of Washington;* Robert P. King, "Lincoln in Numismatics: A Descriptive List"; and Edward C. Rochette, *The Medallic Portraits of John F. Kennedy: A Study of Kennediana.*

RESEARCH COLLECTIONS

Generally speaking, it is unlikely that even the best university libraries will have extensive holdings in philatelic or numismatic literature. (In fact, major public libraries generally have better collections.) Even rarer are institutions that can make specimens available to the scholar. Researchers who desire more contact than either Scott's or the Red Book can provide will seek out the libraries and specimens of strong philatelic or numismatic collections. Although the best are located in the East, useful collections can be found in the Midwest and West.

Stamps

The three best research collections are the National Philatelic Collection, located in the Smithsonian's Museum of History and Technology, Washington, D.C.; the Collectors Club of New York; and the American Philatelic Research Library in State College, Pennsylvania. Once a part of the Library of Congress, the National Philatelic Collection is both library and archive. It maintains an extensive but uncataloged collection of philatelic literature and a massive stamp collection which includes all but one of the American issues and numerous essays. Its photographic collection of over 6,000 prints and slides is indispensable. The collection also maintains a postal history clipping file, statistics, paraphernalia, postmaster correspondence on all commemoratives, and a tape and film library. Here you can listen to Tim Healey's radio program, "Ivory Stamp Club of the Air." The collection is open to the public weekdays from ten to five. Nearly 300 philatelists use the facility each year, so an appointment with the excellent staff is advised.

The Collectors Club of New York maintains a limited membership of about 1,100 people, but its excellent library (only recently surpassed by the Smithsonian) is open by appointment to scholars. Its John N. Luff Reference Collection is extensive, and the J. Bruce Chittenden Memorial Library, with 140,000 items, is particularly strong in pre-twentieth-century material, including postmasters' reports. The American Philatelic Research Library is the research wing of the American Philatelic Society. Its holdings include 7,000 books and monographs, 400 periodicals, and 150 catalogs but no stamp specimens or slides of American stamps. An important aid to scholars is the library's extensive but as yet unpublished index of early philatelic literature. The library is open to the public and material is circulated to non-APS members through interlibrary loan.

Other major collections can be found in the B. K. Miller Collection of the New York Library; the Philatelic Foundation, New York; the George Linn Memorial Research Library, Sidney, Ohio, which holds 3,000 volumes and one hundred periodicals; and the Western Philatelic Library of the Sunnyvale (California) Public Library, which maintains a collection of 2,500 books. Furthermore, the public libraries of Chicago, Cleveland, Los Angeles, Milwaukee, Newark (New Jersey), and Pomona (California), and the free libraries of Philadelphia and Baltimore have considerable holdings.

Specialized collections holding philatelic literature and stamps are also attractive to scholars. The Lincoln Shrine in Redlands, California, has philatelic materials relating to Old Abe. Eisenhower's collection can be found in the Cardinal Spellman Philatelic Museum along with the cardinal's personal collection of stamps and 8,000 volumes of philatelic literature. FDR's collection and related materials are located at the FDR Library and Museum in Hyde Park, New York. Finally, the Wiltsee Memorial Collection of Western Stamps in the Wells Fargo Bank History Room, San Francisco, houses stamps of 235 different companies including the Pony Express.

Coins

The two major numismatic organizations maintain fine libraries. The American Numismatic Society, located near Broadway and West 155 Street in New York, has the smaller membership but a larger output of scholastic publication. Its library of 50,000 items, described earlier, is the nation's best. The American Numismatic Association, located in Colorado Springs, Colorado, has a much smaller library of 3,000 volumes, but it is likely to meet the needs of most researchers. Both institutions are open to scholars and lend books through interlibrary loan. As in philately, numismatic libraries can be found in major public libraries. Richard H. Rosichan reports in *Stamps and Coins* that the public libraries of New York and Minneapolis and the Free Library of Philadelphia have good collections. Major university collections of numismatic literature are found at Glassboro (New Jersey) State College, Yale, Washington, and New York universities, and the universities of Chicago and Colorado.

While both ANS and ANA maintain superb numismatic museums, the best specimen collection continues to be the National Numismatic Collection housed in the Smithsonian's Museum of History and Technology, Washington, D.C. The collection began when the U.S. Mint transferred its collection to the Smithsonian in 1923. Since then, and with the help of the ANA and ANS, the collection has grown from about 40,000 to over 150,000 pieces. The Smithsonian, as well as the ANA and ANS, displays many of its specimens, and visitors to all three collections may view vaulted material upon request. An excellent history and description of the National Collection is Vladimir Clain-Stefanelli's monograph *History of the National Numismatic Collections*. The author's appendixes also provide interesting information for those researching the early growth of American numismatics. Some banks such as Detroit National also maintain excellent coin displays.

Like any stamp or coin collection, university coin collections are likely to change hands frequently. Any listing of such collections is bound to be dated. Elvira Clain-Stefanelli reports that major collections can be found at Yale, Dartmouth, Johns Hopkins (although it has just sold its J. W. Garrett Collection), Princeton, Columbia, Vassar, St. Louis, and the universities of Wisconsin, Chicago, and California at Berkeley.

HISTORY AND CRITICISM

To my knowledge, no book-length work of scholarship on the history of stamp collecting or the cultural significance of stamps exists. Some scholarly articles have appeared in the past three decades, but, generally speaking, the ideas and controversies related to philately have been limited to popular magazines and journals. Coins present a slightly different picture. Since numismatics is rooted in traditional scholarship, studies of ancient and some modern coins as cultural artifacts can be found. American coins, however, have only recently received proper attention. To a certain extent, then, what can be said for stamps may apply to coins: much study remains to be done.

Stamps

Critical works pertaining to philately may be broken down into three groups: those treating the growth of philately as a hobby or business, those exploring the artistic merit of stamps themselves, and those concerning stamps as social icons. It is with the latter issue that I will discuss what I consider to be this essay's major problem: whether the postage stamp can serve as a reliable cultural indicator.

The scores of philatelic guides and memoirs of prominent collectors constitute a major resource of primary material for the student hoping to trace the development of collecting. Frederick Booty's *Stamp Collector's Guide* is probably the first philatelic handbook. Like Bellar's *Standard Guide,* already mentioned, it is nothing more than an introduction to the hobby and a price list. Today, the beginner's guide has dispensed with the price list and become a form of "companion literature" which speculates on why people collect; explains modes of collecting, hobby technique, investment, and clubs; relates hobby lore; and lists philatelic literature and terminology. Philatelic glossaries, which include such locutions as "aerophilately" and "stampic," seem designed to pique the interest of sociolinguists on the trail of the deep structure of hobby language.

Themes in stamp guides often reflect the anxieties of a predominantly male leisure class. Early artifacts, for instance, adopt an apologetic tone which strongly argues that the hobby is not idle play but that it engenders care, method, and neatness. As late as the 1930s noted philatelist Ellis P. Butler in *The Young Stamp Collector's Own Book* felt compelled to remind his young, obviously male, readership that collecting is a "form of play" that encompasses adventure, exploration, and hunting and that it is emphatically not a "sissy" pastime. (Evidence that the rank and file of philately are broadening to include more women can be found in Barbara Mueller's *Common Sense Philately*, which points out that as of 1958 women made up about 10 percent of the New York Collectors Club membership, a considerable increase over Butler's era.) The fear that philately is childish or sissified is frequently countered in such guides as *Stamps for Fun and Profit*, by Henry M. Ellis and *Everybody's Guide to Stamp Investment*, by Joseph E. Granville by the notion that stamps stimulate the manly endeavor of finance. Why philately still seems to be a predominantly male mode of collecting is a problem that may lead the feminist critic to fruitful speculations.

Popular magazines in nearly every decade have promoted the ideas that stamps are both educational and lucrative. Philately has been seen as an aid to teachers of geography, history, language, and literature. *Parents Magazine* argues that a child's "early collecting instinct should be encouraged."[5] *School Life* states that postage stamps can "stimulate patriotism."[6] The *Journal of Educational Method* instructs us on how to make a "stamp map."[7] Since the 1920s, articles gauging philately's investment potential have appeared in such periodicals as *Business Week*, the *Economist*, *Nation's Business*, *Newsweek*, *Popular Mechanics*, and *Time*. Other nonphilatelic periodicals that have published articles measuring the pulse of the hobby are *Hobbies*, *Popular Science*, *Profitable Hobbies*, *St. Nicholas*, and *Scientific American*.

Of course, the best resource for recent hobby developments is the trade weekly. *Linn's Stamp News* is probably the largest. *Stamps* (published by Lindquist) and *Mekeel's Weekly Stamp News* are also newspapers of considerable heft. Deeper speculations and more arcane scholarship can be found in the hobby journals. Widely distributed is the *American Philatelist*, the monthly house organ for the American Philatelic Society. Indexed every December, it is an attractive amalgam of trade notes, book reviews, committee reports, news of current stamp issues, specialized departments on taxes, and other collecting problems, and a good deal of scholarship on stamp variants and the cultural history of stamps (international). More modest yet more scholarly is the *SPA Journal*, edited by the Society of Philatelic Americans (the number-two national stamp organization). Other specialized journals are the *United States Specialist*, put out by the Bureau Issues Association, which focuses on issues produced by the Bureau of Engraving and Printing, and the *American Revenuer*. These and the *Essay-Proof Journal* are likely to offer the cultural historian important material on U.S. postal history and iconography.

A recurring issue in many hobby publications is the problem of why people collect in the first place. Do we collect in order to touch the past and thereby escape the present, thus making collecting a form of nostalgia? Do we collect in order to classify, to take a slice of a proliferating world, organize it, and create on our own a silent moment of order? Do we collect because we want to know the world, or because we enjoy pretty things? Do we collect, quite simply, because the things, pretty or not, are there in sufficient variety and quantity and are begging to be collected?

What have the psychologists to say of the collecting mania? One philatelist speculates that Freud might categorize the impulse to collect as "repressed imperialism."[8] Lamentably, I have not been able to find any writings by Freud or his immediate brethren substantiating this speculation. Perhaps psychoanalysts find collecting too healthy to worry about. Recently, however, a group of psychologists led by R. T. Walls studied children's collection preferences and found that, when given a choice of collecting a prescribed set of objects or collecting several copies of one member of that set, children of ages four and ten overwhelmingly prefer to fill out a set. At best, this evidence may explain the popularity of topical over traditional stamp collecting. It may also prove the infantilism of collecting.

Clearly, the psychological aspects of collecting require more systematic study. For the time being the student of the phenomenon must be satisfied with the thin speculations of magazine writers. According to *Literary Digest,* for instance, the parameters of the impulse to collect range "from relaxation to big business."[9] Trimming those limits neatly are F. Neilson, who calls for a "cultural avocation" in the nation,[10] and A. Repplier, who discusses the "pleasure of possession."[11]

Deeper speculations have come from a group of magazine writers in the 1930s who explored what might be called the myth of nostalgia in collecting. For Y.Y. of the *New Statesman and Nation,* philately signaled a return to childhood. In one Wordsworthian recollection, "Grand Passion," he discusses his childhood stamp collection and the loss of innocence inherent in the recent development of philately into a science. Even more sentimental is Guy Boas's belletristic piece "The Mysterious Hobby of Stamp Collecting," which argues that stamps, "like poetry, are a link with salvation."

For every escapist there is a cynic and for every enthusiast a naysayer. Dissenting opinions on the psychic needs and relevance of collecting come from Thomas H. Uzzell, whose "Postage Stamp Psychosis" lightly satirizes philatelists. Far from being an escape, stamp collecting, he says, is only a metaphor for the complexity of modern living. Indeed, "the real trouble with this country is its stamp collectors," because, for lack of anything else to do, they have overexamined stamps and found a maddening number of microscopic varieties to collect. Philately does not release us from such modern trends as overspecialization: it adds to them. Philately's biggest naysayer is Harold Nicolson, who in his "Marginal Comments" for *Spectator* issues a scathing denunciation of the hobby. To be a philatelist is "to become excited by objects which are totally unworthy of man's unconquerable mind." Nicolson wants a hobby that will make contributions "to useful knowledge."

Presumably, art is the tacit object most worthy of man's unconquerable mind, and yet, as if to confound Nicolson, some classify the postage stamp as art and worthy of study for its own sake. During the 1950s and 1960s a recurring discussion on the artistic merit of stamps was conducted in the pages of the *New York Times Magazine* (see A. B. Louchheim, "Our Stamps Could Be Artistic, Too," and A. Shuster, "Stamps for Art's Sake"). Adding to this discussion is Barbara Moore's *The Art of Postage Stamps,* and Sam Iker's "World's Richest Art Competition" reminds us that stamps more than ever are an important arena in the field of art and design.

Pursuing the aesthetic potentials of postage, the artist Donald Evans, in *The World of Donald Evans,* has used stamp design motifs to express his comic, somewhat odd, vision. Here, it may be said, the stamp becomes art in and of itself. Art historian A. Hyatt Mayor devotes barely a paragraph to the postage stamp in his *Print and People: A Social History of Printed Pictures,* but his characterization of the engraved, mass-produced "miniature print," or stamp, is significant. It "is published in the largest of all editions and exposes a country's taste to global criticism." Notions of taste aside, Mayor clearly sees stamps as a reflection of a nation's culture, and his observation provides us with a simple transition from the problems of the art of collecting and the art of the stamp to a third and yet perhaps most important focus: the problem of the stamp as icon and reliable cultural indicator.

The postage stamp is not only an obvious engine of propaganda but a potential symbol maker. It can sell an idea, and by placing a portrait or object in a perforated frame it can transform that portrait or object into an icon that presumably reflects the sentiments and acceptance of the people. But the critical dilemma is whether these images are forced by the few upon the many or whether the few who issue the stamps are responding genuinely to the pulse of the many. Most likely, postal authorities shape our stamps to what they think is acceptable to the many. Furthermore, any of a number of extraneous factors may enter into the selection of a stamp design. George Washington provides a good example. It is safe to say that the fifty-three stamps that bear the first president's likeness confirm Washington as an American icon, but in fact not every stamp derives from the man's popularity. Four of five essays submitted for one early Washington stamp bore likenesses of Indians; the fifth, accepted essay was simply better executed than the others. Also, the ninety-cent Washington stamp of 1861 was issued simply because the postmaster general wanted the likeness of the president on a stamp of high value. To be sure, these two examples do not undercut the general acceptance of Washington as an icon. But it is clear that with respect to other less-revered figures the cultural historian must not depend too heavily upon the assumption that whatever appears on a stamp is necessarily an icon.

Distribution figures for a stamp may indicate the visibility or familiarity of a stamp, but a widely distributed stamp may not necessarily mean that the stamp is an accepted icon. Only eight stamps (excluding Christmas stamps) have exceeded the billion mark in distribution. To be sure, four of those stamps, depicting Columbus, Harding, and Washington, are likely candidates as stamps with a popular appeal. The remaining four, however, are clearly propagandistic. The National Recovery Act stamp issued during the Depression and the Allied Nations and Four Freedoms stamps issued during World War II promote distinct political ideologies. And, as H. H. Tennant and S. Hershey argue in the *American Mercury,* the 1952 NATO stamp with a distribution of nearly 2.8 billion was issued to help shore up the pact's shaky reputation in its third year. The distribution of a stamp then, is not necessarily a function of the stamp icon's popularity. An approach to this problem must be ironed out. Two recent articles, W. E. Hensley's "Increasing Response Rate by Choice of Postage Stamps" and Paul Schnitzel's "Note on the Philatelic Demand for Postage Stamps," indicate that the problems are only just beginning to be recognized. Also of help in the area of propaganda may be O. Carlos Stoetzer's *Postage Stamps as Propaganda.*

The only systematic cultural history of stamps in the academic arena is David C. Skagg's essay, "The Postage Stamp as Icon." Inspired by the recent issue of Bicentennial stamps, Professor Skaggs focuses on the one event that is depicted most often in American philately, the Revolution, and compares past and present stamps to determine any trends. His essay is brief but generally accurate as to detail (although he designates Martha Washington as the first woman to appear on an American stamp when in fact Queen Isabella of Spain has that honor). Skaggs discusses five categories of stamp vignettes (depicting individuals, battles, documents, symbols, and groupings). His general thesis is that although today's stamps reveal a trend toward "democratization" and symbolism (more commoners and liberty bells are featured than statesmen and heroes), the postal service has continued to be fairly "uncontroversial" in its selection of designs. The author looks forward to a time when Americans can recognize that 1776 was as much a civil war as a revolt and will therefore honor on their stamps the defeated and exiled Royalists as much as the standard heroes. "Only time will tell," he concludes, "if iconography can approach reality."

While Skaggs has made some basic observations, his essay is polemical and his methodology lacks rigor. I do not believe that we can be quite as confident as Skaggs is in assuming that the postage stamp "symbolizes the nation's popular self-image." If anything, a stamp is likely to reflect primarily the notions of a select and decidedly unrepresentative group of Americans including federal officials, artists, and artisans, not to mention the members of the Citizens Stamp Advisory Committee, which for decades has approved the nation's stamp topics. Furthermore, Skaggs's article implies that the predominant iconography on stamps stems from the Revolution, when, in fact, a wide range of categories including New World discovery, western expansion and statehood, the history of flight and technology, and the postal system itself far outweigh the year 1776 and suggest a nation obsessed with growth, progress, and power. By emphasizing the stamp portraits of such revolutionaries as Washington, Franklin, and Jefferson, Skaggs necessarily excludes significant iconography relating to Jackson and Lincoln.

Although Skaggs is correct in stating that the recent Bicentennial issues emphasize the common man rather than the familiar heroes, he overgeneralizes in asserting that these stamps are also more symbolic than early issues. Perhaps a more accurate observation would be that recent stamps are artistically more "stylized" and less allegorical. Finally, Skaggs suggests that the cause for changes in philatelic imagery is our hero-less age, shaped by television's "fuzzy images" of "transitory celebrities." This perfunctory jab at television directs our attention away from more relevant causes. To begin with, today's stamps clearly reflect recent trends in art and design. More important, in the past two decades postal authorities have consciously introduced new printing techniques, flashier colors, more varied designs, and innovative stamp arrangements in order to make U.S. stamps more attractive to collectors. It is quite likely that more Bicentennial stamps have been put in albums than on letters. Thus, in dealing with recent stamps as cultural indicators, we must assume that a stamp is as much a reflection of the philatelist's demands as of the people's "self-image."

Despite its methodological shortcoming, Skaggs's article has initiated a legitimate field of study that can yield an abundance of knowledge which, if properly applied, can serve as an intellectual handmaiden to other fields R. D. Roberts, for instance, in an attempt to derive a fair cross-section of names to determine American surname frequency, compiled a list from the thousands of people who bought stamps from his mail order stamp dealership. The results are questionable since there is no guarantee that certain minorities will be accurately polled: nevertheless, Roberts's technique, which yields a wide sampling of middle America, may be of interest to the sociologist. (If anything, the list provides an excellent surname profile of the mid-1950s philatelist.)

More intriguing is H. A. Fischel's aforementioned article, "Philatelic Portrait of the Modern Jew," which asserts that the stamp is "a significant medium of recognition in modern society." Unlike Skaggs, who assumes that any portrait or object appearing on a stamp is necessarily an icon, Fischel uses philately as evidence of the growing acceptance of Jews since World War II. Fischel's main problem is determining who can be classified as a Jew. As of 1958 Marx and Heine were the world's most frequently depicted Jews. Given the growth of the Israeli state, persecution of Soviet Jews, and the loosening of postal restrictions in the United States, we can expect some fascinating modulations in Fischel's findings since 1960. An update of this study is clearly required. Most important, however, is that Fischel's method can serve as a model for similar treatments of the acceptance of other minorities or the evolution of social attitudes. Of particular interest, of course, is the Black Heritage series of stamps issued throughout the racially problematic 1980s. Also, John Bryant's brief analysis of the 1984 Melville issue (an overdue supplement to the Famous American series of 1940) notes the lethargy with which the post office moves in acknowledging even the most widely accepted of our "literary" heroes.

Scholars can and should turn more frequently to the postage stamp as a useful investigative tool. Handled properly, philatelic material can yield new insights into the myths, symbols, and icons that shape and reflect our lives. Comparative philatelic studies of Washington, Franklin, Jefferson, Jackson, and Lincoln seem to be the most obvious scholastic endeavors. The role of women and minorities in stamps is an equally significant problem. A study of philatelic landscapes might add a chapter to the "pastoral myth." But before we proceed with these projects, it is clear that the cultural historian must examine the work of philatelic researchers, learn the fundamentals of how a stamp is produced, determine the relevance of distribution figures, and distinguish between stamp icons and propaganda. Until a methodology is established, our conclusions will remain shallow and useless.

Coins

Numismatic literature, when it is not overly embroiled in gold and silver market trends, generally achieves a higher degree of scholastic merit than its philatelic counterpart. Numismatists have given us some book-length and many monographic studies that approach coins aesthetically and socially, but to my knowledge academic aestheticians and social historians have not examined the topic. Those embarking upon the field of numismatics would do well to seek models in the works of Walter Breen, Elvira and Vladimir Clain-Stefanelli, Don Taxay, and Cornelius Vermeule.

Important material on the nascent age of the coin-collecting hobby can be found in the *Proceedings* of the Numismatic and Antiquarian Society of Philadelphia (1865–67, 1877–1936), the American Numismatic and Archaeological Society (1878–1914), and the American Numismatic Society (1908–). Other important early periodicals are the *American Journal of Numismatics* (1866–1924) and J. W. Scott's *American Journal of Philately and Coin Advertisers* (1879–1886). An interesting nineteenth-century monograph that sheds light on the hobby's early days is Elizabeth B. Johnston's *A Visit to the Cabinet of the United States Mint at Philadelphia*. Since numismatics did not become fully "democratized" until the 1930s, early guidebooks did not, generally speaking, address themselves to juveniles. Since World War II, however, numismatists have learned a great deal from philatelists on how to "push" their hobby, and the more recent guidebooks may be worth analyzing. Rosichan's section on juvenile literature in *Stamps and Coins* is a suitable starting point in this field. Various popular magazines have, of course, kept abreast of recent events in hobby development. Of interest are Charles French's "Changes in Coin Collecting" and G. Rayner's "History of the Coin Investment Market," both found in *Hobbies*. The weekly column on numismatics in the *New York Times* provides excellent and readable analysis of the hobby's rapid growth. Hobby magazines and news weeklies are a major resource for hobby trends. *Coin World,* a weekly, and *Coins,* a monthly, are both market-oriented publications. *Calcoin News Quarterly Magazine,* the organ for the California State Numismatic Association, includes articles on coin history and biography. Articles on numismatics as a collecting phenomenon as well as trade news may also be found in the *Numismatist.*

Turning to the cultural analysis of numismatics, the best treatments focus on coins as art objects rather than social icons. Traditional numismatic studies of ancient specimens have used coins to clarify or even rectify notions of ancient architecture and portraiture. Aesthetic studies of modern coinage are Carol H. Sutherland's *Art in Coinage: The Aesthetics of Money from Greece to the Present Day*, and Thomas W. Becker's *The Coin Makers*. For decades U.S. coins have been derided for their comparative artlessness. Cornelius C. Vermeule's excellent study, *Numismatic Art in America: Aesthetics of the United States Coinage,* sets out to overcome that prejudice by examining coins in the context of American sculpture. Also of interest is Lynn Glaser's series of articles on "Art in American Coinage" in the *Numismatic Scrapbook Magazine.* Vermeule's *Bibliography of Applied Numismatics in the Fields of Greek and Roman Archaeology and Fine Arts,* while not dealing with American art or coinage, will lead the researcher to model works in the field of coin aesthetics.

There is something holy about money that makes coins and paper money better candidates for social icons than stamps. Coins are tokens of social confidence and political power; they last longer and circulate more than stamps. Apparently their influence goes even deeper. According to William H. Desmonde in *Magic, Myth, and Money,* an anthropological study of coins and coin iconography, money is a part of religious ritual. Also of interest here is Giovanni Gorini's article "Coin as Blazon or Talisman: Paramonetary Function of Money." As with stamps, though, the iconic power of coins is necessarily lessened when we realize the propagandistic uses of money designs. F. C. Ross in "Numismatic Thoughts" argues, for instance, that "currencies, from almost the beginning, have been propagandists." Finally, journals that generally publish scholarly works relating to the aesthetic and iconographic aspects of both coins and paper money are the *Numismatist, Paper Money* (quarterly for the Society of Paper Money Collectors), and the *Essay-Proof Journal.*

NOTES

1. Wilbert D. Newgold, "Hobbies," *Encyclopedia Britannica: Macropaedia,* 15th ed. (Chicago: Encyclopaedia Britannica, 1978), p. 973.
2. Henry John Bellars, *The Standard Guide to Postage Stamp Collecting* (London: John Camden Hotter, 1864), n.p.
3. Ed Reiter, "Numismatics: College Level Training," *New York Times.* December 23, 1979, Sec. D, p. 36.
4. Ed Reiter, "Numismatics: Is the Hobby Suffering from Growing Pains?" *New York Times,* December 30, 1979, Sec. D, p. 36.
5. R. T. Fuller, "Collector's Luck: Early Collecting Instincts Should Be Encouraged," *Parents Magazine,* 10 (June 1935), 19.
6. H. S. New, "Postage Stamp Promotes Popular Education and Stimulates Patriotism." *School Life,* 11 (September 1925), 1.
7. R. M. Adams, "Making a Stamp Map," *Journal of Educational Method,* 4 (October 1924), 63.
8. Mauritze Hallgreen, *All About Stamps: Their History and the Art of Collecting Them* (New York: Alfred A. Knopf, 1940), p. 10.
9. "Collecting: Impulse Ranges from Relaxation to Big Business," *Literary Digest,* 123 (February 27, 1937), 30.
10. F. Neilson, "Need for a Cultural Avocation." *American Journal of Economics,* 16 (January 1957), 145.
11. A. Repplier, "Pleasures of Possession." *Commonweal,* 13 (December 17, 1930), 181.

BIBLIOGRAPHY

Books and Articles

Stamps

Adams, R. M. "Making a Stamp Map." *Journal of Educational Method,* 4 (October 1924), 63–69.
Allen, E. M. "America's Best-selling Portrait: Franklin." *American Artist,* 20 (April 1956), 70.
Ashbrook, Stanley B. *The Types and Plates of the United States One-cent Stamp of 1851–57.* New York: Lindquist, 1938.
———. *The United States Ten-cent Stamp of 1855–57.* New York: Lindquist, 1936.
Bacon, E. D. *Catalogue of the Philatelic Library of the Earl of Crawford, K. T.* London: Philatelic Literature Society, 1911.
Bellars, Henry John. *The Standard Guide to Postage Stamp Collecting.* London: John Camden Hotter, 1864.

Boas, Guy. "The Mysterious Hobby of Stamp Collecting." *Cornhill,* 160 (July 1939), 46–64.

Booty, Frederick. *Stamp Collector's Guide.* London: Hamilton, Adams, 1862.

Brazer, Clarence. *Essays for United States Adhesive Postage Stamps.* New York: American Philatelic Society, 1941.

Brookman, Lester G. *Nineteenth Century Postage Stamps of the United States.* 2 vols. New York: Lindquist, 1947.

Bryant, John. "Herman Melville: His Real and Stamped Face." *Melville Society Extracts,* No. 58 (September 1984), 4–5.

Butler, Ellis P. *The Young Stamp Collector's Own Book.* Indianapolis: Bobbs-Merrill, 1933.

Carline, Richard. *Pictures in the Post: The Story of the Picture Postcard and Its Place in the History of Popular Art.* London: Gordon Fraser Gallery, 1971.

Catalogue of the Philatelic Collection. Johannesburg, South Africa: Johannesburg Public Library, 1960.

Catalogue of the Philatelic Library of the Collectors Club. New York: Collectors Club, 1917.

"Collecting: Impulse Ranges from Relaxation to Big Business." *Literary Digest,* 123 (February 27, 1937), 30–32.

Collecting: United States. Cambridge, Mass.: Stamps Information, 1972.

Dietz, August. *The Postal Service of the Confederate States of America.* Richmond, Va.: Dietz Press, 1929.

Ellis, Henry M. *Stamps for Fun and Profit.* New York: Funk and Wagnalls, 1953.

Evans, Donald. *The World of Donald Evans.* New York: Delacorte Press, 1980.

Fischel, H. A. "Philatelic Portrait of the Modern Jew." *Jewish Social Studies,* 23 (July 1961), 187–208.

Freehafer, John, and Helen K. Zirkle. "A Selective List of Philatelic Handbooks, with a List of Libraries in Which They May Be Found." In *The Congress Book 1956.* Philadelphia: American Philatelic Congress, 1956, pp. 93–106.

Fuller, R. T. "Collector's Luck: Early Collecting Instinct Should Be Encouraged." *Parents Magazine,* 10 (June 1935), 19.

Fuller, Wayne E. *The American Mail: Enlarger of the Common Life.* Chicago: University of Chicago Press, 1972.

———. *RFD: The Changing Face of Rural America.* Indianapolis: Indiana University Press, 1964.

Glass, Sol. *United States Postage Stamps, 1945–52.* West Somerville, Mass.: Bureau Issue Association, 1954.

Grant, Robert W. *Handbook of Civil War Patriotic Envelopes and Postal History.* Hanover, Mass.: Robert W. Grant, 1977.

Granville, Joseph E. *Everybody's Guide to Stamp Investment.* New York: Heritage, 1952.

Green, P. D. "Postage Stamp Stampede." *Nation's Business,* 32 (July 1944), 40.

Hahn, G. C. *United States Famous American Series of 1940.* State College, Pa.: American Philatelic Research Library, 1950.

Hallgreen, Mauritze. *All About Stamps: Their History and the Art of Collecting Them.* New York: Alfred A. Knopf, 1940.

Harlow, Alvin. *Old Post Bags: The Story of the Sending of a Letter in Ancient and Modern Times.* New York: Holt, 1928.

Hensley, W. E. "Increasing Response Rate by Choice of Postage Stamp." *Public Opinion Quarterly*, 38 (Summer 1974), 280–83.

Herst, Herman, Jr. "The Mistake of Approaching Your Hobby as Speculative Economic Investments." *Hobbies*, 71 (August 1966), 99.

Horowicz. Kay, and Robson Lowe. *Colonial Posts in the United States of America, 1606–1783.* London: Lowe, 1967.

Iker, Sam. "World's Richest Art Competition." *National Wildlife,* 17 (December 1978), 40–43.

Johl, Max. *United States Commemoratives of the Twentieth Century.* 2 vols. New York: Lindquist, 1947.

Johl, Max, and Beverly S. King. *United States Stamps of the Twentieth Century.* 5 vols. New York: Lindquist, 1938.

Kaduck, John M. *Patriotic Postcards.* Des Moines, Iowa: Wallace-Homestead, 1974.

Kaiser, John B. "Bibliography: The Basis of Philatelic Research." In *The Congress Book 1953.* Newark, N.J.: American Philatelic Congress, 1953, pp. 37–54.

Kelen, Emery. *Stamps Tell The Story of John F. Kennedy.* New York: Meredith, 1968.

Kimble, Ralph A. *Commemorative Postage Stamps of the United States.* New York: Grosset and Dunlap, 1936.

Klamkin, Marian. *Picture Postcards.* New York: Dodd, Mead, 1974.

Konwiser, Henry M. *The American Stamp Collector's Dictionary.* New York: Minkus, 1949.

Lane, Mary B., and Elliott Perry. *The Harry F. Allen Collection of Black Jacks.* State College, Pa.: American Philatelic Research Library, 1969.

Laurence, Robert. *The George Walcott Collection of Used Civil War Patriotic Covers.* New York: R. Laurence, 1934.

Lindenbaum, Arieh. *Great Jews and Stamps.* New York: Sabra Press, 1970.

Linn's World Stamp Almanac. Sidney, Ohio: Amos Press, 1977.

Louchheim, A. B. "Our Stamps Could Be Artistic, Too." *New York Times Magazine,* May 27, June 10, June 17, 1951.

Lowe, James. *Bibliography of Postcard Literature.* Folsom, Pa.: J. Lowe, 1969.

Luff, Moe. *United States Postal Slogan Cancel Catalog.* Spring Valley, N.Y.: M. Luff, 1975.

McCluer, Margaret N. *Women as Presented on United States Stamps.* Kansas City, Mo.: n.p., 1936.

A Master List of Philatelic Literature. North Miami, Fla.: HJMR, 1979.

Mayor, A. Hyatt. *Print and People: A Social History of Printed Pictures.* New York: Metropolitan Museum, 1971.

Moore, Barbara. *The Art of Postage Stamps.* New York: Walker, 1979.

Mueller, Barbara. *Common Sense Philately.* New York: Van Nostrand, 1956.

Negus, James. "A List of Cumulative Indexes to Single Periodicals." *Philatelic Literature Review,* 23 (June 1974), 100–107.

Neilson, F. "Need for a Cultural Avocation." *American Journal of Economics,* 16 (January 1957), 145–49.

New, H. S. "Postage Stamp Promotes Popular Education and Stimulates Patriotism." *School Life,* 11 (September 1925), 1–4.

Newgold, Wilbert D. "Hobbies." *Encyclopaedia Britannica: Macropaedia.* 15th ed. Chicago: Encyclopaedia Britannica, 1978, VIII, 937–81.

Nicolson, Harold. "Marginal Comments." *Spectators,* 176 (June 21, 1946), 634.

Norona, Delf. *Cyclopedia of United States Postmarks and Postal History.* Lawrence, Mass.: Quarterman, 1975.

"Personal Business: Stamp Collecting." *Business Week* (March 3, 1962), 101–2.

"Philatelic Boom." *Newsweek,* 22 (November 8, 1943), 64.

Philately of Tomorrow. New York: Philatelic Research Laboratory, 1940.

Postage Stamps: A Selective Checklist of Books on Philately in the Library of Congress. Washington, D.C.: Library of Congress, 1940.

Postage Stamps of the United States. Washington, D.C.: Government Printing Office, 1973.

Preliminary Inventories of the United States Archives, nos. 63, 82, 114. Washington, D.C.: Government Printing Office, 1953, 1955, 1959.

Reinfeld, Fred. *Commemorative Stamps of the United States of America.* W. Somerville, Mass.: Bramhall, 1956.

Repplier, A. "Pleasures of Possession." *Commonweal,* 13 (December 17, 1930), 181–88.

Ricketts, William R. *The Philatelic Literature Bibliography Index.* Forty-Fort, Pa.: n.p., 1912.

Roberts, R. D. "Surname Frequency and Stamp Collectors." *Names,* 3 (September 1955), 172–84.

Rosichan, Richard H. *Stamps and Coins.* Littleton, Colo.: Libraries Unlimited, 1974.

Scheele, Carl H. *A Short History of the Mail Service.* Washington, D.C.: Smithsonian, 1970.

Schnitzel, Paul. "Note on the Philatelic Demand for Postage Stamps." *Southern Economics Journal,* 45 (April 1979), 1261–65.

Scott's New Handbook for Philatelists, New York: J. W. Scott, 1967.

Scott's Specialized Catalogue of United States Stamps. New York: J. W. Scott, 1979.

"Search for Freak Stamps Yields Fortune." *Popular Mechanics,* 46 (December 1926), 924–25.

"Selling Coloured Paper." *Economist,* 211 (May 9, 1964), 585.

Shuster, A. "Stamps for Art's Sake." *New York Times Magazine,* September 20, 1961.

Skaggs, David C. "The Postage Stamp as Icon." In *Icons of America.* Edited by Ray B. Browne and Marshall Fishwick. Bowling Green, Ohio: Popular Culture Press, 1978.

Smith, Chester. *American Philatelic Periodicals.* State College. Pa.: American Philatelic Research Library, 1978.

Staff, Frank. *The Picture Postcard and Its Origins.* New York: Praeger, 1966.

"Stamps: No Gold Mine." *Changing Times,* 17 (February 1963), 19–20.

Stiles, Kent B. *Postal Saints and Sinners: Who's Who on Stamps.* Brooklyn, N.Y.: T. Gaus Sons, 1964.

Stoetzer, O. Carlos. *Postage Stamps as Propaganda.* Washington, D.C.: Public Affairs Press, 1953.

Sutton, R. J., and K. W. Anthony. *The Stamp Collector's Encyclopedia.* New York: Arco, 1973.

Tennant, H. H., and S. Hershey. "Nearly Everybody Wants to Get in the Stamp Act." *American Mercury,* 76 (February 1953), 79–83.

Thompson, Edmund B. *Portraits on Our Postage Stamps.* Windham, Conn.: E. B. Thompson, 1933.

Thorp, Prescott H., ed. *Thorp-Bartel's Catalogue of the Stamped Envelopes and Wrappers of the United States.* Netcong, N.J.: Thorp, 1954.

Tiffany, John K. *The Philatelical Library: A Catalogue of Stamp Publications.* St. Louis, Mo.: John K. Tiffany, 1874.

Turner, George T. *Essays and Proofs of United States Internal Revenue Stamps.* Arlington, Mass.: Bureau Issues Association, 1974.

———. "Trends in United States Philatelic Literature." In *The Congress Book 1945.* Cleveland: American Philatelic Congress, 1945, pp. 145–52.

Uzzell, Thomas H. "Postage Stamp Psychosis." *Scribners Magazine,* 97 (June 1935), 368–70.

van Peursem, J. H. *George Washington.* S-Gravenhage, Holland: Philatelie en Geschiedenis, 1932.

Walls, R. T., et al. "Collection Preferences of Children." *Child Development,* 46 (September 1975), 783–85.

"Worldwide Market." *Time,* 81 (June 7, 1963), 96.

Y. Y. "Grand Passion." *The New Statesman and Nation,* n.s. 24 (September 26, 1942), 204.

Zareski, Michel, and Herman Herst, Jr. *Fancy Cancellations on 19th Century United States Postage Stamps.* Shrub Oak, N.Y.: Herst, 1963.

Coins

Adams, Edgar H., and William H. Woodin. *United States Patterns, Trial and Experimental Pieces.* New York: American Numismatic Society, 1913.

American Numismatic Society. *Dictionary Catalogue of the Library of the American Numismatic Society.* New York: Hall, 1972.

Attinelli, Emmanuel J. *Numisgraphics, or a List of Catalogues, Price Lists and Various Publications of More or Less Interest to Numismatologists.* New York: Attinelli, 1876.

Baker, William S. *Medallic Portraits of Washington.* Iola, Wis.: Krause, 1965.

Becker, Thomas W. *The Coin Makers.* Garden City, N.Y.: Doubleday, 1969.

Beistle, Martin Luther. *A Register of Half Dollar Varieties and Sub-Varieties.* Omaha: Beebe's, 1964.

Belden, Bauman L. *Indian Peace Medals Issued in the United States, 1789–1889.* New Milford, Conn.: N. Flayderman, 1966.

Betts, Charles W. *American Colonial History Illustrated by Contemporary Medals.* Lawrence, Mass.: Quarterman, 1972.

Bradfield, Elston G. "Benjamin Franklin: A Numismatic Summary." Numismatist, 69 (1956), 1347–53.

Breen, Walter. *Brasher and Bailey, Pioneer New York Coiners.* New York: American Numismatic Society, 1958.

———. *The Secret History of the Gobrecht Coinages (1836–1840).* Coin Collectors Journal, no. 157. New York: Scott Stamp and Coin, 1954.

Buttrey, Theodore V., Jr., ed. *Coinage of the Americas.* New York: American Numismatic Society, 1973.

Carothers, Neil. *Fractional Money: A History of the Small Coins and Fractional Paper Currency of the United States.* New York: Kelley, 1967.

Catalogue of the Numismatic Books in the Library of the American Numismatic and Archaeological Society. Boston: American Numismatic and Archaeological Society, 1883.

Chamberlain, Georgia S. *American Medals and Medalists.* Annandale, Va.: Turnpike, 1963.

Clain-Stefanelli, Elvira E. *Numismatics—An Ancient Science: A Survey of Its History.* Washington, D.C.: Government Printing Office, 1965.

————. *Select Numismatic Bibliography.* New York: Stacks, 1965.

Clain-Stefanelli, Vladimir. *History of the National Numismatic Collections.* Washington, D.C.: Government Printing Office, 1968.

Cohen, Roger S., et al. *American Half Cents, the "Little Half Sisters" : A Reference Book on the United States Half Cent Coined from 1793 to 1857.* Bethesda, Md.: N.p., 1971.

Coin World Almanac. Sidney, Ohio: Amos Press, 1979.

Criswell, Grover, and Clarence. *Confederate and Southern States Currency.* New York: House of Collectibles, 1961.

Desmonde, William H. *Magic, Myth, and Money.* New York: Free Press, 1962.

Dikeson, Montroville W. *The American Numismatic Manual.* Philadelphia: J. B. Lippincott, 1860.

Forrer, Leonard. *Biographical Dictionary of Medalists.* New York: Franklin, 1971.

Franklin and Numismatics. Colorado Springs, Colo.: American Numismatic Association, n.d.

French, Charles. "Changes in Coin Collecting." *Hobbies,* 67 (February 1963), 102.

Frey, Albert. *Dictionary of Numismatic Names.* New York: Barnes and Noble, 1947.

Friedberg, Robert. *Paper Money of the United States.* New York: Coin and Currency Institute, 1972.

Glaser, Lynn. "Art in American Coinage." *Numismatic Scrapbook Magazine (1962),* 2462–79, 2792–2800, 3092–3101.

Gorini, Giovanni. "Coin as Blazon or Talisman: Paramonetary Function of Money." *Diogenes* (Spring-Summer 1978), 77–88.

Grierson, Philip. *Numismatics.* New York: Oxford University Press, 1975.

Griffiths, William H. *The Story of the American Bank Note Company.* New York: N.p., 1959.

Grosvenor, Gilbert, et al. *Insignia and Decorations of the United States Armed Forces.* Washington, D.C.: National Geographic Society, 1944.

Hepburn, A. Barton. *A History of Currency in the United States.* Clifton, N.J.: Kelley, 1968.

History of the Bureau of Engraving and Printing (1862–1962). Washington, D.C.: Government Printing Office, 1962.

Hood, Jennings, and Charles J. Young. *American Orders and Societies and Their Decorations.* Philadelphia: Bailey, Banks and Biddle, 1917.

Jamieson, Melvill Allan. *Medals Awarded to North American Indian Chiefs, 1714–1922.* London: Spink, 1961.

Johnston, Elizabeth B. *A Visit to the Cabinet of the United States Mint at Philadelphia.* Philadelphia: J. B. Lippincott, 1876.

Judd, J. Hewitt, and Walter Breen. *United States Patterns, Experimental and Trial Pieces.* Racine, Wis.: Whitman, 1962.

Kappen, Charles V., and Ralph A. Mitchell. *Depression Scrip of the United States.* San Jose, Calif.: Globe, 1961.

Kenney, Richard D. *Early American Medalists and Die-Sinkers.* New York: W. Raymond, 1954.

Kerrigan, Evans E. *American War Medals and Decorations.* New York: Viking, 1964.

King, Robert P. "Lincoln in Numismatics: A Descriptive List." *Numismatist,* 37 (1924), 55–74; 40 (1927), 193–204; 46 (1933), 481–97.

Kosoff, Abe. *An Illustrated History of United States Coins: Proposed Designs as Well as the Standard Types.* Encino, Calif.: N.p., 1962.

Library Catalogue of the American Numismatic Association. Colorado Springs, Colo.: American Numismatic Association, 1972.

Loubat, Joseph F. *The Medallic History of the United States of America, 1776–1876.* New Milford, Conn.: N. Flayderman, 1967.

Low, Lyman H. *Hard Times Tokens.* San Jose, Calif.: Globe, 1955.

Massey, J. Earl. *America's Money: The Story of Coins and Currency.* New York: Crowell, 1968.

Mishler, Clifford. *United States and Canadian Commemorative Medals and Tokens.* Vandalia, Mich.: Mishler, 1959.

Muscalus, John A. *Famous Paintings Reproduced on Paper Money of State Banks, 1800–1866.* Bridgeport, Conn.: Muscalus, 1938.

———. *Index of State Bank Notes that Illustrate Characters and Events.* Bridgeport, Conn.: Muscalus, 1938.

———. *Index of State Bank Notes that Illustrate Presidents.* Bridgeport, Conn.: Muscalus, 1939.

———. *Index of State Bank Notes that Illustrate Washington and Franklin.* Bridgeport, Conn.: Muscalus, 1939.

———. *The Views of Towns, Cities, Falls, and Buildings Illustrated on 1800–1866 Bank Paper Money.* Bridgeport, Conn.: Muscalus, 1939.

Nussbaum, Arthur. *A History of the Dollar.* New York: Columbia University Press, 1957.

Rayner, G. "History of the Coin Investment Market." *Hobbies,* 82 (October 1977), 131.

Reed, Mort. *Cowles' Complete Encyclopedia of United States Coins.* New York: Cowles', 1969.

Reiter, Ed. "Numismatics: College Level Training." *New York Times,* December 23, 1979; December 30, 1979.

Rochette, Edward C. *The Medallic Portraits of John F. Kennedy: A Study of Kennediana.* Iola, Wis.: Krause, 1966.

Roosevelt and Numismatics. Colorado Springs, Colo.: American Numismatic Association, n.d.

Ross, F. C. "Numismatic Thoughts." *Hobbies,* 46 (June 1941), 90–92.

Rothert, Matt. *A Guidebook of United States Fractional Currency.* Racine. Wis.: Whitman, 1963.

Ruby, Warren A. *Commemorative Coins of the United States.* Lake Mills, Iowa: Graphic, 1961.

Salton, Mark. *Glossary of Numismatic Terms.* New York: Barnes and Noble, 1947.

Sheldon, William H., et al. *Penny Whimsey.* New York: Harper, 1958.

Slaubaugh, Arlie. *United States Commemorative Coins: The Drama of America as Told by Our Coins*. Racine, Wis.: Western, 1975.

Snowden, James Ross. *A Description of Ancient and Modern Coins in the Cabinet Collection at the United States Mint*. Philadelphia: J. B. Lippincott, 1860.

Sutherland, Carol H. *Art in Coinage: The Aesthetics of Money from Greece to the Present Day*. New York: Philosophical Library, 1956.

Taxay, Don. *Comprehensive Catalogue and Encyclopedia of United States Coins*. New York: Scott, 1971.

———. *An Illustrated History of United States Commemorative Coins*. New York: Arco, 1967.

———. *Money of the American Indian and Other Primitive Currencies of the Americas*. New York: Nummis, 1970.

———. *The United States Mint and Coinage: An Illustrated History from 1776 to the Present*. New York: Arco, 1966.

Todd, Richard Cecil. *Confederate Finance*. Athens: University of Georgia Press, 1954.

Unger, Irwin. *The Greenback Era: A Social and Political History of American Finance, 1865–1879*. Princeton: Princeton University Press, 1964.

Van Allen, Leroy C., and A. George Mallis. *Guide to Morgan and Peace Dollars: A Complete Guide and Reference Book on United States Silver Dollars*. Silver Springs, Md.: Katen, 1971.

Vermeule, Cornelius C. *Bibliography of Applied Numismatics in the Fields of Greek and Roman Archaeology and Fine Arts*. London: Spink, 1956.

———. *Numismatic Art in America: Aesthetics of the United States Coinage*. Cambridge, Mass.: Harvard University Press, 1971.

Yeoman, Richard S. *Guidebook of United States Coins*. Racine, Wis.: Western, 1988.

———. *Handbook of United States Coins*. Racine, Wis.: Western, 1978.

Periodicals

Stamps

Aero Philatelist Annals. New York, 1953–71.

Airpost Journal. Albion, Pa., 1929–72.

American Philatelist. State College, Pa., 1909–.

American Philatelist and Year Book of the American Philatelic Association. Springfield, Mass., 1894–1908.

American Revenuer. New York, 1954–.

Essay-Proof Journal. Jefferson, Wis., 1944–.

JAPOS Bulletin. Clinton Corners, N.Y., 1975–.

Let's Talk Parachutes. Fort Worth, Tex., 1976–.

Linn's Stamp News. Sidney, Ohio, 1928–.

Mekeel's Weekly Stamp News. Portland, Me., 1905–.

1869 Times. Memphis, 1975–.

Philatelic Literature Review. Canajoharie, N.Y., 1942–.

SPA Journal. Cincinnati, 1932–.

Stamps. Hornell, N.Y., 1932–.

Topical Times. Milwaukee, 1949–.

United States Official Postal Guide. Washington, D.C., 1847–.
United States Specialist. West Somerville, Mass., 1930–.

Coins

American Journal of Numismatics. New York, 1866–1924.
Calcoin News Quarterly Magazine. San Jose, Calif., 1947–.
Coins. Iola, Wis., 1962–.
Coin World. Sidney, Ohio, 1960–.
Numismatic Literature. New York, 1947–.
Numismatic Scrapbook Magazine. Chicago, 1935–.
The Numismatist. Monroe, Mich., 1888–.
Paper Money. Jefferson, Wis., 1962–.
Proceedings of the American Numismatic and Archaeological Society. New York, 1878–
     1914.
Proceedings of the American Numismatic Society. New York, 1908–.
Proceedings of the Numismatic and Antiquarian Society. Philadelphia, 1865–1936.

Stamps and Coins (Journals specializing in both fields and popular magazines that often publish articles or columns on either or both.)

American Journal of Philately and Coin Advertisers. New York, 1879–86.
Essay-Proof Journal. Jefferson, Wis., 1944–.
Hobbies. Chicago, 1931–.
Popular Science Monthly. New York, 1872–.
Profitable Hobbies. Kansas City, Mo., 1945–.
St. Nicholas. Darien, Conn., 1873–1940.
Scientific American. New York; check files from 1890 to 1930.

Television

ROBERT S. ALLEY

The angle of vision with which one approaches television will have a marked impact upon the way in which its history is recorded. There is the option of writing a totally technological history with reference to those developments that have taken the television set from the crude model created by John L. Baird in 1926 to the new color consoles that will instantly record broadcasts for replay on twenty-five-inch screens. It is also possible to see television as a form of entertainment and examine its history via its stars, drama, and comedy. Alternatively, as a means of communicating news, television may legitimately be weighed and compared with other news media regarding accuracy and influence. Social scientists have a valid concern for television as a social force and its influences on both children and adults. Indeed, it is in this area that the largest number of monographs have surfaced over the past two decades. Of course, television is a business, and its history may be examined in terms of the rise and success of competing networks. Finally, Marshall McLuhan and others have made us aware of television as an appropriate topic for philosophical discourse. I give notice to significant contributions in all these areas. However, for the purpose of this chapter I describe the history of television in humanistic terms, with attention to the ways in which it has become preeminently *the* popular culture and a primary purveyor of values and ideas. It is only recently that the long-held reticence of the humanities to see the medium as a proper target of inquiry has been successfully challenged, which accounts for the small amount of literature in several important areas. Nell Eurich noted some fifteen years ago that the materials of the humanities are hardly neutral . . . even in the humanities we see some teachers, in a desperate attempt to ape the "hard sciences," avoiding the difficult, but critical, issue of values. . . . humanists have retreated from the front line of creative and original thought and become priests of the past.

Today film is a primary medium in which the creative arts are united. Together the writer, musician, artistic director, and actor have made film the means with which to capture the innuendos as well as the reality of human experience. . . . With TV, the combined power (visual and audible) has entered the home and become a formidable antagonist—and potential ally—for the teacher relying on words in the classroom.

Still the humanist has not invited the new creative expressions of artists into his sanctuary. Nor have we, by and large, entertained the large questions that must be raised, if the humanities are to have any influence on the quality of our lives today, much less tomorrow.

To remain ignorant of or aloof to science and technology and the directions they are carrying us, to assume that the past alone can enlighten, is to cripple the humanities and shrink the chances for human survival.[1]

HISTORIC OUTLINE

In the year 1926 there were practical demonstrations of living scenes viewed the instant they took place by audiences removed from the events. (A full discussion of this early history, combined with a thorough bibliography, is to be found in Joseph Udelson's *The Great Television Race: A History of the Television Industry, 1925–1941.* Articles detailing the growth of the medium may be read in Lichty and Topping, *American Broadcasting: A Source Book on the History of Radio and Television.*) In London, Paris, and New York, the technology was similar and impressive. In 1927 the *New York Times* noted that television "outruns the imagination of all the wizards of prophecy." In that year the movies conquered the sound barrier with *The Jazz Singer.* Radio emerged at the same time as a startling source of instant information and live entertainment. Depression, war, and technical difficulties combined to deter the development of television even as its two media partners flourished. The irony was that television, maturing in the 1950s, radically changed the face of both radio and cinema, thereby challenging the existence of each. Only as the two accommodated themselves to the young upstart did they find hope for survival.

By 1951 the commercial television networks had established their hegemony and were developing means of transmitting signals coast to coast. Beer sales rose as baseball invaded the medium, and at least one doctor dolefully predicted that children would have stunted feet from too little walking. By 1953, television had attracted the likes of Bob Hope, Groucho Marx, Lucille Ball, Fred Allen, Jack Benny, Edgar Bergen, and George Burns and Gracie Allen. Thus radio, which had been a way of life for two generations of children, evaporated by the mid-1950s as quickly as it had burst upon them in the 1930s. Gone were the comedians and the dramas of a rainy afternoon. We were to discover that words, which had carried considerable weight, became conditioned by the visual.

The early 1950s was the era of television hearings—Estes Kefauver and Joseph McCarthy—and of the so-called golden age of television. That age lasted only a few brief years as it claimed the talents of writers, such as Paddy Chayefsky, Reginald Rose, and Rod Serling; directors, such as Delbert Mann, Arthur Penn, and Sidney Lumet; and a luxury of talent including Paul Newman, Sidney Poitier, Kim Stanley, Rod Steiger, and Joanne Woodward. The remarkable success of the live anthological drama series that emerged with these personalities was all too short-lived. In the first place, the social comment of a play like *Marty* was in sharp contrast with the shiny world of the burgeoning number of eager sponsors. Second, the very success of television prompted a new breath of fresh air for cinema, which began to drain talent from New York and consequently to eliminate live television drama. Finally, the growing fear of both network executives and advertisers concerning controversial drama tended to stifle talent. Erik Barnouw dates the decline of these anthologies in the year 1955. Delbert Mann concurs. (See in particular Karen Sue Foley, *The Political Blacklist in the Broadcast Industry.*) In a 1975 interview Mann noted that the early television dramas, starting in the late 1940s, appealed to small, specialized audiences. As sets increased in number, the nature of the audience changed. The need to appeal to the mass audience was stimulated by the growing interest of manufacturers in advertising in the new medium. This coincided with the McCarthy era and the blacklisting of performers and writers. Mann noted that there was a pressure not to offend. Thus was developed an inevitable pattern of restricting the kind of material that could be used. Mann, like many other persons in the profession, left television for film by the end of the 1950s.

A great deal more was involved for television in the 1950s than fiction. The accident of technological discovery gave control of the television networks to the radio people. Radio, while deeply involved in entertainment, was a news-oriented medium for much of the public. And it was centered in New York. Quite naturally, then, the use of television after 1950 included a considerable emphasis upon public events. Had the motion picture industry controlled the medium, it is not altogether certain that such emphasis would have been as strong. Located on the East Coast and in close proximity to political and social phenomena which were shaping the nation, network executives promoted the beginnings of a vast news network. (For CBS that meant Edward R. Murrow, whose contributions are noted in two books: Bliss, *In Search of Light,* and Kendrick, *Prime Time.*) In an excellent early study of CBS, David Halberstam noted:

Television arrived simultaneously with the height of McCarthyism [which] probably helped to narrow the parameters of journalistic freedom, but it was bound to happen anyway. Politically, television was simply too powerful a force, too fast, too immediate, with too large an audience, for the kind of easy journalistic freedom that radio and print reporters had enjoyed.[2]

He expanded upon this in his later book, *The Powers That Be:*

Almost from the start of television there was an unconscious decision at the networks to limit the autonomy of the network news show. . . . [There was] a desire among network executives not to do anything that might offend either the government or Madison Avenue.[3]

Even in its restricted form, television brought living drama into American homes regularly in its first decade. The Estes Kefauver Senate hearings on crime catapulted the senator into the Democratic nomination for vice president by 1956. ABC moved quickly to televise the activities of the Army-McCarthy hearings in 1953. Concurrently millions of citizens had become more aware of the political process through the televising of the two party conventions of the previous year.

The first pronouncements of Richard Nixon were televised, and his classic "Checkers" speech was delivered in 1952. Many Americans heard about "old soldiers" from General Douglas MacArthur in that same year. In the aftermath of the Supreme Court's decision in *Brown vs. Board of Education* in 1954 came Little Rock and Governor Orville Faubus, and a changing domestic scene. From Sputnik to the 1959 "kitchen debate," television provided a window on the world beyond the United States.

The American public felt the influence of television entertainment through language, cosmic heroes, and classic portrayals. The phenomenon of families gathered silently around a small box to watch Milton Berle or Sid Caesar exploded in the 1950s in a dozen different directions. The culture of postwar America was straining under the old melting-pot philosophy, and much of the comedy of that decade sought to reestablish the mentality of a secure, middle-class, picket-fence community of the 1930s.

The 1940s gave the American viewer its most enduring television figure, Ed Sullivan, in 1948. A less remembered role was that played by E. G. Marshall in "Mary Poppins" in the year 1949. The next year the crucial decade began with Sid Caesar, Jack Benny, Burns and Allen, and "Broadway Open House" (forerunner of "Tonight"). Live drama was highlighted by Helen Hayes in *Victoria Regina*. In the early years American cultural roots remained in the radio era, a phenomenon that would disappear by 1955. The classics "I Love Lucy" and *Amahl and the Night Visitors* were produced early in 1951. The next year there were more comedians—Ozzie and Harriet, "Mr. Peepers," "Our Miss Brooks," and "My Little Margie." Sunday became the preserve of that special niche of television history called "Omnibus," and the "sweaty" hand of the forge became as well known as Snap, Crackle, and Pop with the arrival of the Mark VII production, "Dragnet."

Along with the inauguration of President Eisenhower, Red Skelton, Steve Allen, and Danny Thomas took to television. *Marty,* deftly directed by Delbert Mann and consistently described as a high point in television drama, was also produced in 1953. That same year viewers might have caught James Dean in *A Long Time till Dawn* and Richard Kiley in *P.O.W.,* a drama about brainwashing and the Korean War. The heart of the picket-fence era was probably 1954. The new offerings included "Father Knows Best," "Lassie," "Walt Disney Presents," "Love That Bob" (Bob Cummings), and "Private Secretary" with Ann Sothern. Live drama prospered in such offerings as *Twelve Angry Men,* written by Reginald Rose.

Little in 1955 programming warned Americans that their world was changing. Alfred Hitchcock entertained, as did "The Honeymooners" and "Sergeant Bilko." "Captain Kangaroo" entered and became a traditional CBS figure for generations of children with Mr. Green Jeans, Dancing Bear, and Bun Rabbit. Meanwhile, American viewers focused on the past in dramatic series. "Wyatt Earp" was the first, but "Gunsmoke" made it official; 1955 was the year the Westerns began. Single dramatic offerings were outstanding—Sidney Poitier in *A Man Is Ten Feet Tall,* Raymond Massey and Lillian Gish in *The Day Lincoln Was Shot,* with Jack Lemmon as John Wilkes Booth, Barry Sullivan in *The Caine Mutiny,* Maurice Evans in *The Devil's Disciple,* Michael Redgrave in *She Stoops to Conquer,* Lee Grant in *Shadow of the Champ,* and Humphrey Bogart in Delbert Mann's production of *The Petrified Forest.* Rod Serling contributed *Patterns.* Perhaps "never again on this stage" was the television epitaph for 1955.

The election year of 1956 saw the movement to Hollywood gather momentum. Film was replacing live drama, not always directly to its detriment, but other effects were more subtle. Dramatically, 1956 belonged to Rod Serling and his *Requiem for a Heavyweight.*

In 1957 television offered "Maverick," "Perry Mason," "Wagon Train," "Leave It to Beaver," and "Have Gun, Will Travel." The Westerns were on their way, as was Jack Paar, who replaced Steve Allen that year on the "Tonight " show. Avid viewers may recall the maudlin conversations that Paar had with Hollywood personalities about bomb shelters and whether having one was cowardly.

Drama, now mostly on film, continued with high quality in 1958 with *The Bridge of San Luis Rey, The Days of Wine and Roses,* and *Little Moon of Alban.* Perhaps the most controversial dramatic series was "The Untouchables," a product of Desilu. It was heavily criticized for its Italian stereotyping and high level of violence. The era of anthological dramatic shows was coming to an end with the television-film phase of 1955 and the practical use of videotape beginning in 1957. "Studio One" moved to Hollywood in 1958; most other similar ventures faded and died. Even so, the last year of the decade offered some reason for hope that drama was not dead. There was Jason Robards in *For Whom the Bell Tolls,* George C. Scott in *Winterset,*

Ingrid Bergman in *The Turn of the Screw,* and Laurence Olivier and Judith Anderson in *The Moon and Sixpence.* However, perhaps a greater harbinger of the 1960s was the debut of "Bonanza" that same year.

In the 1960s the stunning social dramas of the earlier decade were replaced by live newscasts, which made television fiction pale in comparison. The 1960 television debates between Richard Nixon and John Kennedy heralded the beginning of the decade of the newsman. A barrage of newsmaking events assailed the television viewer. If the event was not presented "live," it reached us within minutes thereafter—the Berlin Wall, the missile crisis, the assassination of John Kennedy and the subsequent killing of Lee Harvey Oswald "before our eyes," the reality of the war in Vietnam, which every night on the news became more unreal, again assassination—Martin Luther King, Jr., and Robert F. Kennedy—riots at home from Watts in Los Angeles to Washington, D.C., men landing on the moon, and always the war in Southeast Asia. Historians may determine that the Vietnam years were more devastating to our culture than any other event in our past. Distrust of government was rampant, with arrogance of power, depression, and discontent among the dispossessed, fear and loathing among and toward youth, and destruction of decent models for children. Narcotics became a way of life for men called upon to commit mayhem abroad. Rising expectations and white stupidity created civil disorder from Watts to Washington. Television was there, and it recorded a rare second chance in New Hampshire in February 1968, but America, after losing Robert Kennedy and Martin Luther King, Jr., to assassins, chose Richard Nixon. After that came Cambodia, Kent State, Attica, Spiro Agnew, John Mitchell, Watergate, and pardons. In June 1977 Johnny Carson gave voice to many pent-up feelings when he noted upon the sentencing of John Mitchell and H. R. Haldeman to minimum security prisons in Alabama that had it been you or I, we would have been put in a cell with Charles Manson. Clearly, dramatic and comedic television had considerable competition in those years.

The enduring nature of television series comedy, often lumped together as "sitcoms," requires special attention. The earliest comedy was the personality—Milton Berle, or Jack Benny, or George Burns. The gentle comedy of "The Goldbergs" and "Mama" was joined by the outlandish antics of Lucille Ball in "I Love Lucy." By the close of the fifties situation comedies included "Leave It to Beaver," "Father Knows Best," and "The Adventures of Ozzie and Harriet." Mild doses of fun were sprinkled among basic Puritan moralisms. Male blue-collar workers usually found themselves less mentally alert, as in "The Honeymooners" and "The Life of Riley." The bucolic humor to be enshrined in "The Beverly Hillbillies" first appeared in "The Real McCoys."

Women were generally stereotyped, seldom portrayed as other than housewives if married; teachers, nurses, and secretaries chasing men, if single. There was an important shift in emphasis in "Beaver," where the father and mother shared, as friends and companions, the role of rearing children. After the demise of the offensive put-down of blacks in "Amos 'n' Andy" in 1953, it was not until 1966 that a network featured a black actor as a star in a series, "I Spy."

The 1960s saw the flowering of an odd genre with "Car 54 Where Are You?," "Gilligan's Island," and "My Mother the Car." Many of the sitcoms of the sixties poked fun at authority symbols—the law, the scientist, the socialite, or the banking profession. Some, such as the "The Munsters" and "The Addams Family," seemed to take on all social conventions, but it would be foolish to make too much out of this because each show was also designed quite obviously to match the public mood, which increasingly seemed to desire escape. Lucille Ball interestingly reversed the trend. Her early shows were slapstick. Her comedy of the 1960s was similar to the earlier Ann Sothern efforts. Family comedies were more and more styled around the single parent, usually a man. Since divorce was a forbidden subject for the networks, death of the departed spouse was mandatory. From "Andy Griffith" to "The Courtship of Eddie's Father" to "My Three Sons" to "Family Affair" this style prevailed.

Topical humor and sex entered the scene in the late sixties with "The Smothers Brothers," "Laugh-In," and "Love, American Style." Social drama was developing with "The Defenders" and "The Bold Ones."

The year 1970 marks a major shift for series comedy. Garry Marshall introduced "The Odd Couple" on ABC, and CBS began its reign in comedy with "The Mary Tyler Moore Show," followed quickly by "All in the Family" and "M*A*S*H." The social and political humor contained in a rising number of series owed much to the Smothers Brothers and to Dan Rowan and Dick Martin.

As the history of the 1970s is being written, the attention devoted to television will undoubtedly emphasize the enormous success of a new comedy art in the business. Norman Lear, Grant Tinker, Garry Marshall, Paul Witt, Susan Harris, James Brooks, Allan Burns, and Larry Gelbart will carry the credits along with Carroll O'Connor, Jean Stapleton, Bea Arthur, Mary Tyler Moore, Cloris Leachman, and Alan Alda. The similarities between "M*A*S*H" and "Maude" are more felt than defined, but the commonality was expressed both by audiences and actors. The flowering of the television comic short story may well be a most important cultural phenomenon. Beginning in 1971 the American public became conscious of Archie and Mary and Hawkeye. Every week these and other characters filled the screen with social bite in comic form. We laughed, often with a tear, and experienced what many knew finally to be reality joining hands with fantasy. The style and class and a social consciousness, coupled with a dominant humanism, characterized these shows and their companions—

"The Bob Newhart Show," "Good Times," "The Jeffersons," "One Day at a Time," "Phyllis," "Happy Days," "SOAP," "Laverne and Shirley," "Mork and Mindy," and "The Odd Couple."

The Reagan years in television began with "Dallas" and "The Dukes of Hazzard" leading an undistinguished collection of series. The rash of evening serials continued, and violence returned as mayhem and over-charged weaponry took their toll even on the young with "The A-Team." Somewhere in that mix there appeared in the year 1984 a new style of comedy effectively led by "Family Ties," "The Cosby Show," "Kate and Allie," "Newhart," "Cheers," and "Night Court." In two significant cases, audience reactions to series about women, the award-winning "Cagney and Lacey" and the delightful comedy "Designing Women," had a great deal to do with keeping them on the air. If any-thing characterized the last part of the eighties it was a more forceful representation of women and the rise of women to significant positions in behind-the-camera work. Some of the finest social drama in made-for-television films came at the hands of a new generation of highly mo-tivated young women and men.

The independent female, first effectively addressed in "That Girl," be-came more pronounced with "Julia" in 1968 and the successors to Mary Richards in the seventies: "One Day at a Time," "Maude," "Laverne and Shirley," "Rhoda," and "SOAP." As noted, the eighties built upon these foundations to create a new level of representation of the feminine per-spective.

Even so, the early independence did not stretch to include much change in series drama, and, in fact, the comedy was gentle in relation to the realities of the women's movement. Likewise, black participation in the medium was almost totally confined to comedy—"Good Times," "The Jeffersons," and "Sanford and Son." Aside from the "Cosby" phenomenon, little evi-dence exists suggesting any perceptible shift in old network attitudes.

The decade of the sixties was notable for three types of drama—police, Western, and medical. Apart from them, there were only a few dramatic series that survived long enough to remember—"The Defenders" (1962), "Combat" (1962), "Outer Limits" (1963), "East Side, West Side" (1963), "Mr. Novak" (1963), "Slattery's People" (1964), "Twelve O'Clock High" (1964), "Star Trek" (1966), "The Bold Ones" (1969), "Room ZZZ" (1969)—an average of one new series per year.

From their beginnings in 1955 the Westerns expanded to number fifteen by 1960. That number was reduced to five by 1965. By the end of the decade it had diminished to three, including "Bonanza" and "Gunsmoke." The history of police-detective drama is less consistent. When Americans entered their second ten years with television, they were watching "Naked City," "Peter Gunn," "Hawaiian Eye," "The Untouchables," and "The Detectives." "Dragnet" appeared and reappeared on the schedule during the same period. By 1964 there was not a single drama of this genre represented in network scheduling. In 1965 Quinn Martin, the most persistent purveyor of the police motif, introduced the long-running "FBI," and by 1969 the schedule included no less than seven police–private eye shows. The 1970s saw that proliferate into over twenty in the 1975–76 season. The police dramas have been dominated by three producing giants—Martin, Jack Webb, and Spelling and Goldberg.

We were deluged in the sixties by an ever increasing assortment of gun-toting enforcers. Television always upholds the law. It may be violent and sometimes in poor taste, but right does prevail. Not so in the movies or on the stage or in novels and magazines—these all offer alternatives to the triumph of the system. Television sustains it. Not without criticism, to be sure, but support there is, nonetheless. Baretta may condone small-time crime, and Kojak may bend the rules, but from Starsky and Hutch to Barnaby Jones to Charlie's Angels, the message is the same. Television has obviated certain cultural differences and leveled our language and dress. History may also affirm that it was the glue that held the clue to societal survival in the present decade. Certainly we all had television in common, and it has been affirming traditional social values. As early as 1968 the National Advisory Commission on Civil Disorders, commenting upon television coverage in 1967, noted:

Content analysis of television film footage shows that the tone of the coverage studied was more calm and "factual" than "emotional" and rumor-laden. . . . Television newscasts during the periods of actual disorder in 1967 tended to emphasize law enforcement activities, thereby overshadowing underlying grievances and tensions. . . . In contrast to what some of its critics have charged, television sometimes may have leaned over too far backward in seeking balance and restraint.[4]

By the end of the seventies forces concerned about violence had significantly reduced network offerings in this arena. (The debate over the so-called family hour triggered a bitter struggle between networks and independent producers, detailed in Geoffrey Cowan's See No Evil.) A decade later, in 1988, with the rise in popularity of sophisticated weapons, space stories, and the horror genre, television has recovered much of its violent nature. The gritty realism of "Hill Street Blues" was at one end of a spectrum that included, at the other, the short-lived Clint Eastwood look-alike, "Lady Blue."

Medical drama moved in and out of the television scene in the sixties and seventies, beginning with the two long-running series "Ben Casey" and "Dr. Kildare," debuting in 1961 and departing in 1966. By 1969 a new set, "Marcus Welby," "Medical Center," and "The Bold Ones," gave viewers three opportunities to experience vicariously the treatment of obscure and not so obscure diseases. Medicine became a topic for television critique by the mid-seventies with "Medical Story," and later "Trapper John, M.D." The long-running "St. Elsewhere" has provided a new realism to medical drama in the past few years. (See in particular "Medical Melodrama" by Robert Alley in Rose's *TV Genres*.)

Documentaries burgeoned in the 1960s. The networks, spurred on by an obvious interest in public events, focused on social issues (national and international) for material, from migrant workers to Vietnam. Simultaneously, domestic unrest bubbled to the surface and cascaded across the land in 1967 and 1968.

The task of calling the nation's conscience to attention fell more and more after 1970 to mini-series, such as *Roots,* and to movies for television with a social message, such as *The Autobiography of Miss Jane Pittman* and the impressive work of Richard Levinson and William Link, including *My Sweet Charlie, That Certain Summer, The Execution of Private Slovik, Crisis at Central High, The Guardian* (HBO), and the 1988 drama concerning an Arab terrorist. (See Levinson and Link, *Stay Tuned*.) In this area the effective dramas produced by women like Marian Rees and Blue Andre have made a significant difference in recent years.

Television has massive power of promotion and persuasion, and its immediacy to our every thought makes it a likely target when cultural leaders search for a culprit for which to blame the general tone of our society. It is new; we presume it is beyond our control; it is electronic. Television is popular culture. Although many social critics condemn and deride what television offers, for the majority of American people television is a friend, and has become, as well, a critic in comedy and, less often, in drama, of the flaws in our society. James Brown has written:

The fact that the medium [television] produced several outstanding multi-hour presentations a month deserves more praise than the meager annual productivity of Broadway. Books have been with us since movable type for over 600 years. How many books of true significance and public acceptance are published annually? Daily newspapers have been around for more than a century. Movies have been on the scene three-quarters of a century. But radio was first heard clearly in the land in 1920. Television has elbowed its way through exuberant adolescence and is now just beyond its teens. As a mid-twenty-year-old, it continues to try to find itself, to achieve its proper identity in society.[5]

In the early days the term *educational television* was used to apply to those stations normally expected to be unaffiliated with a commercial network. It was not until February 1950 that the first non-commercial station, WOI-TV in Ames, Iowa, was licensed and began operation. It was the one-hundredth station to begin television broadcasting in America. Because of the slow beginning of educational television, most of the stations occupied UHF channels, which the Federal Communications Commission (FCC) had begun to assign in 1952. As late as 1956 there were only twenty-four non-commercial, educational channels on the air, and most of those were struggling. Television set manufacturers completely ignored UHF on early sets, and it was not until a decree from Congress required it that all sets began to be sold with UHF tuners incorporated. Even then, the technology that allowed snap-lock tuning of VHF channels was not installed with the UHF tuner, and this meant long years of invidious comparison with the ease of tuning channels 2 through 13. This problem was coupled with the fact that the UHF signal was usually more difficult to receive and had a much more restricted range. As late as 1968 only 55 percent of American families could receive UHF. In 1977 most hotels and motels were still not equipped with sets capable of receiving UHF broadcasts. A decade later the expansion of cable systems into major markets had altered this markedly.

The original National Educational Television (NET) network survived through grit and grants from a small number of major foundations. Finally, in 1967, Congress took direct action and established the Public Broadcasting System (PBS) with federal funding. It still required substantial fund-raising by the local stations in order to guarantee survival. Since 1967, commercial networks have been quite guarded in their reactions to their new colleagues. Publications such as *TV Guide* have, until recently, generally ignored PBS activities except in the most obvious instances. Trade papers have tended to focus more attention on public policy regarding the new network than on the contributions it was making to television offerings.

Nevertheless, by 1975, with greater ease of reception becoming a reality for more and more of the viewing public, PBS began to attract more attention. There were two clear reasons—the huge success of "Sesame Street" and the prestige garnered from British offerings, such as "Masterpiece Theatre" and "Upstairs, Downstairs." However, the financial difficulties of PBS affiliates did not abate. Inadequate staffing and generally poor pay characterized many of the less affluent PBS members in comparison with the more prosperous channels in New York, Los Angeles, Pittsburgh, San Francisco, and Boston. Most of the new programming sprang from these more fortunate affiliates. Auctions and scrambling for grants of any size became a way of life for most stations. Threatened with economic collapse, the temptation has been real to emulate the commercial networks in their quest for ratings. Furthermore, there is the constant danger of government interference in the affairs of PBS, even though every effort is made to eliminate politics from the system. There has been considerable pressure from some lawmakers for PBS to serve broader publics since it uses tax dollars. Nevertheless, PBS has continued to offer excellent quality programming to a solid minority of citizens. Properly funded, it can provide a healthy stimulus not only to the three major commercial networks, but to the current plethora of cable companies and movie channels like Home Box Office (HBO), as it serves a significant public of its own.

A brief, unscientific comment is appropriate on the chaotic state of network broadcasting at present. Declining dramatically in number of viewers, the three networks have serious dilemmas confronting them. Indeed, the very appearance of cable and pay television threatens the three-network trinopoly severely, and financial strain has been evident in layoffs and cutbacks since 1986. Takeovers of NBC and ABC by General Electric (GE) and Capital Cities brought in new, leaner management headed by men who had little concern for the unique character of broadcasting as a popular art form. This also happened at CBS, despite the continued presence of William Paley. The quality of cable offerings, in spite of the promise, has been pathetically poor. Apart from movies and sports, little has changed except with the Arts and Entertainment (A&E) offerings of a greater variety of British-made fare.

REFERENCE WORKS

Even though directed toward "scientific" study of television, and now dated by ten years, an absolute essential for any research in the area, from whatever perspective, is the three-volume work from the Rand Corporation bearing the general title *Television and Human Behavior: The Key Studies.* The first carries the subtitle *A Guide to the Pertinent Scientific Literature.* It, like the other two volumes, is under the general editorship of George Comstock. The first task of the study was to list some 2,300 citations with a single-word description of any area a particular citation might touch. While focused upon social and behavioral science, most of the important contributions by humanists, critics, and columnists are noted. Unfortunately and predictably, the *Key Studies,* an expanded description of 450 of the most significant "scientific" works, includes almost none of the material on content analysis and ignores writings by humanists and interpreters of popular culture. While it would be foolish to fault the Rand study for its omissions, given its purpose, it is legitimate to call to the attention of social scientists the growing literature on television as art and culture.

George Comstock and others brought the bibliography up to date in 1978 with the publication of his interpretations of the material by Columbia University Press, *Television and Human Behavior.* Again, the emphasis is "scientific," but Comstock, who was the senior research coordinator for the 1972 Report of the Surgeon General's Scientific Advisory Committee on Television and Social Behavior, is a well-balanced scholar whose interpretations of the data point toward the need for content analysis. His writings reflect a recognition of the limitations of interpretation by social scientists of their collected information. He points further to the lack of substantive answers and reminds his readers that alternative methods of examination of the medium are appropriate. Comstock's writings could become a bridge for communication among academics concerned with the study of television. He wrote in 1976: "It is tempting to conclude that television violence makes viewers more anti-socially aggressive, somewhat callous, and generally more fearful of the society in which they live. It may, but the social and behavioral science evidence does not support such a broad indictment."[6] Comstock has reassessed some of his thinking in a newer volume, *Television in America,* published in 1980.

Another, less elaborate listing, but perhaps of equal significance for the humanities, is *Broadcasting and Mass Media: A Survey Bibliography,* compiled by Christopher Sterling. More restricted in scope, but useful, with 619 entries, is an appended bibliography to *Television Economics* by Bruce M. Owen, Jack H. Beebe, and Willard G. Manning, Jr. *Television and Social Behavior: An Annotated Bibliography of Research Focusing on Television's Impact on Children,* by C. K. Atkin, J. P. Murray, and O. B. Nayman, is helpful in the same way as the Rand study, but far less thorough. The most recent and useful bibliography is that offered in 1985 by Mary Cassata and Thomas Skill, *Television: A Guide to the Literature,* in which judicious selection and intelligent categorizing make it an essential tool for the student of the medium. See as well Thomas F. Gordon and Mary Ellen Verna, *Mass Communication Effects and Processes: A Comprehensive Bibliography, 1950–1975.*

As previously stated, this chapter will concentrate on contributions to television research by humanists and critics of the culture. A primary emphasis is writing in the area of content analysis. Other citations will be offered that might assist a student of popular culture in new investigations, and some "scientific" works will be cited. However, it should be understood that the vast majority of such inquiries have been omitted. The reader is referred to the growing number of books from Sage Publications that attempt to cover the ever-widening field of social science research into television. A major trend, yet to be charted, is the rise of communications schools that fall comfortably under neither social science nor the humanities, but are developing a language and style of their own, heavily weighted with semiotics. A harbinger of this "new school" is *Reading Television* by John Fiske and John Hartley, published in 1978. This new criticism is best outlined in the words of that volume:

We shall try to show how the television message, as an extension of our spoken language, is itself subject to many of the rules that have been shown to apply to language. We shall introduce some of the terms, originally developed in linguistics and semiotics, that can help us to identify and successfully decode the sequence of encoded signs that constitutes any television programme.[7]

Fiske's disciples, and that is in fact what they are, reject content analysis and origination as irrelevant. To that extent the school of thought almost borders on a determinism antithetical to the humanities endeavor. Time will tell to what degree this approach to the medium will remain primarily linguistic.

HISTORY AND CRITICISM

Erik Barnouw's *The Image Empire* and *Tube of Plenty* are classics. One of the most effective presentations is Barnouw's treatment of the days of television blacklisting and the harassment of the creative talent in the medium. This has now been augmented by J. Fred MacDonald's *Television and the Red Menace*. Barnouw is effectively illustrated and fulfills the glowing promise of the publisher's jacket. Other authors to explore the early years include Christopher Sterling, who, with John M. Kitross, has produced an effective volume, *Stay Tuned*. Two fascinating early glimpses of television in the forties come from Robert E. Lee, *Television: The Revolution*, and Herbert L. Marx, Jr., *Television and Radio in American Life*.

A large number of books now flood the market detailing the programming on the commercial networks. Special attention to the DuMont Network by Gary Hess deserves mention. Tim Brooks and Earl Marsh have edited a third edition of *The Complete Directory to Prime Time Network TV Shows: 1946-Present*, and it joins the second effort of Vincent Terrace, *The Complete Encyclopedia of Television Programs: 1947-1979*. In 1980 Alexander McNeil compiled *Total Television*, similar in nature to the Brooks-Marsh volumes. Paul Michael and Robert Parish developed an interesting trivia book, *The Emmy Awards*, and Parish, with the help of Terrace and Mark Trost, has published the three-volume *Actors' Television Credits* ranging from 1950 through 1982. Brooks has recently authored *The Complete Directory to Prime Time TV Stars: 1946-Present*, a partially successful though incomplete work.

An ambitious pictorial record was complied by Jeff Greenfield in 1977, and it is augmented by several other works by Jay Harris, Jeff Rovin, and Steven Scheuer. Together these works offer an overview of prime-time programming. Larry Gianokos provides a look at content with *Television Drama Series Programming: A Comprehensive Chronicle*, which extends from 1947 to the mid-eighties. Les Brown in his *New York Times Encyclopedia of Television* provides a quick reference guide. A listing of all episodes, with a brief description of plot, of 153 sitcoms now in syndication is a helpful source published by Joel Eisner and David Krinsky. An overview of special programming is presented in Robert Bailey's *An Examination of Prime Time Network Special Programs, 1948-1966*. Other noteworthy contributions to this genre are Vince Waldron's *Classic Sitcoms* and the earlier *Cavalcade of Broadcasting*, by Curtis Mitchell.

The stories of several successful series have been recorded well either by the participants or by historians of the popular arts. In the former category are included books by Desi Arnaz, Gertrude Berg, Milton Berle, Frank Blair, Dick Cavett, Jack Webb, and Gene Roddenberry (with Stephen Whitfield). Among the growing number of special books on specific series, some of the best are Richard Adler on "All in the Family," Bart Andrews on "I

Love Lucy," Irwyn Applebaum on "Leave It to Beaver," Jane Feuer, Paul Kerr, and Tisa Vahimagi on the MTM Company, Richard Kelly on "The Andy Griffith Show," John McCarthy and Brian Kelleher on "Alfred Hitchcock Presents," Robert Metz on the "Today" show, Ted Sennett on "Your Show of Shows," Ginny Weissman and Coyne Steven Sanders on "The Dick Van Dyke Show," and Donna McCrohan on "The Honeymooners."

Overviews of television history are handled well by Ralph Brauer in his analysis of the Television Western. A more recent study of the same subject is Donald Kirkley's examination of Westerns from 1955 to 1963. Documentaries receive intelligent notice from Charles Hammond in *The Image Decade*. An early, fundamental source on documentaries is A. William Bluem's *Documentary in American Television*. Margaret Scobey joined Phillip and Beatrice Kalisch in a serious look at one profession in *Images of Nurses on Television*. Robert LaGuardia offers the big-book approach in *Soap World*, while Manuela Soares provides sharp insights in *The Soap Opera Book*. Muriel Cantor and Suzanne Pingree's *The Soap Opera* seeks to sample the product with a degree of content analysis, while Mary Cassata and Thomas Skill have done the most thorough study under the auspices of Project Daytime, entitled *Life on Daytime Television*. Donald F. Glut and Jim Harmon offer a popular treatment of heroes in *The Great Television Heroes*. The genre of the private detective is the focus of a fine study, *Television's Private Eye*, by Robert Larka.

In the area of women and the medium, little work has yet been offered. Diana Meehan has the best overview in her *Ladies of the Evening*. From Canada has come a publication by the Canadian Broadcasting Corporation entitled *Portrayal of Women in Programming*. And of course there is Gaye Tuchman's *Hearth and Home*. Sexism in the medium is the target of Matilda Butler and William Paisley in *Women and the Mass Media*. A forthcoming volume on the role of women in the medium by Robert S. Alley and Irby Brown will offer a comprehensive look at this issue.

The black experience on commercial television is examined by J. Fred MacDonald in *Blacks and White TV*. He deals with negative stereotyping, blacks and the civil rights movement, and the subordinate roles blacks have received since the movement began. Anthony Jackson in *Black Families and the Medium of Television* approaches a basic issue in a medium so devoted to the family theme in programming. Randall Miller's *Ethnic Images in American Film and Television* deals not only with blacks but with seven other ethnic minorities as well.

Less ambitious than Greenfield but highly informative in its concentration upon nostalgia and popular appeal is *How Sweet It Was*, by Arthur Shulman and Roger Youman. Arranged topically, interlaced with 1,435 photographs, and quite well written, the book provides a visual display of television history. The chief problem with the work is that it concludes in 1966. The same authors returned to the task in 1972 with *The Television Years*, a less ambitious undertaking with only a few pages devoted to each year and made up primarily of photographs. It is not in a class with the initial effort. Irving Settel and William Laas are the authors of *A Pictorial History of Television*. Arranged chronologically, the text is not nearly so illuminating as *How Sweet It Was*. The quality of the paper and photographs is inferior, but it is a good reference with correct information. More recent efforts of similar character are Judy Fireman, *TV Book: The Ultimate Television Book* (1977), Rick Mitz, *The Great TV Sitcom Book* (1980), and Harry Castleman and Walter J. Podrazik, *Watching TV: Four Decades of American Television* (1982).

Newspapers and news magazines provide a primary source for the progress of television since World War II. The single best source for programming is *TV Guide*, which has, since 1952, chronicled every schedule shift on a weekly basis. In addition, the magazine is a gold mine of opinion on television over its history. Through the late utilization of microfilm, the magazine is now widely available, but its index remains several years in arrears. Barry Cole has produced two collections of *TV Guide* articles, and the twenty-fifth anniversary issue is a handsome addition to the literature.

Three other works are worthy of mention in passing. Paul Michael and Robert Parish have compiled a handy resource, *The Emmy Awards*, that has encyclopedic value. Finally, there is the totally disappointing *International Television Almanac*, now in its thirty-third year. It contains so many omissions that its use is somewhat questionable. For example, in the 1976 edition listing television personalities, Norman Lear was not included. In other sections the failure to be complete erases the value of the volume. Unfortunately, more and more libraries appear to be ordering it under the assumption that it is what it advertises itself to be.

The Center for Cassette Studies in North Hollywood has collected a large selection of taped conversations about the medium, many dating to the early 1960s. Many appear to have been taped from television panel discussions held in New York. There are a growing number of videotapes dealing with the medium and offering extended interviews with makers of television.

The Roper Organization has published *What People Think of Television and Other Mass Media: 1959–1972* and has continued to keep it current. From 1959 to 1974 the percentage of persons considering television performance excellent or good rose from 59 to 71 percent. In 1963 Gary Steiner wrote *The People Look at Television*, a study at the Bureau of Applied Research of Columbia University that makes some interesting data available on the different viewing habits of college and non-college graduates. Ten years later Robert T. Bower wrote *Television and the Public*, an effort to pose the same questions as the Steiner book in order to understand possible shifts in public attitudes. The findings proved inconclusive, offering very little new information.

Variety and the *Hollywood Reporter* contain daily information about the happenings in the entire television industry as well as columns interpreting events. Both are trade papers, and as such tend toward advocacy, but are indispensable for the serious historian of television. The archives of NBC, ABC, and CBS are not open to the public, and there is little information as to the amount of material that has been saved, particularly from the 1950s. Rumors persist that most of the memorable moments from those early days have been lost. The networks have not taken seriously a responsibility to establish a central library and indexing facility. Some of the funds expended by them each year on "research" could well be diverted to such an enterprise as an investment in future study. Since 1968, Vanderbilt University has maintained a complete videotape library of all network news broadcasts. The collection is available for study either in Nashville or, at a nominal charge, through interlibrary loan. The Vanderbilt authorities maintain that no such record exists anywhere else in the world, including the major networks. The collection is maintained by the Vanderbilt Television News Archives. Three archives now exist that are open for research and/or public use: the American Film Institute, the UCLA Archives, and the Museum of Broadcasting in New York. The museum, the brainchild of William Paley, has begun to fill that enormous gap in television research so long ignored by the industry itself.

Arno Press has preserved two excellent collections through reprints. Christopher Sterling, editor of the *Journal of Broadcasting,* is also the editor of the *History of Broadcasting: Radio to Television,* a collection of thirty-two reprint titles including such vintage works as *First Principles of Television* (1932), *The Outlook for Television* (1932), and *Television: A Struggle for Power* (1938). The second series, also edited by Sterling, is entitled *Telecommunications* and contains some interesting early titles on the technology of the medium.

History begins to blend into criticism and analysis in Robert Metz's *CBS: Reflections in a Bloodshot Eye,* David Halberstam's *The Powers That Be,* Sally Bedell's *Up the Tube: Prime-Time TV and the Silverman Years,* Geoffrey Cowan's *See No Evil: The Backstage Battle over Sex and Violence on Television,* Herbert Gans's *Deciding What's News,* Gary Gates's *Air Time: The Inside Story of CBS News,* and William Paley's *As It Happened: A Memoir.* The primary emphasis seems to have been on CBS so far, and comprehensive analysis of the other two networks remains a needed addition to the literature.

Metz presents a congenial, if critical, picture of the CBS network. It is a nicely illustrated book of both events and personalities, centering on William Paley. The narrative flows effectively, with facts about growth, censorship, and programming strewn across the pages in journalistic style with no concern about identification of sources. It is a useful book. Halberstam's is better. To be sure, he concentrates on the news and the profits, but his analysis is more thoughtful, his evidence more convincing. His study of the Murrow days of "See It Now" weaves a far more complex web of personal involvements, resulting in a stunning presentation that is at once fair and vigorously critical. Paley's book is an excellent opportunity to examine one of the two giants of television's birth. The biography by Eugene Lyon of David Sarnoff provides glimpses of Paley's NBC peer.

Among the critical analyses of television, *The TV Establishment* by Gaye Tuchman, *Media Power* by David L. Altheide, *Look Now, Pay Later: The Rise of Network Broadcasting* by Laurence Bergreen, *Telegarbage* by Gregg Lewis, *Four Arguments for the Elimination of Television* by Jerry Mander, *The Cool Fire: How to Make It in Television* by Bob Shanks, *The View from Sunset Boulevard: America as Brought to You by the People Who Make Television* by Ben Stein, and *The Mind Managers* by Herbert I. Schiller are important and offer thoughtful comment.

Writing on the subject of television news has been quite popular for over a decade. Many of these studies have attacked alleged television news bias. Chief among those who have addressed that subject from the conservative perspective have been Edith Efron, *The News Twisters,* Ernest Lefever, *TV and National Defense,* and Joseph Keeley, *The Left-Leaning Antenna. TV Guide* inaugurated "Newswatch" several years ago to offer conservative criticism of the news systems in the networks. When authors of an ultra-liberal point of view take up the pen against network news, the same arguments are turned in the opposite direction. In fact, the evidence supports the contention that moderation is the goal of most news reporting. The highly acclaimed volumes edited by Marvin Barrett, the DuPont-Columbia University Broadcast Journalism series, are extremely helpful as a means of interpreting events as viewed by television. In one essay therein Michael Novak has included some helpful insights on news:

The accusations that the national news is not "objective," has a liberal bias, or a Northeastern bias, are, then, wide of the mark. What really is at stake is that the national news is geared to too high and general a focus. It assumes that there is a national, homogeneous point of view. It does not adequately focus on America's real diversity of soul—a profound diversity of perception and point of view.[8]

An informative, critical study of news and opinion in the networks, *Due to Circumstances Beyond Our Control . . .* by Fred Friendly is a personal vindication of his rupture of relations with CBS in 1966. He followed this in 1976 with *The Good Guys and the First Amendment: Free Speech vs. Fairness in Broadcasting.* Edward Epstein has done a detailed investigation of the news-gathering activities of NBC in *News from Nowhere.* The thesis is that television news is largely controlled by organizational factors. A more satisfying investigation has come from M. L. Stein, author of *Shaping the News.* He points to the many problems that plague reporters and the media in general. A companion volume that should be read in conjunction with the two previously mentioned works is *Power to Persuade* by Robert Cirino. It is a presentation of dozens of case studies relating to decision making and the news. While not restricted to television, it addresses the medium extremely well. Robert MacNeil, a practicing television journalist, has written a highly critical study of television news reporting, *The People Machine*. He concludes with a call for some government control over network news, a risky suggestion in light of his own discussion on presidential access to television in a previous chapter of his book. There is an intriguing effort to forecast the future role of news through examination of past history in Edwin Diamond's *The Tin Kazoo*. One of its chief values lies in the account of the activities of television reporters in the later Nixon years. A few other books on the news are of special interest. A thoroughly engaging, well-documented work, *Media Ethics: In the Newsroom and Beyond,* has recently been issued by Conrad Fink. The same issues respecting ethics were earlier examined by John Hulteng in *The Messenger's Motives*. Ron Powers approaches the problems inherent in making the television news show business in *The Newscasters*.

Documents on news and politics are available from several sources, including many accounts of the Watergate scandal. Two collections from the Nixon years seem particularly useful: Edward Knappman's *Government and the Media in Conflict/1970–74* and a compilation from Arno entitled *The Mass Media and Politics*.

The Aspen Institute has sponsored a series of workshops that have inspired at least three excellent considerations of the news. Paul Weaver and Michael Robinson each contributed an essay to *Television as a Social Force*, edited by Richard Adler and Douglass Cater. Sharon Sperry provided an outstanding chapter "Television News as Narrative," to *Television as a Cultural Force,* edited by Richard Adler. She views news as an extension of the entertainment medium.

Television as a political force has attracted sufficient attention to provide at least a few first-rate works. The classic is Joe McGinniss's *The Selling of the President, 1968*. The author writes from firsthand experience with the Nixon campaign in the fall of 1968 and makes a strong case for the proposition that politicians are being packaged for consumers like soap and toothpaste, and just as effectively. Thomas Patterson and Robert McClure have challenged the effect of television on elections in *The Unseeing Eye*. The book jacket states that the authors will dispute the contention that "television elected John F. Kennedy." In fact the writers do no such thing. They have concentrated on the most unlikely election in many decades—McGovern-Nixon—without any real attention to Watergate-related activities. The book fails to examine either the 1960 or 1968 presidential elections, when most observers believe that television had a marked impact on the outcome. It is unlikely that McGinniss would argue that any amount of neat packaging could have sold McGovern in 1972. In the end, the study cannot carry the weight of its rather pretentious subtitle, *The Myth of Television Power in National Elections.* (Patterson has done a far better job with his later analysis in *The Mass Media Election,* published in 1980.) A more plausible, less polemical work is that of Sig Mickelson, *The Electric Mirror.* It is a thoughtful, well-documented study that poses pertinent questions related to politics in the age of television. For comparison, the book by Jay Blumler and Denis McQuail, *Television in Politics,* offers a thoroughly engrossing look at television in British politics. A much needed area of inquiry was addressed by Newton Minow, John Martin, and Lee Mitchell in *Presidential Television.* Serious problems are identified respecting the power of the president to control television and turn it to his advantage. Specific focus makes for interesting reading in Peter Braestrup's *Big Story,* which details press reporting of Tet in Vietnam. Todd Gitlin sought to examine how the mass media dealt with the new left in *The Whole World is Watching.* The 1980 election has received first-rate coverage from Michael Robinson and Margaret Sheehan in *Over the Wire and on TV.*

Any appreciation of television as a force in the culture cannot afford to eliminate the business side of the industry. While numerous sources already referred to touch upon that aspect, there are some that concentrate directly on the economics of the medium. One of the best and most informative is *Television Economics* by Bruce Owen, Jack Beebe, and Willard Manning, Jr. It is intended to elaborate for the general public the economic theory and policy for television. Another excellent tool is *Broadcast Management: Radio and Television,* edited by James Brown and Ward Quaal. A particularly thorny problem for broadcasters involves government regulations; the Brookings Institution has sponsored a study entitled *Economic Aspects of Television Regulations,* by Roger Noll, Merton Peck, and John McGowan, that is exceptionally well balanced in its treatment of a most difficult subject. A book by Erwin Krasnow and Lawrence Longley that addresses itself to the specific regulations involving the FCC bears the title *The Politics of Broadcast Regulations.* Sydney Head's *Broadcasting in America* is something of a classic in the industry and is thoroughly reliable as a major source of information on the business of broadcasting. Alan Pearce, former staff member of the House Committee on Interstate and Foreign Commerce and the Federal Communications Commission, has written a first-rate analysis, "The Television Networks." Erik Barnouw focuses on advertisers in *The Sponsor,* another fine contribution from the historian. Two recent works on the use of language in advertising are noteworthy: Michael Geis's *The Language of Television Advertising* and Martin Esslin's *The Age of Television.*

There are some other excellent books that attempt to deal with the economic aspects of television within the broader framework of the society. One of the best of these is Les Brown's impressive account, *Television: The Business Behind the Box.* The personal knowledge brought to the book by this veteran journalist adds life and sparkle to the accounts of the rating wars of the 1960s. It is a New York insight into the network operations. While critical, Brown is sympathetic to the problems he addresses. In a similar vein, with a bit more polemic, is Martin Mayer's *About Television,* an engaging inquiry into the entire range of activities that compose the business, along with a well-directed barb or two at the academic critics of the medium. It is good reading. From an author directly involved in television administration, Bob Shanks, has come a how-to book entitled *The Cool Fire.* An instruction manual for anyone interested in pursuing television as a career, it is, as well, a fine primer for anyone wishing to understand the workings of the networks.

As early as 1956 William Y. Elliott was raising significant questions about the medium in a cultural context. He wrote:

More than any other medium of communication, [television is] symbolic in its own development and trends of much that is of basic importance to American culture, and serves more than the movies to reflect that culture—even if the mirror is distorted. Can it serve to educate as well as to entertain? How?[9]

While Elliott's volume, *Television's Impact on American Culture,* has most to do with educational television, the study is suggestive for students of culture. One essay by Eugene Glynn, a psychiatrist, points to most of the issues that were to emerge in the succeeding two decades. He asserted:

Television can produce a people wider in knowledge, more alert and aware of the world, prepared to be much more actively interested in the life of their times. Television can be the great destroyer of provincialism. Television can produce a nation of people who really live in the world, not in just their own hamlets.[10]

More recent critics, such as Michael Novak, or Herbert Gans in *Popular Culture and High Culture,* have challenged this trend as to its desirability in what continues to be a primary debate about the role of television for the future.

Neil Postman, who has a habit of being on the mark before most other observers, published an exciting volume in 1960 titled *Television and the Teaching of English,* in which he wrote:

But beyond the products of "high culture" which television made available, what are the effects on society of the more typical programs, the western, the "private eyes," the family shows, the adventures? Although these programs do not have the same status or high purpose of classic literature, we may discover, in the best of them, a "literature" that may be used in much the same way as traditional forms have been and are used. We may use these programs as pleasant and intelligent entertainments or diversions, as a means of increasing our knowledge of ourselves and other people, as criticisms of the social order, and, perhaps most important of all, as forms which call forth satisfying aesthetic responses.[11]

In a more recent effort, *Amusing Ourselves to Death,* Postman is far less optimistic and sees television nearly as an enemy.

Marshall McLuhan took the center of the stage in the early 1960s with his *Understanding Media.* There he developed his thoughts about television as a "cool" medium, one into which the viewer is drawn as a participant. His emphasis upon the literate quality of Western culture and the consequent revolutionary effects of television upon it won him the distinction of becoming for many the first "seer" of television. There have been many critics of McLuhan since, often offering devastating arguments against his theory. Yet he continues to hover over the television scene. Gerald Stearn edited a "critical symposium" that attempted to analyze him in *McLuhan: Hot and Cold.* Raymond Rosenthal did the same in 1968 in *McLuhan: Pro & Con.* Individual reflections have often been more effective, as in the comments by Brian Groombridge in *Television and the People* and the crisp remarks of Raymond Williams in *Television: Technology and Cultural Form.* Williams notes:

The particular rhetoric of McLuhan's theory of communications is unlikely to last long. But it is significant mainly as an example of an ideological representation of technology as a cause, and in this sense it will have successors, as particular formulations lose their force.[12]

By the mid-1960s Harry Skornia had established himself as a recognized critic of television, quite severe in his judgments. In his *Television and Society,* he struck vigorously against the excessive commercial influences on the medium. He then turned to an agenda for change, including a suggestion that there be created a profession of television broadcasting that would encourage stiff opposition to the largely economic demands of the top executives. In 1966 Patrick D. Hazard edited *TV as Art,* an excellent apologia for television as a work of art.

An important contributor through the years to literate humanistic interpretation of television has been Michael Arlen, both in the *New Yorker* and in several volumes, including *The Living Room War, The View from Highway 1, The Camera Age: Essays on Television,* and *Thirty Seconds.* Arlen gave poignant expression to the common cultic experience of vietnam, and a later book offered some stunning essays on a diversity of topics from Norman Lear to television violence. His final essay on violence includes this observation:

But if anyone truly wishes to lessen violence in this country, it is hard to believe that more than a cosmetic alteration will be produced by censoring gunfights in television entertainment; or even, or especially, by relying on the "higher realism" of the classic American literary imagination.[13]

Perhaps this is the appropriate place to cite those "scientific" contributions that have led to so much debate over the subject of the social impact of violence. Chief among the many television critics concerned with the medium's impact is George Gerbner, director of the Annenberg School of Communications at the University of Pennsylvania. Gerbner is knowledgeable and urbane. He is sincerely convinced of the rightness of his views on the role of television violence and its impact on viewers, a perspective that can be examined in a dozen journal essays. Perhaps the best source for understanding the Gerbner thesis is "Living with Television: The Violence Profile," which appeared in the *Journal of Communications;* its co-author was Larry Gross. Several recent studies have challenged his conclusions; among them see Robert S. Alley, *Television: Ethics for Hire?*

If one is to understand the violence debate, it is imperative that the Surgeon General's Report be examined as well as the five volumes of research data collected by George Comstock, Eli Rubinstein, and John Murray in *Television and Social Behavior.* There are at least three schools of thought on violence, all based upon "scientific" data. A. Bandura, Leo Bogart, and L. Berkowitz are convinced of the deleterious effects of television violence, while Seymour Feshback and Robert Singer argue that violence has a cathartic, favorable effect. Dennis Howitt and G. Cumberbatch, two British researchers, believe that "the effect of mass media violence on attitudes, if anything, is very slight in terms of the adverse influences." Selected works by each of these individuals are found in the bibliography of this chapter. Comstock has sought to find a rational way through the extreme differences expressed by researchers. All of this suggests an important role for the humanities in addressing television as a popular literary form and investigating the content of programming with humanistic tools.

Perhaps as a result of the changing patterns of comedy programming and the admitted significance of television in relation to the war in Southeast Asia and Watergate, practitioners of the humanities began to be concerned about television as a source of popular culture. One of the earliest, and most provocative, studies was that of Horace Newcomb. In 1974 he wrote *TV: The Most Popular Art.* Well versed in American studies and capable of examining the medium's content from a literary and ethical perspective, Newcomb subjected a whole array of television fare to scrutiny. He pioneered in this area, and professionals such as Earl Hamner have expressed admiration for his work. What Newcomb did was to take seriously the television drama and comedy as products of men and women who might quite correctly be described as humanists. He sought to do what Postman had urged over a decade before: see television scripts as art. He, along with academics like David Thorburn of the Massachusetts Institute of Technology, has provided a structure for serious investigation by the humanities of this new art form. Thorburn expressed the sentiments of a growing group of television critics when he wrote:

The aesthetic and human claims of most television melodrama would surely be much weakened, if not completely obliterated, in any other medium, and I have come to believe that the species of melodrama to be found on television today is a unique dramatic form offering an especially persuasive resolution of the contradiction or tension that has been inherent in melodrama since the time of Euripides.[14]

A second volume from Newcomb, a collection of essays entitled *Television: The Critical View*, offers opportunity for the reader to sample some of the better examples of cultural criticism focused on television. Most of the chapters have appeared previously in other formats. Perhaps the best contribution, apart from Newcomb's, is one by John R. Silber, "Television: A Personal View," reprinted from a 1967 publication. Silber describes McLuhan as "surely the funniest stand-up comic in the Western Hemisphere." He calls "Bonanza" "the perfect antidote to 'Father Knows Best' and other idiotic shows." He says of "The Beverly Hillbillies" that it is "a wholesome corrective to Goldwater Republicanism and the pseudo thought of Ayn Rand." And concerning the other popular Westerns of the 1960s, "Wagon Train" is "very good on religion and race," while "Gunsmoke" is a reminder that "it is far easier for a racial bigot to accept enlightenment from Matt Dillon than from Martin Luther King."

Coincident with the work of Newcomb was a series of workshops sponsored by the Aspen Institute for Humanistic Studies and funded in large part by the National Endowment for the Humanities. Resulting from these gatherings were two collections edited by Richard Adler: *Television as a Social Force* (with Douglas Cater) and *Television as a Cultural Force*. Essays in these collections range from examination of news to comedy and drama.

In more recent years several other analyses of television and its structure have appeared, authored by academics and journalists, the best of which are the following: Les Brown, *Keeping Your Eye on Television;* Muriel Cantor, *The Hollywood Television Producer* and *Prime-Time Television: Content and Control;* Gregor Goethals, *The TV Ritual;* Rose Goldsen, *The Show and Tell Machine;* Allan and Linda Kirschner, *Radio and Television: Readings in the Mass Media;* Frank Mankiewicz and Joel Swerdlow, *Remote Control;* David Marc, *Democratic Vistas;* James Monaco, *Media Culture;* John O'Connor, *American History, American Television: Interpreting the Video Past;* Michael Real, *Mass-Mediated Culture;* Brian Rose, *Television and the Performing Arts* and *TV Genres;* and Martin Williams, *TV: The Casual Art.*

Of particular interest to historians of the medium are several collections of essays by television critics, the best of which are Gilbert Seldes, *The*

Great Audience; Tom Shales, *On the Air!;* Bob Shanks, *The Primal Screen;* Robert Shayon, *The Crowd-Catchers, The Eighth Art,* and *Open to Criticism;* and Robert Sklar, *Prime-Time America.*

Two volumes previously noted as being British contributions—Brian Groombridge and Raymond Williams—provide valuable insights about an alternative system and suggest applications for American television. Williams offers a strong case for television content as contrasted with McLuhan.

Inherent in much television criticism has been a note of distance between the medium and the writers. Richard Levinson and William Link, writer/ producers, offer an inside view that reflects a sympathetic understanding in *Stay Tuned* and *Off Camera.* Some of the same empathy may be noted in the Alley/Newcomb volume, *The Producers' Medium,* and in Alley's earlier work, *Television: Ethics for Hire?*

Apart from the massive literature of the social sciences on the effect of television on children, there have been some important efforts to discuss content and effect. William Melody has done a fine service with his study of the economics of children's television. Evelyn Kaye expressed serious concerns in *The Family Guide to Children's Television.* F. Earle Barcus has expanded the vision as a critic of children's television to explore the various components of a child's environment in *Images of Life on Children's Television.* Two works that explore the extant research in the area are *The Early Window* by Liebert, Sprafkin and Davidson, and *Children and Television,* edited by Ray Brown.

In 1981 Joseph Turow offered a content analysis oriented look at children's programming in *Entertainment, Education, and the Hard Sell.* Two years earlier Ellen Wartella edited *Children Communicating,* a look at the cognitive growth of children in relation to viewing. An oversimplified connection between television and children's behavior may lead to unbalanced treatments of an anecdotal type such as Marie Winn's *Plug-In Drug.*

Sesame Street has attracted several good studies including one by Richard Polsky that details the organization of the Children's Television Workshop and Gerald Lesser's personal record in *Children and Television.* Gary Grossman's thoroughly documented history, *Saturday Morning TV,* is a fine tool for research. Peggy Charren, has produced a study, *Changing Channels* (co-authored by Martin Sandler), that provides a particular kind of personal insight by a crusader. Two positive approaches to children's television viewing come from Leland Howe and Bernard Solomon, *How to Raise Children in a TV World,* and Frederick Williams, Robert LaRose, and Frederica Frost, *Children, Television, and Sex-Role Stereotyping.* Concerning Jerome Johnson and James Ettema's book, *Positive Images: Breaking Stereotypes with Children's TV,* Cassata says, "This work may well serve as the model for planned prosocial television programming in the future."[15]

A classic, after thirty years, is the Himmelweit, Oppenheim, and Vince book *Television and the Child*. It details the study of two groups of children in Britain in 1958, one exposed to television, the other denied it. The results pointed to a far less significant effect than many modern observers suggest.

There have been numerous efforts to recount the activities of PBS and its predecessor, National Educational Television. Some of the best work has been done by Wilbur Schramm in *The Financing of Public Television* (co-authored by L. Nelson), *The Impact of Educational Television, The People Look at Educational Television* (co-authored by J. Lyle and I deSola Pool), and *Quality in Instructional Television*. The foundations of PBS are best understood by reading the report of the Carnegie Commission on Educational Television, *Public Television: A Program for Action*. In 1969 Koenig and Hill edited a volume entitled *The Farther Vision* that sought to set an agenda for the future of educational television. In 1980 Sheila Mahoney, Nick DeMartino, and Robert Stengel examined means of supporting public television in the future in *Keeping Pace with the New Television*.

No longer the frontier, some serious study of the current state of cable is in order. Adler and Baer edited *The Electronic Box Office*, and the Sloan Commission published the optimistic *On the Cable: The Television of Abundance*. Rightfully, Monroe Price and John Wicklein demonstrated concern for public involvement in the new arena. Kirsten Beck has posed important questions about the future in *Cultivating the Wasteland: Can Cable Put the Vision Back in TV?*

One area has exploded in the past decade, that of religious television. Little of help has been done to aid understanding of this phenomenon other than in articles in various publications. Jeffrey Hadden's work in cooperation with Charles Swann, *Prime Time Preachers: The Rising Power of Televangelism*, was the first serious attempt to deal with the phenomenon. Peter Horsfeld has addressed the phenomenon as a minister and likewise speculates on the future of religious broadcasting. See also Robert Alley, "The Television Church," in Rose's *TV Genres*. An early warning about the use of television by religious fanatics entitled *The Television-Radio Audience and Religion* was published by Everett Parker, David Barry, and Dallas Smythe in 1955.

Some of the most interesting and able writing on television has been appearing in journals and newspapers over the last forty years. Columns by critics in the *New Yorker*, the *Saturday Review of Literature*, *Playboy*, the *Washington Post*, the *Los Angeles Times*, and the *New York Times* have sparked lively debate during the medium's growth. The journals listed in the bibliography offer added means to explore current commentary on the rapidly changing face of television.

Commercial television continues to falter in its obligation of self-evaluation. This failure of self-criticism has important implications, as a recent editorial in the April 23, 1988, *TV Guide* suggests. Nevertheless, the concerned viewer has more than ample material from which to choose in assessing the past and current condition of what Horace Newcomb has called "the most popular art."

NOTES

1. Nell Eurich, "The Humanities Face Tomorrow," in Alvin Toffler, ed., *Learning for Tomorrow* (New York: Random House, 1974), pp. 150–51.
2. David Halberstam, "The Network and the News and the Power and the Profits," *Atlantic Monthly,* 237 (January 1976), p. 63.
3. David Halberstam, *The Powers That Be* (New York: Alfred A. Knopf, 1979), p. 15.
4. *Report of the National Advisory Commission on Civil Disorders* (New York: New York Times, 1968), p. 373.
5. James Brown and Ward Quaal, *Broadcast Management:Radio and Television* (New York: Hastings House, 1975), p. 440.
6. George Comstock, *The Evidence on Television Violence* (Santa Monica, Calif.: Rand Corporation, 1976), p. 5.
7. John Fiske and John Hartley, *Reading Television* (London: Methuen, 1978), p. 16.
8. Michael Novak, "The People and the News," in Marvin Barrett, ed., *Moment of Truth* (New York: Crowell, 1975), p. 200.
9. William Y. Elliott, *Television's Impact on American Culture* (East Lansing: Michigan State University Press, 1956), p. xvi.
10. Ibid., p. 181.
11. Neil Postman, *Television and the Teaching of English* (New York: Appleton-Century-Crofts, 1961), p. 38.
12. Raymond Williams, *Television: Technology and Cultural Form* (New York: Schocken Books, 1975), p. 128.
13. Michael Arlen, *The View from Highway 1* (New York: Farrar, Straus and Giroux, 1976), p. 293.
14. David Thorburn, "Television Melodrama," in Richard Adler, ed., *Television as a Cultural Force* (New York: Praeger, 1976), p. 87.
15. Mary Cassata and Thomas Skill, *Television: A Guide to the Literature* (Phoenix: Oryx Press, 1985), p. 69.

BIBLIOGRAPHY

Books and Articles

Adler, Richard. *All in the Family: A Critical Appraisal.* New York: Praeger, 1979.
———. *Understanding Television: Essays on Television as a Social and Cultural Force.* New York: Praeger, 1981.
Adler, Richard, ed. *Television as a Cultural Force.* New York: Praeger, 1976.
Adler, Richard, and Walter S. Baer, eds. *The Electronic Box Office: Humanities and Arts on the Cable.* New York: Praeger, 1974.

Adler, Richard, and Douglass Cater, eds. *Television as a Social Force*. New York: Praeger, 1975.

Alley, Robert. *Television: Ethics for Hire?* Nashville: Abingdon Press, 1977.

Alley, Robert, and Horace Newcomb. *The Producer's Medium: Conversations with Creators of American TV*. New York: Oxford University Press, 1983.

Altheide, David L. *Media Power*. Beverly Hills, Calif.: Sage, 1985.

Andrews, Bart. *Lucy & Ricky & Fred & Ethel: The Story of "I Love Lucy."* New York: E. P. Dutton, 1976.

Applebaum, Irwyn. *The World According to Beaver*. New York: Bantam Books, 1984.

Arlen, Michael. *The Camera Age: Essays on Television*. New York: Farrar, Straus and Giroux, 1981.

———. *The Living Room War*. New York: Tower Publications, 1969.

———. *Thirty Seconds*. New York: Farrar, Straus and Giroux, 1980.

———. *The View from Highway 1: Essays on Television*. New York: Farrar, Straus and Giroux, 1976.

Arnaz, Desi. *A Book*. New York: Warner Books, 1976.

Atkin, C. K., J. P. Murray, and O. B. Nayman. *Television and Social Behavior: An Annotated Bibliography of Research Focusing on Television's Impact on Children*. Washington: Government Printing Office, 1972.

Bailey, Robert Lee. *An Examination of Prime Time Network Television Special Programs, 1948–1966*. New York: Arno, 1979.

Bandura, A. *Aggression: A Social Learning Analysis*. Englewood Cliffs, N.J.: Prentice-Hall, 1973.

Barcus, F. Earle. *Images of Life on Children's Television: Sex Roles, Minorities, and Families*. New York: Praeger, 1983.

Barnouw, Erik. *The Image Empire: A History of Broadcasting in the United States from 1953*. New York: Oxford University Press, 1970.

———. *The Sponsor*. New York: Oxford University Press, 1978.

———. *Tube of Plenty: The Evolution of American Television*. New York: Oxford University Press, 1975.

Barrett, Marvin, ed. *The Alfred I. duPont-Columbia University Survey of Broadcast Journalism*. Vol. 1, *Survey of Broadcast Journalism, 1968–1969*. New York: Grosset and Dunlap, 1969; Vol. 2, *Survey of Broadcast Journalism, 1969–1970: Year of Challenge, Year of Crisis*. Grosset and Dunlap, 1970; Vol. 3, *Survey of Broadcast Journalism, 1970–1971: A State of Siege*. New York: Grosset and Dunlap, 1971; Vol. 4, *The Politics of Broadcasting, 1970–1972*. New York: Crowell, 1973; Vol. 5, *Moment of Truth?* New York: Crowell, 1975; Vol. 6, *Rich News, Poor News*. New York: Crowell, 1978; Vol. 7, *The Eye of the Storm*. New York: Lippincott and Crowell, 1980; Vol. 8, *Broadcast Journalism, 1979–1981*. New York: Dodd, Mead, 1982.

Beck, Kirsten. *Cultivating the Wasteland: Can Cable Put the Vision Back in TV?* New York: American Council for the Arts, 1983.

Bedell, Sally. *Up the Tube: Prime-Time TV and the Silverman Years*. New York: Viking, 1981.

Berg, Gertrude. *Molly and Me*. New York: McGraw-Hill, 1961.

Berger, Arthur Asa. *Media Analysis Techniques*. Beverly Hills, Calif.: Sage, 1982.

———. *The TV-Guided American*. New York: Walker, 1976.

Bergreen, Laurence. *Look Now, Pay Later: The Rise of Network Broadcasting*. New York: Doubleday, 1980.

Berkowitz, L. *Aggression: A Social Psychological Analysis*. New York: McGraw-Hill, 1962.

Berle, Milton. *An Autobiography*. New York: Delacorte Press, 1974.

Berman, Ronald. *How Television Sees Its Audience*. Beverly Hills, Calif.: Sage, 1987.

Blair, Frank. *Let's Be Frank About It*. Garden City, N.Y.: Doubleday, 1979.

Bliss, Edward, Jr. *In Search of Light: The Broadcasts of Edward R. Murrow, 1938–1961*. New York: Alfred A. Knopf, 1967.

Bluem, A. William. *Documentary in American Television*. New York: Hastings House, 1965.

Bluem, A. William, and Roger Manvell, eds. *Television: The Creative Experience. A Survey of Anglo-American Progress*. New York: Hastings House, 1967.

Blumler, Jay G., and Denis McQuail. *Television in Politics*. Chicago: University of Chicago Press, 1969.

Bogart, Leo. *The Age of Television*. 3rd ed. New York: Frederick Ungar, 1972.

Bower, Robert T. *Television and the Public*. New York: Holt, Rinehart and Winston, 1973.

Braestrup, Peter. *Big Story: How the American Press and Television Reported and Interpreted the Crisis of Tet in Vietnam and Washington*. Boulder, Colo.: Westview Press, 1977.

Brauer, Ralph. *The Horse, the Gun, and the Piece of Property: Changing Images of the TV Western*. Bowling Green, Ohio: Bowling Green University Popular Press, 1975.

Brooks, Tim. *The Complete Directory to Prime Time TV Stars: 1946-Present*. New York: Ballantine Books, 1987.

Brooks, Tim, and Earl Marsh. *The Complete Directory to Prime Time Network TV Shows: 1946-Present*. 3rd ed. New York: Ballantine Books, 1985.

Brown, James A., and Ward L. Quaal. *Broadcast Management: Radio and Television*. New York: Hastings House, 1975.

Brown, Les. *Keeping Your Eye on Television*. New York: Pilgrim, 1979.

———. *The New York Times Encyclopedia of Television*. New York: Times Books, 1977.

———. *Television: The Business Behind the Box*. New York: Harcourt Brace Jovanovich, 1971.

Brown, Ray, ed. *Children and Television*. Beverly Hills, Calif.: Sage, 1976.

Browne, Ray B., Marshall Fishwick, and Michael T. Marsden. *Heroes of Popular Culture*. Bowling Green, Ohio: Bowling Green University Popular Press, 1972.

Butler, Matilda, and William Paisley. *Women and the Mass Media: Sourcebook for Research and Action*. New York: Human Science Press, 1980.

Cantor, Muriel G. *The Hollywood Television Producer: His Work and His Audience*. New York: Basic Books, 1971.

———. *Prime-Time Television: Content and Control*. Beverly Hills, Calif.: Sage, 1980.

Cantor, Muriel G., and Suzanne Pingree. *The Soap Opera*. Beverly Hills, Calif.: Sage, 1983.

Cassata, Mary, and Thomas Skill. *Life on Daytime Television: Tuning-In American Serial Drama*. Norwood, N.J.: Ablex, 1983.

————. *Television: A Guide to the Literature*. Phoenix: Oryx Press, 1985.

Castleman, Harry, and Walter J. Podrazik. *Watching TV: Four Decades of American Television*. New York: McGraw-Hill, 1982.

Cavett, Dick, and Christopher Porterfield. *Cavett*. New York: Bantam Books, 1975.

Charren, Peggy, and Martin Sandler. *Changing Channels*. Reading, Mass.: Addison-Wesley, 1983.

Cirino, Robert. *Power to Persuade: Mass Media and the News*. New York: Bantam Books, 1974.

Cole, Barry, ed. *Television: A Selection of Readings from TV Guide Magazine*. New York: Free Press, 1970.

————, ed. *Television Today: A Close-Up View, Readings from TV Guide*. New York: Oxford University Press, 1981.

Comstock, George. *Effects of Television on Children: What Is the Evidence?* Santa Monica, Calif.: Rand Corporation, 1975, Paper #P–5412.

————. *The Evidence on Television Violence*. Santa Monica, Calif.: Rand Corporation, 1976, Paper #P–5730.

————. *The Long Range Impact of Television*. Santa Monica, Calif.: Rand Corporation, 1976, Paper #P–5750.

————. *Television and the Teacher*. Santa Monica, Calif.: Rand Corporation, 1976, Paper #P–5734.

————. *Television in America*. Beverly Hills, Calif.: Sage, 1980.

————. *Television and Its Viewers: What Social Science Sees*. Santa Monica, Calif.: Rand Corporation, 1976, Paper #5632.

Comstock, George, Steven Chaffee, Natan Katzman, and Maxwell McCombs, eds. *Television and Human Behavior*. New York: Columbia University Press, 1978.

Comstock, George, and F. G. Christen, eds. *Television and Human Behavior: The Key Studies*. Santa Monica, Calif.: Rand Corporation, 1975.

Comstock, George, and Marilyn Fisher, eds. *Television and Human Behavior: A Guide to the Pertinent Scientific Literature*. Santa Monica, Calif.: Rand Corporation, 1975.

Comstock, George, and George Lindsey, eds. *Television and Human Behavior: The Research Horizon, Future and Present*. Santa Monica, Calif.: Rand Corporation, 1975.

Comstock, George, Eli Rubinstein, and John P. Murray, eds. *Television and Social Behavior: Media Content and Control*. Vol. 1. Washington, D.C.: Government Printing Office, 1972.

————. *Television and Social Behavior: Television and Social Learning*. Vol. 2. Washington, D.C.: Government Printing Office, 1972.

————. *Television and Social Behavior: Television and Adolescent Aggressiveness*. Vol. 3. Washington, D.C.: Government Printing Office, 1972.

————. *Television and Social Behavior: Television in Day-to-Day Life, Patterns of Use*. Vol. 4. Washington, D.C.: Government Printing Office, 1972.

————. *Television and Social Behavior: Television's Effects, Further Explorations*. Vol. 5. Washington, D.C.: Government Printing Office, 1972.

Cowan, Geoffrey. *See No Evil: The Backstage Battle over Sex and Violence on Television*. New York: Simon and Schuster, 1979.

Diamond, Edwin. *The Tin Kazoo: Television, Politics and the News*. Cambridge, Mass.: MIT Press, 1975.

Edmondson, Madeleine, and David Rounds. *The Soaps: Daytime Serials of Radio and TV.* New York: Stein and Day, 1973.

Efron, Edith. *The News Twisters.* Los Angeles: Nash, 1971.

Eisner, Joel, and David Krinsky. *Television Comedy Series: An Episodic Guide to 153 TV Sit-Coms in Syndication.* Jefferson, N.C.: McFarland, 1984.

Elliott, P. *The Making of a Television Series: A Case Study in the Sociology of Culture.* New York: Hastings House, 1973.

Elliott, William Y. *Television's Impact on American Culture.* East Lansing: Michigan State University Press, 1956.

Epstein, Edward Jay. *News from Nowhere: Television and the News.* New York: Random House, 1973.

Esslin, Martin. *The Age of Television.* San Francisco: W. H. Freeman, 1982.

Feshbach, Seymour, and Robert Singer. *Television and Aggression.* San Francisco: Jossey-Bass, 1971.

Feuer, Jane, Paul Kerr, and Tise Vahimagi, eds. *MTM "Quality Television."* London: BFI Books, 1984.

Fink, Conrad C. *Media Ethics: In the Newsroom and Beyond.* New York: McGraw-Hill, 1988.

Fireman, Judy, ed. *TV Book: The Ultimate Television Book.* New York: Workman, 1977.

Fiske, John, and John Hartley. *Reading Television.* London: Methuen, 1978.

Foley, Karen Sue. *The Political Blacklist in the Broadcast Industry: The Decade of the 1950's.* New York: Arno, 1979.

Friendly, Fred W. *Due to Circumstances Beyond Our Control . . . .* New York: Random House, 1968.

———. *The Good Guys, the Bad Guys and the First Amendment: Free Speech vs. Fairness in Broadcasting.* New York: Random House, 1976.

Gans, Herbert J. *Deciding What's News.* New York: Pantheon, 1979.

———. *Popular Culture and High Culture: An Analysis and Evaluation of Taste.* New York: Basic Books, 1974.

Gates, Gary Paul. *Air Time: The Inside Story of CBS News.* New York: Harper and Row, 1978.

Geis, Michael L. *The Language of Television Advertising.* New York: Academic Press, 1982.

Gerbner, George, and Larry Gross. "Living with Television: The Violence Profile." *Journal of Communications,* 26 (Spring 1976), 172–99.

Gianokos, Larry James. *Television Drama Series Programming: A Comprehensive Chronicle, 1947–1959.* Metuchen, N.J.: Scarecrow Press, 1980.

———. *Television Drama Series Programming: A Comprehensive Chronicle, 1959–1975.* Metuchen, N.J.: Scarecrow Press, 1978.

———. *Television Drama Series Programming: A Comprehensive Chronicle, 1975–1980.* Metuchen, N.J.: Scarecrow Press, 1981.

———. *Television Drama Series Programming: A Comprehensive Chronicle, 1980–1982.* Metuchen, N.J.: Scarecrow Press, 1983.

Gitlin, Todd. *The Whole World Is Watching: Mass Media in the Making and Unmaking of the New Left.* Berkeley: University of California Press, 1980.

Glut, Donald F., and Jim Harmon. *The Great Television Heroes.* New York: Doubleday, 1975.

Goethals, Gregor. *The TV Ritual*. Boston: Beacon, 1981.

Goldsen, Rose K. *The Show and Tell Machine: How Television Works and Works You Over*. New York: Delta Books, 1977.

Gordon, Thomas F., and Mary Ellen Verna. *Mass Communication Effects and Processes: A Comprehensive Bibliography, 1950–1975*. Beverly Hills, Calif.: Sage, 1978.

Greenfield, Jeff. *Television: The First Fifty Years*. New York: Harry N. Abrams, 1977.

Groombridge, Brian. *Television and the People: A Programme for Democratic Participation*. New York: Penguin Books, 1972.

Grossman, Gary H. *Saturday Morning TV*. New York: Dell, 1981.

Hadden, Jeffrey, and Charles E. Swann. *Prime Time Preachers: The Rising Power of Televangelism*. Reading, Mass.: Addison-Wesley, 1981.

Halberstam, David. *The Powers That Be*. New York: Alfred A. Knopf, 1979.

Hammel, W. M., ed. *The Popular Arts in America: A Reader*. New York: Harcourt Brace Jovanovich, 1972.

Hammond, Charles M. *The Image Decade: Television Documentary 1965–1975*. New York: Hastings House, 1981.

Harris, Jay S., ed. *TV Guide: The First 25 Years*. New York: Simon and Schuster, 1978.

Haselden, Kyle. *Morality and the Mass Media*. Nashville: Broadman, 1968.

Hazard, Patrick D., ed. *TV as Art: Some Essays in Criticism*. Champaign, Ill.: National Council of Teachers of English, 1966.

Head, Sydney. *Broadcasting in America: A Survey of Television and Radio*. 2nd ed. Boston: Houghton Mifflin, 1972.

Hess, Gary Newton. *An Historical Study of the DuMont Television Network*. New York: Arno, 1979.

Himmelweit, Hilde T., A. N. Oppenheim, and Pamela Vince. *Television and the Child: An Empirical Study of the Effect of Television on the Young*. London: Oxford University Press, 1958.

Horsfeld, Peter. *Religious Television: The Experience in America*. New York: Longman, 1984.

Howe, Leland W., and Bernard Solomon. *How to Raise Children in a TV World*. New York: Hart, 1979.

Howitt, Dennis. *The Mass Media and Social Problems*. Elmsford, N.Y.: Pergamon Press, 1982.

———. "Television and Aggression: A Counterargument." *American Psychologist*, 27 (October 1972), 969–70.

Howitt, Dennis, and G. Cumberbatch. *Mass Media Violence and Society*. New York: Wiley, 1975.

Hulteng, John L. *The Messenger's Motives . . . Ethical Problems of the News Media*. Englewood Cliffs, N.J.: Prentice-Hall, 1976.

The International Television Almanac. New York: Quigley, 1955-.

Jackson, Anthony W. *Black Families and the Medium of Television*. Ann Arbor: Bush Program in Child Development, University of Michigan, 1982.

Johnson, Jerome, and James Ettema. *Positive Images: Breaking Stereotypes with Children's TV*. Beverly Hills, Calif.: Sage, 1982.

Johnson, Nicholas. *How to Talk Back to Your Television Set*. New York: Bantam Books, 1970.

Kalisch, Phillip, Beatrice J. Kalisch, and Margaret Scobey. *Images of Nurses on Television*. New York: Springer, 1983.

Kaye, Evelyn. *The Family Guide to Children's Television: What to Watch, What to Miss, What to Change and How to Do it*. New York: Pantheon, 1974.

Keeley, Joseph. *The Left-Leaning Antenna: Political Bias in Television*. New Rochelle, N.Y.: Arlington House, 1971.

Kelly, Richard. *The Andy Griffith Show*. Winston-Salem, N.C.: John F. Blair, 1981.

Kendrick, Alexander. *Prime Time: The Life of Edward R. Murrow*. Boston: Little, Brown, 1969.

Kirkley, Donald H. *A Descriptive Study of the Network Television Western During the Seasons 1955–56–1962–63*. New York: Arno, 1979.

Kirschner, Allen, and Linda Kirschner. *Radio and Television: Readings in the Mass Media*. Indianapolis: Bobbs-Merrill, 1978.

Knappman, Edward W., ed. *Government and the Media in Conflict/1970–74*. New York: Facts on File, 1974.

Koenig, Allen E., and Ruane B. Hill, eds. *The Farther Vision: Educational Television Today*. Madison: University of Wisconsin Press, 1969.

Krasnow, Erwin G., and Lawrence D. Longley. *The Politics of Broadcast Regulation*. New York: St. Martin's Press, 1973.

LaGuardia, Robert. *Soap World*. New York: Arbor House, 1983.

Larka, Robert. *Television's Private Eye: An Examination of Twenty Years of Programming of a Particular Genre, 1949–1969*. New York: Arno, 1979.

Learning While They Laugh: Studies of Five Children's Programs on the CBS Television Network. New York: CBS Broadcast Group, 1976.

Lee, Robert E. *Television: The Revolution*. New York: Essential Books, 1944.

Lefever, Ernst. *TV and National Defense: An Analysis of CBS News, 1972–1973*. Boston, Va.: Institute for American Strategy Press, 1974.

Lesser, Gerald S. *Children and Television: Lessons from Sesame Street*. New York: Random House, 1974.

Levinson, Richard, and William Link. *Off Camera: Conversations with the Makers of Prime-Time Television*. New York: New American Library, 1986.

———. *Stay Tuned: An Inside Look at the Making of Prime-Time Television*. New York: St. Martin's Press, 1981.

Lewis, Gregg A. *Telegarbage*. Nashville: Thomas Nelson, 1977.

Lichty, Laurence W., and Malachi Topping. *American Broadcasting: A Source Book on the History of Radio and Television*. New York: Hastings House, 1975.

Liebert, Robert M., Joyce Sprafkin, and Emily Davidson. *The Early Window: Effects of Television on Children and Youth*. Elmsford, N.Y.: Pergamon Press, 1982.

Lyon, Eugene. *David Sarnoff*. New York: Harper and Row, 1966.

McCarthy, John, and Brian Kelleher. *Alfred Hitchcock Presents*. New York: St. Martin's Press, 1985.

McCrohan, Donna. *The Honeymooners' Companion: The Kramdens and the Nortons Revisited*. New York: Workman, 1978.

MacDonald, J. Fred. *Blacks and White TV: Afro-Americans in Television Since 1948*. Chicago: Nelson Hall, 1979.

———. *Television and the Red Menace*. New York: Praeger, 1985.

McGinniss, Joe. *The Selling of the President, 1968*. New York: Pocket Books, 1970.

McLuhan, Marshall. *Understanding Media: The Extensions of Man*. New York: McGraw-Hill, 1964.

McNeil, Alexander. *Total Television: A Comprehensive Guide to Programming from 1948–1980*. New York: Penguin Books, 1980.

MacNeil, Robert. *The People Machine: The Influence of Television on American Politics*. New York: Harper and Row, 1968.

Mahoney, Sheila, Nick DeMartino, and Robert Stengel. *Keeping Pace with the New Television: Public Television and Changing Technology*. New York: VNU Books, 1980.

Mander, Jerry. *Four Arguments for the Elimination of Television*. New York: William Morrow, 1978.

Mankiewicz, Frank, and Joel Swerdlow. *Remote Control: Television and the Manipulation of American Life*. New York: Times Books, 1978.

Marc, David. *Democratic Vistas: Television in American Culture*. Philadelphia: University of Pennsylvania Press, 1984.

Marsh, Spencer. *God, Man, and Archie Bunker*. New York: Harper and Row, 1975.

Marx, Herbert L., Jr., ed. *Television and Radio in American Life*. New York: H. W. Wilson, 1953.

Mass Communication Review Yearbook. Beverly Hills, Calif.: Sage, 1980-.

The Mass Media and Politics. New York: New York Times/Arno, 1972.

Mayer, Martin. *About Television*. New York: Harper and Row, 1972.

Meehan, Diana M. *Ladies of the Evening: Women Characters of Prime-Time Television*. Metuchen, N.J.: Scarecrow Press, 1983.

Melody, William. *Children's Television: The Economics of Exploitation*. New Haven: Yale University Press, 1973.

Metz, Robert. *CBS: Reflections in a Bloodshot Eye*. Chicago: Playboy Press, 1975.

———. *The Today Show*. Chicago: Playboy Press, 1977.

Michael, Paul, and Robert Parish. *The Emmy Awards: A Pictorial History*. New York: Crown, 1971.

Mickelson, Sig. *The Electric Mirror: Politics in an Age of Television*. New York: Dodd, Mead, 1972.

Miller, Merle, and Evan Rhodes. *Only You Dick Darling! or How to Write One Television Script and Make $50,000,000, a True-Life Adventure*. New York: William Sloan, 1964.

Miller, Randall N. *Ethnic Images in American Film and Television*. Philadelphia: Balch Institute, 1978.

Minow, Newton N., John Bartlow Martin, and Lee M. Mitchell. *Presidential Television*. New York: Basic Books, 1973.

Mitchell, Curtis. *Cavalcade of Broadcasting*. Chicago: Follett, 1970.

Mitz, Rick. *The Great TV Sitcom Book*. New York: Richard Marek, 1980.

Monaco, James. *Media Culture*. New York: Delta Books, 1978.

Newcomb, Horace. *TV: The Most Popular Art*. New York: Doubleday, 1974.

———, ed. *Television: The Critical View*. 4th ed. New York: Oxford University Press 1988.

Noll, Roger G., Merton J. Peck, and John J. McGowan. *Economic Aspects of Television Regulation*. Washington, D.C.: Brookings Institution, 1973.

O'Connor, John E., ed. *American History, American Television: Interpreting the Video Past*. New York: Frederick Ungar, 1983.

Owen, Bruce M., Jack H. Beebe, and Willard G. Manning, Jr. *Television Economics.* Lexington, Mass.: D.C. Heath, 1974.

Paley, William S. *As It Happened: A Memoir.* Garden City, N.Y.: Doubleday, 1979.

Parish, James Robert. *Actors' Television Credits: 1950–1972.* Metuchen, N.J.: Scarecrow Press, 1973.

Parish James Robert, with Vincent Terrace. *Actors' Television Credits: Supplement II.* Metuchen, N.J.: Scarecrow Press, 1982.

Parish, James Robert, with Mark Trost. *Actor's Television Credits: Supplement I.* Metuchen, N.J.: Scarecrow Press, 1978.

Parker, Everrett C., David W. Barry, and Dallas W. Smythe. *The Television-Radio Audience and Religion.* New York: Harper Brothers, 1955.

Patterson, Thomas. *The Mass Media Election: How Americans Choose Their President.* New York: Praeger, 1980.

Patterson, Thomas, and Robert D. McClure. *The Unseeing Eye: The Myth of Television Power in National Elections.* New York: Putnam's, 1976.

Pearce, Alan. "The Television Networks." Paper presented at the National Conference of Black Lawyers Convention, Washington, D.C., 1975.

Perry, Jeb. *Universal Television: The Studio and Its Programs, 1950–1980.* Metuchen, N.J.: Scarecrow press, 1983.

Polsky, Richard M. *Getting to Sesame Street: The Origins of the Children's Television Workshop.* New York: Praeger, 1974.

Portrayal of Women in Programming. Toronto: Canadian Broadcasting Corp., 1984.

Post, Joyce A. *TV Guide 25 Year Index, 1953–1977: By Author and Subject.* Radnor, Pa.: Triangle Publications, 1979.

Postman, Neil. *Amusing Ourselves to Death.* New York: Viking, 1985.

———. *Television and the Teaching of English.* New York: Appleton-Century-Crofts, 1961.

Powers, Ron. *The Newscasters.* New York: St. Martin's Press, 1978.

Price, Monroe E., and John Wicklein. *Cable Television: A Guide for Citizen Action.* Philadelphia: Pilgrim Press, 1972.

Public Television: A Program for Action. Report of the Carnegie Commission on Educational Television. New York: Bantam Books, 1967.

Rather, Dan, with Mickey Herskowitz. *The Camera Never Blinks: Adventures of a TV Journalist.* New York: William Morrow, 1977.

Real, Michael R. *Mass-Mediated Culture.* Englewood Cliffs, N.J.: Prentice-Hall, 1977.

Red Channels: The Report of Communist Influence in Radio and Television. N.p., 1950.

Rissover, F., and D. C. Birch, eds. *Mass Media and the Popular Arts.* New York: McGraw-Hill, 1971.

Robinson, Michael J., and Margaret Sheehan. *Over the Wire and on TV: CBS and UPI in Campaign '80.* New York: Russell Sage Foundation, 1983.

The Roper Organization. *What People Think of Television and Other Mass Media: 1959–1972.* New York: Television Information Office, 1973.

Rose, Brian. *Television and the Performing Arts.* Westport, Conn.: Greenwood Press, 1986.

———, ed. *TV Genres: A Handbook and Reference Guide.* Westport, Conn.: Greenwood Press, 1985.

Rosenthal, Raymond, ed. *McLuhan: Pro and Con*. New York: Funk and Wagnalls, 1968.

Rovin, Jeff. *The Great Television Series*. New York: A. S. Barnes, 1977.

Scheuer, Steven H., ed. *The Television Annual, 1978–79: A Complete Record of American Television from June 1, 1978 Through May 31, 1979*. New York: Macmillan, 1979.

Schiller, Herbert I. *The Mind Managers*. Boston: Beacon Press, 1973.

Schorr, Daniel. *Clearing the Air*. Boston: Houghton Mifflin, 1977.

Schramm, Wilbur. *The Impact of Educational Television*. Urbana: University of Illinois Press, 1960.

———, ed. *Quality in Instructional Television*. Honolulu: University of Hawaii Press, 1973.

Schramm, Wilbur, J. Lyle, and I. deSola Pool. *The People Look at Educational Television*. Stanford: Stanford University Press, 1963.

Schramm, Wilbur, and L. Nelson. *The Financing of Public Television*. Palo Alto, Calif.: Aspen institute, 1972.

Seldes, Gilbert V. *The Great Audience*. New York: Viking, 1950.

Sennett, Ted. *Your Show of Shows*. New York: Macmillan, 1977.

Settel, Irving, and William Laas. *A Pictorial History of Television*. New York: Grosset and Dunlap, 1969.

Shales, Tom. *On the Air!* New York: Summit Books, 1982.

Shanks, Bob. *The Cool Fire: How to Make It in Television*. New York: W. W. Norton, 1976.

———. *The Primal Screen*. New York: W. W. Norton, 1986.

Shayon, Robert Lewis. *The Crowd-Catchers*. New York: Saturday Review Press, 1973.

———. *Open to Criticism*. Boston: Beacon Press, 1971.

———, ed. *The Eighth Art*. New York: Holt, Rinehart and Winston, 1962.

Shulman, Arthur, and Roger Youman. *How Sweet It Was. Television: A Pictorial Commentary*. New York: Bonanza Books, 1966.

———. *The Television Years*. New York: Popular Library, 1973.

Singer, Dorothy G., Jerome L. Singer, and Diana M. Zuckerman. *Teaching Television*. New York: Dial Press, 1981.

Sklar, Robert. *Prime-Time America: Life on and Behind the Television Screen*. New York: Oxford University Press, 1980.

Skornia, Harry J. *Television and Society: An Inquest and Agenda for Improvement*. New York: McGraw-Hill, 1965.

Sloan Commission on Cable Communications. *On the Cable: The Television of Abundance*. New York: McGraw-Hill, 1971.

Soares, Manuela. *The Soap Opera Book*. New York: Harmony Books, 1978.

Stearn, Gerald. *McLuhan: Hot and Cold*. New York: Dial Press, 1967.

Stein, Ben. *The View from Sunset Boulevard: America as Brought to You by the People Who Make Television*. New York: Basic Books, 1979.

Stein, M. L. *Shaping the News: How The Media Function in Today's World*. New York: Washington Square Press, 1974.

Steiner, Gary A. *The People Look at Television*. New York: Alfred A. Knopf, 1963.

Sterling, Christopher, ed. *Broadcasting and Mass Media: A Survey Bibliography*. Philadelphia: Temple University Press, 1974.

————. ed. *The History of Broadcasting: Radio to Television*. Reprint of 32 vols. New York: New York Times/Arno, 1972.

————, ed. *Telecommunications*. Reprint of 34 books. New York: New York Times/Arno Press, 1974.

Sterling, Christopher, and Timothy R. Haight. *The Mass Media: Aspen Institute Guide to Communication Industry Trends*. New York: Praeger, 1978.

Sterling, Christopher, and John M. Kitross. *Stay Tuned: A Concise History of American Broadcasting*. Belmont, Calif.: Wadsworth 1978.

Television and Growing Up: The Impact of Televised Violence. Report to the Surgeon General. Washington, D. C.: Government Printing Office, 1972.

Terrace, Vincent. *The Complete Encyclopedia of Television Programs: 1947–1979*. 2nd ed. New York: A. S. Barnes, 1980.

Tuchman, Gaye, ed. *The TV Establishment: Programming for Power and Profit*. Englewood Cliffs, N.J.: Prentice-Hall, 1974.

Tuchman, Gaye, Arlene Kaplan, and James Benet. *Hearth and Home: Images of Women in the Mass Media*. New York: Oxford University Press, 1978.

Turow, Joseph. *Entertainment, Education, and the Hard Sell: Three Decades of Network Children's Television*. New York: Praeger, 1981.

Udelson, Joseph H. *The Great Television Race: A History of the American Television Industry, 1925–1941*. University, Ala: University of Alabama Press, 1982.

Waldron, Vince. *Classic Sitcoms*. New York: Macmillan, 1988.

Wartella, Ellen, ed. *Children Communicating: Media and Development of Thought, Speech, Understanding*. Beverly Hills, Calif.: Sage, 1979.

Webb, Jack. *The Badge*. Englewood Cliffs, N.J.: Prentice-Hall, 1958.

Weissman, Ginny, and Coyne Steven Sanders. *The Dick Van Dyke Show: Anatomy of a Classic*. New York: St. Martin's Press, 1983.

White, David M., and Richard Averson, eds. *Sound and Society: Motion Pictures and Television in America*. Boston: Beacon Press, 1968.

Whitfield, Stephen, and Gene Roddenberry. *The Making of Star Trek*. New York: Ballantine Books, 1968.

Wilk, Max. *The Golden Age of Television: Notes from the Survivors*. New York: Delacorte Press, 1976.

Williams, Frederick, Robert LaRose, and Frederica Frost. *Children, Television, and Sex-Role Stereotyping*. New York: Praeger, 1981.

Williams, Martin. *TV: The Casual Art*. New York: Oxford University Press, 1982.

Williams, Raymond. *Television: Technology and Cultural Form*. New York: Schocken Books, 1975.

Winn, Marie. *The Plug-In Drug*. New York: Viking, 1977.

Zettl, Herbert. *Sight, Sound, Motion: Applied Media Aesthetics*. Belmont, Calif.: Wadsworth, 1973.

Periodicals

access. Washington, D.C., 1969-.

American Film: Journal of the Film and Television Arts. Washington, D.C., 1975–.

Arts in Context. New York, 1974–.

Broadcasting: The Businessweekly of Television and Radio. Washington, D.C., 1931–.

The Caucus Quarterly. Los Angeles: Caucus for Producers, Writers and Directors, 1983–.

Channels: The Business of Communications. New York, 1980–.

Columbia Journalism Review. New York, 1962–.

Critical Studies in Mass Communication. Annandale, Va.: Speech Communication Association, 1984–.

EMMY. Los Angeles: Television Academy of Arts and Sciences, 1978–.

The Hollywood Reporter. Los Angeles, 1930–.

Journalism Quarterly. Minneapolis, 1924–.

Journal of Broadcasting. Philadelphia, 1956–.

Journal of Communications. Philadelphia, 1951–.

Journal of Popular Culture. Bowling Green, Ohio, 1967–.

Los Angeles Times. Los Angeles, 1881–.

New Yorker. New York, 1925–.

New York Times. New York, 1851–.

Playboy. Chicago, 1953–.

Public Opinion Quarterly. New York, 1937–.

Saturday Review. New York, 1924–84.

Television Quarterly: The Journal of the National Academy of Television Arts and Sciences. Beverly Hills, Calif., 1963–78, and sporadically thereafter.

TV Guide. Radnor, Pa., 1953–.

Variety. New York, 1905–.

Washington Post. Washington, D.C., 1877–.

Trains and Railroading

ARTHUR H. MILLER, JR.

For the eminent historian and former Librarian of Congress, Daniel Boorstin, the "Age of the Railroad is perhaps the most romantic" in the history of American life.[1] This romance is best found in Lucius Beebe's books, which appeared from the 1930s to the 1960s. In introducing his first rail book, *High Iron,* in 1938, Beebe sounded his clarion call: "The most herioc of American legends is the chronicle of Railroading."[2] Its epic scale and its relation to the national destiny is further recognized by B. A. Botkin in his introduction to *A Treasury of Railroad Folklore:* "The impact of the railroad on the American imagination has been greater than that of any other industry."[3] In the 1950s Barton K. Davis observed that model railroading alone was the "absorbing interest of more than 100,000 Americans."[4] In the 1980s railroad enthusiasts have provided the focus for their own micro-industry: publishers of magazines and books, museums and preserved short lines, memorabilia, modeling, and associations and clubs across the country. Trains and railroading have a long history and a vital present and future in American popular culture.

A first step in understanding railroading in the context of popular culture comes in attempting to describe the range of interest of railfans, dedicated railroad hobbyists, in the words of Paul B. Cors, whose 1975 *Railroads* is the standard reference bibliography on the topic. According to Cors, railfans (mostly male) resemble one another little except in their "fascination with and devotion to railroading."[5] Two common characteristics seem to be railfans' tendency to be both photographers and book collectors. Beyond these traits, railfan interests tend to be specialized and partisan. A railroad buff may concentrate on steam or diesel locomotives, on traction (electric railroad and rapid transit) or narrow-gauge railroads, on short lines, on a particular railroad company, on railroad general history and literature, on cars, on stations, on models, on live steam (except scale engines run by real steam and large enough to ride upon), or on collecting toy trains, railroad art, and railroad memorabilia. A list based on recent memorabilia advertisements gives a sense of the range of collectables: timetables, cap and hat badges, stocks and bonds, passes and tickets, engine plates, calendars, dining car china and silverware, lanterns and lamps, posters and signs, brass whistles, annual and trip passes, engine builder's plates, telegraph instruments, depot phones, keys and locks, and pocket watches. In addition, Paul Cors's reference guide lists six pages of publishers who specialize in books for railfans or else cater to them significantly. Pictures, too, are collected, most often of locomotives and in all formats—from postcards and slides to glass negatives, stereopticon views, and steel engravings. Ephemeral material, preferably illustrated, is highly sought: manufacturer's catalogs, travel brochures, name-train folders, and the like. The railfan's most valued pictures or ephemera will record personal experiences, such as snapshots of out-of-the-way and/or endangered lines or handouts from rail museums visited. Enthusiasts endeavor to visit and then ride (or, if too late, walk over) new railroads. These may range from mainline railroads to the most obscure interurban line. In sum, railfan interest is specialized, passionate, cumulative, and oriented toward travel and printed material.

But the railfan phenomenon is only the central core of popular interest in trains and railroading. As Daniel Boorstin has observed and as the very popular Beebe demonstrated, the romance of railroading appeals to a much wider audience—the general public—which is drawn by nostalgia. An example here is a magnificent coffee-table book called *Decade of the Trains: The 1940s,* by Don Ball, Jr., and Rogers E. M. Whitaker ("E. M. Frimbo"). In the preface Ball draws a clear connection between life in the late 1970s and that three decades earlier:

I hope this book captures the spirit of railroading in the forties and also the unique character . . . of America during the war and the rest of the decade. During the 1940s, America "worked." It seemed to be an era of good times and almost innocent merriment-even with the dark and terrible war.[6]

According to the jacket, here "the reader becomes an eyewitness. This trip *is* necessary—for everyone who remembers the war years and [of course] for every railroad fan." This nostalgia for a simpler era and for the values of the era—innocence, for example—provides the bridge from railfans' special passions to more general currents of popular interest.

There has been considerable academic and professional interest in the literature of railroading. For the railfan this is delightfully specialized and detailed. Historical material (primary and secondary), company literature, government reports and surveys, technical manuals, and investment information all reach the hobbyist or popular perception at some point.

Important background, too, for viewing America's romance with railroading is the awareness that this is part of an international phenomenon. Particularly in Britain the literature on the subject is well developed and the level of interest intense. Railroads (or railways) began there, first captured the popular imagination there, and first experienced significant abandonment, nostalgia, and comprehensive railfan activity. Thus British popular interest in railroading has provided a context for the development and continuation of Americans' preoccupation with their rail heritage.

HISTORIC OUTLINE

"Historically," according to Archie Robertson, "the railfan is at least as old as railroads." In his *Slow Train to Yesterday* Robertson provides a charming look at the railfan phenomenon:

The Charleston & Hamburg, . . . earliest American railroad, ran its first trains for enthusiasts who just couldn't wait for the public opening. Before the Civil War the B&O ran excursions for camera fans from Washington to Harper's Ferry. . . . Fan trips were commonplace throughout the nineteenth century although no one called them that.[7]

The history of American railroading cannot, indeed, be separated from the public enthusiasm for rail travel or for the advancement and progress of the railroad industry. In the 1820s the railroad had taken hold in England, and by Christmas 1830 the first scheduled steam-railroad train run in America took place on the Charleston & Hamburg, carrying 141 passengers. The engine, the "Best Friend of Charleston," was the first commercially built U.S. locomotive. The expansion westward from the coast in the early nineteenth century led to rapid deployment of the railroad, at first in what might seem like unusual locations. The new technology captured the imagination and backing first of southerners, whose seaports were suffering as the water routes further north—particularly the Erie Canal—drew trade to New York and the Northeast. Laying track to the interior offered a new chance for ports such as Charleston and Baltimore to compete. Boston, too, coveted New York's success and in the early 1830s wisely decided to build not more canals but railroads. The nation's first Railway Exhibit was in Boston in 1827, to which enthusiastic crowds paid admission to view the display of English locomotives.

By the 1850s the rail system reached to the Mississippi, as the various coastal establishments tied themselves to Western settlements. Already the call for Manifest Destiny was to be heard, to build a railroad to the Pacific.

Sectional rivalry, at first, was a stimulus to discussion: should the transcontinental line go across from a more northerly or southerly route, building from slave states or free? In the end the struggle's intensity was so great that it served to delay the transcontinental route until after the Civil War. The North's by then superior rail system contributed significantly to the preservation of the Union, and railroading today forms a key subgrouping of Civil War buff interest. As a result, in the 1950s the "Great Locomotive Chase" was a popular story and film topic. But before this climactic encounter western cities had hosted railroad conventions to crystallize interest in a line—west from Memphis, St. Louis, or Chicago. As with the earlier Boston exhibition, these special events reflected and served to stimulate popular interest and support. Throughout the century the opening of new lines, anniversaries, and the great fairs of 1876 and 1893 were occasions for celebrating the progress, both geographical and technical, of the railroads.

After the Civil War forces were mobilized quickly, thanks to government incentives, creative management and engineering, and no little corruption, to forge the link to the Pacific. In 1869 the Union Pacific and the Central Pacific met at Promontory Point, Utah, ending the "Great Race." This epic feat was followed in rapid order by the completion of other lines to the north and south. By the end of the century the West was covered by a complete (often redundant) rail network, the Indians had been subdued, and the frontier (according to Frederick Jackson Turner) was closed.

From the end of the war to the closing of the frontier popular interest in the railroads was at a peak. The mighty task of crossing the continent was great by every measure: the profits, the speed at which track could be laid, the iniquity of life on the work gangs ("Hell on Wheels" and boom towns), the tall tales, the personalities (General Dodge, Jack Casement, and Charles Crocker), and the celebrations. In the years that immediately followed, easterners and travelers from abroad made the trip across the plains and the mountains to San Francisco from Council Bluffs, Iowa, through prairie dog villages, mountain gorges, Indian lands, and deserts. Their accounts and the pictures by the illustrators and photographers who went along were printed and widely distributed, testifying to the railroad's popular appeal.

By the end of this period the railroads had begun to reach beyond opening new possibilities for Americans and immigrants. By the close of the century railroad domination had become a major issue, particularly in the transMississippi West. Popular support waned as reports of scandals such as the Credit Mobilier matter, which concerned Union Pacific corruption, reached the public. Land prices, freight rates, and the continuing stock manipulations of what popularly became known as the "robber baron" period turned first the western farmers and later a majority of the public against railroad excesses. The Granger movement reflected the farmers' attempt to organize against the power of the railroads. And train robbers appeared as Robin Hoods in the popular imagination, dime novels, and the mass press. The spectacular exploits of Christopher Evans and John Sontag in the San Joaquin Valley of California are reflected in Frank Norris's ambitious novel of 1901, *The Octopus*. In general, *The Octopus* best characterizes the popular perception of the western railroads at the end of the nineteenth century: greed, corruption, impersonality, manipulation, and oppression.

Interestingly, "the best scholarship of late suggests" that the notion of a "'robber baron' period" is "dead wrong," according to railroad historian H. Roger Grant.[8] An example of the kind of detailed research on which this new perspective is based is Maury Klein's 1986 *The Life and Legend of Jay Gould*. Klein's book is as much a study of the popular image of "the most hated man in America" as it is a story of one man's life.[9] An industrialization swept across the land, "Gould was not only part of this revolution, but one of its prime movers."[10] Not only successful, but bluntly honest in an era still rooted in earlier conventions, Gould offended many. In a time of transition this mighty, visible harbinger of a new order was reviled by a public mind still rooted in a simpler age and susceptible to the influence of a hostile press.

The railfan disappeared after the first blush of transcontinental travel. Archie Robertson reports that his return is first noted some half-century later, by the *Railway Age* in 1927.[11] By the late 1920s automobiles were no longer a novelty, and trains had gained the dignity of age and tradition and, says Robertson, "the sympathy which belongs to the underdog." This respected position has prevailed through much of the last half-century. Cors observes that "in the thirties . . . the rail hobbyist came into his own," with 1938 being a watershed year: the "first real railfan book," *Along the Iron Trail* by Frederick Richardson and F. Nelson Blount, appeared, along with Lucius Beebe's first rail book, *High Iron*. *Railroad Magazine* now served the railroad enthusiast as much as the working railroaders. In 1940 Kambach Publishing Company introduced *Trains*, the first "unequivocally" hobbyist periodical.[12] The war brought new reliance on the rail system, but this was short-lived. In the late 1940s further growth in automobile and air travel gave rail travel for passengers permanent underdog status and provided challenges for freight service as well. A new wave of nostalgia boosted modeling and other railfan occupations to record levels in the mid-1950s. The 1960s—with the space program, war, and social change—once again eclipsed railroading in the popular mind. But by the end of the 1970s the railfan had been "born again," as one hobby dealer reported.[13] The reason echoed the heyday of the 1940s: gasoline shortages and a much-heralded return to the rails, nostalgia for a simpler and more personalized era of travel, and a sense of national tradition and destiny. In the 1980s, a century and a half of popular fascination with railroading continues.

According to John Shedd Reed, retired Chair of Santa Fe Industries, railfans of the 1920s and 1930s were slightly different from those of today.[14] Then they "were strong supporters of progessive railroading . . . always looking at new developments." These contrast with more recent railfans, who seem to be more inclined to be sentimentalists, seeking a return to the past. With the demise of both the steam locomotive and the passenger train, by the 1970s the railroad industry "found itself attacked by the great body of fans who in earlier days had been their supporters." In an era of change and competition, the survival of traditional rail travel, which was championed by fans, was in conflict with the survival of the railroad industry itself.

Both the late nineteenth century and the late twentieth century have been periods of major change for railroads. These times particularly have seen a complex relationship between railfans and the rail industry. In times like the 1860s and the 1940s, the glamour of rail travel cast a glow over these ties. But perhaps more often fans have been critical of and hostile toward railroad leadership.

REFERENCE WORKS

A number of reference and bibliographic tools exist on trains and railroading. For an overview of American railroading—reading beyond the quite useful articles in such encyclopedias as the *Britannica* or the *Americana*—the general reader should turn to two now somewhat venerable titles: Stewart H. Holbrook, *The Story of American Railroads*, and John F. Stover, *American Railroads*. Holbrook provides more business and engineering coverage, while Stover gives more emphasis to social history. A more popular approach is found in Lamont Buchanan's 1955 *Steel Trains and Iron Horses: A Pageant of American Railroads*.

The relation of railroading to culture is explored in *Railroad: Trains and Train People in American Culture*, edited by James Alan McPherson and Miller Williams. This collection of excerpts and illustrations opens with an essay by McPherson entitled "Some Observations on the Railroad and American Culture." The excerpts range from scholarly essays and poetry (Emily Dickinson, Karl Shapiro, William Stafford) to early pamphlet material and advertisements for escaped slaves. This attractive, illustrated trade publication missed being reviewed in the academic press, but the hint of regret in the *Library Journal* review is worth noting: "The compilers are, in sum, more successful in raising important questions about political matters, working conditions, and the like than in capturing the romance of steam locomotives, faraway places, and lonely whistles in the night.[15] *Railroad* provides a direct, rich visual and literary experience of the same material covered more formally by Holbrook, Stover, and Buchanan.

Narrower in coverage but providing a firm foundation for academic study are two classic American studies texts: Henry Nash Smith, *The Virgin Land*, and Leo Marx, *The Machine in the Garden*. Smith reviews the popular pressure to build the rail link to the Pacific and the Orient and the subsequent problems of the railroad's domination. The campaigning for a transcontinental route by Thomas Hart Benton, Eli Whitney, and others plays a prominent role, and the sense of the original documents comes through clearly. Marx extends this view of the railroad, relating it more to the literary culture and art.

A landmark railroad book is John R. Stigloe's 1983 *Metropolitan Corridor: Railroads and the American Scene*. Stigloe, associate professor of landscape architecture and visual and enviromental studies at Harvard, follows Smith and Nash, relating railroads in the era of their dominance in America (about 1880–1930) to the development of the physical world of that time: terminals, viaducts, crossings, and industrial zones. For his sources he turned often to the material of popular culture: fiction (often illustrated), Lionel catalogs, photographs, postcards, and advertisements. Grant suggests that "this may be one of the most important railroad books ever published."[16]

The literature of railroading is, to repeat, vast; fortunately, two very useful guides are available. Most important for the study of trains and railroading in America is *Railroads* by Paul B. Cors, published by Libraries Unlimited in their series Spare Time Guides: Information Sources for Hobbies and Recreation. As a guide to railfan literature, Cors's volume begins with an introduction which relates briefly the history and definition of the genre and describes the railfan as well. The railfan has been treated above, but Cors's "identifying characteristics common to most railfan literature" are necessary at this point. Books often are published by small or specialist firms, in small editions that quickly become scarce and highly sought. There is great attention to "precise, technical detail" based on patient research. Emphasis is on equipment operations rather than corporate and financial matters. Books written for railfans are heavily illustrated: photographs, maps, ephemera, and so forth. More highly priced items contain one or more specially commissioned paintings by one of a group of well-regarded railroad artists.[17] In his guide, Cors goes beyond this body of literature to cover more technical professional material as well as work by scholars. As a handbook to twentieth-century serious popular interest in trains, this guide is indispensable.

Beyond the scope of Cors's interest lies non-North American literature of railroading as well as writing on modeling. These topics—along with a good selection on U.S. railroads—are covered by the English librarian E. T. Bryant in his *Railways: A Readers' Guide*. Introducing his brief American coverage, Bryant points out that "the number of books on American railways probably rivals that on British companies."[18] The publication of books and periodicals outside the United States does center in England, and the resulting body of materials has been made easily accessible in this country. A number of U.S. and Canadian book dealers regularly channel British titles to railfan collectors, and their catalogs include nearly as many British and foreign titles as American. This literature, then, has provided a foundation for American interest in locomotive and station preservation, short lines, and unusual railroads (or railways, in British parlance), and modeling. Thus, Bryant's guide is essential to gaining an overall sense of railroad literature.

A very useful survey for the researcher is Carl Condit's "The Literature of the Railroad Buff: A Historian's View," which appeared in the Spring 1980 issue of *Railroad History*. Condit's aim is to open the specialized vernacular literature accessible to historians of technology, and he focuses on seventy representative titles: pictorial albums, railroad histories, and motive power catalogs. Noteworthy, too, for the student of popular culture is the suggestive introductory section.

The World of Model Trains, by Guy R. Williams, a 1970 British publication distributed in the United States by Putnam, provides an international perspective on making models, constructing layouts, garden railroads, and so on. American examples are included. The classic work in this country is Louis H. Hertz, *The Complete Book of Model Railroading*. An extensive chapter on the model railroad hobby provides a useful and relatively early survey of this aspect of railroad popularity.

These overviews and guides provide, then, a basic reference perspective on the subject. In addition, there are a number of more specialized reference and bibliographic tools on railroading that are useful to the study of railroading in popular culture and give a clue of the range of popular railroad interest. Both Cors and Bryant provide coverage here, but with an emphasis on more recent material. This sketch, therefore, will be highly selective.

The *Railway Directory and Yearbook,* published in London, is a classic reference tool, which can be traced back to 1898, and which provides current international information on rail routes, companies, and personnel. Recent volumes devote forty pages to the United States. Even more basic is *Jane's World Railways,* according to Cors "the single most complete source of data.[19] More specialized but a delight to the railfan is the *Car and Locomotive Cyclopedia*. The 1970 edition bears a resemblance to earlier volumes dating back to 1879. An extensive "dictionary of car and locomotive terms" is included, along with an exhaustive catalog of current rolling stock.

More specifically designed for the railfan is John Marshall's *Rail Facts and Feats*. Though undocumented and probably requiring verification in more standard or specialized sources, it gives a good sense of the range of superlatives of most interest to railroad enthusiasts. Also, one cannot go far in railroading literature without recourse to a specialized glossary. The language of romantic railroading is made accessible by two guides: *The Language of the Railroader*, by Ramon F. Adams and *Rail Talk: A Lexicon of Railroad Language,* collected and edited by James H. Beck in 1978. Reaching back to the heritage of Casey Jones and Steel Drivin' Men, the language of railroad builders and workers was and is "imaginative, emotional, sensitive, humorous, earthy, literal." Much of it is a permanent, colorful part of our modern speech: "double-header," "highball," "called on the carpet," "side-tracked," and many more such terms.[20]

A number of guides exist to serve the traveling needs of railfans. An annual (including even discount coupons) is the *Steam Passenger Service Directory Including Electric Lines and Museums,* published since 1966. For the person more interested in "high iron" (a main line), there is *Travel by Train,* by Edward J. Wojtas. Here the emphasis is on major Amtrak routes, but shorter routes—including non-Amtrak lines—earn coverage. Brief mention is made of Canada, Mexico, "auto train," and tourist railroads. The discussion of "America's Trains Today" provides a recent overview designed for a broader general public. For a more specialized group is *Right-of-Way: A Guide to Abandoned Railroads in the United States,* by Waldo Nielsen. Requiring perhaps less hiking are local train watchers' guides. A fine example is *The New Train Watcher's Guide to Chicago,* by John Szwajkart, which is accompanied by a large map. Indicated are what is to be found at a location, the best times to see it, and how to get there. This listing is preceded by capsule descriptions of each line and a discussion of passenger operations in Chicago.

Very briefly, two useful charts deserve mention for the nonspecialist librarian or student of the railfan subculture. The first and most readily available is the table of "Railway Systems of Selected Countries" found under "Railroads and Locomotives" in the *New Encyclopedia Britannica,* 15th edition. Given here is a listing of the gauges for each country, standard or otherwise. At a glance, one can see whether or not a book on the rails of Taiwan would appeal to a narrow-gauge enthusiast. The second aims to aid the reader of literature on locomotives who encounters a series of numbers like the following: 2–4–0 or 2–8–4. These numbers represent the three groupings of locomotive wheels by diameters: the front-end, drivers, and truck wheels. The Whyte Classification is illustrated on a chart by Frederic Shaw in his 1959 *Casey Jones' Locker* (p.174), along with a brief discussion of the locomotive's evolution.

In addition to the guides by Cors and Bryant, a number of bibliographies are available. To support these guides, reference can be made to the *Railbook Bibliography, 1948–1972: A Comprehensive Guide to the Most Important Railbooks, Publications and Reports,* compiled by F. K. Hudson, which, though unannotated, attempts to list all U.S. and Canadian railroad books and government documents.

For more current information, searches should be made of standard bibliographical and index sources. A good selected list, "Railroads, Interurbans and Highways," appears in *The Frontier and the American West,* compiled by Rodman W. Paul and Richard W. Etulain. In the same series Robert H. Bremner's *American Social History Since 1860* includes a list of works on "Mining, Transportation, and Lumbering" which treats railroading. But more comprehensive is the "Railroads" listings in the *Harvard Guide to*

American History, edited by Frank Freidel. *America: History and Life*, a periodical index, provides good ongoing coverage of scholarship. More popular material is available in the *Readers' Guide (Poole's Index* for the last century) and the *New York Times Index*.

Some specialized bibliographies are available. By far the most important here is Frank P. Donovan, Jr.'s landmark work, *The Railroad in Literature: Brief Survey of Railroad Fiction, Poetry, Songs, Bibliography, Essays, Travel and Drama in the English Language and Particularly Emphasizing Its Place in American Literature*. Donovan's survey puts a structure on a very substantial body of material and is a high point in the bibliographic control of American popular culture. Another listing of importance for earlier material is *A List of References to Literature Relating to the Union Pacific System* from the library of the Bureau of Railway Economics. The coverage is broad, encompassing the debates from the 1830s and 1840s, later travel literature, and government documents; it is a sweeping overview of a central element of the American rail phenomenon. Finally, the rail historian, the railfan, and the student of popular culture all can use *Railroads of the Trans-Mississippi West: A Selected Bibliography*, compiled by Donovan L. Hofsommer. Thorough but selective, three chapters indicate the level of usefulness for social and cultural study: "Regulation and Reaction to Railroad Excesses," "The Captains of Industry/The Robber Barons," and "Railroad Labor/Employees."

Finally, periodicals represent an important part of railfan literature. Two periodicals provide regular surveys of railroad historical literature, the *Lexington Newsletter* and *Railroad History*. Also, available from the National Model Railroad Association is an annual index to model railroad magazines. This last item is reported in an article on model making (with a section on railroads and live steam) by Frederick A. Schlipf in *Magazines for Libraries*, edited by Bill and Linda Sternberg Katz.[21] Much more than just a list of periodical titles, Schlipf's article describes the problem areas of model periodicals—thin coverage by libraries, lack of indexing, damage to precise drawings by library binding, and lack of microform availablity. These problems plague researchers in many areas of popular culture study, of course. In addition, Schlipf describes for his librarian audience the activities and needs of modelers and relates these to the structure of the literature. Schlipf's observations are directly relevant to understanding a key aspect of the railfan phenomenon.

RESEARCH COLLECTIONS

In this century libraries and archives have provided much leadership in the serious study of all aspects of railroading. Even more significant than the Bureau of Railway Economics' Union Pacific list of 1922 was its 1912 *Railway Economics: A Collective Catalogue of Books in Fourteen American Libraries*. Because few comprehensive studies existed, the bureau's list sought to bring together from several collections the materials needed by the "student of railway transportation."[22] Included are materials from periodicals, collections of miscellaneous essays, and general works, as well as technical information of "historical or economic significance." Most documents and laws, guides, maps and atlases, and timetables are excluded. Still, the listing is massive: a specialized catalog for the bureau plus the Interstate Commerce Commission, the Library of Congress, the New York Public Library, the Crerar, and collections at Columbia, Stanford, Harvard, Chicago, Illinois, Michigan, Pennsylvania, Wisconsin, and Yale universities. Although the coverage may be more selective in some areas, guides, informal narratives, and maps are presented for many categories.

The best overview of library research collections today is found in Lee Ash's *Subject Collections,* which shows that the great library collectors of the turn of the century have been joined by a number of others. Southern Methodist University's DeGolyer Library reports having one of the world's largest collections of railroad photographs, about 230,000 prints. In addition, there is a 12,000-volume collection of railroadiana. Northwestern University's Transportation Library also is a major resource, for the railfan phenomenon as well as for the specialist technical literature. Many local and regional libraries have comprehensive collections now, relating to more local developments: Bowdoin College, the Maryland and Minnesota historical societies (for example), and the Denver Public Library. Specialized collections can be found at the Connecticut Electric Railway Association, the Baltimore Streetcar Museum, Harvard's Baker Library, and—to savor the very earliest—the American Antiquarian Society. For some of the collections there are special catalogs or guides. In 1935 Columbia University Library published *The William Barclay Parsons Railroad Prints: An Appreciation and Check List.* A popular and important collection is chronicled in the Smithsonian's *The First Quarter Century of Steam Locomotives in North America: Remaining Relics and Operable Replicas with a Catalog of Locomotive Models in the U.S. National Museum,* by Smith Hempstone Oliver. A 1978 Smithsonian publication, *Guide to Manuscript Collections in the National Museum of History and Technology,* records vast holdings of material on railroad companies, individuals, and railroad preservation. Railroad maps have been drawn since the first U.S. tracks were laid in response to Americans' intense interest in routes. The motivating force of popular interest opens the preface to Andrew M. Modelski's *Railroad Maps of the United States: A Selective Annotated Bibliography of Original 19th Century Maps in the Library of Congress.* The thorough scholarly introduction provides a context which is a useful guide to other, smaller map collections. A list of railroads covered in their extensive files of reports, etc., is available from the Center for Research Libraries in Chicago (researchers should inquire through their home libraries).

Like the Columbia railroad prints checklist, exhibit catalogs can call attention to promising material. A good example is *From Train to Plane: Travelers in the American West, 1866–1936,* the catalog for a 1979 exhibit at Yale's Beinecke Library. In their preface, Archibald Hanna, Jr., and William S. Reese sound the call:

> The travel literature of the American West in the pre–Civil War era has been more closely examined than any other group of material on the Trans-Mississippi region. The opposite is true of the post-1865 era, when travel opened to the multitude rather than the hardy few. An extensive body of material on later travellers and tourists exists, but it remains largely untapped by researchers.[23]

A particular vision and desire to reach a range of publics is found at the Newberry Library. There, for the serious researcher, are housed the Illinois Central, Burlington, and Pullman archives, and a printed *Guide to the Illinois Central Archives in the Newberry Library, 1851–1906* by Carolyn Curtis Mohr. But popular interest in railroad history was stimulated by the publication in 1949 of Lloyd Lewis and Stanley Pargellis's *Granger Country: A Pictorial Social History of the Burlington Railroad.* In a format attractive to general and railfan readers, the book calls attention to the collection and makes some of its riches widely accessible. Newberry "marketing" also resulted in serious but accessible scholarship, such as works by historian Richard Overton. Since Pargellis, Newberry librarian Lawrence Towner has added both the Pullman archives (rich in material on the porters) and also collections of railroad lithographs which testify to nineteenth-century popular enthusiasm for the locomotive particularly.

Some libraries have stimulated research and popular appreciation of railroading because their partners and backers have been private collectors. The Newberry, again, provides an example with its Everett D. Graff Collection of Western Americana. Colton Storm's catalog of this originally private library includes a substantial number of materials that either affected or reflected early popular interest in trains: guides to railroad land sales, travel accounts, reminiscences, and other ephemeral material. Similarly, the Thomas Streeter Collection is an important foundation for the American Antiquarian Society's railroad holdings.

Many collections of more recent railroad materials remain in private hands. Some of these are now coming into institutional collections. In the last few years the Saint Louis Mercantile Library Association has received the collection on American railroads (1913–76) of John W. Barriger III. The Donnelley Library, Lake Forest College, provides a good example of this process. In the 1970s the family of the late Elliott Donnelley—an important figure in railway preservation and in live steam—gave to Lake Forest his collection. Built between 1940 and 1975, this collection reflects the era of the railfan; it encompasses steam, modeling, live steam, short lines, western railroads, narrow gauge, railroadiana, and international topics—including many British imprints, especially. Through family generosity the collection has continued to grow and includes over twenty periodical subscriptions. In the 1980s gifts by Professor James Sloss of MIT's Transportation Department have complemented the Elliott Donnelley material. In addition to enriching the coverage, timetables, rule books, maps, and travel literature have been added, often with an East Coast emphasis that complements Donnelley's collecting. These examples point to the general problem facing the researcher, the difficulty of locating broad, consistently built holdings of more modern material.

HISTORY AND CRITICISM

Much of the history of trains and railroading in the United States is a blend of hope and enthusiasm with frustration and criticism. Albro Martin's *Enterprise Denied: Origins of the Decline of American Railroads, 1897–1917* exemplifies this situation. In the preface the author speaks of his awareness as a child in the 1930s of the "American Railroad Problem." Martin finds the roots in early twentieth-century government regulation and, in the words of the jacket blurb, the book "chronicles a tragedy for the American people whose hopes for a superb . . . system . . . were permanently blighted." The literature on American railroads either centers on epic moments or on blighted hopes and thus reflects a nostalgic tone reminiscent of the ambiance of classic southern fiction. This special character can be traced from academic to more popular historical writings.

The history and study of railroads began in the last century. The Bureau of Library Economics' catalog and list on the Union Pacific both testify to this. Early writing reflected the epic quality of railroading. An example is *Memoir of Henry Farnum* by Henry W. Farnum. This key figure in the early trans-Mississippi railway construction, and partner of Thomas C. Durant, is celebrated here by his son. Nevertheless, the material is still useful: Dee Brown drew on it for *Hear That Lonesome Whistle Blow*, an account of the celebration in 1854 at the linking of the Atlantic to the Mississippi at Rock Island, Illinois. Brown drew on many such contemporary and firsthand accounts for his very useful study.

A unique study from early in the century is *North American Railroads: Their Administration and Economic Policy*, by W. Hoff and F. Schwabach. The report of a comprehensive, official German survey of the U.S. rail system, it provides a remarkable view of life behind the railroads' operations. For example: "The principle prevails in general with American business life that the payment of wages for services rendered constitutes the complete settlement between employee and employer.[24] Elsewhere the Germans marvel at companies which deal through ticket "scalpers."[25] Overall, the report gives a view of Americans' railroad expectations through European eyes.

By the 1920s academic studies were more common. One such study is Orville Thrasher Gooden's doctoral dissertation, "The Missouri and North Arkansas Railroad Strike." Gooden deals with the relation of public opinion to one moment of crisis between a railroad and its workers.

Railroad historical scholarship came of age in Richard C. Overton's *Burlington West: A Colonization History of the Burlington Railroad*. In its scope and accomplishment it opened a new era of study and, through its bibliography, pointed to new sources and approaches. An example is the late nineteenth-century popular local history. Overton has continued to set a high standard in *Gulf to Rockies: The Heritage of the Fort Worth and Denver-Colorado and Southern Railways, 1861–1898; Burlington Route: A History of the Burlington Lines;* and many other works. As consulting editor of Macmillan's Railroads of America series, he has overseen the production of works covering the B & O, the Canadian Pacific and National, the Santa Fe, the Illinois Central, and others.

Personalities have been critical in the popular perception of railroads. Thomas C. Cochran, at the beginning of his *Railroad Leaders, 1845–1890*, notes that "our popular heroes have normally been politicians and businessmen."[26] He continues by observing that historians have been too ignorant of the psychology of these figures.

Thus a number of recent biographies have looked anew at how the great railroad moguls were successful. This revision appears graphically in Stanley P. Hirshson's *Grenville M. Dodge: Soldier, Politician, Railroad Pioneer*. Hirshson finds Jacob R. Perkins's 1929 biography of Dodge inadequate because it sought to make his subject a "demi-god" and failed to capture his spirit or his energy, which was the source of his magnetism. Like Richard Overton, Albro Martin went directly to archival material for his *James J. Hill and the Opening of the Northwest*. Among available published material Martin had found relatively little, and what he did find closely fit the robber baron stereotype.

In addition to studies of companies and individuals, modern scholarship has turned its interest to other subgroupings of railroad history. A classic of American sociology is W. Fred Cottrell's *The Railroader*, which gives the railroader's world in a well-defined hierarchy. At higher levels Cottrell found skills to be monopolized, by which he meant that trainmen maintained their superiority over the company, fellow railroaders, and the public. Even by 1940 the demise of this monopoly and, with it, the railroaders' proud community could be seen. The study provides a classic view of "romantic heroes" caught in change and obsolescence.

The field of urban history has also looked in detail at the railroad. Carl W. Condit sees the railroad as center to one development phase of the city, prior to the automobile. His *The Railroad and the City* focuses on Cincinnati and shows how fundamental the railroad was to the social organization of urban culture. George W. Hilton and John F. Due describe the important but brief role the interurban railway played in the development of intercity transport in *The Electric Interurban Railways in America*. In spite of the coincident appearance of the automobile, this peculiarly American institution was responsible for greatly increased passenger mobility. One recent dissertation points the way to a link between urban and popular cultural history in this area: David Lynn Snowden's "Rail Passenger Service in the United States Since the Nineteen Thirties: Its Decline, Nostalgia and Esthetics (With Emphasis on Greater St. Louis)."

The notion of taking a more conscious look at rail nostalgia has begun to interest serious students. Rail literature is a primary source for George H. Douglas's article, "Lucius Beebe: Popular Railroad History as Social Nostalgia." Douglas finds that Beebe's books, such as *When Beauty Rode the Rails* or *Hear the Train Blow,* recall that "the railroad in its best days offered the American public an unbeatable combination of eccentric individuality, snob appeal, and high style." The railroad era, as found in Beebe's scores of books and articles, "still evokes fond memories . . . of an America that once was and doubtless still lies buried just underneath the surface of our consciousness."[27]

As mentioned above, special paintings have accompanied many railfan books. The wide appeal of this specialized kind of art is considered in the introduction to *Great Railroad Paintings,* edited by Robert Goldsborough. Growing out of the pioneer efforts of urban realists such as Reginald Marsh and Edward Hopper, a group of illustrators accepted commissions from railroads for calendars in the 1920s. Out of this development, based in advertising, has come this particular nostalgia and the preservation of a genre, one which was in eclipse in the two decades after 1950. Today, the Santa Fe has commissioned Howard Fogg to paint current scenes, and Amtrak has brought back calendar paintings. Goldsborough's collection reproduces a selection demonstrating the range, from 1923 to the 1970s.

In rounding out this survey of literature relating to railroading in popular culture, a return to the railfan is inevitable. Cors's and Bryant's guides provide a good view, as does Archie Robertson's chapter on the movement in *Slow Train to Yesterday.* This "indefinable affection"[28] which affects so many is discussed, too, by Frederic Shaw in a chapter entitled "Genus Railroadiac" in *Casey Jones' Locker.* Shaw, Robertson, and Cors all examine in detail the various railfan organizations, the vernacular, and the pioneers of the history of trains and railroading. The Railway and Locomotive Historical Society, based at Harvard's Baker Library, is the most scholarly of these organizations, publishing *Railroad History* (Carl Condit is among the contributors), which preserves, documents, and focuses on the industry. Largest is the National Railway Historical Society, which, in conjunction with local chapters, sponsors "fantrips." The oldest group is the Railroad Enthusiasts. Other specialized groups include the Central Electric Railfans' Association, the National Association of Timetable Collectors, the Railroadiana Collectors' Association, and the Railroad Station Historical Society. Perhaps most arcane is the American Vecturists' Association, many of whose members specialize in collecting railroad or streetcar tokens. The variety is endless. In Archie Robertson's words: "The fan deserves a closer scrutiny than I have given him. He shares many of the surface characteristics of all hobbyists, with one basic difference: he is essentially selfless. He just wants to be around trains and, if possible, to help them out when they get in trouble."[29]

NOTES

1. Daniel J. Boorstin, "Editor's Preface," in *American Railroads,* by John F. Stover (Chicago: University of Chicago Press, 1961), p. v.

2. Lucius Beebe, *High Iron: A Book of Trains* (New York: Appleton-Century, 1938), p. 3.

3. B. A. Botkin, "Introduction," in *A Treasury of Railroad Folklore: The Stories, Tall Tales, Traditions, Ballads and Songs of the American Railroad Man,* ed. B. A. Botkin and Alvin F. Harlow (New York: Bonanza Books, 1953), p. xi.

4. Barton K. Davis, *How to Build Model Railroads and Equipment* (New York: Crown, 1956), p. 4.

5. Paul B. Cors, *Railroads,* Spare Time Guides: Information Sources for Hobbies and Recreation, no. 8 (Littleton, Colo.: Libraries Unlimited, 1975), p. 12.

6. Don Ball, Jr., "Preface," in *Decade of the Trains: The 1940s,* by Don Ball, Jr., and Rogers E. M. Whitaker ("E. M. Frimbo") (Boston: New York Graphics Society, 1977), p. 11.

7. Archie Robertson, *Slow Train to Yesterday: A Last Glance at the Local* (Boston: Houghton Mifflin, 1945), pp. 151–52.

8. H. Roger Grant to the author, January 16, 1987. Grant, professor of history at the University of Akron, is the author of *The Corn Belt Route: A History of the Chicago Great Western Railroad Company* (Northern Illinois Press, 1984) and (with Charles Bohi) *The Country Railroad Station in America* (Pruett, 1978).

9. Maury Klein, *The Life and Legend of Jay Gould* (Baltimore: Johns Hopkins University Press, 1986), p. 3.

10. Ibid., p. 492.

11. Robertson, p. 152.

12. Cors, pp. 11–12.

13. Charles R. Day, Jr., "All Aboard for a Lifelong Hobby." *Industry Week,* 203 (December 10, 1979), 98.

14. John Shedd Reed to the author, January 17, 1987.

15. W. C. Robinson, review of *Railroad: Trains and Train People in American Culture,* ed. James Alan McPherson and Miller Williams, in *Library Journal,* 101 (December 15, 1976), 2573.

16. Grant to author, 1/16/87.

17. Cors, p. 13.

18. E. T. Bryant, *Railways: A Readers' Guide* (Hamden, Conn.: Archon, 1968), p. 116.

19. Cors, p. 15.

20. See Preface in James H. Beck, ed., *Rail Talk: A Lexicon of Railroad Language* (Gretna, Nebr.: James Publications, 1978).

21. Frederick A. Schlipf, "Model Making," in Bill Katz and Linda Sternberg Katz, *Magazines for Libraries*, 5th ed. (New York: R. R. Bowker, 1986), pp. 715–27.

22. Bureau of Railway Economics, *Railway Economics: A Collective Catalogue of Books in Fourteen American Libraries* (Chicago: University of Chicago Press, 1912), p.v.

23. See Preface in *From Train to Plane: Travelers in the American West, 1866–1936* (New Haven: Yale University Library, 1979).

24. W. Hoff and F. Schwabach, *North American Railroads: Their Administration and Economic Policy* (New York: Germania Press, 1906), p. 213.

25. Ibid., pp. 245–50.

26. Thomas C. Cochran, *Railroad Leaders, 1845–1890: The Business Mind in Action* (New York: Russell and Russell, 1965), p. 1.

27. George H. Douglas, "Lucius Beebe: Popular Railroad History as Social Nostalgia." *Journal of Popular Culture,* 4 (Spring 1971), 907.

28. Frederic Shaw, *Casey Jones' Locker: Railroad Historiana* (San Francisco: Hesperian House, 1959), p. 165.

29. Robertson, pp. 162–63.

BIBLIOGRAPHY

Books and Articles

Adams, Ramon F. *The Language of the Railroader.* Norman: University of Oklahoma Press, 1977.

Ash, Lee, ed. *Subject Collections: A Guide to Special Book Collections and Subject Emphases as Reported by University, College, Public and Special Libraries, and Museums in the United States and Canada.* 6th ed. New York: R. R. Bowker, 1985.

Ball, Don, Jr., and Rogers E. M. Whitaker. *Decade of the Trains: The 1940s.* Boston: New York Graphics Society, 1977.

Beck, James H., ed. *Rail Talk: A Lexicon of Railroad Language.* Gretna, Nebr.: James Publications, 1978.

Beebe, Lucius. *Hear the Train Blow: A Pictorial Epic of America in the Railroad Age.* New York: E. P. Dutton, 1952.

———. *High Iron: A Book of Trains.* New York: Appleton-Century, 1938.

———. *When Beauty Rode the Rails.* Garden City, N.Y.: Doubleday, 1962.

Botkin, B. A., and Alvin F. Harlow, eds. *A Treasury of Railroad Folklore: The Stories, Tall Tales, Traditions, Ballads and Songs of the American Railroad Man.* New York: Bonanza Books, 1953.

Bremner, Robert H. *American Social History Since 1860.* New York: Appleton-Century-Crofts, 1971.

Brown, Dee. *Hear That Lonesome Whistle Blow: Railroads in the West.* New York: Holt, Rinehart and Winston, 1977.

Bryant, E. T. *Railways: A Readers' Guide.* Hamden, Conn.: Archon Books, 1968.

Buchanan, Lamont. *Steel Trains and Iron Horses: A Pageant of American Railroads.* New York: Putnam's, 1955.

Bureau of Railway Economics. *A List of References to Literature Relating to the Union Pacific System.* Newton, Mass.: Crofton, n.d. (reprint of 1922 edition).

———. *Railway Economics: A Collective Catalogue of Books in Fourteen American Libraries.* Chicago: University of Chicago Press, 1912.

Car and Locomotive Cyclopedia. New York: Car and Locomotive Cyclopedia, 1879– . Quadrennial.

Cochran, Thomas C. *Railroad Leaders, 1845–1890: The Business Mind in Action.* New York: Russell and Russell, 1965.

Condit, Carl W. "The Literature of the Railroad Buff: A Historian's View." *Railroad History,* 142 (Spring 1980), 7–26.

———. *The Railroad and the City: A Technological and Urbanistic History of Cincinnati.* Columbus: Ohio State University Press, 1977.

Cors, Paul B. *Railroads.* Spare Times Guides: Information Sources for Hobbies and Recreation, no. 8. Littleton. Colo.: Libraries Unlimited, 1975.

Cottrell, W. Fred. *The Railroader.* Stanford, Calif.: Stanford University Press, 1940. Reprint. With an introduction by Scott Greer. Dubuque, Iowa: Brown Reprints, 1971.

Davis, Barton K. *How to Build Model Railroads and Equipment.* New York: Crown, 1956.

Day, Charles R., Jr. "All Aboard for a Lifelong Hobby." *Industry Week,* 203 (December 10, 1979), 98–100.

Donovan, Frank P., Jr. *The Railroad in Literature: Brief Survey of Railroad Fiction, Poetry, Songs, Biography, Essays, Travel and Drama in the English Language and Particularly Emphasizing Its Place in American Literature.* Boston: Railway and Locomotive Historical Society, 1940.

Douglas, George H. "Lucius Beebe: Popular Railroad History as Social Nostalgia." *Journal of Popular Culture,* 4 (Spring 1971), 893–910.

Farnum, Henry W. *Memoir of Henry Farnum.* New Haven: N.p., 1889.

Freidel, Frank, ed. *Harvard Guide to American History.* Rev. ed. 2 vols. Cambridge, Mass.: Harvard University Press, 1974.

From Train to Plane: Travelers in the American West, 1866–1936. New Haven: Yale University Library, 1979.

Goldsborough, Robert, ed. *Great Railroad Paintings.* New York: Peacock Press/ Bantam, 1976.

Gooden, Orville Thrasher. "The Missouri and North Arkansas Railroad Strike." Ph.D. dissertation, Columbia University, 1926.

Grant, H. Roger. *The Corn Belt Route: A History of the Chicago Great Western Railroad Company.* Dekalb: Northern Illinois University Press, 1984.

Grant, H. Roger, and Charles Bohi. *The Country Railroad Station in America.* Boulder, Colo.: Pruett, 1978.

Guide to Manuscript Collections in the National Museum of History and Technology. Washington, D.C.: Smithsonian Institution Press, 1978.

Hertz, Louis H. *The Complete Book of Model Railroading.* New York: Simmons-Boardman, 1951.

Hilton, George W., and John F. Due. *The Electric Interurban Railways in America.* Stanford, Calif.: Stanford University Press, 1960.

Hirshson, Stanley P. *Grenville M. Dodge: Soldier, Politician, Railroad Pioneer.* Bloomington: Indiana University Press, 1967.

Hoff, W., and F. Schwabach. *North American Railroads: Their Administration and Economic Policy.* New York: Germania Press, 1906.

Hofsommer, Donovan L. *Railroads of the Trans-Mississippi West: A Selected Bibliography.* Plainview, Tex.: Wayland College, 1974.

Holbrook, Stewart H. *The Story of American Railroads.* New York: Crown, 1947.

Hudson, F. K., comp. *Railbook Bibliography, 1948–1972: A Comprehensive Guide to the Most Important Railbooks, Publications and Reports.* Ocean, N.J.: Specialty Press, 1972.

Jane's World Railways. London: Macdonald and Jane's, 1966–. Annual.

Klein, Maury. *The Life and Legend of Jay Gould.* Baltimore: Johns Hopkins University Press, 1986.

Lewis, Lloyd, and Stanley Pargellis, eds. *Granger Country: A Pictorial Social History of the Burlington Railroad.* Boston: Little, Brown, 1949.

McPherson, James Alan, and Miller Williams, eds. *Railroad: Trains and Train People in American Culture.* New York: Random House, 1976.

Marshall, John. *Rail Facts and Feats.* New York: Two Continents, 1974.

Martin, Albro. *Enterprise Denied: Origins of the Decline of American Railroads 1897–1917.* New York: Columbia University Press, 1971.

———. *James J. Hill and the Opening of the Northwest.* New York: Oxford University Press, 1976.

Marx, Leo. *The Machine in the Garden.* New York: Oxford University Press, 1964.

Modelski, Andrew M., comp. *Railroad Maps of the United States: A Selective Annotated Bibliography of Original 19th Century Maps in the Library of Congress.* Washington, D.C.: Library of Congress, 1975.

Mohr, Carolyn Curtis. *Guide to the Illinois Central Archives in the Newberry Library, 1851–1906.* Chicago: Newberry Library, 1951.

New York Times Index. New York: New York Times, 1856–.

Nielsen, Waldo. *Right-of-Way: A Guide to Abandoned Railroads in the United States.* Bend, Ore.: Old Bottle Magazine, 1972.

Norris, Frank. *The Octopus.* Cambridge, Mass.: Robert Bently, 1971.

Oliver, Smith Hempstone. *The First Quarter Century of Steam Locomotives in North America: Remaining Relics and Operable Replicas with a Catalog of Locomotive Models in the U.S. National Museum.* Washington, D.C. Smithsonian Institution, 1956.

Overton, Richard C. *Burlington Route: A History of the Burlington Lines.* New York: Alfred A. Knopf, 1965.

———. *Burlington West: A Colonization History of the Burlington Railroad.* Cambridge, Mass.: Harvard University Press, 1941.

———. *Gulf to Rockies: The Heritage of the Fort Worth and Denver-Colorado and Southern Railways, 1861–1898.* Austin: University of Texas Press, 1953.

Paul, Rodman W., and Richard W. Etulain, comps. *The Frontier and the American West.* Arlington Heights, Ill.: AHM, 1977.

Perkins, Jacob R. *Trails, Rails and War: The Life of General G. M. Dodge.* Indianapolis: Bobbs-Merrill, 1929.

"Railroads." In *Encyclopedia Americana.* International ed. Vol. 23. Danbury, Conn.: Americana, 1979, pp. 152–69.

"Railroads and Locomotives." In *New Encyclopaedia Britannica*. 15th ed. Vol. 15. Chicago: Encyclopaedia Britannica, 1974, pp. 477–91.

Railway Directory and Yearbook. London, Transport Press, 1898–. Annual.

Readers' Guide to Periodical Literature. New York: H. W. Wilson, 1900–. Annual.

Richardson, Frederick H., and F. Nelson Blount. *Along the Iron Trail*. 2nd ed. Rutland, Vt.: Sharp Offset, 1966.

Robertson, Archie. *Slow Train to Yesterday: A Last Glance at the Local*. Boston: Houghton Mifflin, 1945.

Robinson, W. C. Review of *Railroad: Trains and Train People in American Culture*, edited by James Alan McPherson and Miller Williams. *Library Journal*, 101 (December 15, 1976), 2573.

Schlipf, Frederick A. "Model Making." In Bill Katz and Linda Sternberg Katz, *Magazines for Libraries*. 5th ed. New York: R. R. Bowker, 1986, pp. 715–27.

Shaw, Frederic. *Casey Jones' Locker: Railroad Historiana*. San Francisco: Hesperian House, 1959.

Smith, Henry Nash. *The Virgin Land*. Cambridge, Mass.: Harvard University Press, 1950.

Snowden, David Lynn. "Rail Passenger Service in the United States Since the Nineteen Thirties: Its Decline, Nostalgia and Esthetics (With Emphasis on Greater St. Louis)." Ph.D. dissertation, St. Louis University, 1975.

Steam Passenger Service Directory Including Electric Lines and Museums. New York: Empire State Railway Museum, 1966–. Annual.

Stigloe, John R. *Metropolitan Corridor: Railroads and the American Scene*. New Haven: Yale University Press, 1983.

Storm, Colton, comp. *A Catalogue of the Everett D. Graff Collection of Western Americana*. Chicago: University of Chicago Press, 1968.

Stover, John F. *American Railroads*. Chicago: University of Chicago Press, 1961.

Szwajkart, John. *The New Train Watcher's Guide to Chicago*. Brookfield, Ill.: John Szwajkart, 1976.

The William Barclay Parsons Railroad Prints: An Appreciation and a Check List. New York: Columbia University Library, 1935.

Williams, Guy R. *The World of Model Trains*. New York: Putnam's, 1970.

Wojtas, Edward J. *Travel by Train*. New York: Rand McNally, 1974.

Periodicals

America: History and Life. Santa Barbara, Calif., 1964–.

Lexington Newsletter. Plainview, Tex., 1942–.

Railroad History. Westford, Mass., 1921–. (Formerly *Railway and Locomotive Historical Society Bulletin*.)

Railroad Magazine. New York, 1906–.

Railway Age. Bristol, Conn., 1856–.

Trains: The Magazine of Railroading. Milwaukee, 1940–.

Women

JEANIE K. FORTE
and KATHERINE FISHBURN

The study of women in popular culture has mushroomed in the few years since the first edition of this handbook to the extent that a comprehensive and detailed survey of the literature would be massive. However, certain issues have emerged in relation to this field that bear particular examination, especially since they have wider implications for the general study of popular culture.

Specifically, women "in" popular culture must be re-articulated within three categorical distinctions: women can be seen variously as producers of popular culture; as its consumers; and, for some scholars, as its very basis or conceptual foundation. Both as producers and consumers, women can occupy one of three positions (to borrow terminology from Stuart Hall): a dominant one, reading a mass cultural text at face value and/or contributing to mass culture, which would demonstrate their support of the dominant ideology (which assumes a certain understanding of the relations of culture and ideologies, via neo-Marxian thought); negotiated, in which certain aspects of received culture are questioned but the overall system accepted; or oppositional, either through critique or the production of alternatives, which may or may not also be associated with feminism. Thus women are no longer perceived, as they once were, as the passive (and homogeneous) recipients of culture, but as interactive participants within it, whose responses depend on their specific, historically grounded circumstances, necessarily including questions of race, class, and political beliefs.

Another, related branch of analysis, influenced by post-structuralist and psychoanalytic theory, cites Woman as the conceptual foundation of mass culture—the term *Woman,* as Teresa de Lauretis notes, here designating a fictional construct, one elaborated by cultural practices, distinct from actual, historical women. In addition, the term *mass culture* is preferred by some scholars because it more specifically identifies cultural forms which are "imposed from above," generated by the dominant system, rather than "popular" art, which arises from the people. Tania Modleski points out that such a distinction enables discussions of power and profit inherently problematic in studies of culture. It would seem self-evident that these distinctions especially pertain to studies of the relations of women to culture. Indeed, this school argues that studies of mass culture cannot now be undertaken without an understanding of the contemporary feminist critique of gender construction, precisely because of the "privileged" relationship of Woman and women to mass culture. In contemporary postmodern parlance, derived from the intersections of post-structural, psychoanalytic, and feminist theory, Woman is constructed as the Other, the object, in relation to the male subject, existing only to reflect male desire, her own desire having been denied existence. According to Michele Montrelay, women thus exist as the potential "ruin of representation," owing to their special position and the possibilities for subversion from within. This perspective has particular currency with regard to studies of "popular" culture—as Modleski notes, recognition of the misogynism underlying the split between high culture and mass culture (which is devalued for its association with "the feminine") necessitates new theoretical paradigms that incorporate gender. For De Lauretis, the psychoanalytic paradigm, as a descriptive model of a culture's psyche, is irrevocably bound to studies of mass culture and readings of practices (such as film) pointing up the continuing need for a feminist politics of the unconscious. Since the apparatuses which produce our popular images exert their most powerful influence in the unconscious realm, the effort to make these processes conscious and expose them to critical view becomes a crucial feminist strategy.

Thus the study of women in popular culture now encompasses extremely far-ranging and necessarily interdisciplinary material, and presumably could include any and all studies of women as producers/consumers of an inexhaustible variety of cultural forms, as well as general treatises on particular arenas of activity. For the bibliographic purposes of this chapter, I have included a short historical outline focusing on literature, magazines, and film, incorporating basic introductions to the theory and issues currently under debate, and brief notes on reference works, collections, and selected important works, with emphasis on recent issues.

HISTORIC OUTLINE

No one would dispute that women have long been active producers and consumers of various cultural forms that are labeled "popular," insofar as women have routinely been denied or discouraged access to the conventional forms of "high" culture. Although women painters and sculptors have existed throughout history, confinement to the domestic sphere and active (often punitive) discouragement from the pursuit of un-"ladylike" activities has meant that most women have sought alternative means of expression, means which have generally been devalued. Journal writing, the private recorded thoughts of women, is now being recognized as one of the few places where women could find voice; but the more public venue of popular novels and/or magazines has been a particularly fruitful avenue for American women, albeit fraught with controversy, since the 1600s.

As early as 1682, American colonists affirmed their beliefs in white supremacy and manifest destiny through reading Mrs. Mary Rowlandson's account of a woman's Indian captivity. Immensely popular, running to thirty-one editions, *The Sovereignty and Goodness of God . . . , Being a Narrative of the Captivity and Restoration of Mrs. Mary Rowlandson* proved a prototype for later popular novels. These early works were already predicated on a female protagonist who experiences a crisis in relation to her "home" culture, and is generally either rescued, thereby reasserting her religious faith and essential goodness, or punished (usually by death) for her fall from goodness. The so-called sentimental novel emphasized the latter, serving as a moral lesson for women in the New Land. One of the earliest examples was Susanna Haswell Rowson's *Charlotte Temple: A Tale of Truth* (1791). While she herself provided the example of a strong businesswoman, her heroine demonstrated the stereotype of feminine weakness and poor judgment, becoming pregnant without benefit of marriage and ultimately dying while giving birth. In her failure to escape the wages of sin, Charlotte Temple sets a pattern for the heroines in large numbers of contemporary novels of the gothic and romance varieties.

It is also important to recognize the link of popular literature's emergence (with women both as erstwhile writers and habitual consumers) to publishing practices. As outlined by Janice Radway and John Tebbel, throughout America's early period book production and distribution were limited to primarily private publication for a recognizable, sometimes even sponsoring, audience. Publishers initially prided themselves on the variety and breadth of their offerings to readers, emphasizing the particularity of books intended for specific audiences. But as the nineteenth century began, technological innovations in communications and printing, as well as liberal postal regulations, combined to make publishers aware of the possibilities of presenting a series of formulaic books or stories on a continuous basis to a growing nationwide audience. Attempting to avoid losses and predict profits, publishers such as the Beadle brothers and Theophilus B. Peterson capitalized on the success of single best sellers through imitation, using repetitive formulas to create mass-produced fiction. In 1839, New York publishers Benjamin and Wilmot combined early serials with "news," tak-

ing advantage of cheap mailing costs—thus heralding a new era in the
concept of popular book production and distribution. In spite of such advances, the production of serial books underwent setbacks in the latter half
of the nineteenth century, after a brief literary boom faded when publishers
failed to develop useful ways to survey and predict public taste. By 1940,
however, improvements in printing and binding techniques made mass
production cost-efficient, and new distribution ideas brought paperbacks
to newsstands, combining publishing acumen with an easily accessible audience. In the 1950s, publishers Gerald Gross at Ace Books and Patricia
Myrer at Appleton launched the women's "gothic" novel, with Phyllis
Whitney's *Thunder Heights* and Victoria Holt's *Mistress of Merlyn*. The sudden and immediate popularity of women's gothics, reaching as they did an
already "captive" audience in food and drug stores, was followed in 1972
by the emergence of a new style dubbed the "sweet savage romance,"
epitomized in Kathleen Woodiwiss's *The Flame and the Flower* and Rosemary
Rogers's *Sweet Savage Love*. Quickly surpassing even the gothics in popularity, these new works, also known as "erotic historicals," "bodice-
rippers," and "slave sagas," included explicit sexuality, travel, adventure,
captivity and subjugation, and romantic interludes, and ended with rescues
by heartthrob heroes. Avon Books and Harlequin Enterprises, two of the
leading publishers in the genre, now claim readerships of over sixteen million American women, and their success has depended at least in part on
the innovative marketing and distributing techniques developed in recent
decades; to what extent the content of the books provides a necessary outlet/
message/escape/or reinforcement of dominant ideology for their female
readers remains highly debatable. Certainly, as Radway suggests, the mar-
ketability of the texts serves an important function in their selection by
readers—looking at her survey of inveterate romance readers, the emphasis
on size, access, and ease of reading makes the books seem like mental
"snacks" which the readers rely on for momentary respite from their daily
routine, but it is a snack with more weighty significance. Her "ethnographic
investigation" provides a picture of romance-reading as a "combative and
compensatory" act, one which is allied with folkloric practices in its refusal
of "the hegemonic imposition of bourgeois culture." Tania Modleski, on
the other hand, cautions against "invoking analogies based on older cultural
forms in order to explain the functioning of mass cultural artifacts," arguing
that such an approach ignores the more complex nature of contemporary
culture. The rise of the romance requires examination on its own terms, in
present context, as the production of certain conventions and expectations
within its distinct sphere. A study of the romance and its meteoric ascen-
dence to popularity at precisely the same time as the emergence of the
contemporary women's movement would provide a most compelling challenge, indeed; and although there is much scholarship already available on
the subject, it is by no means exhausted.

The earliest American magazines recognized the power of women as consumers and catered to their perceived needs with special columns and features. Richard Steele's *Tatler* (founded 1709) carried a women's column, and Noah Webster's *American Magazine* (1787) promised to care for its "fair readers," publishing sentimental and gothic fiction as well as helpful hints for homemaking. To the same end, the *Saturday Evening Post* in 1821 began a feature called "The Ladies' Friend," publishing poetry and articles that both reflected and helped to define woman's position within culture. As the first purveyors of advertising and fashion, these works are valuable resources for the study of early American popular culture.

The *Ladies' Magazine,* founded in 1828 by Boston businesswoman Sarah Josepha Hale, was the first to fully capitalize on the consumer power of women, and began setting the standard for all such magazines to come. The limited status of women, who were largely confined to housekeeping and discouraged from other pursuits, was reinforced through the glorification of domesticity as the proper sphere.

The *Ladies' Magazine* was to become the foundation for the multibillion-dollar business of selling American housewives an image to emulate. These magazines focused on housekeeping hints and "feminine" endeavors, excluding or actively campaigning against any pursuits considered unladylike. Louis Antoine Godey's *Lady's Book,* founded in Philadelphia in 1830, was another popular example of the form; Godey made the best of a business when he purchased *Ladies' Magazine* in 1837 and hired Sarah Hale as editor of the new *Godey's Lady's Book,* which reigned as purveyor of women's interests until 1898. During Hale's tenure as editor, from 1837 to 1877, she increased circulation, promoted women's education, and encouraged female contributors to sign their names (instead of remaining anonymous), while ignoring politics. The magazine featured recipes, health and beauty aids, embroidery patterns, and "embellishments"—ornate illustrations and hand-painted fashion plates which made the periodical famous.

The main contender with *Godey's* for the woman's attention was the *Ladies' Home Journal,* founded by Cyris H. K. Curtis in 1883. (It was originally entitled *Ladies' Journal and Practical Housekeeper,* but the confusing masthead gave rise to the shortened name.) For editor, Curtis hired Edward Bok, whose policy was to "uplift" and "inspire" his readers. He wrote one advice column under the pseudonym "Ruth Ashmore" called "Side Talk to Girls," and another, more boldly, under his own name called "At Home with the Editor." He discouraged women from entering business because there they would "lose their gentleness and womanliness." He also campaigned against patent medicines, Paris fashions, cigarettes, and venereal disease (this last which lost him thousands of subscribers). In 1897 he expanded the domestic coverage of the *Journal* to include architectural plans and interior shots of homes, broadening the scope of its critique and taste-setting standards.

Godey's and the *Journal* were admittedly the "big two" of the early ladies' magazines, but not alone. Fashion magazines, begun primarily as pattern catalogs, included the *Delineator* (1873–1937), *Harper's Bazar* (1867, then *Harper's Bazaar* in 1929), and *Vogue* (1892). Other more general titles were *McCall's* (1870), *Women's Home Companion* (1873), and *Good Housekeeping* (1885). All directed their material exclusively at women, particularly the "homemakers," the mothers and nurturers of a largely white (immigrant), burgeoning middle class in a rapidly growing America. They went un-challenged until World War II, at which time other emerging media— particularly television—took over much of the task of "educating" the American woman in her role and guiding her purchasing power. While most women's magazines floundered for their audience and few publishers dared introduce a new magazine concept, *Ms.* magazine, founded in 1972 with an explicitly feminist agenda, proved an exception, riding the crest of the women's movement of the late 1960s and early 1970s. In the 1980s, with backlash against feminism and a more conservative political climate, *Ms.* has undertaken changes in format and emphasis, presumably to reach a wider audience. The recent resurgence of homemaker and mothering journals as well as the renewed popularity of "glamour" (*Cosmopolitan*) and "career" (*Working Woman*) magazines for women testifies to the industry's ability to target a market and address a specific audience successfully. Fish-burn points out the similarity between women's and men's magazines, in that an exploration of the neighborhood newsstand readily reveals that it is still the images of women that sell—the female body, the images of femininity—and deliver products for the consumer's purvue, from cars to vacations to tampons. Michele Barrett, in her discussion of "Ideology and the Cultural Production of Gender," notes that the representation of women is part of a larger system of signification, linked to historically constituted real relations. We can only understand how female images are more per-suasive if we take into account an already existing commodification of women's bodies. Judith Williamson, discussing both British and American trends in magazine advertising, argues that femininity represents notions of leisure and personal relations (as opposed to work) for consumers, which is perceived as the only sphere of control wherein the "worker" can exercise "freedom of choice." Women (or images of women) carry these values for society—feeling, caring, and interpersonal relations—in direct proportion to their exclusion from the economic and social spheres. Williamson's Marx-ist analysis of the constructed difference of femininity and its function within capitalist society moves studies of advertising iconography into a new the-oretical realm, but nevertheless she does not account in a specific way for the popularity of women's magazines with female readers—presenting problems similar to those of the romance novel. This area of research re-mains relatively untouched.

The advent of film in the twentieth century has provided another apparatus for the dissemination of cultural tastes and standards regarding the roles and functions of women. As various critics have noted, the story of women and film is primarily one of how men have presented them, as men have dominated the industry. From the earliest images of Mary Pickford as the neophyte child-woman to present-day sex goddesses and career women, representations of women in film have reflected cultural stereotypes and male fantasies in a complex interweave of signifying systems and social context. From the start, however, small numbers of women have also fought to be filmmakers, almost always presenting alternative viewpoints of women and their experience in opposition to the dominant cinema. In recent years, some women filmmakers have also pursued the possibility of nonpatriarchal cinematic techniques.

Shortly after the turn of the century, Mary Pickford made the image of the Victorian child-woman the ideal, seemingly ageless and sexless in films such as *A Poor Little Rich Girl* (1917) and *Little Annie Rooney* (1925). While Pickford fulfilled the roles, the images were engineered by David Wark Griffith, producer and filmmaker, who built an entire industry around his girlish actresses. Other stars in his films included Lillian and Dorothy Gish (sixteen and fourteen) and Mae Marsh (seventeen). In *The Birth of a Nation* (1915), Elsie Stoneman (Lillian Gish) presents a picture of white purity and innocence, is threatened with rape by a black man, and suffers the suicide of her little sister (Mae Marsh), who throws herself off a cliff when similarly threatened. In *Broken Blossoms* (1919), a Chinese man lusts after a twelve-year-old girl but never acts on his desire; thus the audience is assured that "his love remains a pure and holy thing."

Griffith's pandering to the Victorian conscience and thwarted sexuality faded with the rise of the easy sexuality of the Roaring Twenties. America shifted its focus from virgins to vamps such as Theda Bara and Tallulah Bankhead, whose vulgar (for the times) and voracious sexuality served both as titillation and as a caution against the price of wantonness. The simultaneous entrance of greater numbers of women into work and the boom economy of the twenties combined to give the flapper/vamp great appeal—newly enfranchised, with spending money, these female characters reflected more freedom to choose, in terms of behavior, dress, and even men. Movies reflected the high spirits of the times (*Jazzmania, The Flappers, Our Dancing Daughters, Wine of Youth*) but still glorified women who were ready to give up everything for a good man. Clara Bow won and married her wealthy boss because she had IT (in *It,* 1927); but unrepentant vamps or "bad girls" still got punished, as did Joan Crawford, dying in a car wreck after mistreating a millionaire in *Sally, Irene and Mary* (1925).

The Depression buried the flapper—women lost jobs almost twice as fast as men, and movies turned to escapism in fantasy worlds and Shirley Temple happy endings. Another factor in the vamp's demise was the implementation of the Production Code, which severely censored sex in films and thus limited even further the already slim roles available to women. The vamp was replaced by "clever" women—detectives, reporters, molls, and spies, exemplified by elegant Myrna Loy in the series of *Thin Man* films. After the war years and a brief flirtation with *Rosie the Riveter,* soldiers returned home seeking stability in home and family, and American film once again focused on the twin images of woman: sex goddess (Marilyn Monroe, Jayne Mansfield, Jane Russell) and innocent, the latter personified in the dutiful and subservient housewife (Doris Day, Debbie Reynolds, Natalie Wood). The girl-next-door merged with worldly sophistication (for boys who had seen Paree) in Audrey Hepburn's *Roman Holiday* (1953) or Leslie Caron's *An American in Paris* (1951).

The 1960s and 1970s saw an increased loosening of the Production Code, influenced in part by foreign imports and by the so-called sexual revolution; but women's roles, although now more open to a variety of occupations, personality types, and life situations, continued to focus on female sexuality—the threat of it, the lack of it, or the pursuit of it. Also, roles for men far outnumbered roles for women, revealing an industrywide imbalance in all facets of film production—from writers to producers—that still bodes ill for actresses. After a few promising developments in the early 1970s with dominant cinema successes such as *The Turning Point, Julia,* and *An Unmarried Woman,* films that deal with non-stereotypical women and/ or focus on women's experiences have dwindled considerably, reflecting the conservative backlash of the Reagan years. Women of color have, of course, fared much worse, suffering confinement to stereotypes and tokenism in the shamelessly blatant racism of Hollywood. From "pickaninnies" dancing in the streets in *Birth of a Nation* to the empty-headed Prissy in *Gone With the Wind* (1939), black women have been relegated to the most simplistic and degrading roles. The occasional films that attempt an honest exploration of black women's experience—*Lady Sings the Blues* (1972), *Sounder* (1972), *Cotton Club* (1984)—serve as glaring exceptions to the rule. Steven Spielberg's *The Color Purple* (1986), although laudable in its employment of large numbers of blacks both on and off-screen, was ironically billed as a film "about US," indicating its appropriation of the text and black culture for a universalizing white viewpoint; an erasure of difference in spite of the text's obvious grounding in a specific culture. The lesbian relationship in the novel all but disappeared in the film, providing an example of Hollywood's equally blatant homophobia. At its best, Hollywood still poses difficult tradeoffs for black actresses. Latina and Asian-American women, by comparison, must rely primarily on foreign imports for anything other than superficial or stereotypical portrayals.

Women directors and screenwriters have struggled to make inroads into production and distribution systems that have persistently excluded women, and some have managed a degree of success in a man's world. During Hollywood's formative years, Lois Weber produced and directed, Anita

Loos and Frances Marion wrote screenplays, and some actresses, such as Gish and Pickford, even directed themselves on some occasions (but without screen credit). With the emergence of sound, only one woman survived as director: Dorothy Arzner directed Katharine Hepburn, Rosalind Russell, Claudette Colbert, and others from 1927 to 1943, using conventional techniques to critique the standard representations of women. Among her better-known films today are *Working Girls* (1930), *Merrily We Go To Hell* (1932), *Craig's Wife* (1936), and *Dance, Girl, Dance* (1940). By the late 1940s, American women were virtually shut out of the industry and turned to 16mm equipment for alternative filmmaking. Filmmakers such as Maya Deren, Marie Menken, and Shirley Clarke are credited with inspiring the women's independent cinema movement in the United States. Deren's *Meshes in the Afternoon* (1943) and her later dance films influenced a whole generation of young avant-garde artists with her experimental techniques. Apart from the few who have managed to direct for Hollywood studios (Elaine May, Ida Lupino), American women have tended to work in highly experimental modes. Perhaps the best known of these is Yvonne Rainer, whose features—*A Film About a Woman Who . . .* (1974) and *The Man Who Loved Women* (1984), among others—particularly explore alternatives to traditional narrative in an attempt to wrest women from the strictures of dominant representations.

As women continue to insist on the manipulation of film as a feminist tool, feminist film critics have simultaneously provided some of the most far-reaching advances in feminist theory, analyzing not only the dominant cinema and its stereotypes, but also the cinematic apparatus itself and its implications vis-à-vis narrative structure, the construction of gender, and spectator response. Much of this theory has reference to other studies besides film, including television, theater, and performance art.

REFERENCE WORKS

Although there are a number of useful reference materials available for studies of women in general, most of them are limited in particular ways, and few have "popular culture" as an index entry. Also, very little has changed since 1982 in the way of additional bibliographic resources. There is still a crying need for more scholarly endeavor in this area.

Katherine Fishburn's reference work, *Women in Popular Culture,* is perhaps the most comprehensive to date, combining historical narrative with extensive annotation of bibliographic information. Topic headings include histories, popular literature, magazines, film, television, and a section on theory that is especially wide-ranging, covering almost any extant text on women in relation to their culture. Her text has become an extremely useful starting point for scholars in the field. Other recent additions to research on women include *Studies on Women Abstracts,* out of Lady Spencer Churchill

College at Oxford Polytechnic, England, issued bimonthly since 1983. It catalogs both European and U.S. journals (primarily English-speaking), with some books and book abstracts as well. The cumulative subject index in the year's end issue provides a guide to specific topics such as "media," "television," "musical comedy performers," "women's culture," and so on. The journal *National Women's Studies Perspectives* ran a special issue in Winter 1986 (Vol. 4, nos. 23–24) on "Sources and Resources," compiling a substantial bibliography under a variety of headings. Also, the *Women's Review of Books*, started in the summer of 1983 by the Wellesley Center for Research on Women, has rapidly become a substantial source of information about new publications in women's studies, covering an interdisciplinary selection of subjects; each year's reviews are indexed in a special issue.

One of the more valuable early bibliographies still is Albert Krichmar's *The Women's Movement in the Seventies: An International English-Language Bibliography*. The entries, most of them annotated, are accurate and arranged alphabetically according to subject headings and by country. The most pertinent heading is "North America—U.S.: Cultural and Literary Studies," which contains nearly 200 items; included are books, articles, and dissertations completed in the 1970s on women in literature, film, music, art, education, and other related fields.

A more specialized and much briefer bibliography is entitled "Popular Culture," appearing in Barbara Friedman et al., *Women's Work and Women's Studies/1973–1974, A Bibliography*. Again, this work is limited to studies published only very recently. Intended primarily as a working list, it also contains information on work in progress as of 1974. Only occasionally annotated, the seventy entries are helpful mainly because the editors have restricted themselves to the topic of women in popular culture. Other sections of the book of some interest are "History," "Literary Criticism," and "Bibliographies and Resources." The book includes an appendix of bibliographical sources and an index of authors.

Another source that is limited to current work is Carol F. Meyers's *Women in Literature: Criticism of the Seventies*, which catalogs material appearing in print from January 1970 to Spring 1976. International in scope, it is alphabetized in part one according to topics; part two is a general bibliography. The critics and editors are indexed.

A more sweeping work is Albert Krichmar's *The Women's Rights Movement in the United States, 1848–1970, A Bibliography and Sourcebook*. The bibliography itself contains 5,170 entries; a separate section on manuscript sources contains 402 entries. These latter sources are arranged by state and indexed by content. Although the bibliography is not annotated, it is organized by subjects and indexed by both author and subject. Relevant headings include "General," "Economic Status," "Education," "Religion," and "Biography." Included also is a list of women's-liberation serials.

Another resource is Helen Wheeler's *Womanhood Media: Current Resources*

About Women, which contains 318 annotated entries with categories and subcategories such as "The Arts," "Literature and Rhetoric," and "Fiction." Wheeler also includes titles of pamphlets, movement periodicals, and special issues on the woman. (For instructors interested in establishing a feminist curriculum, she also includes what she calls "a basic book collection," pp. 105–96, of nonsexist writings.) Three years after the appearance of this work, Wheeler published *Womanhood Media Supplement: Additional Current Resources About Women,* which, as she says in the preface, will be her last attempt to keep up with the burgeoning field of women's studies.

A highly specialized work is *The Black Family and the Black Woman: A Bibliography,* which was prepared by the library staff and the Afro-American Studies Department of Indiana University. The material documented is held by the university; it includes lists of primary material written by black women ("Anthologies with Black Women as Editors," "Other Anthologies with Writings by Black Women," "Works by Individual Authors") and a section of "Bio/Criticism." A companion work in this field would be Lenwood G. Davis's *The Black Woman in American Society: A Selected Annotated Bibliography,* which contains 562 annotated entries of books and articles on the American black woman. There is also a helpful list of U.S. libraries with major black history collections. The book is indexed by subject and author.

Ora Williams has also published "A Bibliography of Works Written by American Black Women," which is divided into several useful categories such as "Bibliographies and Guides to Collections," "Novels," "Short Stories," and so on. George P. Rawick's *From Sundown to Sunup: The Making of the Black Community* contains a bibliography of slave narratives, including those written by women; Rawick also lists his secondary sources. Russell C. Brignano's *Black Americans in Autobiography* is an annotated compendium of autobiographies and autobiographical books written since the Civil War, arranged alphabetically by author; the titles are indexed, and the book contains a list of locations and institutions for cross-reference. Another pertinent work, albeit rapidly becoming outdated, is *A Selected Bibliography of Works by Chicanas and Other Women Interested in Chicana Culture,* issued by Vance Bibliographies in 1979. Clearly much work remains to be done regarding women of color in relation to popular culture.

A specialized bibliography in the field of wilderness literature is Dawn Lander Gherman's "Frontier and Wilderness: American Women Authors," which is a working, annotated checklist of American prose literature by and about women in the American wilderness, documenting material on red, black, and white women. It includes both primary and secondary sources, a list of bibliographies consulted, and brief discussions of captivity narratives and fiction. Two specialized bibliographies in the area of film are *Women and Film: A Bibliography,* by Rosemary Ribich Kowalski, which is primarily useful for material prior to 1976; and *Women and Film: A Resource*

Handbook, compiled by Project on the Status and Education of Women, also from the 1970s.

In 1975 Jayne Loader compiled "Women in the Left, 1906–1941: A Bibliography of Primary Sources," providing an index, table of contents, and annotated entries. In the same year, the Michigan Department of State published *Bibliography of Sources Relating to Women,* which contains information about unpublished sources for women's studies in various Michigan institutions.

Women Studies Abstracts, issued quarterly, covers a wide range of periodicals and books; each volume is accompanied by a cumulative index, and a lead section lists special journal issues by subject. Another source for theme issues of periodicals is Susan Cardinale's *Special Issues of Serials About Women, 1965–1975,* although it excludes all women's periodicals per se. See also *Womanhood Media* by Helen Wheeler. The *Standard Periodical Directory* indexes women's periodicals under "Women's Liberation" and "Women's Fashions." *Ulrich's International Periodicals Directory* indexes "Women's Interests"; especially helpful is the section on cessations, providing the publishing history of defunct periodicals.

The following resources provide information on individual women. *Notable American Women, 1607–1950: A Biographical Dictionary* contains brief biographies of women who were born after 1607 and who died before 1950 (with only five exceptions). This is a mammoth scholarly work of 1,337 articles (22 of which include two or more figures), which also contains a brief historical survey of America and its women written by Janet Wilson James. Frances E. Willard and Mary A. Livermore's *American Women: Fifteen Hundred Biographies with over 1,400 Portraits* is a comprehensive encyclopedia of nineteenth-century women, arranged alphabetically, and indexed by professional contributions. An earlier version of this work, entitled *A Woman of the Century,* is available in a facsimile reprint of the 1893 edition.

Information on living authors appears in the latest edition of *Who's Who of American Women: A Biographical Dictionary of Notable Living American Women, 1977–1978.* Tamar Berkowitz's *Who's Who and Where in Women's Studies* is an educational directory that lists the names of women's-studies instructors and their courses. It is not annotated. In 1973 the Sense and Sensibility Collective published *Women and Literature: An Annotated Bibliography of Women Writers,* a revised and expanded version of one that first appeared in Susan Cornillon's *Images of Women in Fiction.* All the authors included write fiction, and most are contemporary. Except for occasional brief biographies, the entries are composed almost exclusively of lists of books these authors have written; each novel is annotated. *Women and Literature* is arranged alphabetically by author and contains a fairly comprehensive subject index. (Other checklists can be found in the discussion of the several popular culture genres that follows.)

Although a start has been made, there is still much work to be done in women's bibliographies, as Patricia K. Ballou observes in her review essay, "Bibliographies for Research on Women." In this article, Ballou surveys a wide variety but, confined by her subject, a small number of checklists. Her topics range from the general to history and literature. She also mentions several bibliographies in the social sciences that she has categorized by specific discipline. A less successful attempt to gather bibliographies is Margrit Eichler's *An Annotated Selected Bibliography of Bibliographies on Women*. It is very brief and covers mostly those lists that would be of interest to students of feminism or politics rather than students of popular culture. The standard resource in this area, the *Bibliographic Index,* catalogs published bibliographies under "Women: Fiction," "Women: History," and "Women: United States."

For lists of periodicals that have dedicated entire issues to women, there are several reasonably complete sources for recent years. In its own way, Susan Cardinale's *Special Issues of Serials About Women, 1965–1975* is quite thorough, but it excludes all women's periodicals per se. It is annotated and arranged alphabetically by serial title. See also *Womanhood Media* by Helen Wheeler and *Women Studies Abstracts* (discussed above) and the section below on women's periodicals and special issues for more information on this topic.

RESEARCH COLLECTIONS

As women contribute to all forms of popular culture, either as its authors or as its subjects, any major collection of primary resources would certainly include some material relevant to them. But because the serious study of women per se is a fairly recent activity, many of the available collections remain hidden. Exceptions to this situation are the letters and diaries of early American women, which are cataloged by several major research libraries. The New York Public Library and the Houghton Library of Harvard University, for example, house the correspondence of Mary Louise Booth, Lydia Maria Child, and Elizabeth Palmer Peabody. In its extensive archives, the Schlesinger Library of Radcliffe College houses the papers of Antoinette Brown Blackwell, Caroline Wells Healey Dall, and Elizabeth Cady Stanton and the Lydia Maria Child correspondence. It also contains documents on medicine, law, and the women's liberation movement. Founded in 1943, the library holds more than 13,000 volumes, in addition to its collection of journals and newsletters. The Sophia Smith Collection in the William Allan Neilson Library of Smith College contains over one million manuscript pieces on the social and intellectual history of women, with an emphasis on Americans. Its subjects include Lucretia Mott, Lucy Stone, and Sojourner Truth. The 1971 *Catalog of the Sophia Smith Collection,* produced by the Smith College Library, describes the collection's major primary and secondary sources. The Boston Public Library's Galatea Collection, founded by Thomas Wentworth Higginson, features material on women in history and the suffragette movement. The University of Nevada Library, Reno, has amassed a substantial Women in the West Collection, including diaries, letters, autobiographies, and biographies, from both the nineteenth and twentieth centuries.

The letters of Mrs. E.D.E.N. Southworth are held by Duke University Library, the Louisa May Alcott manuscripts by the Harvard University Library, and miscellaneous information on women writers in the American Woman's Collection of Connecticut College Library (mostly uncataloged). The Walter Clinton Jackson Library at the University of North Carolina–Greensboro houses a special collection on women from the sixteenth to the twentieth centuries.

Pine Manor Junior College in Chestnut Hill, Massachusetts, lists 298 volumes of first editions of distinguished women writers from 1833 to 1932. The UCLA Research Library's Social Sciences Collection contains a comprehensive collection of literature by and about women and makes available a printed guide. The Kresge Library of Oakland University, Rochester, Michigan, contains the Hicks Collection of approximately 1,000 English-language volumes written by and about women, dating from the seventeenth to the nineteenth century. The Hamilton Library of Elmira College, in Elmira, New York, holds a 100-volume collection of Genteel Women's Reading from 1855 to 1955. The books and manuscripts of Edna Ferber are held by the University of Wisconsin Library at Madison. The Russel B. Nye Popular Culture Collection of the Michigan State University Library houses about 600 books in girls' detective fiction, such as Nancy Drew, the Bobbsey Twins, and Cherry Ames. This collection also contains a substantial holding of Harlequin romances (about 2,000) and small samples of other romances and gothic novels; related romance and confession magazines number about 1,000. The Watkinson Library of Trinity College, Hartford, Connecticut, is particularly strong in women's periodicals of the nineteenth century. Both the Brooklyn Public Library and the Drexel Institute of Technology library have collections on clothing, dress, and fashions in women's history.

A few collections on black American women have been established. Some of these are the Afro-American Woman's Collection in the Bennett College Library, mentioned above; founded in 1946, this collection contains information from the eighteenth to the twentieth centuries. The Schlesinger Library, also mentioned above, houses the Charlotte Hawkins Brown Papers. The Library of Congress has the Mary Church Terrell Papers and the Booker T. Washington Papers, the latter making references to Mary Margaret Washington. For reference books and articles describing the holdings on black women, see Ora Williams's "A Bibliography of Works Written by American Black Women."

Other topical collections that contain contributions by women are the

Ayer Collection at Chicago's Newberry Library, which is one of the most extensive collections of Indian captivity tales in the country. (Others are held by the New York Historical Society and the New York State Library.) Some noteworthy dime novel collections are held at the Denver Public Library, Western History Department, Colorado (over 50,000 volumes); the University of South Florida, Tampa (over 8,000 volumes); Northern Illinois University, Dekalb, in the Founders Memorial Library (over 7,000 volumes); the University of Rochester, New York (12,000 volumes); and New York University's Division of Special Collections (1,000 volumes in the Edward G. Levy Collection of Dime Novels).

The Alverna College Research Center on Women (Milwaukee, Wisconsin) maintains files on sex stereotyping, images of women, and examples of sexism in the media; also available are bibliographies and seminar reports on the status of women. The Women's History Research Center, Inc. (Berkeley, California), manages the International Women's History Archive and a Topical Research Library. In cooperation with Bell & Howell, it publishes *Herstory*, a collection of microfilm volumes of contemporary women's journals and newsletters. The center also publishes directories of women's periodicals and films. The Woman's Educational Equity Communications Network (Bethesda, Maryland) is developing a repository of materials devoted to women in education, including papers on women in literature such as those presented at Modern Language Association conferences.

The Library of Congress, of course, contains invaluable resources on and by women. Lee Ash's *Subject Collections* indexes several topics relating to women and can be useful in locating major collections of material on women. Unfortunately, it does not index popular culture as a category. *Research Guide in Women's Studies* by Naomi B. Lynn et al., lists a few collections. In *Women's Movement Media: A Source Guide,* Cynthia Ellen Harrison includes a thoroughly annotated listing of libraries and their holdings on women; she even includes addresses and telephone numbers.

HISTORY AND CRITICISM

General

A number of useful books have come along in the 1980s to provide important historical data and theoretical developments in women's popular culture. Kathryn Weibel's *Mirror, Mirror: Images of Women Reflected in Popular Culture* still stands as a thorough overview of media representation; however, its 1977 publication date renders it somewhat dated, not only in history, but also in critical approach. With chapters on fiction, television, movies, women's magazines and advertising, and fashion, combining an examination of the reflections of women and critical assessments of the motivations and values behind these reflections, Weibel nevertheless provides a practical guide to dominant trends in the portrayal of women in popular culture; it has particular relevance as a historical document of the seventies. Another work on the seventies which looks more at women as producers is *Women's Culture: The Women's Renaissance of the Seventies,* edited by Gayle Kimball. Sections on "Definitions," "The Visual Arts" (including Judy Chicago, underground women's comics, ritual performance, women's theater, film, and fashion), "Music," "Literature and Dreams," "Religion," and "Organizations" make visible a wide range of women's activities that are mostly considered "popular" culture; there are also bibliographies at the end of each essay. Its theoretical slant is decidedly "cultural feminist," assuming an essential difference between men and women: "Women have distinctive experiences and values and . . . these must be studied as unique contributions to culture." The clash between this view and more recent theory will be noted later. A recent book that focuses on actual cultural artifacts is *Images of Women in American Popular Culture,* edited by Angela G. Dorenkamp and others. It pulls together an amazing variety of essays, excerpts from fiction, critical writings, and advertisements, intended for use in the classroom or as an introduction to materials available for research. While the use of excerpts is sometimes annoying to the scholar already familiar with the material, the book does present a lot of information in a short space and would be useful for generating discussion in the classroom.

Other books that provide historical backgrounds include Jean E. Friedman and William G. Shade's *Our American Sisters: Women in American Life and Thought;* Barbara Welter's *Dimity Convictions: The American Woman in the Nineteenth Century;* Ann Douglas's *The Feminization of American Culture;* Nancy F. Cott's *The Bonds of Womanhood: "Woman's Sphere" in New England, 1780–1835;* Susan Phinney Conrad's *Perish the Thought: Intellectual Women in Romantic America, 1830–1860;* Janet Wilson James's *Changing Ideas About Women in the U.S., 1776–1825;* and Benita Eisler's *Private Lives: Men and Women of the Fifties.*

Friedman and Shade's book is an interdisciplinary collection of essays on both black and white women organized into historical periods, each essay prefaced and followed by suggestions for further reading. Barbara Welter's *Dimity Convictions* is also a collection of essays with the general focus of rediscovering women's history. Hers is a useful sourcebook for sociological, historical, and medical information, and includes the landmark essay, "The Cult of True Womanhood, 1800–1860."

Ann Douglas's *The Feminization of American Culture* investigates the relationship between the contemporaneous disestablishment of the American clergy and the American woman. Carefully argued and painstakingly documented, this book offers a wealth of bibliographical and biographical detail. For Nancy Cott, the domestic fiction of the late eighteenth and early nineteenth century was popular because it reassured those women who, for lack of an alternative vision, were forced to believe in the myth of home and hearth. Based on sermons, magazines, secondary sources, and the unpublished letters and diaries of one hundred women, the book is also indexed and well documented. In *Perish the Thought,* Susan Conrad examines the women intellectuals' interpretation of the nineteenth-century feminine ideal and how they tried to transform it via romanticism. It includes an index and selected bibliography.

In *Changing Ideas About Women in the U.S., 1776–1825,* Janet James relates attitudes to the intellectual and social milieu, "even that limited milieu inhabited by people who wrote books." In eighteenth-and nineteenth-century climates of opinion, James examines the creation and reflection of the English ideal of the decorative and virtuous lady, the radical feminist thought of the Enlightenment, and the moral reformism of the religious revival known in America as the Second Great Awakening. A particularly valuable chapter covers the rise of the woman author. Jumping ahead, Benita Eisler's *Private Lives* follows the fifties generation coming of age in the United States, contrasting images in popular culture with actual experiences of the middle-class white postwar family. In an anecdotal style, Eisler discusses popular public figures created by the media; the sections on Marilyn Monroe and Sylvia Plath in particular connect cultural images with their influence on women's lives and the conflict between image and reality.

Three other books provide historical information on different subcultures: the American South and blacks. Anne Firor Scott's *The Southern Lady: From Pedestal to Politics 1830–1930* is useful as a portrait of what the upper-class southern white woman was like and what she became as a result of the Civil War. She, too, quotes from diaries, letters, magazines, and unpublished manuscripts and spends some time on popular literature and its authors. Scott's footnotes are informative, and she includes a supplemental bibliographical essay. Gerda Lerner's impressive collection of papers, *Black Women in White America,* documents the history of black women from the early nineteenth century to the present. Her materials range from diaries to newspaper articles and court transcripts. Two valuable essays supplement the text: a discussion of the location of her primary sources and a series of bibliographical notes containing information on secondary sources. In *Black Rage,* William H. Grier and Price M. Cobbs describe the pernicious effects of slavery on black women (see their chapter, "Achieving Womanhood," in particular).

Various works are interested in theoretical elaborations of women's position within popular culture and take a much more material stand, looking at relationships of production and consumption from a socioeconomic perspective. One of the most significant works in this area is *Studies in Entertainment: Critical Approaches to Mass Culture,* edited by Tania Modleski. While providing a crucial redirection and reevaluation of mass culture criticism since the Frankfurt School, Modleski's introduction also makes clear the importance of a feminist perspective in current research—her contention, along with the other essayists in the book, is that one cannot undertake an examination of mass culture today without an understanding of the implications of gender and the cultural construction of Woman as Other. Covering a wide variety of cultural phenomena in the various essays, the book is primarily useful for its considerable contributions to theory and methodology. Other important texts would have to include Betty Friedan's *The Feminine Mystique,* a landmark text exploring the origins and consequences of the American mystification of woman. In her investigation, she discusses the role of the mass media in promulgating the myth of the happy housewife. Adrienne Rich's *Of Woman Born: Motherhood as Experience and Institution* takes on the culture's construction of women as mothers, and what mothering signifies alongside the systematic oppression of other possibilities for women. The anthology *Building Feminist Theory: Essays from Quest* provides an excellent introduction to issues of politics, race, and class in contemporary feminism, including sections on "Power and Practice," "The Politics of Everyday Life," and "Feminist Perspectives on Class"; many of the essays directly address issues in popular culture studies. Judith Williamson's *Consuming Passions: The Dynamics of Popular Culture* also develops brief but incisive analyses of various aspects of mass culture, including advertising, fashion, diet, sex, art, education, film, and the nuclear family, and always with a feminist slant; an entire section is devoted to women and pop culture. Although British, Williamson writes about U.S. culture as well, and her theory is equally relevant to both countries.

Related, more general works might include Janice Delaney, Mary Jane Lupton, and Emily Toth's *The Curse: A Cultural History of Menstruation,* Phyllis Chesler's *Women and Madness,* Kim Chernin's *The Obsession: Reflections on the Tyranny of Slenderness,* and Vivian Gornick and Barbara K. Moran's *Woman in Sexist Society.*

Two books that are composed primarily of illustrations are Agnes Rogers's *Women Are Here to Stay: The Durable Sex in Its Infinite Variety Through Half a Century of American Life,* a collection of photographs, paintings, fashion illustrations, and cartoons; and Carol Wald's *Myth America: Picturing Women 1865–1945,* a portfolio of popular art published in the form of prints, advertisements, and postcards. A work that intermixes interviews and commentaries with illustrations is Maxine Nunes and Deanna White's *The Lace Ghetto;* although it emphasizes Canadian popular culture, its contents are not irrelevant to America's history.

Popular Fiction

Popular fiction continues to retain its appeal, for both readers and scholars, and several new works of analysis have appeared in recent years, including Tania Modleski's *Loving With a Vengeance: Mass-Produced Fantasies for*

Women, Janice Radway's *Reading the Romance: Women, Patriarchy and Popular Literature,* Kay Mussell's *Women's Gothic and Romantic Fiction,* and Leslie Rabine's *Reading the Romantic Heroine: Text, History, and Ideology.* Each of these works tackles the thorny phenomenon of women reading romance narratives that would seem to reinforce patriarchal values, and each comes up with a different understanding of why this activity takes place and what it signifies for women and feminist thought. Modleski and Rabine both combine contemporary critical theories with materialist viewpoints, but come up with differing results; Radway calls herself an "ethnographic" critic, basing her analysis on interviews with readers; and Mussell focuses on textual readings and what they tell us about women's daily lives, "hopes, aspirations, values and world view." Any serious scholar in this field would be well advised to consult all four works for an understanding of the complex issues and problems involved in investigations of popular fiction.

Useful histories abound, most of them general and not woman-specific. A recent addition is Mary Kelley's *Private Woman, Public Stage: Literary Domesticity in 19th Century America.* Kelley calls the women writers of this time "literary domestics" and asserts that in both their published prose and their now discovered letters and diaries they reported as unwitting witnesses the public event and their own private experiences; chapters then examine the individual lives and works of over a dozen writers. A truly original approach is that of Helen Waite Papashvily's *All the Happy Endings: A Study of the Domestic Novel in America, the Women Who Wrote It, the Women Who Read It, in the Nineteenth Century.* Papashvily maintains that nineteenth-century domestic novels are cryptic political tracts, written and read by women who chafed under their repressive social conditions, finding patterns of female behavior in the books that she labels subversive to patriarchy. She provides substantial biographical, sociological, and political backgrounds in her discussions of the books that are particularly helpful.

A general history of the development of sentimental fiction is Herbert Ross Brown's *The Sentimental Novel in America 1789–1860,* which traces the influence of Samuel Richardson and Laurence Sterne on the American novel. The most relevant chapters for women and literature are "Sex and Sensibility," in which Brown discusses the female novelists and describes the sentimental heroines; "The Sentimental Formula," in which he provides a paradigmatic description of the genre; and "Home, Sweet Home," in which he discusses the imagery and themes of the domestic novelists. Although it is rather repetitious since Brown has organized his work by ideas rather than by authors, the book is carefully and thoroughly documented and is regarded as an important introduction to sentimental fiction.

Other studies that give attention to women's fiction are three that focus on the phenomenon of best sellers. Frank Luther Mott's *Golden Multitudes: The Story of Best Sellers in the United States* covers the period from colonial times to 1945. In describing these popular books, Mott discusses their publishing history, offers some background material on their authors, and speculates on the reason for their success. The text is indexed and contains three appendixes that list overall best sellers in the United States, better sellers, and annual best sellers in the bookstores. Mott also gives a working definition of the term *best seller*.

Working from the foundation that Mott laid, James D. Hart published his more scholarly investigation of the subject in 1950. His study, *The Popular Book: A History of America's Literary Taste,* is an attempt to explain the success of popular books in terms of historical and sociological data; it covers the period from 1561 to 1949. In his book, Hart devotes considerable space to the women novelists (although he is quite critical of their works) and indexes several women's topics. Another helpful feature is his bibliographical checklist, in which he describes the secondary sources he used to write each chapter. Hart's text is illustrated and includes a chronological index of all the books he discusses.

A more recent examination of best sellers is Suzanne Ellery Greene's 1974 study, *Books for Pleasure: Popular Fiction 1914–1945.* Greene's method is to list the best sellers in a given time span at the beginning of a chapter and then discuss their characteristic contents and formulas. Although this approach often verges on simplistic summarization, it is interesting to follow the social patterns they seem to project from decade to decade, and Greene emphasizes the roles of women and the family in her investigation of these books.

A perennial source of information on what books are selling well is Alice Payne Hackett's series, whose latest compendium now bears the title *80 Years of Best-Sellers 1895–1975;* this volume brings up to date *70 Years of Best Sellers* and is co-authored by James Henry Burke. Lily Deming Loshe's *The Early American Novel* provides useful plot summaries of difficult-to-locate books. Although her summaries can be trusted, some of her other information is no longer valid since the book was published in 1907 before certain facts were available about early American fiction (she attributes *The Power of Sympathy* to Sarah Wentworth Morton, for example, when it has since been determined that its author is William Hill Brown).

A specialized field of growing interest to scholars is that of women's science fiction. *The Feminine Eye: Science Fiction and the Women Who Write It,* edited by Tom Staicar, collects a number of essays of conventional literary criticism on female sci-fi writers, including Leigh Brakett, C. L. Moore, Suzy McKee Charnas, and Joan D. Vinge, among others. The essays expressly investigate "sex roles and attitudes prevalent in the societies of the future," with a nod toward contemporary feminist analysis. Betty King's *Women of the Future: The Female Main Character in Science Fiction* looks at works both by and about women from the early twentieth century to the present, tracking the evolution of female images to today's diverse portrayals. Mostly synopsis with very little analysis, King's text is especially useful for its appendixes: collections and anthologies, women characters in erotic sci-fi, and amazon women.

Earlier works, still of considerable interest, include Dorothy Yost Deegan's 1951 book, *The Stereotype of the Single Woman in American Novels,* which samples American fiction to discern a pattern of description of single females, albeit with some obvious interpretive biases; Katharine Rogers's *The Troublesome Helpmate: A History of Misogyny in Literature,* wherein she surveys a variety of works from classics to contemporaries to trace misogynist attitudes; and Mary Ellmann's *Thinking About Women,* also focusing on misogynist stereotypes in literature. Ernest Earnest's *The American Eve in Fact and Fiction, 1775–1914* argues that literature is not an accurate measure of women's accomplishments, interests, intelligence, and activities of this period, paving the way for recent theories on the relationship between image and ideology. Despite some bibliographic errors, the book is well documented and persuasive.

Still other books that are relevant to women and popular literature are William Wasserstrom's *Heiress of All the Ages: Sex and Sentiment in the Genteel Tradition,* an examination of the relationship between literature and society in America from the 1830s to World War I; Judith Fryer's *The Faces of Eve: Women in the Nineteenth-Century American Novel,* which concentrates, with the lone exception of Kate Chopin, on male novelists; and Kathryn Weibel's *Mirror, Mirror,* which contains a chapter on images of women in fiction. Russel B. Nye, in his extensive history, *The Unembarrassed Muse: The Popular Arts in America,* surveys women's literature as part of his discussion of the development of popular fiction and poetry. Leslie Fiedler's *Love and Death in the American Novel* explores the peculiarly American sexual milieu that keeps the male's positive sexual relationships with women out of its literature. Annette Kolodny's *The Lay of the Land: Metaphor as Experience and History in American Life and Letters* documents the overt and covert sexual imagery of American male authors, which she compares to that of rape. A rather uneven collection of essays is Susan Koppelman Cornillon's *Images of Women in Fiction: Feminist Perspectives;* the best essays are those that explore the influence of society on literature, such as Joanna Russ's "The Image of Women in Science Fiction," Kathleen Conway McGrath's "Popular Literature as Social Reinforcement: The Case of *Charlotte Temple,*" and Cornillon's own contribution, "The Fiction of Fiction."

Magazines

Of all the women involved in magazine publishing, Sarah Josepha Hale continues to attract the most attention. Two early works on this remarkable woman are Ruth E. Finley's *The Lady of Godey's: Sarah Josepha Hale* and Isabelle Webb Entrikin's *Sarah Josepha Hale and Godey's Lady's Book.* Both works are well-documented biographies (the latter is a dissertation), and both reflect the esteem in which she is held by these two writers, an admiration that occasionally interferes with their ability to estimate her worth. More recent evaluations of Hale's accomplishments (such as that found in Ann Douglas's *The Feminization of American Culture*) regarding her in less favorable light, finding her apolitical stance reactionary and hardly mitigated by her interest in women's education. No one, however, tries to underestimate her power and her influence on American magazines and mores.

Four histories of magazines contain information about women's periodicals. Helen Woodward's *The Lady Persuaders,* although it contains a wealth of information about such magazines as *Godey's, McCall's, Ladies' Home Journal,* and *Cosmopolitan,* is virtually undocumented, and her facts are not always to be trusted. It has few footnotes, no bibliography, and is without an index. Much of Woodward's information is firsthand since she worked for years at *Cosmopolitan;* much is also taken from others' research. Woodward's admitted dislike of women's magazines must also be considered. A recent supplement to this field is Trevor Millum's *Images of Woman: Advertising in Women's Magazines.* Replete with illustrations, Millum's text makes some early efforts to correlate images and influence on readers.

A more scholarly and reliable study is Frank Luther Mott's *A History of American Magazines 1741–1930.* Familiar to students of the genre, this important work is especially valuable in that it is thoroughly indexed. Each of the first four volumes has its own index, and the final volume includes a cumulative index for the entire work. In all five indexes, there are extensive entries on women and women's subjects. Volumes I through IV contain essays on various topics in magazine history, which are followed by a section entitled "Sketches of Important Magazines." Volume V is exclusively sketches. Since women's magazines played a crucial role in the development of the American periodical, they are given careful consideration in Mott's *History.* His essays cover such subjects as female education and the woman question. He also quotes liberally from the prospectus of each magazine he highlights, giving its publishing history in the form of publisher, editor, name changes, and important dates. All five volumes are illustrated.

Another less extensive, general history is James Playsted Wood's *Magazines in the United States,* third edition. This single-volume history does not index the topic of women, only the names of the journals and the major figures in the field. It contains a brief general bibliography, however, and the table of contents is fairly descriptive, featuring, among other topics, women's magazines. A final survey is Theodore Peterson's *Magazines in the Twentieth Century,* which is a study of recent periodicals (not all of which have survived into the 1970s). Its most relevant chapters are "Advertising: Its Growth and Effects" and "The Old Leaders that Survived" (*McCall's, Ladies' Home Journal,* and others). It, too, is illustrated.

A book that is composed almost entirely of illustrations is Jane Trahey's *Harper's Bazaar: 100 Years of the American Female.* There is no interpretative text, only sixteen literary selections purporting to reveal *Harper's* contributions to American female culture; many of these selections, however, were not even written by an "American female." It is fun to browse through, but it is less than scholarly. Other attempts to illustrate the relationship between American women and their magazines are more substantial: Dominic Ricciotti's "Popular Art in *Godey's Lady's Book*: An Image of the American Woman, 1830–1860" and Phyllis Tortora's "Fashion Magazines Mirror Changing Role of Women" are examples. A fine essay on this subject, "Images of Women in Women's Magazines and Magazine Advertising," appears in Kathryn Weibel's *Mirror, Mirror*. Images of women found in men's magazines are discussed in Richard A. Kallan and Robert D. Brook's "The Playmate of the Month: Naked But Nice" and in Lee D. Rossi's "The Whore vs. The Girl-Next-Door: Stereotypes of Woman in *Playboy, Penthouse*, and *Oui*". Cornelia Butler Flora's "The Passive Female: Her Comparative Image by Class and Culture in Women's Magazine Fiction" is a study of the image of women in magazine short stories.

Film

Undoubtedly film is the area of greatest growth in studies of women and popular culture; this field now includes numerous full-length histories, theoretical studies, journals, and bibliographies.

Recent works have primarily focused on the intersections of feminist theory and film practice, providing sophisticated models for understanding relationships of representation, ideology, apparatus, and resistive strategies. Teresa de Lauretis has contributed two landmark texts to this study since her first, a collaboration with Stephen Heath called *The Cinematic Apparatus*. In *Alice Doesn't: Feminism, Semiotics and Cinema,* de Lauretis sets up a complex interweave of theory concerning image, narrative, desire, and the viewing subject using the latest developments in feminism, psychoanalysis, and semiotics. Although she applies her theoretical models to specific films, the work is read primarily for its theory and the implications for other studies of women in relationship to their culture; any work on women and representation must now acknowledge this ground-breaking text. More recently, *Technologies of Gender: Essays on Theory, Film and Fiction* gathers together essays written since *Alice Doesn't,* continuing in a similar examination but with more specific applications. Of particular interest are the opening essay, "The Technology of Gender," and the two concluding essays on feminism and women's cinema. Annette Kuhn has also been prolific: her earlier book, *Women's Pictures: Feminism and Cinema,* provides a well-developed, pragmatic approach to feminist film criticism, combining psychoanalytic theory with issues of production and distribution, looking first at dominant (male-directed) cinema and then at women's films, raising important questions about what constitutes feminist film practice. It includes a useful glossary and appendix on film availability as well as a substantial bibliography. Her latest work, *The Power of the Image: Essays on Representation and Sexuality,* brings the latest advances in feminist theory to bear on pornography, dominant cinema, and sexual education/propaganda films. Among other things, her discussion of the problems confronting a feminist analysis of pornography is stunningly lucid, avoiding simplistic reductivism. Again, there is included a bibliography for further reading. E. Ann Kaplan's *Women and Film: Both Sides of the Camera* (1983) also provides crucial explorations of the workings of representation and the construction of the spectator via the cinematic apparatus. An earlier work that combines history, theory, and practice is *Sexual Stratagems: The World of Women in Film,* edited by Patricia Erens. The number of essays is impressive, and the work is structurally organized to consider the male-directed cinema separately from women's cinema. Individual filmmakers and their oeuvre are examined as well as individual films. Useful filmographies and a bibliography are included. In terms of progenitors, all of the above works are deeply indebted to Laura Mulvey's stunning essay, "Visual Pleasure and Narrative Cinema" (1975), which deftly laid out many of the concerns and theoretical parameters that are still being discussed today, particularly in terms of the fetishization of the female body and the replication of the male viewpoint in cinematic technique.

Specialized works include *Home Is Where the Heart Is: Studies in Melodrama and the Woman's Film,* edited by Christine Gledhill, a compilation which addresses the problematic genre of melodrama within the context of white Hollywood cinema. In particular these essays examine the relationship of women—through studies of production and consumption—to the genre historically seen as the "woman's domain." Its superb bibliography focuses on women and feminist criticism. Jan Rosenberg historicizes the woman's film in *Women's Reflections: The Feminist Film Movement.* This sociological study of filmmaking by women, based on numerous interviews, audience questionnaires, and historical data, observes the activity within the context of political movements such as the National Organization for Women (NOW), discussing attitudes toward dominant as well as women's cinema and debates on the political relevance of the avant-garde women's film. It contains useful appendixes and a bibliography. Louise Heck-Rabi relies on countless reviews and interviews culled from books, newspapers, magazines, and journals in *Women Filmmakers: A Critical Reception.* She uses these materials to explore the major works of eleven recognized women filmmakers from the 1920s to the present, providing a comprehensive critical overview but relatively little analysis. Tania Modleski, in *The Women Who Knew Too Much,* reassesses the women in Alfred Hitchcock's films from a materialist-feminist perspective, often in glaring contradiction to earlier critical interpretations, providing a corollary understanding of the covert sexism in much film criticism.

Of the seventies, four books stand out as historical surveys, with varying degrees of comprehensiveness and readability: Marjorie Rosen's *Popcorn Venus: Women, Movies and the American Dream;* Molly Haskell's *From Reverence to Rape: The Treatment of Women in the Movies;* Joan Mellen's *Women and Their Sexuality in the New Film*; and Marsha McCreadie's *The American Movie Goddess.* Rosen and Haskell, both widely available in paperback, particularly mobilized more in-depth studies of dominant cinema; both, basically sociopolitical in outlook, search for cause-and-effect relationships between the images of women in cinema and the social context in which they emerged. Of the two, Rosen is decidedly more readable and better organized. Mellen focuses on U.S. and continental films and filmmakers; of particular interest are her essays on the bourgeois woman, female sexuality, and lesbianism in the film. She also attempts a feminist recuperation of Mae West's films. McCreadie's text is intended as sourcebook for a college-level introductory writing course.

An earlier scholarly collection of critical essays is *Women and the Cinema: A Critical Anthology,* compiled by Karyn Kay and Gerald Peary. The book ranges from feminist perspectives and theory to interviews with women in film production, and contains several helpful bibliographies. A compendium of very brief filmographies is Ian and Elizabeth Cameron's *Dames,* which includes seventy-four actresses whom the editors consider "female heavies," "tarts," or "singers."

Because most critics discuss primarily the role of women when they discuss sexuality in the films, it is not surprising that at least one book that investigates this topic actually focuses almost exclusively on women's sexuality. Alexander Walker's method in *Sex in the Movies: The Celluloid Sacrifice,* like that of most critics of this topic, is to compare the on-screen images of movie stars with their off-screen experiences. As a result, Walker provides biographies of most of the major American sex goddesses, from Theda Bara to Elizabeth Taylor. Of particular interest is his essay on the decline of American cinematic censorship, in which he explores the relationship between the Production Code and the Catholic Legion of Decency. One cavil: Walker, a Britisher, is convinced that the United States is a matriarchy and quotes from certain comedies of the 1960s to prove that the American male has been castrated by the likes of Doris Day and other American females.

In *Sex Psyche Etcetera in the Film,* Parker Tyler offers a rather glib assessment of the decline and fall of famous actresses ("The Awful Fate of the Sex Goddess"). Although he strives for ironic disapproval of their treatment, his own essay smacks of misogyny and is, ultimately, superficial. An anthology of more thoughtful essays on the subject is *Sexuality in the Movies,* edited by Thomas R. Atkins, which includes chapters on social backgrounds, sexual theory, and interpretations of individual films. The book is liberally illustrated.

In *Movies: A Psychological Study,* Martha Wolfenstein and Nathan Leites describe the various guises of "the Good-Bad Girl" as she appears in American films. The essay is reprinted in Bernard Rosenberg and David Manning White's *Mass Culture: The Popular Arts in America.* It is, disappointingly, more descriptive than interpretative. Although it contains no specific topics on women, Lewis Jacobs's *The Rise of the American Film: A Critical History* is useful as a general guide to the contributions of women to American film. Another book that discusses the role of women in a larger framework is Donald Bogle's *Toms, Coons, Mulattoes, Mammies, and Bucks: An Interpretative History of Blacks in American Films.* Since most studies of the film concentrate on white heroines, this book is a necessary corrective to their somewhat narrow perspective. One author who does mention blacks in her general survey, "Images of Women in Movies," is Kathryn Weibel (*Mirror, Mirror*).

Sharon Smith's *Women Who Make Movies* is a directory of bibliographical information on U.S. and foreign women filmmakers since 1896 and contains a current listing of U.S. women filmmakers. Jeanne Betancourt's *Women in Focus* is an alphabetical compendium of more than seventy-five films about women—some written and directed by women, others by men, all with a feminist perspective. The films are thoroughly annotated, and the book contains a bibliography of film periodicals and secondary sources about women. The Women's Film Co-Op publishes a catalog describing short and feature films by, and/or about women that can be ordered from the Co-Op at 200 Main Street, Northampton, Massachusetts 01060. The Women's History Research Center, Inc., sells a catalog entitled *Films by and/or About Women,* which lists hundreds of films, filmmakers, and distributors. The catalog itself is annotated and provides complete rental information. It can be ordered from the Research Center at 2325 Oak Street, Berkeley, California 94708.

Several journals in the field now routinely focus on women in film and as filmmakers, demonstrating the wide variety of feminist perspectives and the extent of scholarly enquiry in feminist film studies. Of particular interest are *Camera Obscura, Screen, Wide Angle,* and *AfterImage. Women and Film* ran from 1972 to 1976 and is available on microfilm. Special issues on women and film include (but are by no means limited to): *Jump Cut,* no. 24/25 (1981), "Lesbians and Film"; *Isis International Bulletin,* no. 18 (1981), "Women and the Media"; *Film Library Quarterly* (Winter 1971–72), "Women in Film"; and *Take One* (January 1972), "Women and Film."

Other journals that have devoted special issues to women in recent years are *Chicago Journalism Review* (July 1971), "Women and the Media" (articles on women in newspaper work); *College English* (May 1971); *Futures* (October 1975), "Women and the Future"; *Journal of Communication* (Spring 1974), on images of women in television; and (Spring 1975) "Women in Detective Fiction: Symposium"; *Journal of American Folklore* (January–March

1975), "Women and Folklore" (including rap groups, black women, images of women); *The Drama Review* (June 1980), "Women and Performance"; *Heresies,* no. 10 (1980), "Women and Music"; *Journal of the West* (April 1982), "Women in the West"; *Frontiers* (Fall 1981), "Native American Women"; *Women and History* (Summer/Fall 1982), "The Empire of the Mother: American Writing About Domesticity, 1830–1860"; *Seminar* (August 1984), "The Sexist Media"; *New Directions for Women* (September/ October 1986), "Women in the Arts" (including lesbians in film and television); and *Women's Studies International Forum,* no. 4 (1986), "Political Fiction."

Because of the recent resurgence of scholarly interest in women's studies, a number of specialized journals have been founded—some still going strong, others lasting only a few issues. The following is a selective list of those that are either easily available or particularly appropriate to women in popular culture: *Feminist Studies,* a journal dedicated to opening "new areas of feminist research and critique"; *Quest: A Feminist Quarterly*—each issue carries a special title; of interest are "Future Visions and Fantasies" (Vol. 2, no. 1) and "Race, Class and Culture" (Vol. 3, no. 4); *Regionalism and the Female Imagination* (continuation of *The Kate Chopin Newsletter*), short articles on women regionalists; *Signs, Journal of Women in Culture and Society,* an interdisciplinary journal typically containing articles, review essays, letters, and "Archives," a list of lost or forgotten documents written before 1950; *University of Michigan Papers in Women's Studies,* and interdisciplinary feminist journal that carries articles, monographs, reviews, and annotated bibliographies; *Women and Literature,* a "scholarly journal of women writers and the literary treatment of women up to 1900," containing notes on work in progress and an annual bibliography of women in English and American literature before the twentieth century in addition to articles; and *Women's Studies,* an interdisciplinary journal that has featured a special issue on androgyny (Vol. 2, no. 2).

BIBLIOGRAPHY

Books and Articles

Ash, Lee. *Subject Collections: A Guide to Special Book Collections and Subject Emphases as Reported by University, College, Public and Special Libraries and Museums in the United States and Canada.* 6th ed. New York: R. R. Bowker, 1985.

Atkins, Thomas R., ed. *Sexuality in the Movies.* Bloomington: Indiana University Press, 1975.

Ballou, Patricia K. "Bibliographies for Research on Women" (review essay). *Signs, Journal of Women in Culture and Society,* 3 (Winter 1977), 436–50.

Banta, Martha. *Imaging American Women.* New York: Columbia University Press, 1987.

Barrett, Michele, ed. *Ideology and Cultural Production*. New York: St. Martin's Press, 1979.

Berkowitz, Tamar, ed. *Who's Who and Where in Women's Studies*. Old Westbury, N.Y.: Feminist Press, 1974.

Betancourt, Jeanne. *Women in Focus*. Dayton, Ohio: Pflaum Publishing, 1974.

Bibliographic Index: A Cumulative Bibliography of Bibliographies. New York: H. W. Wilson, 1978.

Bibliography of Sources Relating to Women. Lansing: Michigan History Division, Michigan Department of State, 1975.

The Black Family and the Black Woman: A Bibliography. Bloomington: Prepared by library staff and the Afro-American Studies Department, Indiana University, 1972.

Bogle, Donald. *Toms, Coons, Mulattoes, Mammies, and Bucks: An Interpretative History of Blacks in American Films*. New York: Viking Press, 1973.

Brignano, Russell C. *Black Americans in Autobiography: An Annotated Bibliography of Autobiographies and Autobiographical Books, Written Since the Civil War*. Durham, N.C.: Duke University Press, 1974.

Brown, Herbert Ross. *The Sentimental Novel in America 1789–1860*. Durham, N.C.: Duke University Press, 1940.

Building Feminist Theory: Essays from Quest, a Feminist Quarterly. New York: Longman Press, 1981.

Cameron, Ian, and Elizabeth Cameron. *Dames*. New York: Praeger, 1969.

Cardinale, Susan. *Special Issues of Serials About Women, 1965–1975*. Monticello, Ill.: Council of Planning Librarians, 1976.

Chernin, Kim. *The Obsession: Reflections on the Tyranny of Slenderness*. New York: Harper and Row, 1981.

Chesler, Phyllis. *Women and Madness*. Garden City, N.Y.: Doubleday, 1972.

College English, 32 (May 1971). Special issue devoted to women.

Conrad, Susan Phinney. *Perish the Thought: Intellectual Women in Romantic America, 1830–1860*. New York: Oxford University Press, 1976.

Cornillon, Susan Koppelman. "The Fiction of Fiction." In *Images of Women in Fiction: Feminist Perspectives*. Edited by Susan Koppelman Cornillon. Bowling Green, Ohio: Bowling Green University Popular Press, 1972, pp. 113–30.

———, ed. *Images of Women in Fiction: Feminist Perspectives*. Bowling Green, Ohio: Bowling Green University Popular Press, 1972.

Cott, Nancy F. *The Bonds of Womanhood: "Woman's Sphere" in New England, 1780–1835*. New Haven: Yale University Press, 1977.

Davis, Lenwood G. *The Black Woman in American Society: A Selected Annotated Bibliography*. Boston: G. K. Hall, 1975.

Deegan, Dorothy Yost. *The Stereotype of the Single Woman in American Novels: A Social Study with Implcations for the Education of Women*. New York: King's Crown Press, Columbia University, 1951.

Delaney, Janice, Mary Jane Lupton, and Emily Toth. *The Curse: A Cultural History of Menstruation*. New York: Mentor Books, 1976.

De Lauretis, Teresa. *Alice Doesn't: Feminism, Semiotics and Cinema*. Bloomington: Indiana University Press, 1984.

———. *Technologies of Gender: Essays on Theory, Film and Fiction*. Bloomington: Indiana University Press, 1987.

De Lauretis, Teresa, and Stephen Heath, eds. *The Cinematic Apparatus.* New York: St. Martin's Press, 1980.

Dorenkamp, Angela G., John F. McClymer, Mary M. Moynihan, and Arlene C. Vadum. *Images of Women in American Popular Culture.* San Diego: Harcourt Brace Jovanovich, 1985.

Douglas, Ann. *The Feminization of American Culture.* New York: Alfred A. Knopf, 1977.

Earnest, Ernest. *The American Eve in Fact and Fiction, 1775–1914.* Urbana: University of Illinois Press, 1974.

Eichler, Margrit. *An Annotated Selected Bibliography of Bibliographies on Women.* Waterloo, Ottawa: University of Waterloo, Department of Sociology, 1973. Printed by the AUCL Committee on the Status of Women, Ottawa, Canada.

Eisler, Benita. *Private Lives: Men and Women of the Fifties.* New York: Franklin Watts, 1986.

Ellmann, Mary. *Thinking About Women.* New York: Harcourt Brace Jovanovich, 1968.

"The Empire of the Mother: American Writing About Domesticity, 1830–1860." *Women and History,* nos. 2/3 (Summer/Fall 1982). Special issue.

Entrikin, Isabelle Webb. *Sarah Josepha Hale and Godey's Lady's Book.* Philadelphia: Lancaster Press, 1946.

Erens, Patricia, ed. *Sexual Stratagems: The World of Women in Film.* New York: Horizon Press, 1979.

Fiedler, Leslie. *Love and Death in the American Novel.* New York: Criterion Books, 1960.

Finley, Ruth E. *The Lady of Godey's: Sarah Josepha Hale.* Philadelphia: J. B. Lippincott, 1931.

Fishburn, Katherine. *Women in Popular Culture: A Reference Guide.* Westport, Conn.: Greenwood Press, 1982.

Flora, Cornelia Butler. "The Passive Female: Her Comparative Image by Class and Culture in Women's Magazine Fiction." *Journal of Marriage and the Family,* 33 (August 1971), 435–44.

Friedan, Betty. *The Feminine Mystique.* New York: W. W. Norton, 1963.

Friedman, Barbara, et al., eds. *Women's Work and Women's Studies/1973–1974: A Bibliography.* New York: Barnard College Women's Center, 1975.

Friedman, Jean E., and William G. Shade, eds. *Our American Sisters: Women in American Life and Thought.* 2nd ed. Boston: Allyn and Bacon, 1973.

Fryer, Judith. *The Faces of Eve: Women in the Nineteenth-Century American Novel.* New York: Oxford University Press, 1976.

Gherman, Dawn Lander. "Frontier and Wilderness: American Women Authors," *University of Michigan Papers in Women's Studies,* 2 (1975), 7–38.

Gledhill, Christine, ed. *Home Is Where the Heart Is: Studies in Melodrama and the Woman's Film.* London: British Film Institute, 1987.

Gornick, Vivian, and Barbara K. Moran, eds. *Woman in Sexist Society.* New York: Basic Books, 1971.

Graubard, Steven R., ed. "The Woman in America." *Daedalus,* 93 (Spring 1964), 577–803. Special issue. Later published in book form; see Robert Jay Lifton, ed., *The Woman in America.*

Greene, Suzanne Ellery. *Books for Pleasure: Popular Fiction 1914–1945.* Bowling Green, Ohio: Bowling Green University Popular Press, 1974.

Greer, Germaine. *The Female Eunuch.* New York: McGraw-Hill, 1970.

Grier, William H., and Price M. Cobbs. *Black Rage.* New York: Basic Books, 1968.

Hackett, Alice Payne, and James Henry Burke. *80 Years of Best-Sellers 1895–1975.* New York: R. R. Bowker, 1977.

Hall, Stuart. *The Popular Arts.* New York: Pantheon Books, 1965.

Harrison, Cynthia Ellen. *Women's Movement Media: A Source Guide.* New York: R. R. Bowker, 1975.

Hart, James D. *The Popular Book: A History of America's Literary Taste.* New York: Oxford University Press, 1950.

Haskell, Molly. *From Reverence to Rape: The Treatment of Women in the Movies.* New York: Holt, Rinehart and Winston, 1973.

Hays, H[offman] R[eynolds]. *The Dangerous Sex: The Myth of Feminine Evil.* New York: G. P. Putnam's Sons, 1964.

Heck-Rabi, Louise. *Women Filmmakers: A Critical Reception.* Metuchen, N.J.: Scarecrow Press, 1984.

Jacobs, Lewis. *The Rise of the American Film: A Critical History.* Rev. ed., with an essay "Experimental Cinema in America 1921–1947." New York: Teachers College Press, 1967.

James, Janet Wilson. *Changing Ideas About Women in the U.S., 1776–1825.* New York: Garland, 1981.

Journal of Communication, 24 (Spring 1974). Special issue on women.

Kallan, Richard A., and Robert D. Brooks. "The Playmate of the Month: Naked but Nice." *Journal of Popular Culture,* 8 (Fall 1974), 328–36.

Kaplan, E. Ann. *Women and Film: Both Sides of the Camera.* New York: Methuen, 1983.

Kay, Karyn, and Gerald Peary, eds. *Women and the Cinema: A Critical Anthology.* New York: E. P. Dutton, 1977.

Kelley, Mary. *Private Woman, Public Stage: Literary Domesticity in Nineteenth Century America.* New York: Oxford University Press, 1984.

Kimball, Gayle, ed. *Women's Culture: The Women's Renaissance of the Seventies.* Metuchen, N.J.: Scarecrow Press, 1981.

King, Betty. *Women of the Future: The Female Main Character in Science Fiction.* Metuchen, N.J.: Scarecrow Press, 1984.

Kolodny, Annette. *The Lay of the Land: Metaphor as Experience and History in American Life and Letters.* Chapel Hill: University of North Carolina Press, 1975.

Kowalski, Rosemary Ribich. *Women and Film: A Bibliography.* Metuchen, N.J.: Scarecrow Press, 1976.

Krichmar, Albert. *The Women's Rights Movement in the United States, 1848–1970: A Bibliography and Sourcebook.* Metuchen, N.J.: Scarecrow Press, 1972.

———. *The Women's Movement in the Seventies: An International English-Language Bibliography.* Metuchen, N.J.: Scarecrow Press, 1977.

Kuhn, Annette. *The Power of the Image: Essays on Representation and Sexuality.* London: Routledge and Kegan Paul, 1985.

———. *Women's Pictures: Feminism & Cinema.* London: Routledge and Kegan Paul, 1982.

Lerner, Gerda, ed. *Black Women in White America: A Documentary History*. New York: Vintage Books, 1972.

"Lesbians and Film." *Jump Cut*, no. 24/25 (1981). Special issue.

Lifton, Robert Jay, ed. *The Woman in America*. Boston: Houghton Mifflin, 1965. Originally published as special issue of *Daedalus*, Spring 1964.

Loader, Jayne. "Women in the Left, 1906–1941: A Bibliography of Primary Sources." *University of Michigan Papers in Women's Studies*, 2 (September 1975), 9–82.

Loshe, Lily Deming. *The Early American Novel*. New York: Columbia University Press, 1907.

Lynn, Naomi B., Ann B. Matasar, and Marie Barovic Rosenberg. *Research Guide in Women's Studies*. Morristown, N.J.: General Learning Press, 1974.

McCreadie, Marsha, ed. *The American Movie Goddess*. New York: John Wiley and Sons, 1973.

McGrath, Kathleen Conway. "Popular Literature as Social Reinforcement: The Case of *Charlotte Temple*." In *Images of Women in Fiction: Feminist Perspectives*. Edited by Susan Koppelman Cornillon. Bowling Green, Ohio: Bowling Green University Popular Press, 1972, pp. 21–27.

Mason, Bobbie Ann. *The Girl Sleuth: A Feminist Guide*. Old Westbury, N.Y.: Feminist Press, 1975.

Mellen, Joan. *Women and Their Sexuality in the New Film*. New York: Horizon Press, 1973.

Meyers, Carol Fairbanks. *Women in Literature: Criticism of the Seventies*. Metuchen, N.J.: Scarecrow Press, 1976.

Millum, Trevor. *Images of Woman: Advertising in Women's Magazines*. Totowa, N.J.: Rowan and Littlefield, 1975.

Modleski, Tania. *Loving with a Vengeance: Mass-Produced Fantasies for Women*. Hamden, Conn.: Shoestring Press, 1982. Reprint. New York: Methuen, 1984.

———. *The Women Who Knew Too Much*. New York: Routledge, 1987.

———, ed. *Studies in Entertainment: Critical Approaches to Mass Culture*. Bloomington: Indiana University Press, 1986.

Montagu, Ashley. *The Natural Superiority of Women*. Rev. ed. New York: Collier Books, 1968.

Montrelay, Michele. *L'Ombre et le nom: sur la feminité*. Paris Editions de Minuit, 1977.

Mott, Frank Luther. *Golden Multitudes: The Story of Best Sellers in the United States*. New York: R. R. Bowker, 1960.

———. *A History of American Magazines 1741–1930*. 5 vols. Cambridge, Mass.: Belknap Press of Harvard University Press, 1938–39, 1957, 1966.

Mulvey, Laura. "Visual Pleasure and Narrative Cinema." *Screen*, 16, (Autumn 1975), 14–22.

Mussell, Kay. *Women's Gothic and Romantic Fiction:* Westport, Conn.: Greenwood Press, 1981.

"Native American Women." Frontiers, 6 (Fall 1981). Special issue.

Notable American Women, 1607–1950: A Bibliographical Dictionary. Cambridge, Mass.: Belknap Press of Harvard University Press, 1971.

Nunes, Maxine, and Deanna White. *The Lace Ghetto*. Toronto: New Press, 1972.

Nye, Russel B. *The Unembarrassed Muse: The Popular Arts in America*. New York: Dial Press, 1970.

Papashvily, Helen Waite. *All the Happy Endings: A Study of the Domestic Novel in America, the Women Who Wrote It, the Women Who Read It, in the Nineteenth Century*. New York: Harper and Brothers, 1956.

Peterson, Theodore. *Magazines in the Twentieth Century*. 2nd ed. Urbana: University of Illinois Press, 1964.

"Political Fiction." *Women's Studies International Forum*, 9 (1986). Special issue.

Project on the Status and Education of Women. *Women and Film: A Resource Handbook*. Washington, D.C.: Project on the Status and Education of Women, 1974.

Rabine, Leslie W. *Reading the Romantic Heroine: Text, History, and Ideology*. Ann Arbor: University of Michigan Press, 1985.

Radway, Janice A. *Reading the Romance: Women, Patriarchy, and Popular Literature*. Chapel Hill: University of North Carolina Press, 1984.

Rawick, George P. *From Sundown to Sunup: The Making of the Black Community*. Westport, Conn.: Greenwood Press, 1972.

Ricciotti, Dominic. "Popular Art in *Godey's Lady's Book:* An Image of the American Woman, 1830–1860." *History of New Hampshire*, 27 (1972), 3–26.

Rich, Adrienne. *Of Woman Born: Motherhood as Experience and Institution*. New York: W. W. Norton, 1976.

Rogers, Agnes. *Women Are Here to Stay: The Durable Sex in Its Infinite Variety Through Half a Century of American Life*. New York: Harper and Brothers, 1949.

Rogers, Katherine M. *The Troublesome Helpmate: A History of Misogyny in Literature*. Seattle: University of Washington Press, 1966.

Rosen, Marjorie. *Popcorn Venus: Women, Movies and the American Dream*. New York: Coward, McCann and Geoghegan, 1973.

Rosenberg, Bernard, and David Manning White, eds. *Mass Culture: The Popular Arts in America*. Glencoe. Ill.: Free Press, 1963.

Rosenberg, Jan. *Women's Reflections: The Feminist Film Movement*. Ann Arbor: UMI Research Press, 1983.

Rossi, Lee D. "The Whore vs. The Girl-Next-Door: Stereotypes of Woman in *Playboy, Penthouse,* and *Oui.*" *Journal of Popular Culture*, 9 (Summer 1975), 90–94.

Scott, Anne Firor. *The Southern Lady: From Pedestal to Politics 1830–1930*. Chicago: University of Chicago Press, 1970.

A Selected Bibliography of Works by Chicanas and Other Women Interested in Chicana Culture. Monticello, Ill.: Vance Bibliographies, 1979.

Sense and Sensibility Collective. *Women and Literature: An Annotated Bibliography of Women Writers*. 2nd ed., rev. and exp. Cambridge Mass.: Sense and Sensibility Collective, 1973.

"The Sexist Media." *Seminar*, no. 30 (August 1984). Special issue.

Smith, Sharon. *Women Who Make Movies*. New York: Hopkinson and Blake, 1975.

Smith College Library. *Catalog of the Sophia Smith Collection*. Northampton, Mass.: Smith College, 1976.

Staicar, Tom, ed. *The Feminine Eye: Science Fiction and the Women Who Write It*. New York: Frederick Ungar, 1982.

Standard Periodical Directory. 5th ed. New York: Oxbridge Communications, 1977.

Tebbell, John William. *A History of Book Publishing in the United States.* 4 vols. New York: R. R. Bowker, 1972–81.

Tortora, Phyllis. "Fashion Magazines Mirror Changing Role of Women." *Journal of Home Economics,* 65 (March 1973), 19–23.

Trahey, Jane, ed. *Harper's Bazaar: 100 Years of the American Female.* New York: Random House, 1967.

Tyler, Parker. *Sex Psyche Etcetera in the Film.* New York: Horizon Press, 1969.

Ulrich's International Periodicals Directory. 17th ed., 1977–78. New York: R. R. Bowker, 1977.

Wald, Carol. *Myth America: Picturing Women 1865–1945.* Text by Judith Papachriston. New York: Pantheon Books, 1975.

Walker, Alexander. *Sex in the Movies: The Celluloid Sacrifice.* Baltimore: Penguin Books, 1968.

Wasserstrom, William. *Heiress of All the Ages: Sex and Sentiment in the Genteel Tradition.* Minneapolis: University of Minnesota Press, 1959.

Weibel, Kathryn. *Mirror, Mirror: Images of Women Reflected in Popular Culture.* Garden City, N.Y.: Anchor Books-Doubleday, 1977.

Welter, Barbara. *Dimity Convictions: The American Woman in the Nineteenth Century.* Athens: Ohio University Press, 1976.

Wheeler, Helen. *Womanhood Media: Current Resources About Women.* Metuchen, N.J.: Scarecrow Press, 1972. *Supplement,* 1975.

Who's Who of American Women: A Biographical Dictionary of Notable Living American Women, 1977–1978. Chicago: A. N. N. Marquis, 1977–78.

Willard, Frances E., and Mary A. Livermore. *American Women: Fifteen Hundred Biographies with over 1,400 Portraits.* Rev. ed. 2 vols. New York: Mast, Crowell and Kirkpatrick, 1897.

Williams, Ora. "A Bibliography of Works Written by American Black Women." *CLA Journal,* 15 (March 1972), 354–77.

Williamson, Judith. *Consuming Passions: The Dynamics of Popular Culture.* London: M. Boyars, 1986.

Wolfenstein, Martha, and Nathan Leites. *Movies: A Psychological Study.* Glencoe, Ill.: Free Press, 1950.

"Women and Film." *Take One,* 3 (January 1972). Special issue.

"Women and Folklore." *Journal of American Folklore,* 88 (January-March 1975). Special issue.

"Women and Music." *Heresies,* no. 10 (1980). Special issue.

"Women and Performance." *The Drama Review,* 24 (June 1980). Special issue.

"Women and the Future." *Futures,* 7 (October 1975). Special issue.

"Women and the Media." *Chicago Journalism Review,* 4 (July 1971). Special issue.

"Women and the Media." *Isis International Bulletin,* no. 18 (1981). Special issue.

"Women in Detective Fiction: Symposium." *Journal of Communication,* 25 (Spring 1975), 98–119. Special issue.

"Women in Film." *Film Library Quarterly,* 5 (Winter 1971–72). Special issue.

"Women in the Arts." *New Directions for Women,* 15 (September/October 1986). Special issue.

"Women in the West." *Journal of the West,* (April 1982). Special issue.

Women's Film Co-op. *1972 Catalogue.* Northampton, Mass.: Women's Film Co-op, 1972.

Women's History Research Center. *Films by and/or About Women*. Berkeley, Calif.: Women's History Research Center, 1972.

Wood, James Playsted. *Magazines in the United States*. 3rd ed. New York: Ronald Press, 1971.

Woodward, Helen. *The Lady Persuaders*. New York: Ivan Obolensky, 1960.

Periodicals

AfterImage. Rochester, N.Y., 1972–.

Camera Obscura. Berkeley, Calif., 1976–.

Feminist Studies. College Park, Md., 1972.

National Women's Studies Perspectives. Old Westbury, N.Y., 1983–.

Quest: A Feminist Quarterly. Washington, D.C., 1974–.

Regionalism and the Female Imagination (formerly *Kate Chopin Newsletter*). State College, Pa., 1977–79.

Screen. London, 1950.

Signs, Journal of Women in Culture and Society. Chicago, 1975–.

Studies on Women Abstracts. Oxford, England, 1983–.

University of Michigan Papers in Women's Studies. Ann Arbor, Mich., 1974–.

Wide Angle. Baltimore, 1978–.

Women and Film. Berkeley, Calif., 1972–76.

Women and Literature. New Brunswick, N.J., 1975–.

Women Studies Abstracts. Rush, N.Y., 1972–.

Women's Review of Books. Wellesley, Mass., 1983–.

Women's Studies. Flushing, N.Y., 1972–.

Appendix: The Study of Popular Culture

MICHAEL J. BELL

At first glance, popular culture seems to be exclusively modern. If the idea brings anything to mind, it is probably images of television, movies, popular music, automobiles, comic books, or fast food, all of which, by their very nature, seem to depend upon an extremely diverse, technological world to explain their existence and to justify their impact upon human life. Such appearances, however, are deceiving. In truth, there has always been a popular culture. Something is popular, after all, if it succeeds in reaching and pleasing as many people as possible. And popular culture attempts precisely that, no more, no less. At its simplest popular culture is the culture of mass appeal. A creation is popular when it is created to respond to the experiences and values of the majority, when it is produced in such a way that the majority of the people have easy access to it, and when it can be understood and interpreted by that majority without the aid of special knowledge or experience. Every human society at every stage of human history has had artists and craftsmen who have produced such materials. Artisans have always sought to fashion objects and ideas which appealed to a select few and to fashion others which delighted audiences as wide as could be imagined. Equally, human communities have long recognized that their productivity and vitality rested not only on their ability to create for small groups with distinctive interests but also upon their ability to satisfy the concerns and desires of broad majorities of people. Still, it is not unreasonable to see popular culture as somehow especially modern. For while that world did not produce the first popular culture, it was the first to define its nature, its worth, and its difference.

Popular, elite, and folk culture are different because they define different experiences. But their differences are not ones of quality. The three are different because they describe different kinds of relationships between producers and consumers. Elite culture is exclusive. Its artists define their task as the creation of something different, something which has never existed before, and yet something which can be evaluated in relation to the known great works of previous times. Elite creators seek to produce "classics" in which the mixture of the subjective part, the artist's personal self, and the objective part, the accepted rules for the production of aesthetic experiences, are combined to produce new ways of confronting and experiencing the human condition. Elite audiences, likewise, accept the idea of creation as a consciously aesthetic act and expect that they will be provided with products and entertainments which will be novel and daring. They know their creators; they expect them to seek out complexity and use it as an end in itself. Elite creations, therefore, even when they are intended for some useful purpose, tend to exist for their own sake. They are appreciated for what they are, for how they compare to the creations of the past, and not for what they might do.

Folk culture is personal. It is the culture of everyday life. Folk creators work with the facts of ordinary experience and with the most regular and routine relations of social life. They and their audiences are immediately present to each other, and they are bound together by the fund of traditional knowledge and practice through which communities hold themselves together from generation to generation. This tradition sets the boundaries by which social life proceeds from moment to moment and by which individuals in that life find and orient themselves with one another. Those who create folk culture, therefore, work with and within the tried and true patterns of experience, and those who are its audience expect that their experiences will reflect the conventions of what has gone before and served them well in the past. Folk culture, accordingly, is a culture of continuity, governed by traditions and the expectation that the experience of daily life, lived as most people do most of the time, will continue largely as it has gone before.

Popular culture is comprehensive. Unlike either folk or elite culture, its creators are seldom known by or know their audiences. They work for the large mass of people, and they seek to satisfy as many and offend as few of those people as possible. Their concern, therefore, is not complexity or profundity, though both may result, but that they will reach, be understood by, and perhaps even move their audiences. The audience for popular culture seeks most of all to be entertained or to have a product that will serve a purpose. They want their values, their expectations, and their experiences to be validated. In a sense, they want novelty, but they do not want that novelty to be overwhelming. The audience for popular art or products wants to recognize themselves in what is being presented to them. They want it to conform to their personal set of critical standards, to be what they like. Popular culture thus tends to be responsive to the marketplace. It aims for a consensus among its public and for the possibility that in reaching out to the majority of the community it can affirm what is already valuable in their lives and offer direction toward what ought and might become important in their world.

One way of visualizing this relationship is to see it not as a jumble of elements randomly piled one on top of another but as an integrated whole in which each component is dependent upon all the others for its existence and meaning. In such a relationship, the whole is greater than the individual parts. The pieces which make up the system are subject to the same rules. They do not simply exist in the presence of each other but continually interact and exchange information. Thus, they are always mutually influencing each other, producing change. And this change produced in any one part in turn produces change in all the other parts. In this way the elements in the relationship take on distinctive features which they could never have on their own. They become bearers of information about themselves and about how they have interacted, are interacting, and will interact with the other components in the system. In sum, they communicate.

A working model of this communication can be diagrammed, drawing on the work of Roman Jakobson, in the following manner:

context

text

creator(s)..............audience(s)

media

Each element in this model represents one of the essential elements out of which a communication develops. For such an exchange to take place, someone must convey something to someone in a certain way under certain conditions. A creator, in this case, offers a text to an audience. That act happens at a specific time and place, a context, and is transmitted by specific means. For popular culture, such a communicative relationship might involve a movie director producing a movie which is literally turned into a film to be shown to an audience in a theater, or a cartoonist producing a comic book which will be printed and sold in stores. Specifics aside, however, what is important is that all of these individual components only become meaningful because they are involved with each other and because that involvement adds important, new information to the whole that no single part could acquire on its own.

Each element in this model also represents a vantage point from which contemporary critical analysis attempts to describe, define, and explain cultural phenomena. Since each component is dependent upon the others, each stands as a way into the whole cultural meaning and significance present in the relationship. They act as refined perspectives from which the others can be watched. By focusing on one feature, it is possible to use it as a window through which the other features can be observed. The text, held constant, or privileged, to use the modern term, can lead the analyst back to its creator or forward to its audience. Equally well, it can speak to its historical times, and depending on whether it is oral or written or filmed, to the available methods for transmission that exist for its presentation to the world. Critical methodology, the way one examines a cultural phenomenon, and critical theory, the justifications for such examinations, therefore, are simply ways of perceiving through one feature to the meaning of the whole event. Not by any means, however, does this mean that either theory or method is itself a simple idea or a simple procedure. What it means is that despite their complexity both remain ways of seeing and interpreting.

The best starting point in the model for describing the various ways of studying popular culture is the text. Texts are easily recognizable. They seem somehow to have substance, to be real, tangible objects that can be held and touched. People can hold a book, see a movie, drive a car, or listen to a song. Seldom, however, can they have as direct a contact with the people who produce such products or who create them. Moreover, texts are usually the first classroom objects that students are asked to criticize. They hold that book in their hands, or are shown that film, or even take that car apart, all in order to explain how it is put together and what makes it work. In terms of the model and popular culture studies, however, the idea of a text refers to more than just the most obvious associations. Text here defines any self-contained product presented by a creator to an audience. It can be the traditional book, but it could also be a car, or a television show, or an actor's performance, or a comic's routine. A text is anything that is presented as a manufactured whole. It can be as simple as the words on a page or as complex as the performance of a play.

Not surprisingly, texts are the component around which the most well-developed body of method and technique has developed. Like ordinary people, scholars, too, have recognized the high visibility of the self-contained object, and they have responded with a number of different means for discovering what such objects are attempting to communicate. The simplest of these approaches, known as the *rhetorical*, is concerned with analyzing the basic components of the surface of a text. It is based on two assumptions. The first states that the text is intended to do something. It does not just exist; it has a definite purpose. The second is that that purpose can be discovered through a careful analysis of the relationships out of which the immediate presence of the text is constructed. Whatever the text is designed to do, it asserts, can be found in the words, the characters, their relationships, the plot, the style, the very techniques out of which the work is made. Once these assumptions are accepted, however, rhetorical analysis divides into two different forms, New Critical and dramaturgical.

New Critical approaches to the text argue that the self-contained quality of the text is so powerful that such objects can be said to exist apart from the world and from their creators. Texts, for the New Critics, stand alone. Arguing that the author's intentions are unknowable and the audience's perceptions untrustworthy, they treat the text as understandable on its own terms. The author's intentions are unknowable because they are not in the text. Regardless of what an author/creator thought he was doing, there is no final way of determining if that is in fact what he did. He might have thought he was doing one thing and, in the end, produced quite another. Moreover, an author/creator's own description of intention is unreliable because there is no guarantee that he is telling the truth. He might be telling the truth as he believed it, but whether it was the only truth or the whole truth can never be known. Similarly, audiences could not be trusted to respond in precisely the same ways or in reliable ways. Knowing what one liked was not a substitute in New Critical analysis for knowing the most correct meaning that could be drawn from the text. Hence, New Critics rely on what the text reveals about itself. Texts are seen as powerfully defined, very specific cultural events whose design contains some special meaning. There is a message in the surface construction of the text, in the immediately observable choices made to unify the text, in the ideas it portrays and the solutions it produces. How does the plot move its characters forward? What happens in these relationships? Do they represent human complexity, or do they act out events and situations in a simplified and conventional manner? All of these questions seek to draw from the text any and all of the potential messages that it can offer up. For the practice of New Critical analysis, the formal relations of these features of the text constitute a logically circumscribed artifact directed toward a goal which succeeds or fails solely in terms of its internal construction. The analyst's task becomes to trace that logic and to determine if it fulfills the intended meaning. What the text means, therefore, is in the end a function of the messages that can be read out of its surface. The more complexly and richly detailed that surface is, the more numerous will be its meanings.

Dramaturgical analysis differs from New Critical over the question of intentionality. Like the New Critics, those who approach a text dramaturgically begin with the text as a self-contained artifact containing a message to be deciphered. They see the text, however, as still within the world. For dramaturgical analysis the text is a performance. It is constructed by someone with a specific purpose in mind, and it contains in its organization and use the evidence of that purpose. The object of inquiry, therefore, is to discover how this purpose is performed. What specific events and situations, symbols and activities, roles and words are used to create what kind of impression? What does that impression convey to those for whom it is presented? In dramaturgical analysis, the goal is to take apart the specific arrangement of information inside the text and measure how that particular information moves its audience from one point of view to another. Overall, then, it does not matter for dramaturgical analysis what the limits of the text are. Objects small enough to be held and whole cultural events can be treated in exactly the same fashion. The parts out of which they are made stand as strategies used by the creator to develop certain images. Granted, the impact of these strategic manipulations cannot be precisely predicted. As before, authorial intention can be frustrated. Despite careful construction, audiences can still see different things than they were intended to see. Nonetheless, the assumption of dramaturgical analysis is that the text is trying to do something to its audience and that that goal is discoverable and describable. A dramaturgical approach, therefore, is as interested in the effect of the text as it is in the message presented. Texts are evaluated not only on their order but on their success. The question is not only how is intention presented but also did it accomplish anything. Texts succeed when they motivate their audiences, and they succeed best when those motives bring the audience to new understandings. Another way of saying this is that texts promise, and their value depends upon how and how well their promises are kept.

A second critical approach which takes the text as its subject is formalist analysis. Unlike the rhetorical approaches, which evolved as almost natural responses to the visibility and availability of the text, formalism began as a particular methodological attempt to solve a specific textual problem. It resulted from the attempts by a group of Russian linguists and folklorists, particularly the latter, to discover if there were any precise limits to the objects they studied. Their problem was that the texts that interested them seemed to be extraordinarily diverse. Folktales, costumes, even spoken language can display a wide range of differences even when they are arguably the same text. One word can be spoken in a variety of ways; two tales can tell exactly the same story and yet have characters and locations that do not at all match. How then, they questioned, was it possible to form scientific opinions about the meaning and use of such objects when they appeared to show contradictory messages about themselves? Their answer was to search for some method of classification which was capable of accounting for the bewildering variety of individual examples which any one cultural form could create. The major initial success of this movement was the work of Vladimir Propp. Through an approach which he characterized as *morphological,* Propp was able to demonstrate that there existed a distinctive, specific, and regular set of features which underlay the construction of all folktales and which made stories as diverse as Snow White and Little Red Riding Hood fundamentally the same. In his *Morphology of the Folktale,* Propp argued that the analysis of folktales could not proceed from the examination of their surface features. These were obviously too diverse for careful study. Instead he began by analyzing a character who did something, in terms of what that action did to advance the flow of the narrative. From this, he determined that these character-action relationships were of a limited number and, more important, followed a rigorous pattern of occurrence. Ultimately, he showed that folktales consisted of thirty-one functions, as he defined these relationships, following only two distinct patterns.

Growing from Propp's work, modern formalist analysis takes as its task the discovery of the underlying fundamental pattern or patterns which give any text its particular form. For formalists, texts are understood as the surface reflections of a deeper set of rules for their production. These rules stand behind the actual texts and govern how they are to be manufactured. They act, therefore, as a formal scaffolding, holding the text together and allowing its audience to recognize that it is like other texts of the same type. Rules are discovered through the application of several fairly basic methodological steps. First, the formalist attempts to discover the component parts out of which the text is constructed. These abstract units of construction are then analyzed in order to determine if they follow any logical pattern and if that pattern is consistent for other texts sharing the same surface similarities. Finally, the formalist attempts to formulate a single consistent pattern of function and action which can account for all the real and potential texts which might occur within a single form.

Accordingly, formalism can be said to be concerned primarily with the discovery and analysis of textual convention. Its central questions, therefore, are defined in terms of the essential organization of form and genre. What are the conventions, the component parts, of specific texts? What is it that makes detective stories alike, or Westerns similar, or situation comedies the same? What are the relationships of these parts to each other? Does the appearance of a hard-boiled detective demand a specific kind of villain and make it impossible that any other kind should appear? Does one kind of hero push all other types off the page? Is there a logical and necessary order to the appearance of actions within an event, and does that order determine the meaning any specific action can have? Can a threat to a hero's life be as real, with only twenty minutes left in an hour television drama, as one occurring in the first twenty minutes of the same show? In an even more obvious example, can the hero of a continuous series ever really be threatened? These questions, in turn, make it possible for the formalist to discover the true differences which make one cultural form or event different from any other. With this information, they argue, it is then possible to discover what is truly meaningful and what is simply the product of the formal rules for creation. In the end, therefore, the formalists assert that form determines both content and meaning. Component parts, the relationship of such parts, the wholistic ordering of those relationships, all these combine, argue the formalists, to produce single examples, the individual texts, that are spoken, or read, or worn. These in their turn open the door to meaning. Insofar as an individual creator follows the necessities of pattern, the text defines itself as within a known form. Insofar as that creator introduces special information and insight, the text acquires its specialness and its character.

The last form of textual analysis is *structuralism*. Like formalism, structural analysis is concerned with getting beyond the surface of the text to the basic organizing principles which make the text possible. Unlike formalism, however, these rules and patterns are not seen as abstractions from the text. For the structuralist, the formal meaning of the text grows from the actual surface of content. This difference in orientation is immediately evident in the manner in which structuralists approach the systematic nature of the text. Like the formalists, the structural analysts consider the text to be an organized whole whose meaning is greater than the sum of its parts. They, however, are more explicit in defining the nature of that wholeness. For the structuralists, texts are understood to function as languages. They are ordered in the way language is, and they are best analyzed in the manner in which linguists analyze their languages. Thus, structuralists draw their assumptions and their procedures from linguistics.

In particular, they begin with the assumption that there is a fundamental difference between language and speech. The former, they argue, is what communities share in order to produce speech. It is the system of rules which permits individuals to speak and understand each other. Speech is what is produced from a knowledge of those rules. Speech, therefore, is an expression of personal freedom. It is what an individual speaker can produce, sometimes imperfectly, when the rules of language are brought into play. Language, however, extends beyond the acts of any individual. It is a social institution, a competence, shared by all the members of the community, which stands apart from individual action and intention. Moreover, this social competence means that language is not a random or free phenomenon. Language is coded. It makes its individual sense because the ideas communicated, if they are to be understood, have to be expressed in a form that the community recognizes and understands. Thus, if a speaker of English wishes to speak to a speaker of French, they either must both be able to speak the same language or they must be capable of developing between them a third language in which to speak their ideas. If they cannot discover such a means of encoding their ideas, then no matter how urgently they need to speak *to* each other they will only be able to talk *at* each other.

Within this linguistic model, meaning is produced through the interaction of two distinct relationships. The first is called syntagmatic. A syntagmatic relationship is one which exists between any linguistic element in a grammatical construction and those other elements immediately next to it. For example, "David" and "runs" can be placed next to each other in English and produce a conventional construction in a way that "David" and "tree" cannot. The first, thus, is a possible syntagmatic relationship, while the second is not, and, obviously, the first means, while the second does not.

One element of meaning, therefore, is dependent upon the number and kinds of syntagmatic relationships which are possible and practical in a given language system. The second kind of relationship is called paradigmatic. A paradigmatic relationship is one which exists between those linguistic elements which can replace one another in syntagmatic relationships without destroying their sense. Thus, in the previous example, any noun could replace "David" and any verb could replace "runs" and the two elements would still be in a syntagmatic relationship. This would stay the case even if the two replacements made no ordinary sense. "Frog philosophizes" is not an ordinary English construction and probably would never occur in conversation, but it still conforms to the syntagmatic expectation of a noun-verb relationship. Accordingly, language is represented as a system of difference, of presence and absence, in which any single element, no matter how large or small, develops its identity in terms of what it is, of what it can replace or be replaced by, and by what it may or may not be placed next to.

For structural analysis, meaning in texts grows out of this system of association and replacement. Like language itself, the texts are built out of codes which are themselves the products of syntagmatic and paradigmatic relationships. These codes may be as simple as the rules and procedures by which sentences and paragraphs are produced, or they may be as complex as the rules and procedures by which fashion, myth, or culture itself is produced and made meaningful. Within these codes, and, more important, from these codes, individual creators construct texts whose meaning is a function not only of what is present and given to the audience but also of what might be there and instead is absent. The text, therefore, speaks as a statement of social intentions. In its organization are the coded relationships, the interplay between the various parts that are present and those which might have served as appropriate substitutes: from these are constructed the basic, acceptable, cultural meanings of the text, the structures out of which the rules of social experience grow.

The undertaking of a structuralist analysis, therefore, follows certain predictable steps. Initially, structural study begins with the distinctive features out of which a text or a collection of similar texts are constructed. Once these patterns are established, then the analyst traces the syntagmatic relationships which exist between the distinctive features, and these in their turn make it possible to isolate the possible alternatives which might have been constructed. More specifically, the analyst begins by attempting to discover a pattern which explains how the text has its particular effect on its audience. What is the outline of relations between characters in a story or set of stories? How do 'A' and 'B' interact, and how does their relationship affect the flow of the narrative? With this pattern, the analyst then examines the process by which it is used to produce critical meanings. How, in the immediate contents of the text, is this pattern articulated, and what does this articulation speak to social codes by which the community forms its ideas about itself and the world? Finally, the analyst attempts to discover the play of contrasts against which these codes and conventions can be read. What else might have occurred without making nonsense of the whole, and what does the presence of one choice and the absence of another say about the immediate text and the culture which produced it? Once this is completed, it is possible to describe the internal relationships which permit the text to say something significant to those communities that know and preserve them.

Another perspective from which the popular culture relationship can be studied is that of the author. In the same way that the idea of the text defined something more than the limited notion of single, constrained object, the idea of the author represents more than the commonsense perception of a single individual who creates a single event from whole cloth. In popular culture, author covers the possibility of a single individual working alone, but it also describes a whole other range of different behaviors. In fact, in popular culture single authorship is not the norm. Most popular cultural forms are produced in several stages, and at each stage of the process several individuals may be directly affecting the creative structure. Movies are the perfect example. They begin with a script which may have been produced by a single author and then rewritten by several more; they then become the concern of a director and an entire production crew, any one of which might affect how the words are transformed into images and sounds, and they then still remain incomplete until they are realized in an actor's performances. Even then movies remain incomplete until they are cut and edited into the product that audiences see when they go to their local theater. Still, despite this potential complexity, examining the popular cultural relationship from the perspective of the author offers some interesting and productive information.

Methodologically, authorial analysis is *biographical*. Its main concern is to recover from the text or event at hand the intentions of the creator. These intentions are seen as the key to the text's meaning and as a reflection of the creator's internal state at the time of creation. Author-oriented criticism, therefore, assumes a direct relationship between what an author desires and what an author produces. The final text is what its creator intended it to be. It is a closed book that the audience can only receive and respond to. In this sense, there is the further assumption that the author is always more powerful than the reader. Not only do readers receive, they fail at their task if they are incapable of discovering and interpreting what the author wants them to know. Thus, authorial criticism is always a process of puzzle solving. The text has been given a right order, and only that order "correctly" explains the content of the work.

Within these critical assumptions, there are two perspectives from which the intentions of the author can be considered. The first concentrates on the external features of the author's life and interests and questions the relationship of these experiences to the created work. What does an author know? What unique or particular events have formed his point of view? Are there social, political, cultural or philosophical problems that have interested a particular creator or have been central to the world in which a creator lived and worked? How have any or all of these entered into the creative process, and how have they molded or altered the final work? In essence, the questions grow from the belief that creativity cannot feed on anything but what an author knows, believes, or experiences. It is this reservoir that supplies the basic building blocks from which any and every creation must be formed. Hence, the contents of the work, no matter how they are finally transformed, begin as an outgrowth of the known world of the creator. The task of the analyst is thus one of interpretation and of the validation of interpretation. The critic is faced with the responsibility of discovering what it is that the creator wants to stand as the message of the work and then of discovering how that message is related to the life experiences of the individual who produced it.

The second biographical approach focuses on the internal, or *psychological,* features of authorial intention. Psychological criticism is concerned with the relationship between conscious intent and unconscious desire. The psychological critic argues that the text is more than just a composite of the biographical "facts" of its creator's life. These, of course, are fundamental. But they are only half of experience. Equally important, for psychological criticism, are the subjective feelings and attitudes which shape how a creative individual responds to the facts of the world. These mold the personality of the individual, they argue, and thus stand as a screen between the world and any individual's experience of the world. Moreover, the psychological critic argues that these patterns of subjective response and reaction between the self and the world are formed in the very first processes of human life. They begin in infancy as each human being learns to cope with reality through interacting with the members of his or her immediate family. Thus, psychological criticism asserts that these early life experiences, many of which occur before an individual is even aware of the social rules for defining what experience is, will act to determine how a creative individual will perceive the world. Accordingly, the text for the psychological critic is a projective device. In it, the creator has constructed from the traditional, public symbols of his society an object which is neither wholly objective nor wholly subjective. Instead, it is a creative sharing of his own private interpretation of the way the world is ordered and the public expectation of the way the world is and ought to be. Thus, the final product displays information which is simultaneously more personal than intended and more universal than expected. It is more personal because the creator is largely unaware, as is any individual, of the patterns of relationship which have produced his or her individual self, and hence unaware of the particular patterns which have gone into organizing the facts of life presented in his or her work. It is more universal because, at an abstract level, every individual in a community has had to undergo a similar process of socialization to the world if they are to be counted as appropriate members of the group. Thus, in finding an audience, the text will touch in some way the unconscious organization by which each individual accounts himself or herself as different from others.

The ability to say something about what a creator "really meant" is very appealing, but it is also what makes the psychological approach the most difficult form of critical analysis. Those who undertake such analyses must not only know the necessary biographical facts of a creator's life and the necessary historical facts of a creator's times which make sense of that biography, but they must also be working with a psychology of the human mind that provides some insight into how a functioning personality is formed and maintained in the world. The great danger, therefore, is that a failure in any one of these areas will make the critic's conclusions, at best, incorrect, and, at worst, ridiculous and dangerous. Psychological criticism should be approached with caution, therefore. It can be done. It does provide important insight. But it demands the highest concentration to make it work properly.

The third facet of the model which can be taken as a perspective for analyzing the popular cultural relationship is that of the audience. In one sense, audience-oriented criticism reverses the major assumptions of authorial analysis. Critical studies that concentrate on the audience begin with the assumption that the created expression is somehow incomplete until it is received and interpreted by someone. They argue that the audience completes the text by making it mean. Before an object or event has been received, they believe, it has nothing but the potential to reach and affect. After it has been received, it has only the effects that its audience creates for it. Hence, audience-based criticism starts by declaring the freedom of those who receive a text to make of it what they will. The audience is thus seen as the final arbiter of taste. It decides what the contents of an object or experience explain, and it determines if these messages mean anything to the world at large. In their most extreme, audience approaches argue that there can be no wrong interpretation of any text since each individual experience is a valid one for the person who is having it. By and large, however, audience-oriented criticism is not naive or simplistic. Rather, it falls into two distinct categories, depending on whether or not the concern is with the individual receiver of a text or with the overall effect of a text on its widest audience.

Critics concerned with how the individual responds to the text are interested basically in the discovery of the conditions under which readers create meaning. Texts, they argue, are multiple realities. They are full of information. One reading may introduce an individual to one particular theme or interest, and a second reading might call attention to a wholly different perspective within the work. One viewing may do even more, since, of course, as the number of senses brought into the process increases, the amount of information which has to be processed increases rapidly and geometrically. Thus, such critics assert that the relationship between creator and audience is open-ended, and itself creative. Many different interpretations exist, accordingly, because no single act of interpretation can ever hope to exhaust all that the text has to say. Given this, individual-oriented critics ask, What are the constraints that control the nature of the reception process? These they define in four different ways. First, it may be that the text cannot say all it might because the author is not aware of all that has been included or of all the ways in which his or her intentions might misdirect the audience. Second, in creating the work, the creator might have intentionally or accidentally misinterpreted a source. Perhaps a source is too painful or too obvious, and thus has to be disguised or distorted in order that the author's originality can shine through. Third, it may be that the text is so controlled by convention that it is incapable of allowing the audience any freedom in its interpretation. Perhaps it is so commonplace that it does not leave any room for thinking and reduces its audience to the role of passive observers. Finally, it may be that the audience is itself blind to the potentials of the text. They may through their culture be incapable of perceiving the differences in a text as anything but aberrations. Thus, the text that attempts to go beyond the ordinary boundaries of social expectation is seen as too radical, or too strange, or too repugnant to qualify as something of value. In the last analysis, therefore, the critic's task is to sort between these various possibilities until one or several succeed in opening the text to interpretation. This is aided, of course, by the recognition that the critical process is also subject to the same constraints as the "reading" process, and hence open to the same forms of interplay.

The approach to the broadly defined audience operates within the same methodological universe as do those which are concerned with individual response. Here, however, the focus is shifted from the qualitative to the quantitative impact of the work. How widely is the work received? Are there any differences in the types and kinds of receptions? What constraints are involved in the reception? The assumption is, thus, that there is a direct relationship between the distribution of a creative work and the effect it has on a community. The methodological task becomes, therefore, to create effective techniques which can examine this problem of distribution. Surveys of audience awareness or of consumption, how many know of or have used the product, are the central procedures through which such information is gathered. Beyond this, those interested in the broad audience response are also concerned with the impact of the various ways of distributing information on the audience's ability to see and value products. What are the relationships between the appeal of a work or object and the various methods in which it can be presented to the public? Does the multidimensional presentation of an image or message increase or decrease the value of an event? Here, accordingly, the concern is broadened to include the problem of availability and its effects on the amount and kind of information an audience has when it acts to interpret a message. Can a message be experienced in more than one way, and do these various experiences reinforce or contradict each other? The broadly focused audience perspective, then, seeks to locate the effects of a product within the network of its presentation. Those who know it constitute the body of people who can be affected by it. Thus, the meaning of the work can only be known and measured in terms of the patterned reception it did or did not receive from the public world into which it was launched and within which it has existed.

Though these last questions derive from a concern with the audience's perspective, they reflect equally well another of the perspectives from which the popular cultural relationship can be studied, that of *media*. Media studies focus on the relationship between the form of a message and its impact. They argue that there is a direct relationship between the formal method in which information is communicated and the response it brings forth from its audience. For media studies, print, television, radio, oral speech, dance, and the like constitute methods of encoding and transmitting information. They represent distinct and wholly individual ways in which the same message can be presented. Accordingly, media specialists are concerned with the problem of choice. Since the different media present and represent information in different ways, the choice of one way of transmitting an idea or image over another determines in the most basic manner how the message can be perceived. Knowing, therefore, what choices were made, why they were made, and what effects they had on the nature, quality, and distribution of the message allows media analysts to describe not only what was experienced by the audience but also how that particular experience was actually created.

Media analysis approaches these problems from the perspectives of capacity and constraint. Capacity, at its most technical level, refers to the absolute quantity of information a particular channel can carry. It is the analysis of what a communication relationship, for example a speaker and a hearer, can tolerate before the messages dissolve into nonsense. Thus, though the human voice can speak much faster than 150 words per minute, the human ear can only absorb sound at or near that rate. If a speaker wants to be understood, therefore, he or she should not exceed that rate. In popular culture studies, capacity is treated less technically. Analysts begin with the technical information on how much any sensory system of the human mind can deal with and, using that as a guide, question the particular cultural constraints which expand or limit a particular channel of mass communication. Cable television is a particularly good example of a form upon which such an analysis is conducted. The ability of television to transmit information is nearly limitless. It can use the full range of verbal and visual codes to entertain an audience, to persuade them to buy a product, to believe an idea, or to take a "fact" for granted. Moreover, though it is a public medium, television creates a private relationship between creator and audience. Millions may be watching at any one time but most do so in their own homes, alone or with family. Cable television expands even this enormous capacity. Through its use of satellite transmissions and its vast expansion of the number of individual channels, it offers the possibility of transmitting anything that can be created and for which an audience exists. Some cable systems, in fact, already transmit everything imaginable. Still, most communities are much less liberal in what they will allow their cable systems to transmit. They establish boards of review and constantly monitor what is being presented. Thus, an unlimited capacity to communicate is brought under the control of community standards, and these determine the kind and quality of events which can be viewed.

This focus on capacity can be even more refined. Instead of examining a medium in revolution, it can be used to draw attention to the cultural constraints which affect the transmission of single ideas or themes. Thus, media analysis can focus on the transmission of violence or sex through a single medium, examining the kinds which can be transmitted, the contexts in which it can appear, the results it produces in the audience. Using television, again, media analysts have examined the violence in children's programming or sex in soap operas, or the stereotypic characterizations of women and minorities in comedies. In these cases, the analyst begins by establishing the criteria which frame the form to be constructed. What kinds of characters or relations are used to create particular messages? How do the limits of time organize what can be presented? If a story has to be ready for the 6 o'clock news, it might have to be reduced to its bare essentials, while if it is for the next day's newspaper, it might contain all sorts of extra detail. Within these criteria, the analyst next attempts to determine how the particular ideas or images are formulated against the background of the method in which they are to be presented. How, they ask, for example, does the use of one ethnic type as villains affect the public's perception of that group, or conversely, how does the continued use of another type as heroic characters affect that group's image? The key in each case is a concentration on the conditions under which the idea or image is experienced. How is what is given made meaningful by the manner in which it is given?

The analysis of the cultural capacity of particular media can even be further refined through a focus not on what is intentionally given, but rather on what is unconsciously or unintentionally presented. Here what is questioned is the relationship between the ability of certain mass communication techniques to overwhelm the audience with information and the audience's selective acceptance of that information. Thus, what is examined is, for example, the organization of messages within an advertisement and the impact it has. Where is the announcement of the hazardous effects of smoking in relation to all the other "facts" in the advertisement? Alternatively, how does the display of information within a news broadcast affect the audience's perception of the quality of life within its community? Do people see the world as violent or safe because the order of stories emphasizes "bad" news over "good"? Overall, then, media analysis discusses the convergence between the pattern of input, what is put into the text, and the pattern of output, what is taken out by the audience. Its subject, accordingly, is human linkage. It seeks to explain the ties that bind people together, the conditions under which messages can be exchanged, in order to answer how those ties make people into what they are.

The final perspective from which the popular culture relationship can be examined is that of *context*. The goal of contextual analysis is to locate the text in some place. It assumes that objects, events, and even ideas cannot exist in isolation from the constraints of the real world. They happen in time and space; that is what makes them real, that is how people know they exist, that is the only way they can be reacted to by an audience. The environment, therefore, provides the boundaries in which experiences quite literally happen. Accordingly, the problem for contextual analysis is twofold. First, it is necessary to determine the limits of the event. What, to use Erving Goffman's term, are the *frames* of experience? Where do objects or events begin and end? For example, defining the limits of a football game would seem a simple proposition. Football is what happens on the field between the opposing teams. This behavior is monitored by the referees and controlled by the rules of the game. Finally, it is limited by the size of the field, one hundred yards by fifty yards, and the length of time the game can be played, four quarters of fifteen minutes each. This context of football, however, does not take into consideration what happens on the sidelines, the place of coaching, or any of the other immediate activities which can be part of the "game." Neither does it consider the relationship between what happens on the field and what goes on in the stands among the fans whose cheering or booing might directly affect the play of the game.

Even when the frames are well defined, contextual analysis is still faced with determining the relationships between the individual boundaries and with describing their effects on each other. To continue the same example, imagine that the context of the football game is drawn to include everything that happens inside the stadium from the moment the game begins until the moment it ends and that the boundaries between each individual frame, playing field, sidelines, grandstands, behind the stands, are precisely delineated. The question still remains as to how each individually bounded event connects to the others. Are the players responding to the activities of the fans in the stands when they accomplish something unexpected, or do they motivate their own behaviors? What are the lines of influence and responsibility? How is the power to control or command distributed? Each of these questions, then, seeks to expand on the nesting of context within context to inquire into the location of meaning.

In terms of its practice, contextual analysis operates at three distinct levels. The first is concerned with the immediate *frame* of an object or event. A story, as an example, does not not just come out of the blue. Usually, someone wants to tell it, someone is there to listen, there is a reason for its telling, and it happens in some particular place at some particular time. The immediate level of contextual analysis is concerned with these last phenomena. Are the contexts of stories individualized? Can, for example, the same kind of joke be told at a party as could be told in a church? How do the different contexts of experience—classrooms, hallways, bars, babershops, offices—expand or contract the abilities of individuals to think certain ways, to say certain things, or to feel different emotions? Can such places contain the same events and acts, and can those experiences be interpreted in the same way?

The second level of contextual analysis is *cultural*. At this level, the concern shifts from the experience as it is actually lived, from a participation in the event, to the social community which makes the event possible. Culture is concerned with group. It is generally defined as the knowledge an individual needs to be a functioning member of a specific enclave. It takes as its subject the conditions under which group membership is possible. What does being Irish, or Polish, or German mean? How does membership in such a community (or any other type of social community that might be defined) affect individual response to an idea, object, or event? How does one group's understanding of its own identity affect its ability to evaluate another group? In popular cultural studies, cultural analysis is particularly important because so much of the popular nature of the materials is constructed out of the conventional images and ideas that make up American society. Thus, often, the texts of popular culture deal in the stereotypes one community has of itself and of the other communities in its world. These, in turn, evoke expected responses such as the beliefs that the "others" are really like their presentations in popular culture, that the media misrepresent the real identities of the communities they draw their images from, but they also serve to raise questions about how culture itself molds and operates through the lives of individuals. Thus, cultural analysis of popular culture permits the examination of how the various structures of identification that individuals use to define themselves as alike and different from the others around them create meaning out of the artifacts of the social world.

The final level of contextual analysis is the *historical*. Historical analysis is concerned with the problems of origin and change. Its goal is to discover where something came from, how it got to be the way it is, and what it went through to get that way. Historical analysis seeks to understand the social, political, and intellectual constraints that permit one kind of object to arise and not another. What is it about the times of an event that make

the choice of one cultural form appropriate? For example, what is the relationship between the rise of a particular genre of popular literature such
as science fiction or Western novels and the world in which they are created?
Can they only exist in a world of a certain type and experience, or can they
transcend their context and exist under any conditions? Certainly, science
fiction has survived for a hundred years as a popular form, but an enormous
amount of such fiction is hopelessly outdated and unread. Did these works
by limiting themselves to the science of their times, and thus doing what
they needed to do in order not to be seen as nonsense, also make it impossible
for them to be seen as sensible at any other time? As well, historical analysis
seeks to map out the progress of such change through time. The Western
novel, for example, began at a time when the presence of the American
Indian was not perceived as a threat to the white settling of the New World.
It also arose at a time when those native Americans were seen by some
romantic thinkers as Noble Savages, somehow apart from the destructive
influences of civilization. Indian characters were varied in their presentations, therefore, with a surprising number actually being shown as more
honest and moral than their than white counterparts. As the availability of
land became a question and the Indian presence an impediment to its occupation, Indian characters were increasingly portrayed as vicious savages
incapable of any human virtues, suitable only to be exterminated. This
image continued well into the twentieth century, long after the settlement
of America was complete, and only shifted in the last decades under pressure
from Indian activists rightfully offended by their unfair, biased presentation
in the media. Thus, a historical analysis of this process would seek to
discover the relationship between these "facts" and the different times they
represented.

Accordingly, contextual analysis, at whatever level it is practiced, argues
that the social surroundings of an activity influence the perceptions of the
people within its boundaries. Within the walls, literal, cultural, and historical, of such social organizations, it attempts to explain how events are
defined and how such definitions of situation create meaning for the moment, for the community, and for the times. And, in this, it asserts that
the sense of identity and community shared by the members of a social
group arises not only from what the members know and do but also from
the social situation that holds such knowledge and action together.

Knowing the kinds of questions and the reasons why they are important
are only the first steps in research. It is also necessary to know what else
has been written on the same subject. Research, after all, is not just a process
of solving an interesting problem. That is a legitimate beginning, but it is
of little use if the problem has been solved already, or if the new solution
fails to say all that it could because it does not take into account the ideas
and discoveries of previous researchers. Accordingly, the starting point of
research, of studying popular culture in this case, is to examine the basic

bibliography of the topic that has been chosen. This material can be found in the individual bibliographies at the end of each of the chapters in these volumes. They contain the major articles and books on each particular topic and provide the necessary information about the kinds of studies that have been done. By examining them and using their information, it is possible to see concrete examples of how individual scholars in specific areas have approached a popular cultural topic and attempted to say something significant about it.

The bibliographic essay that follows attempts to do much the same for the practice of critical analysis, with some differences. It, too, is designed to provide the basic introductory texts, collections of essays, and articles for each approach that has been described, but it does not attempt or pretend to be comprehensive. There are an enormous number of works that use each of the methods described, and any number of these could be included in this survey. Long lists of theoretical and methodological discussions, however, can sometimes be overwhelming to the nonspecialist, as they often are for the specialist. Accordingly, rather than overpower with lists of texts for each approach, this bibliographic survey contains only a selection of each critical practice. The individual choices, therefore, do not tell the whole story on any one method of analysis. They are intended to open the doors to each method in the simplest and easiest manner, but more reading will be required if any particular method is to be used. The choices, then, are mini-introductions. Each section is designed to point up what each critical practice hopes to accomplish, to point out where other relevant information can be found, and, finally, to serve as a model of how a successful use of a particular method might look when it is finished.

Because it is the oldest method discussed, New Criticism has the broadest and most established bibliography. Still, for the beginning student, the best starting points are the essays and arguments that initiated the approach. Several of these can be found in William K. Wimsatt, Jr., and Monroe C. Beardsley, *The Verbal Icon: Studies in the Meaning of Poetry* (Lexington: University of Kentucky Press, 1953). As well, an insight into the working out of the approach can be found in Cleanth Brooks, *A Shaping Joy: Studies in the Writer's Craft* (London: Methuen 1971), and Elder Olson, *Tragedy and the Theory of Drama* (Detroit: Wayne State University Press, 1961). A nonliterary approach similar to that of the above works can be found in E.H. Gombrich, *Art and Illusion* (Princeton, N.J.: Princeton University Press, 1961).

The most accessible examples of dramaturgical analysis can be found in the writings of its founder, Kenneth Burke, of Hugh D. Duncan, and of the sociologist Erving Goffman and his followers. Burke's output is wide and varied, and nearly any of his works provides an excellent introduction to this approach. One of his best, however, remains the collection of essays, *The Philosophy of Literary Form: Studies in Symbolic Action* (Baton Rouge:

Louisiana University Press, 1941). Duncan's use of the dramaturgical approach can be found in his *Communication and Social Order* (New York: Oxford University Press, 1968). Like Burke, Erving Goffman has produced a remarkable body of work. Two of his works that best exemplify his use of dramaturgical concepts are *The Presentation of Self in Everyday Life* (Garden City, N.Y.: Doubleday, 1959) and *Frame Analysis* (New York: Harper and Row, 1974). Three other books that extend Goffman's work are Lyn H. Lofland, *A World of Strangers: Order and Action in an Urban Public Space* (Prospect Heights, Ill.: Waveland Press, 1985 [reissued]), Michael J. Bell, *The World from Brown's Lounge: An Ethnography of Black Middle Class Play* (Urbana: University of Illinois Press, 1983), and Gary Alan Fine, *With the Boys: Little League Baseball and Preadolescent Culture* (Chicago: University of Chicago Press, 1987).

Though it can, at times, be complex, one of the best starting points for understanding formalist analysis is Victor Erlich, *Russian Formalism: History, Doctrine* 3rd ed. (New Haven: Yale University Press, 1972). There are so many other good introductions to the formalist approach that choosing representative texts has become almost impossible; still, three very useful texts are Jan Mukarovsky, *Aesthetic Function, Norm and Values as Social Facts,* translated by Mark E. Suino (Ann Arbor: University of Michigan Press, 1979), P.N. Medvedev and Mikhail Bakhtin, *The Formal Method in Literary Scholarship,* translated by A.J. Wehrle (Baltimore: Johns Hopkins University Press, 1978), and Fredric Jameson, *The Prison-House of Language: A Critical Account of Structuralism and Russian Formalism* (Princeton, N.J.: Princeton University Press, 1972). Of course, to observe the formalist method in action it is still best to begin with Vladimir Propp's *Morphology of the Folktale* (Austin: University of Texas Press, 1968). Propp was one of the first formalist critics, and his work continues to be a marvelous introduction to how formalist technique can be applied. A more concise explanation of the method can be found in Alan Dundes, "From Etic to Emic Units in the Structural Study of Folktales," *Journal of American Folklore,* 75, 95–105. As well, Dundes's "On Game Morphology: A Study of the Structure of Non-Verbal Folklore," *New York Folklore Quarterly,* 20, 165–74, offers an interesting use of the approach with nonnarrative materials. Lastly, Tzvetan Todorov's *The Fantastic: A Structural Approach to a Literary Genre,* translated by Richard Howard (Cleveland: Case Western University Press, 1973), provides an informative and readable example of the manner in which the method can be developed and the kinds of new insights that such developments can provide.

Like formalist analysis, structuralism has an identifiable beginning in the work of a single individual, the French anthropologist Claude Lévi-Strauss. His works, *Structual Anthropology* (New York: Basic Books, 1963) and *The Savage Mind* (Chicago: University of Chicago Press, 1966), are the best statements of his very complex approach. However, the beginning reader is better off starting with less formidable introductions. Several collections of essays and interpretations which provide such entry are Michael Lane, ed., *Structuralism: A Reader* (London: Jonathan Cape, 1970), especially Lane's introduction, pp. 11–43; Terence Hawkes, *Structuralism and Semiotics* (London: Methuen, 1977); Jonathan Culler, *Structuralist Poetics: Structuralism, Linguistics and the Study of Literature* (London: Routledge and Kegan Paul, 1975); and, finally, Ino Rossi, ed., *The Unconscious in Culture: The Structuralism of Claude Levi-Strauss in Perspective* (New York: E.P. Dutton, 1974). Two works that exemplify structuralist analysis in different and special ways are Henry Glassie, *Folk Housing in Middle Virginia: A Structural Analysis of Historic Artifacts* (Knoxville: University of Tennessee Press, 1975), and Roland Barthes, *Mythologies* (Paris: Editions du Seuil, 1957), which remains even today the most witty and literate introduction to the practice of structural analysis.

The practice of biographical criticism depends upon exactly what facts are or can be known about the individual under analysis. Its starting point, therefore, has to be a gathering of all the basic facts of the individual's life and work. Only then can the work of relating the two begin in earnest. This means, however, that each example of such analysis is as unique as the life it attempts to describe. Some readable and potentially useful examples of how biography might be accomplished are Phyllis Rose, *Parallel Lives: Five Victorian Marriages* (New York: Vintage Books, 1984), Martha Saxon, *Louisa May: A Modern Biography of Louisa May Alcott* (Boston: Little, Brown, 1977), and John Edgar Wideman, *Brothers and Keepers* (New York: Holt, Rinehart and Winston, 1984). Realistically, however, most students will be asked not to produce a full-length biography but what is commonly called a biographical-bibliographical essay in which the task is to relate portions of an individual's life to some work or activity they accomplished. Here, the task depends on the particular relationship that can be established between individuals, their ideas, and events. Some examples of how this biographical practice can be accomplished are Peter Conrad, *Imagining America* (New York: Oxford University Press, 1980), and Donald E. Pease, *Visionary Compacts: American Renaissance Writings in Cultural Context* (Madison: University of Wisconsin Press, 1987).

As noted earlier in this essay, psychological criticism is the most difficult of all methods described and must be undertaken with the greatest restraint. For those interested in examining this approach, the best starting point is still a collection of essays edited by Hendrik M. Ruitenbeek titled *Psychoanalysis and Literature* (New York: E.P. Dutton, 1964). These offer an intelligent introduction to the terminology of psychological criticism as well as a variety of well-documented, well-written analyses of the relationship between the individual mind of a creator and the creations that it produces. Another excellent collection of psychoanalytically oriented essays is *The Practice of Psychoanalytic Criticism* (Detroit: Wayne State University Press,

1976), edited by Leonard Tennenhouse. Two useful works by Norman Holland that employ psychoanalytic methodology and that are also excellent as introductions to psychoanalytic criticism are *The Dynamics of Literary Response* (New York: Oxford University Press, 1968), and *5 Readers Reading* (New Haven: Yale University Press, 1975). As well, Martin Grotjahn's *Beyond Laughter* (New York: McGraw-Hill, 1958) and Alan Dundes's collection of essays, *Parsing Through Customs: Essays of a Freudian Folklorist* (Madison: University of Wisconsin Press, 1987), are excellent examples of the strengths and weaknesses of the psychoanalytic method. Finally, Joseph Natioi and Frederik L. Rusch's *Psychocriticism: An Annotated Bibliography* (Westport: Greenwood Press, 1984) provides a useful compilation of the most recent work in the area.

Audience-oriented critical approaches that focus on the individual's particular response to the text in question come in a wide variety and with extreme differences in difficulty. Students interested in this approach, therefore, should take their time and move slowly through this potentially complicated methodological terrain. A good starting point is Wolfgang Iser's essay, "The Reading Process: A Phenomenological Process," *New Literary History* 3:278–99. Another potential beginning can be found in Maurice Merleau-Ponty's essay, "Cezanne's Doubt," found in his collection of essays, *Sense and Non-Sense,* translated by Hubert L. Dryfus and Patricia Allen Dryfus (Evanston, Ill.: Northwestern University Press, 1964, pp. 9–24). Other seminal works in reception theory are Iser's *The Art of Reading* (Baltimore: Johns Hopkins University Press, 1966) and *The Implied Reader* (Baltimore: Johns Hopkins University Press, 1972), Marc Eli Blanchard's *Description: Sign, Self, Desire* (The Hague: Mouton, 1980), Hans Robert Jauss, *Towards an Aesthetic of Reception,* translated by T. Bahti (Minneapolis: University of Minnesota Press, 1982), and Umberto Eco, *The Role of the Reader: Explorations in the Semiotics of Texts* (Bloomington: University of Indiana Press, 1979). Two useful collections of essays and a good critical introduction to the method of response criticism are Susan Suleiman and Inge Crosman, eds., *The Reader in the Text: Essays on Audience and Interpretation* (Princeton: Princeton University Press, 1980), Jane P. Tompkins, ed., *Reader-Response Criticism: From Formalism to Post-Structuralism* (Baltimore: Johns Hopkins University Press, 1980), and Robert C. Holub, *Reception Theory: A Critical Introduction* (New York: Methuen, 1984). Sociological approaches to the audience's involvement in the creation of meaning, often grouped under the rubrics of cognitive anthropology and ethnomethodology, can be found in Alfred Schutz, *The Phenomenology of the Social World* (London: Heinemann, 1974), Harold Garfinkel, *Studies in Ethnomethodology* (Englewood Cliffs, N.J.: Prentice-Hall, 1967), and Aaron Cicourel, *Cognitive Sociology* (New York: Basic Books, 1973). Four excellent enthnographic examples of the method at work are Kenneth Kusterer, *Know-How on the Job: The Important Working Knowledge of "Unskilled" Work-*

ers (Boulder, Colo.: Westview Press, 1978), Mihaly Csikszentmihaili and Eugend Rochberg-Halton, *The Meaning of Things: Domestic Symbols and the Self* (Cambridge, England: Cambridge University Press, 1981), Robert McCarl, *The District of Columbia Fire Fighters' Project: A Case Study in Occupational Folklife* (Washington; D.C.: Smithsonian Institution, 1985), and Patricia Adler, *Wheeling and Dealing: An Ethnography of an Upper-Level Drug Dealing and Smuggling Community* (New York: Columbia University Press, 1985). Finally, an excellent translation of this sociolgical approach into practical techniques for data gathering and analysis can be found in John Lofland's *Analyzing Social Situations* (Belmont, Calif.: Wadsworth, 1971).

Approaches that use the broadly conceived audience model can be found in Russel B. Nye, *The Unembarrassed Muse* (New York: Dial Press, 1970). This work is a classic in popular culture studies and remains a useful survey of how popular tastes have been transformed in different historical contexts. Other, older works that cover the same ground are James D. Hart's *The Popular Book: A History of America's Literary Taste* (Berkeley: University of California Press, 1950) and Luther Mott's *Golden Multitudes* (New York: Macmillan, 1947). Useful newer studies include Marshall Berman, *All That Is Solid Melts into Air: The Experience of Modernity* (New York: Penguin Books, 1985), Werner Sollors, *Beyond Ethnicity: Consent and Descent in American Culture* (New York: Oxford University Press, 1986), and Cecelia Tichi, *Shifting Gears: Technology, Literature and Culture in Modernist America* (Chapel Hill: University of North Carolina Press, 1987).

Marshall McLuhan's *Understanding Media* (New York: McGraw-Hill, 1964), and Russell Lynes's *The Tastemakers* (New York: Harper and Row, 1971) are still excellent, if quirky, introductions to media studies. Several other interesting and helpful works that explore the theory and process of media analysis in a variety of forms are Joshua Meyrowitz's *No Sense of Place: The Impact of Electronic Media on Social Behavior* (New York: Oxford University Press, 1985), *The Myths of Information: Technology and Post-Industrial Culture* (Madison: University of Wisconsin Press, 1980), edited by Kathleen Woodward, and Andreas Huyssen's *After the Great Divide: Modernism, Mass Culture, Postmodernism* (Bloomington: University of Indiana Press, 1986). For the ambitious reader, Elizabeth L. Eisenstein, *The Printing Press as an Agent of Change: Communications and Cultural Transformations in Early Modern Europe,* 2 vols.(New York: Cambridge University Press, 1979), is a superb analysis of the impact of media on culture. Three recent and highly readable analyses of specific media are Dick Hebdige's *Cut 'N' Mix: Culture, Identity and Caribbean Music* (New York: Methuen, 1987), E. Ann Kaplan's *Rocking Around the Clock: Music Television, Postmodernism and Consumer Culture* (New York: Methuen, 1987), and Janice Winship, *Inside Women's Magazines* (London: Pandora, 1987). Finally, though not directly concerned with the media themselves, two works by

Raymond Williams, *Culture and Society: 1780–1950* (New York: Columbia University Press, 1958) and *The Long Revolution* (London: Chatto and Windus, 1960), continue to provide marvelous insight into how changes in technology and the creation of new communicative media act to transform both popular taste and the structure of society itself.

There are a number of excellent works that offer an introduction to the practice of contextual analysis. Dell Hymes has written a series of articles that explore the why and how of the ethnography of context. Among the best are his "Towards Ethnographies of Communication," in *The Ethnography of Communication,* edited by John J. Gumperz and Dell Hymes (American Anthropologist, 1964, pp. 1–34), "The Ethnography of Speaking," in *Anthropology and Human Behavior,* edited by T. Gladwin and W.C. Sturtevant (Washington, D.C.: Anthropological Society of Washington, 1962, pp. 13–53), and "Models of the Interaction of Language and Social Setting," *Journal of Social Issues,* 33, 8–28. As well, Joel Sherzer and Regna Darnell provide a good working outline to the practice of contextual ethnography in their "Outline Guide for the Ethnographic Study of Speech Use," in *Directions in Sociolingusitics: The Ethnography of Communication,* edited by John Gumperz and Dell Hymes (New York: Holt, Rinehart and Winston, 1972). Good examples of the ethnography of context abound; among some of the best are Richard Bauman's "Quaker Folk Linguistics and Folklore," in *Folklore: Performance and Communication,* edited by Dan Ben-Amos and Kenneth   Goldstein   (The Hague: Mouton, 1975), and "The Le Havre General Store: Sociability and Verbal Art in a Nova Scotia Community," *Journal of American Folklore,* 85, 330–43, which explore the uses of this method with historical/memory culture; and Jennifer Coate's *Women, Men and Language: A Sociolinguistic Account of Sex Differences in Language* (New York: Longman, 1986) and Susan Kalcik's " '. . . Like Ann's gynecologist or the time I was almost raped': Personal Narratives in Woman's Rap Groups," in *Women and Folklore,* edited by Claire R. Farrer (Austin: University of Texas Press, 1975), which demonstrate the method in use with contemporary performance.

Analyses that focus on the cultural context of a particular subject, form, or institution, since they constitute the domain of the discipline of anthropology, are so numerous as to be overwhelming. Two extremely helpful introductions that make this material manageable are Edmund Leach, *Culture and Communication: The Logic by Which Symbols Are Connected: An Introduction to the Use of Structural Analysis in Social Anthropology* (New York: Cambridge University Press, 1976), and James P. Spradley and David W. McCurdy, eds., *The Cultural Experience: Ethnography in a Complex Society* (Chicago: Science Research Associates, 1972). Also useful in understanding the practice of broad cultural analysis are Roger D. Abrahams, *The Man of Words in the West Indies* (Baltimore: Johns Hopkins University Press, 1984), and Henry Glassie, *Passing in the Time in Balleymenone* (Philadelphia: University of Pennsylvania Press, 1982).

Two good, solid examples of a mainstream historical analysis with specific popular culture orientations are Norman Cantor and Michael Wetham, eds., *The History of Popular Culture* (New York: Macmillan, 1968), and Thomas Hine's *Populuxe* (New York: Alfred A. Knopf, 1986). Equally useful contemporary works are Ruth Schwartz Cowan, *More Work for Mother: The Ironies of Household Technology from the Open Hearth to the Modern Kitchen* (New York: Basic Books, 1983), and Susan Porter Benson, *Counter Culture:Saleswomen, Managers and Customers in the American Department Store 1940–1980* (New Haven: Yale University Press, 1986). Beyond these, examples of historical analysis are as varied as the people, places, and events that can be described. The best approach to historical analysis is to find topics that are of interest and to examine the different ways in which individual historians have handled the same material. It is important to remember that there will be differences. History is never cut and dried, and seldom do historians agree on what history means or even what history was. Accordingly, it is important always to explore more than one text and one historian's point of view. Several works that offer excellent examples of what can be accomplished through the use of the historical approach are Lawrence W. Levine, *Black Culture and Black Consciousness: Afro-American Folk Thought from Slavery to Freedom* (New York: Oxford University Press, 1977), Richard Price, *First-Time: The History of an Afro-American People* (Baltimore: Johns Hopkins University Press, 1983), and E. G. Alderfer, *The Ephrata Commune: An Early American Counterculture* (Pittsburgh: University of Pittsburgh Press, 1985).

A final word. It may seem at this point that research in popular culture, or in anything, for that matter, is overly concerned with method. That is not the case. Method is important. It determines the final quality of the work in question. It permits scholars to validate their work, to say to one another: this is the manner in which I gathered my data; these are the procedures I used to discover my facts; and these are the conclusions I have drawn. But it is not why scholars ask questions, nor is it why it is important to know how something can be studied. Knowing about methodology is important because that knowledge makes it possible for anyone, beginning student, interested amateur, or professional scholar, to make a genuine contribution to the advancement of knowledge. That may sound far-fetched and even corny, but truly it is not. In fact, it is particularly true in the field of popular culture studies. The idea of a discipline of popular culture is relatively new, and the number of active scholars, though growing, is not that large. Students at all levels, therefore, have the opportunity of participating in making the discipline into what it can become. But this can only happen if these beginning contributions try to follow the rules of the scholarship, try to say what they have to say in some coherent and intelligible way, and, above all else, try to operate within the consistent universe that a method provides. Scholarship works because it tries to inform its reader, and, in the process, to see aspects of the world that were hidden from view.

Method helps because it ensures that the writer and the audience understand the rules for seeing what is intended. In the end, however, both depend for their success upon the person doing the research. The choice, therefore, to do research cannot be only a choice of an interesting way to proceed. The researcher also has to want to think, to reflect, and to say something about something that has not been said or seen in the same way. Research, then, is not only the desire to discover. It is also an insistence on showing what has been found in order that others may know.

Name Index

Subject Index

450, 463; in magazines, 210-11, 389, 646; recordings of, 1168; regionalistic, 1196. *See also* Caricature; Cartoons, editorial; Comics, stand-up; Comic strips

Illustration, 567-89; in advertisements, 6, 13, 17, 577; of books, 519, 573; of fashions, 430, 431; in magazines, 569, 571, 581-82, 645; women depicted in, 569, 570

Indians, American, 746-48, 755, 756-58; almanacs published for, 45; art of, 758; captivity stories of, 44, 746-47, 963, 1427, 1439; dances of, 259, 268; depicted in literature, 757; games of, 506; and gardening, 527, 529; literature of, 757-58; and magic, 672; medicine of, 758; music of, 758; news coverage of, 837; oratory of, 343, 352, 747-48; publications for, 650; shamanism of, 855; stories of in almanacs, 44; treatment of death by, 280. *See also* Minorities

Intelligence: and disinformation, 1058-59; and propaganda, 1056-58

Jazz, 591-614, 762, 773, 774; and dance, 261, 262, 271-72; recordings of, 597-98, 599, 608, 1158, 1159, 1168, 1169, 1175

Jews: depicted in editorial cartoons, 397; depicted on postage stamps, 1354-55; dietary habits of, 485; propaganda about, 1088

Jogging. *See* Running

Journalism. *See* Magazines; Newspapers; Yellow journalism

Korean War: gardening during, 532; physical fitness of inductees during, 932; propaganda during, 1051, 1052, 1081

Latin America: propaganda aimed at, 1054-56

Latin music and dances, 263-64, 1176

Leisure activities. *See* Games and toys;

Outdoor entertainment; Recreational vehicles; Sports; Stage entertainment

Literature: American Indian tradition of, 757-58; and automobiles, 115-16; black tradition in, 756; death depicted in, 724; made into films, 464-65; about magazines, 657-58; in magazines, 649, 657; and magic, 703; medicine depicted in, 722-23, 727-28, 729-33, 738; minorities depicted in, 757, 759-60, 761; regionalism in, 1186, 1187, 1188, 1190, 1191, 1194, 1195-97; on religion, 1259, 1261-62; about sports, 1282, 1285-86, 1290; about trains, 1414; westerns, 1188-89, 1196; women depicted in, 1427-28, 1434, 1436, 1442-45

Local color movement. *See* Regionalism

Lyceums. *See* Chautauquas and lyceums

Magazines, 641-69; advertising in, 8, 24, 644, 645-46, 647-48, 658; on agriculture, 657, 1207; almanacs as forerunners of, 41; on architecture, 83-84; for automobile buffs, 111-12; on boating, 617, 618, 627; on business, 148-49; for children, 644, 1207; on comic art, 219, 393-96; for computer users, 233, 239; on dance, 273; on death and dying, 291-92; editorial cartoons in, 369, 370, 371; ethnic, 650; and fashions, 419, 430-31, 645; on films, 453-54; on food, 487-89; on gardening, 543-44; for humor, 210-11, 389, 646; illustration of, 569, 571, 581-82, 645; on jazz, 607-8; literature about, 657-58; on magic, 701; movie reviews in, 467; for photographers, 893; photography in, 8, 656; on physical fitness, 944; pornography in, 658, 957, 964, 967, 969-70, 979, 985, 993; publications about, 651, 652; for railfans, 1414; regionalistic, 657; science coverage in, 1204, 1206-7, 1210, 1216; on science fiction, 240, 573; sports de-